AF248691

NOTEBOOKS OF A
WANDERING MONK

NOTEBOOKS OF
A WANDERING MONK

MATTHIEU RICARD

TRANSLATED BY JESSE BROWNER

THE MIT PRESS   CAMBRIDGE, MASSACHUSETTS   LONDON, ENGLAND

© 2023 Massachusetts Institute of Technology

Originally published as *Carnets d'un moine errant.* © Allary Éditions 2021. Published by special arrangement with Allary Éditions in conjunction with their duly appointed agent 2 Seas Literary Agency.

All rights reserved. No part of this book may be reproduced in any form by any electronic or mechanical means (including photocopying, recording, or information storage and retrieval) without permission in writing from the publisher.

The MIT Press would like to thank the anonymous peer reviewers who provided comments on drafts of this book. The generous work of academic experts is essential for establishing the authority and quality of our publications. We acknowledge with gratitude the contributions of these otherwise uncredited readers.

This book was set in Stone Serif by Westchester Publishing Services. Printed and bound in the United States of America.

Library of Congress Cataloging-in-Publication Data

Names: Ricard, Matthieu, author. | Browner, Jesse, translator. | Ricard, Matthieu Carnets d'un moine errant.
Title: Notebooks of a wandering Monk / Matthieu Ricard ; translated by Jesse Browner.
Other titles: Carnets d'un moine errant. English
Description: Cambridge, Massachusetts : The MIT Press, [2023] | "Originally published as Carnets d'un moine errant. Allary Éditions, 2021." | Includes bibliographical references.
Identifiers: LCCN 2022054775 (print) | LCCN 2022054776 (ebook) | ISBN 9780262048293 | ISBN 9780262375658 (epub) | ISBN 9780262375641 (pdf)
Subjects: LCSH: Ricard, Matthieu. | Buddhist monks—France—Biography. | Religious life—Buddhism.
Classification: LCC BQ982.I23 A3 2023 (print) | LCC BQ982.I23 (ebook) | DDC 294.3/657092 [B]—dc23/eng/20230213
LC record available at https://lccn.loc.gov/2022054775
LC ebook record available at https://lccn.loc.gov/2022054776

10   9   8   7   6   5   4   3   2

Do not forget your teacher;
Pray to him at all times.

Do not let your mind be distracted;
Look into its very nature.

Do not forget death;
Let it spur you on to Dharma.

Do not forget sentient beings;
Pray for them with compassion.

Dilgo Khyentse Rinpoche

CONTENTS

AUTHOR'S NOTE

It's strange and a little unnatural to write your memoirs when you have spent much of your life shunning the self-centered and individualistic point of view. I have always held up selfless love as my guiding star; the ego cannot point the way. That is why this book is not so much a traditional autobiography as a testament to a life inspired at all moments by the spiritual masters I have met along the way.

I have little interest in making myself the subject of a book. Within these pages, therefore, I am merely an intermediary, a ferryman, to those men and women who have nourished my spiritual journey, guided me, enlightened me, encouraged me, spurring me on to become a better human being and, to the best of my abilities, to serve others.

Starting with my first trip to India and my meeting with my root master, I kept a little yellow notebook in which I jotted down my thoughts— and a few ornithological observations. Other entries followed, until I began recording my brief daily notes in a succession of Tibetan calendars. That is the source of the primary materials from which I have drawn, supplemented by my recollections and those of my friends, to bring to life the world of those remarkable human beings who were my teachers. I have tried in this way to offer a glimpse of the rich teachings that I have witnessed and of which I have been a privileged recipient, and to retrace the major stages of my inner journey, free from possessions and attachment to a specific place. For fifty years, I have been a monk errant in its earliest sense: "errant," from the Latin *iterare*, meaning wandering, traveling, searching.

I hope this testament will inspire you and that some of the light that I have absorbed from those who have been dear to me will shine through these pages to you.

I

MEETING THE MASTER

1

JUNE 12, 1967

In Darjeeling, near the border with Tibet, I meet the spiritual teacher who is to guide my life: Kangyur Rinpoche.

I was born on June 12, 1967, at the age of twenty-one. That was the day I met Kangyur Rinpoche, my spiritual teacher.

Two miles of winding, bumpy road led in a steep descent to Lebong, a little village below Darjeeling. To the north, at the border of Sikkim, Nepal, and Tibet, the snow-capped summits of the Kanchenjunga, "the five treasures of the great snow mountain," rose more than five miles into the sky.[1] The driver turned off the ignition on the descent. In a country where much of the population lives on the equivalent of two or three dollars a day, you soon learn how to economize. That day, like all others, the expedition was basically one long, acrobatic downhill coast. A dozen villagers and I were crammed together with bales of merchandise, a few hens, and two goats in the jury-rigged Land Rover that provided the regular shuttle service. A little plaque near the steering wheel, "Progressively manufactured by Mahindra and Mahindra," accurately described the way things are done in India—little by little and by as many people as possible. Outside, three or four passengers standing on the rear bumper did their best to stay on board as we careened around the bends in the road, clinging to their multicolored umbrellas as they sought shelter from the downpours.

Before heading down to Lebong, we had stopped at a market to buy fruit and a few other items to present as offerings to Kangyur Rinpoche and his family. I was accompanied by Tulku Pema Wangyal, his eldest son, who was my first spiritual friend and interpreter. My rudimentary English and total ignorance of Tibetan prevented me from conversing directly with Kangyur Rinpoche, who would soon become my teacher despite the language barrier. By chance, Tulku Pema Wangyal had gone up to Darjeeling to pay a visit on Father Vincent Curmi, a Canadian Jesuit whose address I had been given and who had offered me a place to stay the previous evening.

After passing through a forest of Japanese cedars, whose majestic trunks rose more than sixty feet high, the Land Rover dropped us at the side of the road a few miles outside the village of Lebong. Stairs of slippery stone, green with moss, and a path rutted by erosion led us up to a hamlet of some ten little wooden cottages roofed with sheets of corrugated metal painted brown or green, beneath which great barrels collected the rainwater that cascaded down the gutters. Swiftly filled by the torrential rains of the monsoon, they overflowed into a culvert. Children scampered here and there, making a joyful racket. Above the low doorway of one cottage, a cloth banner of blue, red, and yellow stripes indicated the dwelling of a Tibetan family in a village populated mainly by Nepalese.

Passing through the low doorway, I went down a short flight of wooden steps into a small room of worm-eaten floorboards that served as both kitchen and antechamber. I half-glimpsed some smiling faces, but my mind was intent on the imminent encounter, and I have few clear memories of how I was greeted. In the next room, which was only slightly bigger, Kangyur Rinpoche sat on a makeshift plank bed covered by a Tibetan rug in faded tones of yellow and red. Along the walls, some fifty heavy leather bundles were piled up to the ceiling. As I would later learn, they contained the precious library that Kangyur Rinpoche had taken great pains to bring with him from Tibet, saving them from certain destruction at the hands of the Red Guards of the "Great Cultural Revolution" and the "peaceful liberation of Tibet"—Chinese propaganda slogans that, in reality, refer to the invasion of Tibet by Mao's People's Republic of China in 1950, leading to the Dalai Lama's exile in 1959. A square table, a few chests, a second bed, and a big clock made up the rest of the furnishings.

I presented my modest offerings to the master and, not quite knowing what to do, sat at his feet on a small rug spread on the floor.

Thus began the adventure that was to inspire the rest of my existence.

I had read the biographies of sages, saints, and hermits, followers of various philosophies and religions; I had seen photographs of contemporary masters and listened to tales told by travelers. That path had led me to this moment. For the first time, I was in the presence of a spiritual master.

As he prayed, Kangyur Rinpoche exuded a peaceable and benevolent strength, and his mere presence created an aura of calm that I had never felt before. It was as if every object, every moment was pervaded by the master's serenity. The only sound was the rustling of the *mala* beads, a Buddhist rosary that slowly slid between his fingers, its little wooden pearls polished by the chanting of a million mantras.[2] Prayer came as naturally to him as breathing.

With the passage of the years, I have come to see that this meeting was one of such simplicity, dazzling clarity, and peaceful strength that words are powerless to describe it. We sometimes find ourselves in circumstances of such powerfully obvious perfection that language becomes incapable of depicting them. Only by experiencing them can we grasp their measure, and then but imperfectly, according to the limits of our understanding. And yet, in seeking to describe even the tiniest part of what I was able to retain of that wonderful moment, all I have is words, dull reflections of the substance of that encounter as they are: love, wisdom, knowledge, beauty, nobility, simplicity, fortitude, dignity, consistency of thought and action—these, among others, were what I sensed in that first meeting with my teacher, the "precious one," as translated from the honorific "Rinpoche."

In the presence of exceptional human beings, the best we can hope to do is open our heart and our mind, allow ourselves to be pervaded by their qualities, and then to keep at it for months, for years, for our entire life. Certain Buddhist texts that I was to discover later speak of an ordinary log lying in a forest of sandalwood trees; as it absorbs the raindrops that fall from that precious wood, the log is eventually imbued by their fragrance.

An encounter with a genuine master shines a light on our deepest sense of vulnerability and perplexity in the face of existence. Does life have a meaning? Or, more modestly, can I give meaning to my life? Now, however, you are not brooding over dark worries, keeping score of old wounds, or entertaining dreams of the future—you are savoring, here and now, the sweetness of a beneficent balm.

It is impossible to exhaust the presence of such a master. You want to merge with the master and never be separated again. That which you have long desired without fully knowing it is at your disposal, within arm's reach. The sterile flight of minutes and hours is at an end; in such a luminous presence, time expands within us and enfolds us in its boundless space. A single instant would suffice, but better yet, it opens out, grows more abundant day after day and gives itself to us so that we may drink at its source.

Kangyur Rinpoche's wife, Jetsün Jampa Chökyi, whom we all respectfully and affectionately referred to as Amala, "Mother," was the radiant embodiment of gentleness. Her spiritual realization was equal to that of the greatest masters. Kangyur Rinpoche shone like the sun; she glowed like a serene moon. I have never seen such a gentle gaze. And once her gaze had penetrated you, she broke into a smile that suspended time in a space of unconditional benevolence.

Her oldest son, Pema, a young man of boundless kindness, would go on to become the interpreter, companion, guide, and, finally, the spiritual teacher of his father's students, including me. Although his qualities were self-evident, his earliest Western students were unaware that he was the incarnation of a great master of the past, Taklung Tsetrul Rinpoche. This deeply humble young man, who was always ready with a smile on his face to help anyone in need, would have been the venerated abbot of an important monastery in Tibet had he stayed there. His temporary anonymity was the perfect counterpart to his modesty. He had received spiritual instruction from his father from the earliest age and studied many texts at his side; at the time of my first visits, he was spending part of the year with his younger brother, Rangdrol Dorje, at the Central Institute of Higher Tibetan Studies, near Varanasi, where several hundred students, refugees like they were, bore the burden of preserving the fragile heritage of the traditional philosophy and knowledge of Tibetan Buddhism.

The youngest son, Jigme Dorje, three and a half years old at that time— and also destined to become one of my most cherished masters who became later known as Jigme Khyentse Rinpoche—was a child with an astonishingly penetrating gaze. He spent most of his time at his father's side and even slept beside him.

Kangyur Rinpoche's eldest daughter, Rigdzin Chödrön, lived in a neighboring hamlet with her husband, her three-year-old daughter, Dawa, and her newborn daughter, Dekyi. She came to visit her parents every day. Her two younger sisters, Yangchen Chödzom and Pema Chökyi, were students at the Tibetan school in the Darjeeling refugee camp. The harmony that reigned and continues to reign in Kangyur Rinpoche's family has always been one of the most inspiring illustrations of the teachings he shared with us. The passing days were practically identical to one another, and yet rich in new discoveries.

Kangyur Rinpoche and his family woke long before dawn, but no one moved for the first hour or two. Seated on their pallets, they whispered their prayers, fingering their *malas*, or remained in silent contemplation. Soon, the soft crackling of the fire being lit in the kitchen could be heard, followed by the sound of brick tea being churned. Using a long handle that ended in a cap and rose and fell like a piston through a wooden tube bound by copper rings, a section of tea brick was mixed with boiling water, to which butter and salt were added. The tea was accompanied by wheat round breads cooked over a wood fire in a hearth of rammed earth. Brass ladles, a few casseroles, and an Indian calendar depicting the child Krishna hung from the soot-blackened walls of the kitchen.

My teacher remained seated, silent, and serene, like a mountain of wisdom and kindheartedness, splendid yet accessible. He meditated or prayed for most of the day, murmuring mantras, perched before a window that opened onto a sea of clouds through which an occasional glimpse of the haughty Kangchenjunga mountains emerged. His gaze, unfathomably deep, reflected an immutable enlightenment. The tick-tock of the clock accentuated the silence and counted off the passing hours, resonant with the teacher's openness and the student's aspirations.

In the entry room that also served as a kitchen, sitting cross-legged on a bed level with the window, Lama Wangchen, a wonderful calligrapher, copied out precious manuscripts with a sharpened bamboo stick and ink made with soot from the hearth, finely crushed and mixed with glue. He often shook with silent laughter that furrowed his entire face, pulled his head down between his shoulders, and gently stuck his tongue out, as Tibetans sometimes do as a sign of politeness.

From the very earliest days, my meditation consisted principally of merging my mind with that of my teacher, a union that would remain at the heart of my practice for the rest of my life. This simple yet profound experience consists of joining one's mind, narrow and confused, to that of the teacher's, vast, free, and clear, just as the space that is confined within a vase merges with the immensity of the sky once the dividing barrier is removed. In my novice's eagerness, I was sometimes able to detect the peaceful rhythm of Kangyur Rinpoche's breathing and to synchronize my own with it. I naively imagined that this would allow me to become one with him. At other times, my mind rested in the quiet simplicity that pervaded the room. But all of this was little more than the straining of a beginner's mind taking its first tentative steps into the expanse of consciousness. I had launched a quest whose destination was still unknown to me.

Alone with my teacher, I meditated all morning—or at least tried to—and a good part of the afternoon. Around 11 a.m., Kangyur Rinpoche's wife or one of his daughters would bring in a wooden tray bearing a plate of rice, a bowl of vegetables cooked in mustard oil and flavored with Indian spices, and a cup of tea. This meal marked the end of the morning meditation.

In the afternoon, I sometimes went up to Darjeeling, which was not much more than an overgrown village in those days, but more often than not I stayed and meditated until twilight, especially since it was full-blown monsoon season at the time. The hours spent sitting cross-legged, a posture that was relatively new to me, eventually gave rise to aches that tended to take center stage during my meditation. And yet I noticed that, beyond the pain, the nature of mind did not change; it did not depend on comfort or discomfort, on joy or sadness. The feelings and thoughts that these states generate merely color the edges of the mind, whose nature remains immutable, just as the fundamental quality of light—its ability to illuminate objects—is not altered by whether it falls on a pile of garbage or a mound of precious stones. When night fell, Kangyur Rinpoche recited prayers out loud, then we switched on the light bulb that hung from a wire nailed to the ceiling. The evening soup

was served. The household went to bed around nine. I was given one of
the two remaining beds—that of the elder son, Pema, I was later to learn.
The family slept here and there on flat, square cushions stuffed with rice
bran and placed side by side to form a mattress. I see now that it was very
brash of me to move in with my teacher that way, but Tibetan hospitality
is discreet, natural, and unlimited.

The intensity and depth of those days living in the presence of Kangyur
Rinpoche in no way precluded simplicity and good humor. At mealtimes,
or at the arrival of a family member or visitor, conversation quietly sprang
to life and there was much laughter. These exchanges, like all activities
of everyday life, were infused with the calm and serenity born of daily
meditation. The imprint of their spiritual accomplishment was so strong
that contemplation seemed to be finely interwoven into every act, every
gesture, every word, as if it were impossible to deviate from the path of
wisdom.

What struck me most about these "ordinary" moments was the subtle, timeless, and even delightful harmony that reigned around Kangyur
Rinpoche. The concept of "spiritual nourishment" was fully manifest
here: every instant, every gesture, ever word seemed to assist, inspire,
guide, remind, and comfort.

The time spent in Kangyur Rinpoche's presence was like the welcome
relief experienced by a traveler who, after wandering for years, has found
a safe harbor and can set down his burden. I felt as if I had finally found
a home at the heart of my existence. Everything arose and found its
place without artifice or complication. Not once did I feel the weight of
time dragging on or the boredom that it can entail; something essential,
rich, and precious was happening here. Until now, I had known what I
didn't want—a vain, insipid, meaningless, distracted, disenchanted life—
without knowing what it was I had been truly seeking. Things were now
becoming clear: I wanted to follow the path that led from confusion to
clarity, from ignorance to understanding, from suffering to happiness,
and from servitude to freedom.

Fifty years later, I can still remember certain salient moments of my
first visit. One afternoon, Kangyur Rinpoche took a bell, rang it, and
held it in the air until its crystalline tone faded away into silence. Then,
through his eldest son, he asked me, with a playful look in his eye, "What

is making the sound? The bell? The clapper? The hand?" Puzzled, but aware that there was an important point to be understood here, I tried to formulate a response. "Is it not the mind that produces the sound?" I was well aware that my answer was too intellectual and did not reflect an intimate understanding of what I was trying to say. Kangyur Rinpoche fixed me with a cheerful look, laughed, and said nothing further. It was not really clear to me at that moment, but this was the first time that Kangyur Rinpoche had introduced me to the nature of my own mind. He had tried to show me the indescribable aspect of its luminous nature, stripped of all conceptual contrivance and ever-present behind the screen of thought.

Sometimes, at the right moment, the teacher will ask the student to examine and observe his own thoughts. Where do they come from? Where do they abide? Where do they disappear to? We are compelled to acknowledge our inability to locate the origin of our thoughts or to recognize any inherent qualities in them—form, nature, location. They don't go anywhere once they are done; they simply dissolve into the emptiness from which they emerged, the way waves arise out of the ocean and subside back into it. One day, I took a little notebook and jotted down a thought that had occurred to me: "Foam bursts from the sea without ceasing to be the sea and is reabsorbed into the ocean's vastness without affecting it in any way." Other than these improvised yet incredibly precious lessons, Kangyur Rinpoche offered me no formal instruction on the path to Buddhism during this first stay.

On another day, I sensed the omnipresence of the teacher in everything I perceived, and I wrote down some reflections in my daybook: "The teacher's mind is at the heart of all things, my own heart, Pema's heart, the table, the entire world. This presence is not altered by the unfolding of daily events or by the thoughts that obscure it. The ego only has the power that we grant it, and the student obtains results according to his diligence." In rereading these notes today, I see that I had a kind of intuition about the practice of what is called "pure vision"—the perception of the presence of the teacher in all things. As the days passed, I noticed that every meditation that began with devotion flourished more naturally than the others.

When his son was absent and he had no interpreter, Kangyur Rinpoche pointed to various objects and, with the aid of gestures, asked me what they were called in my mother tongue. As I responded, he had great fun repeating the word in French. He took up a notepad and wrote them down in phonetic Tibetan: "spoon," "fork," "table," "sun," "moon."

One day many years later, after he had moved to the Orgyen Kunzang Chökhorling Monastery, south of Darjeeling, Kangyur Rinpoche reached under his pillow, produced that same old notepad, and with the same playfulness read out this little French vocabulary.

One afternoon, when I was deep in my meditation, Kangyur Rinpoche suddenly clapped his hands to draw me out of my absorption. An eminent master, Pawo Rinpoche, had just arrived. Eager to observe the etiquette required in such circumstances, I leaped to my feet and went to stand quietly in a corner of the room. A meeting between two masters always offers an astonishing spectacle, the wonderment of seeing the same quality of being in two different faces. Far from being formal or solemn, these reunions sparkle with joy, spontaneity, and humor. Suddenly, two suns are ablaze in the room. At certain times, they shine on one another; at other times, they merge. For the student as witness to such meetings, they confirm that enlightenment is not an isolated phenomenon or an unobtainable goal but the culmination of a path that others have trodden. It strengthens us in the conviction that if we dedicate ourselves with tireless resolve to spiritual practice, we will reach our destination: complete inner freedom. In one another's presence, the masters vie with each other in perfectly authentic humility, the way the branches of a tree laden with fruit bend toward the earth—a good lesson for those who believe that acquiring knowledge and virtue is a cause for vanity or even arrogance. Needless to say, this lesson is all the more relevant when it comes to the celebrity, power, wealth, intellectual prowess, or physical beauty by which success is sometimes measured. Humility is one of the distinctive qualities of a true master. When you find it lacking in someone you had considered taking as your teacher, it's probably best to just move on.

I had several opportunities to meet up again with Pawo Rinpoche at the monastery where he lived, Bhutia Basti. He had a special warmth and laughed a great deal, and when he did, his entire face seemed to be one great smile topped by two eyes twinkling with kindness.

Kangyur Rinpoche's son, Tulku Pema Wangyal, took me to meet another highly respected master who lived in Kalimpong, some two hours' travel from Darjeeling: Dudjom Rinpoche ("Rinpoche" is a term of respect given to Tibetan spiritual masters, meaning "precious one" or "venerable one"). The winding road passed through immense forests of Japanese cedar then plunged into the valley of the powerful Teesta River, which is spanned by a concrete beam bridge, before rising up again 5,000 feet toward Kalimpong, a pleasant haven that enjoys more sunshine than Darjeeling, with views of the foothills of Bhutan to the east and Sikkim to the north. Tulku Pema Wangyal had the deepest respect for Dudjom Rinpoche, one of the most impressive masters I have ever met, yet a man of great and abiding simplicity. He radiated goodness, the living embodiment of the awareness that shone from his face at all times. He explained that there are two kinds of meditation: one active, centered on concentration; the other without a focal object, which purifies and clarifies the mind, making it appear like an immaculate sky.

While Tibetan Buddhism is not built around a formal hierarchy, Dudjom Rinpoche was considered to be the head of the Nyingmapa school, and Tibetans held him in the highest respect. This tradition, the oldest within Tibetan Buddhism, dates back to the period when the canonical texts of Buddhism were first translated from Sanskrit into Tibetan, in the eighth and the ninth centuries, when Guru Padmasambhava—"Born from a Lotus"—came to Tibet.

Three weeks had passed. The moment when I had to return to Darjeeling and pursue my travels across India arrived sooner than I would have liked. Before taking my leave, I asked Kangyur Rinpoche the questions that had been weighing on me.

"Should I come to live with you?"

"First finish the studies you have begun," he replied, before adding, "It is not expedient to interrupt a task on the verge of being achieved."

"Should I start a family?"

"Make no decisions before you turn thirty, and things will become clear," he advised me.

He told me that I should live between seventy and eighty years if I practiced meditation. Our goodbyes were very moving. Kangyur Rinpoche gave me his blessing—he held my hands, touched my head against his for ten seconds that felt as if they were outside the regular flow of time, draped a white scarf around my neck, and enjoined me to continue practicing. I backed away, my eyes overflowing with tears. So much had been given to me! How could I assimilate all this new abundance? Finally, I said farewell to Amala and the monk-calligrapher.

As there were no cars on the road, I left on foot with my backpack. Tulku Pema Wangyal walked with me as far as the Lebong Racecourse, about half a mile away, where horses had once competed in the time of the British Raj. He told me that the spiritual teacher could perceive the student's fervor, even from a great distance. "He sees his student as a little flame, brighter or dimmer according to his devotion." This proposition was a source of great inspiration and peace of mind for me when I was far away, in the dreary grind of Parisian life. As we said goodbye and I prepared to take the shortcut to Darjeeling through the forest, Tulku Pema Wangyal had one last suggestion for me: "Keep your teacher constantly in mind, merge your mind with his and he will never be apart from you." Then he added, "Don't forget me!" There was little risk of that.

2

FROM VARANASI TO KASHMIR

Portraits of Tibetan masters in a documentary about India by Arnaud Desjardins.

A few months earlier, in early spring 1967, Arnaud Desjardins and his wife Denise invited me to their home to watch the documentary *The Message of the Tibetans*, which they had shot over the course of six months of travels through India, accompanied by Sonam Kazi, an interpreter for the Dalai Lama. Arnaud was a friend of my mother and a television producer with a passion for spirituality and the Hindu masters; he would go on to write a number of books with a very wide readership. He had filmed the Tibetan masters who had fled the communist Chinese invasion of Tibet and taken refuge on the Indian and Bhutanese sides of the Himalayas. In the second half of the film,[1] over the course of three long, silent minutes, the faces of some twenty hermits and spiritual masters appeared one after the other, looking directly into the camera. To me, it was like suddenly finding myself face-to-face with twenty living versions of Socrates or Saint Francis of Assisi. Although they were very different from one another in face and physical appearance, they all exuded the same spiritual strength. No sequence of images had ever had such a powerful effect on my mind. A friend of Arnaud's and my mother's, Frédérick Leboyer—an obstetrician famous for his gentle birthing practice known as "birth without violence"—had also traveled to Darjeeling and shown me photographic portraits that he had taken there.[2] He and Arnaud told me that, of all the masters they had met, the one who had most impressed them was named Kangyur Rinpoche, and indeed, the vision of that face of unfathomable depth and overflowing with goodness struck me like a revelation. I decided to leave for India.

In the end, it was a film and a portrait that proved to be the catalysts for my change of life. They resonated in me like an irresistible call. Why had the generous and welcoming strength that emanated from my teacher in particular, setting him apart from all the others, struck me so forcefully? I later learned that such deep-rooted affinities sometimes arise between a teacher and his students. With experience and hindsight, I have come to see that a teacher's face expresses something unique that photography is able to reveal, becoming the medium of a genuine encounter.

The beauty of these exceptional humans, glowing from within, corresponds very poorly with the aesthetic criteria of the Greek or Hollywood ideal. According to such codes, some of these faces might even be seen as "ugly," yet they offer the observer the purest and most elemental of experiences: a window onto the qualities of enlightenment. Such beauty is not a facade and cannot conceal a heart of stone behind an angel's countenance. Upon seeing a sage, a face that radiates the harmony of wisdom and selfless love, you understand intuitively that you are in the presence of someone who can help you to actualize the very best of the nature that slumbers in each and every one of us.

On June 2, 1967, the day of my grand departure for India was at hand. A friend, Christine O., dropped me at a Paris city gate, and I stuck out my thumb, destination Munich, where a charter flight on Syrian Arab Airlines was scheduled to leave for Delhi on June 6. I dawdled a little on the way, stopping overnight at, among other places, a youth hostel on the shores of the lovely Lake Starnberg. In Munich, I visited the Pinakothek Museum, which my mother had often told me about, and then went to a renowned harpsichord dealer who had built the instrument used by Helmut Walcha, my favorite interpreter of the works of J. S. Bach. On reaching the airport on June 6, I learned that the Six-Day War had just broken out and that my flight had been cancelled. While I weighed the pros and cons of hitchhiking all the way to India, the other passengers and I were transferred to a flight on BOAC, the British national airline at the time. We left at six in the evening and arrived in Delhi at daybreak on June 7. With only 650 rupees in my pocket,[3] and despite the fact that it was 110°F in the shade, I was compelled by necessity to cross the city on foot, rucksack on my back, to the home of Narayan Menon, the director of Indian national radio and a friend of Frédérick's, who had informed me that Narayan was a wonderful player of the veena, a stringed instrument related to the sitar. I had some trouble finding the address in the labyrinth of Delhi. Narayan offered me a place to stay and helped me buy a train ticket for Darjeeling. On the morning I left, at my request, he was kind enough to play, beautifully, a raga, a traditional form of classical Hindu music whose name means "passion"—a passion entirely enwrapped in the profundity of the complex harmonies of this music, which I had first heard on recordings in France. The standard performance of a raga takes almost an hour, starting very slowly then progressing to a crescendo, brilliantly showcasing the player's virtuosity.

After forty-eight hours on the train, at 11 p.m. I arrived at Siliguri, a market town at the foot of the mountains and the unavoidable crossroads between India, Nepal, and Bhutan. The train for Darjeeling was to leave the next morning, and I spent a rather spartan night on the station platform. But I was not alone—far from it!

After the torrid plains of India, the slow climb to Darjeeling was enchanting. I was told that the "toy train," as some called it, was the oldest train in service in the world. Its great age was proudly engraved in large characters on the very body of the engine: "Built in 1879." The train soon gained altitude. When the slope steepened, one of the engineer's assistants positioned himself astride the front bumper and, when necessary, poured sand onto the rails to prevent the wheels from skidding in the climb. When the slope grew too steep, a switch allowed the train to back up onto a side track on a gentler gradient, where it built up a head of steam to tackle the steeper one. Overlooking the luxuriant undulations of tea plantations, we slipped past little waterfalls in the midst of towering trees and exotic flowers. An eagle kept pace beside the train for a few moments, just ten yards from my window. At times we plowed through thick banks of fog from which we emerged, dazzled, to a vision of hillsides rising from the sea of clouds.

The train was made up of four little cars. People got on and got off pretty much anywhere, not only in the stations. Children on their way home from school jumped onto the exterior steps as the train rolled, and held on joyfully for the next few miles. Announcing its presence with great blasts of its whistle, the train barreled its way straight up the main streets of the villages it passed through. I was struck by the gentleness of the place and its inhabitants, in contrast to the harshness of their living conditions.

We came to the end of the line at the little Darjeeling train station, located on a square lined with homes, shops, and warehouses. Piles of coal to fuel the locomotives rose here and there. My mind now turned its full attention to my imminent meeting with Kangyur Rinpoche, the object of my voyage to India. I was calm but galvanized by an event whose importance I could not yet grasp, yet which I sensed would be like no other I had ever experienced. And indeed, this remarkable encounter, the precious and incommensurable time I was to spend in the serenity of Kangyur Rinpoche's "hermitage-cabin," would unleash an ineluctable and irreversible change in me.

The journey that I took through India afterward was to enrich my mind in an altogether different way. I plunged from an internal exploration into an intense immersion in the kaleidoscopic whirlwind of the subcontinent's cultures, from the holy city of Varanasi to the mountains of Kashmir, crossing the Ganges at Haridwar, only to end up in a hospital in Delhi with typhoid. I had wanted to explore other spiritual traditions, but that aspiration had lost all its urgency after it had been fulfilled beyond all hope by my meeting with Kangyur Rinpoche. But there was still a fertile voyage of discovery ahead in a country rich with new sights and revelations for a curious and open-minded young Westerner like me. I struck out eagerly for adventure.

In India, traveling by train is the ultimate in railroad experiences. Imagine a journey of two days and two nights (that's how long it took to get from Delhi to Darjeeling) in a carriage of compartments without doors—first class was beyond my means—where everybody talks with everyone else and no seat belongs to anyone in particular, not even to the person occupying it. No matter how well you may plan ahead, it is perfectly acceptable for a bench that has been reserved for a night's sleep to be used by anyone who wants to sit on it during the day. Once they have settled in, passengers begin by unrolling their bedding, a thin mattress rolled up in a sturdy canvas sack that also contains a pillow, pajamas, toiletries, and the other usual items. Even in third class, which was not abolished until 1977, bathrooms were generally equipped with a showerhead in the ceiling—a godsend during long journeys, especially as the dog days approached.

In this atmosphere of joyful commotion, conversation is lively and soon turns to politics—the preferred subject of Indian debate. Everyone jumps in, sometimes from one compartment to the next. Every stop—and they are many and long—is the occasion for a boisterous hustle and bustle of passengers getting on and off, not only when they are beginning or ending their travels, but just to get some air, take a cup of tea, or grab a bite to eat on the platform crowded with little stalls and street vendors with their kettles of scalding tea and cups of sun-dried clay that you throw away after use. Puri, delicious crepes fried in oil and served with potatoes in a spicy sauce, make the best breakfast. The station rings with full-throated sales pitches: *Chai garam*—hot tea! *Munphali*—peanuts! At last, the engineer blasts the signal for departure. In 1967, the locomotives were still powered by steam, and as the train slowly gathered speed, we had plenty of time to hop on board.

Train station platforms are also holiday spots. It is not uncommon for trains to run six or seven hours late, and you sometimes have to wait half a day to make a connection. Many passengers spread a length of fabric on the ground to rest on, using their baggage as pillows. The arrival of a train, announced by loudspeaker, is a real event for those who have waited so long. Years later, I was on the platform at the Gaya station, heading for Delhi. The train was due at 4:30 p.m. Shortly before that time, its imminent arrival was announced—the Tinsukia Mail, originating in Assam. The waiting travelers were caught up in a sudden tumult, gathering their bags as they prepared to embark, which is never an easy matter. The fact that the train was on time, for once, was subject of much commentary. A moment later, a second announcement was broadcast. The excitement abated forthwith. I asked what had happened. "It's yesterday's train," I was told. Ours was not expected until late in the evening.

In the morning, a clerk passes through the cars with a notebook, taking orders for lunch. There are several options—vegetarian or not, rice or *chapati* (a flatbread made of wheat). The clerk gets off at the next station, where he transmits the orders via telegraphic relays to another station where the meals are prepared. At midday, when the train arrives at that station, an army of deliverymen swarms the carriages, bearing towers of *thali*, round or rectangular aluminum platters with hollow compartments containing the individual dishes, protected by a cover. I've always wondered how the workers manage to deliver every customer what he ordered, without ever making a mistake.

India—endearing, inspiring, and disconcerting all at once. One navigates between the functional chaos of cities bustling with crowds day and night and the rusticity of villages that seem to have emerged straight out of the distant past; between generally peaceful coexistence among countless spiritual traditions and the strict observance of rules defined by a caste system that remains very current within the Hindu population. "Melting pot of civilizations" is an expression that applies perfectly to India. Peoples come together and live side by side, but they don't combine. The markers and modes of expression of the various cultures and religions are everywhere, multifarious, and noisy. It would be unthinkable in India to prohibit the wearing of turbans, veils, or religious vestments, much less to ban public nudity as practiced, among others, by Jain monks of the Digambara ("sky-clad") school and certain Hindu sadhus. I once saw a man stroll completely naked along the crowded platforms of the Kolkata train station, without attracting any particular attention. The concept of "private life" has not yet taken hold. One day, I was reading a letter on a street in old Delhi when I found myself immediately surrounded by five or six curious souls reading over my shoulder, seeking to decipher the missive alongside me. As for noise, loudspeakers on the streets of cities and towns compete in volume with one another to ensure that everyone can hear, often at the same time, the hymns coming from the Hindu temple, the muezzin's call to prayer (in Muslim quarters one often hears several at a time from the various neighborhood mosques), and the chants of a Sikh *gurdwara*. If you set up a sound system on the streets of any of these neighborhoods to broadcast movie music at full blast at nine in the evening, you will be considered a benefactor of humankind.

My first destination after returning to Darjeeling was Benares, the renowned holy city of Hinduism, now having been restored to its true Sanskrit name, Varanasi. I am at a loss for words to describe the wonders of this unique and fascinating place, the majestic beauty of the ghats—the banks of the Ganges built up into flights of sacred stairs below rows of temples, where the faithful go at dawn to bathe in the river, animated by ecstatic fervor.[4] The ghats are a meeting place, a place to socialize, that offers all sorts of activities: open-air chess clubs, gymnasts doing their morning exercises, temple hawkers selling rafts of trinkets with good-natured insistence. The old city, which runs along the Ganges, is traversed by a maze of alleys that bustle with activity pretty much all day and all night: artisans, who often work in the street itself; street vendors and beggars; sadhus, Hindu holy men who have renounced society and all possessions and live exclusively on handouts; pilgrims next to deliverymen pushing handcarts brimming with merchandise at full speed, all mingling in a motley crowd and a most invigorating bedlam. Stalls offer rosewater *lassi*, the best in India, they say—a drink made of whipped yogurt, rose syrup, and ice water—or tea scented with cinnamon or other spices. Huge textile workshops, run mostly by Muslims, manufacture the renowned silk goods prized throughout India, saris and shawls, as well as magnificent brocades purchased by folk from the Himalayas to decorate their Buddhist temples.

The flood of pilgrims heading to the river for their sacred ablutions begins well before dawn. Majestic, highly venerated sadhus have their own appointed places along the ghats. Beside them, a trident planted in the ground and a little brass bowl indicate their membership in the cult of Shiva. They wear their long hair knotted in a capacious chignon at the top of their heads; their half-naked bodies are covered in ashes, the symbol of death and rebirth and an ever-present reminder of human mortality. Horizontal stripes of red, yellow, or black powder streak their foreheads.

Further along, pyres consume the bodies of the dead—people who often set off on their journey to Varanasi as death approaches so as to be cremated in this holiest of holy cities. Blind river dolphins occasionally surface into the golden reflections of the rising sun.

Some six miles from Varanasi, I found Sarnath, the deer park where the Buddha gave his first teachings after attaining enlightenment. There he set forth the Four Noble Truths for his five former ascetic companions: the truth of suffering that must be recognized; the truth of the causes of suffering that must be eliminated; the truth of the cessation of suffering that must be actualized; and the truth of the path leading to the end of suffering, which must be taken. The contrast is vast between the perpetual feverish bustle of Varanasi and the immutable serenity of the park, of the great Dhamek Stupa commemorating that first sermon—a monument whose architecture symbolizes the *dharmakaya*, the absolute dimension of the Buddha and his awakening.

I mingled with the pilgrims who strolled or meditated in silence, while others sat studying texts for hours in the shade of a tree. I also visited the Central Institute of Higher Tibetan Studies, where the older sons of Kangyur Rinpoche had studied for years with some of the great Tibetan scholars who had been able to flee the Chinese invasion and were striving to preserve the philosophical heritage of Tibetan Buddhism. I also reconnected with Tarthang Tulku, whom I had met in Darjeeling and who had devoted his life, in India and in the United States, to publishing hundreds of precious volumes so as to make them available to all.

Out of curiosity, I also set out to find an ashram where I might meet with swamis of the various Hindu philosophical traditions. The Sanskrit word *swami*, which means "he who is one with himself," is a title given to Hindu ascetics. I went to the Ananda Marga ashram, which, as I later discovered, turned out to be a somewhat sulfurous organization. A haughty young student, whose long hair, glistening with coconut oil, hung to his shoulders, came to the door and asked me what I wanted. "To receive *darshana*," I replied, hoping to arrange an inspiring encounter with the spiritual master of the place.[5] *Darshana* means "philosophy," the young man told me in a somewhat condescending tone. If I was merely passing through, he concluded, I could not meet with the swami. I left feeling a little mortified, comparing this icy reception to the very warm welcome I had received from the Tibetans.

After Varanasi and Sarnath, I decided to go to Kashmir, a region of great beauty whose capital, Srinagar, lies on the shores of a large lake dappled with water gardens of lotus blossom.

Thanks to the Indologist Lilian Silburn, a friend of my mother who was living in Srinagar at the time, I was able to meet Swami Lakshman Joo, a scholar of Kashmir Shivaism, a school of Hindu philosophy that teaches many methods of meditation based on the nondualism of subject and object. The swami, an affable and straightforward man, was engaged in a textual study with several students, including Lilian. I didn't wish to disturb him, and, having briefly introduced myself, I simply asked his permission to sit in a corner of the room and meditate in his presence. I didn't have the opportunity to ask him any questions of a spiritual nature, but I was moved by the peaceable atmosphere of the place.

Certain inspiring meditation instructions discovered in the texts translated by Lilian Silburn—who dedicated her life to the study and practice of that very particular discipline—recall the techniques of Tibetan Buddhism, although these two traditions differ in many other respects. In the light of the explanations provided by her teacher, she offered the following commentary on a verse that encourages the practitioner to meditate on the moment at which the sound produced by a string instrument disappears: "At the end of the last extended sound, thought loses all support and is absorbed into the emptiness."[6] That principle echoed the question that Kangyur Rinpoche had asked me about the chiming of his bell.

At twilight, the immense Lake Dal reflects all the subtle changes of light. It is blanketed by a thin layer of fog, from which a smiling fisherman slowly emerges to offer me some lotuses. This beguiling scene, of such powerful simplicity, is typical of the ten serene days I spent on the lakeshore, which in those days was sparsely inhabited once you left Srinagar. The time came when I had to head back down to the plains of India. I intended to go to Haridwar, another holy city and pilgrimage destination on the banks of the Ganges. On the bus to the nearest train station, I met a friendly Englishman who, like me, was passionate about classical music. We were headed in the same direction. In Pathankot, we were told that there were no seats available on the train for the next ten days. Bereft at the idea of being stuck on this station platform for the foreseeable future, expedience got the better of our probity and we decided to travel unticketed, like sadhus, and to sleep in the train corridor. We imagined that fortune had smiled upon us when we found a compartment that was strangely empty. We entered and closed the door, very pleased with ourselves. But our delight was short-lived. With blows that started out tentative and intensified to furious, accompanied by colorful imprecations, the ticket collector and his assistants made it more than clear that they did not share our enthusiasm. Grasping at snippets of their conversation, we understood that the local police would be waiting for us at the next station. As their voices receded down the corridor, we decided to take advantage of the lull by abandoning the compartment and leaping from the moving train at a spot where it slowed down. We went sprawling headlong down the rocky embankment. Grabbing our backpacks, we followed the train tracks for a few hundred yards before reaching a level crossing where several dozen rickshaws—those notorious tricycle cabs—were waiting for the barrier to rise. We flagged one down, and the driver agreed to convey us in that most traditional of vehicles to the nearest town, where we would take a bus to Haridwar. This foray into the world of freeloading cost us skinned elbows and knees, but taught us a valuable lesson about instant karmic retribution for our behavior.

Haridwar is one of the four holy places of India. Every twelve years, alternating from one site to another, it is the host of the Kumbh Mela, an unparalleled pilgrimage during which several million devotees come to bathe in the river. The largest Kumbh Mela, in Allahabad, at the confluence of the Ganges and the Yamuna Rivers, was attended by sixty million people in 2001, in what was considered at the time to be the greatest gathering in the history of humankind. It is about sixty miles as the crow flies from the source of the Ganges, and the water is still icy there. I went for a swim but underestimated the strength of the current; in no time, I had been swept a hundred yards downstream. In Rishikesh, some dozen miles from Haridwar, I paid a visit to the ashram of the late Swami Sivananda, the renowned Hindu master who had synthesized the various forms of yoga and taught the philosophy of Vedanta.[7] In a temple at the ashram, groups of the faithful sang devotional songs, the *bhajan*, to the rhythm of tambourines. The swami in charge informed me that the ashram could not accommodate me for the night and that no study program was currently being offered. In the garden was a bust of Swami Sivananda, at the base of which was inscribed the epigram "Be good, do good."

I have always thought these four words are the simplest and best advice it is possible to give.

I started back for Delhi and decided to return to France by road. But by the time I got to Haridwar I was already beginning to feel unwell, and as the days progressed, I developed a powerful fever. At the suggestion of Adrien Dufour, a minister counselor at the French embassy to whom I had been referred by mutual friends, I went to the Holy Family Hospital.

"Are you sick?" the doctor asked me.

But because I wore a beard at the time, and my English was lacking, I thought that he had asked me, "Are you a Sikh?"[8]

To which I responded, "No, I'm French."

This did little to impress him with my ability to think clearly but was not enough to tip him off. The doctor told me to take vitamins and took the opportunity to advise me that the hospital was not a hotel. Very fortunately, I almost passed out when I stood up; I turned out to have a fever of 104°F, which convinced him in extremis to keep me under observation. The sisters who worked at the hospital brought me in a wheelchair to a group ward. The next morning, a priest came to ask me if I wished to receive communion and the holy sacraments. I think it can wait, I told him. I was first treated for malaria, then given shots for typhus and who knows what to rid me of "liver flukes." The final diagnosis was that I was suffering from typhoid. While the experience of being sick was hardly pleasant, the sisters and the doctors treated me with great care.

Burning with fever, bathed in sweat, and unable to eat, I slept fitfully. The two weeks I spent in the hospital felt like a time of renewal, yet strangely, my memory has reduced them to a few difficult days, dull and confused, in strong contrast to my two weeks in Darjeeling, which, rich in substance as they had been, felt as if they had lasted a lifetime and marked the beginning of my true rebirth. Some twenty-five pounds lighter (I weighed 120 by the time I left the hospital), I spent a few days at the home of Adrien Dufour, whose family had touched me with their warmhearted visits to the hospital, bearing fruit and reading materials. They staunchly advised me to return home by plane.

3

FROM DAMASCUS TO PARIS

Back in France with my family, I come to appreciate the significance of the days I had spent with Kangyur Rinpoche. My mother decides to make her own journey to India.

The return flight on Syrian Arab Airways made a half-day stopover in Damascus, where we were required to claim our luggage, which in my case meant my backpack and a sitar purchased at the renowned Lahore Music House in Delhi. Once I got off the plane, I decided to take the opportunity to explore the countries that I would otherwise have seen only from above the clouds. I felt my appetite for the open road rekindled, and I let the flight for Paris leave without me to pursue my travels by train and car. In Damascus, where French was still spoken everywhere, I was struck by the kindness and hospitality of the people. I visited the tomb of the great Sufi master Ibn Arabi, whose work is considered the crowning glory of Sufi Islamic esotericism and of whom my uncle, the navigator Jacques-Yves Le Toumelin, often spoke. I then took the train for Istanbul, passing the impressive Krak des Chevaliers fortress, and marveled at the superb countryside of Syria and Turkey. In Istanbul, I spent a few quiet moments of meditation in the great Blue Mosque and saw the wonders of the Topkapi museum. Then I set off to hitchhike to France.

After a speedy crossing of the Balkans, the driver who had been kind enough to pick me up dropped me off in Tournus. I was still very weak after my recovery from typhoid, overflowing with vivid and varied experiences, intoxicated by the intense sensations of the past two and a half months. My parents had told me of the Romanesque abbey of Tournus, so I decided to stop there to investigate and replenish my strength. It was empty, or almost, and perfectly silent. I sat a long while on a pew in the church, allowing my mind to rest in the tranquility of a place imbued with a thousand years of spiritual life. When this moment of release had passed, I understood that my journey was truly at an end. The last leg of my trip to Paris was just a formality. On my arrival, I learned that my mother and sister were spending several days in the grand home of our friend Gérard Godet, near Nemours. Without pausing, I took the train to Nemours, then strolled along the canal to the house in Fromonville, arriving unannounced on the porch with my backpack and sitar, wrapped in a red satin cloth. Our reunion was tender, and Frédérick Leboyer was among the good friends gathered there for the weekend. I can't remember what stories I told them about my travels, but the important thing was that I was back home and able to share, with far more than mere words, all the wealth of experience I had accumulated.

Returning to Paris, I moved back into our family apartment with my sister Ève, who was studying to be a speech therapist and had become interested in Orthodox Christianity, inspired by an encounter with a monk of that tradition. Back in the thick of Parisian life, which now felt very stale to me, I began to understand the profound impact that my meeting with Kangyur Rinpoche had had on me. My daily meditation, while still tentative, was continuously permeated with his vast and luminous presence. Frédérick Leboyer, who had become a kind of adopted uncle to me, lived nearby and I sometimes joined him for a silent meditation at his home.

My mother, Yahne Le Toumelin, had always been interested in the myriad forms of spirituality, from Meister Eckhart and other Christian mystics all the way to the Vedanta. They fueled her readings and discussions within her circle of friends. But she had not found a direct connection to a living tradition that she could put into practice. On my return from

India, I suggested that if she wished to engage in a spiritual practice, it might be an excellent thing if she, too, went to meet Kangyur Rinpoche and the other great teachers living in Darjeeling, Kalimpong, and Sikkim. In 1968, she embarked on that journey, which lasted several months and was, for her too, a turning point in her life. In India, she met with Mother Teresa in Kolkata and with the great Indian sage Anandamayi Ma. She, too, became a student of Kangyur Rinpoche. When she met the sixteenth Karmapa, another renowned master who lived at the Rumtek Monastery in Sikkim, he advised her to take the vows of a nun. My mother explained that she had a family. "If you can sign a guarantee that you will still be alive next year, then you can wait," the Karmapa replied. My mother understood that it would be best to take the monastic vows immediately, and she did.

On her return, she put her painting career on pause for many years. She had been given her first break by André Breton, a father of Surrealism, who had shown her works in his gallery and devoted a chapter to her in his book *Surrealism and Painting*. Jean Cocteau, another admirer of her work, had written to her: "Thank you for placing a landscape at my window and a path at my feet. Nothing is as admirable as the marriage of chance and talent." My mother's canvases had been shown in several galleries and at the painting salons held each year in Paris, such as the Salon de Mai. Her metamorphosis into a Buddhist nun upset a number of intellectuals and artists among her friends, who, unfortunately, snubbed her more or less openly. A famous art dealer, Daniel Cordier, who had predicted a brilliant career for her in the art world, told her, "You're screwed!" She also told me that the philosopher Cioran, with whom she was acquainted, once crossed the street when he saw her walking toward him! But other friends stuck with her, among them Maurice Béjart, for whom she had painted the scenery for his Buddhist-inspired ballet *Les Vainqueurs* and who remained her friend until his death, as did his principal dancer Jorge Donn. He even considered going to Darjeeling with my mother at the time. Of her painting, he wrote, "The labels 'abstraction' and 'realism' cease to exist before the authenticity of a painting that shimmers like an illumination."

Coming home from school one day—I must have been about fifteen at the time—I saw my mother painting on the floor, as was her habit, in the only spacious room of the apartment, which served her as both studio and bedroom. Armed with a rag soaked in turpentine, she was preparing to destroy a blue painting, some six feet tall, that she was not happy with. I, however, thought it beautiful enough to be worth saving. "I'll buy it," I shouted. "One franc!" The painting survived. It is now the sole large canvas to adorn her little bungalow in Dordogne. I'm afraid to say that I may never have paid her the franc in question, which, with interest, must surely amount today to a hefty debt I owe my one-hundred-year-old mother!

4

A NOMADIC CHILDHOOD

Savoy, Algeria, Mexico, Valmondois, Paris. My uncle, the navigator Jacques-Yves Le Toumelin, gives me a foretaste of the spiritual life.

The essence of what I wish to share does not lie in the ordinary events of what was, all told, a typical childhood. Like anyone else, I learned to ride a bike when I was little. I think that as a teenager I was less prone to the torments that afflicted other young people of my age. I was more romantic than passionate, more idealistic than obsessed with sex, more in love with nature than with the parties that my peers attended. The only time I ever entered a nightclub, I left again a few minutes later. In retrospect, I don't see anything particularly cautionary in my adolescent wanderings, a theme dear to the heart of many a writer more talented than I am.

My oldest memory, oddly enough, is of a cow. A very big cow in a manger in Savoy. To my child's eyes, it was the size of what I would now attribute to an elephant. I must have been two or maybe three. After that, nothing else for some time. My first memory lapse.

My father was assigned to a teaching position in a village in Algeria, near Tlemcen, for about a year, I believe, but I recall nothing about it. My next and more coherent memories after that were about crossing the Atlantic in the ocean liner *Île-de-France* with my mother and Ève. I was four. We were on our way to join my father, who had been appointed philosophy teacher in the French Lycée in Mexico City. What an adventure! There was so much to discover on the ship: the lifeboats, the immense smokestacks, all the different decks and the immensity of the ocean stretching out day after day before my amazed eyes. In the evenings, in the restaurant, I found it funny that everything we were about to eat had been elegantly inscribed in advance on sheets of white paper left on our table. In my cabin at night, with the lights out, I lay for ages with my eyes wide open, enjoying the motley clouds of luminous, multicolored points of light created by retinal persistence drifting slowly through the dark, fascinated by the shapes and colors.

I was expecting a long voyage, so vast did the ocean seem to me. And yet, a week later, there was New York on the horizon. The skyscrapers gradually revealed their majestic height as we approached. To my great regret, we were compelled to disembark. In the great city, I was especially awed by the countless bright signs that covered the buildings lining the streets and broad avenues. Because of my myopia, which had not yet been diagnosed, this patchwork of colored smudges bled into magnificent impressionist landscapes.

We flew to Mexico City on a Super Constellation. I thought that was a very pretty name. When we landed, my father came to pick us up in a long red convertible with cream-colored seats, which made a big impression on us.

We stayed in Mexico City for two years. I went to the Lycée kindergarten. We lived in a lovely house with a garden that was our playground. I retain a number of random memories of those days. One day, armed with a slingshot, I launched the few jewels my mother had inherited from her mom out the window to the poor children playing in the street. This well-intentioned bit of foolishness provoked neither drama nor punishment, but merely the commentary of an understanding mother. On birthdays, we hung piñatas from a beam—animals made of straw and a clay vase, which the children joyfully whacked with sticks until the vase broke and spilled a shower of multicolored candies over the group. I also remember a total eclipse of the sun. We observed its reflection on the surface of a pail filled with water through a shard of tinted glass that served as makeshift sunglasses.

On Sundays, my father sometimes took me to a bullfight in a nearby arena. I loved the sound of the trumpets and the shimmering colors of the toreadors' costumes, but the barbarity of that grim entertainment was not yet obvious to my young mind. The child very often considers whatever his parents do and show him to be normal. That is how he is taught to watch an animal being tortured to death without flinching. Everybody seemed to be overjoyed by it. As for the bull, he had no opinion on the matter. He had been killed. For the pleasure of the spectators. Some call it an art. The art of causing pain and death.

Among our family friends, Leonora Carrington, the famous surrealist painter who had once been married to Max Ernst, became my mother's best friend and inspired her style of painting at that time. They talked about going to Tibet together, a plan that their respective spouses, my father and Csiki Weisz, Leonora's second husband, ruled out as a harmless artistic pipe dream. During the Second World War, Csiki, a Hungarian photographer, had rescued thousands of negatives by the great photographers Robert Capa, whose work he printed; David Seymour, who would go on to found the Magnum Agency; and Gerda Taro. These negatives, unique and essential documentation of the Spanish Civil War and the birth of photojournalism, had a colorful and somewhat obscure story that has gone down in history under the legendary title "The Mexican Suitcase." It was indeed in Mexico that they reappeared three-quarters of a century after Robert Capa, a Jew and a communist, confided them to Csiki Weisz before fleeing Paris. Having traveled hither and yon, the precious photos eventually found their way to Cornell Capa, Robert's brother.[1]

And then there was Luis Buñuel, whose big dark eyes beneath thick black eyebrows intimidated me a little, although they masked a deep kindness, and Jomi Ascott, a young poet who comanaged the film library of the French Institute with my father and used to call me pretending to be the president of the Republic, Miguel Alemán. We had some very serious conversations, but I was not informed until years later that it had not actually been the president at the other end of the line. A neighbor, Helen, sometimes invited me over to her place. She instructed me to hold an egg-shaped stone between my hands and to close my eyes, and together we set out on a space journey across the immensity of the universe. I loved those interplanetary odysseys. The only ones I have ever taken to this day.

For holidays, we went to Acapulco, on the Pacific coast. We stayed in a cabana on the heights, under palm trees, next to a swimming pool. My mother says that, at night, under the stars, I would challenge her with philosophical riddles, such as, "All in all, mama, one day more is one day less," or "At the moment of death, the body stops. Consciousness goes on, of course, but what happens to speech?" My career as a philosopher ended there.

With a child's facility for assimilation, I soon learned Spanish, which I used to converse with my sister Ève. I'm sorry to say that I soon forgot it after we returned to France in 1952, despite the occasional chat with the Spanish grocer on the corner. My father was posted to Florence, Italy, and moved there with my mother and Ève. I was sent to live with my paternal grandmother, France Ricard, who lived in a suburb of Chambéry, in Savoy. She was a doting grandmother to whom I owe a great emotional debt, but she was also a very "proper" lady. We lived a very orderly life, and the house was kept impeccably tidy. When I had a cold, she treated me with vapor inhalations and wrapped my chest in mustard poultices that I had to endure for more than an hour at a stretch. I have been careful to avoid such treatment ever since.

Although I believe that I was a rather well-behaved child, I made more than my share of mistakes. Some have stayed with me, of course, like when, with my pal Jeannot, I used an air rifle to shoot a potato pellet into the rear end of a fat gentlemen digging in his garden, which earned us a fierce scolding from said gentleman and a good comeuppance at home. Another time, I was similarly punished when I used a bow made from an ash bough and homemade arrows to shoot at the frozen bedsheets hanging from the laundry line. The arrows made nice little round holes that looked very pretty to me, but which pleased my grandmother rather less. I remember that Jeannot and I used clothespins to attach pieces of cardboard to the frames of our bikes, which sounded like backfiring mopeds when they flicked against the spokes. I also remember a lady we sometimes passed in the street, pushing a cart and calling: "Rabbit skins . . . yop!" I never figured out if she was selling or buying.

As a widow, although of middle-class origins, my grandmother had financial troubles. Sometimes, a wealthy great-uncle from whom she had borrowed money came to visit from Marseille. I was sent from the room. "We have business to discuss," my grandmother told me. I was very impressed.

In 1953, I reunited with my mother and Ève and we moved with my paternal grandmother to the far more picturesque village of Valmondois, in the Seine-et-Oise department. We lived in an old two-story house. My father, who stayed in Florence until 1957, joined us during the school holidays. He lived in a big room upstairs with all his books. He was not to be disturbed while he was working.

Valmondois was the special place where my childhood was able to blossom. Every traditional trade was still practiced in that village from a bygone era. The blacksmith, a colossus of whom we were in awe, hammered away powerfully at red-hot horseshoes on his anvil. Shortly after our arrival, a neighboring farmer's wife came by to offer her wares to my mother: "I am Madame Poulet [meaning "chicken" in French]. I'm here with some eggs." The vegetable merchant came by every two days with his tarp-covered wagon pulled by a horse resigned to its fate. His cousin had gone off to America. "The country that was discovered by Michel Strogoff," he insisted, in a picturesque turn of phrase all his own.

In the late afternoon, we went to the farm to collect our milk in a tin pot. On the bank of the stream that crossed the valley, the Rû, there was a washhouse where the washerwomen gathered, noisily beating their linens with wooden paddles. One of them, old Virgine, bent with age, called out to us with a dazzling smile: "How happy we are! Look how white my linens are!"

At the end of the summer, the moonshiner set up his mobile still beside an earthen path and distilled alcohol from the local potatoes, whose residue accumulated in a heap that gave off a funny smell. The vapors of distilling alcohol remain my closest and sole experience of drink.

The winters were harsh, and we had no central heating. My sister and I curled up in our cold, damp beds. I suffered from joint pain, childhood rheumatism that the country doctor, a very proper gentlemen who always wore a hat and an overcoat, eruditely ascribed to a growth spurt. The kitchen was our gathering place, well warmed by the great stove that we regularly fed with gleaming chunks of coal, anthracite, or coke, which was of lesser quality but more affordable.

In the courtyard of the local school, we loved sliding across sheets of frozen snow before the schoolmaster spread sand or coarse salt to prevent one of us from breaking a bone. The playground was dominated by the three large Dague brothers. You definitely did not want to mess with "Little Dague" if you didn't want to have to answer to the "Big Dagues," who were no joking matter. At first, we had an old schoolmaster whose blonde daughter, who was very proud of her status as the teacher's girl, was the boys' darling. He was replaced by a teacher in glasses who rapped us on the fingers with an oaken ruler when we made mistakes writing with our Sergent Major dip pens. In his first singing class, our stern teacher turned bright red as his falsetto voice rang out: "No Jeanette, don't cry . . .". Most likely, he was embarrassed at having to engage in such a frivolous activity as singing, which did not show him to his best vantage. We also had to memorize "La Marseillaise," a war song that left me perplexed—I couldn't understand how blood could be "impure" and I had no desire to "form my battalions." We also had to learns poems by heart, which I really enjoyed, such as "Little man, pick your apples / Ah, the fine smell of apples! / Ah, the fine smell of fall!"

I tried my hand at poetry, but I had little aptitude for it, so it seemed just as clever to copy out verses I found in the family library. I made my father burst out laughing when I presented him with one of my "compositions," which ended with the following lines: "Leaning forward, in their white caravels, / They watched new stars rise in an unknown sky / From the ocean depths." He, too, had read José-Maria de Heredia.

Ève's talent as a poet announced itself in a more innocent style. In one history assignment, she wrote that "the Gauls lived in beehives and their chief was named Version Hectorix" and "Pasteur inoculated cowboys with rabies." Beyond her fertile imagination, which she has retained her entire life, Ève already showed evidence of the admirable qualities of generosity and selflessness that she would later put to good use in her work at Saint Anne's Hospital. She spontaneously took charge of those who had been abandoned and befriended Boris, a child the social services had fostered with a wet nurse. Boris was always full of joy and liked to say, opening his arms wide, "Life is this big!" and, with implacable logic, "Life is not for dying, since it's life."

On summer nights, I learned the names of the stars with the oldest son of our neighbors, who would go on to become a Jesuit priest.

The most prominent clan in the village was the Geoffroy de Chaume family. In Mexico City, my parents had become friends with one of the sons, François, a diplomat, and his wife Nelita; it was they who had suggested that we go live in Valmondois. "Madame Mother" was a dowager with a cracked voice and a delicate face crowned with white hair drawn up under a scarf. She seemed to be straight out of one of those ancient oil paintings. She had ten children who lived in various countries but often all reunited in the family home. The house was guarded by a tall gate of solid wood painted a washed-out blue. It opened with a shrill creak onto a paved courtyard, at the far end of which a terraced garden rose in tiers. The entry hall was dominated by a telephone that was recessed in a wooden box and operated by a brass crank, one of very few in the village (we ourselves did not have one), from which you could call the operator in L'Isle Adam, the neighboring village, to be connected to the desired party.

The most attractive room in that enormous residence was the music room, situated on the garden floor. That immense chamber, with its worm-eaten floorboards and its purple velvet hangings, was the depository of numerous instruments, from a grand piano to a French horn, not to mention a harp and vast array of recorders, set out here and there or hung on the walls. All the children were excellent musicians. The oldest daughter, Cécile, who lived in Spain, was a concert pianist. Antoine was a harpsichordist and musicologist of renown. Another son, Jean-Pierre, who had lived and married in Laos, played the recorder, as well as all sorts of bizarre instruments, including iron and bamboo mouth harps, Mexican terra-cotta flutes in the shape of a tortoise, and many others that we listened to in delight. I attended the family concerts fascinated, yet saddened and little embarrassed at not knowing how to play any instrument. Years later, as a teenager, I returned to Valmondois and was thrilled to finally have a turn to play for Jean-Pierre and a few friends. It was a transcription of a cello suite by Bach, which I played on the classical guitar that my teacher and luthier Christian Aubin had made for me with his own hands. I also learned how to play a decent mouth harp.

My father's mother had loaned my parents money to buy a little apartment in Paris. They rented it out to help pay off the loan. We moved in once most of the cost had been recouped, while my grandmother went to live in Marseille, near her second son, Michel Ricard, who had been an officer in Indochina during the war, and later in Mauritania, and whom she worried about a great deal, as well as other members of the family. When we were still living in Valmondois, Uncle Michel, whom I loved very much, would come to visit us on his big Puch motorcycle, which fascinated me. The move to Paris came as a shock to me. I was only ten and was forced to abandon the natural world in which I had flourished for the gloom and asphalt of the city. My father wanted to live in the capital and also wanted us to pursue our education there. François Geoffroy-Dechaume had recently turned over one of his houses on the Valmondois hill for several months to two Tibetan monks who had sought refuge in France, and when my mother pleaded to stay in the countryside, my father responded sarcastically by pointing at me and saying, "You'll be wanting him to learn Tibetan now, no doubt!" Little did he know.

In 1956, I entered the sixth grade at the Lycée Janson de Sailly, where I did not distinguish myself. I was bored; I missed the open air and freedom of village life; everything seemed formal there, disembodied and confining. The school wanted me to retake the eighth grade. My mother went to see my homeroom teacher and told him, "But sir, my son is intelligent!" "All the mothers say that," he told her, adding, "When I talk, his eyes glaze over." My father, who taught philosophy at the Lycée Jean-Baptist Say, had me admitted there to avoid such an embarrassing interruption of my education. At my new school, I stood out more for my talents as a soccer goalie than for my academic prowess. I returned to Lycée Janson the following year, and over the course of my final years of schooling I made real progress in certain subjects, for the simple reason that I genuinely liked my teachers in history, geography, and physics. In fact, I often came first in those classes.

We often went to the Alps or to Le Croisic, in Brittany, for the holidays. Because my grandmother went fishing in the company of other "fine people"—including the local Breton ladies, who still wore their lovely white headdresses, all lined up on the harbor quay—I was convinced that this activity was altogether respectable. It wasn't until I was thirteen that

I came to understand its aberrant nature. This about-face was provoked by my best friend's sister, on whom I had a crush (although she paid no attention to my undeclared passion). One day, she looked me straight in the eye and asked, "You fish too?" It was as if a wall had been torn down—I was suddenly aware of the cruelty of an activity that consisted of inflicting pain and ending a life for the sole aim of having fun. I swore off fishing forever. All it took was for me to put myself in the place of the fish for a few seconds, to imagine how I would feel if someone jerked me from the water with a great big hook in my mouth. Without yet knowing the word, I had just discovered "empathy."

I had long wanted to become a doctor, a surgeon even, but once I had passed my baccalaureate exams and been admitted into advanced math, I wavered between medicine and physics. "There are plenty of doctors," my father told me. "Biology is the science of the future." I heeded his advice for once and enrolled in the Jussieu Faculty of Science, majoring in biology, physics, and chemistry. My father had instilled a taste for intellectual rigor in me. He was a hard worker and a journalist who knew and conscientiously verified his sources. If he were still running *L'Express* today, he would have been merciless about "fake news" and other crazy theories. He had an incredible memory and was able to accurately cite a vast number of articles and books that he had read. Born Jean-François Ricard, he adopted a pen name one day as he sat at an outdoor table at a bistro with his good friend, the historian Pierre Nora. He wanted to take a pseudonym so he could write pamphlets critical of the public intellectuals of the day—such as his "Why Do We Need Philosophers?" and "The Cabal of Idolaters"—while preventing his polemics from influencing his lycée students. The bistro was called Chez Revel. He'd found his name: Jean-François Revel.

I was eighteen when my father left my mother. It was the logical conclusion of a process that had begun a good while earlier, and it had little impact on me. My mother reassumed her maiden name, Yahne Le Toumelin, which explains why my sister and I have different family names from both our parents. Shortly before my first trip to India, my father married journalist Claude Sarraute. They had a son, Nicolas. Born in 1966, he was still a little boy at the time, and we lived in different households. We did not grow close until much later. Nowadays, my mother speaks of my father with affection tinged by sadness; he had not treated her very well. Even so, she went to visit him when he was hospitalized in Dordogne, not long before his death, when he was barely conscious, and whispered a few tender words in his ear. My mother, who had always been a kind and generous person, never expressed animosity about anyone and spoke of my father without anger. Even so, at a later date, when I was editing texts for a book devoted to her work, *Lumière, Rire du ciel*, I found some less biddable words, written in her own hand, concerning intellectuals like my father and, by extension, he himself: "He was an intellectual stuffed to the gills with concepts, who drank too much and ran a business making opinion marmalade—a major magazine."[2] My mother always had a knack for aphorisms. "We should do 'girlcotts' instead of 'boycotts,'" I once heard her opine, "and send 'e-females' instead of 'e-males.'" When some serendipitous event occurred, she sometimes said, "Praises to you, Saint-chronization!"

My mother's brother, Jacques-Yves Le Toumelin, was like a second father to me. A pioneer of solo navigation, between 1949 and 1952 he sailed around the world in a thirty-foot Norwegian cutter, the *Kurun*, with no motor. His book about this odyssey, *Kurun, Around the World*, remains a classic in the literature of solitary seafaring. Several decades after his "leisurely jaunt around the world," he was stunned to hear about the records set by navigators sailing nonstop around the globe at speeds barely conceivable in his day. After his second voyage, to the Antilles, he had planned to sail India—a dream that, unfortunately, he was never able to realize.

He was a great inspiration and encouraged me to read many of the metaphysical and spiritual books that occupied the shelves of his library. He was an avid reader of the Vedanta (the Shankaracharya Upanishads), Sufism (Ibn Arabi), and Meister Eckhart and the *Little Russian Philokalia* on the prayer of the heart, and was a great admirer of René Guénon and his metaphysical writings. He loved and admired books and covered each new acquisition with glassine to protect its cover. Immoderately meticulous, he reminded Ève and me that a sailor could not afford to neglect anything on his boat, at the risk of putting himself in danger. Not content to confine this principle to the *Kurun*, he extended it to his twenty-five-acre estate Gwenved, on the Pen Bron peninsula. He enlisted us to spray the herbicide Roundup on the patches of bramble and gorse he had cut down. It is sadly possible that this played a role in sickening my sister, who developed Parkinson's disease at the very young age of forty-three; we now understand the pernicious nature of such products and their connection to that illness. It was on that vast estate, acquired rather late in life, that my maternal grandparents spent their final years. My grandfather, Victor Le Toumelin, was a master commander of three-mast sailing ships, and my grandmother Yvonne, a lively woman, was a nurse in the First World War, alongside her sister. She had plenty of character and knew how to get her own way. At ninety, she was still driving her Citroën 2CV and occasionally ran the red lights in Guérande.

I have many fond memories of dinners around the long family dinner table of solid oak, overlooking the tranquil waters of the Traict du Croisic, with a few good local friends, especially Jean and Nanie Desnos, with whom I sailed every summer on their sailboat, the *Altaïr*. Our conversations went on deep into the night. We talked about faraway lands and explored a variety of spiritual traditions.

Travelers and explorers of varying degrees of eccentricity often stopped by to see my uncle. I remember Marcel Bardiaux, who crossed the Atlantic alone forty times, and Bernard Moitessier, the "vagabond of the seas," as he called himself, and the "Balata King," a jovial little man covered head to toe in tattoos, who showed up with his entire family and who owed his nickname to his art of crafting figurines from the latex produced by the balata tree, which he sold throughout the Antilles. I also recall this great scar-faced oddball decked out in cowboy hat, leather wristband, and boots, arriving straight from Mongolia at the wheel of a bright red American convertible with a Central Asian shepherd dog as big as a calf in the back seat. This was typical of the picaresque circle of friends around my uncle, who once stopped by the home of one of these acquaintances as he was passing through Paris, only to find a terse message pinned to his front door: "Off to Timbuktu on foot."

Every night, in his fine, methodical handwriting, my uncle marked down the salient events of the day—work-related and social—in his datebook. He used an ink pen that he took great care of and kept with him all his life. On his desk he also had a marine chronometer that kept precise time and a photo of the great Indian sage Ramana Maharishi, whose glowing face inspired me in turn. Above it, a magnificent watercolor by the celebrated seascape painter Marin-Marie showed the *Kurun* tossed on a high sea.

In his maturity, he gave up his life as a "solo sailor," both at sea and on land, in order to marry. His wife, Josée, gave birth to three children—Marie-Ange, Victor, and Lucie—who brought him great joy and today oversee the unique heritage of Gwenved, which in Breton means "white land," referring to the "circle of felicity and plenitude," a small and peaceful enclave on the Guérande peninsula, lodged between the 25,000 acres of salt marshes, the Traict du Croisic lagoon, the woods of Pen Bron, and the Atlantic Ocean.

After my trip to Darjeeling, I often invited my uncle whenever any great Tibetan master was visiting. In this way, he was able to meet Kalu Rinpoche, one of the first Tibetan masters to teach in the West, and Dudjom Rinpoche, a very impressive master whom I myself had had the good fortune to meet on my first visit to India. Deeply marked by his encounter with Dudjom Rinpoche, every day until he died, my uncle, with his typical mindfulness, recited the mantra that the master had assigned him, using the rosary he had given him. He had met a person who had achieved the fullest spiritual realization.

In his later years, my uncle and I would sometimes spend long minutes without saying a word, sitting side by side between conversations in the bright great room of his house, with its enormous windows. It held his vast library, his work desk, magnificent antique models of three-masters, a great stuffed blowfish bristling with spines, a long table of solid wood piled high with beautiful books, a granite chimney, and a telescope with which we observed the seabirds that were abundant in those days, barnacle geese and waders from the Great North. Sixty years later, their steep decline is as indisputable as it is heartbreaking. We now know that worldwide populations of wild animals have shrunk by two-thirds since 1970; that is the tragic imprint that the super-predator that we have become has stamped on the wild world.

I was in Nepal when my uncle died at the age of ninety. His daughter told me that, with his dying breath, he spoke the name of the eldest son of Kangyur Rinpoche, Pema—"Lotus"—who had visited him several times at Gwenved. Had he appeared in his deathbed visions?

I think back to my family, my dear ones, with tenderness and realize how lucky I was to have had such a happy childhood, untainted by adversity and surrounded by loving parents and family. I developed a passion for ornithology (I banded birds, one of which, a willow warbler, was found in South Africa!) after meeting André Fatras, a pioneer of animal photography, who also introduced me to photography in general. I also loved astronomy (I even began building my own telescope, a project that I soon abandoned) and classical music, thanks to the records that my father gave me and that I bought with my own pocket money at the store right across the street from the Lyçée Janson. Although there was nothing remarkable about my school career, I received a solid education through which I progressed at my own pace all the way to a degree in biology, a discipline in which I held a sincere and abiding interest. And yet something was missing, there was a void in me that neither the values nor the goals we are offered by contemporary Western culture were able to fill. When the moment came to make the decisive decision that would determine the course of my future, I had no role model for living and no clear sense of direction to give meaning to my life. I knew what I didn't want: a calm and boring career until the end of my days. Deep down, I felt that human life harbored immense potential, but at that I age I was totally incapable of imagining what it might look like.

Hurtling at dawn down immaculate fields of spring snow as lustrous as velvet, sailing under a sweet breeze and a luminous blue sky on a boat belonging to friends of my seafaring uncle—all this gave me exalted feelings of communion with nature and even, sometimes, with the world in its entirety. Deep down, I was far from being sad or unhappy, but the spiritual dimension that makes everything possible and every day worth living was still absent.

In my teenage years, I was lucky to meet a great many people who were all remarkable in their own way. In our family apartment on the rue de la Tour, a parade of Parisian intellectuals, writers, and philosophers such as

Stéphane Lupasco, Louis Althusser, André Fermigier, and Olivier Todd, to name just a few, as well as painters, including Pierre Soulages and his wife Colette, Georges Mathieu, Hans Hartung and Zao Wou-Ki, stopped by to visit with my parents. My mother cooked beautifully for all of them. On vacation, we were sometimes joined by Jean Delsarte, an eminent mathematician from the Bourbaki group. I also met many great musicians. At the age of sixteen, I was privileged to have lunch in a Parisian restaurant with Igor Stravinsky and his assistant, at the invitation of a friend of my parents, a correspondent for the *New York Times* who had arranged to interview him and knew of my passion for classical music. He signed a score for his opus *Agon* that I had brought with me, with the dedication, "To Matthieu, *Agon*, which I am very fond of myself." This ballet contains a brief mandolin section that recalls the most beautiful Bach gavottes.

As rich and instructive as such encounters might be, I was perplexed, confounded by the fact that there seemed to be no correlation between the particular genius of such individuals and whether they were or were not very especially good human beings. No matter how brilliant someone might be, intelligence, creativity, and knowledge seemed to have no direct link to goodness or badness, happiness or misery. Some philosophers were friendly and warm; others were appalling. The same was true for musicians, gardeners, scholars, and carpenters. Someone once asked me who my role model was. I didn't know what to say—the times offered no popular luminary on whom to project myself. Pelé is a great reference point for anyone who plays soccer, Sviatoslav Richter for anyone who wants to play piano, Dostoyevsky for anyone who loves literature, and Bobby Fischer for those who are fond of chess. Perhaps, in those days, I may have wished to possess the particular genius of these exceptional people, but not necessarily their quality of being. Who would want to *be* Bobby Fischer, who, besides being one of the most brilliant chess players ever, was notoriously deranged and obnoxious? We rarely meet anyone who makes us think, "I wish I were like him, or her."

All that changed when I met Kangyur Rinpoche. His quality of being showed me what was waiting at the end of the road—a road of transformation that leads from delusion to wisdom, from suffering to freedom, and from selfishness to unconditional benevolence. An irreversible process would be set in motion—but the moment for changing my life had not yet arrived.

5

THE INSTITUT PASTEUR

Five years of cellular genetics research in the laboratory of Nobel laureate François Jacob. The launch of my scientific career placed on hold after my doctoral thesis.

Upon my return from my first trip to India, I applied to join the laboratory run by François Jacob at the Institut Pasteur. By a happy coincidence, at the very same time a mutual friend, Professor Pierre Aboulker, happened to mention to François Jacob that I was building a harpsichord. Who knows whether François Jacob believed that this demonstrated a broad range of aptitudes or whether the anecdote influenced his decision? However it may be, after a brief interview, he hired me. The truth is, I never had the intention or the ability to build a harpsichord. I had had high hopes of acquiring one from the United Kingdom, built by the famous London craftsman William de Blaise, but I abandoned that idea after my trip to India because it would have exhausted my savings. The fact remains that my admission to the Institut Pasteur may well have rested on a misunderstanding!

I was only twenty-one when I had my first interview with François Jacob; I had graduated from high school at sixteen, then done four and a half years of university. My future boss advised me to take a master's degree in genetics at the French National Centre for Scientific Research in Gif-sur-Yvette to deepen my knowledge in the field before plunging into research. Everything went my way, thanks in particular to the events of May 1968. The universities were mostly shut down because of the prevailing unrest, so I was awarded my degree in genetics based on the recommendation of the faculty, without having to take the final exam. In the fall of 1968, with my mother gone to India for several months, we had the family apartment to ourselves—me, my sister, who had begun her studies as a speech therapist, and Christine Machenaud, my girlfriend, with whom I would live throughout my years of research.

I was very lucky to be part of François Jacob's prestigious cellular genetics unit during those years. In 1965, he, André Lwoff, and Jacques Monod had been awarded the Nobel Prize in Medicine for their work on the mechanism of genetic expression and regulation. Famous as he was, the laboratory was small, five rooms in all: François Jacob's office, and that of his secretary; a large room assigned to the Japanese researcher Yukinori Hirota, with whom I was to work; and another occupied by my colleague and friend Maurice Hofnung, who was a few years older than me and had already begun his thesis work. Jean-Pierre Changeux—a neurobiologist well-known to biologists for his Monod-Wyman-Changeux model—had another room a little farther down the hall. Jacques Monod's laboratory at the far end of the hallway was barely any bigger. I was therefore placed with my immediate mentor, Yukinori Hirota, a demanding scientist with whom I got along very well. Two lab assistants, Chantal and Marie-Claude, whom I also liked very much, helped us with our work. So it was that I launched my doctoral thesis and my brief career as a research scientist.

In our ground-floor digs in the departments of molecular biology and cellular genetics at the Institut Pasteur, there reigned a most stimulating intellectual exuberance. Animated discussions took place in the labs, in the library, and at all times in the long corridor that led to the work rooms.

The atmosphere was one of discovery and creativity, but also of good humor. Moving from one lab to the next, François Jacob whistled the theme of Mozart's quintet for clarinet, while Jean-Pierre Changeux hummed opera melodies. David Perrin, son of the physicist François Perrin, wore two watches, one on each wrist. Why? "No reason," he answered, when I inquired as to the reason for this novelty. My own wrist was adorned with red cords that had been blessed by Kangyur Rinpoche and other teachers; in the neighboring labs, there was a rumor that I had become the "chief of a tribe in Kashmir."

And yet India was very far away, even if I found myself there every day in my thoughts. Early in the morning, before leaving for Pasteur, and again when I got home at night, I never failed to devote at least half an hour to meditation. The morning half-hour in particular imparted a special flavor to the day and put its stamp on my thoughts, like a reference point and a source of inspiration. If circumstances prevented me from practicing, I felt as if something were missing from my spiritual equilibrium, just as something would have been missing from my physical hygiene if I had neglected to wash in the morning or to walk the kilometer to the metro that took me to the Institut Pasteur.

At lunch, André Lwoff, the discreet patriarch whom everyone held in the highest respect, along with Jacob, Monod, and the visiting researchers from abroad and most members of the two laboratories, gathered around a long table under a glass roof behind the library. Each brought his own lunchbox, prepared at home, and conversation proceeded apace, for the most part focused on our work.

Every so often, François Jacob stopped in at our lab to ask about our progress or stuck his head in at the door to invite me into his office. "What's new?" was how he generally began his inquiries into the latest developments. I summarized the state of my research for him. He asked questions and offered suggestions that went straight to the heart of the matter, then, taking a puff or two on his pipe, he would ask, "How is the colossal Hirota?" (although small in stature, Yukinori Hirota had boundless energy), and then he usually ended with, "Okay . . . all good." I enjoyed good personal relations with François Jacob, respectful and nurtured by affection that, I like to believe, was mutual. Gifted with great and generous intelligence, he could nonetheless seem a little distant, as if a shadow of sorrow hovered about him. But he was a keen observer and a pleasant man endowed with a strong sense of humor. He is among those mentors who have left their mark on me.

I was studying cellular division in a bacterium that is widely used in research, *Escherichia coli*, a colon bacillus that divides every thirty minutes. Fate smiled on me—I soon came to see that, by increasing the salt content of the medium in which the bacteria were grown, some mutant strains that stopped dividing in high temperatures and formed long filaments could be made to begin dividing again. I delved further into this "salt effect" and also identified a certain number of genes on the chromosome involved in cellular division. These discoveries allowed me to complete my doctoral thesis rather quickly, at the age of twenty-six.

During the years I spent at the Institut Pasteur, it was fashionable to be a Trotskyite, and like many others I was unaware of the atrocities committed by the Bolsheviks and their successors, or of the horrors perpetrated by the Maoist regime. It was even thought to be in good taste, among some of my young fellow researchers, to leave Mao's *Little Red Book* lying around on the table, at least until Simon Leys, a friend of my father's, published his devastating book on the Great Helmsman, *The Chairman's New Clothes*, in 1971, which nevertheless elicited cries of outrage from the Paris intelligentsia. Aragon thought that Mao was "just great," while Sartre believed that "unlike Stalin, Mao [had] never fallen into error," blind as they were to the fifty million deaths for which he was personally responsible. My best friend, Pierrot, was from a family of ardent communists, and he and I had lively arguments with his parents. At that time, I briefly joined the youth branch of the Unified Socialist Party, of which my father was also a member. One day, I attended a meeting that was so boring that my interest in militant politics evaporated on the spot. Later, as I traveled extensively in the 1970s, I informed my father of all the atrocities committed in Tibet, where one-fifth of the population ended up dying in Chinese forced labor camps, the *laogai*, and of the "cultural genocide" that was perpetrated there. He became one of the first public intellectuals to denounce, in particular on his broadcasts on Europe 1 radio, the brutal stranglehold of the Chinese communist regime over the Roof of the World and the international community's failure to react. Later, in 2000, he published *La Grande Parade*, in which he denounced the perverse submissiveness of many French public intellectuals and politicians to the Stalinist and Maoist regimes.

The five years that I spent at the Pasteur, as a research associate at the National Centre for Scientific Research, turned out to be highly formative. Under the benevolent direction of François Jacob and Yukinori Hirota, I mastered the scientific methodology that later proved to be extremely useful to me.

A scientific hypothesis must lend itself not only to experimental verification, but also to the possibility of being refuted by evidence that, should it emerge, will prove its falsehood. If a theory is formulated in such a way that it is invariably verified, regardless of the facts observed, it does not advance the status of understanding. As Karl Popper explains, a theory that, in principle, cannot be refuted—that is "unfalsifiable"—is not a scientific theory; it is an ideology.

"Science" can be defined as the entirety of knowledge and the means of investigation that permit the acquisition of a correct understanding of reality. Science can be applied to highly varied areas of investigation: logic and mathematics; the measurable data of the physical world; the organization, laws, and dynamics of the interdependent systems that make up our universe; life in general, and the functioning of our brain in particular; the behavior of living things, as well as the modalities of their lived experience; and so on. Science includes every possible and conceivable realm of investigation so long as such investigation is undertaken in a rigorous and conscientious manner that draws us closer to reality and allows us to infer its nature. In no case can or must science alienate us from the real or dismiss or deform it through mental constructs. These reference points are invaluable in a world where the Internet and debate are flooded with fabrications, each more improbable than the last.

I have often been asked—and I have certainly asked myself—whether my interest in Buddhism, its philosophy and practice, has alienated me from the scientific approach. That might well have occurred, but it has not. One of the central tenets of Buddhist philosophy is to bridge the gap between appearances and reality, that is, to verify whether or not our impressions, perceptions, and beliefs are commensurate with reality. Buddhism shows us how, out of delusion, we accept a distorted vision of reality when we fail to question the validity of our perceptions—how we accept as permanent that which is constantly changing and how we see autonomous beings where there is only a dynamic flux of interdependent phenomena. Like science, Buddhism stresses the means of acquiring "valid knowledge"—*pramana* in Sanskrit. That is why the Dalai Lama always insists on the need to tirelessly analyze phenomena until you reach a conclusion that cannot be invalidated by logic or refuted by an impartial and critical audit of reality.

Buddhism calls on us to engage in an analysis of external reality and how we perceive it, but its main focus of investigation is the functioning of the mind. How can the mind create worlds of suffering or, contrarily, free us from error that leads to suffering? The areas investigated by modern science and Buddhism do not overlap entirely, but they share a desire to understand the world of physical and mental phenomena and to apprehend their true nature.

I have therefore never felt any tension between my scientific research in molecular biology alongside François Jacob and his team and my apprenticeship in Buddhism under my teachers. The only divergence I felt in the early 1970s was in the lack of consistency between my deepest aspirations and the way in which I was living my life. As the years passed, punctuated by summer visits to Darjeeling, I came to see that when I was at Pasteur, my mind was constantly drawn to Darjeeling, whereas, once I was in Darjeeling, Pasteur was soon forgotten.

6

SEVEN ROUND TRIPS AND A ONE-WAY

Between 1967 and 1972, I spend my holidays in the presence of my teacher and receive his instructions. I inform my father that I intend to move on from biological research to the path of enlightenment.

Every year between 1968 and 1972, as summer neared, I looked forward with unalloyed joy to my return to my teacher, Kangyur Rinpoche. Once the plane took flight, every hour and every country over which I flew was colored by the knowledge that I was that much closer to Darjeeling. I saw my teacher's house in my mind; I imagined him sitting, glowing with wisdom and compassion; I projected myself into his presence. Every journey deepened my ties to him and heightened my desire to devote myself entirely to my spiritual practice under his guidance.

When I arrived in Darjeeling in 1968, I learned that Kangyur Rinpoche had moved to the hamlet of Rose Bank, south of Darjeeling, to a little two-room wooden house squeezed in among others. The interior, however, was very similar to what I remembered of the other home. My reunion with my teacher was powerfully emotional. I resumed my meditations in his presence, and that year, through the intermediary of his son Tulku Pema Wangyal, he gave me very deep meditation guidance aimed at destroying attachment to the solid reality of phenomena. It wasn't until many years later, when I practiced it again in the context of practice on the gradual path of Tibetan Buddhism—which allows the student to rise through levels depending on his progress—that I truly understood how lucky I had been to receive this guidance so early in my practice.[1] I put it into practice assiduously, sitting across from my teacher in that rather dark little room with the low ceiling. Rinpoche sat with his back to a little window. He wore a red shirt and a thick woolen cape around his waist. There was always a cup of tea and a few other objects on the little wooden table beside him.

As I meditated one day, Rinpoche suddenly threw his *mala* across the room. It landed in my lap, between my legs crossed in the lotus position. Tulku Pema Wangyal, his oldest son, told me simply, "That is Rinpoche's *mala*." I didn't know what to think. This was beyond anything I was able to grasp. A little uneasily, I responded politely but awkwardly, "But Rinpoche uses it all the time. How will he recite his mantras?" Kangyur Rinpoche burst out laughing and showed me how he was also able to count mantras on his fingers: he placed his thumb on the first joint of his index finger, then the second, and so on until he reached the last joint and tip of his ring finger, making ten. Tulku Pema Wangyal later explained that Rinpoche had used this rosary almost his entire life and that he had recited no fewer than three hundred million mantras of his tutelary deity, Vajrakilaya. For a sense of scale, a practicant who recited mantras from morning to night might possibly complete one hundred million mantras (*tongyur* in Tibetan) in three years. The *mala* was made of rudraksha, the red-orange pit of a stone fruit covered with rough bumps. After many years of use, these beads were now completely smooth and dark brown. The two ends of the string on which the beads were strung passed through a hole pierced through a piece of red coral and were then tied together in a knot.

I cherish this *mala* as if it were one of my most precious possessions, and I long wore it around my neck like a sacred relic. But perhaps because of my unworthiness or because it dried out when it was not used in reciting mantras, the beads began to crack one after the other with the passing years. Whenever one broke, I saved it in a reliquary or put it in some high place where no one would find it, making a wish that the bead, laden with the blessings of my teacher, would spread goodness to anyone who happened by. Today, the remains of that *mala* are preserved in a *gao* (a little reliquary) that I wear on my chest.

Some ten days after I arrived for my second stay with Kangyur Rinpoche, he told me that he would be leaving to attend a grand ceremony in Ghum, at the invitation of Dudjom Rinpoche, the highly respected head of the Nyingmapa tradition. It was to last ten days and ten nights, which meant that I would not see my teacher again before I left. When the moment came to say our goodbyes, I was overcome by emotion. I sat close by him on a little stool. My tears began to flow uncontrollably. Kangyur Rinpoche tried to console me; he took my hand in his and repeated a gesture alternating between his chest and mine. Tulku Pema Wangyal told me, "He is giving you his heart," adding, "You will never be apart."

On my trips to Darjeeling, I had the opportunity to meet with several other great teachers. One of them, in 1968, was the sixteenth Karmapa, Rangjung Rigpe Dorje, who radiated an especially majestic aura and unconditional compassion. It was he who had advised my mother to take the vows of a nun. The "Buddha Karmapa," as he was sometimes called, lived in the large monastery of Rumtek, in Sikkim, a little Himalayan kingdom at the foot of Kangchenjunga that was still semi-independent from India at the time. On another occasion, I was staying in Kolkata with a lama when we learned that the Karmapa was passing through that Bengali megalopolis. He met with us in the hotel where he was staying. After our chat, I needed to make a detour to the toilets. As I was leaving, I crossed paths with the Karmapa as he was going in. When he saw me, he graced me with the most luminous smile I have ever seen on a human face. It felt as if the sun had suddenly pierced the clouds and caused an ordinary landscape to shimmer ethereally. The encounter, which lasted only a few seconds, remains etched in my memory.

At Rumtek, I also had the opportunity to attend the black crown ceremony, one of the most solemn events there is, in sharp contrast to the simple and spontaneous way in which the Karmapa welcomed all those who came to him. Preceded by musicians, the Karmapa entered the main temple of the monastery and took his place on a throne. While the monks invoked the masters of their spiritual lineage and made an offering of a mandala depicting the universe, the Karmapa donned the red headdress of the *panditas*, the scholars of India, which lamas wear at crucial moments in their rituals.

Then, to the sound of *gyalings*—double-reeded woodwinds—a monk presented the Karmapa with a small chest, painted with multicolored symbols, containing the precious black crown wrapped in fine silk. Noble and dignified, the Karmapa removed the red headdress and took the black crown in both hands; he placed it delicately on his own head and held it steady with his right hand, perfectly motionless, throughout the rest of the ceremony. It was explained to me that he was visualizing himself in the form of the buddha of compassion, Avalokiteshvara, while silently reciting the six-syllable mantra, *Om mani padme hum. Om* is a syllable of good omen that opens many mantras; *mani* signifies "jewel" and refers to the altruistic wish to attain enlightenment for the good of all beings; *padme* means "lotus" and indicates the Buddha nature present at the heart of our mind, even if we are under the yoke of error, like the immaculate lotus that grows in the mud of a swamp; the last syllable, *hum*, gives the mantra its efficacy.

It is said that, in the twelfth century, the first Karmapa, Düsum Khyenpa, had a vision in which a multitude of *dakinis*—female celestial spirits whose Tibetan name, *khandro*, means "those who move through the sky (of ultimate truth)"—offered him a black crown made from their own hair. Over the course of the centuries, many lamas and advanced practitioners, including the thirteenth Dalai Lama, have seen the black crown appear spontaneously on the Karmapa's head. A physical replica of the crown was presented to the fifth Karmapa and has been used ever since in ceremonies requiring it.

For ten full minutes, the shrill and hieratic sound of two *gyalings* rang out in one uninterrupted note while the Karmapa wore the crown. He manifested the full power of enlightenment without veils. His gaze remained fixed in space, straight ahead, as if he were contemplating infinity. His immutable face lucidly expressed the ultimate aspect of the Buddha state of being, the *dharmakaya*. Time seemed to stand still.

In an audience with the Karmapa, I asked him whether someone who has attained enlightenment sees the world in its entirety as also being "enlightened. "That's right," he answered. "An enlightened person has a perfectly pure vision of beings and phenomena. He sees the Buddha nature in every being and perceives the primordial purity of phenomena, beyond the duality of beautiful and ugly, pleasing and unpleasing, friend and enemy.[2] At the same time, he overflows with boundless compassion for those who are unaware of that essential nature of sentient beings and the world, and who suffer in consequence." That was one of my first introductions to the concept of "pure vision" that is so central to Tibetan Buddhism.

In December 1969, I was so impatient to see Kangyur Rinpoche again that I put all my savings into a plane ticket and instead of waiting for the next summer holiday for my yearly visit spent several days with him during the winter holidays.

In Kolkata, I was told that Indian Airlines was on strike. I could not pursue my journey. Trying to proceed by train would eat into the brief week I had to spend in Darjeeling. I had to find a flight. I heard that a group of American tourists had chartered a plane for Bagdogra Airport, gateway to my final destination, Darjeeling. The aircraft was about to take off. In those days, nobody cared about issues of security and the tarmac was open to anyone. I ran up to the aircraft, an old Dakota DC-3 prop plane. I introduced myself to the Americans at the foot of the stairway and asked if they would be so kind as to take me with them. I offered to pay my full fare, of course, but they categorically refused to allow me on board. I pleaded my case, but in vain. I was left on the tarmac, deflated. An Indian in an old, grease-stained uniform had observed the whole episode. He approached me and asked what was going on. Having heard me out, he said, "I'm the pilot. I'll take you as a member of the crew." I scurried on board, saying nothing as I filed past the American tourists, and followed the pilot as we climbed—DC-3s are steeply sloped when parked—toward the front of the plane. I took my place on the rumble seat behind the pilot and copilot, and we took off. I exulted over my good fortune and the prospect of an exhilarating ride in the cockpit. Ten minutes later, the pilot engaged the automatic pilot, stood up, and gestured for me to take his seat. Somewhat puzzled, I complied with a touch of excitement mixed with nerves. He proceeded to lie down between the two pilot seats, unfolded a newspaper to cover his face, and went to sleep. Stunned, I turned to the copilot. He, too, was asleep. The radio operator, sitting behind me, was bobbing his head and nodding off intermittently. I could just imagine the Americans' reaction if they only knew who the only person in charge of the plane was! An hour later, as we approached Bagdogra, an alarm went off—"bip, bip, bip." The pilot woke up with a start and took control of the instruments, which I had been careful not to touch.

Upon arrival, we disembarked ahead of the passengers. A little table set with tea, cookies, and a sign that said "crew members" awaited us on the lawn beside the landing strip. I was invited to take a seat as a full-fledged crew member. As I enjoyed a nice cup of spiced tea, the American tourists made their way to the terminal. They looked at me with surprise, curiosity, and mild irritation. The pilot refused any monetary contribution from me. I thanked him profusely—he had made it possible for me to reunite with my teacher.

That winter, Kangyur Rinpoche had moved again and was now living in the two upstairs rooms of the home of Tenzing Norgay, the Sherpa who, alongside Edmund Hillary, was the first man to climb Mount Everest and was also a student of Kangyur Rinpoche. In fact, the designation "Sherpa" had been assigned to him incorrectly, as it is to many other guides and porters from the region who accompany mountain climbers on their dangerous ascents. The Sherpas are a Nepali ethnic group from the high Himalayan valleys. Tenzing Norgay was Tibetan. He was very friendly and deeply devoted to Kangyur Rinpoche. This was my first winter stay in Darjeeling, which sits 6,500 feet above sea level. The cold is biting at that time of year, and the windowpanes were frosted with ice in the mornings. Even so, I spent a wonderful week with Kangyur Rinpoche and his family. I meditated beside my teacher every day, making the most of those precious moments in his presence. The vividness of that memory, an especially serene time as I recall it, led me years later to see that a spiritual path is made up of myriad stages that deepen our understanding, enrich our experience, accumulate, and subtly complete one another. This phenomenon is as profound as it is universal, and difficult to describe. And yet, the lived inner experience is limpid, like a delicious tea whose many nuanced flavors merge into one instant of pure delight.

In early 1970, Rinpoche moved into what would turn out to be his final home, a large English colonial house purchased for him by some of his

Western students, whose numbers had grown with the passing years. Situated high up on the Gandhi Road, some two kilometers south of Darjeeling, the house would soon be enlarged with an additional story and refurbished to become the Orgyen Kunzang Chökhorling Monastery. The temple occupied most of the new story, and its windows looked out over the forest below and the tea plantations on the hillsides in the distance. On one side was Kangyur Rinpoche's room and that of Amala; on the other was the library, housing the precious books brought from Tibet, and two bedrooms for visiting lamas. The other members of Kangyur Rinpoche's family lived downstairs and in a cottage in the garden. In the main temple stood altars of sculpted wood, built on-site by craftsmen over the course of several months. These altars contained statues and valuable books and were decorated with traditional motifs painted by disciples who lived at the monastery. The compound was surrounded by a wooded slope on which eight hermitages were later built, including one where, two years later, I would live for seven years.

In the spring of that same year, I received a letter from Tulku Pema Wangyal, informing me that in June, Kangyur Rinpoche was to confer upon several lucky students the "great empowerment"—*maha abhisheka*—which I absolutely must attend. I had read *The Life of Milarepa*, beautifully translated into French by Jacques Bacot in 1925, and fully grasped the importance of such an event in the light of the trials that Milarepa, a great Tibetan saint of the eleventh century, had endured before receiving this empowerment. It was therefore with a mixture of emotion, joyful expectation, and reverence that I undertook this journey in the summer of 1970.

The term "empowerment" is the common translation of the Sanskrit word *abhisheka*, which means literally "to fill and to disperse," neatly describing what is at play here. The empowerment "fills" the student with qualities and then "disperses" the veils and imperfections that conceal the Buddha nature within him. Its Tibetan equivalent is *wang*, connoting a "transference of power" that confers on the student the ability to undertake meditative practices. This is followed by detailed guidance that gives the student a clear understanding of these practices so that he may engage in them without being hampered by doubt or hesitation, as well as personal instructions tailored to each initiate's individual traits.

The empowerment also gives access to the "diamond vehicle," the Vajrayana, and assists in the practice of meditative techniques to advance rapidly along the path of enlightenment. Without empowerment, it is as useless to attempt such methods as it is to try to extract oil from a grain of sand. It is further explained that empowerment brings the student's potential to "maturity" and allows him to actualize the Buddha nature within himself.

Once in the presence of Kangyur Rinpoche, I learned that there would be an empowerment ceremony and contemplative practices set out in the complete works of Jedrung Rinpoche,[3] Kangyur Rinpoche's root teacher. Kangyur Rinpoche had himself received this transmission at Riwoche Monastery, in Tibet. I arrived a few days late, but I was able to receive most of the precious empowerments performed by Kangyur Rinpoche over the course of ten days to a dozen students in an atmosphere imbued with respectful solemnity, as well as sparkling joy.[4] Kangyur Rinpoche was especially delighted to hand down the teachings of his beloved teacher, and his students were amazed and deeply grateful to receive them. Years later, I had the privilege of working on the reprint of eight volumes of Jedrung Rinpoche's works in Delhi, based on a variety of manuscripts assembled by Kangyur Rinpoche, who had had them copied out by hand by two scribes in Darjeeling.

Like me, Frédérick Leboyer often came through Darjeeling, where we would meet in the presence of Kangyur Rinpoche or "in town," where he took me to choose and sample the best teas. Although his primary teacher was Swami Prajnanpad, a highly respected Hindu sage, he also held Kangyur Rinpoche in great veneration and went to see him almost every year. Among his many talents, Frédérick was an excellent photographer. He used his Leica to take some of the loveliest portraits of Kangyur Rinpoche and his wife, Amala.

As the years went by, a growing number of Kangyur Rinpoche's Western students moved to Darjeeling or visited often. These spiritual brothers and sisters have always been cherished companions to me. I would have liked to pay them all the tributes they deserve,[5] but I have room to sketch out only an occasional portrait of some whom I had the joy of getting to know.

Take, for instance, Luc Cholley. The first time I saw that strapping young man with the singsong accent of southern France, he had just landed in Darjeeling dressed to the nines, in suit and tie, carrying an attaché case and, like any self-respecting pilot, a pair of Ray-Ban aviators on his nose. Without introducing himself, he pitched into Kangyur Rinpoche: "I've hit a wall! I don't know where to go. Something has to give!" As he told his story, Kangyur Rinpoche, his wife, and his entire family laughed wholeheartedly, while Luc remained in dead earnest. He was brought a hearty lunch, and when he was more relaxed Kangyur Rinpoche taught him the rudiments of meditation, laid out a vision of life, and showed him the first few steps on a path that would inspire him for the rest of his days.

It was a book written by Arnaud Desjardins that had led Luc to Kangyur Rinpoche. One day during his military service in the navy, the ship librarian, with whom he enjoyed chatting, had handed him a book titled *The Message of the Tibetans*, telling him, "You'll like this one." The book contained a picture of Kangyur Rinpoche, and Luc made a promise to himself: "I am going to meet that man one day." A few years later, when he was working in Indonesia, he used his vacation time to go to Darjeeling. He found the monastery, but Kangyur Rinpoche was not there. He did, however, meet another great teacher, Chatral Rinpoche. The desire to meet the master whose photo he had seen was still with him months later. He asked for leave without pay and returned to Darjeeling. That second visit sealed the deal.

Luc slipped into a tracksuit and spent the next ten days meditating with the teacher before returning to Indonesia. Before Luc left, Kangyur Rinpoche gave him a Tibetan coin of solid silver. Luc made a medallion of it that he always wore around his neck. A few months later, when he was working in the jungle as a team leader, an employee in an advanced stage of inebriation entered his office, knife in hand, and, before Luc even saw the blow coming, tried to stab him. The tip of the knife was stopped by the silver coin. Luc was able to disarm him.

It was also thanks to Arnaud that, one morning in 1969, Christian Bruyat, at that time a student at the prestigious École normale supérieure de Lyon, and later to become, like Luc, one of my very best friends, decided to travel to India. He had heard the last segment of a radio interview with

Arnaud, who had concluded with, "And I think that the last authentic spiritual teachers today are the great Tibetan lamas who sought refuge in India after fleeing the invasion of Tibet." Like me, Christian said to himself there and then, "I'm going!" Which he did, after having reached out to Arnaud for directions on how to find these teachers. A few months after his trip, he came knocking on my door in Paris. "I've just come back from Kangyur Rinpoche, and he suggested I come see you. He told me that you and I were like brothers," he declared openly.

That is how we became true spiritual brothers. Kangyur Rinpoche sometimes called Christian "young Matthieu," since we did bear a certain physical resemblance to each other and because we both wore beards at the time. Having spent some time in India as an assistant with the Bangalore Alliance française—as a way of being able to visit with Kangyur Rinpoche on a regular basis—he moved to Darjeeling once and for all and did not return to France until after the death of our teacher. He became one of the best translators of Tibetan. We enjoyed an intimate friendship before his premature demise from the complications of pulmonary fibrosis. Over the years, Christian was enormously helpful to me in reading the early drafts of most of my books.

In 1971, I ran into Gilles Baratier—brother of the filmmaker Jacques Baratier, an old friend of my mother's—on the plane from Delhi to Bagdogra. He, too, was on his way to see Kangyur Rinpoche. We hired a car to climb the twisting road cut into the side of the mountain that rises from the plains of India to Darjeeling. Night was falling and the driver of our old Ambassador, one of two or three models then available in India, was driving far too fast, ignoring the signs urging caution in humorous and wise adages, such as, "If you drive like hell, you will be there soon." We were none too happy, but we didn't dare say anything. Then suddenly, at a turn, the car sped straight toward the precipice. We never learned if the brakes had given out or if a loose steering wheel had prevented the driver from taking the curve—common problems in those Indian cars patched together with spare parts from who knows where. By amazing good luck, there was a big pile of gravel at the side of the road. The car barreled to the top of the pile and stopped, just before it would have teetered over the precipice.

A great silence fell. It had all happened so quickly that we hadn't had time to be scared. We got out of the vehicle and saw that a bare six inches separated us from the abyss. The driver, who had surely seen the accident coming sooner than we had, was in shock. We reprimanded him a little, for the sake of good form, but our reproaches were softened by our relief at having escaped the hell promised to reckless drivers. We helped him back the car down and set off at reduced speed toward the next town, Kurseong, where we changed rides. My mother, who was in Darjeeling at the time, told me that while awaiting our arrival, Kangyur Rinpoche had made several comments betraying concern over our well-being and had recited prayer upon prayer.

That summer, Kangyur Rinpoche gave me lessons on the nature of the mind. He asked me surprising questions: Does the mind have a shape? A color? A dwelling place? Where do thoughts come from? Where do they go once they have dissipated? I was perplexed. I had never asked myself such questions. In retrospect, I realize that I was privileged to receive these teachings in such an immediate, humane, and profound manner, rather than through readings that would have deadened the effect of the discovery. Kangyur Rinpoche came back to these questions one by one, fixing me with a gaze that was both inquisitive and amused, as did Tulku Pema Wangyal as he translated, while I struggled to respond as best I could. Afterward, Tulku Pema Wangyal told me that I had done pretty well on the test.

One day, I borrowed a tape deck from the French students and asked Kangyur Rinpoche's permission to record some of his words so I could listen to them when I found myself far from him. Looking me straight in the eye, he improvised this chant, which sums up the essence of the spiritual path:

Oh Matthieu,
In the space of the awareness that springs up unbidden,
Dwell in perfect equanimity in the understanding of the absolute dimension,
Without being sullied by the mire of the eight worldly concerns.
That is the incontestable path of ultimate meaning!
If you get caught up in the eight worldly considerations,
You will be imprisoned in the cycle of lives, samsara.

The eight worldly concerns consist of everyone's ordinary hopes and fears—hope for gain and fear of loss; hope for pleasure and fear of pain; hope for praise and fear of blame; hope for fame and fear of disgrace.

In 1972, after seven round trips, the situation was clear—at our first meeting in 1967, Kangyur Rinpoche had advised me to finish what I had started before I came to live with him. Five years later, it was done. At a weekend spent with my father at his country house south of Paris, we took a walk in the forest, where I told him of my wish to go live in Darjeeling after my dissertation defense. He said nothing, visibly shaken and disconcerted, but trying to act as if it were no big deal. He asked me how I hoped to support myself. I wasn't worried about that, I told him, things would work out for themselves. Again, he said nothing. I am infinitely grateful to him for his understanding and his calm demeanor; it would have been very difficult for me to defy him openly. I had done my best to honor my parents' efforts to provide me with a solid education and good prospects, as well as the pains taken by my boss, François Jacob, to guide me through my doctoral studies. I was happy to have spent those formative years at the Pasteur. "Every philosopher dreams of having a son in the sciences," my father would say, while my mother liked to say that I had a "brilliant career ahead of me." I had completed my doctorate, published four or five articles in scientific journals, and I have absolutely no idea how my life would have turned out if I had pursued a career as a researcher.

Later, after we had written *The Monk and the Philosopher* together, my father told a journalist, "Matthieu was twenty-six years old. He was an adult, free to choose his own direction in life." The truth is, he had been more upset than he let on. In 2006, over the course of long hours spent at my father's hospital death bed in the company of his dear friend Olivier Todd, Olivier told me that my father had visited him the day after my announcement, and that he had cried like a child.

My announcement came as only a partial surprise to François Jacob. Whatever his opinion on the subject may have been, he was very open-minded about it, although not above poking a little fun. The day I defended my thesis, titled "Contribution to the Study of Cellular Division in E. Coli K12," the chairman of the jury, Jean-Marie Dubert, of the

Jussieu Science Faculty—François Jacob could not be the chairman of the jury because he was with the National Centre for Scientific Research and not on the faculty—concluded his statement with these words: "Having learned of your interest in Eastern spirituality, I was surprised to note the quality of your research."[6] When his turn came, François Jacob added, laughing, "It's just the opposite with me. Having seen the quality of his work on a daily basis, it's his persistent interest in the East that surprised me!" The atmosphere was jolly. The entire jury knew that I was leaving for the East instead of pursuing postdoctoral research in the United States, as François Jacob had initially envisaged for me. I was happy to have spent those formative years at Pasteur and left on good terms with the team— although some were shocked by my decision or remained dubious. But I had finished my work and my choice was made—I was going to do my "postdoc" in the Himalayas.

My father and a few close friends attended my thesis defense. During the modest celebration that followed, I confided to Arnaud Desjardins: "Now, the real research begins."

Looking back, I think it was the right thing to have allowed circumstances to mature so that my "grand departure" was not a leap into the void but the natural culmination of a process, the crossing of a mountain pass leading to a fertile valley. Having reached that point, if I had waited any longer it would have felt as if I were trapped in a world that no longer corresponded to my aspirations. Now, I would no longer be studying cellular division in bacteria, but the mechanisms of happiness and suffering, ignorance and wisdom. I never had the least doubt about the rightness of my decision.

Later, someone asked me if it had been difficult to undertake such an abrupt change. But its apparent abruptness was deceiving. If you try to pick a piece of fruit that is not yet ripe, you will have to pull so hard that you may snap the branch. When the fruit is ripe, all you have to do is twist it gently and it will fall right into your hand.

In December 1972, the time had come for me to fulfill my dearest wish: to live alongside Kangyur Rinpoche. I left with my backpack, a red sweater knitted by my grandmother and a blue pullover from the Croisic maritime co-op, three shirts, two pairs of brown velvet trousers, a sleeping bag that I would keep with me for the next twenty years, my camera, three lenses, and *The Life and Liberation of Padmasambhava*, the biography of Padmasambhava, a very great saint venerated in Tibet as a "second Buddha," which my father had given to my mother on the day I was born and from which I read a few pages every day. I needed nothing more. This external frugality was in singular contrast to the horn of plenty I was to receive internally.

After seven round trips, the ticket I bought for India was, finally, one way.

II

SEVEN YEARS IN DARJEELING

7

AT HOME WITH MY TEACHER

In late 1972, I finally go to live near Kangyur Rinpoche at the Orgyen Kunzang Chökhorling Monastery and begin my retreats in my first hermitage.

I arrived in India in December 1972, and having secured a long-term visa, in early January I went to Orgyen Kunzang Chökhorling Monastery to settle in at Kangyur Rinpoche's side. François Jacob's very kind secretary, Gisèle, had allowed my National Center salary to run until the end of my contract, six months later. I lived on that modest nest egg for the next seven years. I made a small monthly offering to cover my living expenses at the monastery. I had almost no other expenses in my hermitage and lived perfectly well on the equivalent of $50 a month. Strangely enough, with no source of income on the horizon, I never considered how I would support myself in the years ahead. Youthful insouciance or trust in the future? Either way, at no time did that concern disturb my thoughts.

In those days, it was difficult to stay in Darjeeling for more than a month at a time. The region had been declared a "restricted area" because of its proximity to Sikkim, a region bordering Tibet, which had been taken over by China. The Nathu-La pass, visible in the distance from Darjeeling, was closely guarded by the Chinese and Indian armies on either side of the border. It was very complicated for many of Kangyur Rinpoche's students to arrange long stays. But I seemed to live under a lucky star. My mother, who a year earlier had moved to Darjeeling to be with Kangyur Rinpoche, had made friends with the wife of the chief of police, who was of Tibetan origin. After a lot of back-and-forth, he granted me a residency permit for Darjeeling, renewable annually. But he did recommend that I avoid travel; if I left India, he could not guarantee that I would be able to return with the same privileges. It made no difference to me. I was just happy to be there and did not see France again for seven years.

The chief of police, however, retired two years later. From that point on, when it came time to renew my visa and residency permit every year, I was in an agony of suspense, which was heightened by the junior official in charge of the files of the few Western students who, like me, wished to spend extended periods in Darjeeling. We called him the "young spy." He would come to my hermitage and take sneaky pleasure in telling me gravely, "Oh, this year it's very difficult, very difficult," and then, after a weighty silence, aware that he held my new life in his hands and breaking into the broad smile of one who has played a clever prank, he would pull my new yearly permit from his satchel. He would then take advantage of my joyful relief and heedless gratitude to solicit a little favor: "If you happen to have a friend coming from France, I would be most pleased if by any chance he were able to bring an attaché case" or some other imported item. I was always able to arrange it so that "chance" paid dividends; I was eager to remain in his good graces to protect my situation. Martin Watten, one of Kangyur Rinpoche's close students, had managed live in isolation in a little sheet-metal cabin, painted green, located 200 yards above the monastery, a full year after his permit had expired. He came down discreetly from time to time to receive teachings and participate in the monastery's activities. Otherwise, he moved around as little as possible. Of the "young spy" and his acolytes who came to ask if he had really left, he liked to say, "They can't slow down fast enough to catch me."

I spent part of every day with Kangyur Rinpoche, sitting in his presence to "meditate" or at least attempt to fathom the mysteries of that practice, in which I was still a novice. I took my meals with him and his family.

The room was infused with an atmosphere of warmth, discretion, and inspiration. Warmth, because of the generosity of Kangyur Rinpoche's family in all circumstances. Discretion, because, as is often the case in

Tibetan families, and especially among meditators, all gestures were measured, all movement was unobtrusive, and all words spoken softly. No one raised their voice; nary a shout was heard. Inspiration, thanks to the quality of being displayed by Kangyur Rinpoche and those around him: their very behavior was a kind of teaching. But this harmonious moderation in no way excluded laughter, which rang out in conversations around the table.

Kangyur Rinpoche took his place on the hard bed where he slept, seated on a rug of faded red and yellow, brought from Tibet.[1] The other members of his family sat on cushions on the floor. Very often, when my attention was elsewhere, Kangyur Rinpoche would skillfully throw me a *ti momo*, a Tibetan steam roll, which would land in my lap or which I would catch on the fly. Kangyur Rinpoche would then look away, playing the innocent and laughing wholeheartedly.

It took only took a month to build my hermitage. I did not build it myself. It consisted of simple planks of cedar, known locally as *dhupi*, the soft, light wood of the immense trees that made up most of the forests of the region. I made friends with the Nepali carpenters and sometimes gave them a hand. The sole room—about seven feet by ten—held a low bed and a little wooden box acquired at the local market, which served both as bedside table and a holdall. On the sill of the main window, I set out the traditional offerings: bowls, seven in all, some containing water, others a flower, incense, or food, and in the middle an offering of light, symbolized by a wick burning in a little cup filled with oil or melted margarine. A hatch was set into the ceiling framework, beneath which I hung two little tinplate trunks that held a few books and some clothing. To reach it, I had to climb on to the windowsill, marshal my forces and hoist myself up into the "attic" with acrobatic agility. The door to the cabin led out to a little balcony protected by a solid-wood railing that opened onto a few wooden steps and a narrow path that snaked down to the monastery, some fifty yards below. The slope being very steep, the front of the cabin was held up by concrete pilings. From my window, all I could see were enormous rhododendrons that were covered in crimson flowers in the spring, while I myself could be seen by no one. Through the foliage, I could make out the red brick walls of the monastery, from which there occasionally arose the music of sacred ceremonies.

Such simple and spare dwellings offered none of the modern comforts that we take for granted. With no running water, electricity, or amenities, I developed a taste for a more basic, ascetic way of living. I used candles for lighting, and on the balcony was a bucket of water that a young monk refilled every two or three days if I was in retreat, and which I used to wash myself, with the help of a ladle. Natural toilets had been dug not far away in the forest. I spent some very happy years in that hermitage and learned the essence of true well-being: a happy and serene mind, joyfully following the direction that most inspires it in life.

In the monsoon season, from mid-June to mid-August, it rained almost every day, which gave me little incentive to go wandering about outdoors. Precipitation exceeds ten feet in Darjeeling, where people like to say that when you open the window the room is filled with clouds. Indeed, in those times of perpetual mist, a light drizzle invaded my hermitage the moment I left the window open, making me feel as if I were living inside a fogbank. The humidity was so high that if I left a candy in its wrapper on the table at night, by morning all I would find was a puddle of sugar. This stubborn humidity lasted from one season to the next, so that even when the sky was solid blue, it made the winter chill all that more penetrating. It rarely snowed, as the winter was generally sunny. I had a thick cape in the Tibetan style made from an old sleeping bag lined with wine-red cloth, in which I swaddled myself when I sat down to meditate.

I did not yet speak Tibetan at that time, but Kangyur Rinpoche regularly gave me instructions on the various stages of the spiritual path, via the intermediary of Tulku Pema Wangyal. He first taught me the practices known as "preliminaries"—*ngöndro* in Tibetan—which are so essential and foundational that, like most followers of Tibetan Buddhism, I was to practice them every day for the rest of my life.

We begin the preliminaries with reflection and meditation on four major themes in order to transform our vision of things and turn our mind to the path of liberation: (1) the precious opportunity offered by human existence; (2) its fragility and the ephemeral nature of all things; (3) what we must do and what we must avoid in order to free ourselves from suffering; and (4), the deficiencies of a life focused on ordinary worldly preoccupations. Each reflection must be meditated upon until it has become one with our mind.

Human life can indeed be wasted in vain pursuits or devoted to progressing toward enlightenment. In contrast to those of other species, human capacities give us the power to reflect on the causes of suffering, to learn how to free ourselves of them, and to start down the path to enlightenment.

The vicious circle of samsara, the world of existence conditioned by ignorance and suffering, will not break itself. To extricate ourselves from it, we must develop the same resolve as a prisoner who thinks of nothing but escape, and yet we must not be prepared to go to any ends to do so—every action has consequences that reflect the intention and attitude behind it. If we are to be mindful at all times, we must be fully mindful that suffering arises from harmful acts; it will inevitably increase so long as we continue to do harm. It is important to distinguish between positive acts and negative acts, to engage in the former and avoid the latter, down to the most minute.

I devoted three full days to each of the four reflections. Since then, I have spent a part of every daily meditation on them.

Next come five stages that constitute the core of the preliminaries: taking refuge, the altruistic vow to attain enlightenment for the benefit of all beings (*bodhicitta*), purification through meditation on Vajrasattva, the offering of the mandala representing the universe, and the guru yoga, which is union with the enlightened mind of the teacher. Each of these stages involves 100,000 recitations of a verse or a mantra. As intimidating or even confounding as it may sound, this number is not about passing a test that you will then submit to your spiritual teacher; it serves as an antidote to laziness and encourages the novice practitioner to persevere in her practice.

The five stages of *ngöndro* require about six months for those who devote themselves to it all day long. It took me a little longer. In most cases, with the mandala offering, the fourth stage, we usually begin the practice session by reciting a long text that describes in detail the visualization of the mandala of the universe, and then we focus on repeating the quatrain that summarizes the offering. When Tulku Pema Wangyal asked his father how many times I needed to recite the detailed text, Kangyur Rinpoche said "100,000 times," as well as 100,000 times the Vajrasattva mantra to purify the mandala, 100,000 times the seven-branch offering prayer, and 100,000 times the quatrain concluding the offering. It therefore took me eight months of full-time retreat to thoroughly complete the mandala offering.

Before embarking on the first phase of this long journey, we need to understand that our usual supports—family, friends, instructors—as attentive as they may be, are not able to free us from samsara, in which they themselves are mired. That's why we must begin by taking refuge in that which is capable of leading us from delusion and, as a result, out of samsara: the Buddha, he who has attained enlightenment; his teachings, the Dharma; and the Sangha, the virtuous community of those who follow the path. Together, they constitute the three principal objects of refuge and are also known as "the Three Jewels." The concept of "taking refuge" does not mean that we are invoking the protection of some mysterious power, but that we are committing ourselves to the teachings that lead to enlightenment, that is, the true knowledge of the nature of mind and reality. To that end, it is critical that we rely on those who already possess such wisdom and embody it in their actions.

In effect, she who will be your guide on this long and perilous road must be capable not only of guiding you, but also of protecting you from mistakes, obstacles, and blind alleys. Her role is thus primordial, essential. And your choice of teacher is therefore the very first step of your journey, and perhaps the most important.

That choice is all the more sensitive for us Westerners, in that we may misunderstand Buddhist wisdom and philosophy; the craving to learn and to free ourselves must not lead us into undue haste. In the East, spiritual studies are at the heart of education from the earliest age, and exposure to the texts, teachers, and their disciplines is a daily occurrence. Choosing a teacher is therefore based on knowledge and acquired experience in a society where qualified teachers are renowned and respected points of reference. In such an environment, charlatans have little opportunity to assert themselves and, should they attempt to do so, are soon discredited. It is said, in fact, that a student must consider a teacher's qualifications for years, from afar and by word of mouth at first, and then more closely, before committing to him. Likewise, the teacher will take his time considering the motives and sincerity of the follower before accepting her as a student. Should they fail to do so, say the texts, teacher and follower may run the risk of dragging one another to the precipice of suffering. In the West, however, things may tend to move too fast. People in search of spiritual gratification often make themselves vulnerable and, in their haste, seek teaching and even empowerments and then rush in without allowing their decision the time to reach maturity or anchoring it in valid reasoning.

A false teacher can seduce with the most attractive outward appearances, while possessing none of the wisdom or unfailing compassion of authentic spiritual masters. The latter, it is said, have attained "a spiritual realization as lofty as the sky and an attention to the detail of ethical conduct as fine as flour." Contrarily, false teachers, prisoners of their own ego, their ambition, and their personal interest, use their power over those who trust them to abuse them, unlike true teachers, who have no other concern than to show the follower the way to free herself from suffering and ignorance. Taking refuge in someone who remains under the yoke of mental poisons amounts to seeking safety in a nest of vipers.

And so, I embarked on the first phase of the long journey ahead of me and, to the rhythm of 100,000 prostrations, I recited, in Tibetan, the taking refuge quatrain composed by Kangyur Rinpoche:

Homage! In the teacher, the Three Jewels and the wisdom deities,
In the assembly of dakinis and enlightened Dharma-protectors,
In the spontaneously arising nature, entirely present from the beginning,
Recognizing my own true nature, I take refuge.

The second phase involves cultivating the altruistic vow to attain enlightenment to the benefit of all beings, known as *bodhicitta*. What's the use, ultimately, of freeing oneself alone? From the very depths of our being, therefore, we must nurture the compassion and love that lead to the desire to attain enlightenment in order to acquire the power to free all living beings from suffering and its causes. We must cross the "ocean of suffering" together. The word *bodhicitta*, "enlightenment-mind," has different meanings depending on the level of teaching. We generally distinguish between relative enlightenment-mind and absolute enlightenment-mind. The first has two aspects: the intention of attaining enlightenment for the benefit of all beings, associated with training the mind to acquire a truly altruistic attitude, and the application of that intention through the practice of the six perfections, or "transcendent virtues": generosity, discipline, patience, perseverance, concentration, and wisdom.

To that end, I recited the quatrain of relative *bodhicitta* 100,000 times:

May all sentient beings possess happiness and the causes of happiness;
May they be free from suffering and the causes of suffering;
May they never be parted from the supreme happiness that is without suffering;
May we be impartial without limits, free from attachment to close ones and aversion
  to others.

The second aspect of *bodhicitta*, absolute enlightenment-mind, represents nondualistic wisdom, knowledge of the essential nature of mind and the world of phenomena, beyond all mental fabrication. I therefore recited a page-long text and a quatrain, both 100,000 times:

Alas! These beings whom duality leads astray
And who fill space: all are my kin!
To stir the depths of samsara in original purity,
I generate bodhicitta in the great spontaneous accomplishment.

I then moved on to the practice of Vajrasattva, the buddha of purification, whom I visualized above my head, as bright as a snow-capped mountain lit by a thousand suns. A luminous nectar flows from his body, purifying our imperfections and sweeping aside the veils of ignorance. Meditating in this way, I recited the hundred-syllable mantra of Vajrasattva 100,000 times.

I then came to the practice of mandala offering, the fourth meditation. To the buddhas of the past, the present, and the future I offer the mandala, the symbol of all the marvels of the universe: jewels, forest and mountains, flowers, and medicinal extracts, amassed in space. Here again, I recited a page-long text and a quatrain, both 100,000 times:

Ah! I offer the billionfold universe, the infinite mandala of the manifested body.
Without attachment I offer this illusory body, the mandala of the body of complete
  enjoyment.
I offer original purity free of elaboration, the mandala of the absolute body.
May all beings realize the pure fields of the three bodies!

To accomplish these recitations, we use a small, circular brass platter (or silver, for those who can afford it) that we hold in one hand. With the other hand, we add fistfuls of rice while reciting the text in which we offer the entire universe. As the rice piles up, we place three brass rings on the platter, which allows us to raise the edges and continue to pour the rice while preventing it from overflowing the platter. Finally, we place a brass pinnacle in the form of a jewel at the top. We then empty the entire thing onto a cloth spread across our lap and start over, hundreds of times a day. To the rice, I added a few little jewels purchased in the market—glass replicas of precious stones and a few pieces of turquoise and coral—which I set aside in the evening before emptying the day's rice in the forest. It is traditional to change the rice every day. In preparing for the practice, I had carefully washed a hundred kilos of rice in saffron water, which I had then spread out on fabric to dry in the sun on the monastery terrace. I had then brought it all back to my hermitage and stored it in a great jute sack. Day after day, I delved tirelessly into this stockpile for my daily offerings. By the fourth month, the strain of holding the mandala at arm's length all day long began to cause me problems. One night, I dreamed that strange monks armed with sabers were preparing to cut me into pieces. I prayed to my teacher with all my heart. Suddenly, my hermitage was filled with a golden light at the center of which stood Kangyur Rinpoche, smiling and resplendent. The threatening vision vanished instantly. Things returned to normal and I continued with my practice.

I had not counted on the extreme humidity of Darjeeling's climate. When I reached the bottom third of my great sack, I found that the rice below had gone moldy. I had to obtain a new provision of fresh rice.

The culmination of the five preliminary practices, the guru yoga, consists in uniting our mind with that of the teacher, then abiding as long as possible in the perfect equanimity of that spiritual fusion. On that occasion, I recited a seven-line invocation of Padmasambhava 100,000 times, then another 100,000 times a quatrain on the union with the ultimate nature of the teacher, the Buddha nature, and finally the Padmasambhava mantra one million times, all while merging my mind with that of my teacher and, more specifically, with its ultimate nature.

My teacher accompanied me step by step on this long journey, and I am infinitely grateful to him for that. The gradual method that he taught me to complete these preliminaries, the foundation of meditative practice, allowed me to undertake each phase with fresh resolve and to appreciate the profound impact of each upon me.

In 1973, my father took advantage of a trip to Japan to stop in India and pay me a visit. When he landed in Calcutta, I put him in touch with my friend Christian Bruyat, who happened to be there applying for an extension of his residency permit. Christian took care of purchasing the train tickets and served as my father's guide as far as Darjeeling. The journey was a little hectic. Some passengers were transporting bags of rice on the roof and kept pulling the alarm signal so as to be able to unload them at leisure as they approached their destination. Following their shared adventure, my father and Christian remained friends and saw each other after they returned to France. My father spent three days in Darjeeling. He stayed at the Everest, a hotel in the old English style some fifteen minutes from the monastery via a footpath through the forest, which I took every day to fetch him at lunchtime, which he ate with Kangyur Rinpoche and his family, who gave him a warm welcome, and me. When my father the sophisticated gastronome found himself facing a plate of Tibetan *momos*—steamed dumplings which, it has to be said, are a little bland—he confined himself to a courteous, "Well, this is something new." Kangyur Rinpoche, in turn, could not resist teasing him: "Now that you've come, you can stay here and Matthieu can go home to France." He did not appear entirely convinced; his interest in Buddhism at the time was still moderate, to say the least. I was nevertheless overjoyed that my father had met my teacher. I had hardly expected him to experience some kind of epiphany, but I told myself that, at least once in his life, he had now met a real spiritual master, which could only plant a seed in his mind.

My father was relieved to see me well and thriving in my new environment—what more can any father want for his son? He went home reassured. I myself was thrilled by his visit, a gesture that meant a lot to me, and glad that he had been able to get some idea of what my new life was like.

My relationship with my father had never been effusive; it was, rather, one of restraint and discretion. Of course, he had provided for my needs all the way up through my teenage years, but once I had finished my studies, I never asked him for any material support and he never offered me any. Our relations had always been affectionate, but neither one of us had ever spoken openly about our feelings. Thinking back, it seems to me that my father kept his emotions inside when it came to intimate relationships, whereas I am naturally inclined to serenity and rarely troubled by turbulent feelings. While he was reserved enough on a personal level, my father could be fiery in debate—not to mention a fearsome speaker—and he lost his temper publicly with any number of intellectuals and politicians, sometimes taking months to reconcile with them. His visit to Darjeeling was solemn but very warm, and I was grateful to him for having come all that way to see me.

Days became months, months became years, time flowed on in Darjeeling, tranquil and fecund. My teacher was the common thread of my thoughts and the living source of my daily practice. His presence impregnated the place like a gentle and subtle perfume, a benevolent influence that inspired me but generated none of the meek deference that one might feel toward a powerful man or a celebrity. The teacher does not give orders, he does not try to seduce or impress, much less to manipulate; he offers himself as a guide and welcomes everyone while expecting nothing in return. Any progress the student might make in his practice is the best way to please the teacher. He wants only to help those who wish to escape the mire of samsara. A landmark par excellence for the wayward traveler, the teacher provides her with a map and a compass. It is then up to the student to set off on her journey, equipping herself with the resources necessary for the road ahead. She must practice, practice and practice some more. Swift and easy progress is suspect. Milarepa, the renowned twelfth-century hermit, said as much in a chant: "In the beginning nothing comes; in the middle nothing stays; at the end, nothing goes." Our entrenched habits are stubborn, our mental confusion is a thick and heavy veil; lifting the one and the other is an immense task, and our application fragile. We must therefore galvanize our perseverance any way we can. True progress occurs imperceptibly and withstands the vicissitudes of existence. As one axiom puts it, "It's easy to be a good meditator sitting in the sunshine with a full belly, but your level of accomplishment will soon reveal itself when you are weighed in the scales of adversity."

Kangyur attached the highest importance to extending benevolence to all living things, attentive to the fate of the tiniest insect in the monastery's garden. His eldest son, Tulku Pema Wangyal, once explained to us how his father had taught him the practice of *bodhicitta*, the altruistic desire to attain enlightenment for the benefit of all beings. Kangyur

Rinpoche first asked him to meditate with constancy and focus on the following wish: "May I achieve the well-being of all sentient beings!" and enjoined him to memorize a text spelling out that wish in detail.

A few days later, Tulku Pema Wangyal reported back to his father that he had learned the text by heart and meditated on its significance. Kangyur Rinpoche explained, "That's good, but a mere wish is not enough. You have to put it into action. Instead of 'may I,' from now on you must tell yourself 'I *will* achieve the well-being of all sentient beings.'"

A few more days went by, and Kangyur Rinpoche again asked his son how his *bodhicitta* training was going. Tulku Pema Wangyal described his efforts and his progress.

"That's good, but that's still not what it's about."

"What do I have to do?"

"You must tell yourself, 'I will do it, *no matter what the cost.*'"

Kangyur Rinpoche explained to him that the meaning of *bodhicitta* was to dedicate one's entire life to the well-being of others. To illustrate his point, he told him a great many stories from the past lives of the Buddha Shakyamuni, in the course of which he had offered his life to save the lives of others. Tulku Pema Wangyal persevered in his meditation. His father again came to question him: "That's good. But it is still not enough. Now you must add this to your wish: 'No matter how long it takes.'"

He cited the example of the bodhisattva Manjushri, who vowed to be reborn into samsara so long as there remained even one being to be freed from suffering.

One morning, with great simplicity and an atmosphere of unassuming contemplation, Kangyur gave me the vows of *bodhicitta*, associated with those of refuge, and I received my first Tibetan name, Konchok Tendzin, literally, "He who holds the teachings of the Three Jewels." Tibetan names are considered good omens and indicate what one could become after devoted practice of the teachings while fully embodying the meaning of the name that has been given us. Over the course of her life, a follower of Tibetan Buddhism receives several names, including during monastic ordination for those who take the vows, and after undergoing important empowerments. But it is usually the name given when the student takes refuge that becomes her principal name. I later learned that Jamyang Konchok Tendzin was also one of Kangyur Rinpoche's names, which he received upon taking his bodhisattva vows. As the years passed, I had the opportunity to receive the same vows again and again, a profound and always new experience.

Kangyur Rinpoche's teaching was also rich in wisdom concerning the appropriate response to life's ups and downs: laughter. One day, a strapping man, originally from the rugged province of Golok in northeastern Tibet, came to see Kangyur Rinpoche in tears. His wife had abandoned him without warning, leaving him alone with their two children. The man, a devoted follower of Kangyur Rinpoche and Dudjom Rinpoche, was known for being jovial and chatty. Seeing him weep and wail was quite unexpected. Listening to him tell of his woes, Kangyur Rinpoche began to laugh out loud. The more the man chronicled his grievances, the more Kangyur Rinpoche was overcome with mirth. Soon, Amala and the other family members were caught up in the contagious laughter. Oddly enough, their merriment did not seem at all out of place. In fact, it lightened the atmosphere, no less compassionate than if everyone had assumed an attitude of false commiseration. The scene offered a vibrant illustration of the imperfections of samsara, an idea well known to the poor, bereft husband. No one was making fun of our unfortunate friend, of course; they were laughing at the unpredictable and illusory sideshow of worldly affairs. Our Golok took no offense; on the contrary, the warm spontaneity and benevolent nature of Kangyur Rinpoche and his entourage were of the greatest possible comfort to him. Once the drama had been drained from the situation, they enfolded him with affection and reminded him thoughtfully and simply of what he had been taught about the impermanence of things. He ended up laughing himself, dried his tears, and left with his tranquility restored.

A sense of humor in the face of life's tribulations is another manifestation of inner freedom. Kangyur Rinpoche willfully engaged in playful and cheerful behavior, setting the example of a mindset freed of received ideas, automatic mental responses, and mimetic behavior.

Another day, not long after the Tibetan New Year, we were all sitting on the monastery terrace, watching a young Nepali man climb a tall cedar to hang prayer flags. The long cord to which the flags had been sewn was attached to his belt, allowing him to pull the whole thing up once he had reached the top of the tree. A young Frenchman arrived, wearing a pouch containing his passport and his plane ticket strung from his neck. He set it down on the table next to Kangyur Rinpoche. While my compatriot and I were chatting, Rinpoche decided to play a trick on him. He attached the pouch to the cord and, when the young man next set eyes on his precious item, it was already on its way to the top of the tree. The Nepali, having no idea what was going on, hauled away with gusto. Our French friend held Rinpoche in the highest respect, but he couldn't help letting his anxiety show as he cried out, "Oh, all my papers are in that bag, you know!" He was visibly relieved when his precious pouch was readily restored to him instead of ending up hanging between two trees among the prayer flags. This incident amused Kangyur Rinpoche no end. At no point had the pouch been in any danger of being lost or damaged, but the way in which the mind superimposes our anxieties on circumstance had been clearly revealed. After this rather unusual introduction, the young man, Patrick, became a follower of Kangyur Rinpoche, and although he was only ever able to spend brief spells in Darjeeling, today, fifty years later, he considers Kangyur Rinpoche to be the most inspiring person he has ever met in his life.

Some time later, we were painting the altar of the monastery's main temple. The lower part had many small square doors, each eighteen inches wide, opening into storage spaces. They were magnificently decorated with flowers and other motifs, which took me a couple of days each to paint. But I had painted one of the panels on the wrong side; when I hung it on the hinges in its frame, the decorations were upside down. Tulku Pema Wangyal and I discussed the option of removing the pins and gluing them on the other edge of the panel. In the meanwhile, Kangyur Rinpoche, who had been observing the scene, grabbed a fat paintbrush and covered the door in a coat of fresh paint! When I turned and saw his handiwork, Rinpoche burst out in sly laughter. The solution to the problem had been simple: do the work again on the spot!

With Kangyur Rinpoche, the extraordinary always felt completely natural. One fine day as I was practicing in my hermitage, the memory of the few animals I had killed in my childhood came to mind. While I had used to go fishing before renouncing it once and for all around the age of thirteen, I had never gone hunting and had been firmly opposed to that activity. How many times, in my grandfather's garden on the shores of the Traict du Croisic, in Brittany, had I scared off flocks of plovers and geese when I saw hunters approaching? And yet, when I was fifteen, my uncle had put a rifle in my hands and sent me to shoot the nutria that were running amok in his pond. I stupidly succumbed to his pressure and shot at one of them at the far side of the pond. It leaped into the air and disappeared into the water. I have no idea if I killed it; I hope not. "How could I have done such a thing?" I asked myself in the quiet of my hermitage. A senseless act, undertaken with a complete lack of respect for the life of a fellow creature. I deeply regretted the possibility that I had killed it, and for the inane reason that it had been eating my uncle's water lilies. I decided to offer my confession to Kangyur Rinpoche.

I scurried down to the monastery and entered the large room in which he sat. While I prostrated three times, Rinpoche began to laugh and exchanged a few words with Tulku Pema Wangyal. Before I was even able to open my mouth to make my confession, Tulku Pema Wangyal translated, "Rinpoche asks how many animals you have killed in your life?" It all seemed so simple and natural. No flashing lights, vibrations, or eerie sensations. I smiled and said that I had probably killed one water rat, but also many fish. He laughed again but said nothing else. As astonishing, and perhaps even "paranormal" as this episode may seem, it unfolded in the simplest and most natural manner possible. In that moment, his question, as unusual and unsolicited as it was, and most definitely not a matter of coincidence, appeared no less obvious for all that. I therefore felt no need to wonder over the whys and wherefores of that surprising and inspiring incident.

I later spoke of this episode to my friend Jonathan Cohen, a neuroscientist at Princeton University. He told me, "A million different things occur in your life. On rare occasions, two apparently unrelated things seem to intimately relate to one another, like when two acquaintances run into each other by chance on a street in a foreign country." Countless unlikely coincidences arise in this way, with perfectly simply explanations. The encounters we experience every day in the street, on the train, anywhere, have one chance in a million of occurring, but we pay them no attention unless they have special meaning in our eyes. It happened to me, as it does to everyone.

For instance, years later, I was strolling through the streets of Paris on my way to meet my editor, Nicole Lattès, when a taxi stopped and a man jumped out, letter in hand. "You don't know me, but I just read your book and was on my way to mail this letter to you. Here it is." That's example number one.

From there, Nicole and I went to the television studio, where the journalist and television host Bernard Pivot was to interview Trinh Xuan Thuan and me for his show on the occasion of the publication of *The Quantum and the Lotus*. After the recording, we had dinner at a brasserie. As I was hailing a taxi to go home, a man came up to me. He wanted to talk. It was late, but I suggested that, if we were going in the same direction, we could share the taxi. He got in and we discussed the Pivot show. The driver overheard our conversation and told me, "I picked up a lady who had been at that show just a few hours ago." Out of curiosity, I asked him the address he had taken to her, and it was my sister's. He had driven her home after the show! He told me that there were fourteen thousand taxi drivers in Paris. Here again, the coincidence was uncanny. Example number two.

The causes of each of these incidents were altogether normal and banal. Writing a letter and going to mail it, strolling down the street and running into someone, taking a taxi home—these activities are totally commonplace, yet they can sometimes lead to amazing coincidences. It may seem incredible that these paths should cross at one specific, extraordinary instant, but it's just a matter of probability, like winning the lottery.

That said, Kangyur Rinpoche had had no plausible reason for asking me point-blank how many animals I had killed. In all the years I had known him, he had never asked me about my childhood or my life in France. I had told him a little about my studies and my family, especially about my uncle and my sister, who were very special to me. Nothing else. As for Kangyur Rinpoche, he generally spoke to me only to give me his spiritual instruction, to relate stories of past teachers, or to comment on some aspect of our day-to-day lives. Now, for the first time in seven years, he had asked me an eerily apposite question about an event from my childhood. Nothing had prepared me for it. The question seemed completely disconnected from our lives here in Darjeeling, so distant and anecdotal, and yet it had come at the very moment when a memory had arisen from the depths of my mind and I was about to share it with him. For me, this episode could not be explained away with probabilistic reasoning. Something else, something deep and mysterious, was at play here. The simplest explanation was that he had read my mind. Other, similar events that I was later party to have tended to confirm that hypothesis.

Jigme Khyentse Rinpoche, my teacher's youngest son, once told us a story to which he had been a witness. One day, a very friendly hippie named Dharma Dipo, dressed in an old Tibetan robe, his blond hair twisted into dreadlocks, a cascade of necklaces around his neck, came to sit at Kangyur Rinpoche's feet. He had smoked some hashish before coming to the monastery. He had just sat down when Kangyur Rinpoche made a gesture imitating someone smoking a chillum, then burst into laughter. As he had not eaten that day, Dharma Dipo found himself wracked with hunger after ten minutes of meditating, but he persisted stoically. It was not yet lunchtime, but Kangyur Rinpoche called Amala over and spoke a few words with her. She came back a few minutes later with a platter of rice and vegetables that she offered to the young hippie. Kangyur Rinpoche insisted that he eat every last grain.

The Tibetan tradition holds that this ability to read the minds of others is one of the qualities that naturally arise with a high level of spiritual attainment. Masters never boast of such abilities and do not admit to possessing them when questioned on the subject. They exercise these gifts very naturally and simply at the right moment, when they feel that they will strengthen the follower's confidence in her spiritual practice. It is always done in the spirit of subtle allusion, never as an ostentatious statement.

8

THE LIFE OF KANGYUR RINPOCHE

His retreats, his life as a wandering hermit, his teachings, how he met his wife, Jetsün Jampa Chökyi, his flight from Tibet before the communist invasion and his establishment in Darjeeling. Kangyur Rinpoche passes away—forty-nine days of ceremonies followed by cremation.

Kangyur Rinpoche was born in eastern Tibet in 1898. He was given the name Longchen Yeshe Dorje, "Vast Space of Adamantine Wisdom," long before he became Kangyur Rinpoche. From his earliest childhood, he showed a strong inclination toward the study and practice of the Dharma. His primary teacher, Jedrung Rinpoche (1856–1922), whom he met when he was nine years old, had a large following in the region around Riwoche Monastery in eastern Tibet, well known for its nonsectarian approach.[1] Although he was never enthroned as an incarnate lama (*tulku*), Kangyur Rinpoche was considered to be the manifestation of Namkhai Nyingpo, one of the twenty-five disciples of Guru Padmasambhava, the master who brought Buddhism to Tibet in the eighth and ninth centuries.

Around the age of eleven, Longchen Yeshe Dorje set off on foot among a group of pilgrims to meet Lama Mipham, one of the greatest masters of his age, who was living in a hermitage at the time. Noticing the little boy, Lama Mipham asked who he was. "Oh, he's just a little boy from our village who wanted to come with us," the pilgrims answered. To which Lama

Mipham replied, "Hmm . . . It is from little children that great teachers are born."

He asked the child, "Do you know how to read?"

"Just about," the child answered politely.

Mipham took out his prayer book, *The Chanting of the Names of Manjushri (Manjushri-Nama-Samgiti)* and handed it to Kangyur.

"Let's hear you read this."

Longchen Yeshe Dorje read the entire thing clearly, easily, and fluidly.

"Ho ho! How well he reads!" Mipham Rinpoche exclaimed.

Thrilled, he conferred upon all the pilgrims, and particularly the young Longchen Yeshe Dorje, the blessing of all his writings by placing the volumes on their heads, along with an empowerment for Manjushri, the buddha of wisdom. He then offered Kangyur a gift of his own copy of the *Nama-Samgiti*, some little pills made of medicinal plants and consecrated in a ceremony devoted to Manjushri, and a little saber of yellow wood, the symbol of the wisdom of that buddha, who slashes away the shadows of ignorance. Having received these blessings and sacred objects, Longchen Yeshe Dorje was able to memorize with ease all the many texts he would go on to study.

Longchen Yeshe Dorje experienced powerful spiritual revelations from early childhood. He had visions in which he received the transmission of "hidden treasures" (*terma*). *Termas* are teachings that, for the most part, were handed down by Padmasambhava to some of his disciples, then concealed in specific locations at his direction. These spiritual treasures were destined to be found by *tertöns*, discoverers of ancient texts, following directions received in visions at precisely the moment when they would be of greatest use.

Heeding the advice of his teacher, Longchen Yeshe Dorje took monastic vows and devoted the first part of his life to study and practice with passionate industry. Unable to afford lamp oil, he read late into the night by the light of the incandescent tip of a stick of incense, on which he would blow to revive its glow. In this manner, he acquired a rare erudition and astonished everyone with his knowledge of the various schools of Tibetan Buddhism. His teacher then advised him to undertake two consecutive three-year retreats at Marthang Dorje Den, one of the retreat centers at Riwoche Monastery devoted to the practice of Vajrakilaya, thereby complementing his learning with the experience and realization born of a profound contemplative practice.

One day in 1922, during his second retreat, he was in the cloister courtyard when he had a vision in which his beloved master, Jedrung Rinpoche, appeared to him in multiple forms of varying size within a sparkling light. Rainbows appeared in the sky amid the tolling of clocks and the pulsing of little drums. Longchen Yeshe Dorje intuited that his teacher had left this world, but his companions in retreat felt that this was a dubious premonition. The news came a month later: Jedrung Rinpoche's life on this earth had ended the very day of Longchen Yeshe Dorje's vision.

He undertook other retreats in various isolated locations, including on the slopes of Kawa Karpo, "the White Pillar," a lofty 22,000-foot mountain of eternal snow in Yunnan, at the extreme southeast of Greater Tibet.

His indifference to power and honors led him to leave Riwoche Monastery, where he had been offered powerful offices. He preferred to live the life of an itinerant hermit, traveling through Tibet from east to west to receive instruction from many teachers and to practice it in remote places.

In the 1930s, he began to devote most of his energies to altruistic activities. He offered numerous spiritual teachings and transmissions. As an expert in traditional medicine, he also healed the sick who came to him, tended to the elderly, assisted travelers and pilgrims, and cared for orphans.

He acquired the name Kangyur Rinpoche because he gave thirteen reading transmissions of the three hundred volumes of the *Kangyur*, the entire Buddhist canon translated into Tibetan in the ninth century. He read them twenty-four times in all. We can appreciate the magnitude of such an undertaking when we know that a single transmission of the text requires almost two months of reading, all day every day.

When he was living in Nyemo County, central Tibet, Kangyur Rinpoche decided to leave the monastic life for that of a yogi, and to take Jetsün Jampa Chökyi as his spiritual companion. Born in Nyemo County in 1922, from her very earliest years she had devoted her life to contemplative practice and was renowned for her compassion. She had met Kangyur

Rinpoche in the heights of Chimpu overlooking Samye Monastery, and became his follower, joining him in practicing his teachings in solitary places. In 1941, she joined other followers in accompanying Kangyur Rinpoche on a yearlong pilgrimage to India and Nepal. They married in 1943 and had seven children, but had the misfortune of losing one.

Very early on, Kangyur Rinpoche perceived the threat that loomed over Tibet and decided to leave the Land of Snow with all his family in 1956. His friends and followers tried to dissuade him, arguing that there was no imminent danger, but Kangyur Rinpoche's decision was unshakable. A few years later, in 1959, history sadly proved him right, and the army of Communist China invaded Tibet after having gradually set the stage for seizing power since 1949.

At the time of his departure, he had been living in Nyemo County, a lovely, fertile valley west of Lhasa that was the birthplace of his wife, Jetsün Jampa Chökyi. Foreseeing the impending tragedy, Kangyur Rinpoche was able to make the journey without much risk, bringing with him (and saving from the destruction to come) a great number of valuable books, along with some statues and relics that he transported in large bales. It was a good thing he did, as most of the libraries that housed precious manuscripts were burned to the ground by Chinese soldiers, Red Guards, and Tibetans themselves, who were forced to do so under duress, under the brutal communist yoke, their irreplaceable treasures sometimes flung into the flowing rivers.

Kangyur crossed southern Tibet by truck, then hired a caravan of yaks and mules to cross a high mountain pass in Kongpo province before descending into the hallowed valley of Pemako, "Lotus Array," a sacred region where he lived for four years, from 1956 to 1960, had many visions, and even considered settling, before finally moving on to India and spending the last fifteen years of his life in Darjeeling.

Kangyur Rinpoche's erudition was equaled only by his humility, which was manifest both in his apparel and in his places of residence. The great contemporary masters who knew him held him in the highest respect. Dudjom Rinpoche thought him the equal of the eminent *mahasiddhas*,[2] the great Buddhist yogis of India, while another distinguished master of the Nyingmapa school, Dilgo Khyentse Rinpoche—who would later play a very critical role in my life—told one of his followers, Lama Chöjor, that Kangyur Rinpoche was just like his own root master, Dzongsar Khyentse Chökyi Lodrö, one of the greatest Tibetan sages of the twentieth century.

Wishing to safeguard the transmission of his teachings to future generations, Kangyur Rinpoche built a monastery in Darjeeling, Orgyen Kunzang Chökhorling, where Tibetan children receive a traditional education to this day. Students also came from all over the world to see him there and were always hospitably welcomed, our master being determined to share his teachings with as many people as possible.

His inner freedom allowed him to remain serene in all circumstances. Generous and deeply attached to the values of altruistic love, he reminded us of the particular importance of helping the sick, the elderly, the poor and traveling pilgrims. Kangyur Rinpoche was completely indifferent to worldly concerns. Ignoring ordinary conventions, he could sometimes be uncompromising and firm so as to ensure that, as the proverb says, "a good student makes regular progress under rigorous discipline." Exercising discipline in one's external conduct was just as important as in one's internal conduct, requiring every follower to be at his very best.

Although he never traveled to the West, Kangyur Rinpoche believed that the Dharma needed to grow there. In that conviction, he was tireless in his teachings to the Western followers who came to meet and stay with him, relying on them to spread the precious ancestral wisdom. He told other eminent teachers, including Dudjom Rinpoche, who was then the head of the Nyingmapa school, and Dilgo Khyentse Rinpoche, that it would be very valuable if they could visit Western countries for the benefit of all beings. In late 1975, at the invitation of Tulku Pema Wangyal, Dilgo Khyentse Rinpoche took his first journey to the West. He went to half a dozen European countries, as well as the United States and Canada. Jigme Khyentse Rinpoche and a few others, including me, accompanied him from Darjeeling to Bagdogra airport. This memorable journey was the first of some fifteen visits by Dilgo Khyentse Rinpoche to the West, mostly to the Dordogne region in France, where Kangyur Rinpoche's family, his wife Jetsün Jampa Chökyi and their children, would eventually settle in the late 1970s. This made it possible for many Westerners to study and practice the Dharma, particularly in the context of traditional three-year retreats and seminars organized by the Chanteloube Study Center.

By mid-January 1975, the symptoms of the illness that Kangyur Rinpoche had begun to present toward the end of the preceding year grew worse. He told his loved ones that he would soon be leaving this life. For those of his followers who were far away, he affirmed that distance meant little so long as they remained devoted.

The concept of devotion might seem odd, even suspect, in this day and age. It evokes the idea of blind faith, which is in exact contradiction to the Dalai Lama's insistence that faith and trust must be based on a correct appreciation of the reality and qualities of the Buddha, the Dharma, and the Sangha, the noble community of realized beings. Blind faith is obscured and distorted by the absence of judgment and is akin to irrational belief. Devotion consists not in "believing in something" but in opening yourself to the immensity and depth of the teacher's spiritual realization and boundless love. Once this intimate link has been forged, it leads to respect and admiration, as well as to the ardent desire to realize in yourself the wonderful qualities you have discerned in the teacher. Devotion also allows you to acquire a "pure vision" of the entire world of phenomena; it liberates you from duality, from perception that continually distinguishes between beautiful and ugly, pleasant and unpleasant, harmonious and discordant, friend and enemy. Pure vision allows you to recognize the fundamental purity of phenomena. By "purity," we mean the fact that all phenomena—forms, sounds, and thoughts—are equally devoid of intrinsic existence, which is the meaning of "emptiness" in Buddhism. In that sense, they are "pure," that is, free of all the distortions that our mental fabrications project on reality. The spiritual teacher's body, words, and mind embody the enlightened aspect of forms, sounds, and thoughts. That is why blending our mind with that of the teacher allows us to perceive the primordial purity of all forms, sounds and thoughts. Devotion, or fervent respect, as understood and practiced in Tibetan Buddhism, melts the ice of our concepts and fixations and allows us to apprehend the perfect unity of appearances and emptiness.

It is for that reason that, regardless of the great variety of practices and effective means offered by Vajrayana Buddhism, union with the mind of the teacher—guru yoga—lies at the heart of all these methods.

Guru yoga allows us to gradually rediscover and actualize the Buddha nature within us—a nature that represents the ultimate aspect of the spiritual teacher. As Dilgo Khyentse Rinpoche taught, "Placing one's trust in the spiritual teacher is the surest way to advance towards enlightenment. The heat of his compassion and wisdom melts the ore of our mind to free the gold of our potential enlightenment, the Buddha nature."

Shortly before his earliest symptoms appeared, Kangyur Rinpoche conferred one last great empowerment upon one of his close followers, Soktse Rinpoche, at his request, and a few others, among whom I was lucky enough to find myself. He gave us the gift of the complete cycle of his spiritual treasure, centered upon the wisdom deity Vajrakilaya, who embodies the enlightened activity of all Buddhas to achieve the welfare of all beings and remove the obstacles in their way.

At sunset on Thursday, January 23, 1975, he asked to be alone, and that is how he left this world, sitting in meditation. When his loved ones entered the room, Kangyur Rinpoche had stopped breathing and had entered the meditation of the afterlife, the *thukdam*, which lasted five days. His wife, Jetsün Jampa Chökyi, surrounded by her children, read aloud *The Treasury of Absolute Space* (*Chöying Dzö* in Tibetan), a text written by the great fourteenth-century master Gyalwa Longchen Rabjam, who revealed the ultimate truth in some fifty pages of astonishing depth.

The meditation associated with *thukdam* arouses a very clear sense of the living presence of the deceased. The head remains upright or tilted slightly forward, the skin remains supple and the limbs flexible, with no rigor mortis. The body gives off a sweet and delicate odor, quite different from the unpleasant odor emitted by bodies devoid of all life and on the verge of putrefaction. This meditation can continue for as long as three weeks. If an advanced adept is able to maintain such meditative absorption, it will allow her to rapidly complete the final stages of spiritual realization. Masters who, like Kangyur Rinpoche, have realized the nature of mind in accordance with the teachings on the Great Perfection have no need to engage in such postmortem meditation, but they sometimes do so for the edification of their followers. In Tibet, people of faith who may by chance find themselves in the presence of an adept practitioner of *thukdam* may believe they are observing a meditator absorbed in deep contemplation, without realizing that life, in the ordinary sense of the term, has already left the body. It is of great value to unite one's mind with that of the teacher at such a moment. Specific signs indicate when the meditation has ended: the head sags, white and red liquids seep from the nostrils, and the body begins to change, like that of any other deceased.

When Kangyur Rinpoche began to show signs that his *thukdam* had come to an end, his body was washed in saffron water and bound in strips of white fabric, then placed in his room, in the lotus position, on the bed on which he had begun his meditation. He was adorned with brocades and ornaments symbolizing *sambhogakaya*, the "body of complete enjoyment," that is, the dimension also known as the "subtle body of a Buddha spontaneously manifesting from the absolute body," the *dharmakaya*. His arms were crossed over his chest, his right hand held a *vajra*, a little five-point scepter symbolizing the transformation of the five principal poisons—aversion, attachment, ignorance, pride, and jealousy—into the five wisdoms and compassion, and his left hand held a bell, symbol of the emptiness of phenomena. His head was girded by a crown with five petals painted with the five *dhyani* buddhas, symbolizing the five aspects of primordial wisdom: all-encompassing wisdom, mirror-like wisdom, wisdom of perfect equality, discriminating wisdom, and all-accomplishing wisdom.

His close students present in the monastery were now able to pay him tribute. We prostrated before his body, praying with all our being for him to remain ever-present in our thoughts and to guide us to enlightenment, in this life or in those to come. We were able to gather together in his room for a few minutes every day. I experienced these very particular, emotional moments—my last in the presence of my teacher's physical body—with deep intensity. I pledged myself with greater resolve than ever to devote myself to practicing the teachings that I had received from him.

Kangyur Rinpoche's elder son, Tulku Pema Wangyal, reminded us that the death of a spiritual teacher differs from that of an ordinary person. The teacher will remain forever present to those who call on him with confidence. Another eminent master who lived not far from the monastery, Nyoshul Khen Rinpoche, told us that only fools do not mourn the death of such a teacher, whose life was dedicated to the well-being of all. A teacher of such excellence, he reminded us, is extremely rare. And yet, he added, while his manifested body may break down, his absolute dimension transcends all forms of destruction.

A few hours after Kangyur Rinpoche's death, Tulku Pema Wangyal managed to get a message to Dilgo Khyentse Rinpoche, who was in Sikkim at the time. He reached the monastery a few days later and completed the sacred rites. He also gave some precious advice to the gathered students and reminded us in particular that the teachings of the Buddha were so encompassing that it was impossible for an ordinary follower to assimilate them entirely, which is what gave such inestimable value to finding an authentic teacher capable of drawing out the essence of these teachings and of providing each in turn with the instructions she needs to progress according to her own specific mental abilities and disposition. We should therefore consider ourselves very lucky to have received such teachings and must never imagine that we lacked certain critical instructions. He reminded us of how the *mahasiddhas*—the great adepts of the past—had achieved ultimate realization by meditating persistently on the few core teachings that their master had passed down to them. It felt as if Dilgo Khyentse Rinpoche had gathered Kangyur Rinpoche's followers in the palms of his hands, the way a new mother might embrace orphans with unreserved goodness and generosity.

The "departure" of a spiritual teacher is a moment of depthless sorrow to his followers, as if the sun has suddenly fallen from the sky. But this particular sorrow rises above all feeling, all emotion, to carry us into the heart of what is essential. The teacher remains present in everything we perceive, see, and hear. He is no longer in his body; he inhabits everything around us because he remains at the very source of our thoughts, at one with the fundamental nature of our mind. And he does so not in the guise of an individual presence, but as the clear, enlightened consciousness that abides, unaltered and unalterable, behind the curtain of our thoughts. The master becomes like a space that encompasses all things, the light that illuminates the world, like a sound that reverberates everywhere and forever.

It was in passing into *parinirvana*, death, that the Buddha gave his final lesson on impermanence—a powerful exhortation not to squander our precious human existence, but to engage on the path to liberation. Among all the Buddha's teachings, that on impermanence is like the elephant's footprint in the forest—it is the biggest of all footprints. Keeping the sense of impermanence always in mind is not meant to fill us with anxiety or distress but allows us to keenly recognize the pricelessness of every passing moment. Just as we do not throw gold dust down the drain, it would be deplorable to waste our lives away in illusion and idleness, minute by minute, day by day, year after year, only to leave this treasure island, our human life, empty-handed.

Over the course of forty-nine days, lamas, monks, and nuns from the surrounding area, as well as Western followers of Kangyur Rinpoche who were present at his death, along with many others who had come from afar, paid homage to their teacher. Ceremonies were held all day long in the temple on the second floor of the monastery, centered on the practice of Vajrasattva, the buddha of purification. Forty-nine days is how long it takes for the consciousness to transit through the bardo, the liminal stage between the moment of death and that of rebirth. It's also the time when ceremonies are held to facilitate rebirth in conditions conducive to pursuing the path of enlightenment. In the case of one who has attained the highest degree of spiritual realization and who is in control of the circumstances of his own rebirth, this interval is symbolic and observed largely to give followers the opportunity to pay tribute to their teacher and to pray that he will soon return to this world for the benefit of all beings.

This practice allows the follower to merge her mind with that of the master, which is considered to be inseparable from Vajrasattva, to make material and visualized offerings—to do so, we call to mind all the beauties and perfections of the universe, which multiply to infinity and fill all space with clouds of offerings—and to purify the obscurations that veil the mind, speech, and body of all present so that they can achieve enlightenment. Those assembled slowly read out a text of some thirty pages, twice a day, morning and afternoon. This is a deep guided meditation that begins with taking refuge in the enlightenment of the Buddha and moves on to the vow of the bodhisattva to attain enlightenment in order to liberate all beings from suffering. The main portion is focused on visualizations of the buddha Vajrasattva, which allows one to cultivate "pure vision." All beings without exception, male and female alike, are seen as buddhas, the Buddha nature dwelling within each of them as oil dwells in every sesame seed.

On the night of February 17, 1975, as the ceremonies continued into the third week after the death of Kangyur Rinpoche, his body was placed in the upper part of a bell-shaped stupa with an opening on one side. This particular stupa was built on the upper terrace of the monastery under the supervision of Tulku Pema Wangyal; we had all assisted in its construction. Dilgo Khyentse Rinpoche and Dodrupchen Rinpoche, another eminent master who had settled in Sikkim after fleeing Tibet, directed the ceremony. Shortly before dawn, the juniper and sandalwood pyre was lit and slowly consumed Kangyur Rinpoche's body as the fire offering ritual continued. Throughout the ceremony, participants visualized the master's body, sitting in the lotus position on a dais, swathed in fabric and brocade, in the form of Vajrasattva. A morning rainbow appeared shortly after sunrise. At the end of the three-hour celebration, the opening in the stupa was sealed to allow the ashes to cool slowly. Later that morning, a spectacular halo formed around the sun and remained visible for half an hour. A few days later, Tulku Pema Wangyal opened the stupa, and the ashes were painstakingly assembled. Some of the bone fragments, as well as Kangyur Rinpoche's heart—which, despite the intensity of the flames, had not been reduced to ashes—were incorporated into a statue that now stands in Kangyur Rinpoche's room. Like many students, I was the grateful recipient of a few shards of my dear teacher's bone.

Another portion of the remains were placed in a gold-plated brass stupa that is kept in the monastery's main temple. It sometimes happens, in the case of preeminent adepts, that the heart, eyes, and tongue are found together, as if mummified, among the ashes, without having been charred by the flames. This is considered to be a sign of high accomplishment. In retrospect, this amazing phenomenon makes me think of Cicero's axiom: "Nothing happens unless it can happen. When that which can happen does in fact happen, it cannot be considered a miracle." The thing becomes interesting once the most plausible explanation casts doubt on the dominant paradigms.

Our task now was to put the teachings we had received into practice for the remainder of our days. My mother, who had also lived and practiced in a little hermitage in Darjeeling between 1972 and 1975, and whom I saw almost every day when we took our meals with Kangyur Rinpoche's family, decided to return to France after our teacher's death. In the final months of her stay, she came down with encephalitis and was in very bad shape. With the help of my friends, I spent several weeks at her bedside, sometimes day and night. On her return, she lived first in Brittany, in a lovely cabin in the woods on the estate of her brother, Jacques-Yves Le Toumelin, and then in Dordogne, where she did a three-year retreat. In later years, she occasionally returned to spend several months at a time in India, Nepal, or Bhutan.

When Kangyur Rinpoche was still alive and I used to come every year from France to be with him, knowing that our reunions awaited me gave each trip a special significance. Time and space assumed new dimensions, imbued with the image of my teacher. And then came the long-awaited moment when I arrived at his home, crossed the threshold, greeted the members of his family, and then found myself in his presence. Years later, I learned that when Tibetans speak of the Dalai Lama, they use neither his title nor his personal name, but simply the word Kundun, which means "presence."

Nowadays, when I travel, very often I am simply going from one place to another. Other than in my heart, there is no longer any place on Earth where I can find my teacher. As the great yogi Shabkar said upon the death of his teacher: "Before, no matter how great the distance, I knew that I would see his face. Now, even with the best horse in the world, I have nowhere to go."

9

WHAT IS AN AUTHENTIC TEACHER?

The characteristics of a true spiritual guide. The long journey that must accompany the choice of teacher. The dangers posed by false teachers.

The heart of spiritual transmission lies in the qualities of the teacher: his inner freedom, his compassion, his wisdom, and his disdain for worldly vanities. After five years of travelling to see Kangyur Rinpoche, I lived two years in his presence and then spent thirteen years with Dilgo Khyentse Rinpoche and long stretches with Trulshik Rinpoche and the fourteenth Dalai Lama. In all those years, I never detected in them any thought, speech or act that might harm others. Their sole and unique concern seemed to be to achieve the well-being of all beings, not only their immediate well-being but an ultimate well-being: their liberation from the world conditioned by suffering, samsara.

Some might say that I am naive and blind to their flaws. But a mere façade masking hidden vices does not hold up to the test of time. Faults in the armor always end up being found, no matter how well concealed they may be. That did not occur here. What's more, unlike dissemblers, who are constantly worried about other people's judgment, one trait shared by all these masters is that they have absolutely no concern about their "image," they never try to "keep up appearances," they have no interest in praise or criticism, fame or anonymity.

That's the very least you can expect from a spiritual teacher worthy of the name, you will tell me. For sure, but such consistency is no less exceptional and inspiring for all that. It is also necessary—how indeed could we call someone who behaves dubiously, even harmfully, toward others a "spiritual teacher?"

The fact is, an authentic spiritual teacher has nothing to gain or lose, but everything to give and to share. He could not care less about attracting a few new followers, he seeks no public recognition, no personal advantage, and his way of life tends always to the simple and stripped-down, devoid of all glamor.

A qualified teacher doesn't suddenly appear out of nowhere; he is the depositary of an unbroken line of spiritual transmission and experience acquired over the course of generations. Through him, the enlightenment of the Buddha, the treasury of his teachings, the Dharma, and the lineage of accomplished beings constitute a virtuous community—the Sangha—that perpetuates itself and commands respect.

In Tibet and Bhutan, whenever someone arrives somewhere, he often asks about the presence of wise men or women in the region so that he can call on them. It's hard to imagine someone arriving in Paris and asking the same question to passers-by in the street. We ask instead about the local supermarket, movie theaters, or the nearest gym. The importance attached to a spiritual teacher may seem surprising, even disturbing, in a world that encourages individualism and self-empowerment. And yet we're perfectly willing to admit that if we wish to learn to drive, to climb a vertical rockface, or play a musical instrument, it is wise to make use of the experience of a qualified instructor, who in turn has benefited from experience accumulated over generations. There is no reason why an apprenticeship in wisdom, compassion, inner freedom, and the path to enlightenment should be an exception to that.

If you hope to sail around the world, you might begin by reading about the great navigators, but such bookish knowledge, as educational as it may be, will be of limited utility. It is also essential to acquire practical skills and know-how for ourselves. The path to enlightenment is a far longer proposition than circumnavigating the world. It would be foolish to embark upon the vast ocean with no map or sextant, without knowing how to navigate or having any idea of your final destination. A qualified teacher brings all that, maps and compasses, but better yet, he remains fixed like the North Pole, orienting the follower's compass, preventing her from stumbling, guiding her aspirations and the realization of her potential, and reminding her of the Buddha's words: "I have shown you the path. It's up to you to take it."

As for me, I would never have spent half a century in the Himalayas if I had not met people capable of showing me the path, wisely and kindly. I would have done little more than take a few pictures of the superb landscapes and make myself a meal for mosquitoes. But from my very first visits, I was convinced that while the teachings and practices of Buddhism had nurtured people as remarkable as Kangyur Rinpoche, his wife, his family, and other teachers whom I met along the way,[1] I in turn needed to tap into that treasury of knowledge and incredible opportunity for inner transformation.

Buddhism distinguishes between several kinds of spiritual teachers, according to their function and abilities. First comes the "spiritual friend," who spurs us to virtue, *kalyanamitra* in Sanskrit, who counsels us, shows the path to follow and teaches the basics of practice. There is also the expert, the learned professor—*acharya* in Sanskrit—who explains the content, meaning, and structure of the teachings. The *acharya* may be a philosophy teacher—*khenpo* in Tibetan. The *khenpo* also holds the monastic lineage and confers ordinations.

Next comes the master of the Great Vehicle (the Mahayana), who sets out the teachings on the philosophy and practice centered on wisdom and compassion that lead to buddhahood. She transmits the precepts related to bodhisattva vows, the resolve to attain enlightenment for the good of all beings.

Finally, the spiritual teacher confers the transmission of empowerments into the Diamond Vehicle, the Vajrayana. It is she who introduces us to the nature of our own mind and guides our path toward enlightenment— our "root teacher." For me, Kangyur Rinpoche embodied all these teachers. He was my root teacher. In addition to evoking the notion of "principal" teacher, the phrase also alludes to the fact that Kangyur Rinpoche is always present at the "root" of my thoughts, at the heart of my being, combining in his person the external teacher who shows us the way and the inner teacher, the ultimate nature of our mind. This is not a mere figure of speech. Today, throughout my life and frequently over the course of each day, the presence of Kangyur Rinpoche and his qualities, along with the desire to merge my mind with his wisdom, is at the forefront of my thoughts.

These different teachers elicit different degrees of engagement on the part of the follower. Learning to sail in a little dinghy alongside the beach is not the same thing as training with a seasoned seaman to ply the high seas in all weather. It is up to each individual to make a fully informed decision about the path he wishes to take and what kind of teacher he is prepared to trust himself to, having carefully considered his goals and investigated the authenticity of the teacher in question from all angles.

The texts also alert us to the rarity of qualified teachers. They describe in particular the qualities required of a teacher of Vajrayana. He, or she, must have an excellent command of the teachings, having integrated them into his or her mindstream and attained a high level of spiritual realization. The latter expresses itself, among other things, in tireless compassion for all beings without exception. A teacher's greatest satisfaction lies in her disciple's progress toward freedom from suffering. This is a far cry from the kind of relationships of domination that we see time and again in modern life, and which characterize a false teacher's efforts to gain power over his followers. The teacher's embrace is a gesture of pure, spontaneous generosity, comparable to the assistance offered to a lost traveler or a fugitive in danger. The teacher shares her experience of uprooting herself from ignorance, negative emotions, and the suffering they entail. With full mastery of the methods of spiritual practice, she knows how to identify those that best suit a follower at any given moment of his life. Such qualities can derive only from inner achievement, perceptible both in the deepest of teachings and in the simplest gestures.

The follower is therefore strongly recommended not to put her trust in the first teacher to come along but first to meticulously examine the qualities of the potential teacher, starting with questioning third parties, and then confirming that the opinion she has formed of him corresponds to reality. She is advised to allow several years to go by before putting her faith in him entirely, because putting oneself in the care of an unqualified individual is akin to swallowing poison.

The Dalai Lama strongly counsels everyone, from the East as from the West, to think long and hard before agreeing to study with a teacher so as to spare themselves potential, and potentially bitter, disappointments. On the other hand, no one should take this as license to go on a spiritual junket through every tradition on the planet and among teachers of every stripe. Like my mother Yahne used to say, "When you find a well with really pure water, drink. But don't become a well tourist!"

The Dalai Lama has also frequently asserted that if a self-proclaimed teacher behaves in flagrant contradiction to the teachings of the Buddha and if, in particular, his actions harm those around him, his followers are duty-bound to denounce his activities.

One criterion of assessment is clear and uncontestable: Buddhism seeks to eliminate suffering and its causes. Consequently, anything that does not remediate suffering or, worse, induces it, is not Buddhism. A teacher who knowingly causes deep and lasting suffering in others is not a teacher but a charlatan. Following such a teacher is like jumping off a cliff, when teacher and follower fall together.

In less serious cases, if, having failed to adequately vet a teacher's authenticity, you come to the simple conclusion that he does not have the required qualities, but that despite everything you have benefited from his teachings of the Dharma, and most especially if you have received a Vajrayana empowerment, the best thing to do is simply walk away.

Once the follower has every reason to think that a teacher is authentic, it is appropriate to place in that teacher a degree of trust that transcends the rationalizations of skepticism. The follower becomes a sort of apprentice mountain-climber who, having begun the climb, must have full and complete confidence in her guide. Failing to do so puts them both in danger.

Teachings that unambiguously describe the qualities of teachers to follow and the defects of those to be avoided act as a kind of guardrail. For instance, *The Treasury of Precious Qualities*,[2] written in the eighteenth century by Rigdzin Jigme Lingpa and elucidated by Kangyur Rinpoche in a glowing commentary, sets out these qualities and defects, summarized as follows:

The teacher who embodies all the qualities of supreme Dharma is very hard to find in these times of decadence![3] In the soil of a pure ethic, he has irrigated his mind with the waters of study and great compassion. He is able to disseminate the teachings because his mind is at peace and free. Guided by his boundless compassion, his only concern is to help others. He has few worldly engagements and devotes his thoughts to the Dharma. He is deeply wearied by samsara and inspires the same feelings in others. He who relies on such a teacher will soon become an accomplished being.

As to false teachers, some are like Brahmans who fear losing their homes and their positions, while others speak well but are no more able to turn the minds of their followers to good than a wooden mill can turn grain into flour, while making a lot of noise. Still others, who have no more than the ordinary person, claim and grossly inflate the qualities that others, in their blind faith, see in them. Taking pride in the offerings they receive and the respect that is shown to them, these teachers are like the frog at the bottom of a well who imagines that its well is as vast as the ocean it has never seen. Others, finally, have studied very little and hold their vows and spiritual connections to no account. Their mind is base, but they behave as if they had attained the very highest spiritual states.

With such crazed teachers, whose cord of love and compassion has been severed, harmful acts are bound to ensue.

Lastly, there are others who have no more qualities than ordinary people and no understanding of the altruistic mind of enlightenment. Placing one's trust in them solely on account of their reputation would be a serious mistake. It would be like putting oneself in the hands of a blind sea captain when crossing the ocean. Making such a misjudgment will plunge us into the deepest shadows.

He who recklessly places his trust in a teacher without meticulously establishing his authenticity will throw all his own virtues to waste and the freedoms that he has managed to acquire will be lost. He is like a man who has mistaken a venomous snake for a rope.

Once one has found an authentic teacher, "uniting with the teacher's nature," or guru yoga, becomes an essential practice based on devotion, which, as we have noted, has nothing to do with "blind faith." It emerges from the recognition of the qualities of enlightenment of which the teacher is the living illustration. This practice allows us to break through the confines of our narrow and confused vision. Our inner sphere is then able to merge with the vast space of the teacher's enlightenment and to rediscover the fundamental nature of our own mind, its luminous emptiness, and its original freedom. This process is difficult to reproduce in the absence of a catalyzer like the guru yoga.

The external teacher also allows us to reconnect with the absolute teacher, the Buddha nature present in us all. As Jamgön Kongtrül,[4] an eminent nineteenth-century teacher, wrote,

Externally, the teacher appears in human form and teaches the path of liberation. Then comes a time when, through his instructions and his blessings, one comes to a realization identical to his. Then one sees that the inner, or absolute, teacher has always been present. It is simply the nature of one's own mind.

Guru yoga is also the most effective practice for removing obstacles and making progress. Deep devotion is required to that end, as written by Drikung Kyobpa,[5] a great twelfth-century master:

If the sun of our devotion
Does not shine on the snow-capped summit
Of the guru's four bodies,
The stream of his blessings will not flow.
Arouse devotion in your mind with determination!

In my humble experience, we feel a sense of elevation in the presence of the teacher that draws the best part of ourselves to the surface, then spreads throughout our mental landscape, bringing joy, serenity, and confidence. This presence restores a sense of adequation between us and the world and other people. The word "elevation" also conjures a feeling of lightness, that of clouds forming in the sky and carried along by a rising breeze. Here, it is the warmth of the teacher's qualities that uplifts the ordinary components of our mind. Uncluttered by cerebration, our mind is ready to embark on the adventure of inner transformation. Our confidence grows—such transformation is possible and represents the highest goal we can aspire to.

But committing to a spiritual teacher is a demanding decision. For our own well-being, the teacher will make no compromises in seeking to eliminate the faults that perpetuate our suffering. Why would she go easy on our deeply entrenched negative tendencies? Why would he make accommodations to our ego, that narcissistic trait that causes us so many problems? What good would it do to let us squander our lives away in the routine of barren thinking and dissipation in activities each more pointless than the last? The teacher's compassion obliges her to wrest us from the quagmire of samsara at any cost. With kindness, the sage disrupts the status quo of our misguidance and sweeps away the rubble of mental habits and knee-jerk responses that keep us in a state of chronic dissatisfaction. The teacher can provide both the gentle maternal caress and the cold shower that awakens us from our slumber and clears away our inner confusion.

For all these reasons, spending time in a teacher's presence and seeing her at regular intervals is immensely valuable. It allows us to set our practice back on track if it has subtly drifted off course.

While it is indispensable for an authentic teacher to possess the qualities described above, we can hardly expect the student to be perfect from the get-go. She has embarked on this journey because, aware of her faults and limitations, she wishes to become a better human being. But she will rightly be expected to behave consistently with the goal she has set for herself and to strive tirelessly to stay on course, gradually eliminate her faults, and cultivate the qualities that will eventually free her from samsara and bring her to enlightenment. It makes no sense for the student to consider as normal, acceptable, or even desirable those faults that clearly hinder her own liberation and that of others from the causes of suffering.

The student must invest her full trust, be diligent in her study and practice, renounce ordinary ambitions, learn to content herself with little and advance toward mastery of her own mind. As Khenpo Yönten Gyatso, a great master of the nineteenth and twentieth centuries, explains in his commentary on *The Treasury of Precious Qualities*,[6] a good student resiliently accepts any circumstance, good or bad, as a bridge that allows all comers to cross. Like an anvil, he is not discouraged by harsh conditions, frugality, the heat of summer, or the cold of winter. He meticulously follows the instructions of his teacher and, with as little vanity as a humble street-sweeper, is filled with respect for the latter and for his own spiritual brothers and sisters. Like a belt that one wears without being aware of it, he is a pleasant and collegial companion and is never demanding. Like salt that dissolves in all waters, be they fresh or saline, he adapts easily to everything that arises. He is aware of his own shortcomings and forswears all forms of arrogance, like an old yak with broken horns that takes its place at the back of the herd. He seeks out places conducive to spiritual practice and ceaselessly nourishes the aspiration to progress toward enlightenment, to be useful to others, and to mitigate their suffering.

In this way, should the student find herself adrift in the sea of samsara and extend the mooring ring of her trust and perseverance to a teacher who uses his wisdom and compassion as a gaffer hook, he can tow her to the high ground of liberation from suffering.

10

IN THE HERMITAGE

From 1972 to 1976, I do not spend a single night outside the monastery. I alternate between retreats in my hermitage and artwork in the temples of the monastery.

Kangyur Rinpoche's children were his principal spiritual heirs. It is largely thanks to his oldest son, Pema Wangyal Rinpoche, that I have been able to pursue my spiritual journey to this day, fifty years later. In the beginning, he translated his father's teachings for me, adding some of his own precious advice, sustained by his own experience and deep personal realization. After Kangyur Rinpoche's death, he became a guide for the retreats I undertook in the years to come, in Darjeeling and elsewhere.

We were later to learn that he had been recognized, by his father and the sixteenth Karmapa, as the incarnation of Taklung Tsetrul Rinpoche, a great master of Taklung Monastery in Tibet. Tulku Pema Wangyal grew up and studied with his father, then extended his philosophical studies at the Central Institute of Higher Tibetan Studies, in Sarnath, a branch of Sampurnanand Sanskrit University, in Varanasi. He also received teachings from some of the most eminent teachers, including Kyabje Dudjom Rinpoche, Dilgo Khyentse Rinpoche, Trulshik Rinpoche, Sakya Trizin, and many other others. On top of that, he spent many years in solitary retreat.

His youngest brother, Jigme Dorje, contracted polio at three and remained disabled. As the youngest, and proving himself to be an out-of-the-ordinary child, he enjoyed special attention from his family. At night he slept snuggled up against his father, and spent a great deal of time with him during the day. Of especially lively intelligence, he charmed everyone with the innocent beauty of his face and the quality of being that emanated from him. His family had always made humility and discretion their primary virtues, and everyone simply called him Jigme, which means "fearless" in Tibetan. With him, too, it wasn't until long afterward that we learned that he had been recognized by several great masters, including his father, as an emanation of Dzongsar Khyentse Chökyi Lodrö, one of the most respected twentieth-century masters of Tibet. We have called him Jigme Khyentse Rinpoche ever since.

Toward the end of 1974, when the first signs of illness appeared in Kangyur Rinpoche, his family begged him to go on living. "You must continue your spiritual work." He pointed to the young Jigme, sitting at the foot of the bed. "You have no reason to be concerned. He will take up my spiritual heritage."

After Kangyur Rinpoche died, his eldest son, Pema Wangyal Rinpoche, who had assumed the management of the monastery, guided me in my retreats. There were two main activities in my life at that time. I devoted myself first and foremost to contemplative retreats, alone in my little hermitage, and also helped with the renovation and decoration of the monastery, especially with painting the temple frescoes.

During one of my retreats, Pema Wangyal Rinpoche very generously gave me a *phurba*, a little ritual object in the form of a three-bladed dagger, symbolizing the powers of the three primordial wisdoms: cutting away the three mental poisons of aversion, attachment-desire, and ignorance. This symbolic object is linked to the practice of Vajrakilaya, a wisdom deity whose meditation removes the external and internal obstacles on the path to enlightenment. A sign seen in a vision had allowed Kangyur Rinpoche to find this *phurba* in the vault of the cave of Rong Trakmar ("Ravine of Red Stone") in central Tibet, the very same nearby cave in which Pema Wangyal was born in a tent at a time when his parents and elder sister had been living there for several months. Once he had extracted the *phurba* from the rocky cave ceiling, Kangyur Rinpoche declared simply that all he had found was a "nail" of no value and left it at that. But his eldest daughter, Rigdzin Chödrön, who had discreetly observed the discovery of this precious object, understood the importance of the event. The *phurba* has never left my side.

Throughout these retreats, all my efforts were focused on inner transformation. I pursued my practice of tackling the spiritual path in phases, including visualizations of mandalas and wisdom deities symbolizing the various aspects of enlightenment, as well as the contemplation of the nature of the mind. The specificity of such practices varies from one practitioner to the next and can be assessed only in the intimacy of the relationship between teacher and student. Suffice it to say that each of these practices fosters the gradual elimination of the veils that mask our innate wisdom and opens the mind to new levels of understanding.

"With patience, the orchard turns into jam," as the saying goes. On the spiritual journey, true change comes slowly but surely. It is like ripening fruit or the hands of a clock that appear still when we stare at them, even as they are moving imperceptibly all the while. "Spiritual fireworks," the various intense meditative experiences that occasionally occur in practice, are like the morning fog—they never last long. If we become attached to them, they turn into obstacles. The distance traveled is not measured in rapid progress or extravagant leaps; it is when we compare what we were a few years earlier to what we have become that we understand all that has happened within ourselves. We can see how our egoism and afflictive mental states have diminished as our serenity, inner freedom, and resilience in the face of life's obstacles have flourished. The signs of our progress can also be measured by the yardstick of our altruism, of the harmony and benevolence we are capable of bringing to our relations with others. If after ten years of practice, they are stilling saying about us, "Oh, he's just as grouchy and impossible to live with as ever," that's a sign that our meditation has taken a wrong turn somewhere. The benchmark of a practice moving in the right direction is, they say, "a temperament that has been pacified and brought under control, combined with a diminution of afflictive mental states."

One essayist has written, "Lacking the courage to endure to the end, the hermit suffers from a kind of inner decay."[1] Going by my own experience, exactly the opposite thing occurred to me. During the lengthy periods I spent in solitary retreat, I did not have to "endure" the slow passage of time; I enjoyed every second of it. Once I had closed the door to my hermitage and at last begun to devote myself to the practices I so cherished, the minutes and hours were transmuted into threads of gold that wove the tapestry of awakening. Every creak of the floorboards, every whisper of the wind, every drop of rain gurgling in the roof gutters and every ray of sunlight that penetrated the room and highlighted the patterns in the wooden wall planks seemed to be in harmony with my mind.

In the quiet of the hermitage, outer circumstances change very little; it is we who are changing. The quality of every passing instant makes all the difference as we rise toward the very best in our ourselves and the spiritual teachers who inspire us.

The contrast is vast when we compare these precious moments of plenitude with the inconstancy of ordinary time, hours wasted in meaningless chatter, days frittered away in idle pastimes, draining our lives away like sand trickling through our fingers. The time that a man of the world does not manage to kill ends up killing him with its meaninglessness.[2]

There is nothing material about the riches we discover on such retreats; they are altogether interior, and all the more radiant with splendor for that. The person we become through this process is the product not of myriad circumstances, adventures, and one new encounter after the next, but of the slow ripening of our abilities toward spiritual realization.

Beyond the reach of the world, the hermitage allows us to become one with the world and to sense at the deepest level the interdependence of all things and all beings, instead of remaining trapped in the bubble of the ego. The spluttering of discursive thought gives way to the space of interior silence that gradually comes to be filled with the clarity of awareness, free of mental projections and fabrications. The boundary between internal and external eventually dissolves in the mind's luminosity. I have a very long way to go before reaching enlightenment, but I can say for sure that every step taken in that direction is eminently rewarding.

I am sometimes asked if I ever knew moments of hesitation or intense doubt like the "dark nights" that some mystics are said to experience. I certainly found myself questioning my own ability to overcome the ignorance, afflictive mental states, and entrenched habits that get in the way of our spiritual enlightenment, and which, having accumulated for so long—many lifetimes, according to Buddhism—are stubborn and deep-rooted. But I do not recall ever having doubted for even one minute my choice to live among my spiritual teachers, the value of their teachings, or the validity of the path I chose to take. I have always taken great joy in studying and practicing and have never felt discouraged, although ever aware that I might have devoted myself with even greater resolve to spiritual practice and serving others.

Buddhism clearly defines the concept of enlightenment. It rises before us like an Everest that, bathed in sunlight, stands out in all its splendor against an immaculate sky. Even so, it must be said that this concept is rarely clear from the start to the neophyte just setting off on the path. The novice might think that she is dealing with something supernatural, but her understanding of enlightenment will grow increasingly refined with her spiritual progression, study, and reflection. And, come what may, I may doubt my ability to climb this formidable mountain, but I do not doubt its existence. I may sometimes feel daunted—"This is not for me. I'd be better off lying on a beach somewhere"—but if I am firm in my conviction that I have embarked on a journey to the highest possible spiritual realization, however long it may take, I will find the energy necessary to muster my strength and set off on the road once again. The practice of Buddhism is far from free of obstacles. Some texts spell them out in lists. We can go astray in our meditation, grow weary or disillusioned, become jaded by the teachings, succumb to discouragement. We may imagine that we have attained profound states of inner realization when they are in fact no more than ephemeral experiences. Hence the importance of a qualified guide who can put things back in their proper place. Ultimately, however, it is up to each practicant to actualize the Buddha nature dwelling within each of us.

Tulku Pema Wangyal sometimes came to visit me in my hermitage in the evening to explain a few pages of commentary that Kangyur Rinpoche had written on Jigme Lingpa's *The Treasury of Precious Qualities*, a teaching that sets out the gradual path according to the Nyingmapa school of Tibetan Buddhism. In addition to the fundamentals of Buddhism—including a description of the suffering of samsara, the means of freeing oneself from it, and the importance of the altruistic vow to attain enlightenment for the good of others—the text offers a dense and profound analysis of the four main philosophical systems of Buddhism, culminating with an overview of the "middle way" (*madhyamaka*), which clearly distinguishes between relative or conventional truth, which is the deluded way in which we perceive the phenomenal world, and absolute truth, which establishes the ultimate reality of consciousness and phenomena, refuting both nihilism and naive realism. The four final chapters of the text, which comprises thirteen in all, address the teachings of the Diamond Vehicle (Vajrayana), which arose in India but were greatly refined in Tibet, as well as teachings on the nature of mind, linked to the view of the Great Perfection. Sometime later, I had the opportunity to commission a handwritten copy of this five-hundred-page text from a Bhutanese calligrapher and was able to get it printed in Delhi. It has recently been translated into English and French by my friends at the Padmakara Translation Group.

Thanks to these teachings, I began to familiarize myself with the philosophical bases of Buddhism, which is essentially a path of knowledge leading to an understanding of the nature of phenomena and of our own mind. It is also a therapeutic path offering concrete and effective remedies for the root causes of suffering.

The spiritual path is not a thousand-mile trek through a scorching desert that finally ends at an oasis where you can bathe in a lake of ambrosia. It is a long, slow inner journey that gradually and almost imperceptibly dissipates our confusions under the light of a wisdom that deepens day by day. Every step is worth the effort and rewards us with a wealth of benefits.

To get there, we need to identify the causes of suffering at all levels and recognize that it is possible to free ourselves from them. At the same time, it is not enough to temporarily soothe the mental afflictive states of hatred, desire, pride, or jealousy through specific antidotes, such as using benevolence to counteract aversion, for instance. Such antidotes are in effect powerless to eradicate the prime cause of suffering: ignorance of the true nature of phenomena. The sole and unique remedy for such ignorance is understanding the "ultimate truth" that all things are empty of existence.

Buddhism does not, however, descend into nihilism, as some nineteenth-century thinkers proclaimed. The philosopher Victor Cousin, among others, spoke of the "cult of nothingness"[3] and the "deplorable idea of annihilation at the heart of Buddhism."[4] It would be patently absurd to deny the existence of phenomena, since they clearly manifest themselves in infinite ways through the effect of a multiplicity of interdependent causes and conditions. Phenomena do not arise out nothingness, do not occur haphazardly, and cannot be their own prime cause.

Buddhism offers an alternative path to the two extreme, erroneous philosophies of nihilism and realism, or eternalism. By recognizing the interdependent production of phenomena, Buddhism refutes nihilism. By recognizing through exhaustive analysis that phenomena are devoid of intrinsic existence even as they manifest themselves, naive realism is undermined. Essentially, the correct manner of describing phenomena and their nature is as the union of appearances and emptiness.

In 1976, between two retreats in my hermitage above Darjeeling, I spent six months assisting an artist who had been entrusted with painting the frescoes in the temple where Kangyur Rinpoche's family lived. The structure of the main temple on the first floor of the monastery had been completed in Kangyur Rinpoche's lifetime, but we had yet to paint the frescoes that were to adorn the walls with representations of the Buddha Shakyamuni and his principal disciples, and Guru Padmasambhava surrounded by the most eminent masters of the main schools of Tibetan Buddhism, as well as the wisdom deities corresponding to the spiritual treasures (*termas*) revealed by Kangyur Rinpoche.

When the moment came to begin the frescoes, Tulku Pema Wangyal asked me to assist Konchog Lhadrepa, who is today, fifty years later, the painting master of the Tsering Art School at Shechen Monastery in Nepal, where I currently live. Konchog-la (Tibetans often add the suffix "la" to someone's name as a sign of respect) first sketched out the deities and landscapes in charcoal, then traced their outlines with ink and brush. Then, following instructions, and although I did not know how to draw (I did not inherit my mother's artistic talent and am quite incapable of drawing even a sheep!), I filled in the colors and applied the gradients with as much care as I was able to muster. Martin Watten, an American disciple who later became a monk, joined us for a month.

I drew great satisfaction from this work. The atmosphere was tranquil, and from morning till night, we naturally fell into a state of "flow," total immersion of the mind in which the perception of the self and of passing time fade away.[5] It was also thanks to those six months in the company of Konchog-la, who did not speak a word of English, that I crossed a threshold in my apprenticeship in spoken Tibetan. I soon came to understand the capital advantage of being able to speak with my Tibetan teachers in their own language, especially in my work as a translator of texts.

As indescribably fruitful as these years were for my inner life, seen from the outside they were totally lacking in adventure. In the evening, as I watched the sun go down, it felt as if only a few hours had passed since the last sunset. Yet, there is nothing monotonous about spiritual practice, in which the mind is so fully engaged that its homogeneous and harmonious flow alters our perception of time. Trying to describe it feels like a challenge, given how the inner sense of passing time completely eludes our standard modes of description, and my life during those days of retreat was so devoid of variety that it provides almost no fodder for a compelling narrative.

The only disturbances of any note came from visits by mice of all sizes, gnawing at the attic lumber with a sound that was all the more invasive as the silence was otherwise almost complete. I devised a "nonviolent" trap to catch them. I struck a nail into a small plank, to which I tied a little piece of cheese or other food item with a string. Its other end was attached to a beam and sufficiently tightened to gently lift one side of a Britannia Biscuits tin, which covered the whole contraption. Attracted by the scent, the mouse crawled beneath the box, and once it had eaten the cheese, the string was freed. The box dropped with a rather victorious racket, temporarily trapping the rodent, which struggled in all directions. When the young monk brought me my meals during my retreats, I gave him the biscuit tin so he could liberate the little creature at a respectable distance. Unfortunately, it turned out that I had underestimated either a mouse's sense of direction or the number of them in search of lodgings. In either case, a new candidate for the biscuit tin never took long to present itself.

Years later, in 1978, toward the end of my time in Darjeeling, I caught one of my little visitors just as I was preparing to go to Bodhgaya to meet Dilgo Khyentse Rinpoche, who had given us precious teachings during the month after Kangyur Rinpoche's death. He was soon to become my second primary teacher. I decided to take the mouse with me on my pilgrimage. I was able to transfer it from the biscuit tin into a glass jar, whose lid I riddled with holes so the little traveler could breathe. I added a healthy provision of lettuce and a wad of cotton drenched in water. I put the jar into my canvas satchel and off we went. My friend seemed to thrive during the two days we spent on the train. When we reached the Great Stupa of Bodhgaya, I set it free at the foot of the Bodhi Tree, where the Buddha Shakyamuni had achieved enlightenment two thousand years earlier. A rare destiny for a Himalayan mouse!

There were, of course, minor incidents that punctuated the routine calm and serenity of my retreats in the little hermitage. When earthquakes struck, it would sway on its stilts, sometimes wildly, sometimes less so. One time, a litter of puppies born beneath the hermitage went missing, carried off by a fox. The mother sat for two days without moving, her eyes empty, her gaze absent, prey to a grief that wrenched the heart, beside the corpse of one of her babies, lying where it had been abandoned.

Another time, the young monks who took turns bringing me sustenance forgot to bring me my meals three days in a row. Finally, I flagged one of them down as he was passing nearby and asked him to deliver a brief written note to Kangyur Rinpoche's eldest daughter, who ran the kitchen: "My mind is very happy, but my body is a little indisposed after three days of fasting." A half-hour later, a young monk hustled up, bearing a fine meal on a platter!

Every so often, sounds would rise up from the main road, 200 yards below, linking Darjeeling to the plains of India. The whistle of the little train that had brought me here for my first visit sang out several times a day, and during the season of Hindu holidays—Holi, Dashain, Diwali—loudspeakers blared songs from Bollywood musicals, which I eventually got to know by heart.

Magnificent birds sometimes alighted on the rhododendrons outside my window. During the rainy season, the soundscape was dominated by a species of cicada that nested in the immense cedars, some fifteen to twenty yards tall, and whose shrill drone stridulated through the fog impressively long and impressively loud. These were the nuptial calls of the males engaged in intense competition to attract a mate, inspiring generally a half-dozen responses in my immediate vicinity. The love song ended in a decrescendo several seconds long, when almost immediately afterward another cicada took up the challenge in the next tree. There were also the monotone and more discreet calls of the tree frogs. Big flying squirrels, of a fine reddish color, occasionally glided from one tree to another, while pairs of golden eagles circled high above.

11

A PRINTER IN DELHI

In 1976, I leave the monastery for a few months to publish some fifty volumes prepared from rare manuscripts that Kangyur Rinpoche had taken with him in his flight from Tibet. I meet the renowned Tibet scholar Gene Smith.

In late 1976, I realized that in the four years since my arrival in Darjeeling toward the end of 1972, I was the only resident never to have spent a single night beyond the monastery compound in which the hermitages were located. Even Kangyur Rinpoche and his family had spent time away at the thermal springs of Khandro Sang Phug, in Sikkim, and the other followers had all gone away at one time or another.

In early 1977, Tulku Pema Wangyal asked me to go to Delhi to print the nineteen volumes of the complete works of the great master Ratna Lingpa, as well as several other important texts. He entrusted me to Lama Sangye, an old lama from Sikkim whom he knew well and who printed Tibetan texts on behalf of Dodrupchen Rinpoche, a great master who lived in Sikkim.

Ratna Lingpa lived in the fifteenth century. From an early age, he demonstrated a powerful attraction to the spiritual life. As a child watching over herds of sheep in the mountain pastures, he spent most of his day meditating while the sheep grazed. At twenty-seven, he had a vision of Padmasambhava in the form of a yogi dressed in yellow wild silk. Padmasambhava held out three scrolls—one white, one red, and one blue—and asked him to choose one. Ratna Lingpa answered that he wanted all three. Thanks to the auspicious connection forged by his response, it is said that Ratna Lingpa revealed in one lifetime the hidden treasures (*terma*) that it should have taken him three to find. Afterward, he revealed twenty-five cycles of precious teachings that are still widely practiced today within Tibetan Buddhism. Kangyur Rinpoche was the main holder of that lineage outside of Tibet. Several other great masters, including Dudjom Rinpoche and Dilgo Khyentse Rinpoche, wished to receive the transmission of the complete *terma* of Ratna Lingpa from him. Kangyur Rinpoche therefore gathered the complete works of that master and asked the most skillful calligrapher in the region, Tripa Tenzin, to recopy the entire work in his elegant and perfectly uniform penmanship, which took him several years. The texts were now ready to be reproduced. It was a privilege for me to be taking care of this publishing venture.

Bearing these invaluable manuscripts, I left Kangyur Rinpoche's monastery and Darjeeling for the bustle of the Indian railways and the old city of Delhi. There I found Lama Sangye, a monk in his sixties. He was stocky and wore a beaming smiling but could also be a little gruff, and we quickly became good friends. For several weeks, we shared a room at a welcome center for Buddhist pilgrims, the Ladakh Budh-Vihar, on the banks of the Yamuna River, and then took two adjacent rooms rented from a householder in the heart of old Delhi.

Collections of Tibetan texts are very different from what we Westerners think of as books. They are unbound, oblong, rectangular folios, held within two boards made of wood or stiff cardboard, one on top and one on bottom, keeping the folios in place. The whole thing is then swathed in silk or cotton fabric fitted with a strip that is wrapped around it to fasten and protect it against dust and insects.

First, we had to number the pages of all these tomes in Arabic numerals, since the printers of old Delhi, Muslims for the most part, obviously did not read Tibetan. We therefore had large sheets of paper printed with the series of numbers from 1 to 1,000. We then had to cut them into little strips and make a notch between each digit so that they could be separated easily and glued one by one to the long folios of our Tibetan books. The task requires patience but is not difficult, other than if you make a mistake you need to identify it right away, if you don't want to have to start all over again from the beginning.

On the day after my arrival, Lama Sangye, who was an early riser, woke me up at 3:00 a.m., saying, "Come on, let's glue numbers." I graciously did as I was asked. When two or three volumes were ready, we went to the center of the old town, to Ballimaran Road, a commercial street buzzing with activity where most printers kept storefronts. Like most of the streets in that neighborhood, it was very narrow and had no sidewalks. It is the only place in the world where I have ever seen serious traffic jams with no cars. There were rickshaws—tricycles equipped with a bench for two passengers (although they can carry up to four!), powered by some poor fellow who pedals all day long for a few rupees—carts laden with merchandise, pulled by one or two buffalo, and pedestrians, an ocean of pedestrians. If you wanted to cross the street, which was only four yards wide, you sometimes had to climb over a rickshaw, greeting the passengers as you passed. The risks were greater still when traffic was on the move. I soon learned that if I heard a rickshaw's hand-powered air horn blast a warning, it was best to scramble out of the way immediately without looking to see what was coming full speed from behind. In a similar situation in the West, people would be calling each other all sorts of names. In India, such in extremis self-preservation reflexes are quite efficient, and no one takes offense at these collisions avoided at the last minute. Drivers and pedestrians alike are amazingly skilled at getting around without hurting themselves in this chaotic torrent of men, beasts, and vehicles and a blaring din of horns that is in no way aggressive, as is often the case in Europe, but simply serves to provide a sound marker of one's location vis-à-vis other people. In India, they joke that if your brakes give out you keep going, but if your horn dies, you'd better pull over.

Between two shops, a steep and narrow stairway led to the place that was to be our workshop for the next few months: Mujeeb Press. The printshop belonged to Mujeeb "Sahib" (a courtesy honorific), a witty and intelligent Muslim who, in addition to his printing work, rubbed shoulders with the politicians of the day, including the sons of Indira Gandhi. Even so, the place was hardly spiffy: two rooms on the second floor outfitted with large, glassless openings overlooking the street. The two rooms were separated by a kind of tiny, open-air courtyard. It had been many years since the walls had been whitewashed, and they now bore some resemblance to abstract art. In the back room, Mujeeb held court part of the day in his dilapidated office, generally in the company of two or three guests who were served milky tea with cardamom, heavily sweetened—the famous Indian *chai*. Affable and refined, Mujeeb liked to chitchat about anything and everything.

Four or five of us "printers" from various monasteries set ourselves up in this space. We worked hard all day and went home late. Our printing technology dated from the earliest days of photo-offset. It was a lengthy process. The Tibetan folios were lined up one above the other in groups of six or seven and photographed full size with an enormous wooden box camera. Once the film was developed on-site, we were given the negatives, twenty inches by thirty each, and our work began. The locally made film stock and the chemicals used to develop it were of poor quality. Countless little white spots and larger splotches muddied the black background of the negatives. All these defects had to be retouched one by one by using paintbrush and opacifier on a light table. If the original happened to be a manuscript recently calligraphed on white paper—as were the tomes that I had been sent to print—the work went relatively fast and took about ten minutes per negative. But if the original was an ancient manuscript on rough Tibetan paper, or one printed from wooden blocks, the negative had countless white patches that took hours to retouch.

Next, Suleiman, one of the supervisors, cut the negatives up page by page and mounted them in a frame. He brought each one to the roof to expose plates made of zinc or aluminum coated with photosensitive material to the sunlight. The texts came out black against these metal sheets. Now it was our turn again. We used India ink to retouch all the spots where the letters had not been printed correctly and a pumice to grind off any undesirable black patches. Depending on the quality of the original, you could spend anywhere from ten minutes to two hours on one zinc plate. The plates were then sent off to a printing outfit in a basement in a nearby street, consisting of two Heidelberg offset presses dating from the 1930s, operated by a master printer assisted by three or four kids aged twelve to fifteen. Child labor was still common in India at that time, serving both as professional training and as financial backup for the parents.

Because there were so many people like me working on texts, it wasn't always easy to get your hands on enough zinc plates for one day, so my time in Delhi lasted longer than foreseen and the hot season set in. In Delhi between late April and late June, before the monsoon begins, "hot" means between 105°F and 120°F in the shade during the day, and 95°F at night. As a result, we had a fan continuously blowing hot air in our faces as we retouched the negatives. It was better than nothing. Indeed, whenever it was cut off by one of the frequent blackouts, you had to step back fast or within seconds you'd have great beads of sweat falling onto the film and ruining all your work. I usually prepared a little food in the morning that I brought with me in a plastic container. During the dog days, the food had almost always spoiled by noon. It was better to eat at one of the little restaurants on the street. I was unlikely to go broke: at lunchtime, a plate of curried rice and vegetables cost the equivalent of one dollar, and in the evening a bowl of *dal* (Indian yellow lentils rich in protein) and four *chapatis* (wheat flatbread baked against the wall of a clay oven) ran to seventy-five cents.

Plowing valiantly through the work, and with joyful tenacity, I completed the nineteen volumes, which were duly printed, trimmed with a cutter, and assembled. At the binder's workshop, I painted the volumes' edges in red, in accordance with Tibetan tradition.

Every volume was printed in three hundred copies, a number sufficient to meet the demand and needs of the lamas and monasteries to which we intended to offer these precious texts. We had ordered wooden crates, each one thirty inches square, that had been used to ship tea from the plantations in eastern India, and packed them with books, protecting them with the cuttings left over from the trimming process. Once the crates had been sealed with metal bands, they were sent to a shipping firm, which then trucked them to our monastery.

Old Delhi is a beehive of activity night and day. I once had to cross town at two o'clock in the morning after getting off a late train, and found people in the street hammering away at metal parts, while others chatted away blithely in the middle of the street, as if it was just the right time and place for working and sharing news. One afternoon, I was approached by a man of very modest appearance who insisted that I come home with him for a cup of tea. He wanted to discuss philosophy. I followed him into his dusty and cluttered room, where piles of books reached right up to the ceiling. He talked for half an hour without a break about the differences in perspective between the great Buddhist philosopher Nagarjuna and the renowned Advaita Vedanta theologian Shankaracharya. Anything seemed possible in that maze of medieval streets that never slept.

With no windows, doors, or even any kind of dividing partition, the merchant's stalls opened directly onto the street. When night fell, the owner pulled down a metal shutter and padlocked it at ground level, from the outside. The tradesmen were still organized into guilds in those days. You might find a dozen workshops on one block, all open to the street, where craftsmen used wooden mallets to hammer away all day long at sheets of gold placed between two thin leather sheaths, transforming them into gold leaf so fine you only had to breathe on it to flatten it if it creased. This gold leaf was produced to decorate statues of Hindu divinities, as a symbol of offering and reverence.

But Ballimaran and its old precincts also had their share of suffering: beggars, crippled children recruited by criminal gangs that sent them out into the streets and took all the alms they had collected at the end of the day, young homeless restaurant waiters and shop clerks who slept in their workplaces, untouchable women who silently entered homes to empty and clean the toilets. On cold winter nights, three or four rickshaw operators, whose families generally lived outside Delhi, would gather and build fires from boxes collected in the streets. They argued and laughed cheerfully as they warmed themselves, then wrapped themselves in thin blankets and curled up to sleep on the banquettes of their rickshaws. The torrid summer posed no problem for those who slept outdoors, but every winter the homeless died of cold at night. One of the most heartbreaking sights was that of Muslim widows reduced to begging, crouched against a wall in the street, their hands outstretched. Unlike other Muslim women, they wore a white burqa and never remarried. If they found themselves forced to beg, it was because they had no one to take care of them, for in Indian families all generations live together and the elderly are rarely abandoned. These women watched the world pass by through the mesh of the eye slits in their burqas; it is possible that, for some, no other human being ever returned their gaze.

Over the course of the two years following that first visit, I returned to Delhi for two or three months to print various other books that Tulku

Pema Wangyal had entrusted to me. On my second stay, I lived with the team set up by Lama Ngodrup to print a collection of sixty volumes pursuant to the instructions of Dilgo Khyentse Rinpoche. These volumes contained the main "hidden treasures" (*terma*) revealed between the eleventh century and the first half of the nineteenth, when the collection was first put together. One member of the publishing team was a scholar, Lama Puzi, who, every day after lunch, elucidated for me a text teaching how to harmoniously combine the views and practices of the three main traditions or "vehicles" of Buddhism: Theravada, Mahayana, and Vajrayana.[1] These friends had rented half of a floor occupied by a Muslim family. I was charmed by the contrast between the way the mother and her three daughters remained hidden and discreet under their burqas when they went out, and their sociable, chatty, and joyful behavior at home. The father even suggested that I bring one of them back with me to France, a friendly offer that I politely declined. The mother had almost never left the neighborhood. In her entire life, she had gone only once to the Qutub Minar, the tallest minaret in India, located on the other side of Delhi, and twice to the Lal Qila, the Red Fort, even though it was only a fifteen-minute walk from the alley in which she lived. Although this sedentary lifestyle conformed to the strict Islamic code of conduct for women, she nevertheless reminded me of the aged inhabitants of the little port of the island of Houat, in Brittany, where I had once gone sailing with my uncle and his friends—who, for entirely different reasons, claimed that they had never been to "the continent," only six miles from the island.

I spent my second stay in Delhi printing a collection of thirteen volumes of writings of Gyalwa Longchen Rabjam. Unfortunately, we were missing two volumes that we had been unable to locate in the library before I left the monastery. One day, I received a letter from Darjeeling (the monastery had no phone, and other than letters, its only means of communication was by telegram), informing me that the two volumes had just been found in the library of a lama from Kalimpong, who had been very happy to lend them to us for the printing. An American visitor, who happened to be staying at the monastery at the time, would bring me these rare texts when he passed through Delhi on his way home. On the day of our rendezvous, I left home early in the morning for New Delhi to meet him at the high end hotel where he was staying. He seemed happy to see me and offered me a cup of tea. When I asked him about the books, he told me that, concerned about the excess baggage weight, he had not brought them with him (they weighed four pounds altogether!). I could find no other response than a laconic "Oh well." We obviously lived in two different worlds, and in my heart I could see no use in explaining what this would mean for me. I thanked him for the tea and returned to the old town. The next day, I boarded the train, traveled two days and two nights, climbed up to the Darjeeling monastery, where I spent the night, then grabbed the books and left forthwith in the other direction. I was somewhat comforted by the fact that I felt no irritation or discouragement but was instead confirmed in my belief that the house of samsara really was a strange place. Throughout my life, I have often had occasion to appreciate this sense of relief and to assess the extent to which resentment can relentlessly poison the mind. It is one of the mental toxins that we must guard ourselves against at any cost.

One early afternoon as I was reading in the half-light of the room I shared with two Bhutanese from Lama Ngodrup's team, the presence of Kangyur Rinpoche grew so strong within me that I caught a brief glimpse of what is called "pure vision."[2] I saw the dusty table, the very mundane objects around me, the furniture, and the room as a whole—in a word, everything that could be seen and apprehended—as a manifestation of Kangyur Rinpoche. Every ordinary sound—the ticking of the clock, the distant hubbub and car horns in the street, the murmurs of my companions talking at the far side of the room—resonated with his voice. And all my thoughts swelled with the awakened wisdom of my cherished teacher. Such an experience, as necessarily limited as it was in my case, nevertheless gives a sense of, or an opening into, what for seasoned practitioners is a sustained experience of pure vision that continuously perceives all forms as manifestations of the body of the teacher or the Buddha, all sounds as the reverberation of mantras, and all thought movement as the echo of primordial wisdom. The continuity of this mode of "pure" perception also corresponds to the teaching that when a master has left this world and his physical body, he is present everywhere and at all times.

It was also on my visits to Delhi that I came to know E. Gene Smith, an outstanding scholar who also became a dear friend. Everyone agreed that he was the most learned Tibetologist of the twentieth century and made a major contribution to saving the literary heritage of Tibet. He had been appointed field director of the United States Library of Congress Field Office in India, a job he accepted with the aim of working to preserve Tibetan texts. By a stroke of luck, the Indian government had to repay a debt to the American government but did so in local currency, which allowed Gene Smith to finance the Tibetans' efforts to print the rare and precious texts in their possession. The Library of Congress paid top dollar for fifteen to twenty copies of each volume, which covered the expense of printing two hundred additional copies that the Tibetans were then able to distribute to those in need or sell at cost.

Gene Smith was very kind to me and, on my third visit to Delhi, generously invited me into his home, located in a more well-heeled neighborhood of New Delhi, where I lived in conditions considerably more comfortable than those of my previous stays. Every morning, I took the bus to the printing house on the far side of Delhi.

Gene received a constant flow of Tibetans bearing texts and hoping that the Library of Congress would agree to finance their publication. He had an encyclopedic knowledge of Buddhist traditions and was able to discern immediately whether a book was a rare pearl, a work of use to the heirs of Tibetan culture and scholars, or a manuscript or woodblock print of a work that was already in print. On occasion, he could be heard shouting joyfully on receiving a text that had been feared lost. At other times, he might be heard scolding someone in Tibetan, with his usual outspokenness: "What is this you've brought me? An incomplete manuscript with spelling mistakes on every other line. We have much better versions of this already." Gene had an unrivaled mastery of Tibetan and an especially sharp eye that could instantly spot a spelling or grammatical mistake on the page.

Once a book had been accepted, Gene wrote a preface in English for each tome or collection, confirming its importance, and created a table of contents. The complete edition of his prefaces is a trove of illuminating information on Tibetan literature. Once the texts had been published, the Library of Congress sent copies to the libraries of various American universities and others around the world. Clearly unaware of the importance of these texts, one such institution sent him an astonishing request, asking him to stop sending them these "baseball bats," alluding to the oblong shape of Tibetan books, which did not fit comfortably on its shelves.

Gene was a powerfully built man, fleshy, with a booming voice that some might find intimidating, even though he was extraordinarily kind and helpful in all circumstances. He was a tireless toiler who got up at 4 a.m. and had already completed most of the day's business by breakfast time. His entire family consisted of his butler, Mangal Ram, and two beloved dalmatians. But the doors to his home were always open, and his table was the gathering place for Tibetan scholars passing through India from all over the world. It was there that I met Carisse and Gérard Busquet, who were living in Delhi at the time. Writers and journalists, they became close friends, and, over the years, Carisse faithfully helped me to edit my translations from the Tibetan and other writings.

Not content with possessing a unique mastery of Tibetan literature and history, Gene also knew Indonesian and was able to read Mongolian and other languages. Before moving to Delhi, he had studied with Dezhung Rinpoche, a renowned Tibetan scholar who had emigrated to the United States and whom he considered to be his mentor. In India, Gene also came to hold Dilgo Khyentse Rinpoche in high esteem. He had framed many photographs of this great master, to whom he generously offered his hospitality whenever the latter passed through Delhi—hospitality in which I shared once I was attached to Dilgo Khyentse Rinpoche, beginning in 1979. We were in fact a rather numerous little delegation at that time, and Gene placed his entire household, including his butler Mangal Ram, at Dilgo Khyentse Rinpoche's disposal. He gave his own room to Rinpoche and went to sleep at a hotel. Gene spent the day with us and debated the texts and historical subjects with the master at length. Khyentse Rinpoche was very fond of Gene and affectionately called him Mahapandita Jamyang Namgyal. Mahapandita is the Indian honorific accorded to great scholars, and Jamyang Namgyal, Gene's Tibetan name, meant "Gentle Victorious Glory"—Jamyang, "Gentle Glory," being the Tibetan name of Manjushri, the buddha of wisdom. When Khyentse Rinpoche called him by this name, Gene shrugged it off bashfully and laughed modestly; he was deeply humble and took no vain pride in his immense knowledge.

It was also at Gene's home that I met the Tibetologist Michael Aris and his wife Aung San Suu Kyi, who had lived in Bhutan. Michael had been tutor to the crown prince of that little kingdom for several years. Michael was a colorful character, whereas Suu, who was not well known in those days, was more circumspect by nature. I have no precise memory of our conversations, but I had no idea at that time that she would play a key role in the history of Myanmar. When she spent fifteen years under house arrest, her husband, whom I met again later in Nepal, was not authorized to visit with her. He told me that she had read and reread the teachings of Khyentse Rinpoche, which I had translated and published in English.

In the more than twenty-five years he spent in India, Gene was able to save almost ten thousand volumes of Tibetan texts—the very life's blood of the heritage of the Land of Snow. He informed me, incidentally, that in terms of the sheer number of books, classical Tibetan literature was the third largest in the East, after Sanskrit and Chinese, and larger even than Japanese.

When the funds for buying Tibetan books dried up, Gene decided to return to the United States. He had his entire library shipped to New York, where Mangal Ram spent several months setting it up in his apartment. But Gene was not done yet. With the assistance of the Rubin Museum of Art, he established the Tibetan Buddhist Resource Center (TBRC) and put together a team of Tibetans living in the United States. He then hired programmers to digitize, index, and post all available Tibetan texts on the Internet. These works were soon joined by books recently reprinted by Tibetans in China. TBRC is today the largest virtual depository of Tibetan books in the world. When Gene's entire oeuvre had been scanned, he considered presenting it to the national library of Bhutan or to our monastery, Shechen, in Nepal. Eventually, he chose Chengdu, in China, a city where many Tibetans with origins in the high plateaus had settled and where the Gene Smith Memorial Library was built. Gene died in 2010, but the TBRC—now the Buddhist Digital Resource Center—is valiantly carrying on his work in Boston.

In retrospect, I have a better understanding of the importance of my years as an "apprentice printer" in Delhi. They were formative, to the extent that they actuated my vocation to preserve the Tibetan spiritual patrimony to the best of my abilities. Born in conditions that are best described as artisanal, the experience strengthened my motivation to do everything within my power to disseminate these texts, whose depth and value are inestimable not only to the faithful but, in my opinion, to the world's cultural and spiritual heritage as a whole. As the Dalai Lama has said, "Tibet has no fossil fuels for cars, but it does have fuel for the mind, and the heritage of Tibetan Buddhist culture concerns not only 6 million Tibetans, but all of humankind."

Between 1977 and 1980, I was able to print some fifty precious volumes, each of around six hundred pages.[3] Later, after I joined Shechen Monastery in Nepal, the monastery's team and I continued the publication effort launched by Lama Ngodrup and supervised the digitization and publication of the complete works of Dilgo Khyentse Rinpoche, amounting to about twenty-five volumes, as well another hundred volumes of great significance to the Tibetan tradition and Buddhism in general. The advent of the digital era marked a great leap forward in the preservation and dissemination of texts and artworks.

12

IN THE KATHMANDU VALLEY

My first visit to Nepal to receive several months of teachings and empowerments from two great teachers: Dudjom Rinpoche and Dilgo Khyentse Rinpoche.

In the winter of 1977–1978, Kangyur Rinpoche's family decided to go to Nepal to receive precious teachings that Dudjom Rinpoche and Khyentse Rinpoche planned to offer to a large number of followers over the course of several months. The Western students living in Darjeeling—including my mother, who happened to be in the middle of one of her stays at the monastery, and me—would join in the trip. This was to be was our first visit to Nepal, a very beautiful country where I would later live for many years. The bus ride from Darjeeling to Kathmandu, the capital, took two days. We crossed the eastern part of Nepal's semitropical plains before beginning our climb toward the valley and crossing the small mountain pass, at an altitude of 6,000 feet, that leads to the heart of Nepali civilization, of which Kathmandu was still the jewel in those years.

Sandwiched between the Himalaya mountains, dominated by Everest, and the vast Indo-Gangetic plain of northern India, Nepal is home to diverse populations and a multitude of cultural and spiritual traditions. The mountain peoples of the Himalayas—the Sherpa, the Manangi, the peoples of Dolpo, Humla, Mugu, Mustang, Khumbu, and so on—are for the most part Buddhist and culturally Tibetan, due to the proximity of the high valleys in which they live and the many passes to the high plateaus of Tibet. On the other hand, the inhabitants of the valleys and plains are majority Hindu. The ethnic and cultural blending has given rise to a mutually tolerant coexistence. Nepal is blessed with a rich and varied natural environment, ranging—in the space of a hundred miles from south to north—from semitropical plains and forests that are still home to elephants, tigers, and a few rare Indian rhinoceroses in the Terai to the highest peaks in the world.

We arrived a few weeks before the teachings were due to begin. We found three little peasant cottages to rent near Boudhanath, a village on the outskirts of Kathmandu that is home to the great stupa of Jarung Kashor, not far from where the teachings were to be given. This was still deep in the countryside in those days, whereas today, forty years later, the city of Kathmandu extends unbroken all the way to Boudhanath. Amala, Kangyur Rinpoche's wife, and her daughters occupied one of the cottages, which consisted of two rooms on the second floor and a disused stable on the ground floor. Tulku Pema Wangyal, his brothers, and two young monks from Darjeeling took a similar cottage, while my mother, a few Western students, and I created a kind of dormitory in the third house next door.

During those three weeks, Tulku Pema Wangyal led us on a pilgrimage to all the holy sites in the Kathmandu Valley and its surroundings. One evening, he and I found ourselves standing before the great stupa of Jarung Kashor, one of the three most revered stupas in the region, alongside those of Swayambunath and Namo Buddha. This enormous monument, some 120 feet high, impresses by its size, its majesty, and its serene splendor. It is also of extraordinary historical significance, its construction having been directly linked to the dissemination of Buddhism in Tibet. According to a text discovered by Shakya Zangpo in 1512 in the large red stupa of Samye, in Tibet, a poultry farmer named Samvari was brought before a Nepali king of the Licchavi dynasty (which ruled from the fifth to the eighth or ninth centuries) so that she could ask him to grant her land on which to build a stupa to house relics of the buddha Kashyap.[1] The king granted her wish, admiring the resolve of this woman of humble origin. Sometime later, his ministers reported to the king that the monument raised by Samvari was gigantic. Could a woman of such modest extraction be allowed to build something so big? Did it not reflect ill on His Majesty?

The king responded: "'Let it be done' [*jarung*] slipped from my tongue [*kashor*]. The king speaks but once!" That is how the great stupa of Boudhanath was later named Jarung Kashor. With nothing but a buffalo to help in all their labors, Samvari and her sons worked on its construction without a break, summer and winter, for four years. They completed the main part of the stupa in that time. But then the poor poultry farmer learned that she had little time left to live. She summoned her four sons and their helpmeet, the buffalo, and urged them to finish the construction of the stupa.[2] They fulfilled her request. It is said that at the moment of the stupa's consecration, each of them made a wish. The first son wished, in a future life, to be a master who would bring Buddhism to the Country of Snow; he was reborn as Padmasambhava. The second son asked to be reborn a king so that he could invite the master to Tibet; he became the emperor Trisong Detsen. The third son wished to be the one to go to India to invite Padmasambhava to Tibet; he became the minister Bami Trihzi. And the fourth asked to be reincarnated as the man who would establish the monastic and philosophical tradition in Tibet; he became the Abbot Shantarakshita. But they forgot to honor the buffalo that had worked so hard carrying and hauling all the construction materials. Angered, the buffalo made the wish to be reborn as the king who would destroy all that the sons had accomplished; he returned to life as King Langdarma, who persecuted Buddhists.

Beyond the legend that surrounds it, the stupa has personal meaning for me. I live nearby, just a few hundred yards away, in Shechen Monastery, and the stupa's turbulent history over the centuries bears powerful witness to Buddhist resilience. It went to ruin and was rebuilt in the sixteenth century by Shakya Zangpo and was then renovated in the seventeenth century by Rangrik Repa; in the early nineteenth century, Shabkar, the great yogi of Amdo, gilded it with gold leaf. In the late sixties, its "tree of life"—the trunk of a sandalwood or juniper tree on which relics are hung—was charred by lightning. Dilgo Khyentse Rinpoche replaced it, perching it at the top of the stupa's dome. Then, in 2015, following two powerful earthquakes, the upper part of the stupa was completely rebuilt to restore its former splendor. Devotees regularly whitewash the stupa. Attendants throw saffron water in broad semicircular movements onto the dome, tracing the immense outlines of lotus petals. From the pinnacle to the base of the stupa and in long oblique lines, five-color prayer flags snap in the wind, carrying off prayers for peace, compassion, and love to all sentient beings in the world. Thanks to the determination and engagement of all involved, the holy site is home to precious relics to this very day. For devotees the world over, it is a majestic lighthouse, made resplendent by the thousands of hours of reflection it has inspired.

But an even more personal and profound association connects me with this holy place. Without quite knowing why, on the night of my first visit to the great stupa of Jarung Kashor, while I stood beside Tulku Pema Wangyal with my hands together, I renewed my bodhisattva vows, the precious *bodhicitta*, the mind of awakening, and the altruistic vow to achieve enlightenment. I was animated by an intensity more powerful than I had ever felt as I prayed: "In this life and in all my lives, may my body down to its very last atom, as well as my speech and my mind, be entirely devoted to the service of others." I then stood in silence for several moments, absorbed in this aspiration with unadulterated sincerity. Ever since, every time I walk around the stupa, I stop for a few minutes before moving on, bring my hands together, and renew that vow by reciting these hallowed verses, written by the great Indian scholars Nagarjuna and Shantideva:

With the wish to free all beings
I shall always go for refuge
To the Buddha, Dharma, and Sangha,
Until I reach full enlightenment.

Enthused by wisdom and compassion,
Today in the Buddha's presence
I generate the Mind for Full Awakening
For the benefit of all sentient beings.

The mind of awakening is the most precious of jewels.
Let us generate it if it is not generated;
Once generated, may it never weaken
Or stop growing stronger.

As long as space remains,
As long as sentient beings remain,
Until then, may I too remain
To dispel the miseries of the world.

Our pilgrimages took us, among other places, to Namo Buddha, 6,000 feet above sea level in the hills about thirty miles east of Kathmandu. It is said that in this sacred place, at the end of one of his past lives, he who would become the Buddha Shakyamuni gave his body to a tigress and her three cubs, who were dying of hunger, and prayed that they would all be reborn as his first disciples when he reached enlightenment.

Tulku Pema Wangyal, a few friends, and I began the climb to Namo Buddha. This is done on foot from the village of Panauti, along dirt paths that cross grain fields and rice paddies. We had to be particularly wary at the approach of water buffaloes, which can be unpredictable when faced with strangers. We spent the night at Namo Buddha, where in those days there were only two or three homes around Thrangu Rinpoche's meditation retreat. I had no idea that, thirty years later, I would undertake lengthy retreats in a hermitage on a hill only a mile or two away.

In Boudhanath in late December 1977, the event for which we had come to Nepal was held just a few hundred yards from the Jarung Kashor stupa. Kyabje Dudjom Rinpoche, the head of the Nyingmapa school, spent an entire month conferring upon one thousand devotees the transmission of twenty volumes of writings by his predecessor, Dudjom Lingpa (who lived in the nineteenth century), as well as a few of his own teachings. It was an immense blessing for us to receive such precious transmissions.

What do these twenty rich volumes of teachings contain? At their core are ten complete cycles of practices, beginning with preliminaries designed to orient our minds toward the Dharma and rising to the most elevated teachings of the Great Perfection, including visualization practices and other aspects of the gradual path. Why so many practices? The truth is, a single cycle is perfectly sufficient in and of itself and allows anyone who devotes herself to it with confidence and diligence to attain enlightenment in this one lifetime. However, the mental capacities and dispositions of individual beings are infinitely varied and external conditions differ from one era to the next. The multiplicity of practices therefore responds to the specific needs of respective beings and allows them to advance along the path to freedom.[3]

Such transmissions are essential to keeping the spiritual heritage of Tibetan Buddhism alive. Among the lamas of all ages who receive these transmissions are those who will, in turn, emerge to ensure their continuity. It is through this process that the living tradition has survived from the introduction of Buddhism in Tibet to this very day. Indeed, without transmissions from teacher to student, the teachings and practices become dead letter, and students are no longer able to use them to progress along the path. They become soulless books instead of the living source of their spiritual inspiration.

This was the first time that Dudjom Rinpoche had offered these complete teachings in such a manner outside Tibet. Devotees had gathered from all corners of India and many other countries. Kangyur Rinpoche's family and the Western students who had accompanied them received them with great joy and gratitude.

In Tibetan culture, the sacred lives comfortably side by side with the playful. One day during the teachings, an old monk, seated among hundreds of devotees in the open air, was seized by a pressing urge dictated by nature. Reluctant to get up and leave for fear of missing part of the transmission, which was nearly four hours long, he decided to relieve himself surreptitiously under his robe into a large goblet from which he drank the tea that was distributed two or three times a day. His task complete, he didn't quite know what to do with its outcome. As he happened to be near the enclosure wall, he thought he might be able to discreetly empty the contents over the side. Unfortunately for him, he drew attention to himself when, among all the assembly, he was the only one to stand up, and all the worse when his plan backfired, and he ended up pouring the golden yellow liquid all over his own head! A few laughs broke out when those around him understood what was happening. And to cap it all off, his belt loosened when he stretched to his full height to jettison the liquid, and now his monk's robe fell to his feet, revealing him in his full birthday suit. The entire assembly burst into wild laughter, including Dudjom Rinpoche, who had witnessed the entire thing from his throne. The empowerments were paused until the hilarity subsided.

The last day of the teachings fell at the beginning of January 1978, shortly after Dudjom Rinpoche gave a final word of advice to the devotees. As the crowd was dispersing, the snow began to fall on Boudhanath like a rain of flowers. In all the many years I spent in that area, I never once saw or heard of snowfall in Kathmandu. The capital may be 5,000 feet above sea level, but it's on the same latitude as Morocco, and the temperature rarely falls below 38°F, even during the coldest winter nights. The winter sky is almost always sparkling blue here.

The following winter and spring were particularly splendid. One month after the transmissions conferred by Dudjom Rinpoche, another cycle of equally precious teachings was bestowed by Dilgo Khyentse Rinpoche, from mid-February to late March 1978, in the largest monastery that existed in Boudhanath at the time, Ka-Nying Shedrub Ling, founded by Tulku Urgyen Rinpoche and his sons.

We all moved out between the two teachings, and, for the modest sum of 300 rupees a month, the equivalent of €30 today, I rented a rustic room on the second floor of a traditional Nepali home, one of the houses built in a circle around the Boudhanath stupa, on the cobblestoned alley on which the faithful circumambulated the sacred monument. The room's floor was rammed earth, spread out over beams covered by wooden slats. The walls were whitewashed, and two wood-framed windows, painted blue, gave directly onto the stupa. In the tiny kitchen, I sometimes made dinner on the kerosene stove for friends—Luc, Erik Pema Kunsang, Helena, Juanita, and some others—who came to visit me from Darjeeling. My mother, who had been a nun since 1968, had rented a room with friends in another house facing the stupa. As always, she was extremely generous and hospitable with everyone. In Nepal as in Darjeeling, we were close to each other while remaining independent, following our own respective paths. We sometimes ran into each other at meals shared with Kangyur Rinpoche, or on pilgrimage or at teachings. At other times, particularly when we were on retreat in our hermitages, we did not see each other.

Many lamas had come from other regions of Nepal, India, and even farther afield. Some also gave teachings in the evenings to small groups of Westerners. I often attended such events.

Very early in the morning, long before sunrise, between 5:30 and 7:30, countless faithful came from all the surrounding areas to circumambulate the stupa. This silent crowd rotated respectfully in a clockwise direction, keeping the stupa on their right, counting off their *malas* and reciting mantras and prayers. The morning faithful contrasted with those who circulated around the stupa in the late afternoon, after their day's work, with less contemplation, distracted from their prayers by their gossip. The shops were closed in the morning, but the neighborhood came alive in the evening: retailers selling tea, *malas*, statues and *thangkas*, ritual objects, incense, and medicinal plants brought down from the mountains in great jute sacks, restaurant owners in their tiny storefronts—they all opened shop. The public squares were also overrun by street vendors, peddlers from India, often disabled, and pilgrims and wandering hermits sitting on the ground, reciting their prayers, prayerbook on their knees, and receiving the alms with which they bought their provisions of *tsampa*, tea, and butter, the bare necessities for pursuing an ascetic life in their mountain retreats. More rarely, a mahout led his elephant in a turn around the stupa. A few lanterns came on once the night fell, and the flames from butter lamps offered to the stupa flickered in the breeze; the sound of music produced by a half-dozen officiants conducting a ceremony in a little temple open to the street wafted into the night air. All this gave the place an otherworldly aura. A universe all its own gravitated around that sacred monument.

Sometimes, toward ten at night, when everything had fallen silent, I took three turns around the stupa, not walking, as usual, but prostrating. I put my two hands on the ground and slid them until I was fully outstretched, my arms extended forward as far as they could go; then I stood up, walked three paces to the place where my fingertips had reached, and started over. One circuit of the stupa normally took a little more than five minutes while walking; performed in this manner it took twenty. It will come as no surprise that I was covered in dust by the time I had finished, and I went to wash off in the water gushing from a fountain that flowed day and night from a gargoyle in an alleyway leading to the stupa, where the washerwomen gathered in the daytime. After bathing in the cool water, I returned to my room and continued to gaze at the stupa for a few minutes longer, prayed to my teachers, and went to sleep. In Tibet, many pilgrims prostrate in this manner for months on their way to Lhasa or other great pilgrimage sites. They generally prefer the cold of winter, and bowing down on frozen ground, to the summer, when the rain and mud make it more awkward.

In mid-February, came the time for the transmissions to be conferred by Dilgo Khyentse Rinpoche. These involved the empowerments and instructions contained in the thirty-odd volumes of the complete works of Chokgyur Lingpa, a great nineteenth-century master who was a *tertön* (a discoverer of ancient texts). This was to be the first time since the Tibetans had fled Tibet (around 1959) that this complete cycle of teachings was to be transmitted. As a result, some fifty eminent lamas, a few hundred monks and nuns, and a similar number of lay followers—around a thousand people in all—had come from throughout the Himalayas and Tibetan refugee centers in India and Nepal. About thirty Western students had also made the journey for the privilege of receiving these transmissions.

Dilgo Khyentse Rinpoche prepared the empowerments in the mornings then performed the transmissions in the afternoons. At the end of the day, he offered detailed exegeses of a particularly important text, describing the correct way to practice the successive stages of the path to enlightenment. That text, which has since been translated into several languages, first in English, *The Light of Wisdom*, in 3 volumes,—is a treasury of instructions for those who wish to engage seriously in the practice of Tibetan Buddhism.[4]

Every day after his teachings, Khyentse Rinpoche stayed behind in the temple for a few minutes with a small group of monks to recite prayers dedicating the merits generated by the transmission of teachings and other virtuous practices. Some of the Western students stayed to join in these prayers. One monk confided to me that Khyentse Rinpoche had told him, looking at me, "You see that foreigner, he knows all the prayers by heart! The Dharma is beginning to spread in the West." Little by little, a strong connection was forming between Dilgo Khyentse Rinpoche and me.

In late March, when the transmissions were complete,[5] a celebration was held in the courtyard of Ka-Nying Shedrub Ling Monastery, and then, on a sunny morning, Khyentse Rinpoche and the other main spiritual teachers and young incarnate lamas (*tulkus*) who had received the teachings departed in procession, preceded by musicians and monks carrying banners, to perform a ceremonial circuit of the Boudhanath stupa, some 300 yards away. The main lamas took their places around Khyentse Rinpoche on the first of the stupa's three tiers, which allowed me to immortalize the moment on film.

Overwhelmed by all these blessings and dazzled by the natural beauty of Nepal and our discovery of its sacred places, we set off for Darjeeling by bus, as we had come—two long days of chaotic driving—and returned to the tranquility of Orgyen Kunzang Chökhorling Monastery and, in my case, of my hermitage. I went into retreat for the rest of the year.

III

A SECOND SUN

13

TEACHINGS AND MONASTIC VOWS

I meet with Dilgo Khyentse Rinpoche once again on his visits to Darjeeling. In 1979, he advises me to stay with him. I receive four months of teachings, take vows, and become a monk.

Before leaving this world, Kangyur Rinpoche assured those close to him that the members of his family and his students would find authentic teachers with whom to pursue their spiritual path. His prediction came patently true. Kangyur Rinpoche's family and followers became the students of two eminent masters, Dudjom Rinpoche and Dilgo Khyentse Rinpoche, who had been very close to Kangyur Rinpoche. Then, depending on the circumstances of their lives, their geographic locations and their individual journeys, these students drew closer to one of these two teachers without ever losing their respect for and devotion to both.

It is quite possible to follow the guidance of several teachers at a time, and thus to be the student of both. In fact, we become the student of every teacher who has conferred important teachings and empowerments upon us, and it is only when the teacher becomes the intimate guide of our practice, stage by stage, that a more personal connection develops. That is what would soon happen to me, providing me with thirteen years of deep intimacy with an exceptional teacher. After Kangyur Rinpoche's death, his eldest son, Pema Wangyal Rinpoche, guided my practice and retreats, and continues to do so today, fifty years later. However, a few years after the departure of my root teacher, I would have the great good fortune of being welcomed as a close student of Dilgo Khyentse Rinpoche, who would not only grant me many teachings and help me advance on my path but would also have the immense kindness of allowing me to share in his daily life, in his service. What more could I possibly hope for at that point in my life?

My first meeting with my second teacher, Dilgo Khyentse Rinpoche, took place in Darjeeling in 1972. He spent several days at Orgyen Kunzang Chökhorling, the monastery of my root master Kangyur Rinpoche. These two remarkable beings were very close to one another and had exchanged teachings on a number of occasions.[1] Whenever Dilgo Khyentse Rinpoche passed through Darjeeling, he usually stayed at Kangyur Rinpoche's monastery. This time, the latter had gone to spend two weeks at the thermal springs of Khandro Sang Phug, in Sikkim, but I myself was lucky enough to be present for his visit.

Khyentse Rinpoche was a very impressive person, not only because of his height—he was almost six and a half feet tall—but also because of his majestic bearing, brimming with a goodness that radiated from his being. His amber skin, his big gentle hands, his fingers and long fingernails, his poised gestures, his warm voice, his immeasurably penetrating gaze, the boundless generosity heralded in his smile—everything about him left an indelible mark on all who knew him. The first time I saw him, I was at first surprised to encounter another great teacher in a place that was already entirely illuminated by the presence of Kangyur Rinpoche. Obviously, Khyentse Rinpoche was his own distinct person, but I spontaneously felt the same respect mingled with devotion that I felt for Kangyur Rinpoche. Beyond appearances, I sensed that their respective spiritual realizations were one and the same. It's striking to realize that, beneath their different physical attributes, the great masters share extensive similarities: their qualities of being are identical.

After Kangyur Rinpoche's death in 1975, Dilgo Khyentse Rinpoche returned to Orgyen Kunzang Chökhorling several times. On one such visit, in 1978, in an outpouring of particular devotion, I decided to give him a *pong-dag*, literally "pure renunciation," implying "of all one's possessions." To that end, I gathered together the few objects I had in my hermitage, amounting to seven silver offering bowls, an alarm clock, a watch dating from my teenage years, my camera, a brand-new Bhutanese robe, and a few other odds and ends. One morning, as Khyentse Rinpoche was saying his prayers in his room, I brought it all to him on two large trays, with the help of a monk who was then in his service, and complemented my offering with a long Tibetan scarf of white silk, a symbol of the purity of intention of the person making the offering. Things went very simply—Khyentse Rinpoche accepted my offerings with a smile then redistributed them to the members of his entourage later in the day. He himself, having lived for decades in the humblest manner possible, in caves and hermitages, had made an offering of all his possessions to his spiritual teachers several times and had no attachment whatsoever to material things. A nun received the silver bowls; she continued to use them to make water offerings on her altar every single day until she passed away at the age of ninety-one. Lama Ngodrup, Khyentse Rinpoche's principal attendant—who would later become a close friend of mine—received my Bhutanese robe. He admitted to me that he had heard of the practice of *pong-dag* but that this was his first time witnessing it. As for my camera, Khyentse Rinpoche returned it to me. The device was of no use to anyone he knew—Rabjam Rinpoche, the only potential recipient, was too young to operate it, he told me—and Khyentse Rinpoche probably thought that it would be most useful in my hands. Indeed, he allowed me to continue photographing my spiritual teachers and the world in which they lived, and to make lasting records of many paintings and other treasures of the sacred art of Tibet.

Two days before my *pong-dag*, I had a dream in which Dilgo Khyentse Rinpoche bestowed an empowerment whose principal deity was Mandarava, one of the two principal consorts of the Guru Padmasambhava.[2] During the ceremony, Dilgo Khyentse Rinpoche placed a ritual cup on my head, filled with nectar, of which he gave me a spoonful to drink. When I awoke, I asked him if there were any practices with Mandarava as the central deity. Rinpoche said there were, without offering any details. It wasn't until many years later that I received from him the Mandarava empowerment that is part of the Heart Essence of the Life Practice of the Lotus Born cycle (Pema Tseyi Nyingtig), a mind treasure received in a vision by Khyentse Rinpoche in the 1950s while camping on the shores of the Golden Milk Lake, in eastern Tibet, at an elevation of more than 15,000 feet.[3] The cycle contains a certain number of practices, one of which is centered on Mandarava, a female deity, or *dakini*, who is linked to this cycle and symbolizes the ultimate bliss of ultimate wisdom. Years later, in Nepal, I spent three months in retreat focused on this practice.

On this visit to Darjeeling, out of his great kindness, Khyentse Rinpoche gave me some advice that would determine the path I was to take for the next thirteen years and have a profound impact on my life. Tulku Pema Wangyal—who, in addition to his father, considered Dudjom Rinpoche and Dilgo Khyentse Rinpoche to be his root teachers—had asked Khyentse Rinpoche to go to France in 1976 in order to offer teachings to the Western students of his father, Europeans, North Americans, and South Americans for whom he had organized a retreat of three years and three months, the traditional duration of that type of contemplative retreat. It was to take place in Dordogne, in a building designed as a cloister with an interior garden and built by the students themselves, who included an engineer and two carpenters. As one of Kangyur Rinpoche's earliest Western students, I imagined that I would be a member that group on retreat. I therefore believed that my seven-year sojourn in India was drawing to a close. I raised this prospect with Khyentse Rinpoche. He answered me point-blank:

"So long as I am alive, stay with me. You'll have other opportunities to go on retreat."

This precious counsel, which would allow me to become one of his intimate students, was the most beautiful gift he could ever have given me. I ended up spending thirteen years with him, in Bhutan, Nepal, and India, in the course of which I would accompany him three times to Tibet.

During those thirteen years, while I was first and foremost his student, I also placed myself at his service. Khyentse Rinpoche was elderly and had difficulty getting around on his own. Since I was living by his side, it was only natural that I should serve him day and night to the best of my abilities. Being in the service of a spiritual teacher like Khyentse Rinpoche or the Dalai Lama is nothing like a "job" or some ordinary "occupation." It is, rather, a precious opportunity to live in close proximity to him and benefit from the quality of his presence, while doing your best to help in his daily tasks. It's also an opportunity to attend all his teachings and transmissions. Of course, I was able to request specific teachings from him, but very often all I needed was to wait patiently until he gave those same teachings at someone else's request, which allowed me to receive them as well, while saving his very valuable time. Infrequently, in certain cases, if he wished to offer the teaching exclusively to the person who had requested it, he would ask those present, myself included, to leave the room. But his main gift and blessing to me lay in the profound spiritual realization and compassion that radiated from him at all times, in private as in public, in the presence of kings and of the very humble.

During that same decisive visit in the spring of 1978, Khyentse Rinpoche advised me to come receive the teachings that he was to give at Mindrolling Monastery, near Dehradun, in northern India. Over the course of four months in the winter of 1978–1979, Khyentse Rinpoche was to confer the transmission of sixty-four volumes of *The Treasury of Precious Termas*, the *Rinchen Terdzö*. This collection of teachings and contemplative practices of the Nyingmapa school was put together by the great scholar Jamgön Kongtrul Lodrö Tayé in the nineteenth century, at a time when many spiritual lines were in danger of extinction or of being forgotten. It was at this time that I became a member of Khyentse Rinpoche's entourage.

During the four months of this important transmission, Khyentse Rinpoche rose every morning at four o'clock to perform his daily practices. He went to the temple monastery around 7:30 a.m., assisted by Lama Chöjor, who was responsible for preparing the mandalas and other elements necessary for the transmission of empowerments, a task that ran late into the evening.

Khyentse Rinpoche then practiced one by one all the visualizations, recitations, and meditations linked to the empowerments he was to confer that day. Next came the daily transmission of three to seven empowerments, depending on their length and complexity, and in the late afternoon he delivered the corresponding instructions. It went on this way for four months, except for a few days' pause for the Tibetan New Year and a brief visit by Khyentse Rinpoche to the Dalai Lama in Dharamshala. The many followers who came from afar to receive these transmissions included hundreds of spiritual masters, *tulkus* (reincarnate past masters), *khenpos* (the equivalent of doctors of philosophy), respected lamas, and some fifty foreigners.

After these very busy days, Khyentse Rinpoche left the temple and returned to his residence—a simple room and a foyer—where almost every day he offered supplementary teachings to those who requested them. Two of us took care of his personal needs: a Bhutanese monk, Tsewang Lhundrup, and me. I slept on the floor in my teacher's room so that I would be on hand if he needed to get up in the night. I had several dreams in which a crowd of people came in to see Khyentse Rinpoche and found me asleep and totally bewildered. "Could these be nonhuman beings coming to receive teachings from Khyentse Rinpoche at night?" I joked to myself.

That winter, I began to serve as interpreter for Khyentse Rinpoche and his Western students. Using a tape deck on loan from an American follower, I was also able to record most of the teachings and textual clarifications that he delivered (except for the empowerments, which it is inappropriate to record). Down the years, I have managed to record four hundred hours of precious teachings on a rudimentary tape recorder I have since acquired. The cheap cassettes then available in India were often counterfeit, and the ninety minutes indicated on the packaging actually provided only seventy, at best! But the price of original brands was beyond my modest means. I was often teased about my eagerness to get that old tape deck rolling, despite its increasing dilapidation from overuse, as soon as Rinpoche sat down to teach. My perseverance paid off, because I now get requests from all over the world for copies of these recordings. I later transcribed and translated some of these teachings into English and French, which were published in five books so far: *The Wishfulfilling Jewel*, *The Heart Treasure of the Enlightened Ones*, *The Excellent Path to Enlightenment*, *The Hundred Verses of Advice*, and *The Heart of Compassion*.

On this exceptional occasion, the distinguished abbot Taklung Tsetrul Rinpoche, a former student of Kangyur Rinpoche's in Tibet, came to spend a few weeks at Mindrolling Monastery. Upon his arrival, I was reminded of the advice that Kangyur Rinpoche had given me on my first trip to India in 1967. I had asked him whether it would be the right thing for me to start a family. His answer had been that I should wait until I was thirty and see where I was then. I reported this advice to Khyentse Rinpoche. I was now thirty-three, and both paths, family and monastic, seemed equally possible to me. The fact is that, since I had left France, I had already been living a semi-monastic life and was perfectly willing to cross the threshold from "life with a home to life without a home," in the words of the definition given in the scriptures of the transition to the monastic existence. I wanted to seek his advice, since the time had come. "Tsetrul Rinpoche has just arrived. He will be performing ordinations. It would be an excellent time for you to take your vows," he replied without hesitation. Khyentse Rinpoche himself did not confer such vows because he was not a monk but a married yogi. A few days later, therefore, at the end of the transmission of *The Treasury of Precious Termas*, I was ordained as a monk. Tsetrul Rinpoche was assisted by five monks representing the Sangha, the monastic community. Two other postulants were ordained at the same time as I was. During the ceremony, which lasted about two and a half hours, the abbot, Tsetrul Rinpoche, first asked us a number of questions to confirm the earnestness of our commitment: "Are you ready to observe the vows you are about to take for all time and in all places and circumstances?" We responded together in the affirmative. Then he gradually conferred upon us the five vows of the novice; *upasaka*, the thirty vows of the *samanera*; and the 253 vows of the *bhikkhu* (*gelong* in Tibetan). The four main vows of full ordination are to refrain from killing, to refrain from stealing, to refrain from sexual relations, and to refrain from lying by claiming to have achieved a high level of spiritual realization. If a monk breaks any one of these four vows, the ordination is instantly invalid.

When I returned from the ceremony, my head shaved and wearing my monks' robes, Khyentse Rinpoche was delighted, and told me, "What great good fortune to have taken your vows." Far from feeling constrained by the monastic vows, I felt incredibly light and joyful; I had a sense of enjoying newfound freedom, like a bird that has escaped its cage. A month later, we paid a visit on Kalu Rinpoche, a high master of the Kagyupa school and a dear friend of Khyentse Rinpoche who had spent years in retreat in Tibet and received teachings from Kangyur Rinpoche at Sonada, near Darjeeling. Khyentse Rinpoche told him about me, saying, "He has taken monastic vows. It's a sign that he intends to devote himself entirely to the Dharma."

I am quite certain that a family can be a source of great joy in life and one of the most rewarding of human experiences, yet I know today, with hindsight, that it was not my path. The choice I made offered me the precious freedom to live all those years alongside Khyentse Rinpoche, far from it all, and to spend a total of five years in solitary retreat over the course of the past forty years. This way of life, in which I am fully immersed, would not have been possible if I had had a family. I have no children, but my organization and humanitarian projects under the aegis of Karuna-Shechen have allowed me and my collaborators to offer a basic education and health care to tens of thousands of children and to contribute, in our own way, to the well-being of future generations. Moreover, in the forty-five years since I was ordained as a monk, and although I have felt tender affection for certain women, it has never once occurred to me to renounce my vows. The presence of my teacher in the depth of my heart and the inestimable value I attach to my monk's vows have always accompanied me assuredly on my chosen path.

14

DILGO KHYENTSE RINPOCHE
A MASTER AMONG MASTERS

Born in eastern Tibet, he is given the name Tashi Paljor, "Auspicious Glory." From his very earliest years, he receives many teachings and empowerments, undertakes years of solitary retreat, and becomes a renowned teacher. His life is so rich and accomplished that he appears to have lived several lifetimes in one.

Dilgo Khyentse Rinpoche was born in 1910 in Denkhok, Kham province, the easternmost of the five regions of Greater Tibet.[1] The fourth child of a prominent family named Dilgo, he received the name Tashi Paljor— "Auspicious Glory"—from one of the greatest spiritual masters of his time, Mipham Rinpoche, who was then living in a hermitage a half-hour's hike above Sakar, the Dilgo family's village. Even before Khyentse Rinpoche had seen the light of day, Mipham Rinpoche asked his mother to bring the newborn to him as soon as possible. That is how, before he had even tasted his first drop of mother's milk, the infant was presented to Mipham Rinpoche, who used saffron water to write the letter *dhi*—the seed syllable of the mantra of Manjushri, the buddha of wisdom—on his tongue. Mipham Rinpoche, by the way, was also the master who had identified the exceptional qualities of Kangyur Rinpoche when he was still a child.

From an early age, Tashi Paljor was powerfully attracted to the spiritual life. He wanted to become a monk, and several lamas informed his father that he was an extraordinary child. But his father, Tashi Tsering, wasn't having it; his two older sons were already ordained, and he intended to put the youngest in charge of managing the family estates.

One day while he was playing with his brother, young Tashi Paljor fell into an enormous cauldron in which soup was being prepared for the community during the summer harvest. The lower part of his body was badly burned, and he spent many months in bed. Several lamas, including Shechen Gyaltsap, who would later become Khyentse Rinpoche's primary teacher, warned that the child would not survive for long if he were not allowed to follow his vocation. In despair, the father told the child,

"If there is anything that can save your life, I will do it!"

"Wearing a monk's robes would help me," Tashi Paljor replied.

His father quickly ordered a monastic robe to be made. The son put it on in his sickbed and was overwhelmed with joy. The child began to heal immediately and was on his feet in a few weeks. The only remaining trace of his accident was a long scar in the flesh of his left thigh, from knee to hip. That is when Tashi Paljor received the monastic name Rabsel Dawa, "Brilliant Moon," and was given the vows of a novice (*sramanera*) by the renowned scholar Khenpo Shenga, who also provided him with many teachings.

At the age of ten Tashi Paljor, now named Rabsel Dawa, accompanied his older brother to Shechen Monastery to meet the lama who would become his primary teacher, Shechen Gyaltsap Rinpoche. When Mipham Rinpoche died in 1911, Shechen Gyaltsap had gone to Sakar to lead the funeral rites. He had seen Tashi Paljor, then one year old, and told his father that this child was very different from others and that, sometime in the future, he wanted to take him under his wing. Shechen Gyaltsap lived in a hermitage on a hillside, forty-five minutes above the monastery on foot. From the little hermitage's window, he could see Shechen Monastery, the river down in the valley and snow-capped mountains in the far distance. Below, halfway to the monastery, was the Shechen retreat center, where ten monks regularly undertook the traditional retreat of three years and three months, during which practitioners engage in a series of practices proceeding step by step from preliminaries (*ngöndro*) to visualizations and the chanting of mantras, and culminating in the very deepest meditations on the nature of mind, the Great Perfection. They are guided by a retreat master who has already completed this cycle once or several times or who has considerable experience in spiritual practice. Every three years, a new group of monks applies to go on retreat. Some complete it several times in a row. Such retreats are open to practitioners who have not chosen the monastic way but who wish to engage in contemplative practice.

Although he was a monk, Shechen Gyaltsap Rinpoche wore his hair long over his shoulders, like most of the retreatants. He was inarguably one of the most learned and accomplished lamas of his time. He once began a three-year retreat, but to the surprise of all he reemerged three months later declaring that he had completed it. The next morning, a monk who attended upon him noticed a deep footprint embedded in the stone that served as a threshold to his hermitage. Asked about this mystery, Shechen Gyaltsap Rinpoche shrugged it off: "Oh, it's nothing." Tibet has seen a number of foot- or handprints left in stone by great masters of the past. While the masters in question never boast about such things or, like Shechen Gyaltsap, claim them to be of no significance, some people believe that they perform these marvels to inspire their students and generations to come. However, that may be, it is said that such signs are *siddhis*, or ordinary "achievements"—the ultimate *siddhi* being the achievement of spiritual enlightenment. For all these reasons, these marks, or "imprints," are venerated by followers. That particular stone was later removed and hidden during the Cultural Revolution. Nowadays, it is preserved among the relics of Shechen Monastery; Dilgo Khyentse Rinpoche had it painted with gold powder mixed with glue on the occasion of his first visit to Tibet in 1985.

For several months, Shechen Gyaltsap Rinpoche conveyed to the young Rabsel Dawa, his older brother, and a few other students a great many empowerments, and the most important teachings of the Buddhist canon, and orally transmitted the works of a number of great masters of the past, Mipham Rinpoche in particular.

While Rabsel Dawa was living among the entourage of Shechen Gyaltsap, another master, Dzongsar Khyentse Chökyi Lodrö, came to receive teachings as well. Even the most accomplished masters continue to receive teachings from other masters, mainly so as to become the custodians of teachings held by others, and thus in turn be able to perpetuate them and ensure their continuity. Moreover, Shechen Gyaltsap was one of the most venerated teachers in eastern Tibet. Pointing to the young student, Dzongsar Khyentse Chökyi Lodrö said, "I am firmly convinced that this child is the incarnation of Jamyang Khyentse Wangpo.[2] I would ask you specifically to transmit *The Treasury of Precious Instructions* to him."[3] The work in question consists of thirteen volumes of teachings on the eight principal practice lineages of Tibetan Buddhism, collected in the nineteenth century by Jamgön Kongtrul. Shechen Gyaltsap conveyed its transmission to the child and some twenty other students over the course of three months.

When it was done, Shechen Gyaltsap enthroned Rabsel Dawa as the incarnation of Jamyang Khyentse Wangpo.[4] He added this very powerful conclusion: "If I should die now, I will have no regrets."

Dilgo Khyentse Rinpoche lived with Shechen Gyaltsap for nearly five years and then, at the age of fifteen, returned to his family and spent a year in retreat in a cave converted into a hermitage, located an hour's walk from Sakar. In the winter, without leaving his cave, he received teachings from the great scholar Khenpo Tubga, who came to transmit them to him in person. When his retreat ended, he went to live with Tubga in the neighboring province of Dzachuka in order to pursue his studies with him. It was there that, in 1926, he learned of the death of Shechen Gyaltsap at the young age of fifty-six. Dilgo Khyentse Rinpoche wrote, "I was dumbfounded at first. And then, the memory of my teacher came over me with such force that I began to cry. It felt as if my heart were being torn from my chest. I returned to Sakar and began a retreat in the mountains that was to last for thirteen years." His older brother Shedrup consoled him: "Do not grieve the departure of your teacher as if it were the death of an ordinary person. Join your mind with his and you will receive his blessing, mind to mind." The next morning, Khyentse Rinpoche went to sit in a meadow and, recalling his beloved teacher, his mind was overcome by immeasurable sorrow. Breaking into tears, he wrote this song of lamentation:

Alas, alas, my authentic teacher,
Although you, the Buddha in person,
Took me under your protection,
Not all your teachings are yet clear to me.
How could you go away, leaving me an orphan?

The ordinary eyes of my bad karma
No longer see the smiling eyes in the bright moon of your face
Looking back at me with such tenderness.
Your son cannot bear losing his father!

Your melodious voice, subtle and inspiring,
Brought me the nectar of the Dharma, vast and deep.
Now my ears no longer hear its strength and purity.
Your son is compelled to cry out for help!

The manifestation of your luminous realization
Shone through your limpid gaze.
When will I be before your eyes again?
I cannot help proclaiming that hope!

Though you have dissolved into primordial space,
Extend to me now the thread of your compassion,
As spontaneous as it is immutable,
Draw me into your benevolent presence, oh sole and unique protector!

While taking a brief break from his practice, he climbed to the summit of a rocky mountain. When he sat down to catch his breath, he suddenly experienced a luminous void, as vast as outer space, without center or boundaries. It was an experience such as he had never known; he remained in that state until it vanished.

After he returned to his family, at the age of sixteen, Dilgo Khyentse Rinpoche wrote a letter to his parents in which he explained in carefully chosen language why he was so set on devoting himself to a life of contemplation. The letter said, in part,

Beloved parents, you gave me a precious human life, you took care of me lovingly and helped me find an authentic teacher. Thanks to you, I have found the path of deliverance. . . . When my venerated teacher gave me the Secret Heart Essence empowerment, I vowed to renounce the activities of this life and to devote myself to practicing the Dharma. . . . Mountain retreats are my only destination. Your son is going away to seclude himself in caves and hermitages, but your smiling faces will always be with me. I will never forget the tokens of your love, and if I should manage to reach the citadel of realization, rest assured that I shall repay your kindness!

He spent most of the next thirteen years in retreat in caves and hermitages on the slopes of the wooded hills of the Sakar Valley. He meditated tirelessly on love, compassion, and his resolve to lead all sentient beings toward enlightenment and freedom.

It was at that time that Dilgo Khyentse Rinpoche fell gravely ill. Dzongsar Khyentse Chökyi Lodrö and many other lamas determined that the time had come for him to take a consort, as is customary for *tertöns*, the discoverers of hidden texts.[5] Dilgo Khyentse Rinpoche married Lhamo, a peasant girl from a village near Sakar. From that moment on, his health improved, he had frequent visions, and revealed many *terma*.

Khandro (an honorific applied to eminent female practitioners and the wives of spiritual masters) Lhamo had the strong and courageous disposition typical of women from eastern Tibet. She was three years younger than Khyentse Rinpoche. Whenever Khyentse Rinpoche went on retreat she did the same, at his side, in the company of two or three Sakar natives, in a hermitage not far from his, and went to visit him from time to time even as she devoted herself to spiritual practice and raised the two daughters born from their union, Chime Wangmo, the mother of Rabjam Rinpoche, and Dechen Wangmo, who, like many Tibetans, died of tuberculosis many years later, shortly after their arrival in India after fleeing the Chinese invasion of Tibet. Unlike today, tuberculosis was barely present in Tibet in those days, and Tibetans were especially susceptible to the disease. When not on retreat, they lived and traveled together whenever Khyentse Rinpoche set forth on a journey.

In his youth, Dilgo Khyentse Rinpoche would spend at least one winter in a cave, cut off from the rest of the world by snow, at more than 15,000 feet elevation, near the summit of Bahla, the mountain that dominates the Sakar Valley. Between each retreat, he spent one or two weeks with his family before returning to a hermitage or cave that he was familiar with, some in the forest, some on the high mountain slopes, but all within one to five hours' walk from Sakar. After he finished with his retreats at the age of twenty-eight, he spent many years in the company of Dzongsar Khyentse Chökyi Lodrö, his second primary teacher. Over time, he received teachings from some fifty eminent masters in Tibet, and in exile he continued to collect transmissions of rare texts and teachings that were in danger of being lost so as to preserve their lineage.

After receiving *The Treasury of Precious Termas*, the *Rinchen Terdzö*, from Dzongsar Khyentse Chökyi Lodrö, Dilgo Khyentse Rinpoche professed that he wished to spend the rest of his life in solitary retreat. Dzongsar Khyentse Chökyi Lodrö's response was categorical and not up for discussion: "The time has come for you to teach and transmit to others the teachings you have received." From that day on, Khyentse Rinpoche worked tirelessly for the good of sentient beings with the inexhaustible energy characteristic of the Khyentse lineage.[6]

Around 1957, Dilgo Khyentse Rinpoche, his wife, and their two daughters spent more than a year on pilgrimage in central Tibet. After a stay at Tsurphu Monastery with the sixteenth Karmapa, Khyentse Rinpoche and his family learned that the armies of Communist China had just invaded Kham and Amdo, destroying monasteries and killing or jailing many monks and laypeople. It would now be impossible to return to his birthplace in Kham. In 1959, like the Dalai Lama, Dilgo Khyentse Rinpoche resigned himself to leaving Tibet, accompanied by his wife and two daughters and his second oldest brother, Sangye Nyenpa Rinpoche, the abbot of Benchen Monastery, and a group of followers.

Their escape was eventful. Many Tibetans were seeking to flee Mao Zedong's troops, who shot on sight. A few days before reaching the border with Bhutan, Dilgo Khyentse Rinpoche and his group learned that Chinese troops were dangerously close by. To avoid being detected, they hid by day and traveled by night. When they finally made it to the Monla Karchung pass, they had to wait to obtain authorization to cross the border into Bhutan, where there was a continual influx of refugees. Their provisions had been exhausted for ten days before the Bhutanese government allowed them to cross the border. Fortunately, the government was very hospitable to Tibetans fleeing Chinese oppression. The group led by Khyentse Rinpoche made it in safe and sound, but many other Tibetans lost their lives trying to escape the Chinese army into Bhutan, Nepal, or India, falling under the bullets of the communist army—which hunted them down and captured and executed them summarily—or dying of hunger or cold in the especially harsh conditions of their trek across snow-filled passes. Dilgo Khyentse Rinpoche and his family spent a few days in the beautiful Bumthang Valley, two days' march from the Monla Karchung pass, and were warmly welcomed by a prominent family whose son, a monk, had studied in Tibet. Having regained their strength, they resumed their journey, through immense, leech-infested forests, under relentless rain, walking ten days and almost 200 miles to reach the capital, Thimphu, which in those days had barely ten thousand inhabitants. Dilgo Khyentse Rinpoche wrote a little verse at that time:

A beautiful country is a dream-like illusion,
It's senseless to cling to it.
Unless the inner forces of negative emotions are conquered,
Strife with outer enemies will never end.

Meanwhile, in Kham, having learned of Dilgo Khyentse Rinpoche's flight into Bhutan, a member of his family gathered up his precious writings and books and hid them for safety in a dry cave deep in the mountains. When he returned some time later to check on the books' condition, he found that field mice had taken up residence in the same shelter and shredded the cloth in which the books had been wrapped. He built a fire of juniper branches to fumigate the cave in the hope of chasing the rodents away. After he left, a gust of wind scattered the cinders, which fell on the books, which took fire and were reduced to ashes. Several volumes of works from Dilgo Khyentse Rinpoche's youth were lost forever.

The Chinese invasion was the cause of many other catastrophes. The spiritual teachers of Shechen Monastery who had not escaped met a tragic fate, as did so many monks and lamas. The titular abbot of Shechen, the sixth Shechen Rabjam, with whom Khyentse Rinpoche had studied, died in prison in Derge in 1959, tortured by the Chinese communists. Shechen Kongtrul, another eminent master, had left for Lhasa at the same time as Khyentse Rinpoche, in 1958, and they had spent some time together in the Tibetan capital. But he was unable to escape and he, too, died in a Chinese prison, in 1960. One witness who survived and came to find Khyentse Rinpoche in Nepal testified that a prisoner had overheard a conversation among the prison guards, in which it was said that Shechen Kongtrul would be tortured to death the next day. The prisoner felt that he had to discreetly warn the future victim of the barbarity being planned. One hour later, while the detainees gathered in the prison courtyard, Shechen Kongtrul sat down on a stool in the corner, in meditative posture, initiated the practice known as the "transference of consciousness" (*phowa* in Tibetan), and uttered the syllable "A," symbol of ultimate truth, three times. Then he remained still, in meditation. Not until the prisoners were summoned to return to their cells did anyone noticed that Shechen Kongtrul had breathed his last. As for Gyurme Pema Dorje, the reincarnation of Shechen Gyaltsap, Dilgo Khyentse Rinpoche's root teacher, he too was executed by the Chinese in 1959, in a prison not far from Shechen, when he was only in his thirties.

Shortly after his arrival in Bhutan, as he was passing through the town of Wangdue Phodrang, Dilgo Khyentse Rinpoche learned of the death of his second primary teacher, Dzongsar Khyentse Chökyi Lodrö, who had managed to escape to Sikkim, in India. Khyentse Rinpoche left as soon as possible, but given the state of the roads, it still took him three or four days to cover the 250 miles between Sikkim and Wangdue Phodrang. Even so, he got there in time to preside over the funeral ceremonies and cremation. He then went on to Kalimpong, a town between Sikkim and Darjeeling. His flight from Tibet and the many privations it entailed had severely emaciated him; he was suffering from diarrhea and chronic vomiting as well. His health continued to degenerate, but he refused to take medicine of any kind. Those closest to him had the impression that Khyentse Rinpoche no longer cared to remain in this world now that his teacher was gone. That is when Dilgo Khyentse Rinpoche received a visit from Chagö Namgyal Gonpo, a dignitary in the court of the king of Derge, who ruled over Kham, Khyentse Rinpoche's native province, and who had remained in Tibet. Namgyal Gonpo told him about his last meeting with Dzongsar Khyentse Chökyi Lodrö, who had been living in the temple of the king of Sikkim. After exchanging a few words with his teacher, who was bedridden and clearly very ill, the dignitary could not restrain his tears. "Why are you crying?" Chökyi Lodrö had asked him. "We have lost our country," Namgyal Gonpo answered, "and now it looks as if we are about to lose our beloved teacher too. What will happen to all those precious Dharma teachings? What hope do we have left?" Chökyi Lodrö reassured him. "I've heard that Tulku Salga managed to escape Tibet and has reached India. He'll take care of the Dharma." Tulku

Salga, a short form of Rabsel Dawa, was the name by which Dilgo Khyentse Rinpoche was best known in Tibet.[7] Upon hearing this story from Namgyal Gonpo, Dilgo Khyentse Rinpoche suddenly felt himself fully committed to the responsibility that his teacher had conferred upon him with these words. From that moment on, he agreed to take his medicine, to eat better, and to attend to his health, which quickly improved.

At the invitation of the royal family, Khyentse Rinpoche stayed in Bhutan as a teacher at the school in Simtokha, near Thimphu, the capital, where he taught poetry, Tibetan grammar, and the rudiments of the Dharma. Very soon, his inner realization and his vast knowledge were recognized and attracted numerous students. He became a teacher revered by all, from the royal family to the humblest practitioner. The queen of Bhutan, Ashi Kesang Choeden Wangchuck, was particularly devoted to him and became his principal benefactor in the Land of the Thunder Dragon.

Down the years, most of the great lamas who sought refuge in India, Nepal, and Bhutan received teachings from Dilgo Khyentse Rinpoche, whichever school of Tibetan Buddhism they belonged to. He was comfortable teaching the views of any lineage of Tibetan Buddhism because in his youth he had been taught by more than fifty masters belonging to the various traditions of Tibetan Buddhism. Even His Holiness the Dalai Lama asked him regularly to come spend a week or two at his residence in Dharamshala so that Dilgo Khyentse Rinpoche could offer him the major teachings of the Nyingmapa school. The Dalai Lama once told me, "Dilgo Khyentse Rinpoche is one of the most important teachers. Ever since we first met, I have received clear indications that I have special karmic ties to him. He has given me teachings for which I am very grateful. I especially appreciate his non-sectarian approach. Despite his fame and his countless students, he is still humble and kind. The Buddha described in detail the qualities of an authentic teacher. I have found all those qualities in Khyentse Rinpoche."

Dilgo Khyentse Rinpoche accomplished so much in his life that he appears to have lived several lifetimes in one. He spent, in total, more than thirty years in solitary retreat, devoting most of his time to spiritual practice. And yet, even in his old age, he continued to solicit the transmission of teachings and texts that he had not yet received, in order to preserve their lineage. From this, you might assume that his principal activities were listening and studying, but he seemed to teach nonstop and to spend the greater part of his life transmitting knowledge. And then, if you went through all twenty-five of the six-hundred-page books he drafted, you would conclude that his main occupation was writing. That is, until you realize that he also worked to preserve Tibetan Buddhism by devoting himself to publishing hundreds of volumes of rare texts and erecting monasteries, stupas, and statues. And finally, when you recall his many travels to Bhutan, India, Nepal, Tibet, and throughout the world, you have to assume that he was constantly on the move. And yet, Dilgo Khyentse Rinpoche was the very opposite of a restless man. He never seemed to be working even when spontaneously engaged in countless activities. He was the still center of a universe in constant motion.

He was both available to all who came to see him and immutably immersed in deep contemplation, every bit as serene as if he were alone in his hermitage. Nothing seemed able to trouble the vast space of his serenity, which did not prevent him from being perfectly present to all those who came before him, treating them with inexhaustible solicitude. He laughed readily in conversation, with a laughter that seemed to rise from the very belly of the Earth. He listened to the stories brought to him by each and every visitor, whom he always welcomed with kindness and good cheer, sometimes with a teasing wit but never with sarcasm or mockery. Animosity seemed as alien to his mind as darkness is to sunlight. You had a natural and intimate sense that everything he advised you was meant exclusively for your well-being. That was the source of the boundless trust with which all who lived in his vicinity held him in their hearts and minds.

In transmitting his vast erudition, he was just as happy teaching one person or a small group for half an hour every day as he was teaching thousands over the course of entire days, weeks, or months at a time. If his schedule did not allow him to respond to a request on the spot, he sent for the person concerned as soon as he had a free moment. In a word, he never rejected any request. Shortly before his death, when his strength and his health began to decline, we tried to limit the number of visitors. Having gotten wind of our initiative, Dilgo Khyentse Rinpoche admonished us with these words: "Until my head drops onto my chest, never prevent anyone from coming to see me."

Everyone who met him was struck by his astounding gift for transmission. Barely glancing at the text before him, he spoke effortlessly, without pause or hesitation, as if he were reading an invisible book open in his memory. This continuous stream, delivered in a bass voice, flowed inexhaustibly at a steady pace, with no dramatic emphases. In his mouth, a few very simple words could open the door to a whole series of inner discoveries. His immense knowledge, the warmth of his presence, and the depth of his spiritual realization gave his teachings a unique flavor. In the course of his many travels around the world, Dilgo Khyentse Rinpoche never established any centers—other than the Shechen monasteries in Nepal and India and the nunnery in Bhutan—but he was respectfully welcomed to all centers affiliated with the various schools of Tibetan Buddhism. He was indeed one of the leading lights of Buddhism in the twentieth century, a master among masters.

15

JOURNEY TO FRANCE
THE CHANTELOUBE STUDY CENTER

In 1980, I accompany Dilgo Khyentse Rinpoche when he is invited to convey teachings in Dordogne. I reunite with my loved ones and the family of my root master, Kangyur Rinpoche.

In the spring of 1980, Khyentse Rinpoche went to France at the invitation of Tulku Pema Wangyal, who, after his first visit alongside Khyentse Rinpoche in 1975, had settled in Dordogne around 1978. One of our friends, Bernard Benson, a student of Kangyur Rinpoche and owner of the Château de Chaban, had offered land in the Vézère Valley to several groups of Tibetan lamas and masters, who had established small communities there. These had thrived over the years and given rise to four centers for the teaching and practice of Tibetan Buddhism, which all together counted several hundred members in those days. Two of the centers belonged to the Nyingmapa school, and two to the Kagyu school, which are very similar to each other.[1] Affiliated with the Nyingmapa school, the Chanteloube Study Center—where Dudjom Rinpoche, Khyentse Rinpoche, and many other great masters were invited by Tulku Pema Wangyal—had been built in great part by the retreatants themselves, assisted by a local mason. It was designed as a cloister surrounding a small garden. The individual cells in which retreatants slept each had a door opening on the garden. In the middle of the row of cells, a two-story building contained a temple on the upper floor and a kitchen and dining room on the ground floor. Khyentse Rinpoche lived in the Sonnerie, a lovely house in the Périgord style where Bernard Benson's mother had lived, and which became his primary residence on his visits to France. He baptized it Tashi Pelbar Ling, "The Place of Glowing Auspiciousness."

The other centers were inspired by the sixteenth Karmapa, who made several memorable visits to Dordogne, as well as by Dudjom Rinpoche and Pawo Rinpoche, who lived there for several years—all the great teachers I had met on my first trips to India. The gentle landscapes and forest of the Périgord offered a peaceful environment conducive to the development of Tibetan Buddhism in its most authentic form. Several of my Western friends who had been students of Kangyur Rinpoche in Darjeeling had settled there for that reason. Some have become excellent translators of Tibetan texts within the Padmakara Translation Group. Nothing seemed capable of disturbing the tranquility of that beautiful countryside. In 1991, the visit of the fourteenth Dalai Lama, who taught Shantideva's *The Way of the Bodhisattva* for a week, attracted almost ten thousand people—a first for the region!

I was now a member of Dilgo Khyentse Rinpoche's entourage and traveled with him. It had been seven years since I had last returned to the country of my birth, and it was a great joy to see my father, my sister Ève, my uncle, and, of course, my mother, who now lived in Dordogne. My sister, now a speech therapist at the Saint-Anne hospital, took excellent care of troubled children from disadvantaged backgrounds. Some refused to speak when they first went into treatment, but she knew how to win their trust and help them find their way in life. She also founded a speech therapy unit within the Institut George Eastman for the children of Paris. She later wrote about her career in a moving book, *La Dame des mots* ("The Word Lady"). My father was now director of *L'Express*, and I continued to report back to him, whenever we had an opportunity to get together, about what we knew of the situation in Tibet through the few Tibetans who continued to escape from their occupied land. My mother was living in a small house that Bernard Benson had loaned her and was practicing under the supervision of Tulku Pema Wangyal. She cooked for the family of Dudjom Rinpoche, head of the Nyingmapa school, on his frequent visits to France. He would later settle in Dordogne, where he lived until his death. In the West, the Nyingmapa school is sometimes referred to as the Red Hat Sect, because of the color of its ceremonial headpieces, and my mother, who was never at a loss for a witticism, called herself the "cordon bleu of the red hats." On the advice of Dudjom Rinpoche, to whom she was deeply devoted, she had started to paint again.

During our brief stay in Paris, I found that the city had greatly changed in appearance with the construction of skyscrapers, of which there had been none at the time I had left. I had become perfectly adapted to life in the East, and I experienced the frenetic pace of urban life and the Western lifestyle as more of a culture shock than a return "home."

Dilgo Khyentse Rinpoche and his entourage were hosted in the apartment of Gérard Godet. A graduate of the École Polytechnique, Gérard worked for an oil drilling company founded by his father and lived a very orderly life. He was not, a priori, the kind of man to embrace Tibetan Buddhism and become one of its most fervent Western practitioners. But he had had brother, Robert, who had flown all the way to India at the helm of a little aircraft in 1953 to meet Dzongsar Khyentse Chökyi Lodrö, Dilgo Khyentse Rinpoche's teacher. Robert died tragically on his second trip to India in 1960, in a plane crash as he took off over Varanasi. It was through his adventurous brother that Gérard had met my mother, with whom he had become close. After some of us had spent time with Kangyur Rinpoche and come away deeply inspired, Gérard decided to make the trip himself. I remember watching him set off, his head protected by a pith helmet—because you never know what might happen. He became one of my best friends, a sort of adoptive uncle. Although he was also one of the most generous patrons of Buddhism and charitable causes, he remained very humble and low-key.

When Gérard returned from Darjeeling, his life changed. Little by little, he cut back on his professional duties and devoted himself more and more to meditative practice. Kangyur Rinpoche appreciated this serious and modest student. In late November 1974, shortly before Kangyur Rinpoche's death, he boarded a plane for Calcutta that was hijacked to Tunisia by Palestinian terrorists who, although they were disowned by the PLO, were demanding the release of seven other terrorists imprisoned in Egypt and Holland. One man was killed by the hijackers. Once the passengers had been freed, Gérard returned to Paris. He would never see Kangyur Rinpoche again.

In Dordogne, Khyentse Rinpoche gave many teachings, mostly for the benefit of the twenty students, men and women, who were preparing to begin their first three-year retreat, but also for all those had traveled from countries far and wide to be with him.

Khyentse Rinpoche provided the future retreatants with all the empowerments and explanations they would need to carry out their first year of retreat. They would also receive all their weekly instructions from Tulku Pema Wangyal. Khyentse Rinpoche was scheduled to return the following year to transmit further empowerments and instructions to them. At the Sonnerie, among other things, he explained for all the visitors the *Thirty-Seven Verses on the Practice of a Bodhisattva*, which I interpreted orally and later carefully set down in writing for inclusion in *The Heart of Compassion*, one of the few books that I would take to my "desert island," where only the essential things are allowed.[2] In it, Khyentse Rinpoche captures the quintessence of the path of the Great Vehicle, based on the practice of altruistic love in all circumstances of life, connecting it to the understanding of the fundamental nature of mind.

Khyentse Rinpoche generally taught for ten, fifteen, or even twenty minutes at a time, without pausing. Then he stopped and I interpreted. He had been accustomed to this way of doing things by Tulku Pema Wangyal, an outstanding interpreter who translated for him from Tibetan into English on his first visit in 1975. Tulku Pema Wangyal had a perfect knowledge of the teachings and, with his infallible memory, reconstituted Rinpoche's words with unparalleled precision and ease.

I was very far from possessing a similar expertise, but with the help of Khyentse Rinpoche's blessings I managed to get by all right. I emptied myself out and put myself in a state of complete availability. I let the outline and details of the teachings imprint themselves on my mind, without allowing any other thoughts to interfere, then I rendered them to the best of my ability, first in French and a second time in English. When Khyentse Rinpoche spoke for ten minutes, I interpreted for fifteen or twenty minutes. My brain was young in those days and I took no notes, which have the unfortunate tendency to simplify the discourse, on top of which I found that writing distracted me from my sole task of listening to Rinpoche's words. I remember once, when I was interpreting for Khyentse Rinpoche in Boulder, Colorado, at Trungpa Rinpoche's main center, he divided his teaching into two parts—the first lasted twenty minutes and the second lasted thirty. It took me thirty and forty minutes, respectively, to translate the whole thing. That made up the entire morning session of teachings. Given the length of these presentations, I had jotted down a few key points to remind myself of the order of the themes addressed and then filled them in from memory. As I interpreted, Khyentse Rinpoche calmly read his prayer book. At the end of the teachings, someone asked which text Rinpoche had expounded and what translation I had read from. I answered that Khyentse Rinpoche had taught directly from his own knowledge that day, without any textual support, and that he had been reading his prayer book during the pauses. As for me, I had kept my eyes glued to my sheet of paper in order to concentrate, but it held only a few thematic reference notes. Some time later, when I had become the fourteenth Dalai Lama's French interpreter, I found myself in the same situation. The Dalai Lama also spoke for about ten minutes at a stretch, then glanced over at the interpreter and suddenly seemed to realize, in a loud voice, "Oh, you have to translate, do you?" which drew gales of laughter from the audience, together with a hint of sympathy for the interpreter. In India and Nepal, I generally translated Khyentse Rinpoche into English, so I had spoken very little French during the seven years that preceded my return to Dordogne. Tibetan texts and a few English translations had been the mainstays of my reading. Toward the end of one afternoon of translation, I received a very unexpected compliment. A woman came up to me and congratulated me. "My, you speak quite good French!"—a remark you might make to a foreigner who has managed a little fluency in your language, but not to a native speaker. I suppose my French had become a little rusty and tinged with an Indian accent.

Most of my close spiritual friends from Darjeeling, students of Kangyur Rinpoche, were now preparing to begin a three-year retreat. Some went on to do a second and a third consecutive retreat, thus spending nine years devoting themselves exclusively to spiritual practice, guided by

Tulku Pema Wangyal and the other great teachers who were to come to Dordogne over the years. Among them, Kyabje Dudjom Rinpoche and Dilgo Khyentse Rinpoche held a very special place.

I shared with Tulku Pema Wangyal the advice of Khyentse Rinpoche that I should stay with him, rather than joining my spiritual brothers and sisters in the retreat that was about to begin. He was a little surprised but understood what a stroke of good fortune Khyentse Rinpoche's offer was for me, an opportunity to spend many more years in the presence of a very great spiritual master.

In late April 1980, at the end of our month in France, I returned to India with Khyentse Rinpoche. He had to return to Bhutan, where he lived six to eight months a year, from the spring until late autumn. However, the kingdom was essentially closed to foreigners in those days. On the plane, I asked Khyentse Rinpoche what I should do. "Return to Darjeeling," he told me, "and I will let you know when I'm on my way to India or Nepal."

Without saying a word, however, he had something else in mind for me. When we reached Delhi, Khyentse Rinpoche stayed at the residence of the ambassador of Bhutan. The next morning, when the ambassador came to pay his respects, he told him, "I wish to bring this young monk with me to Bhutan. Please request the Queen Mother to grant him permission."

16

FIRST MEETING WITH THE DALAI LAMA

Return to India. I accompany Dilgo Khyentse Rinpoche to Dharamshala, at the invitation of the Dalai Lama. I witness the deep intimacy binding these two remarkable beings and see for myself the high esteem in which the Dalai Lama holds my teacher.

Although I first went to India in 1967, it was not until 1980 that I met the Dalai Lama. He mostly lived in Dharamshala, the seat of the Tibetan government in exile, in northwestern India, whereas I always stayed in the Darjeeling area, 1,200 miles to the east. In May 1980, the day after our return from France, Khyentse Rinpoche went to Dharamshala to spend a few days with the Dalai Lama.

From their first meeting in Lhasa in 1958, the Dalai Lama had felt a special kinship with Dilgo Khyentse Rinpoche; Khyentse Rinpoche had been visiting Dharamshala regularly since the 1970s to offer him essential empowerments and teachings of the Nyingmapa school. He would stay anywhere from a few days to two weeks. Over the course of these encounters, their spiritual connection grew continually richer and deeper, to the point where, to this very day, the Dalai Lama often refers to Khyentse Rinpoche as one of his primary teachers.

Around 9 a.m. on the morning after our arrival in Dharamshala, we drove to the Dalai Lama's residence. He was waiting for Khyentse Rinpoche at the front door. My teacher got out of the car and approached by leaning, as usual, on the shoulders of his aides, Tsewang Lhundrup and me. As soon as Khyentse Rinpoche reached the threshold, the Dalai Lama quickly prostrated three times toward him, his head bowed all the way down to the ground. Wishing to return this sign of respect, Khyentse Rinpoche did his best to reciprocate. But owing to his age and limited mobility, he barely had time to touch his forehead once to the soil when the Dalai Lama, who had spryly completed his three prostrations, moved to help Khyentse Rinpoche to his feet. He then led him into a small room giving on the large chamber in which he held audience.

The two masters sat face-to-face on little cubical seats made of wood and covered by rugs. The Dalai Lama had taken care to add a thick cushion to Khyentse Rinpoche's seat so as to be lower than him, since he was going to be receiving teachings and not conferring them. Their seats were separated by two little Tibetan tables bearing the books that would be used in the teachings, two cups of tea, and a few other objects. Khyentse Rinpoche introduced me to the Dalai Lama, to whom I briefly related my spiritual education with Kangyur Rinpoche. Tsewang Lhundrup and I then took our leave. The Dalai Lama and Khyentse Rinpoche were to spend the day alone together.

We returned for Khyentse Rinpoche at around five o'clock in the afternoon. The two masters said their goodbyes by touching foreheads, which, in addition to being a gesture of farewell, is also used when meeting a peer, as a sign of deep mutual respect. Then, holding on to our shoulders, Khyentse Rinpoche headed for the car, while the Dalai Lama waited on the threshold. Having helped Khyentse Rinpoche into his seat at the front of the Jeep beside the driver, Tsewang Lhundrup and I hustled to the back of the car and jumped in. Having said a final farewell to Khyentse Rinpoche by raising his hand to his heart, the Dalai Lama looked at us in the open back of the Jeep as it drove away and laughed as he teased us with a military salute.

This scenario was repeated almost identically day after day. Khyentse Rinpoche told us that they remained alone together most of the day, not only during the transmission of teachings but also at mealtimes and in moments of relaxation, when they would chat about many different subjects. When Khyentse Rinpoche's teacup was empty, the Dalai Lama refilled it himself from a thermos.

The Dalai Lama twice invited us to stay for the day, and we were able to witness their sessions. What a gift that was! I did not squander a second of their presence, the way they interacted, their conversations outside the context of the teachings, their occasional exchanges of pleasantries. Sometimes the Dalai Lama would turn to us and ask us questions on particular subjects, but most of the time we simply sat in their presence, thrilled to find ourselves there.

That was especially true when Khyentse Rinpoche conferred an important empowerment and the Dalai Lama, in his great kindness, asked that we receive it too. A third monk from Khyentse Rinpoche's entourage, Damchö, was in charge of preparing the objects and images used during the empowerment ritual. One empowerment involved several hundred images that had to be presented to Khyentse Rinpoche in the correct order as he blessed the Dalai Lama. In such a solemn situation, it was best to avoid any errors, so I assisted Damchö in his task. I was also given permission to take a few photos and to film one of the transmissions, extracts of which can be seen in the documentary that I made on the life of Khyentse Rinpoche, *The Spirit of Tibet*. I don't know if there is any other documentation of the Dalai Lama receiving teachings from one of his spiritual teachers.

Beyond the abundance of blessings we received merely by being present, one of the most important lessons I drew from these very special moments was the incredible humility of these two great masters, who rivaled each other in mutual respect. At one moment, the text indicated that the student must take the teacher's foot and place it on his head. Dilgo Khyentse Rinpoche deliberately skipped over that sentence, not wishing the Dalai Lama to take it literally. But the Dalai Lama was following along in the text and detected the omission. Once the teaching had concluded, he rose without saying a word, approached Khyentse Rinpoche, who sat cross-legged on his seat, bent down, took Khyentse Rinpoche's foot in his hand, and placed it on his head. This was about as far as you can get from the clashing egos and self-infatuation that govern so many human relationships, particularly those of the so-called great men of this world. The humility of these perfect beings was neither feigned nor formal. They were totally unconstrained by convention; their actions demonstrated the pure, natural expression of authentic humility and boundless mutual respect.

Meeting the Dalai Lama in the company of Khyentse Rinpoche was a great privilege; from the moment of my arrival, I had been privy to the most private moments between these two great masters. Some of the Dalai Lama's qualities are perfectly obvious to all, and I did not fail to note his simplicity, his vigor, his sense of humor, his kindness, and the attention he accorded to everyone he spoke to. But as is always the case with spiritual masters, it is much harder to describe the ineffable factor that is the very essence of what sets them apart. You can measure the quality of a gold sample in carats, but how do you describe the Dalai Lama's "quality of being"? The fact of the matter is, I understood from our very first meeting that these moments spent in his presence had awakened the very best in me. I felt the authenticity of the Dalai Lama in every one of his gestures and words as a powerful call to be authentic down to the very core of my being.

The fact that I met the Dalai Lama as a student of his own teacher made him feel special affection for me. As for me, I consider myself to be one of his humble students.

17

IN THE LAND OF THE THUNDER DRAGON

Dilgo Khyentse Rinpoche takes me to his adopted country, Bhutan, where the traditions of Tibetan Buddhism remain intact. I visit the temples of Kurjey, in the Bumthang Valley, and the Paro Taktsang sanctuary, the famous "Tiger's Nest."

After our visit with the Dalai Lama in Dharamshala, in May 1980, we flew from Delhi to Bagdogra, a little airport in western Bengal, then took a detour by car through Darjeeling and Sikkim before reaching the border of Bhutan. In the border town of Phuntsholing, when the soldiers guarding the checkpoint saw Khyentse Rinpoche's car approaching, they immediately dropped their guns and rushed to receive his blessing. That was the first indication that we were entering a country like no other!

Only Indian citizens are allowed to enter Bhutan without a visa, and in those days the country was still closed to foreign tourists. My visa had been authorized as a result of Khyentse Rinpoche's request to the Queen Mother. In addition to this precious access, I needed special permits to travel from one province to another.

Our first significant destination was the Kurjey complex, one of Bhutan's major sacred sites, in the province of Bumthang, three days from the capital, Thimphu. The central valley of Bumthang, located at an altitude of 10,000 feet, is about twelve miles long. This is one of the most enchanting places in Bhutan, dotted with magnificent sanctuaries, often quite ancient, and illustrious pilgrimage sites. A powerful river of crystalline waters runs through this wooded region of rare beauty, bounded by high hills adorned with many little temples and hermitages.

In May 1980, a very special date was approaching—the tenth day of the Month of the Monkey in the Year of the Monkey, an event that comes around only once in twelve years in the lunar calendar based on a sixty-year cycle. The day marks the miraculous birth of Guru Padmasambhava, who appeared on a lotus in the middle of Lake Danakosha in the kingdom of Oddiyana, thought to have been located in a high valley in the Swat region, in what is now Pakistan. On that date, a grand historical festival is held in which a hundred monks dance in sumptuous brocade robes, wearing masks representing Padmasambhava and other characters or deities linked to the sacred dances and ceremonies that run from morning to night.

These ceremonies are of very special importance in the temples of Kurjey. The oldest was built in the eighth century to protect and venerate an imprint left in the stone when Padmasambhava leaned against the wall of a small cave, and was rebuilt in the sixteenth century. Two other, larger, temples were erected in 1900 and in the late 1980s. On this tenth day of the fifth month, an immense *thangka*, a long roll of fabric made of swatches of silk skillfully entwined on a textile backing, representing Padmasambhava and his eight manifestations—a technique that the artists of Bhutan have mastered to perfection—was draped across the three-story façade of the largest temple in Kurjey. That day, we awoke at two in the morning to launch the celebrations in the temple and then on the broad paved parterre in front of the sanctuary. Beginning at 9 a.m., sacred dances were performed one after the other throughout the day. The residents of the valley and surrounding districts came with their entire families to picnic and attend the festival, which is said to confer powerful blessings.

When these great religious festivities were concluded, we remained another ten days in Bumthang, and took advantage of this time to visit the valley's most important pilgrimage sites. With Rabjam Rinpoche, Khyentse Rinpoche's grandson, and a few other monks, we undertook the long day's trek from Kurjey to Tharpaling, "The Place of Deliverance," 12,000 feet above sea level. This is where Gyalwa Longchen Rabjam, one of the greatest teachers in Tibetan history, spent several years in the fourteenth century. Hermits undertake long retreats there to this very day.

On the way, we came across a scene that is quite common in Bhutan—an archery tournament, the favorite sport of the Bhutanese and the only one for which they send a team to the Olympic Games. Although it is the national sport, it is practiced mostly at villages festivals. At either end of a field, two narrow planks are set up about 300 feet from each other, each bearing a small colored target about the size of saucer. After they have taken their shot, the archers gather around the target. Completely oblivious to the danger, they await the arrival of each new arrow, which they dodge with agility if it comes too close. When an arrow hits the target, or better yet the bull's-eye, the members of the winning team do a joyful ritual dance and sing victory songs.

During this happy interlude in Bumthang, I felt completely in my element, enjoying every moment like an elixir, thanks above all to the presence of Khyentse Rinpoche, but also to the sacred nature of the sites, which merged seamlessly with the natural beauty. A deep sense of harmony encompassed the entire valley, which felt as if it had come through the centuries with all its historical character, spiritual qualities, and natural wildness intact. Two dirt roads snaked along each bank of the crystalline river. Vast forests of pine trees and junipers covered the mountain slopes. The inhabitants wore the same traditional attire as their ancestors and spoke their own local dialects. Bear, deer, leopards, and other wild animals freely roamed the forests and the heights. When fruit was in season, the bears regularly came down at night to gorge themselves in the apple orchards. If these visits grew too frequent, the farmers took turns at night on the roof of their main dwellings and banged on pots at the approach of the hungry animals, which usually dissuaded them from pressing their luck. But accidents were not uncommon, and I met several villagers whose faces bore the deep scars of an impromptu encounter with a bear. Later in life, I was always overjoyed to return to the enchanting valleys of Bumthang.

On our way back, we spent several days in Gangteng Valley, which also became one of my favorite spots in Bhutan. At the top of a mountain pass, I first saw that long valley, descending gently to the horizon, whose lightly curved shape recalls its glacial origin. On a promontory in the center of the valley, a little village with one narrow street sits below a magnificent monastery. Further along, semi-marshland strewn with small clumps of mountain bamboo (at the elevation of 10,000 feet) is the habitat of choice for black-necked cranes overwintering from northern Tibet and Siberia. These are the valley's mascots. Gangteng, also known as Phobjika, is the most northerly wintering site for the cranes. To prevent their being disturbed, the government decided to forbid the erection of electricity pylons anywhere in this superb glacial valley; only solar electricity is allowed. Once the cranes arrive in October or November, the residents hold a festival devoted to these large birds. The cranes return to the north in early springtime, and it is said that, before leaving the valley, they fly three times around the monastery in a mark of respect. In the spring, the high slopes of the valley are covered by flowering rhododendrons in a blaze of red, pink, and white.

Following this first pilgrimage, we returned to the western part of the country in July for the tenth day of the sixth month, which, according to an alternative tradition, is also Padmasambhava's birthday. Khyentse Rinpoche spent two weeks at Paro Taktsang, the celebrated "Tiger's Nest," one of the most impressive places in the Himalayas. There are many other vertiginous cliffs in that mountain range of yawning immensity, but none where a monastery clings to the rockface as if by magic, 10,000 feet above sea level, in the middle of a vertical wall 3,000 feet high. When I first saw that dark rampart of stone, the sanctuary looked totally inaccessible. It is said that Padmasambhava flew there on the back of a tigress, giving the place its name.

For us mere mortals, a path winds through a great forest of ancient trees whose branches are hung with long, pale green strands of epiphytic lichens. People say that these are the hairs of a hundred thousand *dakinis*, celestial deities who "soar through the sky of ultimate reality." Khyentse Rinpoche undertook the ascent in a makeshift palanquin built from a crate hung from two long wooden poles, which allowed six strapping lads to carry it on their shoulders.

After climbing for two hours, we reached a little stupa at the side of a mountain pass. From there, we descended a steep, switchback trail carved into the rockface of the cliff opposite Taktsang. We stopped for a rest, and tea was served to Khyentse Rinpoche. A simple but evocative picture I took at that moment shows my master from behind, staring at the temple across the abyss.[1]

In those days, you had to negotiate certain passages of the descent on beams suspended above the void between the crevices in the cliff. A wire rope, affixed to the rock wall from one end of the dangerous passage to the next, at least gave your hands something to cling to. I couldn't help wondering about the age of those blackened, weather beams, and how much longer they would hold up under the weight of hikers. At the bottom of the path, you pass a waterfall cascading from 600 feet overhead, at the foot of which prayer wheels revolve night and day, propelled by the current.

Then came the last, steep climb leading to the monastery entrance. Arrival is as much a relief as it is a wonderment. Stairs of stone rise through a vault, then open out on a complex of temples perched on a ledge beneath enormous overhanging rock formations. The exterior walls of the temples are flush with the cliff, and the know-how needed to build them in the seventeenth century, under the supervision of Tenzin Rabgye—the fourth Druk Desi (secular ruler) of Bhutan and grandson of the great Tibetan yogi Drukpa Kunley—remains a mystery.

In the ninth century, when this place was visited by Guru Padmasambhava, the great master who introduced Buddhism to Tibet and Bhutan, there were only a few caves in which he meditated and conferred spiritual empowerments on his closest students. It is also said that, assuming the wrathful aspect of Dorje Drolo, Padmasambhava concealed numerous teachings in the form of "hidden treasures" in various spots around the complex.[2] These "treasures" were revealed over the course of history by visionary masters, known as *tertöns*, including Kangyur Rinpoche and Dilgo Khyentse Rinpoche.

In normal times, this place was inhabited by a handful of monks, but now it was as buzzing with activity as a beehive. A hundred monks and faithful had made themselves at home wherever they could in the common rooms of the little temples. Khyentse Rinpoche held ceremonies and, in homage to Padmasambhava, offered one hundred thousand lamps—little brass cups, and a few more-valuable silver ones—filled with oil or melted butter and outfitted in the middle with a wick fixed into a small hole. These are typically set out in the hundreds, and even thousands, on tables set up before the temple altar. He also gave some thirty students the complete transmission of the empowerments of the Essence of Vast Expanse Heart (Longchen Nyingthig), which was revealed in the eighteenth century by the great master Jigme Lingpa. During Khyentse Rinpoche's visit, Jigme Lingpa appeared to him in a vision in a dream. He placed his hand on Khyentse Rinpoche's head and told him, "You are the heir to my teachings, and you may use them as you see fit." Jigme Lingpa also prophesized that, to maintain peace in Bhutan and ensure the continuity of Buddhism, it was essential to build four great stupas, each containing one hundred thousand miniature stupas, known as tsatsas, and to offer one hundred thousand butter lamps and one hundred thousand circumambulations of the stupas, once they were built. This was all accomplished with the support of the royal family.

Khyentse Rinpoche did not write a spiritual autobiography in which he might have related his meditative experiences, his dreams, and his vision, and we had only a few glimpses of his profound inner experiences and visions through the few stories, such as these, that he sometimes told his heart students. In that vein, Khyentse Rinpoche once told us that long after the death of Dzongsar Khyentse Chökyi Lodrö, his teacher, his secret autobiography was discovered transcribed in a notebook. Reading it, Khyentse Rinpoche realized that he himself had been present when his master had experienced certain extraordinary visions of the Buddha and Guru Padmasambhava. And yet, he told us, "I was sitting right next to him, but nothing in his demeanor suggested that he was in the middle of receiving a profound vision at that very moment." There is no doubt that Khyentse Rinpoche's visionary experiences were every bit as frequent.

I retain, etched into my memory, so many pictures of that unique stay in the otherworldly precincts of Paro Taktsang. I recall a ceaseless, two-way flow of adepts along its narrow paths, some climbing to meet Khyentse Rinpoche, others returning to the valley. One day, after having come to meet Khyentse Rinpoche, some thirty monks from the Paro *dzong* were returning on the path carved into the stone that zigzags along the cliff-face across from Taktsang. In Bhutan, *dzongs* are fortresses that are part monastery and part seat of local government. I had failed to notice this very striking scene, and for once, Khyentse Rinpoche drew my attention to it and gestured to me to capture it on film. At breakfast, the monks some-times amused themselves by fashioning flying saucers out of *tsampa*—roasted barley flour paste—and flinging them into the abyss. They would glide for thirty seconds or so before reaching the forest below.

Early one morning, from a balcony overlooking the precipice, dressed in brocade robes and wearing the lotus headdress, Khyentse Rinpoche stood and, taking in the landscape with his majestic gaze, performed an impressive ritual intended to revitalize the spiritual power of the complex.

There are nine sacred caves and seven temples at Taktsang and its immediate surroundings. Every hilltop has its own little sanctuary encir-cled by prayer flags wafting on the breeze. The mountains and forests are dotted with hermitages where practitioners devote themselves to medita-tion, coming down only once a year, in the monsoon season, to receive alms. Every farm donates a measure of rice and preserved vegetables, and they are able to collect enough in three months to maintain themselves in solitary retreat for the rest of year. Bhutanese friends have often told me that if I decided to stay here in the mountains, they would be happy to provide for my needs. But at that time, it was far more precious to me to remain in the presence of Khyentse Rinpoche, which was worth more to me than all the retreats in the world.

There are many pilgrimages to take around Taktsang, and one day we set off on an excursion with Rabjam Rinpoche and a few monks. Heading north, near a big waterfall, you first reach the cave of Machig Labdrön, a renowned twelfth-century yogini who left her footprint on the stone floor of her hermitage.[3] If you wish to reach it, you have to climb, one step at a time, some thirty feet up the cliff-face on narrow rungs cut into two trunks leaning against the rock, one after the other, each no more than a foot wide.

Child's play for the Bhutanese, who seem immune to vertigo, this short climb is a little more adventurous for a pilgrim like me, especially when the rungs are slick with rain, you are carrying a backpack, and your monastic robes keep catching under your feet! In such circumstances, it is best to avoid looking down into the chasm yawning directly below.

The climb leads to the top of the cliff, a pleasant little plateau in the middle of which is the temple of Ugyen Tsemo, decorated with lovely frescoes. From there, you can return down another path that leads to the eastern temple of Taktsang Sharma, built near the cave of Dorje Drolo. In the old days, the final stretch leading to this little temple was a ledge barely twenty inches wide etched into the sheer rockface, with no safety railing or anything to grab onto. Adding to the danger and the thrill of the passage that year—my first time there—it had been raining. It would have been no challenge to a mountain climber, but I must admit that I contemplated it with a certain amount of apprehension. Finally, I said to myself, "Okay, enough thinking, let's go for it." The path has now been refurbished, and in any case, tourists no longer take that route. In the past, a walkway of beams allowed you to cross the hundred or so feet of cliff-face between Taktsang Sharma and the main temples of the Taktsang complex, but then one day a beam collapsed, a monk was carried off into the abyss, and the whole thing was dismantled.

From Sharma, we climbed up to Ugyen Tsemo and then continued higher still, passing through a forest of enormous trees. Once past the Özer Gang Monastery, we came to a high mountain meadow and the hermitages of Bumdrak, at 13,000 feet elevation. In the 1970s, this was home to a renowned painter of *thangkas*, the traditional form for representing the Buddha, Buddhist deities, and past teachers in Himalayan sacred art, painted on canvas or embroidered on silk. Bumdrak, literally "Rock of a Hundred Thousand," gets its name from the countless marks in the rocky escarpment below the hermitages, which are said to be the footprints left by *dakinis* dancing while offering a ritual feast.

One day during Khyentse Rinpoche's visit, I twice went to the Paro Valley and back in search of books and other objects that Khyentse Rinpoche required to confer teachings and empowerments. I have gone up to Paro Taktsang twenty times since then. I once had the opportunity to spend a week in retreat in a little wooden cabin next door to a modest dining hall set up midway for visitors. Every morning at dawn, I practiced for a few peaceful hours, facing the temple that clung to the majestic cliff before the first pilgrims of the day appeared. I then withdrew into the serenity of my cabin or went to a quiet place in the forest before reemerging in the afternoon once the pilgrims had returned to the valley. These were precious moments, in which I was able to immerse myself intensively in that holiest of holy places. Such sacred sites are all potent sources of inspiration for spiritual practice. It is said that one month of meditation in a place like Paro Taktsang generates as much spiritual progress as a year of retreat in an ordinary place, and I dreamed of building a tiny hermitage with a big window looking out on the cliff.

A fire broke out in 1998. Its causes remain unknown, as the only person at Taktsang that day died in the flames and the rockslides. The fire devastated some of the temples, whose debris and religious treasures were dashed to the valley floor three thousand feet below. However, one of the most precious statues survived the fall almost fully intact, and a few others were spared by the fire as well. Since then, under the guidance of the king and other patrons, the temples have been magnificently restored in a purely traditional style. The monastery was reconsecrated in 2005.

Khyentse Rinpoche cherished Bhutan, where Buddhist culture had flourished unhindered, and its values are deeply anchored in the minds of the people. There's a reason why it's said that in Bhutan, "the land is Buddhist and the sky is Buddhist." Every hill has its own little temple surrounded by prayer flags snapping in the wind. Prayer wheels driven by its streams turn day and night. Its mountains and forests are bestrewn with hermitages where monks, nuns, and laypeople devote themselves to the many forms of Buddhist practice.

After Guru Padmasambhava, the "lotus-born master," introduced Buddhism to Bhutan in the eighth century, other great masters followed, including Pema Lingpa, the discoverer of spiritual treasurers, in the fourteenth century, and Zhabdrung Ngawang Namgyal in the sixteenth. The latter disseminated the teachings of the Drukpa Kagyu school and unified the country, which until then had been fragmented into regional fiefdoms.[4]

Nowadays, certain large monasteries, such as that in the capital, Thimphu, count more than a thousand monks. The religious calendar is busy with ceremonies and sacred dance festivals. At various times of the year, on the tenth day of the lunar calendar, the largest monasteries celebrate the Festival of Day Ten (Tshechu), devoted to Guru Padmasambhava, so that the religious festivities follow close upon one another.

Although Khyentse Rinpoche was in no way associated with the official institution of Buddhism in Bhutan—which is led by the Je Khenpo, who shares the same protocol ranking as the king—he was the most venerated spiritual teacher in the country. Wherever he went, people began lining up outside his door every morning before dawn. When he had finished his prayers, they came in, bringing him offerings of rice, roasted barley flour, white cheese, and fresh butter in colorful bamboo baskets, and asking him to pray for them and their families. With a broad smile overflowing with kindness, he placed his enormous hands on their heads as he blessed them.

Several times a year, Khyentse Rinpoche performed highly elaborate ceremonies known as *drubchen* ("Great Accomplishment"). These complex ceremonies are centered on one or several deities of Tibetan Buddhism. They consist mainly of meditations guided by a support text and continue uninterrupted, day and night, for seven days, in addition to one day of preparation and one of conclusion. Using colored powders, monks create mandalas with multiple and subtle symbolic meanings that serve as visualization models for the participants. Meditating on a mandala is not an imaginary stroll through an enchanting paradise; it is a deep dive into the very nature of our own mind and the world of phenomena. All forms are perceived as the manifestation of primordial purity, all sounds as the echoes of emptiness, and all thoughts as the play of awareness.

All participants in the *drubchen* are together from seven in the morning until seven in the evening, and then split up into three groups that take turns, three hours apiece, maintaining the continuity of the ritual and meditative practice. These ceremonies, of extraordinary majesty, are accompanied by sacred music, dancing, rituals, and *mudras*, symbolic gestures of offering. Some years, Khyentse Rinpoche presided over as many as seven *drubchen* in Bhutan and Nepal. I occasionally participated, day and night, in two back-to-back *drubchen*, separated by only a three-day pause between the two cycles. By the time those twenty days had gone by, perfect silence reigned over the first night of sleep unbroken by ceremony! Nowadays, Rabjam Rinpoche, the spiritual heir to Khyentse Rinpoche, presides over three *drubchen* in the Shechen Monastery in Nepal and two in Bhutan every year.

In the *drubchen* that took place in Bhutan, during the day I would sit among the monks, taking care to remain clearly in sight of Khyentse Rinpoche, who often called on me to perform all sorts of tasks. Every night, I participated in one of the three-hour sessions—the first night from 9 p.m.

until midnight, the second from midnight until 3 a.m., the third from 3 until 6 a.m., and so on for the seven days of the main segment of the *drubchen*. During these nocturnal sessions, I had asked to be part of the group of monks who continuously recited the mantra of the principal deity. This recitation can never once be interrupted throughout the entire *drubchen*, day or night. During these recitations, when it is time for the new group of reciters to take over, the monk seated at the head of the first row hands his successor a little scepter known as a *vajra*, to which is tied a small cord woven of threads in five colors, symbolizing the five primordial wisdoms. This cord connects the reciter to the mandala at the center of the temple. The reciters must be totally focused on their recitation and sit somewhat apart from the monks performing the main ritual. Hot tea and grains of crushed rice were served to all participants at each session. It was not unusual for the Queen Mother of Bhutan, who held Khyentse Rinpoche in high esteem and sponsored most of these ceremonies, to visit us late at night, with no advance warning, perform many circuits of the mandala, then sit down on the sofa reserved for her to recite her prayers. At times, while we were fully absorbed in our recitation, the scent of her subtle French perfume as she entered the temple was the sign of her arrival among us. Those of us who had dozed off a little quickly sat up straight to look our best before Her Majesty. These moments of practice were particularly intense in the warm atmosphere of that compact little temple, dominated by a majestic fifteen-foot statue of Guru Padmasambhava.

When Khyentse Rinpoche traveled, you would have thought that news of his arrival had spread through the entire country. He could not go twenty miles without running into a delegation of villagers waiting for him at the side of the road. People would light fires that they fed with damp juniper branches, filling the air with swirls of aromatic smoke. Rugs were spread over tables covered with food and hot tea. Rinpoche would sometimes offer blessings from the window of his car; more often, he would get out and sit awhile, offering a prayer of long life to the crowd and taking a rest.

On long drives, while contemplating the landscape, Khyentse Rinpoche practiced nonstop, murmuring his prayers and quietly reciting his prayers while he counted out his *mala*.[5] In Bhutan in the 1980s, districts far from the capital were accessible only by roads of beaten earth or backfilled with crushed stone. Travel was therefore somewhat bumpy. Khyentse Rinpoche, however, pointed out that the constant shaking was good for the digestion!

The convoy usually consisted of the yellow Toyota Land Cruiser of the late 1970s that the Queen Mother had given Khyentse Rinpoche and that bore a royal license plate "Bhutan 48," another car borrowed for the occasion, and an army truck transporting Khyentse Rinpoche's followers and the luggage. Two or three monks, a few *tulkus* and some close disciples whom Khyentse Rinpoche taught on a daily basis made up his immediate entourage. Most of the time, the little convoy was led by an open transport vehicle belonging to the royal guard, there to ensure that the journey went off without a hitch. The escort was more a mark of respect than any real protection. Clearly, Khyentse Rinpoche ran no danger in a country where he was beloved by all, but the lead vehicle sometimes moderated the fervor of impatient drivers or of trucks driving on the wrong side of the mountain roads that we used.

When the convoy approached a village or a *dzong*—one of those renowned monastery-cum-fortresses—Khyentse Rinpoche was invariable greeted by an advance delegation of monks and dignitaries. Preceded by musicians and monks waving brocaded banners, the procession would lead him to his residence, where the mayor, the judge, or some other notable— dressed in his official finery and wearing on his belt a silver-sheathed sword with a finely wrought pommel—prostrated before him and offered him tea and sustenance. Then, hundreds of people would gather in the *dzong* courtyard and line up for Khyentse Rinpoche's benediction.

That first month of the ten years that I would spend in Bhutan immersed me from day one in the heart of the spiritual culture of the Land of the Thunder Dragon, a place unlike any other. I remain filled with immense gratitude to this day. From 1980 to 1991, when Khyentse Rinpoche died, I spent most of the year in Bhutan. I have returned many times since then to see Rabjam Rinpoche, always at the kind invitation of Her Majesty the Royal Grandmother Ashi Kesang Choden Wangchuck, the grandmother of the current monarch.

18

ON RETREAT WITH DILGO KHYENTSE RINPOCHE

I have the great fortune to be included in the inner circle present for Khyentse Rinpoche's four-month silent retreat. Meditating in the highlands of western Bhutan, overlooking the plains of India.

In the winter of 1980–1981, Khyentse Rinpoche went into silent retreat for four months. He had chosen a place above the border town of Phuntsholing, in the highlands overlooking the vast plains of India from Bhutan. This was one of the most precious times of my life with Khyentse Rinpoche. We lived in a low-slung little house built in the Indian style that the Queen Mother had offered to Khyentse Rinpoche.

Khyentse Rinpoche lived in the room at the back of the residence, with windows facing onto the semitropical jungle that covered the steep slope down to Phuntsholing, the border town with India. The only furnishings were an altar of varnished wood, bearing a few statues and photos of spiritual masters wedged into the window frames, a very modest bed on which Rinpoche sat, a wooden table, an old sofa, and an armoire. In the foyer, one wall was covered floor to ceiling with shelves holding hundreds of Tibetan books. This foyer was shared by Khyentse Rinpoche's wife, Khandro, and Ani Sherab, the elder nun who assisted her. They were afforded some privacy by a screen dividing the long room, which faced onto the front of the house, where Tsewang Lhundrup and I, the two monks attending to Rinpoche, sometimes sat during the day on a long bench near the front door. As always, I slept on the floor, on a rug spread out before Khyentse Rinpoche's table. A little kitchen and a room with two beds, which were occupied by two other monks, completed this humble home. Rabjam Rinpoche, Khyentse Rinpoche's grandson, who had lived with him since the age of five, stayed in a little room facing the porch, which led out to the lawn. Outside stood eight white stupas built by another great lama, Chatral Rinpoche. The place was utterly peaceful. A few rare visitors came to circle the stupas and to visit a diminutive temple built atop a mound of earth.

The entire household comprised Tsewang Lhundrup, a Bhutanese monk in service to Khyentse Rinpoche; Tulku Kunga, who served both as scribe and as copyist of manuscripts written by our teacher; Drubthob, an old Nepalese lama who resided permanently in the house and lived on vegetables that he cooked whole in a little clay pot; and I. Khandro often asked if such or such a thing was available in the shops of Phuntsholing. Drubthob, who almost never went into town and was outspoken by nature, once answered, "Other than a father and a mother, you can buy anything in Phuntsholing!"

Five Bhutanese students who were close to Khyentse Rinpoche were also among those allowed to share in his retreat, and lived nearby. They received forty-five-minute daily teachings from our teacher after lunch. During these sessions, he limited himself exclusively to the transmission, without ever venturing into ordinary conversations; the rest of the time, Khyentse Rinpoche kept strict silence. Other than those people who had been included from the outset of the retreat, Khyentse Rinpoche never met with any visitor during those four months.

There were three other lodgers in the house: a white and gray cat, a yellow dog, and a white rabbit. The cat and the dog were great friends and played together all the time. The rabbit was curious about these capers, but as soon as the other two tried a little too hard to include him, he made himself scarce. One of the dog's favorite games was to pick up the cat by the scruff of its neck, as its mother would have done, and drag it across the floor all the way through the house, right up to the porch. The cat blissfully let him do it. Once Khyentse Rinpoche had finished his retreat, he invited a few other monks to join him in his room as he conducted offering ceremonies for the next fifteen days. During these ceremonies, the cat liked to hang out on top of the old sofa, where it watched for the dog. Whenever the latter came within reach, the cat pounced on it like a tiger on its prey. Once it had successfully repeated this ploy several times, we all collapsed in gales of laughter, Khyentse Rinpoche included, to the extent that we had to put the ceremony on pause for several minutes.

I spent one or two hours every morning engaging in my own spiritual practices, sitting on a rug a few yards from Khyentse Rinpoche, who silently meditated and prayed, counting out his crystal *mala*, his gaze open to the infinite as if he were contemplating a vast space that was one with the immensity of his inner realization. Nothing disturbed the serenity of the place. Every so often, the call of a toucan, the song of a laughing thrush, or the cry of a muntjac rang out through the wide-open windows. The forest abounded with mushrooms. The crazy idea of eating one raw gave me the opportunity to enjoy my first and last hallucinatory experience, accompanied by vertigo and vomiting.

One day, I got a postcard from France, depicting a landscape—the only piece of mail I received in those four months, I believe. I showed it to Khyentse Rinpoche, who, a few minutes later, shot me a mischievous, smiling glance and handed me a sheet of paper on which he had written the following verses in Tibetan:

Seeing this superb countryside
Reminds you of your homeland.
Here, you eat potatoes
And find yourself reduced to the role of servant.
Such is the play of karma!

He knew very well that the country of my birth and its gastronomic delights meant very little to me compared to the golden opportunity to live in the company of my teacher, at the very heart of his retreat. A Tibetan proverb puts it well: "Leaving your homeland is already half-way towards accomplishing the dharma." I most definitely had no regrets.

It was also around this time that Khyentse Rinpoche received a photocopy of a letter that a Tibetan had sent from Tibet to members of his refugee family in India. A letter from Tibet was a major event! Photocopies of this missive circulated in all the communities of Tibetans in exile. There was nothing special about its contents, just family news, but no private correspondence had ever arrived from Tibet since the Chinese invasion in 1959. The death of Mao Zedong in 1979 was soon followed by an easing of restrictions—very limited, to be sure, but palpable.

Because he had taken a vow of silence, Khyentse Rinpoche had fallen into the habit of indicating with specific gestures which person he wished to call to him. In the case of Tsewang Lhundrup—the monk who, along with me, attended to his personal needs—he rang a bell that he also used in rituals. He snapped his fingers when he needed me, which I was able to hear clearly even when I was in the foyer studying or taking notes about the teachings we had received. If someone else was with him when he wanted me to come, he made a circle with his thumb and index finger and raised it to his eye, simulating the glasses that I wore. When he required the presence of Tulku Kunga, his scribe, he used his hand to mimic the act of writing. Last, if he wanted us to call his wife, he sketched the outline of a long strand of hair by sweeping his finger from his forehead to behind his ear. When he needed something, such as a book, he wrote it with his fingernail on a little oiled slate dusted with a fine layer of ashes. As his writing was difficult to read, I sometimes had to rush from the room, slate in hand, to ask my companions to help me decipher the message, which allowed me to avoid looking befuddled in his presence as I tried to understand what he had written down.

Over the course of those four months, Khyentse Rinpoche gave us a series of teachings that covered the entire path of Tibetan Buddhism. He began by reading and explaining *Words of My Perfect Teacher*, the celebrated text by Patrul Rinpoche on the preliminary steps of the path. Then he conferred upon us a Padmasambhava empowerment in the tradition of the Heart Essence of the Vast Expanse (Longchen Nyingthig) and explained the visualizations and mantras that accompany this practice. He then spent every day of the next three weeks teaching us one of the twenty-one yoga exercises associated with that tradition. Sitting on his bed, he would explain the exercise of the day, while Gelong Sangye, a student of his who had mastered this practice, gave us a demonstration. At the end of the day, under Gelong Sangye's guidance, we gathered in the temple on the little hill a hundred yards from the house to cycle through all the exercises we had learned over the weeks. Every day, a new exercise was added to the series of twenty-one. When the twenty-one days had elapsed, each student took turns, over the course of a week, presenting the full series of exercises not only to Khyentse Rinpoche but to all the practitioners who had gathered at the time scheduled for teachings. It was a kind of entrance exam! When it was my turn, I did my very best, but as usual I stumbled at a particularly difficult exercise, which consisted of leaping into the air and rapidly crossing my legs before coming back to earth in a perfect lotus position. Rabjam Rinpoche and most of my companions, who were all young and trim at that time, had no problem performing this exercise perfectly. In my case, with my Westerner's legs, which had begun their training in such postures later in life, I only managed to land in a half-lotus. Khyentse Rinpoche went benevolently easy on me and, most unusually during his retreat, added a few words of ordinary conversation to his teachings: "Now you're ready to show these exercises to your friends doing the three-year retreat in France." His words came true the next year, when he gave a more condensed teaching of the exercises to the retreatants at the Chanteloube Study Center in Dordogne and asked me to demonstrate the exercises in detail to them. In Phuntsholing, I had taken detailed notes based on Khyentse Rinpoche's explanations of every aspect of the movements. Those notes proved to be very useful decades later, when students of Khyentse Rinpoche's lineage wanted to learn the exercises.

To conclude the cycle of teachings for the retreat, Khyentse Rinpoche conferred the introduction to the nature of mind and the teachings of the text known as the *Yeshe Lama: The Unsurpassable Primordial Wisdom*, the central teaching of the great master Jigme Lingpa on the Great Perfection.

One sunny morning when the four months were over, Khyentse Rinpoche stood up, bare-chested and dressed as usual in his long skirt of wild yellow silk and, leaning on Tsewang Lhundrup's shoulders and mine, stepped out onto the lawn in front of the house. Breaking his vow of silence, he began to speak, as if nothing had happened. His retreat was over.

The next winter, we returned to Phuntsholing, where, at the request of Drikung Kyabgön Rinpoche, head of the Drikung Kagyu school, Khyentse Rinpoche spent two and a half months conferring the eighteen volumes of *The Treasury of Precious Instructions* (*Damngak Dzö*).[1] A large tent was erected for the occasion by the local authorities on a piece of open ground not far from Khyentse Rinpoche's house to make room for one thousand disciples gathering from all corners, including reincarnate lamas (*tulkus*), scholars, and numerous adepts, monks, nuns, and laypeople.

My mother, Yahne, had been invited by Khyentse Rinpoche to spend six months in Bhutan. Having arrived in the summer, she had many opportunities to meet with the Queen Mother when she visited with Khyentse Rinpoche. They grew close, and the Queen Mother took my mother under her wing, constantly demonstrating her affection for her, among other things by sending her a gift every year to this very day. In Phuntsholing, my mother was housed in a residence belonging to the royal family, located a hundred yards from Khyentse Rinpoche's house. She was thus able to receive the teachings that my master gave that winter.

The Treasury of Precious Instructions, collected in the nineteenth century by the great nineteenth-century teacher Jamgön Kongtrül, contains the essence of the empowerments and instructions of the eight principal lineages of Tibetan Buddhism, also called the Eight Great Chariots of the Practice Lineage.[2] These lineages originated in the ninth and twelfth centuries under the inspiration of their founders, who were highly eminent spiritual teachers. Where they differ is not on the fundamental points of Buddhism, but on the greater or lesser emphasis placed on study and contemplation, and they offer an exhaustive collection of practices that are quite varied in form but allow all to complete the full path leading to enlightenment.

Every day during this cycle of teachings, I prepared the texts that Khyentse Rinpoche was to transmit. The final volume of the *Eight Great Chariots of the Practice Lineage* contained a compendium of one hundred brief teachings given in India and Tibet. Every day in the late afternoon, Khyentse Rinpoche explicated one or several of these teachings. It was my job to identify which of these short texts corresponded to the other teachings that Khyentse Rinpoche was to transmit that day and to present them to him late in the day for transmission, so that all one hundred teachings would be addressed by the end of the two months.

When the exegesis of the *Eight Great Chariots of the Practice Lineage* was complete, Khyentse Rinpoche very generously gifted me the entire set of eighteen volumes that he had used during the teachings, and which contained a few notes written in his hand. He explained, "It is only when one is unaware of everything these teachings contain that one runs the risk of adopting a sectarian perspective. Once you are familiar with them, you understand that they all lead to enlightenment and have the same ultimate meaning." I cherish these volumes, which I keep in the library of my mother's home in Dordogne.

19

THE PALACE OF GREAT BLISS

Annual ceremonies at Dechencholing, in the very special atmosphere of the Queen Mother's palace and the residence of Dilgo Khyentse Rinpoche. The royal family's consideration for us.

Every year, at the request of the Queen Mother, Khyentse Rinpoche, accompanied by a dozen hand-picked monks, spent a week leading ceremonies in the royal palace of Dechencholing, located a few kilometers outside the valley of Thimphu, the capital of Bhutan. The ceremonies took place on the third floor of that large and lovely four-story residence of cut stone. It was reached by a broad wooden stairway whose slippery steps gleamed from constant, assiduous polishing. The full name of the palace, Dechencholing Phodrang, means "Dharma Land of Great Bliss."

When there were no ceremonies, a rarely disturbed silence reigned over these spaces. Conversations were held in lowered voices and footsteps were muted against the floor of long, wide, hand-squared boards that gleamed like mirrors. The Queen Mother's servants polished the floor every day with the foliage of an aromatic plant that imparted a perfect sheen and an elegant, dark-red tint, while leaving the rooms subtly scented like forest undergrowth.

Inside, magnificent woodwork decorated in the traditional Bhutanese style alternated with adobe walls adorned with pastel frescoes, created with natural pigments extracted from plants and minerals from the

Himalayas. One fresco, painted at the suggestion of Khyentse Rinpoche, depicted the sixteenth-century lama Jatsön Nyingpo, "Essence of the Rainbow," sitting in space inside two circles of flame. Along the walls were large painted wooden trunks fitted with cast-iron locks. It was all imbued with great refinement and subtle elegance, lacking any trace of ostentatious luxury.

The palace was surrounded by splendid rose beds, English gardens, and a park inhabited by, among others, two stags and a dozen does. A hundred yards above the palace, at the end of a lovely lawn dotted with apple trees, stood a long, low house built in the traditional style that the Queen Mother had placed at the disposal of Khyentse Rinpoche. This was his main residence in Bhutan, if one can even use that term with respect to a master who had no fixed abode and was constantly on the move because of the teachings he was asked to perform and the retreats he undertook in remote places. Even so, he spent about one month a year in that house, and it was where he kept most of his books and precious objects. In the orchard that surrounded the house stood a rotunda encircled by trees where he sometimes gave his teachings. Students were able to get in through a separate entrance built into the wall enclosing the upper section of the park. That is where he conferred, notably, the transmission of *The Seven Treasures* by Gyalwa Longchen Rabjam, one of the greatest teachers and exegetes of the Nyingmapa school of Tibetan Buddhism.

Khyentse Rinpoche's wife, Khandro Lhamo, also had a room at Dechencholing, but she mostly lived in Sissinang Nunnery, a little monastic center that had been offered to Khyentse Rinpoche shortly after his arrival in the country. She accompanied Khyentse Rinpoche on most of his teachings and ceremonies and whenever he traveled outside Bhutan. She could be distrustful of those who sometimes gravitated around Khyentse Rinpoche for personal advantage, and she knew how to keep these unwelcome visitors at a distance. We all held her in the highest esteem. She always behaved most kindly toward me, and I enjoyed her full confidence. I relished spending time with her, when she would joyfully share stories and anecdotes about their life in Tibet. She also offered me advice on the best way to serve Rinpoche and be of use to him.

The yearly ceremonies performed in the palace were dedicated to sustained peace in the country and the long lives of the king and his family. The first days were devoted to longevity practice focussed on the Tsedrup Sangdu, a hidden spiritual treasure discovered by the great fifteenth-century visionary master Ratna Lingpa. In this ceremony, participants visualize themselves as the buddha of boundless life, Amitayus, and gather in their hearts the quintessence of the natural elements and the blessings of the buddhas and bodhisattvas in the form of a vital regenerative force. The practicants visualize themselves extracting the quintessence of the earth element, that of the mountains, the forests, the medicinal plants, gold, and all the precious gemstones; the quintessence of the water element, that of the oceans and their powerful waves, the rivers, and waterfalls, and the moon; the quintessence of fire, the strength of the sun and the conflagration that will mark the end of the universe; the quintessence of the wind, the energy of great storms and of the wind mandala that sustains the universe; and the quintessence of space, the infinite immensity of absolute truth, the emptiness of intrinsic existence, the ultimate nature of all phenomena. In the form of a glowing nectar, these quintessences dissolve in the heart of the student visualizing herself as Amitayus. In this way, the life force is regenerated. The practitioner then offers this life quintessence to the great spiritual teachers who strive for the good of all, to her loved ones, to the ill, and to all living beings.

Khyentse Rinpoche reminded us that the true meaning of "infinite life" was recognition of the ultimate nature of mind, which is beyond life and death. The very gentle and melodious chanting, the highly evocative visualizations, the stately presence of Khyentse Rinpoche, accompanied by only a dozen monks, the majesty of the great hall in which we found ourselves and the palace's atmosphere of profound contemplation imbued the ceremony with a unique solemnity.

For the duration of the ceremonies, Khyentse Rinpoche stayed in a room adjoining the great hall where the ceremonies took place. As it happens, this was the room in which the king had been born. The Queen Mother's chambers were on the floor above. She lived there with a few faithful, ever-alert attendants. She spoke softly but exuded great authority. At the far end of the large, magnificently decorated reception room, an altar of carved wood held a statue of Guru Padmasambhava, painted with fine gold and flanked by effigies of deities and reliquaries containing precious objects, among them a bracelet that had belonged to Yeshe Tsogyal, Padmasambhava's closest female student.

The Queen Mother and her visitors sat on large banquettes upholstered in brocade, before delicately sculpted tables bearing pyramids of fruit in silver bowls crafted by the best goldsmiths of the region. Her conversation, always very affable, bore largely on the wonders of Bhutan, its history, of which she was smitten, and stories of the lives of the great masters of the past. She attributed the kingdom's peace and prosperity to the benevolence and blessings of Khyentse Rinpoche and remained true to his memory years after our teacher's death.

The Queen Mother gave her mornings over to prayer and recited ten thousand mantras of Padmasambhava a day, her devotion to whom was equaled only by that in which she held Khyentse Rinpoche. She prayed with intensity, her eyes often closed, accompanying her invocation with gestures of her joined hands, while the expression on her face was in constant motion. Occasionally, she spoke in hushed tones to a precious statue or a photograph of Khyentse Rinpoche.

Whenever Khyentse Rinpoche was in residence at his house on the palace grounds, the Queen Mother would call on him every two or three days. She would cross the park, taking a narrow path of flat stones, followed by a few servants bearing gifts—vitamins, pots of turmeric, Bhutanese honey, and all sorts of elixirs—all carefully wrapped in Bhutanese paper handcrafted from the fibers of paperbush bark.

On word of her approach, in order to avoid finding themselves in inappropriate proximity to the Queen Mother, Khyentse Rinpoche's visitors would scatter into the woods, hide behind the house, or wait in the room in which we stored the thousands of books printed in India on Rinpoche's order. No one was supposed to happen upon the Queen Mother unexpectedly within the palace precincts. If you sought the honor of a meeting with her, you had to submit a request in advance. The only people remaining when she arrived were Khyentse Rinpoche and his immediate entourage. After we had greeted the Queen Mother, we withdrew into the antechamber and left them to their lengthy conversations, which reached us in calm and muted whispers. Every so often, we would discreetly lift the hem of the heavy red-and-yellow felt curtain that screened the door and take a peek, just to make sure that they wanted for nothing or to see whether the Queen Mother was preparing to take her leave. In due course, she would stand to receive Rinpoche's blessing, then back out of the room, her palms joined over her heart.

Before going back down to the palace, she would spend a few minutes with us. She would bring us up to date on recent events or describe some temple or sacred place in a neighboring valley that she thought I should visit. Not long after her return to the palace, one of her servants would sometimes return with a dish of food or treat for us. The "clandestine" visitors would then reemerge from hiding, and Khyentse Rinpoche would take up his teachings where he had left off.

As I did not eat meat and, in accordance with my monastic vows, ate nothing after my midday meal, I had begun to look a little skinny. The Queen Mother had taken me under her protection and every so often would send me some *dri* cheese, made of *dri* (the female of the yak) milk, or some pastries, which never failed to elicit the recurrent jokes of the young *tulkus* and Rinpoche's close students. To this very day, Dzongsar Khyentse Rinpoche, the incarnation of Dzongsar Khyentse Chökyi Lodrö, Dilgo Khyentse Rinpoche's second teacher, still teases me about the attentions that the Queen Mother lavished on me. In any case, her favors highlighted the kind of contrasts that illustrate the impermanence of all things. When she accompanied Khyentse Rinpoche on one of his excursions, the Queen Mother invited me once or twice to sit beside her in her Mercedes, but the very next day would find me bouncing around at the back of a truck in the pouring rain because Khyentse Rinpoche had sent me for some books he needed. This was a good demonstration of the "one taste" practice, facilitated by my joy of living with Rinpoche day after day.[1]

Whenever we were preparing to spend time in another province of Bhutan, Khyentse Rinpoche would ask me to locate dozens of volumes from the library that covered an entire wall of his room. Like all Tibetan books, they consisted of unbound folios, wrapped in fabric and identified by a cloth tab bearing the handwritten title of the text. He would then tell me which of them he wanted to bring with him, and we would soon have assembled two or three large bales of reinforced canvas, each containing some thirty books. My daily forays into that vast and rich library soon gave me a good knowledge of what it contained.

One or two days before we were due to leave, I would sometimes go to see the Queen Mother's secretary, Doctor Zangpo—he had been a physician in his youth—who worked out of an office in the park. My mission might consist, for instance, of asking him to make an additional vehicle available to Rinpoche. Whatever I asked, his answer always began with "No, no . . ."; I therefore began to call him Doctor No-No. If I wanted to check on the date of our departure and asked him, "We're leaving tomorrow, right?" I might unfailingly expect, "No, no, no. . . . The departure will take place tomorrow morning at ten." Everyone was afraid of him, but I got along well with him, as I found his personality quite amusing.

Also during our stays at Dechencholing, at Khyentse Rinpoche's request, I was able to photograph the Queen Mother's collection of precious *thangkas*—traditional paintings on fabric hemmed with brocade. One splendid series of twenty-three *thangkas* in particular illustrates the past lives of the Buddha, inspired by a text known as "The Wish-Fulfilling Tree." This exceptional collection of paintings on cloth was executed in the refined style known as Karma Gardri, from eastern Tibet, and was offered to the first king of Bhutan, Ugyen Wangchuk, by the fifteenth Karmapa, Khakyab Dorje, in the late nineteenth century. In addition to my photos of these twenty-three *thangkas*, down the years I was able to take more than 35,000 pictures of Himalayan art, which are preserved in the Shechen Archives, in Nepal, and available to anyone who needs them.[2]

Behind the palace was a wooded hillside crisscrossed with streams. Halfway up was the residence of the mother of the third king, Jigme Dorje Wangchuk, who had died in 1972 at the age of fifty-seven. His mother's name was Ashi Phuntsho Choden, and she too was a great benefactor of Buddhism and fervent student of Dudjom Rinpoche. Khyentse Rinpoche went to see her once or twice a year. Enthroned on her wheelchair, she was a woman of noble and calm demeanor who spent her time on spiritual practice.

I had come to feel a deep connection to Bhutan, its sublime landscapes, its pure air and limpid rivers, its simple, devout, and energetic people, as well its lifestyle, profoundly inspired by Buddhist values.

Intimately tied to the country's history, spirituality is reflected even in its descriptions of the landscape. Mountains are "recumbent elephants," symbols of serene power, or "proudly poised lions" whose roars proclaim the Dharma. The plains are "eight-petaled lotus flowers"; the glimpses of sky against rocky cliff-faces are "wheels of joy" (*gakyil*); lakes are seen as horns of plenty or cups of ambrosia. The entire country is sacred, each valley is a pilgrimage site, and every rock, cave, and river is linked to history. Here a hermit meditated, there a saint left his footprint in the stone, over yonder is the home of a guardian spirit of the soil. This spring is inhabited by a *naga*, half-man half-snake; this forest must never be cut down because it was blessed by a past master.

Up till now, Bhutan has done a remarkable job of synthesizing the preservation of its traditional Buddhist culture with the most useful contributions of Western civilization to environmental protection, improved public health, and education. As once noted by a senior Canadian official who helped Bhutan join the United Nations, "Bhutan could become like any other country on the Asian continent, but none of those countries could ever return to being like Bhutan."

20

A BRIEF SEPARATION

Second journey to France. Dilgo Khyentse Rinpoche returns to Bhutan after teaching in Dordogne. I spend three months at the retreat center orally translating *The Treasury of Precious Qualities*. First time away from my teacher.

In the spring of 1981, Dilgo Khyentse Rinpoche was again invited to France by Tulku Pema Wangyal to give a new series of teachings to the students undertaking a three-year retreat in Dordogne. Ever since I had become his student and entered into his service, I had always been at my teacher's side, along with two or three other monks, to care for him and fulfill any demand or need he might have. I therefore accompanied him on this month-long trip, during which, in addition to his group teachings, he gave personal advice to each of the retreatants. He also taught visitors who came from all over the world to his Périgord residence, now renamed Tashi Palbar Ling.

Shortly before he left to return to Bhutan, Dilgo Khyentse Rinpoche asked me to stay on for a few more months, at the request of Tulku Pema Wangyal, in order to provide the Chanteloube retreatant with an oral translation of a commentary on *The Treasury of Precious Qualities*, written by the great scholar Khenpo Yönten Gyatso, a student of the great nineteenth-century teacher Patrul Rinpoche. My heart was heavy as I watched Khyentse Rinpoche leave, knowing that he was going on to continue his in-depth teaching of that very text. I asked a friend of mine who was leaving with him to record every word of the explanations he was to provide, without missing a single minute. I must admit that once the cars that were taking Khyentse Rinpoche and his entourage to Paris had sped off, leaving me alone in his residence, sitting on my bedroom rug, I found myself feeling deeply frustrated and began to beat my fists against the floor. I still had quite a way to go to achieve perfect patience and equanimity!

On the flight back to Delhi, Khyentse Rinpoche wrote down this advice in verses, which he sent to me once he had reached India.

This humble old man is going to India for a while,
While Konchog Tendzin remains in France.
With unshakable faith, pray that teacher and student will never be separated,
And it is certain that we will soon be reunited.

Take time to observe the joys and pains of different countries
And of those who do not recite a single Mani,[1] precious help for their future lives,
And frenetically engage in the affairs of the world.
Think: Do the activities of samsara have any substance?

At other times, examine your own mind:
If afflictive mental states arise, free them the moment they appear and preserve
    that state.
Remaining in the natural state of things as they appear,
Contemplate the face of primordial continuity
And allow your mind to rest in the encounter with the ultimate teacher,
The unaltered simplicity of the nature of mind.

At other moments still, if you feel euphoric,
Cast off all that has you in its grip
And offer your joy to your root master.
Do not cling to bliss,
Maintain the flow of its spontaneous liberation as it arises.

Sustenance and clothing will come to you spontaneously,
But should, from time to time, misery or illness arise,
Use them to purify your obscurations and enhance your compassion.
Sampling joy and pain in one taste, contemplate the ultimate nature of all things.
Dwell at perfect ease in bliss free of hope and fear.

Do not forget your teacher:
Meditate him at the center of your heart!
Do not forget the essential instructions:
Think of them at critical moments.

Do not forget death:
It will spur you on to virtue.
Do not relax your perseverance:
Fuel it day and night.

All separation is the harbinger of imminent reunion,
And yet, as joyful as reunion may be,
The day will come when separation is inevitable, that is certain.

Contemplate this illusory spectacle with your illusory mind.
Recognizing the illusion, experience the essential meaning.

If you behave in accordance with the Dharma, you will lack nothing in this life.
In the lives to come, you will go from bliss to bliss
And conquer the citadel of ultimate nature that transcends the intellect.
I will pray for you unceasingly, fortunate son!

These instructions were sent on the fly by this chattering old man to dispel your
sadness. Drink your fill of the sparkling droplets of this ambrosia, and as your
experience and realization flourish, may you attain the immutable citadel.[2]

Every cloud has a silver lining. I shared three months of the lives of the
Chanteloube retreatants. Every day after lunch, I spent an hour and a half
orally translating from Tibetan into English a few pages of Khenpo Yönten
Gyatso's luminous commentary on *The Treasury of Precious Qualities*, the
most in-depth exegesis of Jigme Lingpa's text in verse. In this way, I com-
pleted the oral translation of the first of two 700-page volumes. Whenever
I had any doubts about certain passages, I submitted my questions to the
great scholar Nyoshul Khen Rinpoche, who also lived at La Sonnerie, the
Périgord-style house that Dilgo Khyentse Rinpoche had renamed Tashi
Palbar Ling and occupied whenever he came to Dordogne. Khyentse
Rinpoche's room has been preserved as it was to this day.

Khyentse Rinpoche appreciated the sincerity and commitment of his
Western students, especially those who devoted themselves to lengthy
retreats. He considered some to be excellent practitioners. He was also
grateful to Tulku Pema Wangyal and his family for making the path of the
Dharma accessible to so many people who, without them, would never
have had the faintest idea about the path of liberation from suffering
offered by Buddhism. But apart from this essential aspiration, Khyentse
Rinpoche was as little attracted by the glitter of Western society's artificial lights, its frenzied consumption, and the substitutes for happiness
touted by its heralds of hedonism and individualism as a lion is by a tuft

of grass. Whenever we landed in India after a trip, he would often heave a sigh of satisfaction: "Home again!" This might seem surprising when you compare the comforts of the West to the chaos of an Indian city or the rusticity of life in Nepal or Bhutan. But for him, of course, that was irrelevant, and he was particularly fond of Bhutan, and especially of the way the Dharma was safeguarded there.

When my three months in France were up, I finally rejoined Khyentse Rinpoche in Bhutan. He greeted me with a warm and loud "welcome" and placed his large hand on my head. I resumed my life alongside him as if we had never been apart. He continued to teach *The Treasury of Precious Qualities* to Rabjam Rinpoche every day for a year, at the rate of half an hour a day. Because of Khyentse Rinpoche's frequent travels, we two were the only ones to receive these teachings no matter what.

Khyentse Rinpoche's travels throughout the vast world also had intangible benefits linked to his spiritual realization and his mere presence. I was a frequent witness to the way in which simply seeing or meeting Khyentse Rinpoche had the power to transform people's perceptions, taking them by surprise and sometimes having a lasting impact on their lives. Stan Lai, for example, a Taiwanese playwright responsible for the revival of theatre in that country over the past thirty years, came to Dordogne to see his teacher, Dudjom Rinpoche. But he could not find his house. Around the bend of a narrow road, he saw a little sign for "Tashi Palbar Ling" at the side of a path. Thinking that this must be the place he was looking for, he entered the house. The person who greeted him showed him the way to Dudjom Rinpoche's house, adding that, if he wished, he could also meet Khyentse Rinpoche. And so, Stan was ushered into the presence of Khyentse Rinpoche, in his room. He sat down in a corner, content simply to observe the master, overcome and incapable of uttering a word. He spent a half hour in Rinpoche's presence, silently weeping, completely astounded to discover that such a being existed in this world. I later became a good friend of Stan, who kept this first encounter engraved in his heart. He met with Khyentse Rinpoche several times more, including just a few months before his death in Bhutan, and later translated into Chinese several of the teachings that I had had translated into English. He later also translated *The Monk and the Philosopher* and *Happiness* into Chinese.

In the late 1980s, a French ambassador, Roland Barraux, and his wife stopped by our monastery, a good hour's walk from the French residence, almost every Sunday. We got to know them and invited them to meet with Khyentse Rinpoche on a few occasions. The ambassador was greatly impressed and, before leaving Nepal, came to seek spiritual counsel from Khyentse Rinpoche. As he was leaving, he asked Rinpoche to summarize the essence of Buddhism in one word. "Compassion," my teacher answered. He later wrote me that in January 1991, shortly after his assignment as ambassador to Somalia, the embassy was overrun when rebels took control of part of the capital. Luckily, the building was located on the seashore, and he, his wife, and some staff members had just enough time to jump aboard a boat, abandoning everything behind them. He told me that Khyentse Rinpoche's words and kindness came back to him at that trying moment. Later, in his retirement, Roland Barraux wrote a biography of the fourteen Dalai Lamas.[3]

Khyentse Rinpoche's power to attract and inspire was just as manifest in the most mundane circumstances and places. On a trip to Hong Kong, as Khyentse Rinpoche entered the airport arrival hall, where a swarm of people were awaiting incoming passengers, almost everyone turned to look at him. Many of those who had been sitting stood up, even though they had no idea who he was. They watched Khyentse Rinpoche in silence for several moments, as if stunned by his natural majesty.

Chögyam Trungpa Rinpoche—a Tibetan master whose teachings and writings had a major impact on Buddhism in the West, and who considered Khyentse Rinpoche, from whom he had received many teachings in Tibet, to be one of his primary teachers—once said of him, "If the Buddha Shakyamuni were alive today, he would resemble Dilgo Khyentse Rinpoche."

21

THE TRANSMISSION OF THE THREE BASKETS

On my return to Bhutan, in the mountain province of Bumthang, Khyentse confers the transmission of the 103 volumes of the words of the Buddha.

In June 1983, we returned to the Bumthang region, in eastern Bhutan, for an exceptional event: the oral transmission of the 103 volumes of the Buddha's sermons and associated texts, which constitute the Buddhist canon translated from Sanskrit into Tibetan in the ninth century. In the Tibetan tradition, if a text is to be fully alive and impart all the spiritual benefits of studying it, it must be read out loud by a teacher who himself received it orally from a lineage holder, and so on back to the very sources of the texts and teachings. In the case of the volumes of the Buddhist canon, known as *Tripitaka* in Sanskrit ("Three Baskets") and *Kangyur* in Tibetan ("Translation of the Word"), such a transmission has continued uninterrupted from teacher to student since the texts were translated into Tibetan and, before that, down the generations in India.[1] This gives a good idea of the wealth of centuries of successive blessings contained in such transmissions, and of their great power for spiritual transformation.

The apartment where Dilgo Khyentse Rinpoche usually stayed when he was in Kuje was on the upper floor of the temple, which required him to climb a long flight of stone steps several times a day, at an age when it was growing harder and harder for him to walk. And so, as the Bhutanese do so cleverly and fast, a bamboo residence was built for Rinpoche and his entourage in just a few days in the middle of a meadow that stretches out before the Kuje temple, the most sacred site in Bumthang. Not far from the house, an area covered by tarpaulins mounted on bamboo scaffolding was speedily set up by the local authorities for the thousand people who would come from the neighboring valleys and throughout Bhutan to receive this precious transmission.

On the day after our arrival, the 103 volumes of the *Kangyur* were solemnly taken to the teaching tent in a solemn procession of 103 monks, each carrying one volume on his right shoulder, led by musicians and incense bearers. Khyentse Rinpoche would be reading these texts every morning for four hours straight, while one of his close students, Sengdrak Rinpoche, who had received this transmission from him fifteen years earlier in Nepal, would take over in the afternoon. At that pace, the entire collection could be read in two months. Khyentse Rinpoche began with the Fortunate Aeon Sutra, which describes the 1,002 buddhas who have appeared and will appear in our era. Just before returning to Bhutan, Khyentse Rinpoche had gone to Gangtok, in Sikkim, to receive the transmission of this first volume from the wife of his revered teacher, Dzongsar Khyentse Chökyi Lodrö. She herself had received it from Dzongsar Khyentse Chökyi Lodrö, while Khyentse Rinpoche had received it from another lama. Rinpoche was so devoted to his teacher that he had resolved to include his lineage and blessings in the transmissions he was to give in Bhutan.

He also conferred some hundred short empowerments, at the rate of a few each day, drawn from the collection of texts known as *Druptap Gyatsa*, "One Hundred Means of Accomplishment." As usual, he also gave teachings in his room to those students who asked him to do so. In addition, he asked Sengdrak Rinpoche to give him the oral transmission of the works of Gyalwa Götsangpa, a great yogi and hermit of the eleventh and twelfth centuries, of which Sengdrak Rinpoche was one of the very few holders.

Khyentse Rinpoche's entourage also had a lot to do. I was assigned to filling the statues that the faithful brought to Khyentse Rinpoche for consecration with mantras and relics. I filled a good hundred or so during our stay, each one requiring an hour's work.

Receiving the transmission of the *Kangyur* in one of the most sacred places in Bhutan had special resonance for me, since my first teacher, Kangyur Rinpoche, had been given his name for having completed this transmission thirteen times over his lifetime. What odd fate had brought me here, the only Westerner among thousands of students, to immerse myself in the intimacy of such a great teacher!

Every day, the representatives of various monasteries, benefactors, or individual students offered Khyentse Rinpoche a mandala symbolizing the universe, the manifestations of the body, the speech, and the mind of the Three Jewels (the Buddha, the Dharma and the Sangha), respectively, in the form of a statue, a sacred book, and a little brass or silver stupa, as well as other offerings. This was a solemn moment, accompanied by prayers for the master's longevity and the distribution of hot tea, a flatbread, and a small monetary offering to all the assembled monks and students.

There was among us a monk, beloved by all, who accompanied Khyentse Rinpoche almost everywhere he went. He had suffered from a mental disability since birth—he could neither read nor write, his diction was somewhat muddled, his movements unwieldy, his dress notoriously sloppy, and the tip of his nose often dripped. But he was very devoted to Khyentse Rinpoche and jovial by nature, he always found a place in the car or truck so he could come with us, and everyone was very pleased to have him tag along. His name was Pema, "Lotus," to which people added the epithet *tsake*, "Dopey." He had his own way of speaking, plain and spontaneous. One day, the commander-in-chief of the Bhutanese armed forces came to pay his respects to Khyentse Rinpoche. As he was leaving, the general recognized Pema standing in the court, and called out to him, "Ah, there you are, Dopey Lotus," to which Pema responded, tit-for-tat, "And there you are, you old cry-baby face!" The general didn't bat an eyelid.

Another time, Pema decided that it was his turn to offer a mandala to Khyentse Rinpoche. He didn't have a penny to his name, of course. He spoke to everyone about it, and we pooled our resources so he could have his wish. He made his offering with all the solemnity he could muster, and Khyentse Rinpoche welcomed him with a broad smile. I was moved to tears seeing our friend Pema so proud and happy to have been able to express his devotion like that. I soon had my own turn to make this offering of a mandala, tea, bread, and money to Khyentse Rinpoche and to the entire monastic congregation and lay practitioners.

The luminaries of Bumthang and the surrounding valleys presented their own offerings with greater pomp and protocol. Dressed in their finest, the men wore large shawls of wild silk, colored orange, red, blue, or green according to their rank and position—only the king and the Je Khenpo, the chief religious dignitary of Bhutan, were permitted to wear a yellow shawl. Some wore a sword at their sides, in sheaths of engraved silver. The women wore splendid dresses with complex and multicolored patterns, woven by hand by the most talented craftsmen of the valley. Khyentse Rinpoche welcomed all the faithful with perfect equanimity, regardless of their social status.

We were also visited by Heinrich Harrer, the Austrian mountaineer who had been training to climb a Himalayan peak when the Second World War broke out. Taken prisoner in India by the English, he managed to escape the Dehradun internment camp with a fellow mountaineer, Peter Aufschnaiter. They crossed the Himalayas into Tibet and made it to Lhasa, where they lived for several years. Heinrich Harrer regularly gave the Dalai Lama lessons in English and mechanics. He wrote an account of his adventures in a best-selling memoir, *Seven Years in Tibet*, which was made into a film. He had a rather comical encounter in Bumthang. Fritz and Lisina von Schulthess, Swiss friends of the third king of Bhutan who were among the handful of foreigners who had regularly visited the Himalayan kingdom since 1952, had brought over a Swiss farmer, Fritz Maurer, as well as a herd of milk cows, also Swiss. Maurer married a Bhutanese woman, became a citizen, and taught the local peasants how to make delicious cheese, harvest honey, and produce bottled apple juice. When he met Heinrich Harrer, Harrer introduced himself with a touch of self-importance as "Harrer, *Seven Years in Tibet*." Maurer, who had not read the book, didn't catch the reference and responded candidly, "Maurer, thirty-five years in Bhutan."

On the last day of the transmission, the chief lamas performed an elaborate ceremony, dedicated to the longevity of the two masters, to express the immense gratitude of the students for the teachings they had just received.

The next day, Khyentse Rinpoche presided over the cremation of the remains of an eminent teacher, Namkhai Nyingpo. He had died in a

Chinese prison in Tibet, but his followers had managed to conceal his remains. In time, his body had mummified and become significantly reduced in size. His followers were able to transport it to Bhutan and asked Khyentse Rinpoche to conduct the funeral rites that had not been able to be held in Tibet.

To conclude his stay in Bumthang, Khyentse Rinpoche, accompanied by a hundred monks and lay students, held a *drubchen*—a lengthy ceremony that lasts seven straight days and nights—centered on the practice of "boundless life," Tsedrup Sangdu, revealed by Ratna Lingpa, the great fifteenth-century *tertön*.

We then left in procession to conduct other teachings and ceremonies in Thimphu and Paro.

22

THE LAMA OF LION'S ROCK

A portrait of Sengdrak Rinpoche, one of Khyentse Rinpoche's closest students, admired by all, particularly the Dalai Lama, and one who inspired me deeply.

While passing through Paris in 1993, the Dalai Lama received a small group of journalists. One of them asked him to name the person he most admired. "At the general level, it's Mahatma Gandhi," the Dalai Lama answered. "And on the spiritual level?" the journalist pressed on. "I cannot talk about my primary teacher; it is too personal." But then the Dalai Lama perked up suddenly and added in a voice full of conviction, "But other than him, it's Sengdrak Rinpoche, Sengdrak Rinpoche! He is the perfect practitioner of the Dharma, both humble and accomplished, a model for everyone." Of course, the journalists hadn't the slightest idea who he was talking about. I myself, having known Sengdrak Rinpoche well, was totally caught off guard but filled with joy by this answer. Sengdrak Rinpoche was certainly a very great practitioner, but he had met the Dalai Lama only a few times and was always extremely humble and discreet. Clearly, the Dalai Lama had not failed to notice his outstanding qualities.

In India a few years earlier, when Dilgo Khyentse Rinpoche was traveling by car with his grandson, Rabjam Rinpoche, and another lama, the latter had asked him, "When it comes to spiritual practice, who do you consider to be your best student?" Dilgo Khyentse Rinpoche had answered without missing a beat: "Sengdrak Tulku."

In 2003, as she was nearing death at the age of ninety-one, Khandro Lhamo, Dilgo Khyentse Rinpoche's wife, had sent for Sengdrak Rinpoche in his hermitage, on the border between Nepal and Tibet, to bless her before she breathed her last.

Who, then, was this Sengdrak Rinpoche, whom so many eminent masters and remarkable people held in such high esteem? He was neither a high-ranking lama, nor a famous teacher surrounded by a horde of students, nor the abbot of an important monastery. He was one of the most simple, light-hearted, and heart-warming souls I have ever met. Nothing seemed to bother him; the highs and lows of existence slid off him like dew off a rose petal. When he spoke, his eyes sparkled with merriment; he radiated such a sense of lightness that you might have thought he could fly away like a bird. Although he had spent many years in contemplative retreat, guided by the most respected teachers of his time, he behaved as if he were the most ignorant of novices—no mask, none of the falsities of convention that create distance between people tainted his gentle personality.

Sengdrak Rinpoche had completed the so-called preliminaries (*ngöndro*) of Tibetan Buddhism, which some practitioners these days claim to be dispensable, no fewer than fifteen times. His experience represented a minimum of twelve years of meditation. When he was studying with his primary teacher, the latter might ask him to spend six months meditating on a single verse of the Mahamudra ("Great Seal") teaching, which deals with the nature of mind. Then, another verse might be the object of an equally long and exacting meditation.

And yet, despite his many years of practice, his humility led him to turn down an invitation from an Argentinian follower to come teach in the West. "I am not ready. I would need to do a few more *ngöndro*," he responded.

When I knew him, he lived most of the time in Barkhang, a hermitage on a mountainside in Nepal. Over the years, a group of two hundred or so meditators grew around him, men and women, monks, nuns, and laypeople of all ages. He said of them, "If they wish to practice, they may stay as long as they like; if they want to leave, I'm not stopping them."

He confessed to me that, as a teenager, he had had a few very difficult years during his early retreats. His emotions, especially carnal desire, had been so powerful that he had thought he was going crazy. He described his inner turmoil with a broad grin, as if it were a big joke. Little by little, by learning the various methods to calm the mind, he had found perfect inner freedom. Ever since, every moment of his life had been one of pure joy. And it showed through in everything he did!

"Sengdrak" is a contraction of "Senge Drakpa"—"Man of Lion's Rock"—a name drawn from the place where his previous incarnation had lived.

He once told me how he had been recognized as the reincarnation of Senge Drakpa Rinpoche:

I was born into a very poor family. My father was a potter. According to a common Tibetan belief, when a *tulku* is born, his family runs into many obstacles. In my case, my father died a year or two after I was born. Then it was my mother's parents and, within the space of a month, six more people in my family died. Our three heads of cattle died in turn. Finally, my mother and I found ourselves alone. My mother's situation was so precarious she had to ask the village families for assistance. She often had to borrow from one to pay another.

The place known as Senge Drak [Lion's Rock] was more like a hermitage than a monastery. Five candidates had been selected as potential reincarnations of the lama who had run it. Four of them were sons of wealthy families and had personal ties to the previous lama.

As for me, I could not keep my mouth shut! As soon as I had learned to talk, I had said again and again that Senge Drak was my monastery and that I wanted to return there. Whenever I went with my mother to visit anyone who had known the previous Senge Drakpa, as soon as I saw an object that had belonged to him, I grabbed it and said it belonged to me. That happened many times.

When I was very little, I would take off my clothes and improvise yoga exercises that were similar to the Six Yogas of Naropa. Every day, I insisted on climbing onto the roof of our hut carrying a stick that I used like a horn. I pretended to blow into it to alert the hermits that it was time to return to their meditation, which the previous lama had used to do.

When the list of candidates was presented to Drukpa Chögön Rinpoche, an eminent master of our spiritual lineage, the emissaries played up the qualities of the first four—the sons of wealthy families—convinced that the *tulku* (incarnation body) would be found among them. At the very end, they briefly mentioned the "son of Wangdu." After consulting the list, Drukpa Chögön declared that the son of Wangdu was, without any possible error, the incarnation of the Senge Drak lama.

Not long afterwards, Drukpa Chögön paid a visit to the sixteenth Karmapa, Gyalwa Rigpe Dorje. He submitted the list of five candidates to the Karmapa. He said nothing for a few minutes and then, without even bothering to perform a divination, the Karmapa confirmed, "Nowadays, a great many monasteries want an attractive child from a comfortable family as their *tulku*. But if your concern is the wealth of the Buddha's teachings and not that of your monastery, there is no doubt that the son of Wangdu is the true incarnation."

From the age of five, I was able to live in the presence of my primary teacher, Ladakh Tripön Rinpoche. As my monastery had no resources, he cared for me as if I were his own son. I shared his bedroom. He taught me the basics of reading. Every night, he would slowly recite a four-verse prayer for me and ask me to memorize it. The next morning, I would have to recite it.

One day, some benefactors offered Tripön Rinpoche the 103 volumes of the *Kangyur*, the collected teachings of the Buddha, of which the little library of the temple-hermitage did not yet have a copy. Rinpoche asked his disciples to read all the volumes aloud. I was barely able to read and could only sound out the words haltingly, but Rinpoche told me, "Go join the monks and read with them." And he added with a smile, "One day you'll be able to say that you read the *Kangyur* when you were five years old!" I went to the temple and read to the best of my ability for many days. The fact is, I was only able to read about a dozen folios a day.

Many years later, in 1983, when Dilgo Khyentse Rinpoche asked me to assist him in giving the oral transmission of the *Kangyur* in Bhutan, I understood how prophetic those words of Tripön Rinpoche really had been.

I was also five years old when Tripön Rinpoche gave the transmission of the Six Yogas of Naropa. He directed me to attend the teachings and added that I could go back over them in detail with his students. I received the complete transmission, including the most difficult exercises. I don't mean to boast, but I don't think I've ever heard of anyone receiving the Six Yogas at five years old! Tripön Rinpoche surely believed that one day I would make my own contribution, humble as it may be, to perpetuating his spiritual lineage.

Indeed, Sengdrak Rinpoche greatly contributed to it.

As humble as he was, he became a touchstone for everyone in the Drukpa Kagyu lineage. He also held many teachings from the Nyingmapa lineage, which he had received from Dudjom Rinpoche, Dilgo Khyentse Rinpoche, and Trulshik Rinpoche.

I once saw him vie in modesty with another of my spiritual teachers, Tulku Pema Wangyal, who was extremely modest himself, as each sought to prostrate lower than the other. A few minutes later, Sengdrak Rinpoche told me with a cheeky smile that if you wanted to bow lower than Tulku Rinpoche (the title by which many people referred to Tulku Pema Wangyal), you'd have to go through the floorboards!

Another time, while I was on retreat, I learned that he was preparing to go on a yearlong retreat. I sent him a letter in Tibetan, in which I asked him, among other things, "You've already attained Buddhahood once; are you trying to do it a second time?" What I meant to say was that, from the point of view of the beginner I was, it didn't seem necessary for someone so spiritually accomplished as him to go on such lengthy retreats. He would later laughingly remind me of my respectful teasing.

I was lucky to receive many teachings from him, including the transmission of a great many volumes of the *Kangyur* on the occasion when he assisted Khyentse Rinpoche in that task, and of the highly inspiring writings of Gyalwa Götsangpa, which he offered to Khyentse Rinpoche upon request.[1] Gyalwa Götsangpa was a great yogi who lived in the eleventh and early twelfth centuries, spent many years in caves, and was renowned for his consummate renunciation.

But it was above all the quality of his presence, his immutable kindness, his joyful serenity, and his spiritual realization that provided the best possible teaching to others. Sengdrak Rinpoche was at all times the perfect exemplar of a being who had attained the ultimate fruit of an authentic spiritual path.

In 2005, at the age of fifty-eight, Sengdrak Rinpoche contracted leukemia. As his strength dwindled, he acceded to his followers' insistent demands that he come down from the mountain for treatment in a Kathmandu Valley hospital. But the disease was already too far advanced. He asked to see Rabjam Rinpoche, Dilgo Khyentse Rinpoche's grandson. He told him that he would soon be dead and that he wished his body to be transferred to the Shechen Monastery and that it should remain there untouched for several days. Doctor Barry Kerzin, who was also a Buddhist monk and later became one of the Dalai Lama's physicians, was at his side in the hospital. He told me that in the afternoon of the day after Rabjam Rinpoche's visit, Sengdrak Rinpoche had asked Barry, who was monitoring his vital signs, to let him know when the moment had come. When Barry felt that Rinpoche had only a very short time left, he told him so. Sengdrak Rinpoche, who had been prone for several days, sat up in his hospital bed, his back straight, crossed his legs in the lotus position, opened his eyes wide while gazing up into the space before him, and breathed his last while intoning the letter "A," symbol of ultimate reality.

Out of respect for his wishes, his body was carefully transported to Shechen Monastery in its sitting posture. The body exuded a gentle scent for a week. At no time were there any signs of effluvia or decomposition. His limbs remained perfectly supple. Although dead, he gave every appearance of merely meditating, but it was in fact the postmortem meditation known as *thukdam*. Rabjam Rinpoche looked in on the body every day and affirmed that for three days he was able to feel, with the back of his hand, heat emanating from the solar plexus, near the heart. After a week, Sengdrak Rinpoche's head drooped, a little fluid dripped from his nostrils and the body lost its appearance of a person in meditation. The remains were prepared and sent to the Barkhang hermitage. Some time later, Drukchen Rinpoche, the head of the Drukpa Kagyu lineage, came with a group of followers to perform the cremation ceremony. In this way, the life of a remarkable being, dedicated to the essence of spiritual practice, came to an end. A journey into a harmonious death that was the culmination of an edifying, if all too brief life—a model for all practitioners.

23

DAILY LIFE WITH MY TEACHER

A master strict and gentle; precious teachings in deeds.

For thirteen years, I was one of two or three monks who accompanied Khyentse Rinpoche everywhere and took care of him. I was, among other things, the one who slept on the floor in the bedroom so that I would always be there in case he needed help in the night, for instance in going to the toilet, since he had trouble walking. Until his death in 1991, I spent practically every night in his presence. He went to bed around 10 p.m., after finishing his nightly prayers for the protectors of the Buddhist teachings—a ritual of around forty-five minutes in which Rabjam Rinpoche and a monk, who recited the texts out loud, participated. I would then unroll my sleeping bag on one of the Tibetan rugs that covered the bedroom floor. My folded clothing served as a pillow. It was wonderful to be so close to my teacher, cradled by his peaceful breathing. Occasionally, his breath would stop for a few seconds, then resume. There was something extremely soothing in all this: everything was calm, silent, still. Only the breathing of an enlightened being filled the silence. I took this as an opportunity to merge my mind with his, vast and luminous, and to rest in the simplicity of this union. Sleep overtook me as I practiced.

To this very day, I recall the very particular quality that the mere presence of an authentic spiritual teacher can impart to everything around him. There's nothing mystical about it. It's not about "vibrations" or any other paranormal phenomenon, but the simple quality of a shared space; breathing the same air as an accomplished being is an experience that reminds us every moment of the value of the wisdom, goodness, and inner freedom that he embodies. Many years later, after Khyentse Rinpoche's death, I was accompanying the Dalai Lama on a flight from Marseille to Paris when I suddenly had the sensation of being back in that presence; it was palpable, filling the entire plane, a space that is usually totally devoid of any spiritual quality. You can rekindle such a feeling anywhere when you recall your spiritual teacher and merge his mind with your own.

Khyentse Rinpoche woke up between four and five in the morning. He let me know he was awake by sitting up in his bed. I would then rise, roll up my sleeping bag, step out briefly to wash up and get dressed, then return to his side and turn on the light. I prostrated three times before him, then approached to receive his blessing. I removed and folded his blankets and put them away in a cupboard. I then draped Khyentse Rinpoche's shoulders with a cape and brought him his prayer book of several hundred pages, which Rinpoche opened on a cushion placed before him. In the delicate jade cup that he used every day, I served him hot water from a thermos prepared the night before. I then opened a case containing vials filled with little pills made from medicinal plants mixed with the relics of past masters. These pills are prepared with care, placed around a mandala, and consecrated in the course of a *drupchen*, a ceremony that may last several days. If the ceremony is dedicated mainly to progress toward enlightenment, it will also include sections devoted to longevity and other beneficial qualities. The pills are therefore considered to be carrying the blessings generated by the ceremony. I put one of each kind into little vessels arranged on the table for Khyentse Rinpoche, and for his wife and Rabjam Rinpoche, and other lamas who happened to be present. There was one there for me, too.

Rinpoche then silently engaged in various meditative practices for the next two or three hours. I sat on the floor facing him, opened my own book, and applied myself to my daily practices and prayers, while also regularly refilling his teacup. At 7:30, he was brought a bowl of *tsampa*, the roasted barley flour that is a basic part of the Tibetan diet, mixed with salted butter tea. Tsewang Lhundrup then took care of Khyentse Rinpoche's grooming, pulling his long gray hair into a little chignon. I had once tried to do this when we were at Dehradun to receive the *Rinchen Terdzö* teachings, but I was unable to twist the braid correctly so that the chignon would hold by itself. I was relieved of that task after a few days, the Bhutanese being far more dexterous than I am! We conscientiously preserved any long strands of hair that clung to the comb to give as relics to his followers.

Imagine that you were given a tunic worn by Socrates or a lock of Jesus Christ's hair; these objects would certainly evoke the presence of those remarkable beings with great force. When people preserve the hair of someone beloved, this aid tangibly revives his memory. The relics of great sages of the past are not only pleasant keepsakes; they also reanimate in our mind the wisdom and infinite compassion of an enlightened being. According to the Dalai Lama, these blessings derive from an inner opening to a guru's qualities that is generated in the presence of objects that connect us directly to him.

Toward 8:30 a.m., Khyentse Rinpoche would break his silence and go into the larger room to receive the visitors who had gathered at his door. In accordance with their requests, he would offer them spiritual instruction, practical advice, teachings, or a simple blessing. He consecrated sacred statues or paintings and met with visitors who had come from afar—pilgrims or messengers sent by other lamas—and exchange news with them.

When an important ceremony was on the schedule, Rinpoche went to the temple where the monastic community met; he stayed all day long, sitting on the main throne with his legs crossed. He remained seated during lulls in the ceremony and received visitors. When a student requested a teaching, he often asked her or him to return at lunchtime, when he ate his meal from a platter in the temple. While chatting with a visitor, he almost always shared his food, telling them to "eat, eat!" Then, opening the text containing the instructions that the student had requested, he began the teaching. His grasp of the teachings and contemplative practices was such that it was impossible to imagine him being stuck for an enlightening answer to any question I might ask him. And yet, Khyentse Rinpoche never called attention to his vast knowledge or his spiritual realization. Whenever he explained the various stages of the path and described the signs of spiritual accomplishment, he would stipulate, "I have never accomplished any realization myself, but this is how my spiritual teachers spoke of these signs." During empowerments, he often said, "Right up to my own teacher, these teachings have been transmitted by a succession of fully accomplished masters, like the links in a gold chain."

When it came to the advice that every student needs to make progress, everything he proposed went straight to the heart of the matter, dispelled doubt, and opened new ways of seeing. His advice, often offered point-blank, gave us exactly what we required at that very moment, helping us avoid getting lost down blind alleys.

It might include suggestions about life choices, such as when he advised me to take monastic vows or to stay with him rather than take the first three-year retreat held in Dordogne. It was more often of a spiritual bent, directing me to undertake such or such practice at any given moment along my spiritual path. He also offered counsel about everyday affairs. For instance, I had chosen not to take antiparasitic medicine so as not to kill the solitary worm that appeared to have taken up residence in my intestines. Ani Jinpa, a Dutch nun, had gotten wind of this intrusion and reported it to Khyentse Rinpoche, of whom she was a close student. Rinpoche asked her to bring him the appropriate dose of medicine—a tall glass filled with a whitish liquid, which he placed on the table. The next day at dawn, he beckoned to me, held out the glass, and told me, "Drink!" I drank. He added, "Your human life is more precious than that of a worm." The next day, he playfully asked me if we should call a monk to sound the conch that was usually used to summon the community to pray for a woman having trouble giving birth. It was his way of asking whether the worm in question had vacated my bodily frame.

Khyentse Rinpoche was deeply gentle and patient, but his imposing presence inspired respect. You were loath to leave him and eager to return to him. Khenpo Pema Wangyal, a Tibetan spiritual teacher and student of Khyentse Rinpoche, observed that one is naturally attracted to someone whose heart brims with compassion, even as you are in reverential awe of the fact that he has fully realized the emptiness of phenomena. He recalled an anecdote about the great hermit Patrul Rinpoche. A student once said to him, "Some people love you, while others fear you and are barely able to say a word in your presence. Why is that?" Patrul Rinpoche paused a moment before replying: "Perhaps some people love me because I practice compassion and goodness nonstop. I scare others because I believe that the ego and phenomena are empty of inherent existence."

In his wise benevolence, a spiritual teacher has no reason to tolerate the vagaries of students that only perpetrate their own suffering unnecessarily. I had direct experience of that. When Khyentse Rinpoche was kind enough to take me on in 1980, he treated me with uncompromising severity for some time. Nothing I did seemed to find favor with him. He scolded me if I set something down on the left, and if I set it down on the right he did likewise. It got to the point where his wife, Khandro Lhamo, finally said to him, "Why are you so strict with that boy?" Khyentse Rinpoche did not answer. Dabzang Rinpoche, a lama who knew my teacher well, told me, "Khyentse Rinpoche behaves that way with students who he believes can make progress. He never reprimands the others." This "preferential treatment" continued for quite a while. Even if I didn't quite grasp the whys and wherefores of his rigor, I sensed that it held a profound lesson that was beyond my everyday understanding.

Shortly after my arrival in Bhutan, we spent two weeks in Paro Taktsang, the Tiger's Nest, above the Paro Valley. My first teacher, Kangyur Rinpoche, had discovered a *terma*—hidden treasure—here, centered on Vajrakilaya, one of the main wisdom deities practiced in the Nyingmapa tradition. Deeming this to be a highly auspicious opportunity, one morning I asked Khyentse Rinpoche to be so kind as to recite the text of the practice that Kangyur Rinpoche had revealed here. He answered unceremoniously that we did not have enough copies to undertake the recitation. I therefore spent several days making a copy of the text, in my rather awkward Tibetan handwriting, which I kept in my prayerbook. When I had finished, I presented the original to Khyentse Rinpoche and mentioned that I now had a second copy. He said nothing at that time.

The next day, he announced his intention to go sit in Padmasambhava's cave and asked me to bring the texts. It was in that cave—a space about six feet high where you can just barely stand up, the most sacred place in the Tiger's Nest—that Padmasambhava had conferred precious empowerments to the three students who accompanied him.

Khyentse Rinpoche took his place on a chair, and I sat at his feet. There was not enough room in the cave for anyone else, so that the monks who had come with us had to stay outside. As he began his reading, Khyentse Rinpoche took my hand in his and kept it there throughout the practice, which lasted about fifteen minutes. Words fail me in trying to describe the indescribable felicity that seemed to flow from Khyentse Rinpoche's hand into mine and fill my entire body with healing nectar. I do not think that I have ever felt such great gentleness in all my life. I literally dissolved within his goodness.

And yet, Khyentse Rinpoche's enlightened sternness toward me did not let up. When we returned to Bumthang the following year, we stayed in a little cottage of woven bamboo built to house Khyentse Rinpoche, his wife, and his entourage during our visit. One night, I went outside and stood quietly for a few minutes in the depths of the dark night, listening to the sound of the river flowing below. I had been trying to figure out the reasons for Khyentse Rinpoche's severity, but could reach no logical conclusion. Without being able to put it into coherent words, I suddenly understood that something essential was going on here, something indispensable that would allow me to move forward on my spiritual path. I became deeply convinced that it was breaking up strata of the most stubborn obscurations of my mind, atavistic tendencies that perpetuate suffering and attachment to the "self" and to reality. Khyentse Rinpoche's severity had nothing to do with my daily behavior; it was targeting the very roots of my ignorance.

Khyentse Rinpoche was the most loving heart you can imagine, but why would he spare my ego? That would have done me no favors! His ruthless attitude toward that impostor, which had afflicted me since time immemorial, was testimony to his extreme benevolence. Indeed, in Buddhism, attachment to the idea of a unitary, independent, and lasting "self" residing at the core our being is the result of an illusion that leads us to distinguish between "oneself," "others," and the "world." This distinction generates impulses of attraction to or repulsion from whatever seems to favor the "self" or threaten it—impulses that may be felt as hatred, desire, confusion, pride, or jealousy and that give rise to all sorts of suffering. Khyentse Rinpoche's intransigence, which at first sight seemed to have no apparent rationale, was aimed at eradicating the exaggerated sense of the self's importance, a primary source of constantly regenerated suffering. Those who lived with Khyentse Rinpoche were well aware that he saw through all hypocrisy and pretense, and that he did not allow his students to fall into the trap of the distraction and worldly concerns that can easily dominate our lives if we let them.

As time went by, Rinpoche's admonitions grew less frequent. Only when I was negligent or strayed from my spiritual practice did Rinpoche quickly set me straight.

After Kangyur Rinpoche died, when I was printing texts in Delhi, I remember reflecting on the fact that, left to my own devices, I was becoming a bit lax in my spiritual practice; I needed to be taken seriously in hand. That was precisely what Khyentse Rinpoche did. A lapse of this kind can be very subtle. I had certainly not strayed from the path, had not adopted bad habits or neglected my practice, and my devotion to Kangyur Rinpoche was as intense as ever. This was more the kind of backsliding that can happen when we find ourselves reengaged with the ordinary world without having first conquered the citadel of inner freedom. We end up shuffling along our spiritual path while making do with a somewhat careless routine. Khyentse Rinpoche made quick work of shaking me out of my indolence and reviving the vigor and assiduity of my practice.

I later came to understand that my lengthy exposure to the "formidable" presence of my masters—in the etymological sense of the Latin *formidabilis*, "that which inspires fear," not the fear of being hurt, but the compound of respect and awe that one feels before a towering mountain—had ultimately given me a firm sense of inner confidence. Like a piece of steel that is tempered by being heated to high temperature then submerged in ice, Khyentse Rinpoche's treatment forged in me an inner strength that I held very dear. When, later in my life, I found myself in the company of the powerful of this world—heads of state, princes, celebrities, or billionaires—I was never intimidated by their presence, even as I maintained a deferential attitude, as was only right. Some of them seemed almost childish to me, compared to my teachers.

Khyentse Rinpoche always expressed immense respect for his own spiritual teachers. One day, in discussing a collection of verses on the nature of mind that are part of a very common cycle of prayers in seven chapters addressed to Guru Padmasambhava, Khyentse Rinpoche confided to me that although he recited this prayer every day, he did not use it to introduce his students to the nature of mind, and resorted to other texts instead. "The truth is, these verses were cited by my beloved teacher to reveal the nature of mind to me. That lesson was so precious that I would never dare to use these verses in my own teachings." He then referred to Shechen Gyaltsap, his primary teacher. Here is one of the verses:

Thus, all that appears in the mind,
All that arises, thoughts or emotions derived from the five poisons,
Do not invite them in or pursue them,
But let these thoughts rest in their natural manifestation
Let them rest in the absolute dimension.

Whenever he asked me to look for one of the books written by Shechen Gyaltsap, he would say, for example, "Bring me the second volume of the Very Kind One" (Katrinchen in Tibetan), thereby avoiding whenever possible having to utter his teacher's name. When a Tibetan teacher is compelled to refer to his master by name, especially in a teaching, he may often resort to a formula like the following: "He whose name it is difficult for me to say out loud, but whom I will name solely to make it clear who I am talking about."

Everyone is familiar with the tragic conditions in which, starting in 1959, several hundred thousand Tibetans were forced to leave Tibet to escape Communist China's invasion and persecution. With a few exceptions, they were forced to leave many books behind, no matter how precious. That's why, like so many other invaluable books, only two or three of the thirteen volumes of the complete works of Shechen Gyaltsap Rinpoche made it out of Tibet. Thirty years later, as Tibet was beginning to reopen, when a lama brought a volume of an especially important teaching by Shechen Gyaltsap to his room, Khyentse Rinpoche laid it against his head for a while, telling us, "For me, this volume is more precious than all the gold on Earth."[1]

In Sikkim, Khyentse Rinpoche always stayed a day or two in the house where his second primary teacher, Dzongsar Khyentse Chökyi Lodrö, had spent the final months of his life. He held offering ceremonies in his teacher's quarters, where his widow, Khandro Tsering Chödrön, still lived. But Khyentse Rinpoche never sat on the banquette where his teacher used to sit, and he even refused to use the en suite toilet and bathroom of the large room where he stayed. He told us, "I would never sit on the seat where my teacher sat." That is one of the rules of respect that govern relations between teacher and student—a student never sits on the throne, bed, or chair used by his spiritual teacher, nor would he use the everyday objects that his teacher uses or once used. Khyentse Rinpoche extended this mark of respect even to the toilet seat!

In Nepal in January 1990, at the request of Pewar Rinpoche, a close spiritual friend of Khyentse Rinpoche from Tibet who had also been a student of Dzongsar Khyentse Chökyi Lodrö, conferred the Kalachakra (Wheel of Time) empowerment. Only some ten students attended the empowerment, which lasted two days and was held in the large room outside his bedroom where he usually received visitors. At one moment during the transmission, Khyentse Rinpoche paused for a few seconds, maintaining his silence, and we saw tears flowing down his cheeks. After the empowerment, he told Pewar Rinpoche that the memory of his teacher conferring the same empowerment on him had arisen with such force that he could not hold back his tears.

It has happened to me more than once, in my hermitage or elsewhere, that while allowing my mind to fill with the memory of Kangyur Rinpoche or Khyentse Rinpoche, recalling their way of being, the sound of their voice or the expression on their face, they have become so present that I have been overwhelmed with emotion and shed every tear in my body, uncontrollably, for several long minutes. These tears express neither sorrow nor despair, but a fervent communion. While they may be bittersweet, it is the sweetness of the thought of my teacher mingled with bitter yearning, the poignant wish that they were still here among us and that we were still able to hear the sound of their voice. In such exceptional moments, their embodiment is almost palpable.

I had the great good fortune to receive introductory instructions on the nature of mind not only from my root teacher Kangyur Rinpoche, but also several times from Khyentse Rinpoche. He conferred this introduction particularly when teaching Jigme Lingpa's *Supreme Primordial Wisdom* (*Yesha Lama*), which addresses the Great Perfection, and when transmitting the Heart Essence of Chetsun (Chetsun Nyingtik), a very profound empowerment that also belongs to the corpus of teachings on the Great

Perfection. These were always especially impressive events. When Khyentse Rinpoche came to the "manifestation of awareness" (*rigpe tsal wang*), which he accompanied with a bell and a little drum, he sang out with a majestic voice, as if from the very depths of the Earth, an invocation to all the masters of the Great Perfection lineage, asking them to come bless those assembled in that place. The invocation was followed by sublime verses on the ultimate nature of mind, awareness, *rigpa*, that transcends all concepts, the primordial and luminous simplicity of our mind, that primary faculty of knowing, free of mental constructions. When he had finished, Rinpoche suddenly shouted out the interjection *"Phet!"* and then, after a moment of silence, his gaze looking straight ahead into the distance, and making a symbolic gesture, the *mudra*, with his right hand pointing at his students, he asked three times in a deep and powerful voice: "What is the nature of mind? What is the nature of mind? What is the nature of mind?" At such moments, time feels suspended, ordinary thoughts dissipate, and only the luminous limpidity of pristine awareness remains.

I remember the day when Khyentse Rinpoche conferred on three or four students the essential Heart Essence of Chetsun empowerment in his little house in Paro, Bhutan. He sat on a cushion on the floor; we were all gathered around him. When he again asked, "What is the nature of mind?" the intimacy of the setting gave his words an even deeper resonance. That moment will remain forever engraved in my memory as one of the purest introductions to the nature of mind that can be imagined. Merely recalling it brings it all back with great power. Khyentse Rinpoche described better than anyone else that most special of all junctures in a student's life when he told of how he had received this instruction from Shechen Gyaltsap, at the age of thirteen or fourteen:

During the empowerments, I was often overwhelmed by the magnificence of his expressions and his eyes when he revealed the nature of mind and pointed his finger at me. I had the impression that while my feeble devotion made me see him as an ordinary man, there was no difference between him and Padmasambhava giving empowerment to his twenty-five disciples. My confidence in him kept growing and growing, and when he again pointed his finger and fixed his gaze on me as he asked, "What is the nature of mind?" I thought with great devotion, "This is truly a great yogi able to see the absolute nature of reality!" and I began to understand for myself how to meditate.

One afternoon in 1986, I found myself alone with Khyentse in the large and magnificent room that he occupied when staying at the Punakha *dzong*. He was reading his prayers on an armchair; I sat at his feet on the floor of brown wooden planks polished by the passage of time and people. At one moment, he lowered his eyes to me and asked, "Have you recognized *rigpa*, pure awareness?" I answered timidly that yes, I sometimes caught a glimpse of awareness, pure consciousness. I was obviously in no position to assert that I had truly and fully realized the luminous character of the mind, but if I was to answer my master sincerely, I could not claim that I had no experience of it. Khyentse Rinpoche made this comment: "That's right. You don't need to look for anything else." In my modest understanding of this episode, Khyentse Rinpoche was trying to show me that *rigpa* was of great simplicity and always present, even if we lose it behind the scrim of thoughts, just as the sun and the immaculate sky are always there, unchanged, behind the clouds that temporarily conceal them. If the meditator perceives it in a moment of inner openness, he must not look "elsewhere" or expect "anything else" than this unalterable nature of his own mind, pristine awareness free of all mental fabrication. Khyentse Rinpoche makes this point radiantly in his explanations in *The Heart Treasure of the Enlightened Ones*:[2]

Mind has no form, no color, and no substance. This is the void aspect of the mind. Yet the mind can know things and perceive an infinite variety of phenomena. This is the clarity aspect of mind. The inseparability of these two aspects, voidness and clarity, is the primordial continuous mind.

At the moment, the natural clarity of your mind is obscured by delusions. But as this obscuration clears you will begin to uncover the radiance of awareness, until you reach the point where, just as a drawing on water disappears the moment it is made, your thoughts are liberated the moment they arise. To experience mind in this way is to encounter the very source of Buddhahood, the practice of the fourth empowerment. When the nature of mind is recognized it is called nirvana; when it is obscured by delusion it is called samsara. Yet neither samsara nor nirvana has ever departed from the continuum of the absolute. When realization of awareness reaches its full extent, the ramparts of delusion will have been breached and the citadel of Dharmakaya beyond meditation can be seized once and for all.

The room where we stayed at Punakha had tall windows overlooking the river below; beneath these wide bay windows was a wooden platform that held Rinpoche's bed. Rabjam Rinpoche, Tsewang Lhundrup, and I slept on rugs spread out on the floor, under Khyentse Rinpoche's eyes.

One morning, I didn't wake up. Come the dawn, Khyentse Rinpoche sat down to his prayers. When Rabjam Rinpoche got up, he noticed that I was still asleep. He came up to shake me. Khyentse Rinpoche, who never spoke before eight in the morning, signaled with his hand to let me be. When I finally opened my eyes, it didn't take me long to assess the situation. I leaped out of my sleeping bag. In my haste, my long monk's underskirt, whose belt was loose, stayed in the bag. I found myself standing tall, stark naked. I scurried back into my sleeping bag, where I quickly donned the underskirt and knotted the belt appropriately. Khyentse Rinpoche, soon joined by Rabjam Rinpoche, burst into such hearty laughter that he had to interrupt his prayers for several minutes. Over the next few minutes, all he had to do was look at me to set his great, majestic body convulsing with silent laughter.

One day, Rabjam Rinpoche and I were with the Queen Mother of Bhutan when she declared, "Matthieu's father should come visit Bhutan too!" And indeed, in that very year of 1986, she invited my father and his wife Claude to come visit. They accepted the invitation with joy. I went to pick them up when their plane landed at Paro, and we set out for Punakha to meet with the Queen Mother and Khyentse Rinpoche, who was performing a major annual ceremony. Halfway there, a hot lunch awaited us at a mountain pass, set out on the lovely, multicolored woolen blankets, known as *yatra*, which are typical of Bhutan, spread out on the grass by servants of the Queen Mother who had come to meet us. After my father and Claude had been settled into the government guesthouse in Punakha, we went into the immense *dzong* and I brought them to see the ceremony, which is as majestic as it is spectacular for non-initiates: one hundred monks, music rich in sonorities that Western ears may find disconcerting, a three-dimensional mandala. Khyentse Rinpoche and Rabjam Rinpoche presided over the ceremony from their thrones, while the Queen Mother and two of her daughters sat on a banquette covered in brocade. My father and Claude were invited to sit beside the Queen Mother, who welcomed them gently with her usual charm and elegance. My father attended the ceremony throughout the afternoon, culminating in twirling dances to accompany a prayer of invocation to Guru Padmasambhava. A lovely introduction to that wonderful country, which never failed to hold my father and Claude under its spell.

The next day, to avoid overdoing it with the ceremonies, I took them to spend the night in the gorgeous glacial valley of Gangten, where the black-necked cranes spend the winter. We then returned to Paro, where I served as their guide to Paro Taktsang, the Tiger's Nest. My father rode a mule to climb the narrow path to the temples 7,500 feet above sea level. Their trip came to a close with a lunch held in their honor by the Queen Mother at her palace in Thimphu. The trip had been a success—my father had been dazzled by the splendors of Bhutan, which I had been thrilled to showcase for him. We had shared one of those rare and precious moments between father and son, uncomplicated and replete with unspoken emotions. It was a good complement to our earlier get-together in Darjeeling, and I was happy to have been able to give my father a glimpse—an inspiring one, I hope—of my new life.

Khyentse Rinpoche taught in the most surprising places. In Bhutan, ceremonies dedicated to the longevity of the king took place every year in the immense Thimphu *dzong*, an imposing fortress-monastery inhabited half by monks and half by officials of the Bhutanese government. These ceremonies took place in the king's private apartments, and protocol gave access solely to guests on a select list. Khyentse Rinpoche was therefore accompanied only by his immediate entourage and monks in charge of the event. However, not wanting to interrupt his teachings, he had come up with an ingenious solution. At the noonday break, a half dozen students arrived discreetly and made their way, one by one, to the adjacent bathroom, which happened to be quite spacious. Khyentse Rinpoche would then come in and take a seat on the toilet throne, which had been cushioned with a carpet, and went on with the current teaching for the next hour, as if it were all perfectly normal. His students then slipped away as discreetly as they had come.

One winter, Khyentse Rinpoche went to the hot springs in Khandro Sangphuk, in Sikkim, to take a thermal treatment for the bad pains in his knees. He chose that location because the springs had been blessed by past masters. He was accompanied by a few students, including Dzongsar

Khyentse Rinpoche and Rabjam Rinpoche. Khyentse Rinpoche spent several hours a day bathing in hot water held in six-foot-wide basins chiseled into the rock. The overflow trickled down to the river below. On this visit, he conferred on his traveling companions the transmission of six volumes of writings by his spiritual teacher Dzongsar Khyentse Chökyi Lodrö. To that end, they built a wooden float on which Khyentse Rinpoche, who was immersed in the water up to his chest, would set the volume from which he read out loud. That is how he transmitted this teaching to his students, who joined him in the basin. Over five days of bathing, he read out the complete works of Dzongsar Khyentse Chökyi Lodrö. The first part of the trip went well for me, but the day after our arrival we learned that the local authorities had gotten wind of my presence and were on their way to ask me to leave that northeastern state of India, which had long been semi-independent. I had entered Sikkim, as usual, in Khyentse Rinpoche's car, which had been led by an escort of the Royal Bodyguard of Bhutan, so our convoy had not been required to stop at the Sikkim border. As a foreigner, however, I was obligated to have a special pass that needed to be requested weeks in advance; I had never had time to complete the formalities. The captain of the Bhutanese Bodyguard escorted me back over the border on the sly, and I had to wait for Khyentse Rinpoche in Darjeeling, so I missed this "transmission in the water."

Khyentse Rinpoche lived and breathed the teachings of the Buddha. Rising above all specific cultural contexts, he had the power to persuade others to profoundly question their priorities in life, and he had the experience necessary to guide them toward inner freedom. The feeling we all shared in his presence is wonderfully expressed in a prayer written by his predecessor, Jamyang Khyentse Wangpo:

When I see your body, ordinary perceptions cease to be.
When I hear your voice, the primordial wisdom of the great bliss is born.
When I think of you, all the world's fears are swept away.
Oh sole father, I call on you, think of me lovingly.

On June 12, 1967, in Darjeeling, I meet Kangyur Rinpoche, my first spiritual teacher, who would inspire the rest of my life.

At home with my master in Darjeeling

Kangyur Rinpoche's wife, Jetsün Jampa Chökyi, welcomed me into their home on my arrival in India. We called her Amala, which means "mother."

Dudjom Rinpoche in 1966. He was a powerfully impressive, eminent, and respected teacher. It was this photo and Arnaud Desjardins' documentary on Tibetan monks in exile that moved me to travel to India to meet them.

Kangyur Rinpoche in 1968, in the little house he shared with his family in Rose Bank, near Darjeeling.

Pawo Rinpoche in 1967. He was a warm-hearted teacher with an enchanting smile. He lived near Darjeeling, where I met him several times.

At home with my master in Darjeeling

The Orgyen Kunzang Chökhorling Monastery, close by the hermitage in which I lived from 1972 to 1979.

Kangyur Rinpoche with my mother, Yahne, who made her first trip to India shortly after mine, in 1968.

A nomadic childhood

Yahne and Jean-François, my parents, circa 1945.

My sister Ève and I, in Chambéry, following our return from Mexico, in 1952.

A nomadic childhood

My uncle Jacques-Yves le Toumelin aboard the *Kurun*, his motorless 33-foot Norwegian cutter, on which he circumnavigated the world alone between 1949 and 1952.

My uncle was like a second father to me. He gave me a broad introduction to metaphysical and spiritual literature. He sometimes gave me the helm. Circa 1955.

The transitional years

In Kashmir on my first trip to India, in 1967.

At the Institut Pasteur in 1970. I am flanked by Paulette and Chantal, lab assistants to Yukinori Hirota, with whom I worked under Nobel Prize laureate François Jacob.

Following the death of Kangyur Rinpoche in 1975, Dilgo Khyentse Rinpoche became my second spiritual teacher.

Dilgo Khyentse Rinpoche, my second teacher

The oldest known photograph of Dilgo Khyentse Rinpoche, taken between 1935 and 1940, probably in Sakar, Tibet. He is wearing a white shawl, symbol of the ability of a great yogi to practice *tummo*, inner fire, in the coldest temperatures.

Dilgo Khyentse Rinpoche and Trulshik Rinpoche, his closest spiritual friend, at Thubten Choling Monastery, in the Khumbu mountains of Nepal, 1972. Years later, Trulshik Rinpoche would become one of my important teachers.

Dilgo Khyentse Rinpoche, my second teacher

As spiritually accomplished as he is, the Dalai Lama continues to receive instruction from eminent spiritual teachers from all schools of Tibetan Buddhism. In Dharamshala in 1991, he receives the transmission of an empowerment from Dilgo Khyentse Rinpoche, who was one of his primary spiritual teachers.

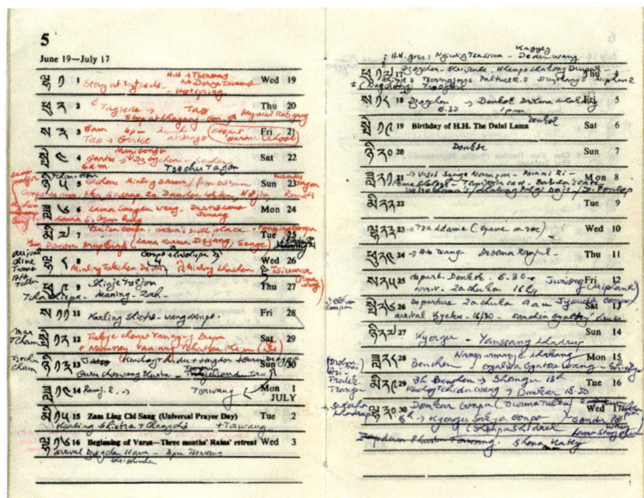

From 1980 to 1990, I used the daily pages of a Tibetan calendar to record all our travels and all the teachings delivered by Dilgo Khyentse Rinpoche.

Dilgo Khyentse Rinpoche, my second teacher

Dilgo Khyentse Rinpoche in his house near the near Paro Kyichu temple. A snapshot from my day-to-day life with my teacher. 1983.

Khandro Lhamo, wife of Dilgo Khyentse Rinpoche, at the age of seventy-five. She helped me serve my teacher better and always gave me her trust and kindness. 1987.

Rabjam Rinpoche, grandson of Dilgo Khyentse Rinpoche and abbot of the Shechen monasteries, whom I have known since he was eight and with whom I have lived for forty years, 2010.

Paro Taktsang (the Tiger's Nest), 10,000 feet above sea level, one of the most sacred sites in Bhutan. It is said that Padmasambhava, the master who introduced Buddhism to Tibet in the eighth and ninth centuries, journeyed there on the back of a flying tigress. The temples atop the sheer cliff were built in the seventeenth century.

In Bhutan

Dilgo Khyentse Rinpoche, en route to the
Bumthang district, rests at the Pelela Pass,
more than 11,000 feet above sea level.
In his lap, he holds a kitten belonging
to his grandson, Rabjam Rinpoche. 1980

In the Paro Kyichu temple, Dilgo Khyentse
Rinpoche prepares to confer a long-life
blessing on the fourth king of Bhutan,
Jigme Singye Wangchuk. 1980.

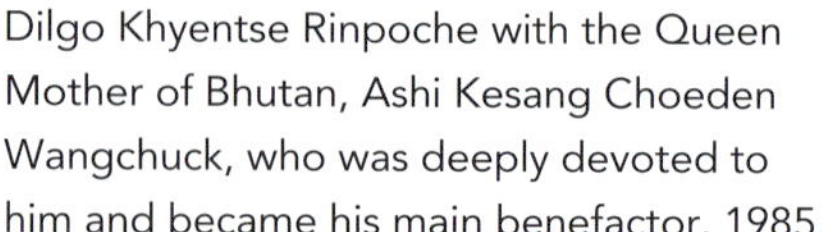

Dilgo Khyentse Rinpoche with the Queen
Mother of Bhutan, Ashi Kesang Choeden
Wangchuck, who was deeply devoted to
him and became his main benefactor. 1985.

On the initiative of Dilgo Khyentse Rinpoche, a new Shechen Monastery was built in Boudhanath, Nepal, in the 1980s, to preserve the legacy of its mother monastery in eastern Tibet, destroyed in the Chinese Cultural Revolution.

At the end of a major ceremony (*drupchen*) lasting nine days, including seven days and seven nights without interruption, the mandala drawn in colored sand (see figure 27) is dispersed to symbolize the ephemeral nature of all things. The sand is then gathered in an urn and carried in procession to the river, into which it is poured.

On their way back, the monks form a "wheel of joy" (*gakyil*), akin to a Chinese yin-yang symbol, in the monastery courtyard, before returning to the temple to conclude the ritual.

Two monks prepare to disperse the colored powders of the mandala that has served as a support for the great *drupchen* ceremony at Shechen Monastery.

Khyentse Rinpoche assigned me the task of filling the 150 clay statues produced at Shechen Monastery, Nepal. Within each statue are placed a "tree of life," saintly relics, hundreds of mantra and prayer scrolls, and minerals, soil, and flowers from numerous holy sites, as well as other sacred objects.

Dilgo Khyentse Rinpoche returns to Tibet in 1985 after thirty years in exile. On the first leg of the journey, we cross central Tibet. Here, we are at Tanggu La Pass, 16,000 feet above sea level, with Noijin Kangsang in the background.

Tulku Pema Wangyal, eldest son of Kangyur Rinpoche, contemplates the ruins of Mindrolling Monastery, once the seat of some of the greatest masters and scholars in Tibet before Communist China ordered its destruction. 1985.

In Tibet

Crossing the Tsangpo (Brahmaputra) River in a flat-bottomed ferry on our way to Samye Monastery, central Tibet. 1985.

In eastern Tibet. Where there is no road, Dilgo Khyentse Rinpoche is carried on a litter. He is preceded by a monk bearing a brocade parasol as a sign of honor. 1985.

24

SOME MANIFESTATIONS
OF ENLIGHTENMENT

The consistent nature of every moment. Spiritual realization made manifest in multiple ways—in one's sense of humor, relationship to pain, or even clairvoyance.

Whether with Kangyur Rinpoche, Dilgo Khyentse Rinpoche, or the fourteenth Dalai Lama when I served as his interpreter, I have never observed the least contradiction between what these remarkable beings advocated and how they behaved. Having borne witness year after year to the consistency between what they taught and what they embodied gave me unwavering trust in them as human beings and in their teaching. If, for example, I am not sure whether a pillar is stable or a rope is strong, I will hesitate to rely on them. But if I have verified their integrity again and again, I will lean against the pillar without fear or apply my full weight to the rope.

I have a tendency to place a priori trust in everyone. Rabjam Rinpoche, Khyentse Rinpoche's grandson and the abbot of the Shechen Monastery, where I live, sometimes jokes that this is my biggest flaw! And yet, even if I believe that it is better to treat others with that attitude rather than to suspect the worst of them, I am well aware that we are often disappointed in the actions of others and have been in that situation a few times myself. But in a half century of living in close proximity to my teachers, I have never once felt such disillusionment with them.

Some may be surprised to hear that authentic spiritual teachers tend to be lighthearted in very humane and benevolent ways, and never exercise their wit to the detriment of others or make fun of or belittle anyone. If a so-called spiritual teacher deeply hurts someone's feelings or causes them pain with a joke, it's a good bet that the teacher in question is a charlatan.

An authentic teacher's sense of humor reflects his freedom from worldly concerns. Being in no way in thrall to the vagaries of profit and loss, the attacks of critics or the praise of flatterers, the hunger for pleasant sensations or the dread of unpleasant situations, the clarion call of fame or the dirge of infamy, a spiritually accomplished being views the ever-changing theater of life's ups and downs with ineluctable levity. He is happy to laugh at its own mishaps, and when he laughs at someone else's, he does so with kindness and empathy. Perceiving the illusory character of all things, the spiritual teacher seeks through his compassion to show us affectionately that worldly success and failure are hardly more serious than a child's game.

An enlightened being will always poke fun at the artificial character of most ordinary concerns. Some people believe that the great spiritual teachers feel they can laugh at the tribulations of mere mortals because they have freed themselves of ordinary contingencies and are untouched by day-to-day worries. Be that as it may, they are far from being insensitive or indifferent to human suffering. Quite the contrary, in the face of tragedy and the many hardships suffered by human beings, their first reaction will be the full force of unconditional compassion.

At a meeting with scientists held at the Dalai Lama's residence in Dharamshala, the latter was informed that a child had just been bitten by a rabid dog. The Dalai Lama's face fell immediately. It took him a moment or two to recover, his gaze slightly lowered, and when he resumed the conversation, his cheeks were wet with tears. The Dalai Lama often weeps, as discreetly as possible, when told of the suffering of others. Once when he was staying at our Shechen Monastery in Bodhgaya, India, he fell gravely ill and had to be driven to Patna, then airlifted by helicopter to the hospital. At one point, he saw a family of beggars on the roadside, traveling through the countryside with their possessions bundled on their heads. He told us later, "I wept for several minutes on seeing their misfortune, but strangely enough, I didn't shed one tear as I suffered intense abdominal pain for hours."

A master could never laugh at the suffering of others, but in particular circumstances, moved by the deepest benevolence, he may lighten the burden of a calamitous situation with liberating laughter. One eyewitness told me of an encounter between Dudjom Rinpoche, one of the greatest teachers of the twentieth century, and a Western student suffering from cancer. She informed Dudjom Rinpoche that her doctor had given her just a few months to live. While fixing her with a gaze laden with terrible pain, Dudjom Rinpoche accompanied his reply with a warm laugh. Speaking no Tibetan, the woman was taken somewhat aback, although it was clear to her that there was no trace of malice in this joyful outburst. The interpreter translated the master's words: "The only difference between you and me is that you have a fairly good sense of when you will die, whereas I have absolutely no idea if I will die today or at some later date. But for both of us, while death is inescapable, its hour is unpredictable." That awareness makes it possible to enjoy every passing moment at its full value, to devote oneself to the essential and to avoid getting lost in thoughts, speech, and activities of secondary importance. Afterward, he offered the patient heartfelt advice on how to live more serenely with her illness until the end.

These days, whenever someone invites me to participate in some event "next year," I always reply: "Maybe, if I'm still alive." My answer never fails to elicit anxious reactions, of the "You're not having health problems, I hope?" sort. I do not do this to cause a stir, but my awareness of the impermanence of things does not allow me to offer any other reply. Furthermore, if we assume that we will be alive next year and that there is no urgency, we continue to put off our spiritual practice.

In Dharamshala in the year 2000, at a conference organized by the Mind & Life Institute[1] to launch a dialogue between high-level scientists and the Dalai Lama and other contemplatives on the theme of destructive emotions, Paul Ekman—one of the world's leading experts on emotion—was among the research scientists participating in the seminary. He did not know the Dalai Lama, had little interest in Buddhism, and had been inclined at first to turn down the invitation. But his daughter Eve, who was eager to meet the Dalai Lama, managed to convince him to come to India and contribute to the five days of dialogue. Halfway through every morning and afternoon session, the participants took a break for tea and an informal chat. For some, this was an opportunity to approach the Dalai Lama and benefit from a few minutes of more intimate conversation and to ask him questions. That is how Paul Ekman and his daughter found themselves sitting on either side of the Dalai Lama, who, as he often does when talking with someone, took their hands in his and held them throughout the conversation. Paul told us later that he was deeply moved by the human warmth emanating from the Dalai Lama. He admitted, "I never would have thought that human goodness could be palpable."

All that week, Paul Ekman held such enlightening discussions with the Dalai Lama, other Buddhist scholars and practitioners, and fellow research scientists on the nature of emotions and how to manage them that, at the end of the event, he announced that he intended to revise half the chapters of the book he had just finished writing, *Emotions Revealed*, a book for the general public that synthesized more than thirty years of research in the study of emotions. Ekman met again with the Dalai Lama on many occasions and published a book of conversations with him.[2] He said that he had found in the Dalai Lama the ideal elder brother that he had never had. Sometime after his return to the United States, his wife, Mary Ann Mason, the first female graduate dean at the University of California Berkeley, told him, "Funny, it's been more than four months since you got angry." Paul is a very good man, but he was known for his brief yet intense outbursts of temper. Now, almost despite himself, they had stopped after his meeting with the Dalai Lama and never recurred thereafter.

Many of us who lived with Khyentse Rinpoche had similar experiences. Sometimes when we were relaxing and sitting around him, on the grass or on a mat, without pausing in what he was saying he would place his hand on someone's head—a hand so large it easily covered the entire skull. I remember one such occasion when the somewhat prosaic nature of the circumstances contrasted greatly with the way I experienced it. Because of his age and limited mobility, when Khyentse Rinpoche went to the toilet, one or two of us always accompanied him. Once we got him seated, we would engage in casual chitchat or even trade jokes. This time, as I crouched to put myself at his level, Khyentse Rinpoche, while talking to another monk, reached out with his soft, hot hand and enclosed the top of my head in his long fingers. He left it there for one or two minutes. To me, it felt like a warm, glowing, and healing nectar flowing from his hand into me and filling my entire body with unparalleled bliss. Time felt suspended within this indescribable peace. I said nothing, not wishing to disturb this precious moment between us. Human goodness is definitely palpable.

Those who were close to Khyentse Rinpoche often noted that his relationship to pain was manifestly different from that of most of us. In Nepal in the 1970s, he went to see the one and only dentist with a practice in the Kathmandu Valley. People spoke of him as "the king's dentist," but king's dentist or not, he was very poorly equipped and unable to offer anesthetic injections to his patients, whose groans could sometimes be heard from the waiting room. We were a little anxious when he treated Khyentse Rinpoche for a tooth with an exposed nerve. But Khyentse Rinpoche remained impassive throughout the entire procedure, his gaze resting in the space before him as if he were quietly contemplating a lovely landscape. On the return journey, one of his students asked how he felt and whether he had been in great pain during the treatment. "Yes, it hurt a bit," Khyentse Rinpoche replied laconically.

During a visit to Dordogne a few years later, a French therapist trained in Eastern techniques, dressed in immaculately white shirt and trousers, offered Khyentse Rinpoche, through Tulku Pema Wangyal, a session of moxibustion. This is a kind of heat-based acupuncture in which a sheaf of mugwort leaves is burned, close to the skin at strategic points on the body, in this case to alleviate a mild digestive problem. Saying his morning prayers in his room, bare-chested as usual, Khyentse Rinpoche agreed, appearing to be neither especially interested nor apprehensive. The therapist began the treatment. Very much the smooth talker, he held the burning end of the sheaf very close to Rinpoche's skin even as he turned to one of us to explain the benefits of the therapy. After a while, he was suddenly brought short by the smell of burning flesh. Finally turning his attention where it belonged, he was horrified to see that he had inflicted a deep burn in Khyentse Rinpoche's abdomen. Deeply embarrassed, he apologized profusely, then sheepishly asked Khyentse Rinpoche why he hadn't said anything. Rinpoche, who had not flinched once during the entire session, replied without raising his eyes from his prayer book, "Oh, I thought that was part of the treatment." I was there, standing behind the doctor, and had watched Khyentse Rinpoche on and off throughout. At no time had I seen him show even the briefest sign of pain or discomfort. And yet we all know how painful a burn can be. The wound caused by the accident took two weeks to heal.

On the path of Tibetan Buddhism, we teach, among other things, the practice of "one taste," which consists in experiencing pleasure and pain, comfort and discomfort, pleasant or unpleasant situations, harmonious or discordant sounds, silky or rough touch, good or bad-tasting food with the same equanimity. This experience has nothing to do with apathy or indifference, nor are the five senses in any way dulled. It is rather a matter of allowing physical sensations to manifest in the vast space of awareness and not in the narrow space of a selective, anxious mind torn between what it likes and does not like, what it desires or rejects on the basis of hope or apprehension. When one is sufficiently trained in this practice, external perceptions and internal sensations are felt with equal clarity, but our mind is not disproportionately disturbed by the nature of these sensations, by attraction or aversion.

I myself have often borne witness to the way in which Khyentse Rinpoche never wavered in his experience of one taste. One day, someone who had offered him a place to stay apologized for the inadequacy of the accommodations. "So long as the roof doesn't leak in the rain, it's all good," Khyentse Rinpoche replied. Having spent thirty years in hermitages and caves, winter and summer, and known the distress and perils of exile, he had experienced every hardship imaginable, and this kind of inconvenience did not rate on the list of his concerns. In fact, in all the years I spent in his presence, I can't remember ever hearing him complain about external conditions.

I try, in my very modest way, to learn from his example and am not very particular about my comforts, noise, temperature, good weather or bad, or fine dining. I know how to appreciate good things and enjoy them happily, but I don't miss them when they are not there. For instance, when we stayed at the Thimphu *dzong*, I sometimes found myself having to make do with very little to eat for days on end. Hunting and fishing are prohibited throughout Bhutan, but most Bhutanese, high-altitude farmers for the large part, are not vegetarians.[3] Whenever we were in Bhutan and staying at the great *dzong* of Thimphu, our meals were not prepared by the nun who usually cooked for Rinpoche and his circle—a nun who, being vegetarian herself, prepared dishes that we shared between the two of us. No question of such preferential treatment here. The only food we were offered contained meat, and I had to make do with a bowl of rice and the chili peppers served with it. I had to strike the right balance: rice alone was too heavy and hard to digest, but too much pepper made it inedible. I barely weighed 130 pounds in those days—far from the 165 I weigh today! It was a good way to maintain my weight and health.

At the end of a meal on a flight from India to France, a young monk prepared Khyentse Rinpoche's tea, adding the contents of a little packet by the side of the teacup. He stirred it all conscientiously and offered it to Khyentse Rinpoche, who slowly sipped from it while contemplating the ocean of clouds below us through the window. He then returned the cup to the young lama. There was a little tea left at the bottom, which the young lama drank as a blessing. His face contorted in a grimace and he turned bright red—without knowing it, he had stirred an entire packet of hot mustard into Rinpoche's tea. The mixture was undrinkable. Confused, he asked Khyentse Rinpoche why he hadn't told him. Just as he had with the distracted therapist, Rinpoche replied, "I thought that's way they make tea around here."

Unfortunately, a far more serious situation arose that left Khyentse Rinpoche in extreme pain. His life was coming to an end, and he knew it without a doubt, but he did not wish to go abroad for the intensive treatment that had been prescribed. He was suffering from a serious illness, that much was clear. He no longer lay down at night but slept sitting up with his head on two pillows placed on a little table before him. He never complained, but when he sometimes closed his eyes and went quiet, it was obvious to us that pain was very present within the space of his inner awakening. We never had the impression, however, that it had engulfed him. He looked like a seasoned sailor watching a storm from the crest of an enormous wave, aware of its power but imperturbable. Of course, these are only assumptions on my part, based on my necessarily limited understanding of the infinite space of inner freedom of someone like Khyentse Rinpoche. For those of us who were close to him, it was nevertheless a moving and very profound lesson.

I have had the opportunity to participate in neuroscience research into the relationship between meditation—mental training—and the perception of pain. We know that anticipation of the gravity or harmlessness of an imminent event plays a major role in our experience of pain. In general, we are better able to endure pain whose duration and intensity are predictable—which allows us to prepare ourselves to push through it and thus be able to manage it—than unanticipated pain whose intensity could last or even increase and whose duration is unknown. The impact of pain therefore depends in large part on our mental attitude. We accept, for example, the painful effects of a medical treatment because we are bolstered by our hope of healing, or of intense sports training so we can excel in our chosen discipline. Many people are willing to donate their blood or an organ to save the life of a loved one. Giving an altruistic meaning to the pain we are about to endure gives us power over it and frees us of distress and the feeling of powerlessness.

Can meditation also influence our perception of pain? Several research laboratories have looked into this question. I had the opportunity to participate in the research conducted by David Perlman and Antoine Lutz in Richard Davidson's lab at the University of Wisconsin. When I entered a state of "open presence" as I was being subject to intense pain, I felt that pain with the same lucidity and acuity than the other, untrained subjects, but its unpleasant aspect was considerably reduced for me.[4] Moreover, I did not anxiously anticipate the pain and, when the painful sensation had abated, I rapidly returned to a normal emotional state. These reactions to pain have been confirmed by numerous long-term meditators, who, it has also been demonstrated, become habituated to it more quickly than novices.[5]

Other studies undertaken by Tania Singer's team at the Max Planck Institute in Leipzig, in which I also participated, show that when experienced practitioners engage in a meditation on compassion for someone who is suffering, and are themselves subjected to physical pain (an electric shock to the wrist, for instance), their compassion for others considerably diminishes the unpleasantness of their own pain. When I opened myself to unconditional compassion for someone who was suffering, without falling into empathetic distress, the sensation of the electric shock took place in a mental space of loving-kindness filled with a deep sense of serenity, in such a way that I found the physical pain far more bearable.

A being like Khyentse Rinpoche, who enjoys perfect inner freedom, has little interest in ordinary conventions. Once, when we were preparing for a ceremony in the king's room in the Queen Mother's palace, Dechencholing, we were missing a piece of red silk that was needed for a burned offering. We were unable to find one, and the city was three miles away. Khyentse Rinpoche asked me to bring him a pair of scissors, which I did. He turned around and, without a moment's hesitation, snipped a good-size piece of red silk from the upholstery at the back of the little throne on which he was sitting. He handed it to me with a mischievous look and said in that deep, warm voice of his, "These are the skillful ways of a yogi of the diamond vehicle!" Laughing silently, and as if nothing were amiss, I carried the precious swatch of red silk to the monks going about their tasks in the next room.

Rinpoche had certainly not behaved this way out of thoughtlessness. He might well have made a different choice and sent me to the shops of Thimphu for the silk. To the best of my humble understanding, he surely believed that taking the silk from the king's room for our ceremony was an auspicious act for the royal family itself.

As for me, I was reminded that relative appearances are like dreams, illusions, and that the notions of "new" and "old," "precious" and "worthless," are merely concepts that hold us to the narrow universe of our ordinary conventions. It is only now, as I write these words, that I offer these explanations. At the time, I asked myself no questions. It all happened in the most natural way, with a touch of humor and joyful complicity.

Those who are spiritually realized are often thought to be endowed with uncommon abilities. I've never seen a yogi levitate or fly through the air, but I've certainly and often borne witness to the capacity of great spiritual masters to read other people's thoughts. I've already described one such incident, when Kangyur Rinpoche asked me how many animals I had killed in my youth at the very moment when I was preparing to confess to him on that subject. But I've experienced that rare ability on more than one occasion.

Once, a young *tulku* was talking with Khyentse Rinpoche, sitting on a rug in his room. As the young *tulku* was getting up to leave, Khyentse Rinpoche gestured with his hand for him to stay a while longer. Ten minutes later, he did the same thing. Finally, after twenty minutes, Khyentse Rinpoche told him laconically, "Well, your movie ticket is useless now." The *tulku* had indeed been planning to go to the movie theater in Kathmandu, without telling anyone (monks are not supposed to go the movies). Khyentse Rinpoche clearly knew what was going on and decided to play a trick on him that would also save him from making a mistake.

When the *tulku* told this story to Rabjam Rinpoche, the latter was not in the least bit surprised; he thought it was perfectly obvious that his grandfather could read our minds. He'd done so to him again and again. Once, for example, when he was about sixteen years old, in the company of a *tulku* of his own age who was his best friend, he rented a motorcycle to go on an adventure. The two of them hit the road for Parphing, a pilgrimage site less than an hour from Kathmandu. They had decided to spend the night there. They had with them two little squares of blotting paper infused with a drop of LSD, which a "generous" soul had had the "great" idea of giving them. They decided to go for it. Rabjam Rinpoche did not have an experience that would turn his world upside down, but it did begin to spin around him, and he could barely get down the stairs of the room they shared in Parphing. The next morning, they returned to the monastery unnoticed. As he did every morning, Rabjam Rinpoche came to greet Khyentse Rinpoche. Reading his prayer book, he let Rabjam Rinpoche have it: "So, now you get dizzy walking down the stairs?" Feeling as if Khyentse Rinpoche had seen right through him, he maintained a shame-faced silence. The incident confirmed his conviction that, although Khyentse Rinpoche rarely let it show, he could read our thoughts like an open book.

In the late 1980s, Trulshik Rinpoche, who was Khyentse Rinpoche's closest spiritual friend, came to visit him at Dechencholing, the Queen Mother's palace in Bhutan. Trulshik Rinpoche was welcomed at the gate by Rabjam

Rinpoche and a few other members of our teacher's entourage, as well as by the Queen Mother. Taking the little path lined with rose bushes, he stopped a moment, looked up at the palace and recited a well-known phrase from a sutra on monastic discipline: "What attraction could I possibly find in a royal palace?" This stanza encourages monks to live a simple, austere life stripped of all external appurtenances of wealth. Trulshik Rinpoche laughed and went on his way, climbed the stairs to the third floor, and arrived in the presence of Khyentse Rinpoche. He had barely crossed the threshold when Khyentse Rinpoche called out to him from across the large room: "So, you recite 'What attraction could I possibly find in a royal palace?' but you come here anyway, I see!" Trulshik Rinpoche laughed heartily and crossed the room to touch foreheads with Khyentse Rinpoche, a gesture of mutual respect made by two great masters when they meet. Then he sat beside Khyentse Rinpoche and launched into an entirely different conversation, as if nothing had happened. Later in the day, Rabjam Rinpoche brought up the incident with Trulshik Rinpoche, who expressed no surprise whatsoever: "Of course he knows everything I think!"

A few weeks later, Khyentse Rinpoche and Trulshik Rinpoche were staying in Kurjey Lhakhang, in the Bumthang district. Dzongsar Khyentse Rinpoche had asked Trulshik Rinpoche to bring some of his monks from Nepal to teach his own how to fill stupas with multiple consecrated objects and to correctly conduct ceremonies, which can be highly complex tasks. Trulshik Rinpoche went to see Rabjam Rinpoche in his room to share his concern: Dzongsar Khyentse's monks had still not arrived, and his own absolutely had to leave for Nepal in a few days so they could attend the start of the summer's monastic retreat. As they were talking, Tsewang Lhundrup, the monk who took care of Khyentse Rinpoche's personal needs with me, came down from upstairs to deliver this message: "Khyentse Rinpoche has asked me to reassure you that Dzongsar Rinpoche's monks are on their way!" The question had been settled.

In 2007, with my friend Wolf Singer, director of the Max Planck Institute for Brain Research in Frankfurt, I spent ten days in our Namo Buddha hermitages, which are spread out across magnificent, wooded hillsides facing the Himalayas, two hours from Kathmandu. Our goal was to continue the dialogue that had led to the publication of our book

Beyond the Self: Conversations between Buddhism and Neuroscience. When we returned to the monastery in Kathmandu Valley, Rabjam Rinpoche invited Wolf to dinner and shared some anecdotes about the clairvoyance of spiritual masters. Those who attended, and I was a part of that small group, related similar stories that they had experienced. At one point, Wolf, a little stunned, ended up exclaiming, "No more, please! If even one of these stories is true, we're in deep trouble!" He explained that he was not questioning our sincerity in any way or challenging our lived experiences, but if thought transmission were an established fact, it would undermine the entire paradigm of the neurosciences, according to which thoughts are exclusively the products of cerebral processes. From that perspective, nothing could explain how one brain could know what was going on in another, aside from deducing and interpreting a person's thoughts on the basis of facial expressions, tone of voice, and other aspects of body language. For two brains to share the same thought at the same time, most of their neural networks would have to be in almost exactly the same state, which is inconceivable. "The problem is," he concluded, "that even if we accept the truth of these accounts, there is no known mechanism whereby a thought can be transferred from one brain to another. What's more, phenomena like these may occur once in a while, but they cannot be reproduced at will in the context of rigorous scientific experimentation, so there's little hope of their being validated by science with the tools available to us."

The obvious question is how many stories, observations, and lived experiences does it take to have the force of proof? As perplexed as Wolf was by our tales of encounters with clairvoyance, in the course of our own conversation he himself shared a troubling experience for which he had never found a plausible explanation.

Wolf had gone to pick up his two young daughters at a carnival party at the far end of town, where he had never been before. He drove an hour through a snowstorm to the address he had been given, which turned out to be wrong. He did not have the phone number, and cell phones were not yet widespread at the time. His only choice was to turn around, spend another hour on the road going home, and wait until his daughters called him with the right address. Very upset, he kept driving, turning first right, then left, leaving it to random luck. He ended up in a cul-de-sac. For reasons he couldn't explain, he decided to park there. Across the street was a building several stories high. He got out and crossed the street to read the names of the residents on the nameplate, when through the door he suddenly saw one of his daughters climbing the stairs from the basement where the party had taken place. Wolf told us, "She opened the door and said, 'You're right on time. The party's just finishing up. Tania will be here in a minute.' When I told them what had happened to me, they weren't surprised at all. "You're our father. Of course you should know where we are," they said. He continued,

Could it be that I had all that data stored subconsciously, and that my subconscious relied on the heuristics that, rather than driving for another three hours, I might do better to wander around a bit, chances being not too low that I might actually find my daughters? But my perception was that I turned at random and that I did not know why I had engaged in such an irrational search process. No. I was furious, I was just driving around, and I had no explicit memory of the street name of the new address. . . . If my daughters' interpretation were valid, we would have to worry about our views on the brain and on nature in general and admit that we are missing something essential. For the time being, however, and despite such experiences and reports, we don't have a strong argument to change the direction of our research because we wouldn't know what to look for.

As our dear departed friend, the neuroscientist Francisco Varela, once told me, "The best attitude is to leave the door open to new answers on the question of the nature of mind."

25

THE SHECHEN MONASTERY IN NEPAL

1980 establishment of the Shechen Monastery, inspired by Dilgo Khyentse Rinpoche to preserve the traditions of the destroyed Tibetan monastery of the same name. Erecting the temple statues and the consecration ceremony.

In 1980, Khandro Lhamo, Dilgo Khyentse Rinpoche's wife, and Trulshik Rinpoche, an eminent master and Khyentse Rinpoche's close student and spiritual friend, suggested that he build a small monastery in Nepal that would become the seat of his grandson, Rabjam Rinpoche. Khyentse Rinpoche gave it a few moments' thought and then replied with a big smile that the monastery would not be small but as big as possible. He decided that it would be located near the Jarung Kashor stupa at Boudhanath, fulfilling the prediction made by his teacher, Dzongsar Khyentse Chökyi Lodrö, that the construction of a monastery of the Nyingmapa school on that site would be a great contribution to preserving Buddhism and promoting peace in the region.

The aim was to perpetuate the spiritual legacy of Tibet as embodied in the original Shechen Monastery, in eastern Tibet. The first Shechen Monastery had been established in the east of Tibet in the seventeenth century. The fifth Dalai Lama (1617–1682) sent three of his main disciples to the province of Kham, charging each of them with founding a monastery of the Nyingmapa order—the "order of the ancient translations," so called because it dated back to the era of the first translations of Sanskrit texts into Tibetan, in the ninth century. Most of the major works were translated at that time, including the *Kangyur*, the 103 volumes of the Buddha's sermons.

Rabjam Tenpai Gyaltsen, born in 1650, was one of the three disciples dispatched by the fifth Dalai Lama. After he reached Kham, he had a vision in which Padmasambhava directed him to build a monastery near a white rock shaped like a bounding lion. "It will have immense benefits for the Buddha's teachings," Padmasambhava predicted. In accordance with these instructions, in 1695 Rabjam Tenpai Gyaltsen built the first Shechen Monastery, Orgyen Chödzong, where he offered teachings to many students. He also expressed the wish for a larger monastery to be built at a later date on the other side of the river that flows through the Shechen Valley.

His wish was fulfilled by the second abbot of Shechen, Rabjam Gyurme Kunzang Namgyal, who founded Shechen Tennyi Dargyeling in 1735. Shechen soon grew into one of the six main monastic centers of the Nyingmapa order. The spiritual eminence of the teachers and hermits who lived there, the high quality of the education offered at its philosophical college, and the authenticity of its sacred art (rituals, songs, music, and dance) secured the reputation of that hub of spirituality. In eastern Tibet, 140 monasteries considered themselves the spiritual affiliates of Shechen. Dilgo Khyentse Rinpoche knew that the monastery had been totally destroyed by the Chinese—indeed, when he returned to Tibet in 1985, after thirty years in exile, he found nothing but ruins—and felt it important to build a monastery in Nepal to preserve the tradition.

Land was purchased, and construction began in 1980. That first year, we soon found ourselves short on funds. A pit of more than forty square yards and twenty feet deep had already been excavated for the foundation. It filled with water during the monsoon season, leading some to joke about the "Shechen swimming pool!" Khyentse Rinpoche asked Kangyur Rinpoche's eldest son, Tulku Pema Wangyal, to raise building funds in the West, which he did diligently. One key donor was Gérard Godet, a close friend whom I often saw when I was in Paris.

As soon as the buildings began to rise, some fifty sculptors, painters, goldsmiths, tailors, mask makers, and other craftsmen—all followers of Dilgo Khyentse Rinpoche—hastened from Bhutan, mostly, but also from Tibet and

India, to contribute to the project. Khyentse Rinpoche insisted that the work be undertaken with great care. These craftsmen worked tirelessly for more than five years to make Shechen one of the most beautiful examples of the Buddhist architectural and artistic tradition outside Tibet.

Throughout their assignment, these artists lived in the accommodations intended for the monastic community. When they had finished their work, they went home and were replaced by monks, me included. From that moment on, the monastery became my primary place of residence.

Khyentse Rinpoche gave me the job of filling the 150 statues crafted at the monastery, ranging in size from a few inches to twenty feet tall. The Nepalis are experts in the technique of lost-wax bronze casting, while the Tibetans excel in copperplate sculpture, but the Bhutanese are known throughout the Himalayas for their skill in clay sculpture. They knead the clay at great length, admixing rice-paper fibers and moistening it with water mixed with consecrated substances. In Nepal, the paper is made from the bark of the daphne shrub (*Daphne papyracea*) and, in Tibet, from the roots of the flowering plant *Stellera chamaejasme*, which grows in profusion in the mountain meadows.

A visitor admiring the statues in a Tibetan temple is usually unaware that they are filled with mantras and prayers printed on paper, relics, and precious material. The act of filling them must adhere to precise rules set down in manuals. Preparing all these contents takes almost as much time as completing the sculpture itself. Over the years, I had learned all the minutiae of this process not only from Khyentse Rinpoche and Trulshik Rinpoche, but also by consulting the manuals, written in Tibetan by great scholars of the past. Preparing the mantras took weeks of work on the part of ten monks, and my turn came when it was time to load them all inside the statues.

At its core, every statue contains a "tree of life," a cross section of a trunk positioned in its natural orientation, that is, the side that faces eastward in nature is turned toward the front inside the statue. The east, the cardinal point of the rising sun, symbolizes rebirth and growth. The tree of life is carefully polished, painted red, and covered in mantras written out in gold in specific places. Relics of saints of the past—hair, bone fragments, or clothes—are affixed to the tree, which is then wrapped in fine yellow silk before being placed inside the statue like its backbone. I prepared them conscientiously, using relics preserved by Khyentse Rinpoche in skillfully decorated wooden coffers, including clothing worn by Padmasambhava and his female disciple Yeshe Tsogyal, a fragment of a meditation belt belonging to the famous eleventh-century hermit Milarepa, and countless others besides. Specific mantras are glued to the interior wall of each part of the body: eyes, ears, hands, and so on. Myriad rolls of mantras and prayers are inserted in such a way as to completely fill the interior space. There are different mantras corresponding to each level. If the statue is six feet tall or more, it will contain a veritable library. I have always enjoyed doing this meticulous work and felt honored by the privilege of seeing and touching these precious relics.

The bases of especially large statues are also filled with vases containing specific plant- or mineral-based substances, as well as mantras to promote local and individual prosperity, the healing of disease, and protection against disaster. Also included are soil, stones, and dried flowers gathered from various sacred sites. At the very bottom, we sometimes place weapons whose symbolic trampling by the statue creates auspicious connections to counter war and armed conflict.

In one of the two satellite temples to the north of Shechen Monastery, a twenty-foot statue of Padmasambhava contains one hundred thousand statuettes of Padmasambhava, the remarkable master who introduced Buddhism to Tibet in the eighth century, as well as the 103 volumes of the *Tripitaka*, or *Three Baskets* (the Buddhist canon translated into Tibetan) that my first teacher Kangyur Rinpoche had managed to smuggle out of Tibet, and which had been offered by Tulku Pema Wangyal to be preserved inside the statue. Various samples of soil, stones, and flowers taken from sacred places, medicinal plants, pieces of gold and silver, turquoise and other objects of value are also stored in the statue's plinth. Once it has been completely filled, the base is sealed.

A few minutes after having put the final touches to the filling of an immense statue of Padmasambhava, a task that had taken a full month to complete, I went to find Khyentse Rinpoche, who was directing a ceremony in the temple, and gave him the news. He placed his big hand on mine and said, *"Katro!"* (an exclamation of affectionate appreciation), adding, "You will see your root master, Kangyur Rinpoche, in this lifetime." I thought he meant that I might one day have a vision of Kangyur Rinpoche, perhaps at the moment of my death, as sometimes happens to practitioners imbued with deep devotion to their spiritual master.

When it comes to the largest clay statues, they are filled in tandem with their construction. During the fabrication of the statues of Padmasambhava and the three buddhas for the main temple—the Shakyamuni Buddha in the middle, with the Kashyapa Buddha to his right, symbolizing the buddhas of the past, and the Maitreya Buddha to his left, symbolizing the buddhas to come—the artists called me in once a week to fill the statue up to the level they had just completed. To top them off, mantras were placed in the statues' heads by means of a hole drilled at the top of the skull, and then they were sealed forever. The statue's face, and even its entire body, may be painted in gold, and the gold surface is polished with an agate to bring out its full luster.

Other sacred objects, such as the Dharma Wheel flanked by two deer (recalling the Buddha's first teaching in the Deer Park at Sarnath) placed in the middle of the edge of the terrace of the top floor at the front of the monastery, are in gilded copper and likewise filled with relics and mantras. The gilding is carried out in the traditional manner. The gold is first rolled out into very thin sheets, then mixed with mercury in a mortar over several days to form an amalgam. I participated in this exercise when I was in Darjeeling; the work dragged on endlessly, hour after hour, day after day. The amalgam is applied to the copper, which is then brought to a high temperature with a blowtorch. The mercury evaporates, leaving a gold precipitate. Mercury vapor is highly toxic, but Tibetan goldsmiths traditionally believe that drinking large quantities of millet beer helps the body secrete the toxin more easily!

Khyentse Rinpoche conducted the ceremony consecrating the statues and frescoes of the monastery's temples no less than one hundred times, whereas only one such ceremony is the norm, which highlights the importance he attached to them. He also consecrated the library on the fourth floor, one of the largest in the Himalayas, which I ran for many years. To this day, I still know where to find most of its books, which number in the thousands. These ceremonies consist in invoking the wisdom, compassion, and power of the deities symbolized by the statues and paintings; in a way, they are giving life to an inert body by infusing it with enlightened mind—these objects then become inseparable from the spiritual qualities they embody.

The walls of the main temple are covered in frescoes illustrating the history of Buddhism in Tibet and include many portraits of the lead masters of the various Tibetan spiritual lineages. The work was undertaken in accordance with Khyentse Rinpoche's precise instructions by two accomplished artists, Konchog Lhadrepa (with whom I painted the frescoes at Kangyur Rinpoche's monastery in Darjeeling) and Wangdu, assisted by a dozen apprentices. Khyentse Rinpoche also consecrated two smaller temples, one dedicated to Padmasambhava, his eight manifestations, and his twenty-five disciples, represented by magnificent statues, and the other to Tara, the female incarnation of compassion who vowed to be reincarnated as a woman until she attained Buddhahood.

An open and lively place, the monastery is home to students and practitioners of all ages, from novices to aged monks. As of this writing, Shechen Monastery has five hundred residents, including a hundred children and teenagers. It is administered by the monks themselves, who take turns every three years assuming a variety of roles, under the inspiration and guidance of Rabjam Rinpoche. Khenpo Gyurme Tsultrim, who entered the monastery at the age of ten in 1980 and later earned a doctorate in philosophy, oversees the administration of all the Shechen monasteries in Nepal and India. The philosophical studies go beyond the framework of what is generally known as "theology." To be sure, they include the major principles of Buddhism and a detailed description of the stages of the path leading to enlightenment, but the curriculum, which can take anywhere from nine to thirteen years to complete, also includes very advanced studies in philosophy. They cover the different philosophical perspectives found within Buddhism and those of Hinduism in India, the birthplace of Buddhism. The study of the *madhyamaka*, the "middle path," among others, seeks to distinguish conventional, or "relative," truth, linked to our perceptions of the world of phenomena, from the ultimate, or "absolute," truth, which, through profound philosophical analysis, elucidates the ultimate nature of "reality" and consciousness. The curriculum also includes treatises on the various categories of mental events (fifty-eight principal categories have been identified), treatises on the theory of perception, the formation of concepts, and many others. Logic is also taught from treatises that rival in complexity and sophistication any Western discourse on logic.

A great monastery always has three or four sections: the main temple, the heart of monastic life, rituals, and sacred music and dance; adjacent buildings where the novices receive an elementary education; the philosophical college, where monks pursue comprehensive studies for a dozen years; and the retreat center, located at a distance, in the serenity of the mountains, where the monks—now hermits—adopt a contemplative life for a certain number of years. In the year 2000, Shechen Monastery acquired a piece of land on an elevated hillside, located at an elevation of 6,500 feet and about a mile and a half from the precious Namo Buddha stupa, the heart of the holy precinct, and there built the Pema Osel Ling, "Lotus Land of Clear Light." It comprises a three-year retreat center, a residence for Rabjam Rinpoche, and half a dozen little individual hermitages—which I use when I do my own retreats—built of sun-dried bricks. I have been doing my retreats there since the year 2000. A shelter for the elderly—monks, nuns, or laypeople who wish to devote themselves to spiritual practice—was later built on the southern slope. The nuns of Shechen, numbering some two hundred, live in the monastery in Bhutan, in the place known as Sissinang, where a retreat center has been set aside for them.

Another vocation of the monastery is to train young people for the spiritual and academic life. Novices are kept extremely busy. Awake at 5:30 a.m., they begin the day with group prayers. They then have breakfast and go to class. Aside from the midday meal and a few rest breaks, they study straight through to the evening prayers, at 5 p.m., and often pursue their studies after dinner. In addition to the traditional subjects associated with Buddhism, they receive a general education modeled on the Nepalese school curriculum. This rhythm is interrupted only for teachings given in the main temple or ceremonies scheduled for specific dates on the lunar calendar. The apparent rigor of their discipline and the fact that they rarely get to see their families, who often live far from the monastery, in no way prevents these children from exhibiting joie de vivre and unusual fortitude.

I have always been struck by the spirit of camaraderie shown by the young novices. Go to any school playground in France and you will see a pandemonium of activity, usually happy and playful. But it's also not uncommon to see children squabbling or even fighting. The very young are bullied as a matter of course. I can sincerely testify that, in twenty years of monastic life, I have never once seen an altercation or violent verbal dispute among the children. The novices are hardly passive or idle, however—as soon as they have a free moment, they play soccer with makeshift balls (often flat), improvise cricket bats out of short planks, and run around like children anywhere in the world. Yet, astonishingly, no nasty arguments. When class is over and they head for the dining hall, for instance, you will see them walking two or three abreast, their arms draped affectionately over their friends' shoulders. In my opinion, the power of example offered by their teachers, monks for the most part, and the emphasis placed by their education and Buddhist culture on kindness, compassion, and humane values is likely to explain this absence of violence.

Certainly, some children enter the novitiate very young (the standard minimum age is twelve, but we sometimes take in orphans or the children of destitute families much earlier). It's very often a parental choice that young children are overjoyed to accept; rather than go to a government school, they prefer studying in the monastery, with which they are already familiar from having attended ceremonies and festivals there. On more than one occasion, parents have decided to bring their children home after a while, for various reasons, but the young ones have run away to return to the monastery. It's an encouraging indication of the welcoming environment available to them!

I remember a diminutive eight-year-old monk whom his family had sent from Bhutan. Every so often in the mornings, he would drop in to visit with Khyentse Rinpoche in his room. Because he tended to look at everything with wide-eyed curiosity, the monks gave him the nickname Ukpa, "Owl."

Almost every monk ends up with a nickname. One goes by the name "Washington" because, when he was little, someone asked him where he was from, and for some unknown reason he claimed to be from that city (he had never left Nepal). A newly admitted young monk who was the spitting image of a resident monk was immediately baptized "Duplicate."

To get back to Ukpa, whenever he came to see Rinpoche, he would stand before him with grave solemnity. One morning, Rinpoche asked him,

"What does your mind look like?"

(Silence)

"Is it blue, green, or white?"

Ukpa shook his head.

"Is it round or square?"

Ukpa thought a moment, then said no.

Khyentse Rinpoche stroked his head with his great hand, and the child left.

On several subsequent occasions, Khyentse Rinpoche continued to question Ukpa on the nature of the mind. Those, like me, who were part of Rinpoche's intimate circle mentioned it to Rabjam Rinpoche, who was naturally intrigued. Years later, Ukpa, whose real name was Gyurme Sangye, studied at the monastery's philosophical college. He then became an excellent meditator, spending six years in retreat at Namo Buddha, in the hills outside the Kathmandu Valley. Today, he serves as retreat master for anyone undertaking the three-year retreat there.

When they turn sixteen, adolescents choose, with their master of studies, either to go on to the philosophical college or to remain within the monastic community and participate in the various daily rituals and those determined by the liturgical calendar. They can also devote themselves to the contemplative life in our retreat center at Namo Buddha, Pema Osel Ling, "Lotus Land of Clear Light." Or, they can also leave the monastery for the secular life. Monastic vows are not taken until the age of twenty, which leaves the novices plenty of time to decide what kind of life they want. Once they have completed their philosophical studies, some students also enter a philological research program, in association with Western universities, focused on ancient manuscripts and the evolution of the divergent philosophical interpretations of Buddhist texts down the centuries.

The abbot of Shechen, Rabjam Rinpoche, Khyentse Rinpoche's grandson, is the seventh incarnation of the founder of Shechen in eastern Tibet. His immediate predecessor was the sixth Shechen Rabjam, who died in 1959 under torture by the communist regime. From the age of five, the

young Rabjam Rinpoche lived mostly with his grandfather and received all his teachings. He always speaks of Khyentse Rinpoche with moving eloquence: "My first impression of Khyentse Rinpoche was that of a wonderfully kind grandfather. As I grew, I began to see him as my spiritual teacher, and I gradually developed an unshakeable faith in him. When I began to study, I realized that he had all the qualities of an authentic teacher, as described in the texts. I've always had complete trust in him, which no ordinary thought could ever undermine."

I met Rabjam Rinpoche when he came to Darjeeling with Khyentse Rinpoche. He was eight years old at the time and proved to be an especially joyful and endearing young *tulku*. I had no idea then that I would live with him for so many years in Bhutan, at Shechen Monastery and elsewhere. We shared many precious moments together and became very close. Rabjam Rinpoche is not only a person of great dignity but also simply and warmly accessible.

The tradition of *tulkus* goes back to the twelfth century in Tibetan Buddhism. The term *tulku* refers to the reincarnation of a great spiritual master who, before he dies, decides to manifest himself once again in human form in the world so as to work for the good of beings. In some cases, shortly before he dies the master leaves intimations concerning his future birthplace, name, family, and so on in the form of letters, poems, or other clues. In other cases, it is the young child himself who clearly indicates, through his behavior and speech, that he is the reincarnation of a dead master. Lastly, in some circumstances, probably the most common, a respected master or hermit receives signs, in dreams or visions, pointing to the place where the child, his parents' name, or other intimations should be sought. Then, armed with these clues, close disciples of the late master go off in search of the young incarnation. Once the *tulku* has been identified with adequate certainty, he is enthroned and begins long years of study and contemplative retreats that will allow him to work to free many from suffering.

Buddhism rejects the notion of personal identity akin to the "soul" as understood in theist religions. For Buddhism, a "person" is defined by a dynamic flow of consciousness in continual change that cannot in itself contain a unitary, autonomous, and permanent "self." The perpetuation of this flow from one mode of existence to another therefore has nothing to do with metempsychosis or any other kind of "transfer" of a personal entity from one body to another, from one life to the next. More than an "individual" per se who comes back to life, what is designated by the ambiguous word "reincarnation" therefore refers here to the continuity of that flow of consciousness. That consciousness remains dominated in ordinary people by delusion and ignorance, while in beings who have freed themselves from the veils of unknowing that obscure the correct and true perception of reality, it is a continuum of wisdom and compassion that is manifest in bodily form capable of achieving the good of beings.

In the late 1970s, on pilgrimage to Namo Buddha in Nepal, Khyentse Rinpoche dreamed that he came to a little temple on a mountain peak. Inside, he saw, sitting side by side, the sixth Shechen Rabjam, Shechen Gyaltsap, and Shechen Kongtrul. He prostrated before them and inquired about the torments they had endured in the Chinese invasion. In one voice, they replied, "For us, birth and death are dreams, illusions; in absolute nature, there is neither growth nor decline."

Khyentse Rinpoche expressed his desire to join them in the pure land of the buddhas, arguing that he saw no purpose in remaining any longer in this world, where the teachings of Buddhism were in decline and so many teachers were charlatans. Shechen Kongtrul stared at him and said, "You must dedicate yourself to the good of beings and perpetuate the teachings of the Buddha until your very last breath. All three of us will incarnate ourselves in one person to help you in that task." Not long afterward, Chime Wangmo, Khyentse Rinpoche's oldest daughter, gave birth to a boy whom the sixteenth Karmapa recognized as the incarnation of the sixth Shechen Rabjam.

I have been an eyewitness to the discovery of a *tulku* on several occasions. One event in particular, in 1983, saw the prediction that my master had made to me come true. Dilgo Khyentse Rinpoche was spending a few days at Ka-Nying Shedrub Ling Monastery, not far from Shechen. Early one morning, as Khyentse Rinpoche was saying his prayers in silence and I was sitting on the floor nearby—trying to say my own without dozing off, I must confess—a young child entered the large room, accompanied by a few people. As soon as he crossed the threshold, he prostrated three times in Khyentse Rinpoche's direction. The latter looked at me and, quite atypically interrupting his usual morning silence, commanded me in an unequivocal tone of voice: "Get up! Don't you recognize your root teacher?" I leaped to my feet and stood aside, stunned, to allow the child to proceed to his meeting with Khyentse Rinpoche.

I realized then that this was the youngest son of Tulku Urgyen Rinpoche, who had just arrived with his mother from Yolmo, a Himalayan region in northeastern Nepal. Without telling anyone, Khyentse Rinpoche had recognized him as the incarnation of my root teacher, Kangyur Rinpoche. I went to pay homage to him later that morning, and for the rest of the day I felt as if I were floating in a space of inner joy, elation such as I had never felt before. Later, Khyentse Rinpoche told me, "If I, an old man, have any ability to recognize a *tulku*, that is undeniably Kangyur Rinpoche." The child was also recognized by the sixteenth Karmapa as the incarnation of Tertön Yongey Mingyur Dorje, a great master who lived in the seventeenth century, long before Kangyur Rinpoche, in eastern Tibet, and whose name he now bears. A whole string of previous incarnations throughout history is often identified in this way. Ever since that memorable dawn, I have always been very close to that child, who now goes by the name of Yongey Mingyur Rinpoche and has become one of the most inspiring teachers of Tibetan Buddhism.

In 2011, I went to see him in Bodhgaya, India, and confided that I had more than once imagined getting off the train at some random little rural station, finding a hut near a village and staying there quietly, cut off from the rest of the world. "But," I added, "It's not always easy to walk away from our pressing responsibilities" (the humanitarian projects of Karuna-Shechen were in full swing at that time). "Not at all, it's very easy," he replied. "It only takes a moment." I had no way of knowing that a few weeks later, he would leave the monastery incognito one night, without money or baggage, to spend the next four years as a wandering hermit, roaming the plains of India and high-altitude Himalayan caves. He reappeared in late 2015 and, more luminous than ever, resumed his teachings and other activities.

The monastic life at Shechen is punctuated by rituals of great magnificence that often last an entire day and, in some cases, can extend for nine days and nine nights without pause. Three of these nine-day ceremonies, or *drupchen*, are held each year. During the ceremonies, the liturgy, sung in low, solemn voices, alternates with periods of silence allowing participants to silently recite their mantras—sacred Sanskrit phrases that act subtly to protect the mind from confusion and to calm it—and musical offerings combining the sounds of long horns, oboes, bells, drums, and cymbals. The ceremonies sometimes end with sacred dances that take place in front of the monastery and are in themselves a kind of choreographic meditation and a spiritual communion with the community of the faithful who come to attend in great number.

During one such ceremony, we had an unexpected visitor. A spotted deer, a chital, endowed with magnificent antlers, wandered into the great paved courtyard of the monastery. It climbed the temple stairs, passed through the door, and went several yards into the interior while the ceremony, conducted by two hundred monks and led by Khyentse Rinpoche, was in full swing. It stayed a few minutes, unmoving, as it observed the proceedings. Then it calmly turned around, left via the portico, crossed the courtyard, and disappeared into the alleys of Boudhanath. In all my forty years in Nepal, I have never seen or heard of a spotted deer roaming freely in a populated area; no one had the slightest idea where it had come from.

A sadhu, an itinerant Hindu ascetic, came every so often to meet with Khyentse Rinpoche. They didn't speak the same language, and their silent exchanges were carried out mostly through smiles and sincere laughter. The sadhu usually asked Khyentse Rinpoche to bless him with his hands, then took a bamboo flute from a bag, played a tune, and left, satisfied and content. Sometimes he also came to the temple during the major ceremonies and stood a few minutes besides Khyentse Rinpoche's seat.

Khyentse Rinpoche gave many teachings at Shechen Monastery in Nepal, some of which lasted several weeks and drew a thousand adepts to the main temple, and thousands more to the great courtyard, where his words were broadcast by loudspeaker. He also invited other teachers to confer on him, and all those present, teachings whose survival he wished to ensure.

A ninety-year-old Sherpa monk came to visit Khyentse Rinpoche from time to time. He was very nice, and we had become good friends. But no one paid him much mind—his clothes were pretty shabby, and his broken voice made little impression. One afternoon, while Khyentse Rinpoche and Trulshik Rinpoche were in a small room all the way at the top of the monastery, this old monk came to see our master. After they had spoken for a few minutes, Khyentse Rinpoche sent me to fetch the Tibetan edition of a biography of Patrul Rinpoche, a great nineteenth-century master. Then he handed it to the old monk and asked him to confer its transmission on him and Trulshik Rinpoche by reading it to them aloud. The old monk had spent many years in eastern Tibet in his youth and had received this transmission from the author of the biography himself. Rabjam Rinpoche came by in the midst of all this and was astonished to see two great masters receiving a teaching from a humble monk.

Whenever Khyentse Rinpoche was in residence at the monastery, the comings and goings of countless visitors made it feel like a beehive abuzz with activity. But he had only to leave for a few hours for the monastery to appear "empty," and not only in the figurative sense. When you crossed the inner courtyard or took the stairs leading to Khyentse Rinpoche's apartments on the third floor, you didn't see a soul. Only the monks went about their usual business.

As I was one of the two monks devoted to assisting Khyentse Rinpoche, my days were generally a constant back-and-forth: summoning someone Rinpoche had asked to see, completing the tasks assigned to me, going up and down the monastery's three flights of stairs to retrieve books he needed from the library. Dennis Tenzin, a rather unconventional American whom everyone affectionately called the "Mad Monk," summed it up with his trademark sense of humor: "Lama Ngodrup [the chief steward monk] runs the monastery, Matthieu runs in the monastery, and I run away from the monastery." I once went to get something for Khyentse Rinpoche, then ran into a few people who asked me to help them with something else, and I came back to Khyentse Rinpoche having forgotten to bring him what he had asked for. Seeing me arrive empty-handed, he asked me laconically, "Is that what is meant by freeing your thoughts without leaving a trace?" He was referring ironically to the method of allowing discursive thoughts to free themselves as they arise in our minds, like a drawing traced on the surface of water. I left again on the spot, embarrassed by my forgetfulness.

As for Dennis, he never had any money, but one day he received a generous gift from one of his many friends and decided to use it to build a little retreat house in Thupten Chöling, in the Solu Khumbu mountains of Nepal, where Trulshik Rinpoche, his primary teacher along with Khyentse Rinpoche, had his monastery. Dennis was very sociable and was in the habit of stopping by to chat and joke with all the lamas. He always had plenty of stories to tell. Once his house was built, he continued to do his rounds, all over Kathmandu and in the vicinity. One day while he was visiting with Khyentse Rinpoche, the teacher quipped, "It's your house that's on retreat, not you!" Dennis realized that it would probably be best to take his decision more seriously and to set aside three years for meditative practice in his new hermitage.

After a year had passed, however, he'd had enough of being cooped up in his room and decided to put an end to his confinement. He prepared himself to leave and conducted the offering ceremonies that usually mark the end of a long retreat. On the eve of his departure, he received the first letter that Khyentse Rinpoche had ever written to him. It said, "I am very pleased that you are on retreat and hope that you will see it through." He didn't have the heart to quit and completed the three years of retreat that he had initially committed himself to.

I did not have my own room at the monastery. At night, I slept in my teacher's room so I could tend to his needs. At dawn, I stowed my belongings away in a little cabinet. After Khyentse Rinpoche's death, I continued for several years to sleep on a rug on the floor of the large hall where he held audience during the day, just outside his room. Then one day, Khenpo Gyurme Tsultrim, the monastery's administrator, invited me to the upper floor, next to the library, and showed me a little room, ten feet by ten, that he had had repainted and furnished without telling me. "This is your room!" he announced. I have to admit that I was thrilled to finally have a room of my own. I had slept in a bed only a handful of times over the past twelve years! I occupied that room until recently. But after the earthquakes of 2015, we had to rebuild the monks' accommodations. When the work was done in 2019, Rabjam Rinpoche "evicted" me from my little room and set me up in a more comfortable one close by his residence. I suddenly realized that, at the venerable age of seventy-four, I had a large room with an en suite bathroom for the first time in my life. All in all, I must say that this new little amenity was highly appreciated!

Whenever he was in Nepal, usually in the winter and spring, Khyentse Rinpoche was often invited to various monasteries, sometimes very far from Kathmandu, the mountainous parts of Nepal being populated mostly by communities that practice Tibetan Buddhism. One of the most memorable of the visits in which I participated took place in 1988. Khyentse Rinpoche was invited to reconsecrate the Tengboche Monastery, in the heart of Sherpa country. The monastery had been severely damaged in a fire and had just been restored. Located on the road to Everest at almost 13,000 feet above sea level, it faces the majestic summits of Thamserku and Ama Dablam, which rise more than 20,000 feet, two or three days' walk from Lukla, the nearest mountain airport. By the way, this airport is very dramatic; it takes a stout heart and cold blood to land and take off from the single little runway, only a hundred yards long, which is located on a slope and surrounded by houses and ends in an abrupt drop-off down a cliff. Helicopters have no problem landing there, but planes must carefully aim for the very front of the landing strip and use the rising slope to brake over such a short distance. Taking off, on the other hand, they can exploit the downward slope to gain sufficient speed and fling themselves into the void at the end of the runway!

Khyentse Rinpoche took the helicopter. But because of the altitude and the weightiness of our group (Khyentse Rinpoche, three of his monks, and the luggage), we landed in Lukla, and from there the aircraft had to make two trips to Tengboche. It was decided that Tsewang Lhundrup and I would go on ahead as scouts, with the luggage, while Rinpoche would follow at his leisure with Lama Ngodrup. As we approached the Tengboche Monastery, a jubilant crowd awaited. As soon as the helicopter hove into view, the procession of monks set off, letting loose on their long horns, *gyalings* (a kind of double-reeded oboe), and cymbals. Juniper bonfires were lit to welcome us with billows of scented smoke. We landed and hopped out to unload the baggage quickly. The music and the shouting instantly stopped. The crowd had realized that Khyentse Rinpoche was not among the new arrivals! Some tourists who had been watching told me, "We thought it a little odd that the great lama was in charge of the luggage." The helicopter took off, and half an hour later, Khyentse Rinpoche arrived with great pomp. Which gave me the chance to take some memorable photos of his arrival.

Today, Shechen Monastery continues to thrive under the guidance of Rabjam Rinpoche, who has established a harmonious and democratic system of governance in which monks take turns serving three-year stints in various leadership positions and meet every week to discuss current matters. After Khyentse Rinpoche died, many masters, including Trulshik Rinpoche and Rabjam Rinpoche, transmitted important teaching cycles. The monastery has thus fulfilled the purpose for which our beloved master had envisioned it: perpetuating and preserving the spiritual heritage of Tibet.

Following two earthquakes in 2015, the main temple had to be entirely restored, under the direction of my friend Luc Cholley. Once the walls had been rebuilt, the artists from the monastery's painting school, the Tsering Art School, which is still led by Konchog Lhadrepa, reproduced the large frescoes exactly like the originals, a demanding task that took them three years.

The monastery and my hermitage at Namo Buddha are my two principal anchorages in this world, given that I have neither home nor property in France, although I am always welcome to stay with my spiritual brothers and sisters in Dordogne, where Kangyur Rinpoche's family live, as do my hundred-year-old mother, my sister Ève, and her husband Yann.

26

FIRST VOYAGE TO TIBET
LHASA AND CENTRAL TIBET

In 1985, I accompany Dilgo Khyentse Rinpoche on his return to Tibet after nearly thirty years in exile. Demonstrations of fervor from the locals. Visits to some of the few sanctuaries spared from the Chinese destruction.

In 1957, Khyentse Rinpoche left his native Kham province to go on a pilgrimage to central Tibet. Two years later, accompanied by his close entourage, he had to flee the Chinese army and seek refuge in Bhutan. In 1985, after nearly thirty years in exile, Dilgo Khyentse Rinpoche returned to Tibet. I had the great good fortune of participating in that adventure, one of the most memorable of my life!

Khyentse Rinpoche had dearly wished to return to Tibet. He therefore asked the king of Bhutan, with whom he had a special relationship—the king considered himself his student—to intercede for him with the Chinese government. At the time, the Chinese wanted Bhutan as an ally to offset India's influence in that Himalayan kingdom, which had been independent from India since 1949 and a member of the United Nations since 1971. After independence, India continued to support Bhutan economically. It built roads and maintained a discreet military presence there to deter any potential aggressor, China first and foremost. In addition, negotiations were under way to finalize the delineation of the border between Bhutan and Tibet, now annexed by China. The government in

Beijing was determined to see these negotiations go smoothly. For all these reasons, the king's request was granted—Khyentse Rinpoche and his entourage were to be received as an official delegation. Still, the Chinese must have been surprised to see that the ten members of the delegation included six Tibetans, three Bhutanese—and one Frenchman. They acted as if it were nothing, however. This exceptional authorization was thrilling for me personally. Tibet had been front and center in my imagination since childhood, fed first by my mother's stories and then, in adolescence, by reading the adventure stories of Alexandra David-Néel and the few extant biographies of the great masters of the past, such as *The Life of Milarepa*, translated in 1925 by Jacques Bacot and, later still, by my own teachers' frequent and vibrant references to it. What could be better than discovering the Land of Snows in the company of Dilgo Khyentse Rinpoche, my revered spiritual teacher? Aware of the privilege I was being given, I envisioned this trip as a unique opportunity to exercise my curiosity and full attention at every moment. To my knowledge, no foreigner had entered Tibet since the Chinese invasion of 1959. The Tibetans I was to meet there confirmed that they had never seen one. I was such an anomaly that some of them even remarked, "Khyentse Rinpoche has come with an Indian!"

But for now, we still had to get there. To that end, our group of eleven travelers flew from New Delhi to Hong Kong, where we stayed for a few days until, on May 26, 1985, we arrived in Chengdu, the capital of the Chinese province of Sichuan, which shares its western border with Tibet.

Khyentse Rinpoche was accompanied by his wife, Khandro Lhamo; his grandson, Shechen Rabjam Rinpoche; Tulku Pema Wangyal, who took care of all of Rinpoche's needs; Lama Ngodrup and Tulku Kunga, his scribe and secretary, respectively; and Amji Sherab Jorden, a Tibetan doctor who lived in Bhutan. Three Bhutanese made up the rest of our group: Tsewang Lhundrup, the monk who, with me, served as personal assistant to Khyentse Rinpoche; Tsering Tenphel, who served Rabjam Rinpoche; and Norbu Gyaltsen, a captain of the Royal Bodyguard of Bhutan assigned by the king to provide Khyentse Rinpoche's security.

On the night we arrived in Chengdu, the governor of Sichuan, Lobsang Dawa, gave a dinner in honor of Khyentse Rinpoche. The governor was a Tibetan who had been raised in China and, like many officials, had only a limited command of his native tongue, being required to use Chinese as his primary language. The atmosphere was festive and many toasts were proposed; our hosts took it all upon themselves, since none of us drank alcohol. The presence of a Frenchman in the garb of a Tibetan monk could not fail to intrigue the officials, who were steeped in propaganda that portrayed Tibetans as backward and lost in the shadows of obscurantism. The word *mongde*, which the Chinese used at that time to refer to Buddhism, literally means "adepts of stupidity." When officials amiably inquired about my background—agreeing among them to call me, in speech and in writing, "Machu Lika," since "R" is pronounced like "L" in Chinese—I took a certain mischievous pleasure in replying, "I had a career in science and obtained a doctorate in cellular genetics. It was fascinating, of course, but at the end of the day I found the study of the philosophy and practice of Buddhism to be more interesting." My questioners were visibly taken aback by this career path, which ran counter to everything they thought they knew. I dare to hope that I managed to sow a little doubt in their minds.

Many Tibetans had gotten wind of Khyentse Rinpoche's arrival; they hurried down from the high plateaus of Kham, which were anywhere from 150 to 500 miles away, depending on the region—which in those days meant one to three day's travel by car—to meet him. They were equally eager to see Rabjam Rinpoche, the reigning abbot of Shechen. The day after our arrival, some twenty visitors assembled in the large room he occupied at the Jinjiang, the only grand hotel in Chengdu at the time. In accordance with tradition, before entering they took off their shoes—mostly old clodhoppers in pitiful condition—which caused a certain amount of anxiety among the hotel staff. Shortly afterward, the telephone rang, and the receptionist asked, "Do you need us to polish the shoes you left outside the door?"

More than mere individuals, it was two very different worlds that came together in that place. When I was in the hotel lobby, two old monks dressed in heavy coats lined with sheepskin asked me where they could find Khyentse Rinpoche. I offered to bring them to him. When the elevator doors opened, they stepped inside, froze in place as they looked about them, turned around in unison and hurried out, noting quite aptly, "It doesn't lead anywhere!" I had to use all my powers of persuasion to convince them that this box with no apparent exit would indeed bring them to Khyentse Rinpoche.

Following the Chinese invasion, Tibet was divided into five parts.[1] The Tibet Autonomous Region, created by the Beijing government in 1965, covers only a third of the territory of Greater Tibet as it was before the 1959 Chinese invasion. Kham, Khyentse Rinpoche's birthplace, which constitutes a major portion of eastern Tibet, has been incorporated into the Chinese province of Sichuan and no longer even goes by the name "Tibet." The functionaries informed Khyentse Rinpoche that they had organized a visit to the Lhasa region, in central Tibet, and that it was impossible to go to Kham because the roads were impassable. Khyentse Rinpoche retorted that central Tibet was not his intended destination on this trip. We pointed out that Kham was the very reason for his visit and that a group of monks from Shechen Monastery, who had arrived that very morning to meet with Khyentse Rinpoche, had assured us that the journey was quite feasible. The official response would suffer no contradiction. We must put stock only in "reliable sources"—in other words, only that which came from the Chinese government was "true." The monks from Shechen must have been the victims of hallucinations on the state of the roads! Tulku Pema Wangyal, who acted as Khyentse Rinpoche's spokesman in these endless negotiations, never lost his cool and continued to press our intentions with tireless tenacity. As for me, I did my best to go unnoticed; the last thing I wanted was to risk compromising the amazing chance I had been given to be a part of this journey.

Finally, Khyentse Rinpoche declared that if he couldn't go to eastern Tibet, he would return to Bhutan without going anywhere. Worried about the possible political consequences vis-à-vis both the king of Bhutan and their own ministry, the shifty bureaucrats broke down and proposed that we go first to central Tibet to give them enough time to "refurbish the roads" and prepare appropriate accommodations. The truth is, the officials in charge of our travels wanted time to meticulously prepare Khyentse Rinpoche's visit to his birthplace so that they could control every single detail. The homecoming of this great master was indeed awaited with fervor and enthusiasm by the people, and the government was determined to ensure that everything unfolded as it intended. Khyentse Rinpoche agreed, and we were told that we would be leaving for Lhasa the next morning.

The government took care of all the preparations and, chaperoned by a few officials, including a high-level functionary assigned by the Ministry for Foreign Affairs, who had flown in from Beijing, we were soon on a domestic flight headed for the capital of Tibet.

I marveled as this first flyover of the Roof the World revealed immense green plateaus that gradually turned ocher as we proceeded west, intersected by mountain ranges, glaciers, and lofty summits. Before landing, we flew over the meanders of the Tsangpo, one of the longest rivers in southern Asia. Arising in western Tibet on Mount Kailash and extending 1,800 miles, it becomes the Brahmaputra River in India before meeting the Ganges and then emptying into the Gulf of Bengal. Gonggar Airport, at almost 12,000 feet elevation, lies on the banks of the Tsangpo. Disembarking from the plane, I was immediately struck by the crisp, thin air that filled my lungs with a sudden cool surge, as well as by the intense blue of the sky.

A convoy of four-by-fours soon brought us to Lhasa, "City of the Gods," the historic and almost mythical capital of Tibet. The road was not paved in those days, and the drive took three hours, first heading west along the sandy banks of the Tsangpo, then northeast into the Kyi Chu River valley. Suddenly, the majestic Potala Palace, the residence of the Dalai Lamas of which I had heard so much, rose before us. Having entered Lhasa without stopping once, we drove straight into a complex of official accommodations with all the charm of a barracks. A great portcullis slammed shut behind us. A few select visitors, given advance warning of Khyentse Rinpoche's arrival, briefly stepped forward. True to form, Khyentse Rinpoche was happy to be there and maintained his usual serenity, characteristic of those who have overcome both hope and fear. Sitting barechested on his bed, a sheepskin-lined cape over his shoulders, he smiled, replied tirelessly to the requests of all who came to him, and offered them advice and teachings, yet briefly and discreetly so as to avoid drawing the attention of the authorities to any sensitive exchanges concerning the worst moments of the Chinese invasion and the repression to which they continued to be subject.

The next morning, rising from a light sleep (the first nights at high altitude often bring on headaches), I found myself in a state of intense excitement—we were going to visit the Jokhang, the main temple of Lhasa and home to the most venerated statue in Tibet, the crowned Buddha known as Jowo, the "Precious Lord." The statue is said to faithfully depict the Buddha at the age of seven. Created in Bengal, it was moved first to China before being brought to Lhasa in the seventh century by the Chinese princess Wencheng, who presented it as a wedding gift to Songtsen Gampo, the first of the great Buddhist kings of Tibet. All Tibetans try to visit it at least once in their lives, and some go so far as to prostrate for months on the long journey from their far-off province to Lhasa, parceling out the distance by the length of their bodies.

Following the Cultural Revolution unleashed by Mao Zedong in 1966, the statue—made of solid bronze and as tall as a man—was banished to a warehouse for twenty years. It miraculously escaped destruction, whereas most of Tibet's precious statues were vandalized, melted down for their metal, or sold on the foreign antiquities markets. The Jokhang itself was used as a prison and as a pigsty for twenty years. During the period of (very relative) liberalization that followed Mao's death, the Jowo was restored to its little temple, newly regilded, topped with a crown of jewels and bedecked in brocade. Only one gash, made above the knee by a red guard with an axe, still bears witness to past abuses. Underlying the moments of peace and blessings experienced in the presence of the Jowo is the paradoxically heightened awareness of the terrible destruction that has been visited upon the spiritual and cultural heritage of Tibet.

Surrounded by officials, we managed to enter the Jokhang discreetly enough, but leaving was a little more animated. A few people had recognized Khyentse Rinpoche upon his arrival, and the news that a great lama, one of the Dalai Lama's own spiritual teachers at that, had come from India had spread like wildfire. When the Jokhang's doors were opened, hundreds of people poured into the esplanade before the temple. They rushed toward Khyentse Rinpoche as soon as they saw him, hoping to receive his blessing or at the very least to get near enough to see his face and be seen by him.

The security agents, somewhat overwhelmed, had to clear a passage through the crowd of faithful so that Rinpoche could get to his car. As for the rest of us, we blazed ourselves a trail as best we could, and in trying to extract myself from the crowd pressing in on me, I lost my monk's shawl. I finally managed to climb into Rinpoche's car. We were drowning in a tide of humanity that was rising on all sides. Some tried to touch the car with their heads to receive Rinpoche's blessing, but all he could offer them was his broad smile brimming with kindness. What a scene! From the back seat, I filmed this extraordinary scene of fervor, which had taken the Chinese officials by surprise. The procession moved off slowly so as not to hit anyone, and we returned to our residence.

At the Jokhang the next day, a consecration was scheduled for a large statue of Guru Padmasambhava, "the Lotus-Born Master," who came from India in the ninth century and established Buddhism in Tibet, where he is venerated as a second Buddha. A few years before the Chinese invasion, Dzongsar Khyentse Chökyi Lodrö, one of Dilgo Khyentse Rinpoche's two primary teachers, predicted that if a large statue of Padmasambhava were built in the Jokhang, facing the Jowo, Tibet would have a chance of preserving its freedom. Unfortunately, because of religious and political intrigues, only a small statue of Padmasambhava—dressed as a pandit, an Indian scholar, and not in the traditional way described in the augury—was set up in the temple. When Dzongsar Khyentse Chökyi Lodrö heard of this, he noted tersely, "Since that's how it is, they'll surely find a place to settle in India." This was his way of prophesying the exodus of all those who would end up fleeing communist persecution.

In order to fulfill Dzongsar Khyentse Chökyi Lodrö's prediction, howsoever belatedly, a man named Lhungtok—a faithful from the province of Amdo, a man of great stature, jovial and resolute—obtained permission to have a sixteen-foot statue of Padmasambhava set up directly across from the Jowo, which is tucked away in a small shrine in the middle the main temple of Jokhang. Lhungtok arranged for the statue to be consecrated on the tenth day of the lunar month, the anniversary of Padmasambhava's birth, which happened to be two days after Khyentse Rinpoche's arrival. Thrilled by this happy coincidence, Lhungtok invited Khyentse Rinpoche to conduct the ceremony. We returned to the Jokhang in the morning, and Khyentse Rinpoche spent several hours consecrating the new statue and renewing the consecration of the Jowo and the temple as a whole. He made an offering of gold paint to gild the entire Jowo, which was applied in half an hour by an official artist while Khyentse Rinpoche prayed for peace in Tibet and throughout the world, giving us the opportunity to see the whole statue, stripped of the trimmings in which it is usually clothed. Khyentse Rinpoche was joined on this occasion by Rigdzin Chenpo from Dorje Drak, an eminent master who, having remained in Tibet, had spent many years in prison and lived quietly in Lhasa since his release, dressed as a layperson. Gen Dawa, an elderly monk who had been forced to renounce his vows during the Cultural Revolution and had accompanied Khyentse Rinpoche in his movements around Lhasa in the late 1950s, was also in attendance.

The spiritual and historic riches of the place were foremost in my mind at every moment, mingling with my powerful sense of the solemnity of the event. This unique experience thus felt especially fraught with meaning, and I absorbed the profusion of blessings emanating from that illustrious temple.

Before leaving Tibet in 1959, Khyentse Rinpoche, sitting in a little recess inside the Jokhang, within sight of the crowned Buddha, had spent several months repeating the lengthy Thirty-Seven Point Mandala Offering one hundred thousand times. One day as he practiced off to the side, the aroma of a very unusual type of incense drew his attention. A few moments later, a smiling, bespectacled young lama entered the temple, accompanied by a few older monks of priestly appearance. It was none other than the fourteenth Dalai Lama, Tenzin Gyatso, who was twenty-three at the time. He asked Khyentse Rinpoche where he was from, chatted with him for a few minutes, and invited him to come see him at the Potala.

We visited the Potala, an immense palace-cum-monastery built under the guidance of the fifth Dalai Lama. Constructed on the slope of a hill, it loftily dominates the city with its immaculately white seven-story façade adorned with hundreds of small windows framed in black and topped with multicolored cloth awnings fluttering in the wind. Shepherded everywhere by our Chinese monitors on our tour through this historic place, I could only imagine what life must have been like in this now-deserted place back in the days of the Dalai Lamas. A few years later, it would be overrun by hordes of Chinese and foreign tourists, huffing and puffing from negotiating its endless stairways and lengthy hallways.

In the chamber that had been the bedroom of many successive Dalai Lamas, I recalled an anecdote that the current fourteenth often tells: "As I child, I used to watch the children of Lhasa playing happy and free way down there on the plaza, while I had to study for hours on end under the iron rule of my tutors. One of them had a whip. The golden handle was wrapped in yellow silk, because I was the Dalai Lama," he says, bursting into laughter, "but the pain was just as bitter!"

We also visited the Norbulingka, the Dalai Lama's summer residence, located in the heart of a beautiful garden and on a more human scale than the massive Potala, and Chakpori, the academy of traditional medicine, as well as the ruins of the great Sera Monastery, which had been home to six thousand monks before the invasion. Throughout these excursions, many of those who had known Khyentse Rinpoche before 1959 managed to meet with him. Some cried as they recounted the tragedies they had experienced over these long years of occupation. Rinpoche listened to them attentively and blessed them, and they went away soothed by the balm of his loving-kindness.

From Lhasa, we were taken west. We crossed the 15,000-foot Khampa pass, which overlooks the sublime vista of the Turquoise Lake of Yamdrok, whose multiple inlets form the silhouette of a scorpion. It takes eighteen days, they say, to walk around the lake, of which only one part is visible from the pass. In the distance rises the majestic 23,000-foot summit of Nöjin Kangsang, covered in perpetual snow. I would have happily stayed a few more hours, absorbing the beauty and majesty of the scene. It was easy to imagine a little hermitage not far from the pass where I could go on retreat, uniting my mind with the immensity of the sky, the mountains, and the lake, putting my masters' teachings into practice.

On the way, we stopped to see the famous Gyantse Kumbum stupa, the oldest and tallest in Tibet, 110 feet in height, divided among six levels, each with its own chapel. We overnighted in Shigatse, at Tashi Lhunpo Monastery, the central institution of the Gelugpa school and the traditional monastic seat of the Panchen Lamas. We then visited Shalu Monastery, founded in the eleventh century. Shalu was an important center of the Sakya tradition. Only the main temple, dating back to the fourteenth century and renowned for its murals, among the most beautiful in Tibet, had been spared by the Cultural Revolution. Shalu was also the seat of the most prolific of Tibetan writers, Buton Rinchen Drub (1290–1364), who wrote no fewer than 227 volumes on the philosophy and practice of Buddhism. We spent the night in Sakya Monastery, of which only its main building, with walls of rammed earth six feet wide, had not been destroyed. The temple is ringed by vast corridors whose walls are lined with thousands of volumes of ancient texts piled all the way up to the thirty-foot ceiling. The monastery library also houses rare manuscripts in Pali and Sanskrit that were brought from India in the twelfth and thirteenth centuries by Sakya Pandita and other illustrious translators.

These monasteries were witnesses to a very rich and vibrant past, but the few that had been partially spared destruction for random and diverse reasons (in some cases, their great age gave pause to certain Red Guard commanders) were the exception. Wherever we went, we saw the sorry ruins of the landmarks of Tibetan Buddhist culture, of which only a few tumbledown walls remained. With a heavy heart, and burdened with the painful awareness of the impermanence of all things, I felt a gnawing sadness over the great suffering endured by the Tibetans. I was appalled by the folly of those who, in the name of sectarian ideologies, had reduced these treasures—the fruit of the patient labor of monks, artists, and craftsmen dedicated to providing the worthiest and most precious settings for the wealth of their spirituality and the profundity of their wisdom—to ashes. And to crown their fanatical cruelty, the Chinese communists had very often forced the Tibetans themselves, under threat of violence, to desecrate and destroy that which they had held most dear.

Dilgo Khyentse Rinpoche, who had known these places at their best and the lamas who had lived in them, experienced this devastation more cruelly than we. Many spiritual masters who had been unable to escape Tibet in time had been executed or had died of hunger, illness, or torture inflicted in Chinese prisons and concentration camps.

I wistfully envisioned the vanished splendor, haunted by the presence of the great teachers of the past.

But Khyentse Rinpoche was too conscious of the ephemeral and illusory nature of things to evince ordinary emotions like anger or resentment. Here and there, Khyentse Rinpoche conferred teachings at the request of monks and lamas who had only recently returned to their monasteries, or what was left of them. He also blessed the faithful who gathered fervently wherever he went.

From Shigatse, we went to Samye, "the Inconceivable," so called because its spiritual dimensions defy all description. It was here, in the eighth century, that Padmasambhava and Abbot Shantarakshita founded the first great monastery of Tibet, under the patronage of King Trisong Detsen. To get to Samye, we had to cross the Tsangpo, which is more than half a mile wide at that point. Fifteen of us crowded onto a long flat-bottomed boat propelled by an outboard motor, reaching the far bank by zigzagging between sandbanks. From there, we all climbed onto a large trailer pulled by a tractor, which chugged along the sandy path that follows the river until it reaches the plain on which Samye Monastery rises, enclosed by a semicircle of hills to the north and bordered by the river to the south.

As a teenager, I had spent years reading and rereading, a few pages a day, *The Life and Liberation of Padmasambhava*, which had been translated from the Tibetan in a wonderfully poetic and inspiring, if somewhat loose, way and published in 1930 by Gustave-Charles Toussaint, a diplomat in China at the time.[2] Oddly enough, my father, who had little interest in spirituality, had found the book in a secondhand bookshop in Aix-les-Bains, in Savoy, and given it to my mother on the day I was born. He obviously had no idea that life would one day lead me to this place, unlike anywhere else in the world and fundamental to the life of Padmasambhava. There, too, under the guidance of Padmasambhava and the great Indian pandit Vimalamitra, a hundred Tibetan translators affiliated with those scholars translated the vast majority of the Buddhist canon extant in India from Sanskrit into Tibetan. I can hardly describe the mix of joy and fervor I felt when my dazzled eyes first saw the monastery.

The monastery, blessed by all the Tibetan masters who taught there for more than twelve centuries, had been horribly abused by the Red Army. There was nothing left of the main temple but the first two stories; only a small number of the many other temples were still standing. The 108 stupas that had topped the outer wall had been dismantled. Within the main temple, just a very few vestiges of the ravaged frescoes bore witness to the beauty of the lost treasures. The statues had been disemboweled or destroyed. By some miracle, a precious statue of Amitayus, the buddha of infinite life, ten feet tall and made of an alloy of five metals known as *lima*, had survived on the second floor. Even the famous full-scale statue of Guru Padmasambhava—known as "Looks Like Me" and modeled from the living "Lotus-Born Master"—had been destroyed. In its place, an old dog-eared photograph attested to its former majesty. A few statues of recent make had been set up on the temple altar. Khyentse Rinpoche abided for a long while, praying for the renewal of Buddhism in the Land of Snows and for the benefit of the Tibetans.

I took many photographs, which earned me an ambiguous jibe from the chief bureaucrat sent from Beijing, accompanied by a knowing smile: "You're supposed to be attending to Dilgo Khyentse, but it seems you're a photographer in your own right, aren't you?"

Before leaving central Tibet, Rinpoche presented a list of requests to the Chinese authorities. He particularly asked that permission be granted for Samye to be restored, stressing its importance to world cultural heritage. The government agreed, and the same Amdo Lhungtok who had worked to erect the Padmasambhava statue at Jokhang raised the funds and the workforce to do the job. Guided by Khyentse Rinpoche, the king of Bhutan, through the intermediary of the Chinese government, also made a large donation for the restoration of the site. In 1990, after a major reconstruction effort, Khyentse Rinpoche would return one last time to Tibet to consecrate the superbly rebuilt temple.

With Tulku Pema Wangyal, we also went up to the famous hermitages of Chimphu, a two-hour walk above Samye, where Guru Padmasambhava taught his twenty-five disciples and where Gyalwa Longchen Rabjam and Rigdzin Jigme Lingpa, two of the most important masters in the history of Tibet, long lived in retreat.

After crossing back over the river, we visited Tsering Jong, the place where, in the eighteenth century, Rigdzin Jigme Lingpa lived at the far end of a little valley, and then we went to Mindrolling Monastery. I can still remember Tulku Pema Wangyal's silhouette perched on top of a ruined wall of what had once been a landmark of the Nyingmapa school of Tibetan Buddhism, contemplating the scene of destruction. A few precious frescoes had been spared, in particular one representing Guru

Padmasambhava that was located in a corridor near the entrance to a temple. It has been said that when Minling Terchen Gyurme Dorje, one of the most respected teachers in the monastery's history, returned from a long voyage, this image of Padmasambhava cried out, *"Ugye!"*, a phrase used to welcome someone who has come from far away and that means "You must be tired!"

In the late afternoon, Rinpoche received a visit from Gangri Lopön, a retreat master who had spent many years in the hermitages and caves of Gangri Thökar, the "White Skull Snow Mountain," where Gyalwa Longchen Rabjam, "Victor of Infinite Space," lived in the fourteenth century in a cave 13,000 feet above sea level and wrote his renowned treatises known as the *Seven Treasuries*, which deal with the most profound aspects of the philosophy and practice of Tibetan Buddhism. Khyentse Rinpoche and Gangri Lopön had not seen each other in thirty years. They spent several hours together in intimate conversation.

Sitting quietly, I did not miss a single minute of that encounter and enjoyed the felicitous calm with which these two spiritually accomplished beings came together without effusive emotion, as if they had seen each other just the day before, and radiated the natural nobility of sages endowed with perfect inner freedom. The next morning, they said their goodbyes without affectation, knowing very well that they would never see each other again.

We returned to Lhasa, where Khyentse Rinpoche conducted more offering ceremonies at the Jokhang. He then went on to Tsurphu, the monastery where successive incarnations of the Karmapa had lived, while I accompanied Tulku Pema Wangyal to Nyemo, a lovely valley dotted with pilgrimage sites and his mother's birthplace, where he still had family.

Fifteen days after our arrival in central Tibet, we returned to Chengdu by air. After such a promising start, I could hardly imagine that the epic voyage to eastern Tibet that awaited us would surpass all my expectations!

27

EASTERN TIBET

Scenes of jubilation along Dilgo Khyentse Rinpoche's journey through eastern Tibet, his native region. I photograph more than ten thousand miniatures that had been hidden away during the Cultural Revolution.

The brief Tibetan summer begins in mid-June, as does the rainy season. We wasted little time, leaving the dreary capital of Sichuan, Chengdu, and the humid heat of the plains for Dartsedo two days later. Before the Chinese invasion, the city of Dartsedo was on the border between China and Tibet. At 8,400 feet elevation, it was a transit point for caravans bearing the bricks of tea used in making the Tibetans' favorite drink, salted butter tea. The Chakzam iron bridge was the symbolic marker of that ancient frontier. It was built in the late fourteenth century by the great yogi Thangtong Gyalpo, who is said to have lived to 125 years of age and to have built 108 bridges in Tibet and Bhutan. He built the bridges by forging long chains of enormous links out of very pure iron, which has not rusted in six centuries. Many of these bridges are still in use today and have become pilgrimage sites. In 1985, Dartsedo was just a small town of Sino-Tibetan architecture. Today, it's a county seat of department stores and luxury hotels.

Leaving the narrow Dartsedo valley, my mind soared, embracing the open space as the road rose toward the pass leading to the Tibetan plateau. Freed from its usual concerns, my mind was fully absorbed in contemplating the majestic landscape, which seemed to go on forever. The silence of thought was in harmony with that of high-altitude nature. At the 13,000-foot Zhara Lhatse pass, Kham suddenly appeared like a revelation. Leaving the gorges and forests behind, we entered an immensity of green plateaus teeming with grazing yak. Nomad tents woven of black yak hair were held up by external tentpoles bound together by garlands of multicolored prayer flags. This new world elated me: women busily churning butter, children staring curiously at unexpected visitors, young yaks kicking up their heels at the passing cars, and mastiffs barking and pulling furiously at their chains around tents from which rose wisps of white smoke.

We passed bands of horsemen making their way across carpets of bright flowers, whistling to summon the yaks from their own herds, and a few sheep, tended by huge dogs. Dressed in thick sheepskins or woolen coats, they and their families were heading out on their seasonal migration to high-altitude pastureland. The women wore coral, amber, and turquoise ornaments in their braided hair, some carrying snugly bundled infants in the folds of their coats, clear of complexion and with cheeks reddened by the wind.

Here and there, untethered horses galloped through the meadows. We drove along rivers of crystal-clear waters and passed through the few remaining pine forests spared from the massive deforestation that had left the mountainsides stripped bare, bristling with jagged stumps. Corridors had been cut to help slide the trunks down to the roads or the rivers. On our trip from Chengdu, we passed countless trucks heavily laden with the trunks of ancient trees felled for the Chinese market, while the great rivers were equally logjammed.

We had to adjust our sense of perspective and adapt to the vast scale. An extraordinary scene came into view in the distance to the south—Minyag Gangkar rising 25,000 feet out of its palace of clouds. Much closer, to the north, looming over green meadows, rose the lofty, eternal snow-covered rocky peak of Minyag Rabgang, one of the six sacred mountains of Tibet.

From June to August, the meadows are carpeted with buttercups, the first to flower, followed by blue gentian and white edelweiss. A fleeting Eden soon to be carried off by the chill of autumn and the ice of winter. A multitude of pikas, little rodents known as *abra* in Tibetan, roam the fields in all directions and abruptly disappear into their burrows at the approach of intruders. Marmots emit strident warning calls at the first sight of an eagle.

On this first trip, the only roads were of beaten earth, along which our vehicles clattered for four days before reaching Shechen Monastery. Today, the same journey can be made in one long day. As widely scattered across the high plateaus as the people were, word-of-mouth had done its job: villagers and nomads came out to greet us in little groups all along the roadside. They had built bonfires and burned pine and juniper branches, filling the air with sweet-scented whorls of white smoke, and threw armfuls of flowers at us as we passed. They set out pitchers of yogurt and copper jars full of pure water, a symbol of good fortune, all along our road.

As our convoy approached, the eager faithful did their best to bring us to a halt and threw themselves at Rinpoche's window to receive his blessing. Children with wind-ruddy cheeks were held up to the vehicle, and Rinpoche placed his hand on their head and enveloped them in his loving gaze, complemented by a sweet smile. For our part, we handed out protective cords that people wore around their necks, as well as substances made of medicinal plants mixed with saintly relics. These brown granules, known as *mendrup* (blessed medicine), had been consecrated in Nepal at a ceremony lasting seven days and seven nights. Some people asked rapid-fire questions or requested a prayer for a dead or ill family member. With such scenes occurring again and again along our way, we made almost no progress that first day in the heights of Kham.

A large crowd greeted us at Tagong Monastery. Khyentse Rinpoche took a seat on a throne set up before the monastery portal and spent half an hour delivering teachings on the basics of the Dharma: how to take refuge in the Buddha's enlightenment, how to cultivate altruistic love and compassion, how to govern one's behavior in such a way as to harm no one and, if possible, to do good to others. He then blessed the crowd as they came before him, one by one. I saw the solemn faces of the attentive audience, their features assertive and their gaze as limpid as the sky. They exuded a trust and an unbending confidence that the long years of Chinese occupation had done nothing to dampen. Their fortitude shone through their bright eyes. Old monks tirelessly spun enormous prayer wheels, their gaze riveted on Khyentse Rinpoche. Some of the faithful held their palms together at chest height for long stretches, their faces aglow with a fervor made all the more intense by the years they had waited to see a lama of such stature in this place.

We spent the night in Dawu, in lodgings set aside for traveling officials. The next morning, before we left, Khyentse Rinpoche offered advice and blessings to the residents of that little town who had gathered in a square.

At midday, a delegation of monks from Shechen Monastery awaited us in the midst of a great flowery meadow near a mountain pass. We took the opportunity to stop and picnic in that enchanting place, while the older monks, who had known Khyentse Rinpoche in the 1950s, engaged him in spirited conversation, overjoyed by this unexpected reunion. Most of them had spent twenty years or more in the forced labor camps that the Chinese had established in the region, but they did not dwell on their past suffering, preferring to focus on the potential opportunities they saw for the monastery's revival. While listening with a broad smile on his face, Khyentse Rinpoche affectionately pulled on the beard worn by the song master (who chants the ritual recitations and has every detail memorized), who was particularly talkative as he sat in the grass before him. The atmosphere was festive. The monks then scrambled into the back of the truck that had brought them, faces to the wind, on the winding road that had led us over two mountain passes and down into verdant valleys.

Two days later, we approached Shechen, our journey's end. In the dazzling sunlight of eastern Tibet, three hundred horsemen—their faces leathery, wearing the white lampshade-like hats known as "welcome hats" and bearing multicolored banners that snapped in the wind—awaited us on the wide plain some six miles before we reached the monastery. The monks had come with great pomp to welcome Khyentse Rinpoche upon his return after an overlong exile. The convoy stopped and the horsemen formed a circle around Dilgo Khyentse Rinpoche's car. Each respectfully doffed his hat as he trotted by, before galloping off so as to reach the monastery before we did. The monks were not alone in coming to meet him; the nomads of the region had come down from the highlands and milled around at the edge of the crowd to witness this great event. As we came around one bend in the river that we were following, we finally reached the gently sloping Shechen Valley, studded with a multitude of white tents housing those who had come from afar to meet Khyentse Rinpoche. Their horses were tiny black, white, and brown dots against the valley slopes.

Of the original monastery, built in the seventeenth century, there remained nothing but ruins. A few tumbledown walls of rammed earth, five feet thick, were reminders that a monastery most highly reputed for its spiritual teachers and scholars had once stood here. The destruction of monasteries in Kham had been especially fearsome. Of the thousands of monasteries that had once existed throughout the region, only half a dozen still stood more or less intact. Of the vast monastic complex of Shechen, the only remnant was a little building that had once been annexed to the philosophical college located a few hundred yards from the ruins of the main temple. Everything else had been razed to the ground.

As Rinpoche's car approached, the shrill sound of oboes, the ringing of cymbals, and the deep lowing of twelve-foot horns exploded from the terrace that still clung to the philosophical college's little temple where Khyentse Rinpoche and we, his entourage, would live for the next two months. A procession of monks and musicians first led Rinpoche to a large white tent in which he took his place, alongside his wife Khandro Lhamo and his grandson Rabjam Rinpoche. As soon as they were seated, a long line of monks and laymen began to proceed past them, their eyes ablaze with intense fervor, offering him white scarves in the traditional Tibetan gesture of respect. At the moment of receiving their blessing, few among them were able to hold back their tears, caught up in a whirlwind of emotion, devotion and joy mixed with the bitter memory of the tragedies they had endured. Some mumbled a few words or spoke their own names to remind Khyentse Rinpoche of who they were—it had been almost thirty years. Khyentse Rinpoche smiled at them, recognizing a familiar face and offering them a few words of comfort. I served Khyentse Rinpoche and took a few snapshots of these moving scenes. After several hours, once the tide of people began to abate, three impressive hillocks of ceremonial scarves had risen before each of the three guests of honor: Khyentse Rinpoche, Rabjam Rinpoche, and Khandro Lhamo. Khyentse Rinpoche was now able to chat with the monastery elders while lashings of salted butter tea were served. They had so much to tell him: the awful tribulations they had endured, news of survivors, the long list of the dead. But that day, priority was given to the joy of reunion. With the return of their spiritual masters, the sun was again rising in their hearts after a long, dark night, banishing at least some of the shadows from their painful memories.

For me too, this was a rare moment, extremely intense and deeply inspiring. I drank from this sparkling spring without trying to conceptualize the experience, which was far beyond my ability to grasp. I kept my mind open to the newness of the moment, allowing events to imprint themselves directly upon it like images onto film. Even today, and despite all the time that has elapsed, words are powerless to capture the intimacy of my experience; reality can sometimes be so raw that it transcends the narrow framework of concepts.

A festival of sacred dances was held over the following days, in which 150 dancers and musicians, all monks from the monastery, took part. This festival is a prominent event on the Shechen annual calendar, but its celebration had been unthinkable under the Chinese occupation. The monks had been banished from the monastery, most of them imprisoned for an average of twenty years or consigned to forced labor. Some were compelled to marry and break their vows. The same was true for convents. During this grim period, monks and nuns were not allowed to wear their monastic habits and anyone caught whispering prayers was subject to severe punishment. A timid relaxation had been under way at Shechen for the past two or three years; the monks had been authorized to regroup and to resume practicing their traditions. Their dance masks and brocade costumes having been destroyed, new ones had been hastily cobbled together. From 1985 until just a few years ago, hesitantly and under government control, Tibet began to enjoy a kind of renaissance that, even under the yoke of a totalitarian regime, was nonetheless greeted with joy. Over the years, most of the monasteries were rebuilt and a limited number of monks and nuns were able to resume their studies and spiritual practices.

When the dances ended, at the request of many local lamas, hermits, visiting scholars, and the monks of Shechen, Khyentse Rinpoche spent a week conferring a series of empowerments, oral transmissions of texts and spiritual instructions.

Khyentse Rinpoche also wanted to spend the night at the high-mountain hermitage where his primary teacher, Shechen Gyaltsap, had lived for many years. As he was no longer able to walk without assistance, he was carried there on a sedan chair. Nothing was left of the hermitage. Rinpoche slept under the stars on the flat ledge, and the others slept where they could, in the forest and nearby caves. Along with Rabjam Rinpoche, I was among those who set up their sleeping bags near Khyentse Rinpoche. He practiced and prayed as usual, reposing imperturbably in the equanimity of enlightenment. The communion of spiritual realization that joined him across time to his teacher, Shechen Gyaltsap, was immeasurable, but was not manifest in the kind of emotional raptures that Western culture often associates with great events. This return to the source, a place where Khyentse Rinpoche had lived with his teacher and learned so much, was both remarkable and truly simple. A hermitage has now been rebuilt on the site of Shechen Gyaltsap's former retreat.

Before leaving Hong Kong, Khyentse Rinpoche—who usually had little interest in my photographic activities—had urged me to buy a large quantity of film. I would soon have the opportunity to photograph precious miniatures, traditional paintings on cloth (the famous *thangkas*), statues, and other sacred objects that had escaped the devastation of Tibet's spiritual heritage. Besides some fifty rolls of slide film that I had taken along (an unusually large number for me, as I had few resources and used them parsimoniously), I had also stocked up on a similar number of negatives that would allow me to make plenty of prints. By my calculations, it should have been more than sufficient, but my count was way off. Once we reached Shechen Monastery, Khyentse Rinpoche asked the leaders of the regional monasteries to bring anything they had been able to save from destruction. These were mostly *tsaglis*, hand-size miniatures usually painted on coated cloth, representing the many deities of Tibetan Buddhism. Each symbolizes a specific aspect of enlightenment, such as wisdom, compassion, or action for the benefit of beings. They are used in rituals empowering students to undertake contemplative practices associated with the principles or qualities they symbolize. The *tsaglis* from Dzongsar Monastery arrived in two full chests—a total of five thousand specimens! I had barely enough film to photograph a third of them. There was neither telephone nor electricity in Shechen back then, but with the help of people traveling between Shechen and Chengdu I was able to order a new stock of film. Wasting no time, I got down to the task of immortalizing these invaluable documents, setting up my workshop on the terrace of the philosophical college's temple. One practical difficulty soon became apparent: the identification of each card was handwritten on its back. Because there were so many, it would have been impossible for me to photograph the front and back of each one. We therefore decided to copy out the information by hand—a task undertaken by Tulku Pema Wangyal and Tulku Kunga, who had elegant handwriting. I cut out and glued the identifying inscriptions to the bottom edge of the images, which are generally framed by a wide red border. I then took pictures in batches and unglued the labels. This project took us many days. There were also several hundred larger mandalas that also had to be recorded on film. All these precious photos are now preserved in the Shechen Archives of Shechen Monastery in Nepal, and available to anyone wishing to make copies. We have also digitized them.

Photographic portraits of spiritual masters were also rare in those days. The family altars in Tibetan homes held at the most one little black-and-white photo of one well-known sage or another. Knowing that they would make welcome gifts, we therefore had one thousand portraits of Khyentse Rinpoche printed in Chengdu to hand out to the faithful. We had no idea how highly they would be prized. We began offering one to every person who came to meet Khyentse Rinpoche. The news soon spread to the surrounding area, and wherever we went we were beset by people clamoring for one.

One day, a nomad promised to spare the lives of one hundred yak and sheep in exchange for a single portrait! Nomad families generally own about twenty animals, sometimes up to a few hundred in more prosperous areas. *Dris* (female yak) and *dzomos* (yak-cow hybrids) are bred for milk, which is used mostly to make butter and cheese. Nomads tend to kill very few of their animals, and recently have begun refusing to sell them to Chinese merchants working for big-city slaughterhouses. Every fall, a nomad family kills one yak and dries its meat for the year's provisions. One tradition requires nomads to promise a lama that they will allow a certain number of animals to die of old age. As a symbol of this commitment, they snip off a little corner of the animal's ear and thread it with a red ribbon, which they remit to the lama as oath keeper. This custom is known as *tsethar*, which literally means "life release."

When the nomad offered to exchange one photo for the lives of one hundred animals, we recognized it as a good deal that would spare the lives of a great many more animals than usual. When the portraits began to run out, we bartered each one against the lives of a growing number of animals. This merciful trade, in addition to other, similar promises that the nomads had made to Khyentse Rinpoche, saved the lives of about three thousand head of cattle in two months. The nomads brought us garlands of ear tips threaded onto cords as tokens of their pledges.

It so happened that we became involved in an even more amusing bargain. Tulku Pema Wangyal and I were bathing in the icy water of the river that winds down the Shechen Valley (there was, of course, neither shower nor bathroom anywhere in the vicinity—not even running water). An old monk watched us as we went about our ablutions and washed our clothes; he seemed to be thinking that these monks from India had some truly bizarre customs. In those days, Tibetans bathed once or twice a year, usually in hot springs—there happened to be one six miles from the monastery. They would spend several hours in the natural steam bath, energetically scrubbing away the year's filth and rubbing each other down, sometimes with flat stones.

As we emerged from the water, we teasingly suggested to the old monk that he take a bath, an idea that he dismissed with a laugh. He explained that if he washed himself in the river using scented Chinese soap, people would gossip and say that his monastic discipline had really deteriorated. We made him an offer he couldn't refuse. "If you get in the water, we'll give you a photo of Khyentse Rinpoche." The old monk wavered for a moment, but the temptation was too strong. He dumped his clothes on the riverbank, got into the water wearing nothing but his underskirt and scoured himself for a few seconds with the soap we had given him. Then he dressed himself in a hurry and left with the precious portrait.

Nowadays, modern times have found their way even into these remote backwaters, and photographs of all sizes are commonplace. Most fortunately, however, the custom of sparing a certain proportion of one's cattle has survived. In 2010, for example, when we returned to Tibet with Dilgo Khyentse Yangsi Rinpoche, the incarnation of Dilgo Khyentse Rinpoche, several hundred yaks were assembled by their owners on the plain of Shechen to be blessed and spared by Yangsi Rinpoche.

On this first trip, in 1985, most of the monasteries in the region invited Khyentse Rinpoche to visit. He did his best to grant their wishes, to the extent that the authorities would allow.

In particular, Khyentse Rinpoche spent several days at Dzogchen Monastery, a neighbor of Shechen. In the seventeenth century, the fifth Dalai Lama appointed two eminent teachers, Dzogchen Pema Rigdzin and Shalam Rabjam Tenpai Gyaltsen, to found two Nyingmapa school monasteries in eastern Tibet. Dzogchen and Shechen were established ten miles from each other. From the main road, a low mountain pass leads to the "Lotus Ground," at the approach to which is the principal Dzogchen Monastery, which is also renowned for its philosophical college, Shri Singha, where the greatest scholars of their time, including Patrul Rinpoche, have taught. Many hermits have undertaken retreats on the valley's wooded slopes and in the uplands leading to the Khang Ziltrom glaciers.

During Khyentse Rinpoche's stay at Dzogchen Monastery, Tulku Pema Wangyal took me to visit these uplands. We were accompanied by Tsering Phuntsok,[1] one of the Tibetan officials supervising our group, who had an excellent knowledge of the area. An easygoing man, he had befriended us. We left, walking stick in hand and a small bag over our shoulders. Tsering Phuntsok also carried a kettle to make tea.

We first climbed up to Ngakchung, a meadowland located at the edge of the steep slope that overlooked the Dzogchen Valley, where Patrul Rinpoche and Mipham Rinpoche, two remarkable teachers of the nineteenth and early twentieth centuries, had lived in retreat.[2] While we were there, Tulku Pema Wangyal told me a story from Patrul Rinpoche's life.[3]

Patrul Rinpoche went off every day to a remote location to perform his practice, while his heart student Nyoshul Lungtok remained at the foot of a tall fir tree, where he did his own practice before preparing the tea. On his return, Patrul sat with him and said,

"Dear Lungtok, didn't you tell me that you still haven't been able to recognize the nature of mind?"

"Yes, I did."

"There's nothing not to know. Come over here." Lungtok did.

"Lie down like this and look up at the sky."

Patrul lay down on his back, and Lungtok did the same.

"Do you see the stars twinkling in the sky?" asked Patrul.

"Yes."

"Do you hear the dogs barking down at Dzogchen Monastery?"

"Yes."

"You hear what we are saying?"

"Yes."

"Well, that's it!"

Lungtok would later tell his own students: "In that very moment, I was introduced directly to the wisdom of naked empty awareness! An unshakable certainty arose from the depths of my being, freeing me of any doubt." His teacher's presence and his own many years of meditation practice created an auspicious coincidence in that moment, producing a profound realization of primordial wisdom, awareness-emptiness inseparably united.

We remained still for several minutes, absorbing the lesson of that profound anecdote, before continuing our ascent.

Above Ngakchung, we came to three lakes in succession: the first in the midst of flowering meadows, the second in an amphitheater of boulders, and the third at the foot of snowbound peaks. By the first lake, Tsering Phuntsok lit a fire and boiled some tea, which allowed us to enjoy a nice bowl of *tsampa*—roasted barley flour mixed with hot tea. We were surrounded by gentian flowers, blue poppies, yellow poppyworts, and a profusion of edelweiss. The latter grow everywhere in the high meadows of Kham, reminding me of how proud we had been, my grandmother and I, to find a lone edelweiss on a steep rocky slope on one of our summer hikes in the Alps.

Around the edge of the second lake were caves that had been used for centuries as retreats by numerous hermits, including the great yogi Kunga Palden, whom Dilgo Khyentse Rinpoche met when he was ten years old. He told us that, one winter's day, Kunga Palden heard someone call out to him. Astonished by this unexpected visit, he left his cave. A man, holding a black horse by its reins, informed him that his old mother lay dying and wished at all costs to see him one last time. Somewhat disconcerted, Kunga Palden followed the man for a dozen yards or so; then, having collected his thoughts, he suddenly realized that it would have been impossible for anyone to have come all this way, especially by horse, at this time of year, the mountain being covered by a thick blanket of snow. He told himself it must be a hallucination brought on by an evil spirit. Closing his eyes, he prayed to his spiritual teacher with intense devotion. When he reopened them, the man and the horse had disappeared. Kunga Palden realized with dread that he was only a few yards from the escarpment that fell straight down to the lake, sixty feet below. Talk about a close call![4]

To reach the upper lake, we had to climb a rocky scree, which was no easy feat in our monastic robes. So Tulku Pema Wangyal and I folded them up and left them under a rock. We hiked our underskirts up to our knees and finally reached the lake, an eternally placid mirror at the foot of snowy peaks. We recited a few prayers, made an offering of incense, immortalized the moment with a few photos, then hurried down without stopping so as to be back before nightfall.

The next day, all three of us went to the far end of the valley to see the Yamantaka Cave, where Patrul Rinpoche wrote his great teaching *Words of My Perfect Teacher*, in which, among other things, he praises places where "disenchantment with samsara, determination to free oneself from it, faith, purity of perception, concentration and absorption arise naturally." I found it difficult to draw a connection between this humble cave and such an essential book, which was first translated into French by my friend Christian Bruyat, and later into several other languages. The cave is located in a quiet setting surrounded by small trees a two-hour walk from the monastery. A few hundred yards away, the turbulent and icy waters of a powerful stream rush down from the glaciers that enclose the far end of the valley a few miles away. The cave mouth opens beneath a massive rock embedded in the mountainside. The interior space is roughly three yards by four. A little altar has been set up on a rocky ledge. The hermit who was living there when we stopped by had made his bed on a thin mattress rolled out on planks. In the nearby forest, small clearings carpeted with flowers were the preferred meditation sites for many yogis. Not far from the cave, a boulder rises from the meadow; Patrul Rinpoche liked to sit on it as he taught.

On the opposite slope to the south was another cave, Tsering Jong, "Grove of the Goddess of Long Life," which we reached by crossing the river on a bridge of rickety logs. Dodrup Thrinle Öser and Do Khyentse Yeshe Dorje, two eighteenth- and nineteenth-century masters, spent many years there in retreat. When Thrinle Öser lived there, his provisions ran out faster than he had anticipated, but he refused to interrupt his retreat and decided to limit himself to eating a single bowl of *tsampa* a day. Legend has it that the Dharma Protector Tseringma personally brought him a bowl of yogurt every day.

Khyentse Rinpoche was also permitted to visit his birthplace, the Denkhok Valley, on the banks of the Drichu (Yangtse) River. The Drichu serves as a natural border between Kham and central Tibet, known today as the Tibet Autonomous Region. Dilgo Khyentse Rinpoche was born in Sakar, "White Land," located on the far bank of the Drichu. In crossing the bridge, which is controlled by the army, one leaves the province of Sichuan and enters the Tibet Autonomous Region, which is governed by a separate administration that did not recognize the travel authorization that had been granted to Khyentse Rinpoche, which was valid solely in Sichuan. Moreover, there was no motor road to Sakar, and Khyentse Rinpoche was therefore not able to go. But as soon as news of his arrival had spread, friends of the Dilgo family, villagers, and local nomads came to meet him in Denkhok, and their reunion was highly emotional.

On this occasion, many lepers—we must have met about twenty of them over the course of two days—came to ask Khyentse Rinpoche to pray for them. The following year, on a visit by Khyentse Rinpoche to France, I suggested to a close friend of mine who spoke Tibetan, Christian Bruyat, that he go to the region with a member of Doctors Without Borders to investigate the possibility of starting a treatment program there. Although the Tibetan part of Sichuan province was off-limits to foreigners at that time, they managed with some difficult to reach Denkhok, where they noted a high incidence of leprosy in the valley. When they offered to help the local authorities establish a treatment and prevention program, they were told that there was no leprosy in the region, that they had no business being there, and that they had better make themselves scarce immediately. Before leaving Kham, Christian managed to visit Dzogchen Monastery and to hike up to the cave where Patrul Rinpoche wrote *Words of My Perfect Teacher*, which he later translated into French.

Khyentse Rinpoche took advantage of our visit to go to the main temple of Denkhok, which houses a very precious little statue to which many pilgrims flock to be blessed. In the seventeenth century, at a time when the valley was being ravaged by floods, a delegation was sent to Lhasa to meet with the fifth Dalai Lama and seek his spiritual protection for those who lived along the Drichu. Having prayed on it during his daily meditations, the Dalai Lama decided to send a statue of Tara—Drölma in Tibetan ("Mother of Liberation" or "She Who Ferries to the Other Shore" of the ocean of samsara)—who vowed to be reborn as a woman until she achieved Buddhahood, enlightenment. The Dalai Lama went into his private temple and assessed all his statues of Tara to select which he would send to Denkhok. At that moment, it is said, one of the statues declared, "I'll go." Ever since, she has been known as the "Talking Tara of Denkhok."

One day, Rabjam Rinpoche, Tulku Pema Wangyal, and I, escorted by a niece and nephew of Khyentse Rinpoche who lived in the valley, took a long walk in the uplands of Denkhok, dotted with caves and hermitages. For three hours, we climbed a steep juniper-lined path and crossed pleasant meadows studded with flowers—including one in which the sixteenth Karmapa was born!—that called out to us to take a rest. We left the Drichu farther and farther behind, down in the valley to which it gives life. We came to one meadow, known as the Lotus Meadow, surrounded by slopes abundant with caves in which a dozen hermits, monks, nuns, and practicing laymen serenely led a contemplative life in a silence that was only occasionally disturbed—as if to emphasize its depth—by the cries of a marmot, the hoarse caw of a raven, or the flutelike song of a *jolmo,* the laughing thrush.[5] As Kalden Gyatso, a Tibetan hermit and poet of the seventeenth century, once wrote,

Do you long for the solitude of the mountains?
Welcoming caves are open in the cliffside
Under summits draped in fog.
Living in such retreats is the source of inexpressible joy, temporal and ultimate.

In the Buddhist tradition, it has always been a privilege for local people of faith to participate in the lives of hermits by subsidizing their modest needs. They stop by for a visit every so often, bringing provisions. If the meditator is in closed retreat, they simply leave victuals at the hermitage entrance. Some hermits go down into the valleys once a year to seek alms in the form of a month's worth of food, then return with their provisions for a year. Sometimes, it is their own families that provide for their needs.

We approached one cave that opened out onto a little sunlit ledge. Our two guides knew that the current occupant did not mind receiving the few pilgrims who were able to make it all the way up there. The site had been arranged very simply; a few stone walls had been built to make it more functional. Bending over to pass through the low doorway, we found ourselves in a tiny antechamber. Its contents were meager: a clay hearth, a pile of dry wood, a kettle, and a few cloth sacks containing provisions. We climbed two steps, pulled aside a heavy canvas curtain, and found ourselves in the presence of the hermit. The austere room was feebly lit by a small opening in the wall, and we were just barely able to stand up at its center. On one side, a little altar had been set up on the rockface. On the other, at ground level, was the hermit's mattress, which also served him as a seat in the daytime. At his bedside, a rustic shelf was piled high with books wrapped in colorful fabric: collections of spiritual instructions, biographies of past masters, and a few philosophical treatises. Such sacred texts are traditionally handwritten or printed using engraved woodblocks.

The hermit welcomed us warmly. He was thirty-six and had been living in retreat in this cave for four years. After studying for many years in a monastery down in the valley, where he had earned the title of *khenpo*, roughly equivalent to doctor of philosophy, he had felt a strong need to devote himself to meditation.

He offered us tea—more accurately, a few tea leaves floating on the surface of hot water. Chitchat felt out of place in this intimate atmosphere. We asked after his health and exchanged a few words about spiritual practice, and I promised to send him a text he had been looking for, which I had had reprinted in India. Silence fell. The aura of contemplation that pervaded the place invited us to share this silence for a few moments rather than break it with hollow chatter. We then took our leave, after making a discreet offering to help him pursue his ascetic life—ironically, a few bank bills bearing the portrait of Mao Zedong!

We began our gentle downhill trek to the cave where, it is said, Guru Padmasambhava meditated when he was establishing Buddhism in Tibet, in the eighth and early ninth centuries. Almost a millennium later, in the nineteenth century, Patrul Rinpoche also spent a few months in retreat there. This sage, as humble as he was learned, who attached the greatest importance to owning nothing, roamed over hill and dale, stopping in caves, forests, and remote hermitages solely to meditate, then went off again with no specific destination in mind. He tirelessly cultivated altruistic love and compassion and told everyone, "Have a good heart and act kindly; nothing is more important." His memory is very much alive, and he is one of the most highly venerated spiritual guides of eastern Tibet.

The time had come to head back down to Denkhok and rejoin Khyentse Rinpoche. We were back in the village an hour and a half later, exhausted, knees trembling, and enjoying the satisfaction of a successful pilgrimage. A few flowers that I had picked at the cave entrance and later dried in a notebook would often help me return there in my thoughts.

The next day, we left the gentle climes of Denkhok for the high plateaus, passing through the ancient kingdom of Ling and other highlands inhabited by nomads. Instead of returning to Shechen, we swung northward for Dzachuka (known by the Chinese today as Serxu), at an altitude of 14,000 feet. Another grand reception awaited us there, with horsemen, musicians, and clouds of incense, and a gathering of lamas and monks from Gemang Monastery, with whom Khyentse Rinpoche had forged strong ties before leaving Tibet.

We then left for Kyerku (now known as Yushu in Chinese), where Khyentse Rinpoche was welcomed by the Prince of Nangchen, a man of about sixty with a delicate and distinguished face. The Chinese had treated him pitilessly during the Cultural Revolution. He had endured the insults and spittle of the Red Guards and endless interrogations and abuse. He was then interned for years in inhumane conditions in a labor camp. He recounted his tribulations to Khyentse Rinpoche, very straightforwardly and with no trace of self-pity or resentment. He ended with a smile that seemed to say, "How could such madness have been possible?" He now lived very modestly with his aged mother. The government had eventually given him a position in the local administration. He was especially pleased to see Khyentse Rinpoche, whom he had known as a child and who listened to his confidences with his customary benevolence.

Throughout our stay, I saw how naturally Khyentse Rinpoche was at his ease everywhere, as if he had never had to leave the country of his birth. He sometimes explained some historical matter connected to the places we visited or told me stories about the remarkable people who had lived there.

We left Yushu and stopped in Dzachuka for the night, and then we made it to Derge in one single push. We passed through Mani Genkok to rest by the shores of one of the most beautiful lakes in eastern Tibet, Yilhung Lhatso, at an altitude of 13,000 feet. The lake's name, "Divine Lake of the Mind's Delight," comes from a local legend. A Tibetan princess was on her way to be married in the Derge region when she was seduced by the beauty of the place and decided to remain there. She sent an ultimatum to her suitor: "Come if you want. I shall go no further." The suitor rushed to her side. This large, fir-lined lake, its colors constantly changing, sparkling dark green one minute and the lightest turquoise the next, is ringed by tall mountains. A glacier descends almost to its banks at the far end of an immense expanse of water. Most of the great granite boulders that frame its shores, sometimes partially immersed in the waves or rising over the gently sloped banks, are engraved with mantras, often painted in colors traditionally associated with each of the syllables contained therein. Countless prayer flags brought by pilgrims hang from the trees. Small, sandy beaches beckon the bold for a swim. But with the water temperature hovering around 50°F, there are few takers, although the plunge can be highly invigorating.

Khyentse Rinpoche took a brief pause in this enchanting place and made an offering of fragrant smoke from juniper branches, accompanied by a ritual invoking the wisdom deities and local deities and asking them to ensure peace in the world and the well-being of all.

From there, we climbed through a magnificent landscape to the Tro La pass. The road is surrounded by glaciers pinned between monumental mountains of black rock whose sharp peaks claw at the intensely blue sky. At the top of the pass, a sign announces the elevation of 16,500 feet. We were driving at an altitude hundreds of feet higher than Mont Blanc!

Beyond the pass, we hurtled into a vertiginous descent on switchbacks snaking along a boundless precipice—a journey that is particularly dangerous in the winter, when the roads are icy. Then, coasting for some time among tranquil pastures, we plunged into deep gorges that led us, two hours later, to Derge, the capital of what was once among the most influential kingdoms of Kham and one of the most important spiritual centers in eastern Tibet. It is today the county seat, a small city nestled among soaring cliffs that echo the roar of a turbulent river day and night.

Derge is home to a treasure unique in the world, a place beyond time: the greatest artisanal printing house in the history of humankind. It contains 270,000 woodblocks engraved with Buddhist texts, books of history, philosophy, traditional medicine and astrology, biographies, grammar, poetry, and more. All the labor, from the xylographic engraving of the woodblocks to the wrapping of the books, including the manufacture of the ink and the paper, is done by hand, using the same techniques passed down over three centuries.

In Buddhism, books are considered to be "supports" for the words of the Buddha and the great scholars. More precious than images or statues, they are never placed on the ground, stepped on, or sat upon. They are stored with respect in a raised area of the temple or the home. Before studying them, you must first have received their oral transmission by a teacher who has inherited them via the same method. You then receive and study commentaries elucidating the meaning of the text. In a country where "learning" is known as "listening," it is sound that transmits knowledge. Reading is intended to draw from the written word the hidden gateway to the meaning, which, from mouth to ear and century to century, links the reader to the Buddha and his principal exegetes.

In 1729, Tenpa Tsering, the tenth king of Derge, inspired by auspicious dreams, directed the establishment of a printing house dedicated to Buddhist texts. His successor, Puntsok Tenpa, continued his good work by ordering the engraving of the 103 volumes of the *Kangyur*—the collection of the words of the Buddha translated into Tibetan. He then erected a more substantial building—the one that remains standing to this day. Anxious that the blocks be engraved with the utmost care, in the case of certain volumes he went so far as to offer each worker the amount of gold powder that could fit in the grooves of each block. The deeper the engraving, the clearer the printing. The mission to which Puntsok Tenpa committed himself was taken up by subsequent generations, and the Derge printing house became the largest enterprise of its sort in the world. Since one skilled craftsman can, at best, engrave a single plate a day, the hundreds of thousands of existing blocks are equal to the output of ten engravers working for 150 years.

Khyentse Rinpoche's host, Pewar Rinpoche, was one of his closest spiritual companions from the old days, both a lama and a great scholar who wore his long hair gathered above his head in a tight chignon, and who himself had been a devoted student of Dzongsar Khyentse Chökyi Lodrö. Pewar Rinpoche was also a *tulku* and abbot of the Sakya Monastery in Pewar, located between Palpung and Dzongsar.

Khyentse Rinpoche was welcomed with great ceremony by a procession alive with color and music that led the way, parting the crowd that pressed in on both sides of the narrow street leading to the printing house. While we explored the many labyrinthine levels of that historic building, Khyentse Rinpoche stayed on the ground floor, leading a ceremony to revive the consecration of the main temple, of which a few very precious statues had escaped destruction. Even as he remained steadily focused on the ceremony, during the pauses he and Pewar Rinpoche traded stories from their shared past with their spiritual teacher.

It is only thanks to the heroic resolve of Pewar Rinpoche and a doctor named Ngawang Sherab that the printing house still exists. In 1966, at the height of the Cultural Revolution, the Red Guards were preparing to destroy it. The two men locked themselves in, blocking the heavy doors and nailing the windows shut. The resulting delay proved critical. The Tibetan district chief, Yarling Dorje, was subjected to a brutal interrogation, receiving four hundred lashes of the whip. Even so, between two torture sessions, he managed to contact Beijing by telegram (there were no telephones in the region at the time). He warned a high-ranking official he knew that the printing house was about to be demolished, like all the monasteries of the region, and asked him to come up with some subterfuge to prevent the disaster.

"Those few days felt like centuries to us," Pewar Rinpoche recalls. "At night, we sneaked the rarest books out the window and concealed them. We also managed to hide one copy each of the 103 volumes of the *Kangyur* so that, if worse came to worse, it could be used as a model to engrave new woodblocks. The Red Guards began destroying the Derge Gonchen Monastery—the great monastery adjacent to the printing house. But a telegram from the then prime minister Zhou Enlai arrived from Beijing three days later: 'Do not destroy the temple or the printing house. We must leave an educational example of the stupidity of the Tibetans, who waste their time on useless spiritual activities.' It was too late for the monastery, but the printing house was saved!"

However, it was not authorized to reopen until 1979. In 1987, Tibetan functionaries working for the Chinese decided to demolish the old building and to build a new one, in concrete, to house the engraved woodblocks. Pewar Rinpoche saved the printing house a second time—he ardently pleaded the cause of the superb ancient edifice, whose rammed-earth walls are two meters wide at their base, arguing that it belonged to world cultural heritage. It should not be destroyed but, on the contrary, restored and reinforced. Aware that his contention was at the very limit of what would be acceptable to the Chinese authorities, he added that the printing house was deeply venerated by the people and that folk came from far and wide to see it. Pewar Rinpoche also paid a whirlwind visit to the Panchen Lama, whom the Chinese still sought to accommodate in those days. And once again, he was successful. The printing house is now protected and has been enshrined by UNESCO as representative of humanity's intangible cultural heritage.

Once inside, one is surprised by the gloom, so unlike the wonderfully luminous exterior. The building has never been electrified for fear of fires, and the traditional windows allow little light inside. The feverish activity within is the first thing to strike the visitor. A hundred workers are hard at work imprinting Tibetan paper on long, finely engraved woodblocks. One by one, the pages of ancient texts on a variety of subjects accumulate around them. The squeak of rollers passing over the paper and the droning whispers of workers counting pages fill the air with the sweet sound of their meticulous labor.

The printers work two by two. Sitting face-to-face, they rock rhythmically back and forth, concentrating on their rapid and precise movements. They use a brush to ink the engraved wood, on which they place a sheet of paper that they then vigorously press with a roller. Each team of printers produces about a thousand pages a day. That may seem like a lot, but when you consider that the *Kangyur* comprises more than 46,000 pages, you can see how much work the printing of even that single collection represents.

The ink is manufactured from mineral pigments, red for the *Kangyur* and black for most of the other texts. The blocks are washed at regular intervals in wooden troughs, and the residue is used in preparing pills believed by pilgrims to be blessed. On the upper floors, plunged in silence, the engraved blocks are catalogued and stored in an endless maze of shelves stretching from floor to ceiling,

In front of the building, on the other side of the forecourt, is the paper factory. The Chinese forbade the use of this handcrafted paper for years, compelling the Tibetans to use industrial paper imported from China. Production has now resumed, albeit on a more modest scale than in the past.

The plant used in its manufacture—*Stellera chamaejasme*—grows in abundance in mountain pastures. The roots are crushed by pestle in a stone trough, the pulp is heated and then brewed in churns similar to those used to make butter tea. It is then poured over a tightly stretched frame of muslin resting on water and allowed to dry, and finally the finished sheet of paper is removed from the frame.

From Derge, our return route led us down off the Tibetan plateau: three days of bumpy roads, over passes and through valleys, passing military convoys and countless trucks carrying heavy loads of lumber to the plains of Sichuan.

In the course of time, we had become friendly with the Tibetan officials accompanying us, while remaining very circumspect with the Chinese delegates, who kept their distance. They wore revolvers on their belts, spoke loudly, and drank copiously at night. One of the Tibetan officials, Alla Truktruk, occupied an important position in the provincial administration and held Khyentse Rinpoche in high esteem that he could never openly express. Once we became friends, he told me that, at the beginning of our journey, the question of my status had been raised at a meeting with the officials to determine whether I was really just a simple monk in the service of Khyentse Rinpoche or some sort of spy. They finally came to the conclusion that I wasn't playing both sides! When we visited a monastery one day, Alla Truktruk discreetly slipped a few bills into my hand and quietly asked me to make a donation on the altar. His position forbade him to do so openly himself.

Toward the end of our journey through Kham, Tsering Puntsok spoke to me of what he knew about contemporary Western history and expressed his outrage at the abominations committed by Hitler, whose name he pronounced "Hi-teu-leu." As we had already spent quite some time together and I felt that I could tease him a little, I replied,

"But there's someone else with just as many deaths on his conscience, if not more."

"Who's that?" he asked, surprised.

"Well, your great uncle," I said somewhat mischievously.

He understood that I was referring to the Great Helmsman, Mao Zedong, whom he held in the greatest reverence. He said nothing, but seemed to process this thoughtfully. I saw him again thirty years later in Chengdu, where he had retired. He now spends his days reading Buddhist texts, praying, and strolling in his neighborhood park. He has cast aside Maoist ideology, whose misdeeds he now recognizes despite the early passion kindled by his indoctrination in a Chinese school.

Another Tibetan official, the regional chief of police, became especially devoted to Khyentse Rinpoche. He later told us that, some years after our memorable visit, he traveled our entire itinerary a second time in a kind of pilgrimage. Returning to Chengdu, we passed through Datsedo, and he invited me to his home. He led me into a little room and opened the doors of a perfectly ordinary wardrobe. With a broad smile and a cunning look, he revealed the Buddhist altar that he had set up within, about which no one outside his immediate family knew a thing. He and I have become great friends since then.

Before leaving Sichuan, we went to Leshan, a few hours from Chengdu, where there is a giant statue of the buddha Maitreya. More than 230 feet tall, it was carved into a cliffside at the confluence of three rivers in the eighth and ninth centuries. The statue faces Mount Emei, one of the four sacred mountains in Chinese Buddhism, dedicated to the bodhisattva Samantabhadra, which was our next destination.

Back in Chengdu, in the open air of the rooftop terrace of our hotel, I photographed the final batch of miniatures, which I had been unable to complete in Shechen, having run out of film. Thrilled and relieved at having been able to accomplish the task that Khyentse Rinpoche had assigned me, I was able to return this precious collection to its owner, and the reproductions continue to be of great use to many lamas and Tibetologists to this day.

Before leaving, and at Khyentse Rinpoche's request, we made a pilgrimage to the Five Terrace Mountain, Wutai Shan, in northeastern China, a sacred place associated with the buddha of wisdom, Manjushri.

And so ended a journey of endless discovery, rich emotion, and unusually profound learning. In those days, lacking resources, I took photographs only when a subject stood out powerfully and prominently. By the end of our three months of travel, I had taken fifty rolls of Kodachrome, a first for me. Today, I can take that many pictures in a few days—at a sacred dance festival, for instance—with my digital camera. What we saw and experienced on that trip was extraordinary, to the extent that when I received the developed negatives, there were almost none to discard. Nowadays, after going through my pictures, I delete three-quarters of them. These pictures are the nucleus of my first book of photographs, *Journey to Enlightenment: The Life and World of Khyentse Rinpoche, Spiritual Teacher from Tibet.*[6]

Wherever he went, Rinpoche taught, comforted, and inspired all those who flocked to him. I came to understand better than ever that Buddhism is not an exotic philosophy of inaccessible ideas, but one based on fundamental principles that distinguish happiness from suffering, knowledge from ignorance. Authentic and lasting development can come only from inner freedom. That freedom, in turn, can be obtained only by cultivating wisdom, love, and compassion and by casting off egoism, aversion, greed, and mental delusion. Khyentse Rinpoche was the living embodiment of all those qualities. He had nothing to lose or win, but all to give.

On this first journey to Tibet, as well as those to follow, Khyentse Rinpoche was greeted with intense fervor. For Tibetans, his visit was immensely meaningful, and they were hardly able to believe their eyes. Many cried out, "It must be a dream!" They had stood fast against great tribulations for thirty years; their faith and their fortitude had never wavered for a moment.

Khyentse Rinpoche received countless offerings: thousands of yaks, hundreds of horses, turquoise, corals, chunks of amber, and many other things besides, including money. He gave away everything he received; the cattle were returned to those who had offered them and the gifts of the faithful were redistributed to 230 monasteries for reconstruction or restoration purposes. But feeling that this generosity was insufficient, he threw in all the money he had had in his possession when he left Bhutan. He submitted the list of everything he gave away to the government authorities. Years later, these officials were still saying that while some lamas hoarded the offerings they received from the faithful, Dilgo Khyentse Rinpoche redistributed his and augmented them with his own funds. It was many qualities like these that made Khyentse Rinpoche an especially beloved lodestar in the region; people were so devoted to him that, after his death, they always welcomed his grandson and spiritual heir Shechen Rabjam Rinpoche with the same deference they had accorded to him.

This journey marked a turning point in my life. I would return to Tibet more than twenty times to do pilgrimages, help monasteries in any way I could, and undertake humanitarian projects that, under Rabjam Rinpoche's guidance, led to the foundation of our humanitarian organization, Karuna-Shechen, whose activities I describe later.

As our plane took off for Hong Kong on August 3, after three marvelous months in Tibet, and we prepared ourselves for the hustle and bustle of that modern city, it seemed to me that the tireless and benevolent availability that Khyentse Rinpoche had manifested day and night throughout our trip were the perfect illustration of the words of Shantideva, one of the great lights of eighth-century Buddhist India:

All the joy the world contains
Has come through wishing happiness for others.
All the misery the world contains
Has come from wanting pleasure for oneself.

28

A HIDDEN MASTER
ZENKAR RINPOCHE

I discover the true face of the Chinese delegation's interpreter, Alak Zenkar Rinpoche, a very discreet yet remarkable master who has always inspired me deeply.

Our first trip to Tibet also gave me the opportunity to meet a spiritual teacher who was just as remarkable in his qualities as he appeared ordinary at first glance.

When we arrived in China and our flight from Hong Kong landed in Chengdu, a delegation of Chinese officials waited at the foot of the stairway to greet Khyentse Rinpoche; some even offered him a long ceremonial scarf of white silk, as was the Tibetan custom. One of them, a short man with a limp and thick glasses, approached with a broad smile and spoke to Khyentse Rinpoche in Tibetan. As he was clearly a member of the official delegation, I couldn't help thinking: "Here we go, another collaborator."

This reaction will remain etched in my memory as the perfect example of a hasty and perfunctory judgement, particularly since it turned out to be totally wrong. This person was far more than the infallible Tibetan-Chinese interpreter who would accompany Khyentse Rinpoche throughout his travels; he was one of the most admirable role models I have ever been lucky enough to meet. He is generally referred to as Alak Zenkar Rinpoche, but he hates titles and prefers his ordinary name, Tudeng Nyima. He is deeply learned, and the work he has done throughout his life to preserve traditional Tibetan texts has been stupendous.

Combining a consistently even temperament with formidable strength of character, Zenkar Rinpoche smiles constantly but resolutely stands his ground when he knows that his position is the optimal one in any given situation. An astute diplomat—as was Tulku Pema Wangyal, with whom he joined up to form an especially effective tag team—he did a great deal to smooth relations between Dilgo Khyentse Rinpoche and the Chinese authorities during the endless confabulations that arose every time Khyentse Rinpoche asked to visit any locale from his past.

Zenkar Rinpoche perfectly embodies that rare blend of humanity, intellect, and the most genuine humility. Buddhist texts compare such people to trees whose branches, heavy with fruit, bow low to the ground, while the self-important, lacking all virtues, point proudly toward the sky like a tree with bare branches.

Among other achievements, Zenkar Rinpoche was the prime mover in the creation of a three-volume encyclopedic Tibetan dictionary that has become the standard of excellence. With the help of his team, he rediscovered and had printed thousands of manuscripts and xylographed texts that were believed to have been lost. Many of these works, generally comprising long, unbound folios, had been abandoned in disorder in warehouses during the Cultural Revolution (while others had been burned or thrown in the river). Once he and his team put them back in order, he had them scanned, often in very difficult circumstances, and then reprinted. They are now available to anyone who wishes to consult them. He somehow managed to maintain a good working relationship with the Chinese authorities and to win their respect, an essential condition for accomplishing the immense task he had assigned himself without having to overcome one obstacle after another.

And yet he himself had endured terrible trials. Like so many others, he was interrogated and tortured at length during the "peaceful liberation of Tibet"—the hallowed phrase that Zenkar Rinpoche never failed to repeat with a knowing smile and special emphasis—and most especially during the Cultural Revolution. Some interrogations lasted ten hours without a break, and he sometimes had to submit to them naked in deepest winter, standing on a stool and forbidden to sit. Whenever he ultimately collapsed onto the frozen concrete, he enjoyed a moment of pure bliss for the half-minute of peace that his interrogators left him lying on the ground, finally able to relax his painful muscles and feeling a sense of immense relief. He had sometimes been hung from the ceiling by a rope tied to his wrists, just high enough to prevent his feet from touching the ground. He recounted all this inhuman abuse, and more besides, with detached humor, as if they were just anecdotes. His jailers made him a particular target—he was guilty of having been recognized as the incarnation of a great nineteenth-century teacher, Do Khyentse Yeshe Dorje. The name given to Tudeng Nyima, Zenkar—which means "white shawl"—refers to the fact that his predecessor wore the white scarf of a yogi rather than the burgundy-colored monastic habit.

Following the very relative liberalization launched in China after the death of Mao Zedong in 1976, Zenkar Rinpoche's erudition and qualities were soon recognized, and the authorities asked him to lead programs to preserve ancient texts and advise the official Sichuan Nationalities Publishing House, which published books in the Tibetan language. He received a salary but continued to live very austerely, sleeping on a mat on the floor of a tiny, narrow room filled with shelves groaning with books. He told me that in those days he divided his meager salary in two. Half went to helping young Tibetans pursue their studies and making modest donations to charitable projects in Africa—surely a first on the part of someone living in China at the time!—while the other half covered his basic needs and telephone bills. "I really like to talk on the phone," he would say mischievously, forgetting to point out that he called not to gossip but to advance his various projects and keep in touch with his many friends and colleagues.

As I slowly came to recognize the immeasurable richness of his inner life, I ended up considering Zenkar Rinpoche one of my precious spiritual teachers.

Zenkar Rinpoche later had the opportunity to travel outside of China, to England and the United States in particular, where he grew very close to Gene Smith, who, as we have seen, was the most highly respected Western expert in Tibetan literature. A rapport based on mutual admiration soon developed between the two men, who shared the same dedication to Tibetan book culture. Each found in the other an ideal, learned, and modest partner for intellectual exchange.

In the West, Zenkar Rinpoche retained his characteristic simplicity and frugal lifestyle. He dressed in clothes purchased in thrift stores or flea markets. Invited to a reception thrown in honor of an English Tibetologist, he arrived wearing a coat that was far too long for him: "It only cost me one pound sterling," he told me with impish pleasure.

It was just about impossible to get him to accept any gift other than something he could turn around and immediately give to or share with others, such as a box of pastries. While he was staying at Shechen Monastery, the Tibetan scholar Tarthang Tulku, who lived in California and was also involved in reprinting Tibetan texts, came to pay him a visit. He wanted to invite Zenkar Rinpoche to the United States to edit books. As he left, he placed a ceremonial scarf and an envelope containing $1,000 on the table and then made himself scarce, deaf to the protests of Zenkar Rinpoche, who leaped up from his seat, chased Tarthang Tulku down the stairs, and stuffed the envelope in his bag. When I ran into him as he returned to his room, he told me what had just happened and concluded delightedly, "I won!"

Another time, when he was living in Dordogne, he needed a new pair of glasses (he suffered from severe myopia). Tulku Pema Wangyal, who knew him intimately, understood that Zenkar Rinpoche would never allow someone else to pay for them. But since, despite this, Pema Wangyal wanted to make a gift of them, he called an optician he knew in Périgueux. He briefly explained the situation and asked him to bill only €30 for the glasses, although their true cost was several hundred euros because of the complex prescription for the lenses, and added that he would pay the balance himself. So Zenkar Rinpoche went to Périgueux with a friend, chose a pair of glasses that suited him, insisted on paying for them, and went home very happy, lavish in his praise for the opticians of Dordogne: "Such good glasses, at such an unbeatable price!" Each player came away very pleased with this happy turn of events.

When Zenkar Rinpoche returned to Paris, Tulku Pema Wangyal surreptitiously slipped a few bills into his carryall as an offering. A few hours later, Zenkar Rinpoche called the guilty party from the airport, complaining that "someone put poison in my bag!"

To this day, despite his fragile health, Zenkar Rinpoche is still pursuing his tireless efforts, in China and elsewhere, to preserve ancient texts, get them published, and make them freely available to all.

Many are those who have been deeply touched by Zenkar Rinpoche's boundless disinterest and selflessness, as well as by his simplicity and lifestyle, which so keenly recall those of Patrul Rinpoche, the great wandering hermit of the nineteenth century, whose complete works he republished at the Sichuan Nationalities Publishing House.

In 2018, Zenkar Rinpoche suggested that I come meet him in Hong Kong, where he goes frequently, to discuss our Tibetan publication projects and spend a few precious moments together. I took full advantage of this opportunity to spend a few days with him at the home of our mutual friend Ingrid, who also works for our Karuna-Shechen organization. We talked about all manner of things, and after dinner, when he seemed to be tiring, Zenkar Rinpoche told me, "Keep talking, even if I look like I'm asleep." So, I asked him questions about some texts that I was translating, overjoyed to find myself in quiet company with such an exalted being! We stayed together from morning till night. When I said my goodbyes at the end of the fourth day, having to catch a flight the next morning, he replied, "Okay, I can see that you're in a hurry!"—his subtle sense of humor always containing the seed of a lesson. As far as he was concerned, we had enough to discuss and texts to study to keep us busy for a week or two, and he was pointing to the fact that Westerners are always in a hurry to go "somewhere" and "somewhere else" to do "something else."

29

THE WHEEL OF TIME EMPOWERMENT
THE KALACHAKRA

In 1985, after a three-day drive, Dilgo Khyentse Rinpoche arrives in Bodhgaya, where two hundred thousand of the faithful have gathered. The Dalai Lama confers the empowerment of the Wheel of Time.

In early December 1985, Khyentse Rinpoche headed out by car for Bodhgaya, India, which would require three days crossing the high-altitude valleys of Bhutan and the plains of India. There, he would receive from the Dalai Lama the transmission of the great empowerment of the Wheel of Time, based on the Kalachakra tantra, one of the most momentous events of all. Once again, I was lucky enough to accompany him.

Five centuries before the birth of Christ, a hermit—significantly emaciated by the exceptionally ascetic life he led—left his place of meditation after spending six years in the forest. He walked unsteadily toward the river Nairanjana and collapsed en route. He revived under the care of a young village girl, Sujata, who offered him milk-rice pudding. Having recovered his strength and bathed in the waters of that wide river lined with silver sands and palm trees, he understood that mortifying the body does not lead to enlightenment, which is to be found within the mind.

He found a majestic tree and sat in down in its shade, vowing not to rise until he had understood the ultimate nature of mind and of what ordinary people call "reality." He spent the night under the *Ficus religiosa*, which would henceforth be known as the Bodhi Tree, or by its common name, pipal. This place would become known as the Vajrasana, or "Diamond Throne," the current-day Bodhgaya. The man was none other than Siddhartha Gautama, who, at dawn, became the Awakened One—the Buddha.

On that cool December day, I sat before the Bodhi Tree and watched thousands of pilgrims from all the Buddhist countries as they meditated nearby, prostrated toward the Great Stupa, or undertook countless circumambulations. I marveled as it suddenly occurred to me that all these people were expressing their admiration not for an emperor, celebrity, billionaire, pyramid-builder, adventurous explorer, or sports champion, but for a being who had transformed his mind. He had achieved enlightenment more than two millennia earlier, and that inner awakening was still being celebrated with great fervor to this day.

These pilgrims are not worshipping a divinity but conveying their respect for the ultimate wisdom of the Buddha. The two thousand to three thousand prostrations they make every day, sliding over smooth wooden planks, are vibrant homage to the awakened body, speech, and mind of the Buddha. They pray in order to purify their own bodies, speech, and mind of all obscurations. For them, the enemy is ignorance, the battlefield is samsara—the world of conditioned existence—and victory is liberation from suffering, ultimate wisdom and unconditional compassion. It is said that not only the Buddha Shakyamuni, but also the 1,002 buddhas of our era—the *kalpa*, or period between the creation of a universe and its final dissolution—have attained and will attain enlightenment in this place, which is thought to be a "hanging garden" in an age when, according to Buddhist cosmology, only the remnants of the golden age survive. The Buddhist poet Asvagosha called it the "navel of the earth's surface."

Archeologists and historians believe that the emperor Ashoka built the first monument commemorating the Buddha's enlightenment by the Bodhi Tree, sometime in the third century BCE.[1] According to the renowned Chinese pilgrim and scholar Xuanzang, who left a detailed account of his travels, a larger edifice was erected in the seventh century. A community of several thousand monks grew up around this monument. The twelfth-century waves of Muslim invasions wiped out Buddhism in India and destroyed the monument. In the fourteenth century, the kings of Myanmar restored the main temple, but it fell into ruin for lack of maintenance.

Over the course of time, it was partially buried in sand deposited by floods and wind. Not until the nineteenth century did a determined Englishman, Alexander Cunningham, undertake to restore it, with the support of the Kingdom of Myanmar, to the state in which it is still seen today. The stupa and the temple within it were revived.

Thirty-five years ago, few pilgrims made the journey to Bodhgaya, rising in the green countryside of Bihar. Today, even as tens of thousands gather from throughout the world at the birthplace of Buddhism, Bodhgaya remains a space of great serenity, in stark contrast to the chaotic bustle of the neighboring town of Gaya.

In that month of December 1985, no fewer than two hundred thousand people came to Bodhgaya. In the West, such an event would have required months of preparation and complex logistics. Here, in the space of ten days, an immense, tarpaulin-covered bamboo shelter, a prettily decorated stage from which the Dalai Lama would confer his teachings, and thousands of tents serving as restaurants by day and dormitories by night sprang up like mushrooms. Indian merchants also attended the gathering—they sold all sorts of goods from makeshift stalls and set up more eateries in the nearby fields.

As a member of Dilgo Khyentse Rinpoche's entourage, and having also been authorized to record the event, I had an ideal vantage point in a little enclave reserved for photographers just opposite the Dalai Lama. I was therefore able to take precious pictures of this historic event, while keeping as low a profile as possible.

Hundreds of faithful had managed to make the journey from Tibet. Crossing snowbound mountain passes, often at altitudes of more than 16,000 feet, they had evaded detection by the border guards, who were under orders by the government to allow no one into India. Their return was no less risky, for that matter, and if caught they ran the risk of reprisal, including months in jail or even severe corporal punishment. It was therefore especially moving to see these Tibetans sitting in the front rows. For ten days, almost without interruption, they were able to rest their gaze intensely on their adored spiritual master, the living symbol of the cause of Tibet, and absorb his inspiring presence. They were in traditional costume, felt boots and sheepskin coats, or threadbare Chinese jackets, poor protection against the biting cold of the Himalayas they had had to cross. Their perspective on things was very different to that of the Tibetan refugees who had been in India for more than thirty years. To these newcomers, everything was new, freedom above all. Their ruggedly beautiful faces, animated by a passion that arose from the very core of their being, stood out amid the rapt audience.

Other than the group of Tibetans who had made the brave journey from their homeland, and were sat to the left of the Dalai Lama, the first fifty rows were entirely occupied by more than ten thousand monks and nuns! To grasp the scale of such an enormous monastic congregation, we need to remember that there were just over one hundred thousand Tibetan refugees in India in those days. That means that 10 percent of their population had taken monastic vows. In Tibet, the percentage was even higher—a unique occurrence in world history.

Leading figures from each of the four main schools of Tibetan Buddhism, having come to receive the empowerment, were seated on small thrones at a right angle to the Dalai Lama, ahead of him to the right and left. On one side sat Dilgo Khyentse Rinpoche, representing the Nyingmapa school; and at his side Taklung Shabdrung, representing the Kagyu school; followed by Minling Dungse, also from the Nyingmapa school. Across from them were, in order, Sakya Trizin, head of the Sakya school; Ganden Tripa, leader of the Gelug school; and Drikung Kyabgön, who also represented the Kagyu school. All the other lamas, *tulkus*, and scholars sat on lower benches extending fifty yards to the right and the left of the Dalai Lama; across from him, the multitude of ordained disciples and laypeople stretched out as far as the eye could see.

About a hundred Western students were also present; a special area had been set aside for them, from which they had a clear view of the Dalai Lama, and they were given little FM transmitters allowing them to listen to the simultaneous interpretation of the teachings.

The Dalai Lama's words resounded clear and bright in the open space, and his voice—relayed by loudspeakers that were, for once, of excellent quality—carried far without interference, as the two hundred thousand listeners maintained a rapt silence.

The Dalai Lama began by establishing a distinction among the members of the vast audience. Some people had come to immerse themselves purposefully in the teachings; others were there out of genuine curiosity; and still others (whom he called the "Hey! Something is going on there!") had heard that something important was happening and simply wanted to see what it was all about. He encouraged each listener to reflect thoughtfully on the teachings. "Otherwise," he said, "if someone asks you what the Dalai Lama taught, all you'll be able to say is, 'Oh, he spoke very well.'"

For the first six days, the Dalai Lama explained *A Guide to the Bodhisattva's Way of Life*, or *Bodhisattvacaryāvatāra* in Sanskrit, one of the most inspiring poems on altruistic love and the fundamental goodness of the human being, written by Shantideva in the eighth century. The text reveals the quintessence of the way of the bodhisattva, based on compassion and transcendent wisdom. Let us recall that the bodhisattva vows to achieve enlightenment for the good of all beings so as to guide them toward the end of suffering. In ten chapters in verse, the text, which is studied in all monasteries and by all practitioners and is the teaching most dear to the Dalai Lama's heart, explains the great value in generating the altruistic mind of enlightenment, like a bolt of lightning that tears through samsara's night of ignorance and delusion. He goes on to explain how to maintain and engage in it diligently, while remaining vigilant and cultivating patience, enthusiastic diligence, and concentration, and, finally, understanding the ultimate wisdom that goes beyond ordinary intellect and concepts.

During these teachings leading up to the great Kalachakra empowerment, the Wheel of Time, the Dalai Lama summarized the teachings of Buddhism in two essential points: view and conduct. The concept of view refers here to understanding the links of interdependence that regulate all phenomena, including happiness and suffering. Ultimately, it refers to emptiness, the lack of intrinsic, independent existence of all phenomena. Conduct consists in avoiding all harmful action; it is the source of benefits to all beings. He explained the concept of interdependence as follows:

We are in the habit of thinking that everything that happens to us, good and bad alike, comes from a unique cause, an independent entity. When the experience is pleasant, we cling to its presumed cause; when it is unpleasant, we feel aversion to it. When we understand that all phenomena arise from the interaction of numberless causes and conditions, external and internal, attraction and aversion can no longer find an obvious object to move towards and cannot arise with the same facility.

He then demonstrated for us how the essence of the Buddha's teachings is clearly summed up in this quatrain from the sutras:

Abandon all negative action;
Practice virtue perfectly;
Tame your own mind.
This is the teaching of the Buddha.

He offered the following commentary on this quatrain:

Our happiness depends on mastering one's mind. It is essential that we pacify our afflictive mental states. We must apply altruistic love as an antidote to hatred. To defeat clinging, we must meditate on the unappealing aspects of the objects of desire. We must annihilate pride by cultivating humility and analyzing the illusory nature of the ego. We must dispel ignorance by meditating on the links of interdependence.

Sometimes, the Dalai Lama embellished his discourse with anecdotes or noticed something unusual in the crowd and burst into loud and spontaneous laughter. He told us the following story, among others:

A Tibetan official owned a parrot that he loved very much. He would feed it by hand and caress its head. The parrot seemed to enjoy these caresses to the highest degree. But whenever I came near it tried to bite me. I finally grew jealous. I said to myself: "I'm the Dalai Lama. Why is the parrot treating me so badly?" The parrot obviously had no idea about any of this. I then spent the next few days trying to win it over by offering it hazelnuts. The parrot accepted them, but reverted to its aggressive behavior immediately afterwards. I lost my cool. I give it a tap on the beak with a twig. There was no chance of our becoming friends after that!

Anecdotes like these, which the Dalai Lama loves to tell, allow him to remind us that he is as human as any of us. He likes to say that he is speaking to us "human being to human being" and not from the perspective of an eminent or dominant figure. His sensibility is so broad and lively that he can go from laughter to tears in an instant—for instance, when reciting these verses by Shantideva:

May I be a guard for those who are protectorless,
A guide for all who journey on the road,
May I be a boat, a raft, bridge,
For those who wish to cross the water.

Just like the earth and space itself
And all the other mighty elements,
For boundless multitudes of beings
May I always be the ground of life, the source of varied sustenance.

He kept silent for a few moments, his face discreetly turned away to avoid making a show of his emotions, then resumed his discourse. At the end of each teaching session, he concluded with this vow by Shantideva:

As long as space endures,
And as long as sentient beings remain,
Until then, may I too remain
To dispel the miseries of the world.

Before dawn and just after dusk, with that promise in their minds, thousands of pilgrims circled the Bodhi Tree and the monumental temple beside it. They murmured their mantras, counted out their *malas*, sang the words of the Buddha, praised his wisdom.

For the next four days, with great focus and a desire to communicate clearly, the Dalai Lama conferred the great Wheel of Time, the Kalachakra empowerment. He guided us with detailed explanations and described the visualizations we should do while receiving the transmission. The Wheel of Time symbolizes the "fourth time," the ultimate truth beyond notions of past, present, and future. Over the course of the numerous and complex stages of the empowerment—based on the Kalachakra tantra and a mandala containing more than seven hundred deities representing diverse mental states that are transmuted into wisdom by enlightenment and the altruistic actions of the buddhas—he introduced us to the notion of "pure vision," which is central to the Diamond Vehicle, the Vajrayana. Pure vision consists of understanding and fully integrating through experience the fact that all phenomena are originally pure within the union of emptiness and manifestation. All things arise forever through the workings of interdependence, while being void of independent existence. Our mental constructs attribute to phenomena an intrinsic reality that they do not possess and provisionally conceal the empty nature of all reality.

And yet, he explained,

Even if negative emotions veil the luminous nature of the mind, they do not penetrate it. The basic nature of the mind is never corrupted. It possesses the capacity to know the entirety of phenomena, external and internal. Nothing can alter that natural quality, which is inherent to the very of the mind. The possibility of sweeping away the extrinsic veils that obscure it has always remained available.

He stressed the fact that ignorance—belief in the reality of things—is the source of the world conditioned by suffering, samsara:

And yet, when you think about it, as powerful as it may be, ignorance is never anything but an error, a mistaken perception. Its opposite, the understanding of the emptiness of phenomena, rests on a natural truth whose proofs are consistent. Let us strive to familiarize ourselves with that understanding and wisdom will thrive and expand, while ignorance will lose its power. In this unequal battle, mistaken concepts, antinomic to wisdom, are doomed to defeat.

Toward the end of the empowerment, the master confers on the one person in the audience whom he considers to be his primary spiritual heir the title of "holder of the teachings," in a ritual not unlike an enthronement. The chosen lama stands beneath a canopy of multicolored silk before the throne of the Dalai Lama, who bestows upon him the symbolic emblems of that spiritual royalty, including a wheel that represents the turning of the Dharma Wheel. In the presence of all the heads of Tibetan Buddhism, the Dalai Lama invested Dilgo Khyentse Rinpoche on this occasion. It was a particularly moving moment for us.

On the last day, an elaborate ceremony of thanksgiving offerings was held in honor of the Dalai Lama. The monks spent an hour reciting the ritual of the offering to the masters of the spiritual line, or Lama Chöpa. Breaking with ancestral tradition, the Dalai Lama asked a Western monk, who had long lived in a Tibetan monastery in India and knew the ritual inside out, to serve as song master, that is, to lead the liturgy that was broadcast to the immense crowd by loudspeaker. The Dalai Lama slipped in a little joke when he announced that it was the day of the *inji goser*, literally, "yellow-headed westerners." "Yellow head" is a nickname widely used by Tibetans for foreigners, as blond hair is totally absent among them.

After the chants, the Dalai Lama concluded the eleven days of teachings with this advice:

From here on out, let us embrace the ideals of the bodhisattvas, let us be good human beings. It does no good for us to stand beneath this tent if we start arguing the minute we leave! Our future depends on our good heart and the purity of our mind. I myself strive to do my best. You should do the same. If we are fundamentally good, we will be happy and all will be well. Our qualities will gradually come to serve as an example to others. That future is in our hands.

Thank you for having listened to me so attentively. I strive at all times to generate the altruistic thought of enlightenment, bodhicitta. That is my practice and I always encourage others to do so. I see it as a practice devoid of all risk, a source of great benefits and powerful blessings.

The two hundred thousand faithful said their goodbyes with these warm words and benevolent wishes. Then, like a cloud of starlings taking wing, they dispersed in all directions, some to undertake the perilous return journey to Tibet. The crowd evaporated as quickly as it had formed. The next day, this place—which had hummed with activity only a few hours earlier, amplified by the presence of the Dalai Lama—was no more than a great empty field, strewn with a few cushions and jute sacks, forgotten or abandoned. Two hundred thousand people had come, stayed, and left. I recalled these verses by Shabkar:

When I saw pilgrims by the tens of thousands
Part from each other and disperse,
It occurred to me that indeed this showed
The impermanence of all phenomena. [. . .]

Like autumn clouds, this life is transient.
Our parents, our relatives, are like passersby met in a marketplace.
Like the dew on grass-tips, wealth is evanescent.
Like a bubble on the surface of water, this body is fragile, ephemeral.

The dharmas of this samsaric world are futile;
The sacred Dharma alone has value.
The chance to practice this Dharma is occurring just once, right now.[2]

30

SECOND JOURNEY TO EASTERN TIBET

In 1988, Dilgo Khyentse Rinpoche again returns to his homeland. Exploring Dzongsar Monastery, where one of his primary teachers once lived. A visit to the caves and hermitages where Dilgo Khyentse Rinpoche spent many years in retreat.

In May 1988, Khyentse Rinpoche wanted to make another visit to eastern Tibet. Following the success of the first, which had come off without a hitch, to the great satisfaction of the people and the local authorities, the Bhutanese government this time asked its Chinese counterpart for the simple authorization for Khyentse Rinpoche and his entourage to return to eastern Tibet on a private visit, and not as an official Bhutanese delegation. In addition to his desire to spend more time in the country of his birth, Khyentse Rinpoche also wished to take advantage of the journey to bring along two young incarnate lamas to visit the places where their predecessors had lived. The first of these *tulkus*, Jamyang Dzongsar Khyentse, had been recognized as the incarnation of Dzongsar Khyentse Chökyi Lodrö, one of Tibet's most highly respected sages and scholars, who had also been one of Dilgo Khyentse Rinpoche's main spiritual teachers. The second, Namkhai Nyingpo Rinpoche, hoped to visit the monastery of his predecessors, in Lhodrag, in southern Tibet. As always, Shechen Rabjam Rinpoche, Khyentse Rinpoche's grandson, accompanied his grandfather and spiritual teacher.

The young lamas could be a bit mischievous, and I was the indulgent victim of their creativity in that domain on more than one occasion. On our flight from Hong Kong to Chengdu, I found myself sitting next to Dilgo Khyentse Rinpoche. I tried to make myself as small as possible in my seat to make as much room as possible for his sizable body. I suddenly felt a burning itch on my neck and back. As I began to wriggle, trapped between Khyentse Rinpoche, who stared out the window as he said his prayers, and a monk asleep to my left, I heard half-stifled giggles erupt from the young rinpoches sitting behind us: Dzongsar Khyentse Rinpoche had had the brilliant idea of pouring an entire packet of itching powder down my neck. Because I had received such a massive dose, the powder caused a burning sensation like that of pepper on irritated skin—far beyond the usual prickling that lends its name to this prank.

When I understood what had happened, I barked a sharp "You think that's funny?" at them, which only confirmed the effectiveness of the powder and set off another burst of laughter that rolled along in frequent waves until we landed an hour later. At least I had the consolation of having given a good laugh to those who later became my spiritual teachers. Thirty years later, Dzongsar Khyentse Rinpoche still tells this story with the same glee.

The authorities organized a meeting between Khyentse Rinpoche and the Panchen Lama, who was living in Beijing.[1] The Panchen Lama represents the second-highest spiritual authority in Tibet, immediately below the Dalai Lama. Khyentse Rinpoche, Rabjam Rinpoche, Tulku Pema Wangyal, Dasho Kesang Dorje (an officer in the Bhutanese army assigned to our teacher's security detail, and who became a close student of Khyentse Rinpoche and an excellent practitioner), and a former Tibetan officer who was also close to Khyentse Rinpoche made a round trip from Chengdu to Beijing in three days.

I was not on that trip, but Rabjam Rinpoche told me that two meetings took place. The first was informal, and Khyentse Rinpoche took that opportunity to ask the Panchen Lama to forge a spiritual connection between them by transmitting to him a text on Manjushri, the buddha of wisdom. They conversed intimately, and the Panchen Lama even made a joke about the respective amounts of time that he and the Buddha Shaky-amuni had spent living ascetically: the Buddha had lived six years on the banks of Nairanjana River, and the Panchen Lama fourteen. He was alluding guardedly to the difficult years he had spent in Chinese prisons and then under house arrest. During his incarceration, he had written a letter every day to the authorities, denouncing the devastation they had inflicted on Tibet and asking that they treat the Tibetans with respect.

The next day, the Panchen Lama threw an official banquet in honor of Khyentse Rinpoche. Six months later, in January 1989, he died of a heart attack in his Tashi Lhunpo Monastery, in Shigatse, Tibet, at the age of fifty. Although no formal evidence was ever produced, many Tibetans believe that he was poisoned for having delivered a speech three days earlier in which he had roundly criticized Chinese policy and affirmed his loyalty to the Dalai Lama—a statement of position more than likely to have irked the Chinese government.[2]

The incarnation of the Panchen Lama was recognized in Tibet by a lama from his monastery, Chatral Rinpoche, and ratified by the Dalai Lama in 1995. The six-year-old child and his family were immediately kidnapped by the Chinese authorities, brought to Beijing, and held in an unknown location. The youngest political prisoner in the world has not been seen since, and nobody knows where he is.

Despite many pleas from the United Nations Committee on the Rights of the Child, various human rights agencies, and political figures, the Chinese government merely replies that the Panchen Lama is well and receiving a "good" education (that's what we're afraid of!), but that, "for his own security," he may not be visited. If he is still alive, he is now over thirty years old.

While Khyentse Rinpoche was in Beijing, the other members of his entourage and I went to Mount Emei, a few hours from Chengdu by car. As we did on our first visit to Tibet, we climbed to the top of the sacred mountain, some 10,000 feet above sea level. In 1988, there were a few Chinese Buddhist temples up there, one of which housed two highly venerated statues of the bodhisattva Samantabhadra. One, in the Tibetan style, was turned toward Tibet; the other, in the Chinese style, was oriented toward

China. Neither survived the Cultural Revolution. Sunrises at the summit of Mount Emei, which often emerges from an ocean of cloud to offer spectacular 360-degree views, are a unique experience. If you stand in a particular place with your back to the sun, your shadow projected onto the clouds below is encircled by a perfectly circular rainbow halo that pilgrims call "the Buddha's halo." We had made the ascent by car along a narrow road but decided to walk back down on the path used by pilgrims in the old days. What an adventure! The path comprises fifty thousand steps, each only about thirty inches wide. After a grueling nine-hour trek, we were barely able to put one foot in front of the other by the time we reached the bottom. For several days, my aching legs refused to tackle even the lowest step head-on; I had to take each one sideways.

Upon his return from Beijing, Khyentse Rinpoche and his now-reunited entourage took the road for Shechen Monastery, where, like the first time, a spectacular reception awaited him. Khyentse Rinpoche conferred teachings for a week, alternating with the young lamas, who were also in high demand among the students, who had come from every monastery in the province.

In Kham, eastern Tibet, the idea of a "private life" barely registers in the vocabulary, especially for spiritual teachers, who receive countless petitioners with diverse expectations: teachings, spiritual counsel, blessings, and so on. On brief visits like this one, those expectations can generate a serious crowd in their room, with a dozen people all pressing forward at the same time, not including the day's public events. Seeking to enjoy a few minutes of peace at the end of the day and in the early morning, the young lamas decided to go camping in a meadow located a ten-minute walk from the monastery. They did not count on Tibetan persistence. Most traditional tents do not use floor coverings, which leaves a gap at the bottom. When Dzongsar Khyentse Rinpoche awoke early next morning and sat up in his sleeping bag, he found fifteen pairs of eyes watching him closely—they belonged to the curious, who had lain down in the grass and stuck their heads under the hem of the tent so as not to miss a minute of the show. Khyentse Rinpoche, who had just been handed a bowl of water, ceremoniously retrieved a can of shaving cream—a product unknown in Tibet at the time—and in a few seconds covered his face in white foam. A collective "oh!" of astonishment rippled through the audience, who had never seen such a thing. It's no easy thing to dodge the zealous Khampas!

The following week, Khyentse Rinpoche returned to the valley of his birth, Denkhok, on the banks of the Drichu. There was still no motor road to Sakar, the village where he had been born, located in the Tibet Autonomous Region on the far side of the Drichu. As in 1985, the official arrangements for Khyentse Rinpoche's visit to eastern Tibet did not include authorization for him to cross that border. Yet again, therefore, he was unable to see his home village. The authorities did, however, grant exceptions to some members of his entourage. Rabjam Rinpoche, Tulku Pema Wangyal, two monks, and I were permitted to cross the river. In the old days, rudimentary boats had been used to reach the far bank; a bridge now spans the river. We then walked for two hours and over a small pass leading down to Sakar, a green valley shaped like an open lotus flower. At an elevation of over 10,000 feet, the land can still be cultivated. At the edge of barley and wheat fields, some fifty houses clustered around the ruins of a small monastery make up the peaceful village where Khyentse Rinpoche spent his childhood. It was here that, at the age of thirteen, he had resolved to leave the comforts of his family home for the austere simplicity of nearby caves and hermitages.

While Rabjam Rinpoche and a few others traveling with us had made the five-mile trip on horseback, Tulku Pema Wangyal and I chose to go on foot. We had to walk so quickly to keep up with the horses that I was on the verge of collapse by the time we got there. But no sooner had we arrived than Tulku Pema Wangyal, who seemed to have been infused with inexhaustible energy, shook me out of my torpor. He wanted to waste no time in undertaking the climb to the hermitage of Gothi, at the top of a hill that overlooks, on one side, the Sakar Valley and, on the other, the lowlands where the sacred waters of the Drichu flow. It was there, in a little temple-hermitage in the middle of a meadow, that the great scholar and hermit Mipham Rinpoche spent the final years of his life and blessed Khyentse Rinpoche at birth.

At dawn the next morning, Jamyang Lodrö, a villager who, in his youth, had sometimes shuttled provisions to Khyentse Rinpoche, served as guide on our pilgrimage to our teacher's retreats. In the middle of a dense forest, we followed the upstream course of a river that we had to cross several times, not without some danger. The "bridges" were made of tree trunks—sometimes just one!—thrown across the stream. We reached Karpo Nang, the "white grove" where Khyentse Rinpoche had built himself a little wooden hermitage where his mother visited him once a month. During his retreats, he lived inside a pine "meditation box," approximately four feet tall by thirty inches deep, in which he meditated day and night, sitting on a flat cushion and wrapped in a woolen cape, leaning against the back of the box. Some practitioners undertake long retreats in this manner, meditating, eating, and sleeping in such boxes so as to maintain the continuity of their practice and enter a state of awareness the moment they arise from sleep. The interior of the hermitage itself, also made of wood, measured about eight-by-eight feet. Khyentse Rinpoche often saw wolves from his one little window; they sometimes even came to rub themselves against the corners of his hermitage. The surroundings also abounded in deer and bharal—large Himalayan blue sheep—and it was even possible to spot leopards from time to time. Khyentse Rinpoche enjoyed feeding the wild birds, some of which allowed themselves to be tamed to the extent that they would perch on him. One such bird was given the name Tsultrim Gyatso, "Ocean of Discipline."

I absorbed the tranquil atmosphere of the place, unbroken by any disturbance—an ideal environment in which to allow spiritual practice to flow and flourish. I visualized my precious teacher Khyentse Rinpoche in retreat, united my mind with his, and opened myself to his blessings.

In the heart of the dark forest, an hour's walk from the white grove, a cliff-face opened out into the cave in which the Indian master Padampa Sangye meditated in the twelfth century. Khyentse Rinpoche lived there in retreat and described it thus:

My cave had a ladder but no door, and bears often came a-growling below. But they couldn't get in. Outside, the forest was teeming with foxes, martens, bears, and all sorts of birds. Leopards lived in the neighborhood, and once caught a little dog that kept me company. In the springtime, a cuckoo served as my alarm clock. As soon as I heard it, around three in the morning, I got up and began to meditate. At five o'clock, I revived the embers of the previous night's fire, which were still hot, and made tea in my sole pot without leaving my meditation box, simply leaning over the wooden partition. I had a lot of books. The cave was roomy—high enough for me to stand up in. Cool in the summer, it retained some heat in the winter. My older brother, Shedrup, lived in a nearby cabin with two monks who made the noonday meal.

Not far away, at the end of a small valley bisected by a stream, was the Tsamkhang Trak cave, embedded in a cliff and opening onto a small rocky ledge accessible by a steep path, where Khyentse Rinpoche spent seven consecutive years. His wife, Khandro Lhamo, and their first daughter, Chime Wangmo, who was born there, lived in a log cabin below the cliff, along with a few other practitioners, and visited him from time to time. In the tranquility of that haven, so conducive to contemplation, Khyentse Rinpoche composed many poems, spiritual instructions, prayers, and songs of realization. He wrote almost a thousand pages, which, unfortunately, were all lost when he was forced to flee Tibet.

Khyentse Rinpoche spent at least one winter alone in a cave, cut off from the rest of the world at an altitude of more than 14,000 feet. The cave nested in a rampart of the imposing rocky mountain known as Bahla, which dominates the Sakar Valley. He went up in the summer, with a few assistants bearing the provisions and fuel (dried yak dung) required for a stay of several months. Once the snow began to fall in late autumn or winter, no one could get up there or leave the mountain until springtime.

A few years later, in 2003, I was able to return in the company of two monks and of Raphaële, a long-standing student of Khyentse Rinpoche and a close friend who works with me on Karuna-Shechen's humanitarian projects in Tibet. After riding for several hours through flower-covered meadows and making a few stops for a cup of tea or a bowl of delicious yogurt in a nomad tent, we spent an hour climbing a steep slope strewn with scree that shifted and slid beneath our feet. Out of breath, we finally came to a rocky ledge, to the rear of which was a cave some twenty feet deep and ten feet high. Other than a few stones arranged as a hearth, on which Khyentse Rinpoche may have brewed his tea seventy years earlier, there was nothing to indicate that the cave had ever been inhabited. No wall protected the entrance, and the fact that a hermit had been able to spend several winters there, in temperatures hovering well below freezing, defied the imagination. Had Khyentse Rinpoche sealed the opening with a barrier of rocks when he lived there?

The cave looked out over a vast landscape. The view encompassed the little Sakar Valley, below to the left, and, beyond a low pass, the majestic Yangtse River flowed through the Denkhok valley. In the distance stretched the mountains and snowy peaks of the Tro Ziltrom range, which rise to almost 20,000 feet. Before such a magnificent vista, the mind easily merged with the immensity of the landscape and attuned itself to the deep silence, in intimate harmony with the lofty cliffs that overhung the valley—a silence occasionally broken by the hoarse croak of a great Tibetan raven or the sharp cries of a brace of eagles soaring through the blue.[3]

We stayed and meditated for a while, devotedly evoking the memory of Khyentse Rinpoche. Then we turned back to the valley, passing nomads busily gathering their yaks for the evening milking. We returned to Sakar exhausted but nourished by precious memories, which continue to live in our hearts.

For the return trip from Sakar to Denkhok, we decided to cross the river and take a car, instead of walking. We boarded a raft made of large pine trunks lashed to one another. The two boatmen rowed with all their might, but the current was so powerful we inexorably began to drift. On top of that, a sandstorm kicked up, turning our crossing into a somewhat alarming adventure. We recited our mantras vigorously, and twenty minutes later we disembarked safe and sound on the far bank, more than half a mile downstream. A car brought us back to Denkhok.

Having spent a week in Denkhok and met with every faithful in the valley who had wanted to meet him, Khyentse Rinpoche returned to Shechen. He spent a month conferring teachings and participating in ceremonies and in the annual sacred dance festival.

For this second visit, Khyentse Rinpoche had specifically asked to be allowed to return to Dzongsar, the monastery of his teacher Dzongsar Khyentse Chökyi Lodrö, where he had lived for many years. He was particularly keen to make this visit because he wanted the Dzongsar Valley faithful to meet the incarnation of Dzongsar Khyentse Chökyi Lodrö, who was traveling with him. He therefore suggested that the young lama accompany him. Such a meeting would be a major event for the inhabitants of the region.

There was no way to get there by car, and it would take three days to reach Dzongsar by foot. The local authorities had made sure that the trail was serviceable and had inspected and reinforced the twenty-odd little bridges that we would use to cross the streams along the way.

After a night spent in the Derge Prefecture, we were dropped off at the foot of a mountain. A major expedition was in store for us. First, it took us all morning to reach the Gosey La pass, at an elevation of more than 16,000 feet. The name of the pass means "white hair," because it is said that if you have dark hair at the start of the climb, it will be white by the time you reach the top! Khyentse Rinpoche traveled in a palanquin carried by a dozen people. All along the way, villagers and nomads jostled to have their turn in fifteen-minute shifts. It was a great honor to porter Khyentse Rinpoche. Although their total burden easily weighed 350 pounds, they walked so fast that, even with no baggage, those of us who had come from India had trouble keeping up.

Near the summit, we came to a meadow where a little tent had been set up by the side of the road by members of the local Dilgo family—Khyentse Rinpoche's own clan. We took a welcome pause to rest and refuel. Some twenty family members of all ages—among whom only the oldest had ever met Khyentse Rinpoche—enjoyed a few minutes in his presence before saying goodbye, almost certainly forever.

Despite his age, seventy-eight, and the primitive and bumpy means of transportation, Khyentse Rinpoche never appeared to be tired by the travel. He wore a sheepskin jacket thrown over his naked shoulders—as usual, he remained bare-chested even at high altitudes. He was happy to see the sacred landscapes and places of his childhood again. At the Gosey La pass, the group stopped to rest and enjoy the scenery—a magnificent vista of hills and mountains rising in tiers into the bluish light as far as the eye could see. The men broke out into joyful cries of *Kihi hi! So so! Lha gyalo!* ("May the gods be victorious!")—a wish Tibetans always express when crossing a mountain pass.

On the far side, a vast landscape of mountain pastures, rocky cliffs and snowcapped peaks came into view. Far down in a valley, the brown dot of Palpung Monastery was just barely visible. After descending a gentle slope for two hours, we set up camp midway for the night. Monks had come up from the monastery to meet us and erected several large tents. As we approached Palpung the next morning, a double rainbow appeared above the monastery's roofs.

On the third day after leaving Palpung, we had to climb another mountain pass, not as high as the others. This one opened out on to wide pastureland on a gentle slope. Suddenly, we came upon no fewer than one thousand horsemen dressed in their ceremonial outfits, standing at the sides of their horses with reins in hand. They had come from the nearby Dzongsar Valley to greet Dilgo Khyentse Rinpoche, and most especially Dzongsar Khyentse Rinpoche, the incarnation of their revered and treasured Dzongsar Khyentse Chökyi Lodrö.

Led by this long cavalcade of horsemen, we descended into the valley, Khyentse Rinpoche borne as ever in his palanquin while the young lamas rode horses caparisoned in brocade. Throughout the valley, the villagers had, in their customary way, lit fires on which they piled juniper branches that sent long swirls of aromatic white smoke billowing skyward.

The entire population awaited us when we reached the valley. They formed a long procession that led us up the winding road to the promontory on which the great Dzongsar Monastery had been built. Sadly, except for a few buildings, all that remained of it was ruins. Before its destruction in 1958, Dzongsar Monastery had been a veritable "monastic village," comprising twenty-three temples, more than a hundred residences for the monks, and many retreat centers.

Before beginning the final stretch to the monastery entrance, everyone raised their eyes to the sky. A glowing halo had formed a ring around the sun, a sign that the Tibetans consider to be highly auspicious. We followed the alleys that crisscross the enormous complex, most of it devastated, to one of the buildings that had survived. This was the former residence of Jamyang Khyentse Wangpo, a teacher who had had a major following in the nineteenth century and made an important contribution to preserving

Tibetan Buddhism at a time when the transmissions of many teachers were in danger of being broken. Dilgo Khyentse Rinpoche and the young Dzongsar Khyentse Rinpoche were both considered to be incarnations of Jamyang Khyentse Wangpo; the first was that of his enlightened mind aspect and the second was that of his body aspect. A great spiritual teacher may sometimes "reincarnate" in the human form of three people, or *tulkus*, each expressing three fundamental aspects of the late teacher: the body, the speech, and the mind.

We stayed in Dzongsar for just under a week. While Khyentse Rinpoche conferred empowerments and teachings on the monks and the people, Tulku Pema Wangyal and a few more of us went on pilgrimages almost every day to the holy places of the region—caves, hermitages, and sacred lakes—guided by monks or villagers sent by Lodrö Puntsok, one of the most amazing people in the Dzongsar Valley. A well-known Tibetan physician, he had spearheaded the rebirth of the Dzongsar Valley and, a few years later, directed the reconstruction of the monastery.

The very day after our arrival, we set out on a twelve-hour hike. We first climbed the steep slope behind the monastery to reach the Khyungdrak caves, "Garuda Rock." We then spent the next hour zigzagging up a hillside bristling with boulders and a few junipers, which can still grow at 13,000 feet. We began to see our first high-altitude flowers, such as the meconopsis. The Tibetans call it *gaochung*, "little reliquary," because of its lovely yellow flower, a poppywort with delicate petals that drape down its long stem like a hanging reliquary. A pair of ravens, a species that has grown extremely rare in Europe (they are twice the size of a common crow) touched down beside us for a few moments then flew away in a concert of deep and resounding caws that echoed off the cliffs. A lammergeyer, its head blazing orange, soared overhead.

Coming to a pass that marked the high point of our ascent, we took in the view of mountain ranges in every direction, the most distant of which blended into the blue of the sky. We then made a sidelong crossing of fields of scree in which rocks of all sizes alternated in jumbled heaps with gleaming drifts of broken slate that shifted beneath our feet, threatening to send us tumbling downhill. Here and there sprouted strange succulents with violet flowers and hairy leaves, patches of emerald-green moss bespeckled with tiny white flowers, and a few rare medicinal plants.

When we neared 16,000 feet, our steps grew heavy and our breathing labored. After an hour of this perilous trekking, we finally reached the entrance to the ring of hills at the foot of which lies "Lion's Roar Turquoise Lake," Seng-ngur Yutsho.

They say that the lake is the home of a *naga*, a semi-divine half man–half snake being that has appeared at its surface several times during the visits of great masters of the past. In sunny weather, the water takes on a turquoise blue color, which may change to pale green or even black if the sky clouds over. The basin is formed of ragged arêtes whose rockslides tumble down into the lake. To the southeast, a rocky dam lined with narrow meadows holds back the water, which overflows into the valleys. A path allows pilgrims to circle the lake while reciting prayers and mantras.

At the far end of the basin, three tiny hermitages built of flat rocks sit on an overhanging ledge sixty feet above the lake. They are so small that there is just enough room for one person to sit inside. Many sages have undertaken retreats in these lofty sacred places, including Jamyang Khyentse Wangpo. Before he left, Lodrö Puntsok told us of a miracle that once took place here. In November 1966, Jamyang Khyentse Wangpo visited the lake in the company of another visionary master, Chogyur Lingpa, the king of Derge, and one hundred adepts. The surface of the lake was frozen over except at its center, where the ice was open like a window around which they formed a circle. That is where the *naga*, the genie of the lake, offered Chogyur Lingpa a gold reliquary containing precious teachings from Padmasambhava.

A few pilgrims had gathered on the flat ground at the entrance to the lake to make an offering of incense. During such an offering, they gaze into the juniper smoke and visualize flowers, jewels, food, and perfumes presented to the buddhas and spirits of the place, praying for beings, in all their infinitude, to be delivered from suffering and enjoy peace and prosperity.

But we could not linger. We hiked down into a long valley that led us, an hour later, to the hermitage of Karmo Taktsang, "The White Tigress Lair." This hermitage consists of a temple surrounded by ten cells clinging to a low cliff deep in the forest. It was here that, among others, the great sage and scholar Mipham Rinpoche spent thirteen years in solitary retreat. He wrote many contemplative tracts here, including the following extract:

When waves of thought
Disturb the mind's serenity
No more than clouds alter the sky,
That is "the liberation of thoughts in their true nature."

A dozen practitioners undertook five-year retreats here. In most retreat centers, the main events of the day—awakening, the start and end times for practice sessions, and bedtime—are marked by a monk with a long blast of a conch shell, a gentle sound that carries far. The same is done at our retreat center in Namo Buddha, where I hear the conch every morning at 4 a.m. (although some retreatants wake up by themselves even earlier). A gong is sometimes used instead. But at Karmo Taktsang, a modest little retreat center, it is a retreatant himself who calls out the hour with a song, beginning softly and gradually growing louder. This is the "Calling the guru from afar," which begins with the words *Lama Khyenno!* ("Teacher, think of me!"), an invocation asking the spiritual teacher to direct his mind and compassion to the student. The monk chants these two words in imitation of the tones of a gong being struck: three distinct strikes, then a certain number of faster strikes in decrescendo, ending with three stronger and more widely spaced strikes. The monk sings, "Lama Khyen . . . Lama Khyen . . . Lama Khyen . . . Lama Khyen, Khyen, Khyen, Khyen, Khyen . . . Lama Khyenno, Lama Khyenno, Lama Khyenno!" thereby endowing the awakening with devotion to the teacher from the very first moment.

Two or three monks also practice here without undertaking the five-year closed retreat. They greet passing pilgrims and tend to the center's material needs. Among other things, they showed us the flat rock on which Mipham Rinpoche enjoyed sitting when meditating outside his hermitage or teaching his students. They offered us a snack, with piping hot cups of reinvigorating salted butter tea. We had to complete the final hour of our descent to the main road on the double in order to reach the monastery before nightfall. Ultimately, having left Dzongsar at dawn, we did not get back until dark, drained yet agog at all we had seen and rich in blessings.

The next morning, we grabbed our pilgrim's staffs and climbed two full hours through flowering meadows to the path leading to Pema Shelpuk, the "Lotus Crystal Cave," one of the most venerated pilgrimage sites in the Dzongsar Valley. The cave, whose vault is covered in rock crystal, is at the center of a huge, sugar-loaf rock in the middle of a green ring of hills. Here, in winter 1856, the two visionary masters Chogyur Lingpa and Jamyang Khyentse Wangpo discovered the spiritual treasury known as *The Three Classes of the Great Perfection*, which contains profound teachings on how to recognize the ultimate nature of mind.[4]

On day three of our wanderings, we made a longer pilgrimage, over the course of forty-eight hours, passing first through Terlung Dilgo, the valley where Jamyang Khyentse was born, and then to the impressive cluster of caves at Dzongshö Deshek Dupa, where Jamgön Kongtrül assembled the sixty volumes of the original edition of *The Treasury of Precious Termas*, the *Rinchen Terdzö*. Tulku Pema Wangyal and I had fallen into the habit of making all these pilgrimages on foot so that we, rather than the horses, could take credit for the journey, and not to inflict on them unnecessary hardships. But we were warned this time that if we did not ride, it would be impossible to reach Dzongshö before nightfall. We set out as a group, accompanied by Khyentse Rinpoche and Rabjam Rinpoche, for once.

When we reached Terlung, a hamlet of a dozen rammed-earth cottages on the banks of a little river, we visited the very modest home where Jamyang Khyentse Wangpo was born. His little room was preserved just as it had been. Lit by two small windows, it contained an altar of dark wood, housing a Buddha statue and a few books and a chest-table set before a square meditation box measuring about four feet on the sides and eighteen inches high, in which Khyentse Wangpo had sat day and night. The heavy cape in which he had swathed himself, lined with long strands of wool, was arranged in the box in such a way as to suggest a person sitting—an evocative intimation of the master who had worn it. After resting for a few minutes, we hurried on our way.

Not until twilight did we reach the imposing group of rocky bluffs containing the Dzongshö caves. The cave where Jamgön Kongtrül had lived was one of the more spacious ones, about twenty feet deep by thirteen high, and furnished in the most rudimentary fashion. There was an altar, low pallets for the two or three monks who might be living there at any given moment, and an earthen hearth located near one of the two windows that had been cut into the stone wall that enclosed the cave's mouth and protected it from intemperate weather. Here Jamgön Kongtrül had lived, practiced, and worked with the scholars who had joined him to collect and edit all the texts that were eventually incorporated into the *Rinchen Terdzö*. We were ushered in and invited to spend the night. The monks had certainly not been expecting a visit from Dzongsar Khyentse Rinpoche and Rabjam Rinpoche, and they scurried about to accommodate them as best as they could and prepare a soup of fresh, handmade noodles, which was very welcome and most fortifying.

The next morning, we toured the eight other caves of the Dzongshö massif, each associated with a particular wisdom deity and available to the hermits who occasionally come to undertake retreats.

As we approached Dzongsar on our return trip, my horse found himself in familiar territory and decided that the sooner he made it home, the better it would be for him. He set off at full tilt, while I, with my minimal skills as a novice rider, was unable to slow him down. Everybody had a good laugh at my look of helpless distress aboard the fiery steed, vainly yanking at the reins while calling for help. One of the Khampa horsemen who were escorting us managed to catch up to me at full gallop, grab my horse's bridle, and bring him to a halt.

The time had come to leave the beautiful Dzongsar Valley and head home. We returned to Chengdu and, from there, flew on to Delhi and Bhutan, where Khyentse Rinpoche resumed his good works.

This second journey to Tibet reinforced the strong sense of affinity I felt for Kham, the eastern part of Greater Tibet, higher and greener than the other regions. So many spiritual masters had taught there! And there are so many eminently inspiring places there which lead directly to the mind's enlightenment! If the government were to relax its iron grip a little and authorize longer visits, I would certainly move there.

31

TWO SCHOLARS

In India, I serve as a guide to the great scholar Khenpo Wanglo through the holy places of Buddhism in his encounter with the Dalai Lama. In Tibet, I grow close to another great scholar, Khenpo Pema Wangyal, who presents me with an amazing gift.

KHENPO WANGLO

In the winter of 1988–1989, Khyentse Rinpoche returned to Bodhgaya to consecrate a new Bhutanese temple. It was on that occasion that he asked me to escort a great scholar from Tibet, Khenpo Wanglo.[1] My job was to serve as his guide to the most important Buddhist holy places of India, and to assist him in a scheduled meeting with His Holiness the Dalai Lama in Dharamshala.

On Khyentse Rinpoche's two visits to Tibet, in 1985 and 1988, a group of six renowned elderly scholars from Gemang Monastery traveled to Shechen Monastery to meet with Khyentse Rinpoche, whom they had known well before the invasion of Tibet.[2] Both times, their reunions were joyful. On the second trip, Khyentse Rinpoche invited them—if they were able to obtain permission to travel outside of China—to visit him in Nepal, which they did in the winter of 1988. Among them was Khenpo Wanglo, a learned sage with a mischievous glint in his eye, a craggy face, and a prominent nose (a rare trait in Tibet), who decided to spend a few months with Khyentse Rinpoche and to follow him to India and Bhutan, to the latter's great pleasure.

In the company of Khenpo Wanglo and three of his monks, we began by visiting Nalanda University, thirty miles from Bodhgaya. Nalanda was established in the fifth century, during the Gupta dynasty (which reigned from the fourth to the sixth centuries BCE). The red-brick complex was once entirely decorated with paintings and sculptures of a level of sophistication unequalled in the Buddhist world. Today, its ruins are spread out over thirty-five acres. Two hundred and fifty years before the Christian era, the Emperor Ashoka had had an enormous stupa built here in memory of Shariputra, one of the Buddha Shakyamuni's chief disciples. The crumbling stupa is today the most imposing remnant of Nalanda. India's most famous Buddhist scholars (the *panditas*), including Nagarjuna, Aryadeva, Chandrakirti, and Shantideva, taught here. At the pinnacle of its glory from the sixth to the eleventh centuries, Nalanda counted ten thousand students and two thousand professors. The university was considered to be an architectural masterpiece, comprising eight building complexes, ten temples, and numerous meditation and study halls. It was surrounded by parks and lakes. The library, known as Dharma Gunj (Mountain of Truth) or Dharmaganja (Treasury of Truth), was renowned throughout Asia for its hundreds of thousands of books. It is said that the terrible fire that destroyed it, set by Muslim invaders led by the Turk Bakhtiyar Khalji in 1203, lasted several months.[3]

The fourteenth Dalai Lama often recalls that Tibetan Buddhism falls within the direct line of the Nalanda tradition and that its current generation of brilliant scholars are the guardians of Nalanda's living tradition. It was very moving to see Khenpo Wanglo, an eminent twentieth-century scholar, sitting among the ruins of what was once the polestar of Buddhist philosophy and one of the premier universities of the world.

Back in Bodhgaya, we visited the Silwe Tsal charnel ground, the "cool grove" where Padmasambhava and other great realized beings engaged in meditation long ago. After crossing the Naranjana River, we trekked a few more miles across a sandy plain. Like Khyentse Rinpoche, Khenpo Wanglo had to lean on the shoulders of two of his monks; his advanced age made it difficult for him to walk long distances. When we reached the charnel ground, which contained a stupa, he said a few prayers then launched into the practice of *chöd* (literally, "cutting through"), which seeks to sever our attachment to our bodies, our egos, and to the phenomenal world at its roots. To that end, practitioners visualize their bodies chopped into bits by a celestial *dakini* and transformed into an ambrosia that they offer to all buddhas, all beings, the protectors of enlightenment (the Dharma), and all those to whom they owe a karmic debt. The yogis who perform this ritual in cemeteries or other remote locations chant a particularly captivating melody, accompanied by a drum. In some traditions, the meditator may even stand up and dance. When he reached that point in the ritual, Khenpo Wanglo was transformed into a vigorous young man, dancing as he circled the stupa and executing wide leaps at regular intervals while beating on his drum. At least fifty children from the village gathered and enjoyed this unusual spectacle, laughing heartily. When he has completed the sequence of leaps, the practitioner emits three powerful cries (*Phet!*) that reverberate like thunderclaps. When Khenpo cried out with all his might, the terrified children scattered like sparrows and ran back to their village.

Khenpo Wanglo had heard that you can catch all sorts of diseases in India. He had therefore decided that he would eat nothing throughout his entire stay except for what he had brought with him from Tibet: a big sack of *tsampa* (roasted barley flour), desiccated cheese powder, and partially rancid butter. That was his diet during our entire pilgrimage. The matter of drinks was more complicated, however. When we were on the train from Gaya to Delhi—almost fifteen hours of travel—Khenpo asked for hot water. The thermos we had filled up at 4 a.m. before boarding the train was now empty. I explained to Khenpo that we could order tea from the vendors who passed through the cars, but that unfortunately there was no hot water because their big aluminum kettles were already filled with sweetened, milky tea when they got on the train. After an hour or two, Khenpo finally agreed to have a cup of tea. As is often the case on Indian trains, it was served in a little cup of sun-dried clay. It's a very hygienic custom because the cups are used only once—after you have finished your tea, you throw them out the window, where they smash on the ballast and return to their original state in the course of time. Khenpo was unaware of this custom and, once he'd finished his tea, he clung tenaciously to his little clay cup. The Indian passengers who shared our third-class compartment on an open corridor tried to make him understand with gestures that he could discard it out the window. Khenpo smiled, thinking that the people from around there had some very odd habits, then handed me the cup to throw away. An hour later, another tea vendor passed by and Khenpo, who was beginning to develop a taste for Indian tea, asked for another cup. This time the tea was served in a real cup with a saucer. Having drained it, Khenpo made ready to throw it out the window. The Indians raised their arms to the sky and cried out, "No, no, we don't throw those cups away!" Khenpo smiled again and returned it to me. "These Indians don't know what they want," he seemed to be thinking.

A little later, Khenpo took out the large wooden bowl he used every day for his meals, filled it with *tsampa* meal, and added a dab of butter. Then, while he waited for hot tea to be found to mix with the *tsampa*, he rested his elbow on the sill of the open window. The hand in which he held his bowl stuck out the window. A moment later, we heard protests rise up from the compartments behind us—the draft produced by the speeding train had emptied the bowl of half its contents, which had spattered the downwind passengers with *tsampa* through the open windows!

We reached Dharamshala at last, bearing a letter from Khyentse Rinpoche to the Dalai Lama, introducing Khenpo Wanglo and asking that he be given an audience. The Dalai Lama was thrilled to meet the respected scholar and spent almost an hour with him. He asked him many questions about the situation in Tibet and the traditions of Gemang Monastery, and in particular about one observance that was unique to that monastery and consisted of a ten-day teaching of the Guhyagarbha Tantra on the basis of the six-hundred-page commentary written by Gyalwa Longchenpa, which the teacher was required to recite by heart as he explicated it. The Dalai Lama was a little surprised that the Gemang scholars memorized the commentary but not the root text of the tantra, which was about fifty pages long.[4] Indeed, in all other philosophical colleges, it is always the root texts that the student must learn by heart before the study masters provide explications based on the commentaries.

While the Dalai Lama could readily understand everything Khenpo Wanglo said, despite the idiosyncrasies of his Dzachuka dialect, Khenpo did not always fully grasp the words of the Dalai Lama, who spoke the purer and more canonical language of Lhasa. He sometimes turned to me to clarify the meaning of these words, so I found myself in the odd situation of being a French monk interpreting for two of the greatest scholars of Tibet in their own language!

A different language problem arose one day between Khyentse Rinpoche and Khenpo Wanglo; although they were both from the same region of Tibet, one had lived in Nepal and Bhutan for thirty years, while the other was newly arrived from the Land of Snows. At Khyentse Rinpoche's request, Khenpo Wanglo gave a ten-day teaching in Shechen, Nepal, of the commentary known as "Dispelling Darkness in the Ten Directions"— the same six-hundred-page commentary of which he had spoken with the Dalai Lama. When Khenpo Wanglo had made the pilgrimage to Nalanda, in India, he had learned that Sunday is a statutory day off, which translates into Hindi as *chutti*. Tibetan refugees in India and Nepal use the same word, *chutti*, to designate holidays or vacations, a notion that is almost unknown in Tibetan culture. However, in the Dzachuka dialect spoken by Khenpo Wanglo, the word *chötri*, meaning "explanation of the Dharma," is pronounced almost exactly like *chutti*. One Saturday in Nepal, as Khyentse Rinpoche and Khenpo Wanglo chatted quietly, Khenpo mentioned that a teaching, *chötri*, would take place the next day. To which Khyentse Rinpoche replied, "No need for a day off (*chutti*)," thinking that Khenpo Wanglo felt obligated to respect the Indian custom of resting on Sundays. Somewhat taken aback, Khenpo Wanglo retorted, "Yes indeed! There surely will be a teaching tomorrow." Khyentse Rinpoche, who still thought they were talking about holidays, appeared a little put out. Luckily, Tsewang Lhundrup and I had understood that they were talking about two different things, and we cleared up the misunderstanding, in the literal sense of the word.

In Nepal, Khenpo was also accompanied by a sixteen-year-old *tulku* from Gemang who had recently finished memorizing Longchenpa's six-hundred-page commentary. To celebrate this accomplishment by making an offering to Khyentse Rinpoche, Khenpo proposed that the young *tulku* recite the text in one go in his presence. This prodigious recitation took place in Khyentse Rinpoche's little bedroom. Khenpo Wanglo and a few of us sat on the rug in a circle around Rinpoche, who was saying his prayers on his bed, while over the next six hours (with one brief interruption) the young *tulku* recited the six hundred pages of the text by heart in a sustained and melodious tone, without once hesitating or making a mistake (a monk followed along in the text at the same time). I marveled not only at the capacity of the human mind to perfectly retain such a rich and complex amalgam of information, but also at the young man's perseverance in bringing this apprenticeship to a successful conclusion. When he was done, Khyentse Rinpoche congratulated him warmly and draped a ceremonial white silk scarf around his neck.

In late 1988, Khyentse Rinpoche invited Khenpo Wanglo to spend several months in Bhutan to undertake a pilgrimage and offer teachings to Rabjam Rinpoche; Jigme Khyentse Rinpoche, the youngest son of Kangyur Rinpoche; Namkhai Nyingpo; and a few other *tulkus*. That is how Khenpo came to spend two months giving daily teachings of *The Treasury of Precious Qualities* and other texts. Khenpo immediately appreciated Jigme Khyentse Rinpoche's qualities and extraordinary intelligence. One day, he said to him, "If you come with me when I return to Tibet, you could acquire an excellent knowledge of the texts." Jigme Khyentse Rinpoche, who was very fond of Khenpo Wanglo, was intrigued by the possibility. "How much time would I have to stay there?" he asked. It's no small thing to go live far from one's family, in the highly austere conditions of the Gemang Monastery, 14,000 feet above sea level. "Oh, thirty years should do it," Khenpo Wanglo replied laconically. A life's work.

In 1969, Bhutan was going through a troubled period following the assassination of the Queen Mother's oldest brother. Khyentse Rinpoche advised her to erect an immense statue of Padmasambhava in Kyichu Temple, in Paro, to ensure peace in the country. Once a year for twenty-three years in a row, Khyentse Rinpoche led a *drupchen*, a long ceremony performed day and night over the course of a week. The Queen Mother attended from the first day to the last. She spent several in the temple, sitting on a brocade-upholstered sofa pushed up against a wall in the little temple. Rabjam Rinpoche and some thirty monks from Trongsar Monastery performed the ceremony. The Queen Mother often invited guests, some of whom had come from far away, to sit at her side. Khenpo Wanglo did not participate in the ceremony, but Khyentse Rinpoche had introduced that great scholar from Tibet to the Queen Mother. One day, she asked him to sit with her for an afternoon. Rabjam Rinpoche had prepared Khenpo by telling him that, in the normal course of events, you were allowed to respond to the Queen Mother if she engaged you in conversation, but that it was customary to keep quiet when she was praying or sitting silently. When speaking to her, decorum required you to lightly bow your head as a sign of respect. The Queen Mother, who spoke Tibetan, asked Khenpo what he thought of Bhutan. Generally, guests would wax extravagant in their praise for that beautiful country, which is incontestably endowed with qualities unique in the world. In eastern Tibet, when you wish to indicate how you feel about something, it is customary to raise the index finger to signify "excellent," the middle finger to mean "average," and the little finger to express a negative opinion. As for Khenpo, having little experience with diplomatic ways and speech, he expressed his sincere conviction that Bhutan was "average." Recalling Rabjam Rinpoche's advice, he bowed lower than necessary, raised his hands to shoulder height and offered the Queen Mother his two superb middle fingers. Rabjam Rinpoche, horrified and totally helpless, could only watch the scene from his throne. With supreme courtesy, the Queen Mother continued chatting with Khenpo Wanglo as if it were nothing. Tea and delicacies were served, and Khenpo took his leave. That night, Rabjam Rinpoche respectfully explained to Khenpo Wanglo what that gesture means in the modern world. "Ah, so that's why my Indian students always burst into laughter when I make it!" Khenpo remarked.

KHENPO PEMA WANGYAL

As great a scholar and practitioner as it has been given me to meet, Khenpo Pema Wangyal ought to have shared the fate of his unfortunate companions upon the arrival of the Chinese invaders in 1959. He owed his freedom to a condition from which he had always suffered: a skin disease that had temporarily flared up, probably owing to the circumstances, which had hit him hard. The Chinese thought he had leprosy and ordered him to get lost. Khenpo was therefore not imprisoned like the other monks and clerics of Gemang. During the ten worst years of the repression, he lived alone, in retreat, in a little hermitage on a mountainside, just below the spot where Patrul Rinpoche's cremation took place in the nineteenth century. Khenpo had studied with a direct student of Patrul Rinpoche, Khenpo Kunpal. As a result, he told me many stories about Patrul that I included in *Enlightened Vagabond*. The valley nomads brought him provisions from time to time. When the political situation eased a little, he returned to Gemang Monastery, resumed teaching, and became the main *khenpo* of Gemang.

Every time I visited eastern Tibet, I spent a few days at Gemang with Khenpo Pema Wangyal and a younger *khenpo*, Khenpo Donnyi, who had come from India with Khenpo Wanglo and now manages the monastery. Khenpo Pema Wangyal had adopted the habit, whenever I was in his presence, of looking at me sidelong and playfully asking the monk who served him: "Who's this guy? Don't know him." Then, with a broad smile, he would touch his head to mine. He always showed me great kindness and gave me precious teachings on the nature of mind. On a visit to Gemang, he once asked me,

"So, you understand what it is, this nature of mind?"[5]

"Occasionally," I replied, not wanting to boast of understanding it fully, while still admitting that I had a vague idea.

"Strange, strange!" Khenpo exclaimed. "How can someone understand the nature of mind occasionally? Either you understand it or you don't."

He burst out laughing.

Khenpo Pema Wangyal also came to Nepal several times to stay with Khyentse Rinpoche. On one of his visits, he was accompanied by another Gemang *khenpo*, Yeshe Gyatso, also a great scholar. They were both sitting on a rug before Khyentse Rinpoche and, in the course of their conversation, the latter said, "While you're at Shechen, be so kind as to transmit some teachings to the philosophical college students." Khenpo Pema Wangyal replied, "But I know nothing!" Then, pointing at his colleague, he added, "And he knows nothing too!" Khenpo Yeshe Gyatso shook his head in agreement. Two eminent scholars, as humble as they were immensely learned.

In Gemang, there were some engraved woodblocks, which had escaped destruction in the Cultural Revolution, of a limpid commentary in a pair of seven-hundred-page volumes written by the famous scholar Khenpo Yonten Gyatso upon Jigme Lingpa's *The Treasury of Precious Qualities*. This was the very text that Khyentse Rinpoche had taught Rabjam Rinpoche and me every day for a year in 1981. I had been able to acquire a copy of the text printed in situ in Tibet, and I knew that Khenpo Wanglo, who was the nephew of Yonten Gyatso, had transcribed, by hand between the lines, the copious explanations delivered orally by his beloved teacher Khenpo Thubga (a student of Yonten Gyatso) when he was teaching this text. Khenpo Wanglo had passed away in 1999.

On a trip to Kham, I had asked Khenpo Pema Wangyal to request that a monk from the monastery transcribe these notes in my copy so that we could duplicate them digitally and publish them in India. I humbly renewed my request the following year. When I accompanied Rabjam Rinpoche on a journey to Kham in 2002, Khenpo Pema Wangyal came to Shechen Monastery to meet him. After having talked with Rabjam Rinpoche, he turned to me, called to one of his monks, and handed me two hefty volumes, about eighteen inches long apiece, printed on Tibetan paper with all the notes beautifully written out by hand. He told me, "This is Khenpo Wanglo's personal copy, with the notes inscribed by his own hand when he was studying with the great Khenpo Thubga." He added impishly: "Will that do?"

I was overwhelmed with gratitude to receive such a precious work.

When I last saw Khenpo Pema Wangyal in 2017, I cried profusely when it was time to leave, as if I had a premonition that I was seeing him for the last time. I was not permitted to return to China in 2018, and Khenpo left this world in April 2019, at the age of ninety. He will always hold a special place in my heart.

32

EXILE IN DARJEELING

As a result of unfortunate rumors about my photographic activities, I am exiled from Bhutan and separated from Dilgo Khyentse Rinpoche. I spend six months in retreat at Kangyur Rinpoche's monastery in Darjeeling. I receive precious letters from my master.

On October 31, 1988, the fourth king of Bhutan, Jigme Singye Wangchuk, married four sisters by whom he already had eight children. A sumptuous ceremony was held in Punakha Dzong—a building that is half monastery, half fortress—in the presence of every dignitary of the kingdom, dressed in their finest regalia, and the entire royal family. Deep in the Chakrasamvara Temple, where Khyentse Rinpoche led ten days of ceremonies every year, the king sat on a splendid throne covered in gold leaf. To his right, on smaller yet equally magnificent thrones, were the Je Khenpo—the chief religious authority of Bhutan, whose rank is equal to that of the king—and two queens. To his left were Dilgo Khyentse Rinpoche and the two other queens. They had arrived in a long procession, preceded by dancers and musicians. Ceremonies to enthrone the queens were held all morning. The atmosphere and decorum made it feel like something out of centuries long past. Every indication of the culture and mores of the twentieth century had totally vanished. In my capacity as Khyentse Rinpoche's attendant, I was the only foreigner present. At one point, the Queen Mother called me over and gave me her little camera, asking me to take a few pictures. No other photographer was present at the ceremony. It occurred to me that if I wanted to best fulfill the Queen Mother's wishes and get high-quality images, I would do well to also take a few pictures with my Nikon FM2, with which I had documented Khyentse Rinpoche's life for many years.

A few days later, in Thimphu, the capital, a second, more sober, affair was organized for the ambassadors, some guests from abroad, and a few journalists. Neither Khyentse Rinpoche nor his entourage were present at this event. Photos of this public marriage wedding appeared in the international press, including *Newsweek*, which showed the king sitting on a sofa, surrounded by his four queens, a setting that had nothing in common with the magnificent ceremonies in Punakha.

Back in Nepal, I sent my diapositives to be developed by Kodak in Bombay, and they were returned to me by mail at Shechen Monastery. I planned to present them to the Queen Mother in person on my return to Bhutan a few months later. But in the meantime, a rumor was circulating in the court that I had sold my photos to the foreign press. The government was furious with me. I sent an explanatory letter along with my slides, believing that the misunderstanding would soon be resolved. But nothing doing. I was banned from the country until further notice. Khyentse Rinpoche interceded on my behalf, but in vain. I was now seen as a duplicitous weasel of the worst sort. The Queen Mother had always treated me with the greatest kindness, but they convinced her that I had betrayed her trust.

Faced with this situation, Khyentse Rinpoche's first idea was to send me to study at the Dzongsar philosophical college, in Himachal Pradesh, in northwestern India. But on waking up one morning, he told me that it would be better for me to go on retreat in Darjeeling, at the monastery where I had spent so many years near Kangyur Rinpoche. He would let me know as soon as he left Bhutan.

Khyentse Rinpoche's wife speculated about the schemers who could have impugned me for no reason, but I preferred to preserve my inner peace. What use would it be to nurse suspicions and animosity? It would be better to use this obstacle as an opportunity to deepen my practice and my devotion to my teachers. Why should I be upset? I had done nothing wrong, and I recalled the Taoist adage: "Favor and disgrace are equally surprising." Of course, I was sorry not to be in Bhutan with Khyentse Rinpoche and to be separated from him for several months, but I would use this time to immerse myself in a contemplative retreat.

Upon reflection, I remain convinced that it is far more comfortable to know that you are blameless and to be at peace with yourself, even if the most derogatory things are being said about you, than to be heaped with praise when you know deep down that you have behaved badly. I feel very lucky to have avoided giving in to bitterness and resentment at the time.

In July 1989, when Khyentse Rinpoche left Nepal, where we had spent the winter, for Bhutan, I headed for Orgyen Kunzang Chökhorling, the monastery of my teacher Kangyur Rinpoche, in Darjeeling. I was welcomed with open arms by Kugno Nyima Sangpo, a very warmhearted old monk with whom I was close. He had also been a dignitary in the Tibetan administration before the Chinese invasion, as well as a student of Kangyur Rinpoche in Tibet. Pema Wangyal Rinpoche, who now lived with his family in France, had left him in charge of the monastery. That first week, I spent some moving moments of recollection in Kangyur Rinpoche's room and enjoyed Kugno Nyima Sangpo's company. I also visited with a few old friends in the little town of Darjeeling, in particular Durga and Mohan Das Pradhan, who owned the town's biggest photo shop. When I had lived in Darjeeling with Kangyur Rinpoche, from 1967 to 1975, whenever I went into town, I always made sure to stop in at their studio, whose walls were covered in large pictures of Himalayan peaks shot in black and white and then painted by hand by local artists. Color photography was prohibitively expensive back then. They owned a collection of precious snapshots of lamas who had stayed in Darjeeling, as well as a picture of the Dalai Lama they had taken in 1959, shortly after his flight from Tibet via the Nathu La pass in Sikkim, which is visible from Darjeeling.

I told Kugno Nyima Sangpo of my wish to go on retreat. He gave me a room right at the top of the monastery, on the terrace that also held the temple of the protectors of the Dharma. My former hermitage was currently occupied by an old monk. The situation was perfect, because no one ever came to the roof except the young monk who set up the offerings in the little temple in the morning and put them away at night. Plus, I would be able to get some exercise by circling the little shrine after nightfall. I took a vow of silence for the coming months and communicated only in writing thereafter.

Having spent eleven years with Khyentse Rinpoche, receiving his teachings and serving him to the best of my abilities, I suddenly found myself idle, and realized that I was physically exhausted. My life during that period had been exceptionally rich and rewarding, beyond all expectations, but also very intense, given the unrelenting hustle and bustle around Khyentse Rinpoche. I began my retreat gently. I took naps and gave myself time to regenerate. Then I gradually increased my hours of practice.

I also took advantage of this time of retreat to devote two or three hours every afternoon to finishing my translation of *The Life of Shabkar*, the autobiography of a great Tibetan yogi (1781–1851), whose life story spans more than a thousand pages. I had already been working on this project for several years, but on retreat in Darjeeling I picked up the pace and was able to translate five pages a day.

The incorporeal presence of Khyentse Rinpoche occupied my thoughts at every moment of the day. I went out onto the terrace at night and prostrated over and over under the starry sky in the direction of Bhutan. I imagined my teacher at dusk, conferring teachings on a few close students in his deep voice, which flowed without a pause like a river, then saying his evening prayers before going to sleep under his heavy coat. I imagined him in the soft morning light, sitting on his bed like an emperor of enlightenment, a cape of orange silk lined with fine white sheepskins over his shoulders, his long hair loose, his chest bare, wearing the agate and turquoise necklace he had inherited from past teachers and his gold reliquary containing a statuette of Manjushri, a legacy from Mipham Rinpoche. I saw him receive the first visitors of the day, holding their hand and caressing their cheek, laughing heartily, giving precious advice. My thoughts of Khyentse Rinpoche mingled with the equally vivid memory of my root teacher, Kangyur Rinpoche, who rests immutably within my heart.

My retreat was nourished twofold by the invisible presence of these two awakened beings, merged into one in my devotion. More than any other form of practice, I engaged in guru yoga, a union with the teacher's nature of ultimate enlightenment—a practice that has always been at the heart of my spiritual path. The union of your own mind with the teacher's allows you to rediscover the primordial simplicity of the nature of mind, in which you need only rest without hope or fear.

The retreat also allowed me to begin assimilating the unbelievable treasury of teachings I had received over the past eleven years. I had enough to practice with for five or six lifetimes! Khyentse Rinpoche sent me several letters with spiritual counsel that were worth all the gold in the world to me. Every time I received one of his missives, I placed it respectfully on top of my head, paused a while without opening it, then unsealed it delicately before reading it with deliberation. I gave each word the time to permeate me to my very core. These very precious letters and poems were certainly worth a few months of exile!

I did my best to compose my replies in Tibetan. I read and understood Tibetan rather fluently, but I often struggled with spelling and grammar, as I do with all languages, being dyslexic. I therefore used a dictionary to compose awkward poems that I knew would make Khyentse Rinpoche laugh. But it warmed my heart to picture his thoughts of love and kindness and his amused smile turning in my direction. One of Khyentse Rinpoche's poems went like this:[1]

In the home of the teacher who achieved the primordial wisdom of the Most Excellent [Kunzang],[2]
The supreme place where the wheel of teachings [Chökhorling] that ripen and liberate was turned,
You exert yourself in your practice, your reading and your writing.[3]
I was very happy to receive your letter, full of affection.

In that peaceful forest, like a hidden land,
Where I dwell quietly in a humble hermitage,
I and those around me were rejoiced by it.
Keep sending me your news again and again, old friend!

Within the pleasant grove of Satsam Chorten,
I have set the outer boundaries of my retreat,
And dwell serenely, at perfect ease,
Like a swine in muck.

Although I do not have the vast certainty of a diamond-like yogi
Who perceives all forms as deities, sounds as mantras
And thoughts as the absolute dimension, the dharmakaya,
With fervent devotion to the masters of the lineage, the holders of awareness,
As if playing a flute I tirelessly let the melodious tones of my prayers ring out.

Brilliant moon [Rabsel Dawa][4] shines in the sky above the Southern Valleys [Bhutan],
While the student's water lily, buoyant with faith and perseverance, flourishes in
    Darjeeling.
But there can be no doubt that through the power of your prayers and karma
You will forever bathe in the moon rays of luminous ambrosia, the source of joy.

When these words reach you,
Delight in the sweet taste of joy and devotion.
Like a deer filled with ease and contentment,
Sketch out a few steps of joyful dance!
Ha ha!

At the end of a long poem sent some time afterward, Khyentse Rinpoche
wrote,

Son, I wrote these lines to delight and surprise you.
The people of the world are fooled by the fantasies of their own minds.
For the yogi who holds the tether of naked awareness-united with emptiness,
The gaudy shimmering of the diverse lands only shed more light on the teachings;
They help you advance your practice and generate deep certainty.

A single glimpse of the primordial simplicity of awareness-emptiness in its pure state
Is enough to reduce to dust the citadels of delusion built in times beyond ken.
Captivated by the spectacle of innate perfection at the heart of the three dimen-
    sions of Buddhahood,
This old man drunk on an excess of the liquor of unseemly livelihood,
Writes these lines during the Gathering of Awareness Holders ceremony.
Thinking over and over of the friend so dear to his heart,
He sends this letter from the grove of medicinal plants where the essence of virtue
    dwells,
Praying that teacher and student will soon be reunited.

I spent five months in retreat, five months of sweet tranquility, combining practice and translation. I also sought to stamp my every ordinary
activity with altruistic aspiration, saying a brief prayer relevant to every
moment of daily life, based on a sutra of the Buddha:

When going to sleep, say to yourself, "May all beings attain enlightenment."
When rising, "May they awaken to Buddha nature."
When rising, "May they attain an enlightened body."
When dressing, "May they retain a sense of modesty and decency."
When lighting a fire, "May the negative emotions of human beings burn."
When eating, "May every being taste the nectar of deep meditation."
When opening a door, "May the door of liberation be open to all beings."
When closing it, "May the gate of the lower realms be closed to all."

When climbing stairs or a hill, "May I lead all beings to the upper realms."
When descending, "May I go and liberate all those who suffer in the lower realms."
On seeing happiness, "May every being attain the happiness of Buddhahood."
On seeing suffering, "May all pain be soothed."

My return to Darjeeling also allowed me to reflect on the most formative times of my life, those that most deeply shaped my mind. More than any others, two high points stand out in particular: the seven years spent in Darjeeling with Kangyur Rinpoche, followed by the months spent in my hermitage after his death, during which I focused on the practices he had taught me; and the thirteen years I had lived with Dilgo Khyentse Rinpoche. During that first period, I had stayed exclusively in Darjeeling, except for a brief trip to Nepal and two visits to Delhi to print books. With Khyentse Rinpoche, on the other hand, I had traveled a great deal and been exposed to new and very often extraordinary situations—ten years in Bhutan and three intense visits to Tibet. An immutable presence at the heart of ceaseless activity, except when on retreat, Dilgo Khyentse Rinpoche often traveled to teach and in response to the requests of myriad teachers and monasteries. But the perfect tranquility of Darjeeling, like the ever-changing circumstances of life with Dilgo Khyentse Rinpoche, were both imbued with what was most important to me: the presence of a spiritual teacher, like an aroma that pervades the mind, a profound unity at the heart of diversity.

Each of these two periods was as formative as the other, each in its own way, and it would be pointless to try to assess their respective impacts. To make a musical analogy, music-lovers consider the chaconne from Bach's *Violin Partita No. 2* to be one of the greatest musical achievements of all time. And yet, in listening to other musical masterpieces, it would seem clearly futile to attempt to establish levels of sublimity in something that already transcends the power of words. In the same way, I can recognize these two periods as having been the most essential of my life, but their virtues and achievements also transcend all basis for comparison. Can you compare two suns, two skies, two freshwater springs, the two wings of the same bird?

In mid-December 1989, Khyentse Rinpoche returned to Nepal. I ended my retreat, said goodbye to my friends, and left to join him.

33

REUNIONS AND FAREWELLS

I reunite with Dilgo Khyentse Rinpoche in Nepal. In the summer of 1990, Dilgo Khyentse Rinpoche journeys one last time to France and then, in the autumn, to Tibet. Our farewells at the Kathmandu airport in April 1991.

One morning in March 1990, after the annual ceremonies that follow the Tibetan New Year, I found myself alone with Khyentse Rinpoche and ventured to tell him that it would be extremely beneficial for everyone if he were to confer the transmission of the complete works of Shechen Gyaltsap, his root teacher. We had collected almost all his writings in Tibet and had them reprinted in India. Khyentse Rinpoche was the last holder of this transmission still alive. He said nothing, but a month later he decided to confer these teachings in the great library on the top floor of the monastery. Some thirty students, including three of his main spiritual heirs—Rabjam Rinpoche, Jigme Khyentse Rinpoche, and Tulku Pema Wangyal (who had also requested the teachings)—received the oral transmission of Shechen Gyaltsap's thirteen volumes of writing over the course of several weeks. These works, composed in clear, simple prose, contain profound commentaries on various aspects of the path.[1]

On the last day, a long-life ceremony was dedicated to Khyentse Rinpoche by his main students.[2] Rabjam Rinpoche describes that moment: "As I was offering the symbols of long life, I was overcome by the feeling that Rinpoche would not live much longer. I burst into tears and left the room. In the stairway, I ran into Ani Jinpa, a Dutch nun and student of Rinpoche's, who asked me, 'What happened? Did Rinpoche say something to upset you?' I did know how to reply." That was last cycle of teachings that Rinpoche ever gave in Nepal. Since then, Rabjam Rinpoche has transmitted it in turn twice—once to the *tulkus* and monks of Shechen Monastery, in eastern Tibet, and once in Bhutan, relayed to many countries through the Internet.

In the summer of that same year, 1990, Khyentse Rinpoche made a six-week journey to France, his fifteenth since 1975. He taught in Dordogne and several Buddhist centers, assisted by his close Tibetan students who had come from Europe and the United States.

In late September 1990, Khyentse Rinpoche returned to Tibet one last time to consecrate Samye Monastery, whose upper floors had been magnificently rebuilt thanks to an appeal he had made to the Chinese government in 1985. The restoration of the main temple was complete, and Khyentse Rinpoche was invited to consecrate it. Only Khyentse Rinpoche and three Bhutanese members of his entourage were permitted to make the journey. But we worked out a scheme to attend this historic event. Tulku Pema Wangyal and Amala (Kangyur Rinpoche's wife), accompanied by their entire family, the eminent scholar Nyoshul Khen Rinpoche, and thirty Western students, including my mother and me, organized an ostensibly touristic visit with the aim of ending up at Samye at the same time as Khyentse Rinpoche. The subterfuge worked, and we were able to join Khyentse Rinpoche at the monastery.

The highly elaborate consecration ceremony lasted three days and was held on the tenth day of the lunar month, dedicated to Padmasambhava, on September 29, 1990. Khyentse Rinpoche also gave teachings and empowerments to the sixty monks of Samye and those who had been invited to attend the consecration.

I did my best to play both parts, traveling with a group of so-called tourists, while also trying, to the extent possible, to stay close to Khyentse Rinpoche. At Samye, Khyentse Rinpoche slept in the main temple, and I attempted to spend my nights, as usual, lying on a rug on the floor nearby.

But the Chinese officials in charge of Khyentse Rinpoche's visit got wind of my presence after the very first attempt, and let me know in no uncertain terms that my place was with the group of tourists camping near the monastery. I was forbidden to mingle with Khyentse Rinpoche's entourage.

The exterior of the main monastery had been restored to its original splendor. The copper roofs, gilded in genuine gold leaf, gleamed with the thousand flames reflected from the morning sun. Inside, new statues replaced those that had been destroyed. Khyentse Rinpoche's daughter, Chime Wangmo, had offered to fund the restoration of a very precious statue of the crowned Buddha, the Jowo Changchub Chenpo, which was on display in the temple on the second floor and whose body had not been completely destroyed. Khyentse Rinpoche asked the king of Bhutan to send the three most talented sculptors in Bhutan, who repaired the statue admirably and remodeled its face with exceptional subtlety.

The vows that Khyentse Rinpoche had made five years earlier had borne fruit, but the restoration of the Samye complex as a whole was far from finished. Still to be rebuilt were the eight subsidiary temples that surrounded the central temple in the eight cardinal and intermediate directions, four giant stupas, and 108 smaller stupas that surmounted the perimeter wall. They have been restored since then.

Khyentse Rinpoche also went to Lhasa, where he offered one hundred thousand butter lamps in the temple of Jowo, the crowned Buddha. Our group was not allowed to follow him on his further travels, including to the Reting Valley, so we decided to accompany Kangyur Rinpoche's family to the various places he had lived, in particular the Rong Drakmar cave, where Tulku Pema Wangyal was born and Kangyur Rinpoche had discovered a spiritual treasure.

Kangyur Rinpoche's family returned to France. As for me, I escorted a core group of the Western students on a pilgrimage through China, to Mounts Emei and Wutaishan, two of China's five sacred mountains, dedicated respectively to the bodhisattva Samantabhadra and the buddha Manjushri, where I had gone previously with Khyentse Rinpoche. Our return flight to France originated in Beijing. On Tiananmen Square, where demonstrations had been suppressed in a bloodbath just over a year earlier, our little group gathered together to recite prayers. Two of us, Martin Watten and I, wore the habits of Tibetan monks. We earned ourselves some smiles and encouragement from passers-by, as well as some irascible looks and words from police officers, who ordered us to move along.

On his return from Tibet, Khyentse Rinpoche made a brief stop in Bhutan, from which I was still banned, then left for Bodhgaya, India, where I joined him. Although he was now eighty years old, he seemed untouched by age, and his charisma was as vibrant as ever. Nevertheless, in mid-December, as he was transmitting the teachings of his predecessor, Jamyang Khyentse Wangpo, he began to show disturbing signs of illness. He was forced to suspend his activities for a few days, which was most unusual for him. The Dalai Lama happened to arrive in Bodhgaya at that time, and visited Khyentse Rinpoche on three occasions, when he asked him to confer a few empowerments.

In early January 1990, Khyentse Rinpoche conferred the Bodhisattva Vow at the foot of the Bodhi Tree, the very place where the Buddha had attained enlightenment. He then presided over the recitation, accompanied by a hundred monks, of one hundred thousand rounds of the Prayer of Perfect Action and the Chanting the Names of Manjushri, which are, respectively, seven and fifteen pages long. In late January, he went to Dharamshala at the invitation of the Dalai Lama and, over the course of eight days, offered him one last series of important empowerments of the Nyingmapa school. On January 28, on the porch of his residence, the Dalai Lama touched foreheads with Khyentse Rinpoche at great length, reciting prayers that they would meet again in many lives to come, and they then took leave of one another—their last farewell.

Upon his return to Nepal, it became clear that Khyentse Rinpoche's health was in inexorable decline. He was losing weight, needed more and more rest, and spent most of his time in prayer or meditation, devoting only a few hours a day, contrary to his normal schedule, to those who had important reasons to seek his company.

In April 1991, Khyentse Rinpoche's stay at Shechen Monastery in Nepal was coming to an end. He was to return to Bhutan. In his bedroom early one morning, he gave a teaching on the preliminary practices of the Heart Essence of the Vast Expanse, the Longchen Nyingthig, to a small group of students. Although I had received these teachings from him at least twenty times before, hearing his explanations oven and again allowed me each time to attain a clearer and more profound understanding. As I drank in his words with full and absolute attention, I was overcome by immense sadness; copious tears were soon flowing from my eyes. I sat silently, far back in the room so that no one noticed my sorrow. I had a veiled suspicion that I was listening to my beloved master for the last time. He was leaving for Bhutan, where I was not allowed; he was very ill; would I ever see him again? I did not formulate these thoughts explicitly, but they were at the heart of the deep sadness that had overwhelmed me.

When the teaching was over and the students had left, it was time for Khyentse Rinpoche to leave. I approached him for his blessing and told him that I would not come to the airport to say my goodbyes, as was customary. He kept his hands on my head for a long while and said nothing, understanding that I preferred to end with this intimate goodbye and avoid the commotion of a public send-off.

Several cars set off for the airport. I found myself unable to resist and hopped into one at the last moment. A Nepalese student with connections to the authorities had arranged for Khyentse Rinpoche to take the car directly to the foot of the plane. It was therefore from the car window, before passing through the gate that led to the runway, that he gave his blessings to those who had come to see him off. I went last, and when he saw me Khyentse Rinpoche laughed, took me by the ear in a familiar gesture of affection, and said with a smile, "So you came after all." Those were the last words I ever heard him speak. My friend Raphaële took a picture at the precise moment that Khyentse Rinpoche pulled me by the ear. A last image of our final moment. As I write these lines, I am gripped by emotion and cannot help crying hot tears.

Khyentse Rinpoche had hoped to make a fourth visit to Tibet, to Shechen Monastery, but he had to abandon that plan. He decided instead to undertake a three-month retreat in Bhutan, across from the Tiger's Nest in Paro Taktsang, one of the holiest places in the Himalayas.

His health seemed to improve after that. He stopped in to see a few of his students who were on retreat and talked to them of the ultimate teacher, beyond birth, death, and all physical manifestations. But his condition soon worsened again.

An accident weakened my beloved teacher even further. One night, the monk who had replaced me at Rinpoche's side went out for a walk instead of going to bed at the same time as him. Meanwhile, Khyentse Rinpoche had to go to the toilet and got up by himself. He slipped, fell on the tiled floor, hit his knee hard, and lay on the ground for quite some time until the monk's return. The latter was horrified by his own negligence, but the damage was done. The state of Khyentse Rinpoche's knee deteriorated to the point of infection, compounding the illness from which he suffered. Sometime later, the Queen Mother asked Lama Ngodrup, the elderly monk who had served Khyentse Rinpoche for thirty years, "This wouldn't have happened if Matthieu had been here, would it?"

Lama Ngodrup agreed, and the Queen Mother burst into tears.

The Queen Mother began to have doubts about the denunciations to which I had been subject and asked the minister for foreign affairs for the incriminating newspaper clippings. There were none, and the minister was unable to explain himself.

Khyentse Rinpoche could neither eat nor drink for twelve days. He sent a message to Trulshik Rinpoche in Nepal, with these few words: "I will leave on the 19th." Trulshik Rinpoche hastened to Bhutan and spent a few days at Khyentse Rinpoche's bedside in Paro.

On the nineteenth day of the ninth lunar month, September 28, 1991, Khyentse Rinpoche was transferred to the Thimphu hospital, at the Queen Mother's request. At dusk, he asked those around him to help him sit up straight, and he then fell into a peaceful slumber. In the early hours of the morning, he stopped breathing and his mind dissolved into absolute space.

That is how Dilgo Khyentse Rinpoche's extraordinary life came to an end—a life devoted to study, practice, and teaching from his very earliest years. Wherever he was, day or night, and with a tireless outpouring of kindness, wisdom, good humor, and dignity, he gave his all to the preservation and practice of Buddhist teaching in all its forms.

I heard the news the next morning in a phone call from Tulku Pema Wangyal, who was in Bangkok on his way to Bhutan. I was at that time in Dordogne, where I had gone in early summer to serve as the Dalai Lama's interpreter for ten days of teaching *The Way of the Bodhisattva*. I don't know how to describe what I felt, as it was so far beyond the scope of ordinary emotions. It was as if the entire universe had suddenly fallen silent. Time stopped, yet at the same time the universe became completely filled by Khyentse Rinpoche's presence—a tangible presence, made not of specific memories but of his quality of being, the ultimate dimension of his wisdom and his gentle compassion, transcending concepts and feeling. The world would never be the same without him, but the presence of Khyentse Rinpoche was no longer subject to time, place, or circumstance. I was staying at the Sonnerie—Tashi Pelbar Ling—at the time, the very place where Khyentse Rinpoche had resided when in Dordogne. He, my beloved teacher, inhabited every inch of space there. I joined a few students who had gathered to say prayers. There was no point in talking among ourselves—words were useless.

The day after Rinpoche's death, Rabjam Rinpoche asked the king of Bhutan if I could be allowed to return. Permission was granted. I took the first plane to India, then on to Bhutan. I participated in all the ensuing ceremonies. Students from all over the world were allowed to come pay tribute to Khyentse Rinpoche's body. He was embalmed according to traditional Tibetan methods, under the supervision of Tulku Pema Wangyal, who had already tended to the bodies of his own father and of Dudjom Rinpoche in the same manner. Khyentse Rinpoche's body was preserved for a year before his cremation so as to give students who had to travel long distances, in particular from Tibet, the time to go all the way to Bhutan and then to Nepal, where his body was brought for three months. Every Friday for the first seven weeks, the Tibetan community in Nepal offered one hundred thousand butter lamps and votive candles that slowly burned down at night on the tiered terraces of the Great Stupa of Boudhanath, near Shechen Monastery.

I briefly returned to France in 1992 to again serve as the Dalai Lama's interpreter in Paris. It was the first time I had seen him since Khyentse Rinpoche's passing. When he entered the hotel lobby, he saw me, came to me, threw his arm across my shoulder, leaned his head against mine, and hugged me silently for several long moments. He said not a word, but anything he might say would have been superfluous—the gesture spoke for his support and his devotion to Khyentse Rinpoche's memory.

In November 1992, Khyentse Rinpoche's body was cremated near Paro, Bhutan, in a three-day ceremony in which one hundred eminent lamas, the king and his entire family, and the government ministers of Bhutan participated, alongside five hundred Western students and a crowd of fifty thousand. It was a gathering unprecedented in the history of that country, which had only six hundred thousand inhabitants at the time. On each of those three days, Rabjam Rinpoche fed nearly ten thousand visitors who had come from afar and were camping in the surrounding countryside. The Dalai Lama had wanted to come to Bhutan for the event; the king had given his approval and everything was organized for his arrival. But having got wind of it, the Chinese government put such heavy pressure on the Bhutanese, threatening to walk away from the talks on drawing the final borderline between Bhutan and China, that the plan had to be scrapped.

A twelve-foot clay funerary stupa was built for the cremation. After a week of ceremonies in which monks from every school of Tibetan Buddhism, including a delegation from the Dalai Lama's monastery, took part, Khyentse Rinpoche's body, wrapped in silks and crowned with the diadem of the Five Wisdom Buddhas, was carried in procession by his closest students to the place of incineration. It was placed in the upper part of the bell-shaped clay edifice, where logs of precious wood, white and red sandalwood, and other essences had been arranged. The pyre was then lit, and for the next three hours the cremation ceremonies were conducted by four groups of monks stationed at the stupa's four cardinal points. Each group was led by a lama from one of the four main schools of Tibetan Buddhism.

The opening of the funerary stupa was then sealed for several days to allow the ashes to cool. During that time, hundreds of the faithful respectfully circled the edifice until late into the night, singing verses of a prayer invoking Khyentse Rinpoche. More ceremonies were held in the daytime. The stupa was eventually opened, and the ashes, remains, and other relics were carefully collected. Despite the intense heat that had raged within the stupa for several hours, Khyentse Rinpoche's heart was almost intact, desiccated by the fire but otherwise undamaged. The upper part of the funerary edifice was then rebuilt to house most of Khyentse Rinpoche's remains. The rest were enshrined in other stupas and statues throughout the world, and fragments were given to the students as objects of devotion.

The enormous stupa at Shechen Monastery, in Bodhgaya, which contains a relic from the Buddha Shakyamuni, received a large part of Dilgo Khyentse Rinpoche's relics; both are now mingled within the same monument, along with many other relics as well.

Never forget that your life passes as quickly as a bolt of lightning through the sky or a gesture of the hand. Now that you have the opportunity to practice, don't waste one minute. Devote all your energy to the spiritual path.

Dilgo Khyentse Rinpoche

One page of Tibetan Buddhism had been turned, but Khyentse Rinpoche's legacy would endure through his teachings. The twenty-five volumes of his work have since been printed and numerous oral teachings translated from Tibetan into many languages. Several hundred hours of sound recordings have been archived. His biography has been published in English, and his life and work have been celebrated in several books of photography. His main students and spiritual heirs continue to perpetuate his lineage today.

His grandson, Rabjam Rinpoche, who was twenty-five at the time, had to assume responsibility for the two Shechen Monasteries in Nepal and Tibet, as well as the nunnery in Bhutan. Together with other close students, I did my best to serve him in this demanding task. To fulfill a wish that Khyentse Rinpoche had often expressed, he completed the building of a Shechen Monastery in Bodhgaya, India, whose construction was overseen by Luc Cholley. Eight more stupas were erected in places that had figured prominently in the life of the Buddha. Rabjam Rinpoche believes that his primary mission is to disseminate the spiritual legacy of his grandfather and spiritual teachers. More than anything, he encourages all those who come to him to be guided by the teachings of Khyentse Rinpoche, which he sums up like so:

He always insisted on the importance of merging our minds with the Dharma and unifying our practice and daily lives. He used to say that it is not when circumstances are favorable, pleasant, and calm that you can judge a true practitioner, but when things begin to go bad. That's when a practice's weak points become apparent. He thought it very important to integrate the meditative aspect into all of life's activities. After years of practice, he used to say, you can assess practitioners' progress by determining if they have become better human beings, developed inner peace, are freer of destructive emotions and less vulnerable to external circumstances. If their mental toxins remain all-powerful and they are overly preoccupied with themselves, they have missed the very point of the path.

In 2010, Rabjam Rinpoche told us:

Even today, almost thirty years after his death, Khyentse Rinpoche is always present in my thoughts, and I often dream of him. One night, for instance, on the road to Bodhgaya, I dreamed that I went into a room and found Khyentse Rinpoche sitting there. Surprised, I asked him, "How is this possible, you are no longer among us?" Rinpoche replied, "You're wrong. I'm always among you." I told him that I'd had a bad dream that he had died and I had searched for his reincarnation. I touched Rinpoche's feet. I cried and clung to him. I woke up with tears in my eyes. The dream had felt so real I couldn't tell if I had had a dream or if life was the dream. So I'm convinced that even if Rinpoche is no longer physically here, his blessings are always with us.

I, too, sometimes dream of Khyentse Rinpoche, whose presence radiates so intensely that I wake up crying. In my dreams, he sometimes asks me, "Where have you been all this time?" And I go back to serving him as I did before. Sometimes, I see him teaching his students.

To this day, I have no other desire than to follow his teachings and to work humbly to perpetuate his vision and his activities for the good of beings.

This prayer, composed by Trulshik Rinpoche, perfectly describes the aspirations of students who have been separated from their teachers by the impermanence of all things and all beings:

Although my eyes no longer see your body, the mere sight of which is liberating,
Bless me so that all appearances manifest themselves as your body.
Although my ears no longer hear your voice, the very sound of which is liberating,
Bless me so that all sounds manifest themselves as your voice.
Although my thoughts are no longer directly linked to your mind, the very memory
    of which is liberating,
Bless me so that all thoughts manifest themselves as your awakened mind.

IV

PRESERVING THE LEGACY

34

ARCHIVIST

At Shechen Monastery, I work to safeguard the treasury of Buddhist culture. I devote myself to publishing the complete works of Dilgo Khyentse Rinpoche and other important texts, including *The Treasury of Precious Termas*. We digitize forty thousand of my photographs on Himalayan art.

Khyentse Rinpoche was often busy writing, be it a commentary or an explanatory guide to various spiritual practices. He always kept blank pages handy, formatted as a Tibetan book, and as soon as he had some free time, he would write several pages. We had no idea what he was working on at any given moment, but once the manuscript was finished, he would hand it off to his secretary, Tulku Kunga. Khyentse Rinpoche's handwriting became increasingly difficult to decipher as he aged. Tulku Kunga, who had become expert at reading it, would copy out a second version by hand that Khyentse Rinpoche would verify. There are three main forms of Tibetan writing: cursive, used to write letters and manuscripts; the so-called headless style—because it lacks the horizontal bar that "caps" words—which favors elegance while facilitating speed; and the "with a head" style, wherein each letter in a word is capped by a horizontal line. This third style can be compared to our capital letters; it is used mainly when engraving text on wooden blocks, xylographs, which then serve for printing books on demand. A few volumes of Khyentse

Rinpoche's work were engraved this way at Thubten Choling Monastery, in Nepal, under the supervision of Trulshik Rinpoche, but most of his compositions were still in manuscript form and amounted to a great many volumes, which we kept very carefully.

After Khyentse Rinpoche's death, I devoted a good part of my time, with a team of four monks, to collecting and computerizing his writings. We had recently been given a high-quality digital Tibetan font crafted by Tony Duff, and the software to format texts in the traditional style. We had also appealed to a scholar and student of Rinpoche's, Lama Puzi, to assist us in this colossal task. He came to us from India to put these writings in order and to carefully reread the texts that had been logged. I took personal charge of entering text from the first volume, which contains biographies of Khyentse Rinpoche's two primary teachers, Shechen Gyaltsap and Dzongsar Khyentse Chökyi Lodrö. I also formatted every single volume and coordinated the project. After three years of hard work, twenty-five volumes, each of six hundred-pages, were ready for printing. They are now the *Collected Works* of Khyentse Rinpoche, published in India by Shechen Publications between 1994 and 1995.

When Dilgo Khyentse Rinpoche's reincarnation was enthroned at the Shechen Monastery, in Nepal, in December 1997, Trulshik Rinpoche conferred, for the first time, the transmission of all twenty-five volumes to the young *tulku* and an assembly of a thousand people. Trulshik Rinpoche had received the transmission himself from Khyentse Rinpoche down the years.

Khyentse Rinpoche also wrote countless letters, poems, and spiritual songs to other lamas, his students, and his nephews and nieces throughout Tibet and India (he was the sole survivor of his parents' ten children). I wrote letters for him in English that he dictated to me in Tibetan. We included in his *Collected Works* all the poems and spiritual guidance we were able to collect. There must be many more scattered throughout the world!

In addition to Khyentse Rinpoche's writing, over the course of some thirty years we managed to reprint more than four hundred volumes,[1] among which almost 150 were digitized and are now available on the website of the Tsadra Foundation,[2] which has generously supported our publication work for the past twenty-five years, and on the website of the Buddhist Digital Resource Center, founded by E. Gene Smith.

The volumes were printed in Delhi by Samdrup Tsering, who currently coordinates the publications of Shechen Publications, the publishing house associated with our monastery in Nepal. They are then made available to many monasteries and libraries, the teachers who hold the transmissions of these texts, and to scholars and practitioners.

These texts, which are critical aids to the transmission of teachings, could have disappeared forever in the devastation wrought by the Cultural Revolution in Tibet. Remember that an untold number of library books were either burned or thrown in the rivers. Mindful of the importance of their spiritual heritage, many Tibetans chose to take books when they fled rather than their personal belongings. A number of works were hidden in caves and other hiding places until Mao's death prompted a relative relaxation of Chinese oppression. But despite the heroic efforts of the Tibetans, many important texts were lost for all time, while others survived in only a few copies, and in some cases only one. That's why Shechen and other monasteries made it their mission to resolutely seek out these works and reissue them.

For my part, I had launched this long-term enterprise in the late 1970s, at the behest of Pema Wangyal Rinpoche, and, as I wrote earlier, had some fifty volumes printed in Delhi on behalf of Kangyur Rinpoche's monastery.

In 2004, when I was in my hermitage at Namo Buddha, Shechen Monastery's retreat center two hours from Kathmandu by car, I asked myself, What project would delight Dilgo Khyentse Rinpoche if he were still alive? Although it would be a massive undertaking, it was clear to me that an elegant edition of the sixty-seven volumes of *The Treasury of Precious Termas*, the *Rinchen Terdzö*, a compilation of texts conceived and annotated by Jamgön Kongtrul Lodrö Tayé in the nineteenth century, would most adequately fulfill Khyentse Rinpoche's vision. Jamgön Kongtrul was a founder of the renowned Rimey movement in Tibet—a movement that might be classified today as nonsectarian, in that he spoke out against the regrettable sectarianism that was gaining force at the time among the various philosophical schools and traditions. Jamgön Kongtrul demonstrated that the spiritual practices and approaches adopted by the main schools that had arisen in Tibet all led to the same ultimate goal: the actualization of Buddhahood. To that end, he assembled the Five Great Treasures, ninety volumes presenting the perspectives and contemplative methods of the different schools and lineages that flourished in Tibet. Not satisfied with collecting the most important writings of various lineages, he also wrote myriad commentaries, practice compendia, and liturgical ritual sequences. One of the Five Treasures is the magisterial encyclopedia of Buddhism in four volumes, *The Treasury of Knowledge*.

The Rimey movement was actively supported by other great nineteenth-century teachers working together, notably Jamyang Khyentse Wangpo and Patrul Rinpoche, but also Lama Mipham, Jamyang Loter Wangpo, and, a bit earlier, Shabkar, the latter being active in Amdo, to the north. This nonsectarian movement was encouraged in the twentieth century by the fourteenth Dalai Lama and Dilgo Khyentse Rinpoche, among others, who made an important contribution to promoting harmony among the followers of the various spiritual schools and philosophies.

The *Rinchen Terdzö* is the largest of the Five Great Treasures composed by Jamgön Kongtrul. It contains not only the principal discovered treasures (*terma*) of Tibetan Buddhism, but also texts outlining the conferral of empowerments and the explanations necessary to practice them. A contemporary of Jamgön Kongtrul, Jamyang Khyentse Wangpo traveled throughout Tibet for thirteen years seeking out many of the texts that were eventually included in the *Rinchen Terdzö*. He also received transmissions that, in some cases, were held by only one or a handful of lamas. He then conferred these to Jamgön Kongtrul and other students.[3] It is thanks to those two eminent masters that these precious works still exist today.

Dilgo Khyentse Rinpoche conferred the transmission of the sixty volumes of the *Rinchen Terdzö* five times, each round taking three to four months. In the 1970s, he marshaled his financial resources and entrusted them to Lama Ngodrup to go to Delhi to print the first edition of the collection outside Tibet, augmented by several volumes of annexes. Khyentse Rinpoche was not especially pleased with the result, however, as most of the originals, printed from engravings on wood, were not clear enough to allow for direct reproduction and had to be recopied by a team of Bhutanese calligraphers using tracing paper, which led to numerous errors and omissions. If it had been a matter of only a few little details, a few basic typos in the texts, we might have been spared those years of toil, but this was about the authenticity of the transmissions that are conferred from teacher to student. Digitizing the texts would ensure their survival and help disseminate them more broadly.

When I returned from Namo Buddha, I told Rabjam Rinpoche about my idea for a new, complete edition of the *Rinchen Terdzö*. He endorsed it enthusiastically on the spot and called together all those who would be involved in the project for a simple ceremony. Rice with raisins and butter tea were served, and we recited prayers invoking the blessings of past masters to favor the project and lead it smoothly to fruition.

We were allocated a large room, and the monks got down to entering the texts shortly afterward. This was the start of thirteen years of painstaking, calm, and focused work. The monks typing the texts into the computer quickly mastered the information technology and appeared to do their work effortlessly. They looked as if they were in a state of "flow," the optimal experience described by the psychologist Mihaly Csikszentmihalyi as an effort that is neither tense nor relaxed, commensurate with the actor's capacities, in which both the sense of passing time and the sense of self are lost. Even visitors who came for a brief chat with one of us would immediately lower his voice and speak in a whisper. Just to be safe, I asked the monks to enter each volume in two copies, each one made by a different "scribe." They would then do a comparison of the two versions using specialized software, and any differences that were detected, down to the letter, were investigated and corrected to conform with the original, thereby eliminating typing mistakes, among other errors. So, in fact it was not 70 but 140 volumes that were digitized!

Six months into the project, Rabjam Rinpoche and I managed to convince Dagpo Tulku, who lived at Mindrolling Monastery, near Dehradun in India, to come oversee this new edition. Dagpo Tulku is recognized today as one of the world's most knowledgeable scholars in textual verification. He set himself up at our retreat center in Namo Buddha, at Rabjam Rinpoche's house, with his assistant, Tsewang Rigdzin, and a young Nepali in charge of the cooking and household tasks. Dagpo Tulku explained to me that it was the memory of his conversations with Dudjom Rinpoche in years gone by that had finally persuaded him to accept this great responsibility, to which he would devote many years of his life. That great teacher and scholar had informed him that it was truly necessary to correct the *Rinchen Terdzö*. Dudjom Rinpochehad planned to supervise the work himself when he still lived in Tibet and had estimated that ten scholarly experts in the matter could finish the job by devoting themselves to it for the four months of the summer season, three years running. As for us, it took that scholar, his assistant, and the monks who entered the text thirteen years to complete this mammoth task. Dagpo Tulku worked tirelessly, taking just one afternoon off every two weeks to go for a walk. He meticulously identified errors, carefully compared the two Tibetan editions, and, in many instances, verified the original sources of the texts contained in the collection. Jamgön Kongtrul had suggested that it would be useful to include in any future edition certain texts that he himself had been unable to obtain or finalize during his lifetime. Dagpo Tulku also took charge of verifying these supplementary texts, which brought the new edition up to seventy-one volumes. When I stayed at Namo Buddha, I often took my midday meal with Dagpo Tulku; he enjoyed pointing out and explaining in detail the mistakes and missing parts he had identified in any volume he was working on. My contribution was to be the general overseer of the project and to coordinate our activities: training the monks who entered and formatted the texts in the Tibetan style (I did it myself for the first few volumes); locating the original texts that Dagpo Tulku needed to finalize his verifications (sometimes as far away as Tibet); and maintaining communications with the Tsadra Foundation and with Samdrup, who was in charge of printing the texts in Delhi, India, on behalf of Shechen Publications. It was also my job to keep up "troop morale" throughout this long-term endeavor.

Konchog Lhadrepa, the painting master at the Shechen Monastery art school, the Tsering Art School, created the illustrations that appear in the volumes and prepared a new series of illustrations that were included, for the first time, in the *Rinchen Terdzö* collection.[4]

At last, on March 29, 2018, a joyful ceremony, led by Shechen Rabjam Rinpoche, was held at Shechen Monastery, Nepal, to celebrate the publication of the *Rinchen Terdzö*. The seventy-one volumes, wrapped in orange cloth, were carried in procession by monks holding one volume apiece on their right shoulder, then deposited on the altar of the great temple. This was followed by a ceremony of offerings and thanks to all those who had participated in the project. A very special tribute was paid to Dagpo Tulku for his perseverance and unparalleled expertise, to the monks who had entered the texts, and to Éric Colombel, president and founder of the Tsadra Foundation, without which the project could never have been undertaken.

To conclude, the assembly recited prayers dedicating the benefits generated by this accomplishment to the good of all beings, the longevity of the spiritual teachers, and the dissemination of the teachings.

For me, it was a moment of immense relief. The project had been brought to fruition, and no obstacle had interrupted it. Following this ambitious but essential undertaking, I decided to step down from my publication functions, and it is now my friend, the English monk Sean Price, who is in charge of coordinating new projects.

I had recorded almost four hundred hours of teachings given by Khyentse Rinpoche since 1979, and I had some fifty hours of film documenting the final years of his life and, notably, his first return to Tibet in 1985. The recordings have now been digitized and catalogued, while the videos provided the main footage for two documentaries: *The Spirit of Tibet*, which I made with Vivian Kurz, and *Brilliant Moon*, a more accomplished film that includes animated scenes of Khyentse Rinpoche's childhood and a few previously unseen sequences. It was made by Neten Chokling Rinpoche for the events celebrating the 2010 centennial of Khyentse Rinpoche's birth.

Down the years, I had photographed countless miniatures, *thangkas*, murals, statues, and other sacred and ritual artistic objects in Tibet, Bhutan, and Nepal. The Shechen Archives, which I run, house all the negatives and transparencies, as well as forty thousand scanned pictures of Himalayan art, for which I have compiled a detailed catalogue. I've done likewise for the collection of photographs that I have had the precious opportunity to take over the course of half a century, documenting the lives of spiritual masters (more than 200,000 images, seven thousand of which form the core collection, all captioned).

These pictures are preserved in the archives of the Shechen Monastery, in Nepal, and available to any who wish to use them. I have also offered twelve thousand scanned images to the Rubin Museum of Art, in New York City, which are posted on its website devoted to Himalayan art.[5] That is my modest material contribution to the spiritual legacy of teachers whose most precious gift is the intangible heritage that dwells in the minds and hearts of their students and spiritual heirs: the teachings that guide us on the path to enlightenment.

35

PRESERVING THE SACRED ARTS

The establishment of the Tsering Art School, an academy for traditional painting, at Shechen Monastery. We perform more than one hundred recitals of sacred dance and music throughout the world, from Venice to São Paulo, not to mention the Cartoucherie de Vincennes theater in Paris.

Buddhist sacred art helps us to penetrate the ultimate nature of reality and allows us to build a bridge between the contemplative life and the active life. Far from inciting passions, it calms them. Sacred art is closely related to meditation on "pure vision," that is, on the perception of the primordial purity of all phenomena. This vision is particular to Vajrayana Buddhism, which recognizes that the Buddha nature is present in every being and that all phenomena appear and yet are empty of independent existence. From that perspective, phenomena are called "pure"—free of all mental distortions and projections that lead us to believe that some things are intrinsically "beautiful" or "ugly," "pleasant" or "unpleasant," "desirable" or "undesirable," and that some people are fundamentally and irremediably "good" or "bad," "friends" or "enemies."

In Tibetan sacred art, the painter and sculptor establish a correspondence among forms, symbols, and the spiritual path. The musician connects the universe of sound to the resonance of prayer and mantra. The works of the writer and contemplative poet teach us the essence of nonattachment that unties the knot of greed, the discipline that rejects any action that might cause suffering, the patience that endures adversity and overcomes anger, the diligence that fosters assiduity in practice without distraction, and, ultimately, the wisdom that reveals the ultimate nature of things and is allied to unconditional compassion for all beings in the thrall of ignorance and suffering.

Khyentse Rinpoche attached great importance to preserving the spiritual heritage of Tibet. Rinpoche's vision inspired me all the more in that I myself was passionate about Tibetan art, the painting of *thangkas* in particular. What's more, as I had had the great good fortune to attend the sacred dances that took place every year in Bhutan, Nepal, and Tibet, I was deeply aware of the richness of the arts associated with Tibetan Buddhist culture.

I therefore explored every possible option for securing the funding necessary to fulfill Khyentse Rinpoche's vision in that sphere. I met with Tom Derksen, the Kathmandu representative of the Netherlands Development Organization (SNV), whose wife was a Buddhist. He approved financing for half the project. The other half was provided by an American benefactor, Jocelyn, in memory of her young daughter, who had wanted to be a painter but had died in an avalanche, and who had the same Tibetan first name, Tsering, as Rabjam Rinpoche's sister, who had also met a tragic end. This was how Tsering Art School, a school for sacred painting, was established within Shechen Monastery that, for the past twenty years, has offered a six-year course of study in traditional painting (*thangkas* and mandalas) to hundreds of students, monks, and laypersons of all nationalities. The Shechen Archives, where I work, was until recently in the same building as the school. Around the same time, I secured financing from the European Commission for the construction, on monastery grounds, of a college of philosophy offering a nine-year curriculum (upon completion of six years of elementary school and three years of monastic studies in the sacred rituals and arts).

One mission of the Tsering Art School is to preserve in its authentic form one of the most beautiful styles of Tibetan painting, that of the Karma Gardri tradition. Prevalent in eastern Tibet, this style is distinguished by its transparency and simplicity and by the beauty of the landscapes surrounding the people and deities represented in the *thangka*. Khyentse Rinpoche asked one of his students, Konchog Lhadrepa, to run the painting school built on the grounds of the monastery. Konchog had been trained by one of best painters in that school, who had managed to escape Tibet and find refuge in Sikkim. It was also Konchog whom I had assisted for several months in painting the frescoes of Kangyur Rinpoche's monastery in 1976. He is today one of the best representatives of the Karma Gardri style living outside Tibet. It is all the more important to preserve the authenticity of this art because of the rise of many, strictly commercial, art workshops catering to the tourist trade that are churning out pseudo-*thangkas* that have more to do with the flights of fancy of poorly trained handicrafters than with ancestral traditions.

Most students who have completed their training remain at the Tsering Art School to teach, as well as to create works commissioned from all over the world. They also work on the restoration of Shechen Monastery' frescoes, which were destroyed in the earthquakes of 2015.

Thangkas and murals are the most significant modes of expression in Himalayan art. *Thangkas* are painted on treated cloth and stretched with string over a wooden frame. The pigments, all natural in accordance with tradition, are mixed with water and glue, then applied like tempera. The deities are depicted on the basis of a strict iconographic canon and their proportions mapped out by a matrix that varies from one deity to the next. These constraints do not prevent the artist from expressing her personal talent through her particular treatment of the subject and the overall technique she applies to the painting; varied landscapes and subtle differences in posture and facial expression are the hallmarks of individual painters. Once the work is finished, the canvas is lined with multicolored brocade.

As she works on her painting, the artist must visualize herself as the deity she is painting. She also imagines her implements—brushes, paint receptacles, and so on—as attributes in the hands of that deity, whose mantra she continually recites as she works. These painters are truly the artists of enlightenment.

Paintings and statues are the symbolic supports of the Buddha's body, just as sacred texts support his speech and stupas support his awakened mind. Sacred painting also has a didactic function, as do frescoes and *thangkas* illustrating the life of the Buddha or the history of his previous lives (Jataka). Other painters depict visions of deities or of buddha-lands experienced by some spiritual masters.

But the main purpose of sacred paintings is to serve as supports for spiritual practice. Tibetan Buddhism has a vast array of meditative practices, some of which involve the visualization of one or several deities and the recitation of their mantras. These deities are thought of not as entities living in various paradises, but as symbols or expressions of diverse aspects of enlightenment, including wisdom, the correct understanding of the ultimate nature of reality, compassion, and actions undertaken for the sake of all beings. In visualizing himself as a deity of wisdom, it will be easier for the practitioner to actualize the "buddha nature" within himself.

The meditator begins by focusing on the deity represented in the *thangka* and absorbs its every detail: shape, colors, attributes, and so on. Once the image is clearly formed in his mind, he stops contemplating it and turns his attention to the inner visualization of the deity, accompanied by the associated mantra. He also tries to recognize the nature of his own mind as being one with the awakened mind of his spiritual teacher, of the deity he is focusing on, and of all buddhas.

Although profane dance and music are proscribed by monastic rule, monks engage in sacred dances—*cham*—as a meditation and spiritual sharing with the lay community that lives in symbiosis with the monastery.

This is the sharing of experience acquired during lengthy ceremonies, then offered in symbolic gestures accompanied by music. Such dances, they say, "liberate" through sight, just as sacred music liberates through hearing, the blessing of a spiritual master through touch, blessed substances through taste, and meditation through thought. Here, "liberate" means throwing off the yoke of the mental toxins—hatred, craving, ignorance, pride, and jealousy—that destroy our inner peace and that of others.

The tradition of sacred dances was established at spiritual feasts known as *ganachakra*. The essential role of these complex and secular ritual offerings, with various levels of meaning, was to gather merit and wisdom. Such sacred feasts once included choreographic sequences accompanied by visualizations intended to cultivate a pure perception of phenomena.

Over the course of time, these dances were taught to certain disciples and their meaning was elaborated and structured. The unbroken transmission from teacher to student, enriched by the visions of great meditators, sustains the tradition.

The origins of sacred dance go all the way back to Padmasambhava, who brought Buddhism to Tibet in the eighth and ninth centuries. The repertory of dances was later augmented by visionary teachers who, down the centuries, breathed new life into the sacred choreography. The most celebrated of these was the great thirteenth-century teacher Guru Chökyi Wangchuk, who had a vision in which he rode a white horse across the sky to the Copper-Colored Mountain of Glory, Padmasambhava's "pure land." There, he found a multitude of celestial beings dancing in space in homage to the master. Following this experience, he initiated the Tenth Day Festival (Tshechu), commemorating Padmasambhava's coming to Tibet.

In the context of sacred art, renewal is the fruit not of personal invention or artistic experiment, but of a profound spiritual realization that opens the gates to great visionary richness. After a teacher has revealed or established a new dance, the role of the custodians of the tradition is then to transmit the content of the sacred choreography as faithfully as possible from generation to generation.

Every year, most of the great monasteries host a festival of sacred dance that attracts the faithful by the hundreds and even the thousands. In Tibet, nomads who come to attend spend several days camped around the monastery. In Bhutan, from dignitary to humble peasant, no one wants to miss these festivals, which can last several days.

The monks' endurance is put to the test by these events. The ceremonies that precede the dancing last almost all night long, and the "dancing monks" then perform various choreographic sequences from nine in the morning until five in the afternoon in the monastery forecourt, adding speech to body movement as the dancer chants nonstop mantras. Body and speech are supplemented by mind—the dancer clearly and without distraction visualizes the deity he embodies.

The symbolism extends to all the accessories used in the ceremonies and sacred dances. The masks worn by the dancers lend themselves to different levels of interpretation; those wearing a peaceful expression symbolize wisdom and altruistic love, while those with a wrathful or impassioned expression depict purification and transcendence over the mental toxins of anger and obsessive desires.

According to the Vajrayana vision that spread throughout India through the outreach of Nalanda University, as well as the influence of the great yogis, or *mahasiddha* ("great adepts"), the Buddha Shakyamuni manifested himself on rare occasions to a few highly qualified disciples, including King Indrabhuti, as a wisdom deity, such as Kalachakra, the "Wheel of Time," and Guhyasamaja, the "Epitome of Secrets." The aim was to allow them to advance rapidly on the spiritual path using uncommon meditative techniques. The main goal of these "skillful means" is in fact to cultivate pure vision, that is, the perception of all forms as being the various manifestations of a wisdom deity, all sounds as mantras, and all thoughts as manifestations of emanations of awareness. The practitioner can also consider forms, sounds, and thoughts as the manifestations of the body, speech, and enlightened mind of the Buddha. While profane dance and song are prohibited by the Vinaya (the rules of monastic discipline), as sacred arts they are glorified in the context of pure vision by practitioners visualizing themselves in the form of a wisdom deity.

I have photographed these sacred dances every year since 1980, and in 1991 I published a book on the subject, *Monk Dancers of Tibet*, but I never imagined that I would one day receive training in this art.[1] And yet, there came a time when I was almost compelled to dance! In Bhutan, a ceremony led by Khyentse Rinpoche in the Punakha Dzong was the setting for a daily sequence of sacred dances that were an integral part of the lengthy ritual. One morning, the Queen Mother suggested that I participate. I confess that I prudently made myself scarce an hour before the fateful moment to avoid flaunting my total incompetence in public and before the entire monastic community!

Between 1995 and 2004, the monks of Shechen gave more than a hundred performances of their sacred dances all over the world. Under the guidance of Rabjam Rinpoche, two friends, Jean-Pierre and Cécile Devorsine, organized some ten tours. The dances usually comprise sequences that are repeated several times. An abridged version was therefore arranged so that the monks could present eight different dances in an hour and quarter. In that regard, Rabjam Rinpoche, who was present for the first tour, told the press, "A spoonful of honey tastes the same as the whole pot." Some twenty monks participated in these tours, each of which took us to fifteen venues in three weeks. I played the role of escort, interpreter, presenter—delivering a ten-minute introduction before each performance on the meaning of the dances and the importance of Tibet's cultural heritage—and even of lighting technician! For our first tours, a designer, François Picard, had developed a "lighting plan" for us, with specific settings for each dance, involving fifty spotlights of varying kinds and colors. But we couldn't bring a specialist in charge of the lights with us everywhere we went. Once we arrived at a venue, a few hours before the show, I wasted no time in getting down to work with the theater's technicians, using the map to arrange the lineup of appropriate spotlights and programming the sequence of desired effects and transitions for each dance into the lighting mixer. In the evening, after introducing the show to the audience, I ran up to the control room just as the gong was rung in the dark and the curtain rose on four musicians playing a prelude to the first dance. I spent the rest of the evening manning the controls. In 1998, a talented lighting designer, Vincent Féron, joined our team for the São Paolo World Music Festival and did an incredible job showcasing the beauty of the dances. Invited by the choreographer Carolyn Carlson, the monks danced under the stars in an ancient theater on San Pietro Island for the Venice Biennale. This was followed by performances in the Court of Honor at the Palais des Papes in Avignon, Montreux; the Cirque Royal in Bruxelles; a train station converted into a theater in Dortmund; and a theater in Lausanne, where Maurice Béjart came to see the dances and meet the monks. In 2001, Ariane Mnouchkine brought us to the Théatre du Soleil in the Cartoucherie de Vincennes, where we stayed in trailers for ten days and celebrated the Tibetan New Year with the theater crew, who introduced the monks to table soccer. Conferences were also organized, including one with the Chinese dissident Harry Wu. We even performed one of the dances for the Trappist monks at Cîteaux Abbey, who invited us to stay the night. A documentary about the monk dancers was also made for television, broadcast first in France and then throughout the world.[2] I took the monks to Dieppe one day—many of them had never seen the sea—where they performed a particularly acrobatic dance on the beach, leaping and touching their foreheads with their pointed toes. That's where I took the picture of the "flying monks" that received a great deal of attention. We went from town to town by bus on these very fun and enjoyable tours, which allowed us to introduce the rich spiritual heritage of these dancing meditations to a broad public. They also turned out to be very demanding, and after performing for ten years, with a final show at the Fez Festival of World Sacred Music in 2004, we decided to take a break.

Instrumental music and song play a fundamental role in ritual and dance. Depending on the circumstances, music can be an offering, an invocation, a call to prayer, an invitation, a rhythmic beat, or an aid to meditation. That is why it, too, can be considered a form of apprenticeship in pure vision, thanks to which all sounds are perceived as mantras, whose ultimate nature is emptiness. In that sense, sacred music contributes to spiritual elevation.

The melodies of certain songs, performed solo or in chorus, are designed to generate fervor. That is particularly true for "Calling the guru from afar," a poignant plea from student to teacher. In other cases, a spiritual teacher or a practitioner may chant an improvised poem, tied to an inspiring melody, that transmits a teaching (on impermanence, renunciation, and the like) or expresses the essence of spiritual realization. The great yogis Milarepa and Shabkar, among many others, were renowned for teaching in this manner.

If art is a natural human expression, it must be said that, in the context of the sacred arts, all forms of expression are harmoniously linked to spiritual progress.

Throughout the fifty years I've spent in the Himalayas, I have always striven to understand and document these different forms of sacred art. Every time I've had the chance, during lengthy *drupchen* ceremonies or monastic dances, I have recorded the sacred music and done what I can to contribute to the research of reknowned musicologists like Mireille Helffer, who studied the rituals and music of Shechen Monastery. I have amassed a vast collection of photographs of Tibetan and Bhutanese painting and sculpture, available to all. Beyond my work as an archivist and documentarian, for me it's always been about helping to preserve the authenticity of the living traditions practiced by the representatives of Tibetan Buddhism.

36

SEARCHING FOR THE REINCARNATION OF DILGO KHYENTSE RINPOCHE

The Yangsi, the reincarnation of Dilgo Khyentse Rinpoche, is recognized thanks to directions given by Trulshik Rinpoche, his closest spiritual friend. Ceremony in the Maratika cave. The Yangsi meets the Dalai Lama. Ceremonial enthronement in Nepal.

After Dilgo Khyentse Rinpoche died, his grandson Rabjam Rinpoche had a dream in which he told Rinpoche what a blow his sudden death had been for him.

"I tried to warn you, but you ignored my messages," Khyentse Rinpoche observed.

"Where will you be reborn?" Rabjam Rinpoche asked.

"Don't you worry, I'll send clear signals."

That was his reply.

Rabjam Rinpoche and Khyentse Rinpoche's main students asked Trulshik Rinpoche, Khyentse Rinpoche's closest spiritual friend, to go in search of his reincarnation. Out of modesty, Trulshik Rinpoche usually declined such missions, but he accepted this one immediately.

Trulshik Rinpoche provided no updates for more than three years. And then, in April 1995, from his Thubten Choling Monastery, located in the Solukhumbu district northeast of Kathmandu, he sent a messenger to Rabjam Rinpoche with a letter. The message described what he said was only a dream: "It was a dream, but I wasn't asleep," he wrote with humility. In what was more akin to a vision, Dilgo Khyentse Rinpoche appeared to him, wearing a severe expression that then turned to one of joy. He sang a song announcing a year of birth, the name of two parents, and the place where a child would be found "who was unquestionably Tashi Paljor [Khyentse Rinpoche's birth name] come back to life [*yangsi* in Tibetan]." Trulshik didn't wish to make too much of this vision, modestly setting it down to his imagination. But instead of vanishing as it had arrived, the vision grew clearer and clearer as the day wore on. Trulshik Rinpoche also received signs that the time had not yet come to divulge the news. He kept the details secret for a year, until April 1995. Only then did he send his letter to Rabjam Rinpoche, containing the poem and explanations.

In the poem, the names of the parents appeared in Sanskrit. The child, who had come into the world "in the year of he who is born in a nest," should be sought northeast of Shechen, a direction that could have sent us looking far afield, all the way to Tibet! Rabjam Rinpoche called me to his home, and we scoured the dictionaries for the Tibetan equivalents of these Sanskrit names. Once we had decoded the poem, the search went quickly. It turned out that the personal name (usually known only to one's intimates) of Tsikey Chokling Rinpoche (Mingyur Dewa'i Dorje, Immutable Diamond Bliss) and that of his wife (Dechen Paldrön, Glorious Torch of Great Bliss) corresponded perfectly to those in the poem. The couple did in fact have a son who had been born, according to the Tibetan calendar, in the Year of the Bird, the tenth day of the fifth lunar month—the birthday of Padmasambhava—that is, June 30, 1993. Ka-Nying Shedrub Ling Monastery, where they lived, was indeed located northeast of Shechen, in Boudhanath. In being born so near at hand, and by giving us such clear directions, Khyentse Rinpoche had spared us a long and far-flung search!

So Rabjam Rinpoche sent a reply to Trulshik Rinpoche, laying out the results of his research and asking if he needed to continue his search. By return messenger, Trulshik Rinpoche confirmed that that would no longer be necessary. In fact, one morning before dawn, even before he had received this new information, he had had a dream. As if on wheels, twenty-five golden stupas rolled across a large field that separated Shechen Monastery from Ka-Nying Shedrub Ling Monastery. He was suddenly quite certain that the stupas contained Dilgo Khyentse Rinpoche's remains. As he wondered which was the main stupa, one came to a stop before him; a marvelous bird of unknown species appeared at the window set in the upper part of the structure and began to sing. Trulshik Rinpoche approached and offered a white ceremonial scarf before the bird. At that moment, the other twenty-four stupas lined up behind the first and set off in procession for Ka-Nying Shedrub Ling Monastery, where they dissolved. Through this dream, Trulshik Rinpoche had confirmed the identity of the young *tulku* even before Rabjam Rinpoche had been able to send him the details of his discovery.

Trulshik Rinpoche then sent a letter to the Dalai Lama, asking him to confirm his intuition. The latter, who attached great importance to this matter, went on a weeklong retreat, hoping to obtain compelling corroboration. When this week of meditation ended, and without offering any further clarifications, he replied, "I have no doubt that this young child is the true incarnation of Dilgo Khyentse Rinpoche."

Trulshik Rinpoche directed Rabjam Rinpoche to keep the secret for a few more months. When the time was right, Rabjam Rinpoche went to meet the child and his parents. I had the opportunity to accompany him. As you might imagine, it was a deeply moving experience; with deep emotion, wonder, and respect, we scrutinized every expression on the toddler's face. The parents were overjoyed to learn that their youngest son had been recognized as the incarnation of their own spiritual master. They informed us that another elderly lama, Chogye Tri Rinpoche, had told them that he, too, had received signs that their son was the incarnation of Khyentse Rinpoche, but that he did not believe it was his place to speak openly about them.

Sometime later, Rabjam Rinpoche, who has a great sense of humor, admitted to us that he had had some trouble picturing Khyentse Rinpoche's enormous body squeezed into that very young child, and that the situation reminded him of the movie *Honey, I Shrunk the Kids*, in which a wacky scientist accidentally shrinks his children.

One incident that had taken place fifteen years earlier suddenly made sense now in the light of this revelation. In the late 1970s, Chokling Rinpoche, the young *tulku*'s father, had come to inform Dilgo Khyentse Rinpoche that, like his previous incarnations, he wished to live the life of a married yogi and not that of a celibate monk. He was considered to be the third incarnation of the great nineteenth-century *tertön*

Chokgyur Dechen Lingpa. He had come to Khyentse Rinpoche for advice, and Rinpoche had told him that he would give it some thought. In 1980, Dilgo Khyentse Rinpoche went to Darjeeling. Among those who came to see him was a young woman, Dechen Paldrön, from the Gyantse family in Tibet. The previous night, Dilgo Khyentse Rinpoche had had a premonitory dream, on the basis of which he asked the young woman and her parents if she wished to become Chokling Rinpoche's wife. After thinking it over, they said yes the next day.

A few months later, in 1981, a ceremony was held at Khyentse Rinpoche's residence in Nepal, a small house set back from the site where Shechen Monastery would soon be built. Chokling Rinpoche and Dechen Paldrön arrived dressed in their finest, accompanied by their families. Dilgo Khyentse Rinpoche performed a ceremony and conferred a longevity blessing on them. Trulshik Rinpoche attended the event and was very surprised because, strictly speaking, there is no wedding ceremony in Tibetan Buddhism; at the most, a blessing for prosperity and long life is offered to the couple and their future children. Trulshik Rinpoche had never seen Dilgo Khyentse Rinpoche behave this way. When the ceremony was over, he asked him why he had made such a fuss over this particular marriage. "You'll see, you'll see . . . all in good time," was his enigmatic reply. The fact was, he had just married the parents of his own reincarnation—in other words, his own future parents!

In accordance with tradition, once the reincarnation had been announced, a series of steps was set in motion: the naming, the first haircut ceremony, and the solemn enthronement.

On December 27, 1995, in eastern Nepal, not far from the border with India and Sikkim, Trulshik Rinpoche stood waiting, staring up at the sky, at the head of a procession of monks and laypersons, each of whom held a stick of incense. The thrum of a heavy Russian helicopter broke the mountain silence. Among the twenty-two passengers was Dilgo Khyentse Rinpoche's young reincarnation; his mother; his older brother, Pachog Rinpoche; Khandro Lhamo (Dilgo Khyentse Rinpoche's widow); Rabjam Rinpoche; and a few more of us. As soon as the aircraft landed, the blades slowing in a cloud of dust, the Yangsi disembarked in the arms of an elderly monk. Trulshik

Rinpoche offered him a ceremonial scarf of immaculate white silk and held his forehead against the boy's for a long while. This was the first time he was meeting his teacher's incarnation, whom he himself had identified in his visions, in the flesh. He then led the Yangsi in procession to the little temple where he would be lodging for the next few days.

The next morning, the immense Maratika cave was crowded with an unusual number of lamas, monks, nuns, and students from various countries. It is a sacred place where, they say, Guru Padmasambhava and his Indian spiritual companion, Mandarava, attained *siddhi*, the supreme accomplishment of "infinite life," the realization of the luminous emptiness of enlightenment that transcends all concepts of birth and death. It is an awe-inspiring place, 3,000 feet above sea level in a semitropical zone. It is located a day's walk from a little mountain airport, or a three-day hike from the main road linking Nepal to India (a paved road has been opened since then). Above a little village of some thirty little houses, a hundred feet of stairs lead down to the broad expanse of an immense rocky cavern. Hundreds of bats flit in and out, clinging to the numberless crags of the vault and walls of this gigantic circular stone sanctuary, more than two hundred feet wide and fifty feet high.

A moving ceremony was held under the vast dome of the cave. Surrounded by other lamas, Trulshik Rinpoche offered the Yangsi the name conferred by the Dalai Lama: Ugyen Tenzin Jigme Lhundrup—"Fearless and Spontaneously Accomplished Holder of the Teachings of Padmasambhava"—and a longevity blessing. Butter lamps and candles burning on the ledges and in the crevices of rock walls cast a golden, shimmering light within the cave. The Yangsi, his family, and that of Khyentse Rinpoche, and the Dalai Lama's representative and a few relatives sat on a low rock platform around makeshift thrones assembled for Trulshik Rinpoche and Yangsi Rinpoche. Around two hundred people sat below on the cave floor; some had come from far away, and on foot, to see the sun rise once more in their hearts. The prayer that the Dalai Lama had written a few days after Khyentse Rinpoche left this world had come true:

The more vulnerable people there are,
The more it is in your nature to love them.
To perfect and liberate all beings in this dark age,
Promptly reveal the brilliant moon of the face of your emanation!

Afterward, Trulshik Rinpoche began to hand out pills that had been blessed in a longevity ceremony. The young Yangsi, age two and a half, watched for a few minutes, then took the dish from Trulshik Rinpoche's hands and insisted on continuing the distribution himself. He gave a pill to Dilgo Khyentse Rinpoche's wife, Khandro Lhamo, then to his own mother and those who were sitting near the throne. When the monk who was attending him in this ritual reached out for the little dish, the Yangsi gestured toward the crowd, indicating that he wished to give a pill to someone in the audience. The monk pointed to several people, but the Yangsi dismissed them with a shake of the head. A monk went down among the crowd in the direction signaled by the child and, keeping his eye on the Yangsi, pointed at different participants. When he came to an elderly Bhutanese, the Yangsi nodded in acquiescence and invited the man to approach. The latter presented himself before the Yangsi, who filled his hand with pills. The man burst into tears. He was Norbu Gyaltsen, a retired captain of the Royal Bodyguard of Bhutan who had served Khyentse Rinpoche for many years. In particular, he had been with us on our first visit to Tibet, in 1985. Having come on foot the evening before with his family and a group of Bhutanese, he was seeing the Yangsi for the first time. Most people could not understand why this man had been chosen over all others, but those who knew who he was were amazed. I had often heard about how young reincarnated lamas were able to spontaneously recognize people they had known in their previous life, but this was the first time I had witnessed it in person.

About six months later, when the Yangsi went to Bhutan, the king wanted to put him to the test. A delegation of monks, government representatives, and members of the royal family awaited him at the airport when he arrived. Without telling us, the king had sent five men, all more or less the same age and wearing the same traditional Bhutanese outfits, but only one had been a member of Dilgo Khyentse Rinpoche's inner circle for about ten years. A vast crowd welcomed the Yangsi on his arrival; an old lama, a trusted assistant of the royal family, drew the Yangsi's attention to the five men, who were lined up together, and asked him ingenuously, "Do you recognize one of your attendants?" The Yangsi, three years old at the time, was chatty by nature but fell silent at the question, stared solemnly at the five men and then, without hesitating, pointed at one of them and asserted categorically, "That one!" Then, playful and laughing, he moved on to the next thing. The old monk hurried off to phone the palace with the news: "He passed the test with flying colors."

Obviously, such incidents can be disconcerting to a Westerner, and I have no explanation or interpretation to offer based on current scientific understanding. I am only reporting what I saw with my own eyes. Buddhism offers the simplest of answers: the Yangsi retained memories from his former life. What else is there to say?

Many similar episodes played out while the Yangsi was between two and a half and five years old. One morning not long after we had met him with his parents, I received a phone call in the monastery office where we were working on inputting texts. A piping voice said, "Matthieu, work hard!" When I realized it was the Yangsi, it was as if an electric current passed through me. I spoke to his mother about it that afternoon, and she told me that it had been his idea to call me. I did my very best to carry out his instructions to the letter!

Another time, in Nepal, we were taking a short drive in the car, the Yangsi sitting up front and Rabjam Rinpoche, a monk, and myself in back. Suddenly, the Yangsi turned around in his seat and grabbed me by the ear, which he tugged gently for a few seconds. As Rabjam Rinpoche observed, "The only person in the world I have ever seen pull Matthieu's ear like that was . . . the former Khyentse Rinpoche." And it was true. Dilgo Khyentse Rinpoche occasionally made this affectionate gesture, most memorably when I said goodbye to him for the last time at Kathmandu airport.

After the Tibetan New Year, in March 1997, we brought the young *tulku* to Dharamshala to meet His Holiness the Dalai Lama, who would be leading the first haircut ceremony. The little boy's hair had never been anywhere near a pair of scissors until that moment. An intimate ceremony was held at the Dalai Lama's residence in the presence of Penor Rinpoche (the head of the Nyingmapa school at that time), Rabjam Rinpoche, the Yangsi's family, and a few others among us. The Dalai Lama, feeling elated by this meeting with the incarnation of one of his main spiritual teachers, affectionately teased the child, recommending that he behave himself and underlining his words with a raised index finger. He advised Rabjam Rinpoche to give him a good education, but to avoid treating him as an "eminence" until he had manifested spiritual qualities of his own. Later that morning, the Tibetan government in exile, accompanied by representatives of various local monasteries, organized a public ceremony in the main temple of Dharamshala, at which many of the faithful presented the Yangsi with ceremonial scarves.

There was unquestionably "something" about the Yangsi that set him apart from other children his age. On this trip to India, I was struck by the impression he made on the people we met. Whenever we were waiting at an airport or on a platform at the train station, and one of us was simply carrying him in our arms while he looked around, it never took long for a little crowd to gather and stare at him curiously. The same thing used to happen, but on a much larger scale, to his predecessor, Dilgo Khyentse Rinpoche. In his ripe old age, whenever he sat in his wheelchair waiting on the platform for the train to arrive, Indians flocked to him, touching his feet with their hands—a traditional gesture of respect—and seeking his blessing, while dozens of others formed a semicircle to gaze at him from a respectful distance. Naturally, we, the members of his entourage, treated Rinpoche with the greatest respect as well, but without any of the ostentatious pomp that might have drawn the attention of passers-by.

In the fall of 1997, in Boudhanath, Nepal, the monks of Shechen Monastery, under the watchful supervision of Rabjam Rinpoche, spent three months busily preparing for the Yangsi's enthronement. It was planned meticulously, and each of the three hundred monks was assigned a specific role in ensuring that this memorable event unfolded without a hitch.

Over the course of the three days preceding the enthronement, Trulshik Rinpoche held a ceremony in the temple located on the third floor of the monastery, which houses an astonishingly realistic statue of Dilgo Khyentse Rinpoche—his face was modeled in wax by an artist from the Grévin waxworks museum in Paris—and a little gilded stupa containing his relics. The exterior of the monastery had been freshly repainted for the occasion; the forecourt was covered in a large yellow tent and decorated with brightly colored flowers.

The great day finally arrived on December 5, 1997. The enthronement of the young Dilgo Khyentse Yangsi was celebrated with great magnificence, attracting more than fifteen thousand people of more than forty nationalities. When the morning fog burned off, the VIP guests and faithful began pouring in. Each was solemnly greeted by Rabjam Rinpoche and led to the temple. The guests included the leaders of the main schools of Tibetan Buddhism;[1] 137 *tulkus*; representatives of the Dalai Lama and the Bhutanese royal family; renowned Western scholars such as E. Gene Smith and Michael Aris, Aung San Suu Ki's husband; the ambassadors of France and the United States; the actor Richard Gere, a friend of the monastery; and countless students from all over the world.

The little Yangsi arrived with his family. Escorted by Rabjam Rinpoche, he crossed the courtyard, on which auspicious symbols had been drawn with colored rice. He was preceded by a procession of musicians and leaping dancers, as well as by two snow lions (large puppets manipulated by two people hidden inside, one for the head and front legs, the other for the rear legs). When he reached the courtyard, to the resounding blast of trumpets and a crescendo of cymbals, a shudder of excited and joyful jubilation ran through the crowd. As many people as would fit were ushered into the temple, while the faithful gathered in the courtyard and outer gardens raptly followed the ceremony broadcast live on screens.

In the temple, the Yangsi sat first on a chair facing the throne that would soon be his, while Trulshik Rinpoche completed the purification ceremony to eliminate any obstacle that could burden his life or impede his actions. The child then took his place on his predecessor's throne. Trulshik Rinpoche offered him a statue, a book, a stupa, a vase, and a ritual object (a three-sided dagger representing the power of the three primordial wisdoms to cut through the three main mental toxins), respectively symbolizing the body, the speech, the mind, the qualities, and the actions of a buddha, and conferred a longevity blessing upon him.

A description of the advent of Buddhism on this Earth and its development in Tibet, as well as an enumeration of the series of Dilgo Khyentse Rinpoche's emanations up to the current Yangsi, were loudly proclaimed by a monk who, as he read, gradually unrolled the six-foot scroll on which Trulshik Rinpoche had inscribed the text. Trulshik Rinpoche then offered the mandala representing the entire universe, as well as the eight symbols and eight auspicious substances that were presented to the Buddha after his enlightenment.

After the enthronement, which lasted about an hour, one by one the eminent lamas made the symbolic offerings of the qualities of the Buddha, each draped with a long scarf of white silk, symbol of the purity of their intentions. Representatives of the major monasteries made 108 different offerings—statues, books, ritual objects, rugs, brocade scrolls, sacks of grain, bales of tea, and so on—borne in by monks in procession. Thousands of students and devotees—Nepalese, Tibetans, Bhutanese, Indians, Westerners, Thais, Chinese, Vietnamese, Japanese, and many others—filed past, in an atmosphere of joyous calm, to present a white scarf and an offering to the Yangsi.

For seven straight hours, with a very short break, the Yangsi, only four and a half years old, sat patiently on his throne, relaxed and dignified. At times playful and giggling—making funny faces as he donned his lotus headdress or blessing the heads of people he knew with a spirited thump—and at other times solemn, he greeted everyone attentively, combining a little boy's cheerful freedom with the innate gravitas of the man whom he incarnated. "A 2,000-Year-Old Child" ran the headline of an article on the Christian magazine *La Vie* following a meeting with the Yangsi. At no time during that long day did he ever behave moodily or give the impression of being unhappy or bored. Rabjam Rinpoche concluded with this wish: "May the qualities of this child flourish until they equal those of our revered teacher in his previous life!" He then added, "The enthronement of a *tulku* creates a favorable connection so that he may benefit beings and preserve the Dharma."

Rabjam Rinpoche wanted me to remain free to assist in the various tasks to be accomplished during the ceremonies. He had therefore asked a doctor friend, Greg Rabolt—who happened to be an excellent photographer—to document the event. To keep things orderly, Greg was the only photographer permitted in the temple, along with a French camera crew led by our friend Jean-Pierre Devorsine. A little vexed, a professional photographer living in Kathmandu quipped, "A doctor as photographer? Fine, give me a call next time you're sick!"

In the late afternoon, a rarely performed Bhutanese sacred dance, the Dramitse Ngacham (now inscribed on UNESCO's list of the "intangible cultural heritage of humanity"), was presented by the Shechen dancers, directed by a Bhutanese dance master. To the crowd's great delight, it was followed by a lively and comic "dance of the snow lions." Every morning for the next three days, the Yangsi received representatives of Nepalese, Indian, and Bhutanese monasteries in the temple. In the afternoons, dancers from various groups performed cultural and religious dances. Among them was the Tibetan Institute for Performing Arts troupe, from Dharamshala; young dancers from the Tibetan Children's Village, in Bir; the Gesar company, from Kalimpong, made up of practitioners from the Riwoche Monastery in Tibet; and several companies from Bhutan. Lunch was offered every day to more than a thousand people during the five days of festivities.

For ten days, starting on December 12, 1997, the empowerments and explanations of the twenty-five volumes of Dilgo Khyentse Rinpoche's *Collected Works* were, for the first time, conferred in their entirety by Trulshik Rinpoche.[2] This was done principally for the benefit of the young Yangsi, but also for the Bhutanese incarnation of Dudjom Rinpoche and the more than a thousand people gathered at the Shechen temple.

Now that the formal ceremonies were complete, it was time for education. Having grown up under the wing of his spiritual teacher and grandfather, Rabjam Rinpoche decided that he would dedicate the years to come to conscientiously watching over the young *tulku*. He accomplished this mission by enveloping him in his affectionate presence and by transmitting to him the teachings that he himself had received from Dilgo Khyentse Rinpoche. The Yangsi also had an excellent tutor in Khenpo Yeshe Gyaltsen, and he studied Buddhist philosophy with two young *tulkus* of his age for several years. On top of that, he learned to speak fluent English thanks to Sally, a young Englishwoman who lived in his entourage in Bhutan.

In 2010, the centennial year of Khyentse Rinpoche's birth, Rabjam Rinpoche took the Yangsi, now seventeen years old, to eastern Tibet to visit the major sites where his predecessor had taught, and then on to France, North America, Malaysia, and Hong Kong.

In December 2010, sixty monks and nuns, along with a group of pilgrims of all nationalities, accompanied Yangsi Rinpoche and Rabjam Rinpoche to the eight main sacred places of Buddhism in India and Nepal.[3] In accordance with the wish expressed by Dilgo Khyentse Rinpoche before his death, a stupa had been consecrated on each of these sites. In such consecration rituals, lamas and monks visualize all the buddhas of the past, present, and future enthroned in the space above the stupa. They then make them material offerings of flowers, lights, perfumes, and food, which they arrange around the stupa and which they visualize multiplying endlessly until they fill the entire universe. The buddhas are then invited to dissolve themselves into the stupa and give it life by their presence of wisdom wed to compassion. Finally, many prayers are said for the benefit of all beings, the longevity of the spiritual masters and the continuity of the Buddha's teachings.

Following this year of travel and celebrations, the Yangsi resumed his studies at the Shechen Philosophical College in Nepal and with his tutor in Bhutan. From 2012 to 2015, during the three years spent by Rabjam Rinpoche in contemplative retreat in Bhutan, the Yangsi assumed the leadership of the three Shechen Monasteries, assisted to perfection by monks trained by Rabjam Rinpoche. Nevertheless, in 2018 he decided to withdraw from monastic affairs for a time to be at the side of his father, Chokling Rinpoche, who endured a lengthy hospitalization in Singapore (he died in December 2020), and to continue his own spiritual practice.

Like a lotus flower revealing its purity as it slowly blossoms, Yangsi Rinpoche is nurturing qualities that makes us hope that he will work for the benefit of beings with as much selflessness and devotion as his predecessor.

37

MONK AND PHOTOGRAPHER

I discover my passion for photography at a very early age. In the East, I record the lives and circumstances of my spiritual teachers. Publication of my first books of photography.

In 1995, I found myself in New York with a selection of my slides on the life of Dilgo Khyentse Rinpoche, many taken on our trips to Tibet. An acquaintance of mine who taught photography at New York University offered to introduce me to Michael Hoffman, the director of Aperture, a highly reputed publisher in the photography world. Over the course of almost thirty years, I had amassed precious images of the life of my teachers and their world, but I had never made any use of them other than to show them to friends and make them available to my fellow students.

A meeting was set up. When I showed up at the reception desk, Michael Hoffman, who was in his office at the time, hardly seemed interested. He confessed to me later that he had told his wife and main associate, Melissa Harris, "Another photographer bringing us pictures of Tibet. Go talk to him and tell him I'm busy." Melissa came down to meet with me in a little conference room, and I started projecting the slides on a screen. After a few minutes, Melissa called up to Michael and told him, "I think you'd better come down." Michael arrived and we found ourselves immediately drawn to one another. We had a warm conversation, but he still didn't seem interested in my pictures. I suggested, "Why don't I show you the slides as well while we talk," and I started the projection from the beginning. The portraits of my teachers and the images of the world that had nurtured them followed one after the other until they finally held Michael's gaze. Five minutes later, he declared, "Very powerful, very powerful. Let's do a book!" That was the beginning of a fine friendship with Michael. One day in his office—where I always dropped in every time I was in New York—he turned to me and joked, "I'm going off to your monastery for a few months. Take my place at Aperture!" Our relationship was fruitful, culminating in the 1996 publication of *Journey to Enlightenment: The Life and World of Khyentse Rinpoche, Spiritual Teacher from Tibet*, which was published in France a few years later under the title *L'Esprit du Tibet*. After that came *Monk Dancers of Tibet*. And that's how I became a "photographer." Labels rarely stick. That said, my karma must not be entirely random, because even today, having published several photography books, I'm still regularly asked, "Your book is very beautiful, but who took the pictures?"

And yet, it's one of my favorite things to do. I've written many books, but I would not call myself a born writer. I have to put my nose to the grindstone and rewrite again and again before the text achieves its final form. In photography, however, I have become well-versed in technique over the years and take great pleasure in taking and sharing my images.

In the year 2000, when I was showing at the Visa pour l'Image festival in Perpignan, I met Hervé de la Martinière, the main publisher of photography books in France, and two well-known fellow photographers, Olivier Föllmi and Yann Arthus-Bertrand. This meeting with Hervé grew into a solid friendship and fertile association that led to the publication, among others, of *Buddhist Himalayas* (with Olivier and Danielle Föllmi); *Tibet, An Inner Journey; Motionless Journey; Bhutan: Land of Sere*; and, in French only, *108 Sourires* ("108 Smiles"); *Visages de paix, terres de sérénité* ("Faces of Peace, Land of Serenity"); *Hymne à la beauté* ("An Ode to Beauty"); *Contemplations* ("Contemplation"); and *Émerveillement* ("Wonderment"). It occurs to me today that my book *Un demi-siècle dans l'Himalaya* ("Half a Century in the Himalayas"), published in 2017, exactly fifty years after my first trip to India, is the perfect counterpart in pictures to the account I am offering here with these "notebooks."

It all began when I was twelve and was given a Foca Sport camera for my birthday. I took pictures of puddles and reflected light. Relatives would say, "Don't count on Matthieu to take family snapshots." I wasn't a city kid and always felt happiest in nature. I began taking my photography more seriously around the age of fifteen, guided by my friend André Fatras, a pioneer of animal photography in France. We met in very unusual circumstances. He ran aground in an inflatable dinghy, very nearly drowning himself, on the beach at La Turballe, in Brittany, not far from my uncle's house. He had navigated down the Loire River with his nineteen-year-old wife and one-year-old baby, hoping to meet my uncle, the solo yachtsman Jacques-Yves le Toumelin. Out of sheer luck, he crossed paths with my mother, who happened to be walking on the beach. My uncle was happy to host them, and they spent several weeks camping on the heath at his estate, Gwenved.

In later years, I often went to visit him in Sologne, where he took pictures of wildlife, especially birds. At André's house, he is Dédé and I'm known as "Mama" or "Waffle Iron" (one of the expletives used by Captain Haddock in Tintin comics). There's no rhyme or reason to the nicknames at Dédé's, everyone just gets saddled with a moniker. I recently sent an email to Martine, nickname "Mati," Dédé's wife, and signed it "Waffle Iron." For the next two weeks, I received an impressive number of ads offering waffle irons at bargain prices! Dédé and Martine led a thrilling life, sailing seven times to the Kerguelen Islands, as well as to Spitsbergen, Amazonian French Guiana, India, Iceland, the Galapagos, and many other exotic destinations besides. *Paris Match* published a memorable picture of their son Benjamin, dressed as an emperor penguin, in the midst of hundreds of thousands of his "peers," with only a small opening for his face to reveal his human identity. We remain close, and I still visit them in Sologne or in their immense vaulted cavern in the Causses, which Dédé and his friends have devoted twenty years of hard labor to making habitable. It's a one-of-a-kind place: a large bay window in the east-facing outlet lets in the rising sun, while another on the opposite end lights up the cavern at sunset.

I continued to learn photography in the field, and by the time I left France in 1972 I had published a few nature photos in various journals, including on the covers of *Réalités* and *Connaissance de la campagne*. My best pictures from those days were lost when TOP-Réalités, the little agency that represented them, went bust in my absence. Once I had made a home for myself in the Himalayas, I mostly photographed my spiritual teachers and their universe. My aim was to share the splendor, power, and depth I saw all around me. I use photography as a source of hope, seeking to restore faith in human nature and to revive the sense of wonder in the wild parts of the world.

Henri Cartier-Bresson studied painting with my mother in André Lhote's workshop just before the Second World War, and remained friends with my parents. I met Henri in my adolescence and showed him my early work, which did not impress him at all! He shared a principle that his painting teacher had taught him: "A well-composed picture should look just as good upside-down as right-side up." Henry applied this method when judging the composition of a photograph.

When *Journey to Enlightenment* was first published, in the United States, I showed the proofs to Cartier-Bresson. This time, he looked through the book's plates in silence, lingering at length over each page, especially the portraits of my spiritual teachers. I left for India the next morning. A fax from Henri was waiting for me when I arrived: "I was strolling through the Luxembourg Gardens when this phrase came to mind: 'Matthieu's spiritual life and his camera are one. From there, spring these images, fleeting yet eternal.'"

As the years went by, I became close to Henri and his wife, Martine Franck, herself a great Magnum photographer. I often visited them when I passed through Paris.

Anyone who spent time with him knows that, in addition to the genius that earned him the sobriquet "Eye of the Century," Henri—HCB in the photo world—was a true original. When dedicating his books, he often signed his name with the pun *"En rit"* ("Laughs about it"). I remember one story among many. In 2007, he came to the opening of a photo exhibit of mine at the Forum des Halles in Paris. When he saw me, he cried out, "What are you doing here? You're never supposed to come to your own openings!" Once, when he had made an appointment with a journalist from *Newsweek* at 8:30 on a Sunday morning—not your standard interview schedule!—he invited me to breakfast. We were already seated with Martine when the journalist arrived. A little intimidated, he sat across from Henri and set his pen and notebook down on the large round table of waxed wood. Pointing to the notebook, Henri asked, "Are you from the police?" Caught off-balance by this opening salvo, the journalist asked the classic question, "What makes a good photograph?" To which Henri replied, "I'm not a photographer. I prefer drawing. Plus, anyone can be a photographer. All you need is a camera." Martine stepped in as moderator: "Come on, Henri, you know very well that's not true!" The rest of the interview proceeded on a more normal track, to the journalist's great relief.

In 1991, Henri, who had long been interested in Buddhism, came to Dordogne to take some pictures of the Dalai Lama, who was spending the week offering teachings to ten thousand people under a great white tent at the top of a hill overlooking the Vézère Valley. At the midday break, I brought Henri to meet the Dalai Lama in the little tent where he was receiving visitors. I introduced Henri as one of the most highly admired photographers of our time. The Dalai Lama asked him what made a good picture. Henri talked about his famous concept of the "decisive moment" and of the importance of living in the present moment. Well-trained in logic, the Dalai Lama said to Henri in a mischievous way, "But when you're taking the photo, you're thinking about the result, which is in the future, and when you're looking at it you return to the past. So, in fact you're *never* in the present moment!" Henri was not usually at a loss for a comeback, but he didn't quite know how to respond.

It was not until the ripe old age of ninety that Henri fully immersed himself in Buddhism. He studied with Dagpo Rinpoche, a respected spiritual teacher who had lived in France since the 1970s and whose teachings he had already been following for several years. He asked Rinpoche to transmit the vows of refuge in the Three Jewels: the Buddha, the Dharma, and the Sangha. Two weeks before his death at ninety-five, in 2004, I spent a few tranquil moments with him. The only things on his bedside table were a little Buddha, which never left his side, and a glass of water.

The power of a vision, of an image, is obvious as soon as you look at it. I inspect it closely to determine the best way to do it justice, enlisting technique to help rekindle the subjective impression I felt when I first encountered the scene. I love rich colors as much as "colorless color": a white bird flying past a waterfall under falling snow. Danielle Föllmi—who, with her then husband Olivier, founded the HOPE Association (the Himalayan Organisation for People and Education), and with both of whom I published *Buddhist Himalayas*—once told me that I "painted with light." I don't see myself as worthy of such a lovely compliment, which I found very touching, but it does at least apply to the ideal I am pursuing through photography.

When I took the pictures for *Motionless Journey: From a Hermitage in the Himalayas*, I sat in the same place for a whole year, as if waiting for the light. But I was not waiting for anything, and I had no plans to make a book. I was simply staying in my hermitage on a retreat. From dawn to dusk, I looked out over a sublime landscape—the Himalayas stretching out majestically beneath my gaze. A fugitive light sometimes briefly ignited the scene unfolding before my dazzled eyes, and I took a few pictures. The "magical moments" that make up this collection, all taken from the terrace of my hermitage or within a few hundred yards of it, are the fruit of that "waiting without expectation," of the harmony of nature mingling with the bliss of meditation.

I sometimes go for months without taking a picture. Then comes a day when people, place, and light seem so lovely to me that I can't resist setting them down on film, an offering to all those who will look at it. Cartier-Bresson used to say, "Pictures take me, I don't take them." That's how I feel about it. The ideal is to live in the place where you photograph, so that time plays in your favor—one exceptional scene offers itself to your eyes, and you are there.

I often study and admire the work of the great photographers of the past: Ansel Adams, Ernst Haas (especially his masterpiece *The Creation*, which I regularly revisit), Galen Rowell, and many others besides. Today, I am friendly with a number of nature photographers I admire: Jim Brandenburg, Vincent Munier, and Yann Arthus-Bertrand, to name just a few.

I am still learning from them. I sometimes look at a particularly striking or inspiring image and find myself thoroughly absorbed in its beauty, its composition, or the message it conveys, an image that will dwell in my memory and enrich my vision. A successful photograph is one that we never tire of looking at and that uplifts us.

Another eminent photographer, Robert Capa, made this observation: "The pictures are there, and you just take them." Indeed, the gaze educates itself over the years, hones itself, and allows us to better see what is before us, to honor what the world and people bring to us, and then to make the colors shiver and the light sing in order to rediscover the sense of being gripped, of interrupted cerebration and of rapture we felt when contemplating a scene, a face, the immensity of the sky, the majesty of a mountain, the evanescence of a reflection, the labyrinth of a tree's bark, or the intimacy of a flower.

Images of violence and suffering are necessary to arouse the conscience and inspire our resolve to intervene, contribute, and remedy injustice. But we must never allow ourselves to overlook the potential for inner beauty in every being. We must keep ourselves in balance so as not to fall into the "wicked world syndrome," persuaded that the human being is fundamentally evil. The truth is, there lies within each of us, like a gold nugget, tremendous potential for goodness, wisdom, and enlightenment. There is nothing Pollyanna-ish or overidealistic about such "original goodness." What do we find at the very core our consciousness? Not hatred, not obsession, not arrogance but pure, luminous consciousness. When my photo book *Visages de paix, terres de sérénité* was published in 2015, the weekly magazine *L'Express* ran an article titled "Reporter of Peace"—an epithet I gladly embrace.

To be sure, translating such values into images is no easy feat. But the photographer can strive to capture the inner beauty of a spiritual teacher, the radiance of his goodness, the sweetness of a doe-eyed child, or the serenity of an old man with a toothless grin. He can share the wonder that overwhelmed him at the sight of a sublime landscape.

I sometimes travel far afield in search of certain images. When I was sixteen, I saw an iconic box-camera photo by Ansel Adams: a lake bordered by rocks in the foreground, with great depth of field and mountains in the background. Forty years later, having seen a picture of the

Tsophu lakes and hoping to find a similar setting, I walked for four days straight in the mountains of Bhutan with some friends from the region to see the lakes for myself. We reached our destination in the afternoon. The wind was blowing, and conditions were not right for photography. I told my friends that I intended to stay the night. We were 14,000 feet above sea level and had left our tents at the Jomolhari base camp, a two-hour walk away. They were not very enthusiastic, but reluctant to leave me to my sorry fate. We met a family of nomads who hosted us in their tent that night. I knew what would happen at sunrise the next day: at 6 a.m., the lake was like a mirror, and the lofty peak of Jichu Drake, more than 22,000 feet high, was perfectly reflected on its surface. I was thrilled to welcome an image in tribute to Ansel Adams to my camera. It was surely worth a four-day hike!

I've spent a lot of time photographing the world's wild places, wide-open spaces, and magnificent landscapes. A sense of wonder before pristine nature will not, in and of itself, solve the ecological crisis, but it can generate awareness of and respect for the extraordinary forces at work in nature. Respect leads to the desire to take care of its object, and such desire can lead to action. For all that, will we be sufficiently affected to do whatever it takes and with the requisite resolve to radically change our loves? Our activities are now causing the sixth mass extinction event since life began on Earth. It is still possible to avert this upheaval, but without the political will and individual engagement, we are not headed in that direction. There is an urgent need to act, and if my photos of natural beauty can contribute to that awakening, even in the most infinitesimal way, that would be reward enough.

If we wish to escape the rut of toothless proposals, we must take full account of the warnings issued by scientists and harness the tide of ideas promoting altruism and true well-being as authentic guides for our decision-making. This is about more than mere survival; it's about living better, in sustainable harmony with our ecosystem. One of the most precious gifts the world has to offer is its beauty, new with every day.

There are also pictures that I regret not having taken. In Kolkata, I once saw a man struggling to pull a carriage roped to a horse that trailed behind it. I can still see that image in my head, but not on film.

I am sometimes reluctant to take pictures, especially in the presence of a spiritual teacher. I'd rather take full advantage of his presence than play at being a reporter. Even so, if the circumstances are right, I'll take a few pictures as discreetly as possible, with a view to sharing with others the spiritual beauty that I have witnessed. You need to be present while remaining invisible, and to work the shutter as quietly as possible, while inwardly and respectfully requesting permission to enter the personal space of these exceptional beings.

One thing leading to another, neither a true professional nor an amateur, I have participated in many exhibitions and published a dozen books of photography, supplemented by texts in French and a few other languages. Maybe someday someone will ask me, "Great pictures, but who wrote the text?"

38

AN IMMENSE HEART
THE DALAI LAMA

As the Dalai Lama's French interpreter, I am fortunate to meet, through him, such remarkable beings as Desmond Tutu, Jody Williams, and Father Pierre Ceyrac. I accompany him to the Grande Chartreuse Monastery, which is normally off-limits to visits of any kind.

So much goodness! So much goodness. Nothing but goodness. These few words suffice to describe the essence of the fourteenth Dalai Lama's qualities. As I was told by Thubten Jinpa, who serves as his principal English interpreter and accompanies him on his many trips all over the world, "I have never met anyone who is so concerned about all humankind." At one of the dialogues organized by the Mind & Life Institute, the Dalai Lama told us that, during his morning practice, there is not one day when he does not shed tears at the thought of the immeasurable suffering of beings.

We can, of course, talk about his wisdom, his vast erudition, his life devoted to the study and teaching of Buddhism, to the sharing of the basic ethical values essential to all human beings, believers and nonbelievers alike, his sincere openness to dialogue with contemporary science, and his many other admirable qualities. But it is really his unconditional benevolence that places the Dalai Lama in a spiritual and human dimension all his own. According to Dudjom Rinpoche, many masters are distinguished by their level of spiritual realization, but an exceptional master is recognized by the magnitude of his love for beings and his compassion for their sufferings.

I have been fortunate to meet with that remarkable being many times, among them in December 1989, when he was passing through Paris on his way to Oslo to receive the Nobel Peace Prize. I happened to be in France at the time and went to greet the Dalai Lama on his arrival at his hotel. Until that time, if the Dalai Lama spoke in Tibetan when he was visiting a French-speaking country, his speech went through two interpreters, Tibetan to English and then English to French. Because I had often accompanied Khyentse Rinpoche on his trips to Dharamshala, the Dalai Lama knew that I spoke Tibetan fluently and that I had a reasonably competent knowledge of Buddhism. During the brief audience he granted me at his hotel, the Dalai Lama told his secretary that it would be more efficient to make use of only one interpreter—me, in this instance—who was just as comfortable translating Tibetan into English as into French. Naturally, I was very honored to be able to be of service in this way, and well aware of the responsibility that he had entrusted to me. From one day to the next, I became his French interpreter for the next thirty years.

I was thus the privileged witness to many edifying instances of the profoundly human nature of that most authentic person, particularly during chance encounters, which were especially revealing of the power of his unconditional love. I recall one evening, when a dialogue with students at the University of Bordeaux was coming to a close. The Dalai Lama had to pass through the dense throng of those who had been unable to find a seat in the amphitheater. An elderly couple stood to the side, not daring to plunge into the bustle; the husband stood behind his wife, who sat, frail and fragile, in a wheelchair. Ever alert, the Dalai Lama caught sight of them. He plowed through the crowd, took the old lady's hands in his, and looked at her with a smile, saying nothing but the inexpressible statement of his boundless kindness. After this brief encounter, which seemed to last forever, I heard the old man tell his wife, "You see, he's a saintly man."

How often have I seen the Dalai Lama go to shake a porter's hand, or that of a switchboard operator behind her partition, or take impish pleasure in giving a hearty backslap to a Republican Guardsman, standing at attention in his superb uniform with his sword drawn, flabbergasted yet delighted to be treated as a full-fledged human being?

On one of his visits to France, the Dalai Lama was received by President François Mitterrand at the Élysée Palace. After their meeting, the president escorted him to the front portico. But instead of getting into the car waiting at the foot of the stairs, the Dalai Lama, having noticed the guards in their gatehouse, threw protocol aside, walked up to the guards, and shook them by the hand, while the president, somewhat dumbfounded, couldn't decide whether to go back inside before his guest's departure or wait until he had finished his little outing. Ultimately, he chose to wait and waved to the Dalai Lama as his convoy finally sped away.

On another trip, the Dalai Lama was invited to speak before the foreign affairs committee of the National Assembly. As we were leaving, we ran into a minister who was emerging from a different chamber, accompanied by a bodyguard. The latter had been in charge of the Dalai Lama's security on an earlier trip and had spent some ten days with us. He remembered that assignment with great fondness and kept a photo of the Dalai Lama in his wallet. The Dalai Lama recognized him immediately and made straight for him. He embraced him and called him "My friend" with deep warmth, barely acknowledging the minister, whom he didn't know and who stood by watching without quite knowing what to do.

Breaking protocol to show interest in those who discreetly keep him safe is standard behavior for the Dalai Lama when he travels. In 2001, we went to the European Parliament in Strasbourg, where the Dalai Lama was to deliver a speech. An official luncheon had been organized with some twenty heads of European delegations. When we entered the hall, the Dalai Lama noticed two or three cooks who were watching the goings on from the partially opened door to the kitchens. Skipping out on the national representatives, he made directly for the kitchens and spent several minutes with those working there. Heading back to the great table, where everyone stood waiting for him, he proclaimed, "Smells good!"

As his interpreter, I also had the opportunity to spend some time alone with him, for instance when we were driving or in his antechamber between two visitors, or once when he spent half a day having a checkup at the Val-de-Grâce Hospital in Paris. I spent that day in his room, interpreting for him when the doctors came by. I took advantage of the situation to discuss spiritual matters with him, to talk about Dilgo Khyentse Rinpoche, and to ask him for advice about my practice. He always stressed the critical importance of compassion, mastering self-control, learning to be content with little, and behaving in conformity with the teachings, especially those on compassion. As we were leaving the hospital, we passed an elderly woman in a wheelchair. The Dalai Lama approached her, gazed at her kindly, paused for a moment, and asked after her health. She was at a loss for words, but the physician who had attended the Dalai Lama wrote me later to say that she had died a month afterward and had told him that her meeting with the Dalai Lama had brightened her final days.

I remember another typical example of the spontaneity with which he expresses his unconditional compassion—an incident that took place at the celebrations commemorating the fiftieth anniversary of the Universal Declaration of Human Rights, held in Paris in December 1998. On that occasion, the Dalai Lama gave a lecture with the highly respected French lawyer Robert Badinter at the Palais des Congrès convention center in Porte Maillot, Paris. Robert Badinter had passionately and successfully advocated for the abolition of the death penalty in France, and subsequently became justice minister under François Mitterrand. He is now considered one the great moral figures in France and had invited the Dalai Lama for the fiftieth anniversary commemorations. It was raining when we left, and as we drove along the highway, an officer of the national gendarmerie who was escorting us on motorcycle skidded and fell. No sooner had we reached our hotel than the Dalai Lama asked for news of the officer. We learned that the officer was a woman and that, despite a nasty blow to her arm, she was doing fine. The Dalai Lama was leaving for India the next morning, and he asked whether she could and would come to the hotel to meet him. The next morning, the officer came to see us, arm in sling, and was received by the Dalai Lama in his antechamber. He hugged her—carefully avoiding her painful arm—then spent several minutes talking to her and gave her one of his books, which he inscribed to her. She was moved to tears. The fate of that motorcycle cop seemed to weigh more on his mind than the memory of all the statesmen he had met on his visit to France.

On that same trip, the Dalai Lama, a surprise guest at an Amnesty International concert in Bercy, stepped onto the stage ablaze with spotlights, between two rock songs. Fifteen thousand young people leaped to their feet and gave a thunderous ovation to the apostle of nonviolence. In a silence rarely heard in such places, they listened intently to the warm words he spoke to them. Some in the audience noisily voiced their approbation but were silenced by the rest with a resounding "Hush!" I'm not very familiar with rock concerts, but does anyone ever cry "Hush!" for silence at such events? I doubt it. I was supposed to interpret, but his speech in English was simple and direct, and it seemed pointless to interrupt. So, I simply stood beside him, just in case—he can sometimes struggle for a word in English, and an interpreter who knows him well can suggest it for him. When the Dalai Lama left the stage, the audience again roared its approval. How do you explain such unanimity, such heartfelt sincerity from a crowd that hadn't even known he would be there? One thinks of Gandhi or Martin Luther King Jr. Those fifteen thousand young people had seen the greatness of his heart. Such spontaneity can be neither artificial nor taught.

When the Dalai Lama is asked why he elicits such warm responses, he replies in all simplicity and humility: "There's nothing special about me. Maybe it's just that I've spent my whole life meditating several hours a day on love and compassion."

Rabjam Rinpoche once innocently asked his grandfather, Dilgo Khyentse Rinpoche, "Who is the greatest spiritual teacher of our times?" Khyentse Rinpoche replied without hesitating, "Gyalwa Rinpoche, no doubt about it." Gyalwa Rinpoche—"Precious Victor"—is one of the names Tibetans use to refer to the Dalai Lama. "Victor" refers here to victory over ignorance and the causes of suffering.

Over time and through the ups and downs of life, his message has remained constant and unwavering. He repeats it to anyone who will listen: "Every individual, even the ill-disposed, is, like me, a living being who fears suffering, wishes to be happy, and has every right to be spared suffering and attain happiness. That consideration helps us to feel deeply concerned for the well-being of others, our friends and our enemies alike. It is the foundation of authentic compassion."

For me, spending a few days or weeks in the Dalai Lama's presence was like bathing in a spring of spiritual and human rejuvenation. One of his most striking qualities is his unflagging authenticity, the benevolent simplicity with which he treats all he meets, be they humble or mighty. He is exactly the same—present, alert, gentle, and curious—with everyone, whatever their position, status, or pedigree.

Greatness of soul and gentleness imbued with humor. A lack of ego does indeed nurture the sense of humor that we often find in great Tibetan masters, and even in the laypeople of the Land of Snows, who are all ever ready with a joke. The Dalai Lama is no exception to that cultural idiosyncrasy; his natural authenticity and dignity are often complemented by spontaneous levity when confronted with an incongruous situation—levity that usually comes with a hearty laugh that the Dalai Lama amplifies with an amused look at his interlocutor.

In that same year of 1989, when he was staying in Paris, the French first lady, Danielle Mitterrand, jointly presented the Dalai Lama and Serge Klarsfeld with the Prix de la Mémoire, in her capacity as head of the jury. The prize was a piece by the sculptor César, who worked by compressing objects in a hydraulic press. The piece in question was a metal object about eight inches square, unidentifiable because of the method of its creation. As he was wrapping up his thank-you speech, the Dalai Lama quipped, "And I also received—" Gazing at the object and not sure quite what to say, he concluded, "—something."

The next morning, after the Dalai Lama and his entourage had left, the members of the Tibet Bureau in Paris were gathering up the various gifts he had received on his visit and were about to leave the sculpture behind. I ventured to inform them that, contrary to appearances, it had some value on the art market and that they would be well advised to take it with them. I have noticed over the years that Tibetans are relatively unmoved by contemporary art. I must admit that, although I highly admire my mother's work, which has been labeled "lyrical abstraction," more often than not I am left blithely mystified by contemporary art.

The next year, Danielle Mitterrand, who had taken up the cause of the legitimate and peaceful aspirations of the Tibetan people, went to see the Dalai Lama in Dharamshala, India. He showed her the sights, and when they came to the great statue of the Buddha housed in the temple of the monastery located below his residence, he pointed at it respectfully and cracked in English, "My boss!"

At a public lecture in Geneva in 1999, a crowd gathered in the Mon Repos Park. There was no screen to broadcast the event. I stood next to the Dalai Lama to interpret, dressed exactly like him, my head shaved and, like him, wearing glasses. Aware that many people were watching from far back, he began with an explanation: "You see, the monk next to me is a body double, so in case anyone tries to kill me he won't know who to shoot," then he burst out in roaring laughter as he slapped me briskly on the shoulder.

Being the Dalai Lama's interpreter was a very special experience for me, but difficult to describe. A sort of osmosis happens, triggered by my respect for my teacher; the Dalai Lama's words directly penetrate my mind, which must be completely free of the thoughts that usually encumber it. Even one moment of distraction can make me completely lose the thread of his discourse. The interpreter must be perfectly present, with clear and optimal attentiveness, although not tense, which would soon exhaust him. After lengthy translation sessions with Khyentse Rinpoche, Tulku Pema Wang-yal would also remind me that the teacher's blessing surely played a role in the interpreter's ability to accurately render his words. When the Dalai Lama spoke for ten minutes straight before giving me the floor, I had to remember the sequence of the main points he had just raised. Above all, I could not lose that thread! It sometimes happened that, at the moment when the Dalai Lama gave me the floor, I would forget the opening words of his statement. Time came to a halt, and I stood mum a moment or two, desperately seeking the very first words he had spoken, the silence awkward and disconcerting. The audience and the Dalai Lama, who were accustomed to hearing me translate these lengthy passages without much difficulty, must have wondered what had happened and why I was suddenly speechless. And then, as luck would have it, the opening would suddenly pop into my head and the rest flow naturally. Failing that, I would translate starting at the point I remembered and, more often than not, the opening would come back to me as I went along. I would then add it to my interpretation, noting that I had omitted one portion.

In 2001, in Strasbourg, during the Dalai Lama's speech before a full house of the European Parliament, I found myself in the interpreters' booth with the professionals who had to translate the Dalai Lama's words directly into the various European languages when he spoke English, or on the basis of my translation when he switched to Tibetan. They asked me if I had a written statement of the Dalai Lama's speech.

"He improvises," I replied.

"Where's your partner?" they asked, the rule being that there must be two interpreters per booth who take turns every twenty minutes.

"Partner? Afraid it's just me," I explained.

The Dalai Lama spoke at a steady pace, half in English, half in Tibetan, and I did my best to interpret simultaneously. It may be surprising, but it's easier to interpret simultaneously because you don't need to remember everything the Dalai Lama said in his lengthy statement before pausing to allow the interpreter to catch up. In any case, by the end of his speech, which lasted about fifty minutes, the interpreters—who had had to rely on my translation when the Dalai Lama spoke Tibetan—were all smiles and told me I'd done alright for myself. I thanked them for the compliment and explained that the Dalai Lama's interpreters were used to it—he sometimes teaches for five or six hours a day.

In 2003, the Dalai Lama gave five days of teachings at the Bercy stadium in Paris, to more than ten thousand people. Avoiding all fiery rhetoric, the Dalai Lama's discourse expounded a profound philosophy, an investigation into the nature of reality and an account of the means available to become better human beings. As usual, he leavened his teachings with practical advice and humor. The Dalai Lama's manner of teaching is deeply pragmatic. The simple things he speaks of are the fruit of his direct experience and a life devoted to spiritual practice.

The first morning, he explained how Buddhist philosophy rejects two points of view that he describes as "extremes" or deviations concerning the nature of phenomena: nihilism and materialism (or naive realism). Among others, he quoted *The Perfection of Transcendent Knowledge* (the *Prajnaparamita*), which specifies,

To talk about the "true existence" of phenomena is eternalism;
To talk about their "non-existence" is nihilism.
To fall into the extreme of eternalism or nihilism
Is to be ignorant.
And ignorance prevents your liberation from samsara.

The Dalai Lama consistently stresses the importance of studying the great texts of Buddhist philosophy, the exegeses of the Buddha's teachings written by such renowned scholars as Nagarjuna, Aryadeva, Asanga,

Chandrakirti, and Shantideva, who lived in India between the first and seventh centuries and are among the greatest thinkers in history. In Tibet, hundreds of commentaries have been written to explicate, with insight and clarity, the philosophical views expounded in these texts. In his view, such advanced studies are an essential foundation of contemplative practice.

He also undertook a thorough deconstruction of the concept of individual identity—an allegedly independent, singular, and enduring "self." It was a demonstration of his profound erudition; he drew on numerous quotations and canonical commentaries. On stage, I translated to the best of my ability while my friends and colleagues the interpreters translated in the English, German, Italian, and Spanish booths, among others. At our midday break, they told me that they sympathized with me, given the complexity of the teachings and knowing that being the primary interpreter must intensify my sense of responsibility to the Dalai Lama and the public.

At the end of the morning session, the Dalai Lama announced that audience members could submit questions in writing that he would answer at the beginning of the afternoon session. I sought him out before the resumption of the teachings and informed him that many participants found the concept of "no-self" hard to grasp. Among other things, they wanted to know how, if the self does not exist, you can be responsible for your own actions. What's the point of talking about karma and successive lives if there's nothing there to be reincarnated? The Dalai Lama threw me an amused glance. "It's your fault!" he said. "You must have translated wrong. I never said that the self doesn't exist *at all*." Then he burst out laughing, knowing that I'd done a good job relaying his presentation, and added, "I'll explain it all again. The self does exist, but only in a conventional way, in the form of a concept attached to the continuum of consciousness. But it is not an entity endowed with independent existence."

My friend Christof Spitz, an excellent Tibetan-German translator with whom I have often worked when the Dalai Lama has taught in Europe, told me that he had had a very bad stomachache that morning and had had to step away for a few minutes. Another German interpreter, less experienced than he, had to sub for him in the interpretation booth. Christof asked him to step in just as the Dalai Lama was elaborating an especially complex philosophical issue. His friend pleaded, "But I don't understand it!" To which Christof replied, "It doesn't matter. Just say something—whatever comes to mind!" But he'd forgotten to turn off his microphone, and the German audience members had a good laugh.

Paul Ekman, one of the world's greatest experts on the psychology of emotions, once said that in all his fifty years of observing facial expressions, he had never met anyone whose feelings were expressed so transparently on his face as the Dalai Lama. The Dalai Lama is a stranger to hypocrisy and has absolutely no interest in his image. His natural simplicity sweeps away all barriers. How often have I seen people approach him with a formal, resolved, and sometimes dubious attitude, only to come away a short while later with tears in their eyes and hearts overflowing with human warmth. It had taken only a few moments for the Dalai Lama's disarming authenticity and goodness to bring the best out in them.

A person like the Dalai Lama, who has freed himself from the dictates of the ego, thinks and acts with a spontaneity and a freedom that contrast triumphantly with the paranoia generated by self-centeredness. Paul Ekman has studied people whom he describes as "endowed with exceptionally human qualities."[1] The remarkable characteristics he has identified in them include "an impression of kindness, a way of being that others can sense and appreciate, and, unlike so many charismatic charlatans, perfect harmony between their private and public lives," but above all, "an absence of ego. These people inspire others by how little they make of their status, their fame—in short, their self. They never give a second thought to whether their position or importance is recognized." Such a lack of egocentricity, he adds, "is altogether perplexing from a psychological point of view." Paul also stresses that "people instinctively want to be in their company. Even if they can't always say why, they find their presence enriching." Such qualities offer a striking contrast to the foibles of the narcissistic champions of the ego, who are too often in important positions in our world these days.

The Dalai Lama himself asserts, "Even in my dreams, I see myself not as the Dalai Lama, but as a simple monk." When he interacts with the world, with the host of humankind, it is as a simple human who wishes to share the values that he believes to be beneficial to one and all. At a public lecture in Brussels at which I served as his interpreter, he began by declaring: "I stand here before you simply as a human being sharing his experience with other human beings. If I think, 'I am Tibetan,' I [establish] a degree of separation; 'I am a monk,' two degrees of separation; 'I am the Dalai Lama,' three degrees of separation. No, I stand here before you simply as a human being."

I recall one story in particular that illustrates just how that quality of being extends to everything about the Dalai Lama. In 1998, I accompanied the French journalist and television producer Michel Denisot to Dharamshala, where he was to interview the Dalai Lama for the television show *À part ça!*, airing on the Canal+ channel.[2] At dinner the night before their meeting, Denisot, who was the director of the Paris Saint-Germain soccer club, was upset because he had just learned that his team had lost a game. The next morning, we set up for the shoot with a crew of five or six. The tension was palpable, and heightened by a blackout that required us to install a backup generator in a hurry. The ban on smoking in any house where the Dalai Lama is present probably didn't help the crew relax.

Everything was finally ready. The Dalai Lama arrived and, from one moment to the next, the jitters died down like boiling milk removed from the heat. We spent more than an hour in fascinating conversation between the Dalai Lama and Michel Denisot, with me doing simultaneous interpretation. When the interview came to an end, a perfect silence descended on the room. The Dalai Lama draped a ceremonial scarf of white silk over the neck of each crew member, and even over the camera lens, laughing and turning around several times to wave goodbye to everyone as he left. The script supervisor, who had a great deal to do and had been especially tense before the shoot, dissolved in tears and said, "What's wrong with me? Why am I crying? It all went so well."

In India, the town of Dharamshala slumbers peacefully at the foot of the dark and imposing mass of the Himalaya mountains. A few lanterns glimmer on the crest of a wooded hill. The fourteenth Dalai Lama wakes up. For one of the most remarkable beings of our time, the day begins with prayer and meditation. Wherever he is and whatever the circumstances, the spiritual guide of the Tibetan people meditates for four hours every morning—meditation that, more than anything else, is a profound prayer for the benefit of beings.

The room is very plain, paneled in varnished wood, bare of the brightly colored decorations that hang in Tibetan temples. A statue of the Buddha, photographs of his spiritual teachers, and sacred texts sit on the little altar. Toward 6 a.m., while listening to the BBC World Service, the Dalai Lama eats his modest breakfast with a hearty appetite because, like all Buddhist monks, he does not eat dinner. Then he continues to meditate until eight or nine o'clock.

The Dalai Lama adheres unfailingly to this discipline, from which he draws the strength he needs to pursue his tireless activities. When he was nominated for the Nobel Peace Prize in 1989, journalists flocked to his home early in the morning to report the Tibetan leaders' first reaction. The only response they were able get out of the affable and discreet monk who had tended to the Dalai Lama's needs for the past thirty years was, "He hasn't heard the news yet. We never disturb him during his spiritual practice." At the conclusion of his meditation, he moves into a room containing precious relics preserved from Tibet. They include a life-size sandalwood statue of the Buddha that had been offered to the Dalai Lama by followers who had saved it from the devastation unleashed by the Chinese invasion. The Dalai Lama prostrates one hundred times before this statue, which he represents to himself as being the Buddha in person—a humble tribute that he pays not to a god, prophet, or saint, but to enlightenment and supreme wisdom.

I'd been told that, upon request, it was possible to see the statue. I shared my wish to do so with the monk who tends to the Dalai Lama day and night, and whom I know well. Two days later, I was told to come early in the morning. When I was admitted to the Dalai Lama's apartments, he was waiting for me, alone. He took me by the hand and led me to his temple, waited while I prostrated three times before the statue of the Buddha, then took me one by one past the priceless statues and relics kept in glass cases along the wall. Finally, he brought me to the precious Buddha statue, before which stood a photo of his root teacher, Ling Rinpoche. He picked up a magnificent rock crystal and handed it to me, saying, "You are a practitioner of the Great Perfection. This crystal is a symbol of the nature of mind." Before taking my leave, I asked him, with all the respect

I feel for him, if he would bless my spiritual practice. I was a good monk, guided by authentic spiritual teachers, he told me. Everything should go well. I left feeling lighthearted, borne up by a wind of joy and plenitude that I will not attempt to describe. "How can a mute describe the taste of wild honey?" asks the Tibetan proverb.

The second half of the Dalai Lama's morning is devoted to external tasks. "I go to my office around nine o'clock if I have people to see. If not, I read philosophy. I recall texts that I've read in the past and I delve deeper into the commentaries of the great masters of the various schools of Tibetan Buddhism. I think about the teachings and I meditate a little. I have lunch around one o'clock. I then go about my daily business and receive visitors until five. I take tea around six. If my stomach is growling, I bow to the Buddha and ask his permission to snack on a few cookies. Finally, I say my evening prayers and go to sleep around seven-thirty, and then . . . eight hours' sleep. Everybody should try it!"

Meetings with Tibetans who have come all the way from the high plateaus of the Land of Snows are always emotional events. To see the Dalai Lama, if only this once in their lifetimes, some have to cross snowbound passes more than 16,000 feet high and dodge the Chinese army guarding the borders, since most Tibetans are unable to get permission to leave China. And yet they somehow manage to defy the proscription and cannot hold back their tears of joy when the Dalai Lama inquires, in his deep, resonant voice, about their personal odyssey and the situation in Tibet. He asked one monk who had spent twenty years in prison and been tortured again and again if he had been afraid. The monk humbly ducked his head: "My greatest fear was that I would come to hate my torturers," he replied.

The Dalai Lama's residence overlooks the vast plains of India, which seem to stretch on forever beneath one's gaze. The Tibetans call it a "palace" (*phodrang*), although it's really just a house with a few annexes for the Dalai Lama's private secretary, an auditorium, and a conference room. It is in that room that, among other things, seminars and dialogues with scientists, philosophers, or representatives of other spiritual and religious traditions take place, sometimes over the course of several days.

To the north, a few peaks remind us that, beyond the massive mountain chain that surrounds the Land of Snows, Tibet is less than a hundred miles away as the crow flies—so close, so far, and inaccessible to the Dalai Lama so long as its people are unable to enjoy their most fundamental freedoms.

A hushed atmosphere and benevolent calm reign in the residence. People speak softly here, conscious of the vanity of unnecessary speech. Not one superfluous gesture or word. And this silence is broken only by raucous, cascading bursts of laughter from Kundun, the "Presence," which is how the Tibetans refer to the Dalai Lama with love and respect. The Presence: he who is never absent whether you are at his side or at a great distance from him. The joyful laughter sometimes gives way to a silent smile when the Dalai Lama goes on retreat for a few weeks, as he does every year, and more often now that he is advanced in years. On retreat, he voices nothing but his prayers. Retreat—the fruitful alliance of inward contemplation and compassion radiating outward continuously and effortlessly. Most definitely, a "palace" of serenity.

Until the Dalai Lama decided, at the age of eighty-five, to give up long-distance travel, the well-ordered routine of his days often gave way to a whirlwind of journeys throughout the world and to the teachings he offered over the course of fifty years to crowds that sometimes ran into the hundreds of thousands of his followers. The need to tend to the hopes of so many people and to uphold the cause of Tibet, crushed under the boot of a totalitarian regime, compelled this tireless pilgrim of peace to work without respite, if only for a few precious minutes a day. Despite this barely sustainable pace, Kundun maintained the same serenity on his mission of compassion, the same sincerity. No matter whom he met—a visitor or a passer-by in the airport—he was totally and immediately present, his benevolent gaze joyfully crossing the threshold of your heart, where he deposited a smile before quietly moving on.

In 2006, when I was just about to begin a yearlong retreat at my hermitage in Nepal, I had the opportunity to ask His Holiness for advice. "In the beginning, practice compassion; in the middle, practice compassion; at the end, practice compassion," he replied. By "compassion," he meant the desire to see all beings find happiness and the causes of happiness (altruism) and the wish to see all beings freed of suffering and the causes of suffering (compassion).

But goodness does not mean weakness, and the orator's strength can sometimes reveal itself unexpectedly. Speaking to the Paris Bar Association, where he was warmly welcomed, in particularly by his friend Robert Badinter, he said, "My fight for the people of Tibet is not one of those battles that end with a winner or a loser, or more often than not two losers; what I am striving with all my strength to win is the victory of truth." What he meant by "truth" in this context was the triumph of the simple and legitimate aspirations of the Tibetans, who—following the Dalai Lama's vision of the "middle way"—do not seek independence for Tibet but simply the ability to preserve their Buddhist culture (whereas a "good" Tibetan is now supposed to fully assimilate into Chinese society and culture); their language, spoken and written (most schools teach in Chinese alone); and their way of life (nomads are often compelled to become sedentary in order to be more easily controlled by the authorities). The "middle way" so frequently championed by the Dalai Lama, before the European Parliament among others, would involve a certain degree of autonomy with respect to language, culture, religion, and lifestyle—essentially, a significant share of domestic affairs, as is often the case in federal states, while remaining within China and deferring to the central government in the management of foreign affairs, health care, and defense.

The Dalai Lama often refers to the idea of "nonviolence" concerning humans, animals, and the environment. When he spent three weeks in France in 1993—his longest visit to date—he went to the peace memorial in Caen. On that occasion, he explained that peace is not merely the absence of war; if peace is to have any meaning, it must involve trust in and respect for others. One must be able to forgive without forgetting, practice nonviolence without weakness, and develop inner disarmament in order to achieve outward disarmament. "The twentieth century was an era of war," he concluded. "It witnessed destruction on a scale never before seen in human history, wars akin to vast pyres for which human beings were the fuel. May the twenty-first century be an era of dialogue." We still have a long way to go.

I am rereading the notes I made that day, when I was interpreting for him: "Why is someone who kills a man considered to be a murderer, while someone who kills many is a hero? Every war begins with ill-will that devolves into hatred. We need to act on the first sign of animosity, otherwise it will be too late. Violence and warfare are only perversions of human nature. What we need is to rediscover our true identity as human beings who cherish happiness and fear suffering and who—every race, religion, language, and culture—have the same rights to know happiness and be spared suffering."

On another visit to France, the Dalai Lama declared, "A country that sells weapons sells its soul. Violence begets violence," he emphasized, "and unleashes a chain reaction." When we know that 95 per cent of the world's weapons are manufactured and sold by the five permanent members of the United Nations Security Council—those that are supposed to ensure peace in the world—the double standards are glaring.

For all that, according to the Dalai Lama, nonviolence is in no way a submission to the aggression of others or to tyranny; that would be a harmful abdication both for the victim and for his executioner. It is, instead, necessary to break the cycle of hatred. Nonviolence consists essentially of respecting others: human beings, animals, the environment, all that is living. Human beings and animals share the same desire to avoid suffering and preserve their lives—that is common natural law. Nature, too, must be respected. According to the Dalai Lama, "Seeking happiness while remaining indifferent to the suffering of others is a tragic error." In this, he is of the same mind as Martin Luther King Jr., who said, "Nonviolence is a powerful and just weapon, which cuts without wounding and ennobles the man who wields it. It is a sword that heals."

Some are surprised to learn that the Dalai Lama is not a strict vegetarian. He was so for several years after he left Tibet. However, when he fell ill and came down with jaundice, his Tibetan doctor directed him to eat a little meat every week, which he has continued to do after his recovery. At a Mind & Life Institute encounter with a group of environmental scientists, I ventured to mention, with the greatest respect, that a balanced vegetarian diet was perfectly suited to the maintenance of a man's health. He looked at me impishly. At a lunch organized in honor of the scientists, we were standing by the buffet when the Dalai Lama turned to some people nearby and said, "You see, I eat a little meat from time to time," adding as he gave me a little slap on the head and burst into laughter, "Not like this monk next to me!"

On the other hand, whenever he's teaching for a week or two in India, and one hundred thousand followers have come from all the neighboring countries and lands, Nepal and Bhutan in particular, to hear him, he asks everyone to observe a vegetarian diet for the duration of the teachings so as to avoid the massacre of animals that such a gathering would undoubtedly entail if the participants consumed meat. The vast majority of Tibetan monasteries in India and Nepal today no longer cook meat.

Of all the Tibetan teachers, the Dalai Lama is without doubt the most widely respected. His teachings and advice—far from being prescriptions, much less orders—are profound sources of inspiration to all. No one goes around the monasteries and Buddhist centers to check whether his advice is being followed. When acts contrary to the Buddha's teaching are committed, only those who live on-site or frequently visit these institutions are qualified to bear witness, and he often encourages the victims of abuse perpetrated in some Buddhist centers to report them openly and to take legal action, if necessary.

Unlike some other religions, Buddhism has no hierarchical organization. The schools of Buddhism that have arisen in various countries are all independent of one another. At the heart of Tibetan Buddhism, the heads of the four main schools are respected spiritual authorities, but they are not involved in the functions and conduct of the monasteries, which administer themselves. The Dalai Lama frequently reminds us that it is the teachings themselves that serve as the true guardrails; they clearly lay out the qualities of the spiritual teachers to be followed and the faults of those to be avoided.

Until 2018, whenever the Dalai Lama taught anywhere in the world, one of the organizers would publicly submit the balance of income and expenses when the teachings ended, sometimes reporting a financial loss. If there was money left over, however, the inviting organization would distribute it among charitable works, chosen in consultation with the Dalai Lama. The Dalai Lama never accepted the gifts he was offered on such occasions. The Dalai Lama's local expenses in India are covered by the Central Tibetan Administration, the equivalent of the Tibetan government in exile, which is headquartered in Dharamshala and represents Tibetan refugees in India before the Indian government.

The establishment of greater harmony among religions is an important issue for the Dalai Lama. Whenever he goes to a foreign country, the Dalai Lama affirms, in his straightforward manner, "I did not come here to make one or two more Buddhists, but to share the experience I have accumulated in a lifetime devoted to cultivating compassion and promoting the basic human values we all need to build a caring world. To be sure, each person must find the path best suited to his aspirations, but in my opinion, it is better to follow the spiritual traditions and customs of his own country—those he was raised in and that were followed by his ancestors. That is the wiser course. That said, we may sometimes search other traditions for the sources of inspiration that will help us strengthen our own religion." While the Dalai Lama naturally wishes to see the teachings of Buddhism thrive, for the benefit of beings, he scrupulously avoids all forms of proselytizing, and I have often heard him privately tell Tibetan lamas living in the West to teach in a manner best adapted to those who wish to practice Buddhism, and to promote human values in general, but to avoid promoting the propagation of Buddhism. In the same spirit, once when he met evangelical missionaries in Mongolia, he thanked them for their charitable activities but asked that they not use them to convert the local populace.

The Dalai Lama deeply deplores the fact that religions have too often been the catalysts of major conflict. Doesn't every denomination profess the notion of love toward all people? According to him, principles deviate from their true nature when religion is brandished like a flag to divide people instead of seeking to understand and practice the deep meaning of its elevated spirituality. He suggests four approaches that could contribute to eliminating such strife. The first consists of promoting encounters among theologians to help them acquire a more correct and in-depth understanding of their respective traditions, which allows them to identify what they have in common and to respectfully acknowledge their differences. The second brings together contemplatives from the various traditions to share their spiritual experiences, thereby stimulating the affiliation that arises naturally among those who have devoted their lives to inner practice. The third way to bridge the gap among the major religions is to invite their representatives on pilgrimage to the holy places of their respective traditions. Indeed, men and women who go on pilgrimage in a spirit of humility and absorb the spiritual power of these remarkable sites usually come away without their former sectarian biases and intellectual roadblocks. Such multidenominational pilgrimages promote a climate of brotherhood and understanding. In that spirit, the Dalai Lama has traveled in the company of representatives of other religions to Jerusalem, Lourdes, Fatima, Varanasi, the Kumbh Mela in Allahabad (where seventy million Hindus gathered in 2002), and many other sacred places around the world. The fourth initiative involves organizing gatherings of religious leaders of all faiths, such as that held in Assisi in 1986 at the invitation of Pope John Paul II, where these leaders are able to foster mutual respect and, through dialogue, find solutions to tensions among different communities.

Early in the morning on October 29, 1993, we were on the high-speed train from Paris to Grenoble, where the Dalai Lama had been invited by Alain Carignon, who was the minister for information and the mayor of the city at that time. I sat across from him as he recited his prayers. As we passed below the Chartreuse Mountains, I told the Dalai Lama that, on the other side of the massif, in an isolated valley, was the Grand Chartreuse Monastery (Great Charterhouse), where Christian contemplatives spent their entire lives in retreat.

When we reached Grenoble, Alain Carignon asked the Dalai Lama if he had any particular request. The Dalai Lama immediately replied that he'd like to visit the Grande Chartreuse. The deputy mayor informed us that visitors were not allowed, and that no important religious leader had ever crossed the Chartreuse threshold, not even Pope John Paul II when he visited the region in 1986, because of the disruption such an important visit would cause. He assured us that he would nevertheless send a message to the prior of the monastery, Dom André Poisson.

The next morning, we were notified that the Dalai Lama was welcome at the monastery, provided that he came with a very small retinue and that no one was informed of the visit. Alain Carignon therefore advised the press that he had invited the Dalai Lama for a private lunch at his home. Instead, we were taken to a police helipad, where a helicopter flew the Dalai Lama, his monk assistant, Alain Carignon, and me to the entrance of the Grand Chartreuse, located in a superb glen overlooked by the Grand Som and surrounded by a lovely forest, at 2,600 feet elevation. The four of us were invited through the great gate.

The prior, Dom André, and another monk were waiting for us. We talked for about an hour in a small room not far from the main entrance. The conversation revolved entirely around the subject of the contemplative life. The prior and the Dalai Lama compared the way in which monks undertake retreats according to the Carthusian and Tibetan traditions. They each described the hours of the day and night when monks prayed, the rituals performed, and the manner of interment when a monk died (at the Chartreuse, he is buried in the earth without a coffin; in Tibet, depending on who the deceased may be, there is sometimes a cremation, more rarely a burial, or, more often than not, the body is left on a rock for the vultures, which is known as a "sky burial").

They then went into greater detail discussing prayer and contemplation—how prayer began with a focus on a support, such as images of saints, then gradually changed into pure contemplation in an unspoken and ineffable union. As they spoke, they came to see that the spirit and modalities of the eremitical life of their respective traditions were very similar. Dom André joked, "Either Christian and Tibetan contemplatives had contact with one another more than a thousand years ago, or they received the same blessing from heaven!" The meeting was both joyful and inspiring. They spoke the same language—that of the contemplative life.

The father prior also told us that the first charterhouse hermitage had been founded by Saint Bruno in 1084, and that, in the past, whenever the number of monks in a charterhouse reached fifty, a new monastery was established elsewhere to accommodate them. Thus, from the fourteenth to the sixteenth centuries, hundreds of charterhouses sprang up throughout Europe, where monks and nuns lived in separate monasteries and remote places. He concluded his presentation by saying somewhat wistfully, "Forty monks live in the Grande Chartreuse today."

When the conversation ended, the Dalai Lama asked if we might gather in the chapel. We walked through a garden, where we saw other buildings that housed the monks' cells and a kitchen garden maintained by the congregation. A serene hush reigned over all. The chapel was empty, and we stayed there in silence for some ten minutes. Before leaving, the Dalai Lama studied the book of hours, decorated with elegant musical notations, which the prior explained to him. Suddenly, a monk in white entered at the far end of the chapel. He clearly had not been forewarned of our visit, and he stopped dead, as if petrified at the sight of these three monks in red surrounding the prior, then turned around and vanished. It should be noted that the monks take a vow of silence, and while they may occasionally speak briefly for practical reasons, they do not engage in conversation. We took our leave. Before saying goodbye, the Dalai Lama and Dom André embraced warmly. We returned to Grenoble.

The secret of the visit eventually got out, and toward the end of the Dalai Lama's three weeks in France, when he met with François Mitterrand, among others, a reported asked him about the highlights of his trip. The Dalai Lama replied that his visit to the Grande Chartreuse had been his most memorable moment. "As I entered the building, I felt a great sense of peace, a vast silence. It's an extraordinary place, but it's a bit cold! We prayed together. All of us were deeply moved. And then we spent some time meditating in the monastic silence."[3]

It was always astonishing to witness a meeting between the Dalai Lama and Desmond Tutu. They constantly joked with each other and laughed like children, while sharing words with their audience that are as simple as they are profound.

On June 1, 2006, in Brussels, the Light of Truth Award, previously presented to Elie Wiesel and Vaclav Havel by the International Campaign for Tibet, was jointly conferred by the Dalai Lama on Archbishop Desmond Tutu, Nobel Peace Prize laureate, for his work on behalf of Tibet, and the Hergé Foundation, represented by Fanny Rodwell, the widow of the Belgian cartoonist Hergé, in honor of the famous comic *Tintin in Tibet*, which in its own way drew attention to Tibet at a time when few people knew or cared about it. The Dalai Lama draped a white silk scarf over the archbishop's neck and handed him a Tibetan butter lamp, symbol of the "light of truth."

Desmond Tutu began his speech by displaying a caricature published in the South African press titled *Tintin and Tutu in Tibet*. Nor did he fail to note that the Dalai Lama sometimes behaved like a naughty boy and often needed to be reprimanded: "You must behave! People are watching us! Don't forget you are supposed to be a holy man!" He went on to say, "I give great thanks to God that he has created a Dalai Lama. You might think that God would be saying, 'This guy is really good. What a pity he's not a Christian!' But you know," Tutu concluded, "God himself is not a Christian."

The Dalai Lama reminded the audience that Tibetan Buddhist culture was not the exclusive heritage of six million Tibetans, but that in our times it could bring great benefits to billions of people. He urged his fellow citizens and supporters not to consider the Chinese as their enemy.

In his own speech, Desmond Tutu drew an explicit connection between the anti-apartheid movement and the campaign for Tibetan autonomy. "It is impossible to halt the march to freedom," he asserted. Tutu also called on the Chinese government to "do the right thing" for the Dalai Lama and Tibet. He expressed the hope that China, as an emerging country and global political force, would become a "superpower champion in promoting freedom in the world, and more particularly in Tibet." He also added, "The evil will never have the last word. Yes, they have power and weapons, but they have already lost. . . . Justice, goodness, compassion, and love will prevail. Nothing can resist freedom."

One day in April 2008, the Dalai Lama and Desmond Tutu were chatting before heading off to Key Arena, in Seattle, Washington, where they were to speak on the importance of compassion in our lives. They were told that sixty thousand people had gathered to hear them. Tutu turned to the Dalai Lama and said, "I'm not jealous, not at all. But even so, sixty thousand people waiting to hear someone who can't even speak proper English?" The Dalai Lama burst out laughing.

In May 2015, when Desmond Tutu went to Dharamshala, India, to celebrate the Dalai Lama's eightieth birthday, they spent a week in private conversation together, discussing joy, fear, anger, loneliness, humility, generosity. The archbishop confided in the Dalai Lama: "I think one of the best things that ever happened to me was meeting you."[4] Speaking to a crowd of Tibetans on the main square, Desmond Tutu weighed his every word, as he did so well: "He is the most saintly person I have ever met." Then, indirectly addressing the Chinese government: "Please! Please! Listen to me. The Dalai Lama loves peace on earth more than anyone else."

On a visit to Switzerland in 1999, the Dalai Lama was invited by the French Catholic priest Abbé Pierre to deliver the Sunday sermon at Geneva Cathedral. The building was packed, and a large crowd had gathered outside. As the great organs boomed, the Dalai Lama and Abbé Pierre entered the building and walked side by side up the central aisle to the altar. I followed behind the Dalai Lama, and tears began to well in my eyes. The Dalai Lama delivered a magnificent sermon on love and our common humanity. When his turn came, Abbé Pierre spoke of the fragility of life and of death, and added, with a spark of humor tinged with lassitude, that as far as he was concerned, one lifetime was more than enough. He had no use for more!

The next morning, Abbé Pierre and the Dalai Lama went to "Farinet's vineyard," the smallest registered vineyard in the world, named after Joseph-Samuel Farinet, a young peasant who had discovered a gold deposit in the mountains and set about producing counterfeit coins that were more valuable than the real thing because of their higher gold content. He used the fortune they earned him to help the neediest, especially children. He was sometimes referred to as "the Swiss Robin Hood." Nowadays, the vineyard's output is mixed with cuvées developed by local winemakers to produce one thousand numbered bottles a year, which are sold to benefit a charitable organization serving children in need. Celebrities from the worlds of art, sports, and politics come to work there every year. The actor Jean-Louis Barrault, who played Farinet in the 1939 movie *L'Or dans la montagne* ("Gold in the Mountains"), created the Friends of Farinet organization and was the vineyard's first owner. It was later entrusted to Abbé Pierre, who in turn donated it to the Dalai Lama in an informal ceremony.

I was delighted to meet Father Pierre Ceyrac when he came to see the Dalai Lama in Paris. In 1937, at the age of twenty-three, with few financial resources but a wealth of boundless good will, this Jesuit priest moved to the Indian subcontinent. Assisted by numerous Indian volunteers and a few French, he built entire villages as home to almost fifty thousand children from disadvantaged families. He was able to feed and educate these disenfranchised youngsters, who are too often rejected by Indian society, and make them "upright citizens." He also built clinics for the neediest, lepers and untouchables.

We met again thanks to our mutual friend Claudine Vernier-Palliez, a notable reporter and follower of the Dalai Lama.[5] Father Ceyrac was coming up from the metro and said, as he reached me, "People are so beautiful. But they just don't know it." That phrase still rings true to me today. "Despite all their turpitude," he went on, "I am struck by their immense goodness, even those who appear to have closed their hearts and their eyes. It's the others, all those others, who constitute the fabric of our lives and the substance of our existence. Each is a 'note in the great concert of the universe,' as the poet Tagore says. No one can resist the call of love. You always give in after a while. I truly believe that man is intrinsically good. You must always see the good, the beautiful in a person, and never destroy."

I replied, in essence, that like him I was convinced that every human being has the potential for unfailing goodness that asked only to be brought to the surface. Those very same people were also capable of the worst by rejecting that original goodness in monstruous ways. Even so, life would have little meaning without that potential for good.

Father Ceyrac knew what he was talking about. For thirteen years, from 1980 to 1993, he worked with Khmer and Vietnamese refugees on the border between Cambodia and Thailand as the bombs fell. Among the refugees were young people who, before coming to live at the camp, had been forcibly recruited by the Khmer Rouge. He told me, "There were young female guards in Maoist uniform, black belts cinched around their waists, billowing trousers, hard, cold, black eyes. Young women as pretty as can be, twenty, twenty-two years old. Nothing could cheer them up. Then, a child suddenly runs up to me and throws himself into my arms, and all these girls break into tender smiles. Another time, I ran into some old women, not a tooth among them. Their noses had also been broken in torture sessions. They must have been between seventy-five and eighty years old, and their skin was all wrinkled. I told them, "How beautiful you are!" They were so pleased that someone could find them beautiful—'Nobody ever tells us that!' one of them exclaimed—that they carried me off in triumph. And as they were very frail, they collapsed under my weight."

I told him that the idea of being happy in a selfish way was probably the worst idea of them all. The pursuit of selfish happiness is dysfunctional and fundamentally doomed to failure. Love must come as naturally as the breath. "That's exactly right," he replied. "We need to love in order to live, just as we need to breathe."

To the word "charity," which has a condescending ring to it, he preferred the word "love." "Our bourgeois charity wants its cake and eats it too. Real charity is the opposite of a piano bar where whoever pays gets to choose the music. Giving is giving. The gift belongs to the one who receives it. In love, if there's no respect, there's no love. If there's no affection, there's no love. Poverty and destitution are two different things. Destitution, like wealth, can dehumanize us. Poverty, never. Our mission is to help our Indian friends to be more, not necessarily to have more. I still have a lot to learn. I'm working overtime in my life to learn how to love more."

"I always try to see what influence other people have on my life," he told me at one of our meetings when he was ninety-seven years old. He went on, "There are some people who have marked me for life, like Mahatma Gandhi. Sometimes it's enough to know someone for three seconds to change your life forever. It's like when two trains pass each other. And now finally, here in the West trains move so fast we don't have time to look at each other. On trains in India, there's enough time for me to blow a kiss to someone on a train passing mine and for them to blow one back. A very long time ago, I met a beautiful twenty-five-year-old French woman, Yvonne, who had landed in India in 1950. Overwhelmed by the wretchedness of the Kolkata slums, she told me, "I have nothing to give them, so I give myself." She had come to India for three months and spent the rest of her life in Bihar, one of the poorest states in the country. I only met her for a few seconds, but I'll remember her forever."

Before Pierre Ceyrac left for India for the last time at the venerable age of ninety-seven, a journalist asked him if it might not be wiser to retire comfortably within the congregation of Jesuits in Paris. "I don't want to end my days with those old prunes!" he declared. When he went to say goodbye to his old Jesuit friends, they challenged him: "We're the old prunes, are we?" and they burst out laughing.

"At my age, the only thing I still know how to do is love," he concluded. Pierre Ceyrac died in India in 2012 at the age of ninety-eight, among those he had so helped and loved, in the quiet of an early Indian morning, "with no pain, relaxed, at peace," according to those who were with him. The title of one of his works sums up his life and message very neatly: *Whatever Is Not Given Away Is Lost.*

It was thanks to the Dalai Lama that I met Jody Williams, in 2009, at a conference on world peace organized in Vancouver by the Dalai Lama Center for Peace, in which she took part alongside three other women Nobel laureates (Mary Robinson, Mairead Maguire, and Betty Williams). I felt an immediate bond with this short-haired blond woman overflowing with energy. She is the professor in peace and social justice at the University of Houston, but she isn't a great fit with the standard image of an academic. She is a hotheaded activist with a willful gaze and an unabashed turn of phrase, who never backs down in the fight against the global scourges in her sights: "I believe that people can do extraordinary things," she asserts, "when they think of the common good."

Don't expect diplomacy from Jody Williams! She does not mince her words when pressing her arguments and can be obstinate and creative on behalf of her cause. She told me how, alongside her colleagues at the International Campaign to Ban Landmines, she hijacked the adoption of the Mine Ban Treaty from the national representatives meeting in Oslo in 1997. She brought in some fifty people who had been disabled by stepping on landmines, more often than not losing their legs. They lined up in their wheelchairs on both sides of the walkway leading to the entrance of the hall where the meeting was taking place, forming a "guard of honor" for each delegate coming or going. Once a minute—the rate at which someone somewhere in the world set off a landmine—Jody and her friends set off a powerful detonation that could clearly be heard throughout the debate.

She challenged the delegates with these words: "Here you are in this assembly hall, quibbling about full stops and commas. But when you go home to your families, to your children, you'll be regular human beings again. So be human beings now and adopt this Convention!"[6] Which they did, on September 18, 1997. In December, Jody Williams accepted the Nobel Peace Prize on behalf of her organization.

Unfortunately, as often happens, Russia, China, the United States, and a few other countries are not among the 164 states signatories. Despite the failure of these unprincipled countries, the convention has been effective. It is broadly in force around the world, and millions of mines have been removed and destroyed. Production has also decreased, and there are fewer and fewer victims every year.

Jody also has a solid, somewhat cheeky sense of humor from which no one, not even the Dalai Lama, is safe. During the lunchtime break on the second day of the conference, the Dalai Lama went to a university to speak to the students and was delayed on his return to the conference. The first roundtable had to begin without him. When he finally got there, Jody scolded the Dalai Lama in her resonant voice, in front of several thousand people: "You're late, Your Holiness!" In the silence that ensued, the Dalai Lama, who always appreciates spontaneous behavior spiced with a little irreverence, came up to Jody with a chuckle and gave her three friendly taps on the cheek. Jody also told me that at one of their many meetings there, the Dalai Lama leaned in and told her quietly, "You know, I practice meditation and prayer." Jody replied, "That's cool but it's not my thing." The Dalai Lama leaned in again: "But it's not meditation or prayer that will solve the world's problems—it's *action!*" That was all Jody wanted to hear, and it led to her emphatic opinion that "His Holiness is really very cool."

For years, the Dalai Lama had wanted to create an international council of sages, Nobel Peace Prize laureates, scientists, eminent thinkers, and social entrepreneurs. The United Nations should play that role, he said, but the representatives there are naturally prone to defend the interests of their own countries and struggle to prioritize the interests of the world's peoples and the planet. Such a council of wise men and women would be able to advise on serious global issues while rising above national interests. He had spoken about it at great length with Vaclav Havel, who made the Dalai Lama his first official guest when he was elected president of the Czech and Slovak Federative Republic once it broke from Soviet domination after the Velvet Revolution. Unfortunately, no one else seemed particularly interested in the proposal. It is to a certain extent, although in a more restrained manner, the purpose behind The Elders organization, whose members have included Mary Robinson, Jimmy Carter, Desmond Tutu, and some dozen other figures. But when they invited the Dalai Lama to join, the Chinese made such a stink over it that they had to back down to maintain their freedom of action. On behalf of everyone, the Dalai Lama advocates what he calls "secular" or universal ethics, which he wrote about in *Ancient Wisdom, Modern World* and *Beyond Religion*—an ethics acceptable to all and of benefit to all humankind. He cites as a model the constitution of India, the world's largest democracy, in which secularism is defined not as opposed to religion but as respectful of all confessions and beliefs, including the nonbelief espoused by agnostics and atheists, without adopting any of them officially. That said, this unique and remarkable tolerance embedded in the Indian constitution has been undermined in recent years by new partisan political tendencies in India.

At a public talk held in Strasbourg in 2016, the Dalai Lama concluded his teachings with these words: "I have shared a few ideas with you. If you find them useful, practice them; if not, leave them be! But I would ask one thing of you—that you understand that the most important thing in life is to have a good heart." Coming from anyone else, such an assertion could sound like a major platitude of great naivety. But when such words come from such an immense heart, and that person and his words are in perfect alignment, they suddenly seem obvious.

V

TWENTY-ONE JOURNEYS
TO THE LAND OF SNOWS

39

ADVENTURES ON THE ROOF
OF THE WORLD

The daily lives of the nomads of Tibet and my travels with Rabjam Rinpoche, abbot of the Shechen Monastery.

From our first visit in 1985 to 2023, I have been to Tibet twenty-one times, nineteen of them in eastern Tibet. On these journeys—usually accompanied by two monks from Shechen Monastery who manage our humanitarian projects and my friend Raphaële, who is also heavily involved in these projects—we almost always took the route from Chengdu, in Sichuan proper, to Shechen Monastery, in Kham. From there, we would look in on humanitarian projects run by Karuna-Shechen (the organization cofounded by Rabjam Rinpoche and me) in various regions and directions, and visit places where Khyentse Rinpoche once lived. Then we would push on to Amdo, in the north, before returning to Chengdu by plane from Xining. Here are a few of our adventures on the Roof of the World.

The eastern Tibetans, the Khampas, are mostly nomads who move from camp to camp as the seasons change. In the early summer, they lead their herds up to elevations of 15,000 feet. As autumn approaches, they descend to lower altitudes, where the grass is more abundant.

Life in the Khampa nomad camps seems unchanging, dictated by daily chores. On a few occasions, we spent some time in one such encampment in the Namdo Valley, fifteen minutes from Shechen. Whorls of smoke rose from about twenty tents of thick black fabric woven from yak fur. The children had just returned with the animals, which had grazed all day on the green slopes. It was the milking hour; the *dris* (female yak) and the *dzomos* (the progeny of crossbreeding between yak and cow) stood in rows, tied up to stakes. The women, mothers and daughters, got down to harvesting the two or three liters of milk that each animal produced every evening, which was mainly used to churn butter and prepare dried cheese. When the milking was done, the newborns—which had been held apart until that moment—were released and rushed to their mothers to suckle greedily at their udders for the share of milk that had been left for them.

When we approached one of the tents, the mother of the household, the sister of a monk from Shechen, invited us in with a broad smile. At the center of the tent was a hearth, whose smoke rose and escaped through an opening in the roof, which is closed only when it pours with rain. Thin, hard cushions covered in woolen rugs were strewn everywhere. Bundles were stacked at the far end. A butter lamp shed its gold light on a statue of the Buddha on the altar, flanked by photos of the Dalai Lama and the spiritual masters of the region.

The silence was broken only by the fire crackling in the hearth, the trickle of a ladleful of water into a large kettle, a little girl calling to the tent next door, the cry of a cuckoo, a shepherd whistling to his herd, a mastiff barking huskily, the slap of a tent cord on which a horse was rubbing itself. As I napped blissfully in one of these tents, I suddenly felt a rough tongue licking the soles of my feet. A young yak had slipped its head beneath the hem of the tent and found the feet of a French monk very much to its taste.

In the winter, some nomads continued to live in their tents, while others chose to move into houses of rammed earth. In the daytime, they would lead their herds to spots where the wind had cleared away the snow, revealing a few tufts of frost-browned grass. They spent much of their winters reciting prayers and mantras and performing thousands of prostrations. Few activities are possible in these harsh winters, when temperatures can sink to −25°F. Because the days are sunny, the dry cold is more bearable than the humid chill of the Himalayan foothills.

In 1995, seven years after accompanying Khyentse Rinpoche on his second visit, Rabjam Rinpoche was authorized to return to eastern Tibet and stay at Shechen. As the monastery's titular abbot, he was received with joy and great pomp. On that occasion, he conferred a partial oral transmission of the thirteen volumes of writings by Shechen Gyaltsap, Dilgo Khyentse Rinpoche's teacher, which he would gradually complete during his subsequent visits, in 2002 and 2010.

Rabjam Rinpoche was always well-liked by the local authorities. Carrying on Khyentse Rinpoche's work, he offered his support to many monasteries and contributed to countless ventures proposed to make the people's lives easier. He also acted as unifier and peacemaker among the clans of the region, which sometimes quarreled over issues related to access to pastureland. In normal times, nomads bring their herds to pasture according to tacit agreements established down the generations. But when abnormal climactic conditions make grass harder to come by, they may sometimes encroach on the territory of neighboring valleys, provoking endless disputes. For the past several years, these arguments have been aggravated by the exploitation of the high-mountain meadows where the cordyceps mushroom—for which the Chinese will pay its weight in gold because of its alleged medicinal powers—grow in abundance. Freebooters often come from afar to dig up the mushrooms in places from which they are not supposed to be harvested.

Toward the end of Rabjam Rinpoche's 1995 visit, on the return trip to Chengdu, after Datsedo, we drove through deep gorges at the bottom of which rushed a powerful and turbulent river whose roar echoed off the rocky ramparts. Torrential rains had fallen and the swollen river had eroded the foundations of the road's shoulders, to the extent that in certain places some sections of the paving jutted out in midair, suspended over the void. We had to hug the cliff wall as we drove to prevent the road from crashing into the river. The fiery sunset ignited the gorges with a bright orange glow. From time to time, stones fell from the cliff and smashed onto the road. Rabjam Rinpoche was rightly concerned for our safety. I did my best to reassure him by reminding him how much he loved adventure movies and that, for once, we were the actors. Somehow, we made it safe and sound to Chengdu.

On our trip to Shechen in 2002, Rabjam Rinpoche received many invitations to dine with this or that lama from the monastery, or with a family from the neighboring village. Since he was busy teaching, and ceremonies and other activities took up a great deal of his time, he decided to accept all the invitations in one go and to cram them all into one day, near the end of his stay. And so it came to pass that in one day, from eight in the morning till nine at night, he was served twenty-one meals in twenty-one different homes! We took part in the celebrations. The menu was the same almost every time: *dri* yogurt with a bowl of wild sweet potatoes, *droma*, dripping in melted butter and dusted with sugar—an auspicious dish served upon the arrival of an important guest—followed by rice with three or four bowls of different vegetables, usually cooked in oil, and dried yak meat. All washed down with salty butter tea. Aware of what awaited us, we ate very moderately from the very first meal, and then less and less as one banquet gave way to the next. But despite it all, we had to do honor to what had been prepared with such care by our hosts—they had awaited this day so eagerly! Meal after meal, we watched with growing alarm as copious platters of food were brought out to us. How could we ever consume all that food? Out of courtesy, we accepted one spoonful of yogurt and tasted each dish. As for me, I threw in the towel at 7 p.m. and returned to our lodgings. Rabjam Rinpoche, ever smiling, bravely stuck it out until the last invitation, at nine. He had to bless every house and confer a longevity empowerment on its residents and the neighbors who scurried over. If I had been able to formally document the day's events, Rabjam Rinpoche would certainly have gone down in the *Guinness Book of World Records* for the greatest number of unsolicited dinner invitations accepted in one day!

On a later visit, in 2017, we found ourselves in a similar situation. Having already participated in a number of dinners from six to ten in the evening, Rabjam Rinpoche was getting ready to go home to bed when a villager arrived, saying that a hundred people were gathered in a field in front of his house in the hope that Rabjam Rinpoche would grace them with a long-life blessing and pray for the sick and the elderly. He agreed, yet again. It began to snow and, by flickering lamplight in the freezing cold, Rabjam Rinpoche completed the transmission by eleven o'clock. In the car bringing us back to the monastery, Rabjam Rinpoche and his entourage laughed heartily as we recalled all the funny situations that the stubborn, yet deeply devout, tenacity of the Kham faithful had gotten us into.

A learned old lama lived in a hermitage a day's walk from Shechen Monastery. His name was Yegyam, a contraction of Yeshe Gyatso, "Ocean of Wisdom."[1] Although he was somewhat skeptical about modern-day lamas, he was strongly devoted to Rabjam Rinpoche and never failed to stop by whenever he knew the latter was in residence. Having struck up a friendship with me, he also came down from his hermitage when he heard that I was around. He often asked me to read him texts that Dilgo Khyentse Rinpoche had transmitted to me, which is not the sort of thing I generally do but which I happily agreed to in the face of his friendly insistence. On one visit, Rabjam Rinpoche presented him with the twenty-five volumes of Dilgo Khyentse Rinpoche's *Collected Works* that we had had printed in India and that had recently been reissued in China by the lamas of Shechen. Yegyam was over the moon. He borrowed a horse to carry the parcel of books back to his hermitage. I bumped into him as he ran barefoot on tiptoe (he hadn't bothered with shoes that day) down the meadow that led to the road at the entrance to the Shechen Valley. What's the rush, I asked him? He was so happy to have been given these precious books that he wanted to get them home as soon as possible, afraid that someone would ask him for them. Better to hotfoot it and take no chances!

In 2002, Rabjam Rinpoche resolved to honor one of Khyentse Rinpoche's last wishes—to gild the statue of the Buddha that adorns the temple of the monastery of Derge, the historical capital of Kham. Having spent ten days at Shechen, we set off, yet again crossing the 16,000-foot Tro La pass. Like many others in Tibet, the pass is reached at the end of a long ascent and offers the unique sight of a continuum between two landscapes coming together—the one you are leaving and the one you are entering. The eye is drawn on forever, nothing obstructs the immensity of the sky. In Tibet, mountain passes are strewn with prayer flags, which travelers hang between rock clusters. These cairns gradually grow taller as pilgrims add stones each time they pass. Opening our hearts to the wonderment before us, we began our descent into the new valley at our feet.

In Derge, the people crowded along the narrow streets of the upper city to welcome Rabjam Rinpoche, who was escorted to the monastery by a procession of monks. He conducted a consecration ceremony for the new statue that had been built to replace the one that had been destroyed by the Red Guards. The next evening, he learned of the sudden death of his only sister, Tsering, with whom he had been very close and who had been a few years younger than him. A student in Delhi, she had died of typhus. Long before dawn, we got in the car and drove until nightfall to reach Chengdu, where he caught a flight. He spent the night laid over in Bangkok. "I was devastated," he said. "That night, I had a very clear dream in which Khyentse Rinpoche held my sister's hand and told me, 'I'll take care of her, don't you worry.' When I woke up, the feeling of loss had vanished."

As for me, I decided to return from Chengdu, where I had accompanied Rabjam Rinpoche, to spend another month at Shechen, in Kham, with two monks and Raphaële. A few years earlier, Raphaële had been an active militant with Greenpeace and taken part in several campaigns on board the first *Rainbow Warrior*; she later joined the Environmental Investigation Agency (EIA). A little worn out by the intensity and harshness of these battles, and having been attracted to Tibet since childhood, she began to practice Tibetan Buddhism after visiting the sixteenth Karmapa's center in Hawai'i, then the Dalai Lama in Bodhgaya, and Dilgo Khyentse Rinpoche in 1984. These meetings gave her the essential inspiration that guides her life to this day. When she became a close student of Khyentse Rinpoche, we discovered that we were distant cousins through our Breton families. In 1986, she was a member of the very first foreign group to be admitted into Tibet. She stayed for nine months and made it all the way to Mount Kailash. She later visited Tibet some thirty times and learned the language. In 1987, she went by herself to Kham, which was still closed to foreigners, and was arrested several times. Her many adventures could fill an entire book, and she accompanied me on a number of mine!

On one trip, we went to the Nangchen region, where Karuna-Shechen had financed the construction of a school in the village of Jamar, a very mountainous place near the border of central Tibet. Lama Chöjor, an elderly lama whom I had known well in India and who had returned to see out his final days in his home country, had asked us to build a school for sixty children. As it happens, Raphaële had also investigated potential projects in the distant province of Amdo. By 2001, she had already spent almost an entire year on-site and succeeded in building a school for eight hundred students, serving twenty-six villages that had no educational institutions of any kind.

We left the main road and chugged along a barely navigable track for two hours until we reached a great river, where the road ended. The cars would clearly have to ford the river, as often occurs in Tibet. These fords are generally prepped in the winter; when the waters are low and transparent, the largest stones are removed so as not to block the vehicles. They can almost always be crossed, as long as you drive without stopping, to prevent water from entering the tailpipe and reaching the motor. We dashed the car, a Chinese four-by-four pick-up, into the water, but unfortunately, we ran into a hole. The rear end went underwater and the gas tank was flooded, the gas cap being far from watertight. As luck would have it, a passing truck pulled us out and towed us to the hamlet on the far bank. Assisted by the villagers, our driver began to siphon the gas by sucking on a tube to start the transfer. The fuel was then decanted into a large basin. The water rose to the surface and was removed. He reverse-siphoned it back into the gas tank, and we managed to restart the car. But our adventures weren't over. A few kilometers later, great billows of smoke began pouring from the hood. We got out in a hurry, afraid that the whole car might be engulfed in flames. Luckily, the smoke dissipated, but when we lifted the hood, we found that the wiring had melted into a big plastic blob. An hour later, our friends from the village, worried about our lateness, came to look for us in another car, and we finally reached our destination safe and sound. Jamar has only about fifty rammed-earth houses, but nomadic children from the area also come to study at the school we built.

I was very fond of Lama Chöjor, who was the perfect exemplar of someone who had dedicated his life to practicing the Dharma. Always even-tempered and smiling, he showed me great kindness at every opportunity. It was he who had officiated as ritual master when Khyentse Rinpoche spent four months conferring the Rinchen Terdzö empowerments at Dehradun in 1979, toiling late into the night every day to prepare the mandalas and ritual objects necessary for the next day's transmissions. He had spent years on retreat and slept sitting up with his legs crossed, reciting mantras the moment he woke up in the middle of the night. He had chanted an impressive number of them—one hundred million repetitions of Padmasambhava's twelve-syllable mantra. To keep track of such staggering numbers—which take years to recite at the pace of several hours a day—the practitioner uses little "counters" attached to his *mala*. A counter has ten slim brass or silver rings threaded onto a woolen cord. Each counter (up to four may be used for high numbers) ends in a little *vajra* or a bell. When the practitioner has completed one *mala*, representing one hundred mantras, he slides one ring from the top to the bottom of the first counter; when ten rings have been moved, he slides one ring to the bottom of the second counter, and so on to the fourth counter. When all the rings of the fourth counter are at the bottom, that represents a million mantras.

Having visited the school in Jamar and enjoyed Lama Chöjor's company, we returned the way we had arrived and found our abandoned vehicle. It was loaded onto the back of a truck and transported to the main road. There, we used another, borrowed, Jeep to tow it to Yushu, thirty miles away. Because of the condition of the road and the stress it placed on the rope connecting the two cars, the rope snapped several times, until it was barely five feet long, so we had to drive very slowly to prevent the two vehicles from colliding. We drove at twelve miles an hour. Night fell. We realized that the headlights on the lead Jeep didn't work. I had to light the way with a flashlight held out the window. At one point, we almost hit two yaks sleeping peacefully on the dark asphalt in the pitch-black night. We reached Yushu at midnight and, after several unsuccessful attempts, finally managed to find shelter for the night.

Again in 2005, on another escapade in the Sinda region, we had to secretly cross the border into the Tibet Autonomous Region, where we were not supposed to be, only to discover that there was no navigable road to the two monasteries of Sinda and Shona, where we were subsidizing the construction of a school and an academy of philosophy. We had to drive on narrow tracks beaten by the villagers and yak herds or, quite often, straight through the grassland. Our driver was a peerless local virtuoso in navigating marshes, descending—or rather, sliding down—steep meadows and crossing apparently impassable rivers. He had had excellent training for such exploits—he was a reformed car thief. But please note, a thief not without his own moral code: he stole only luxury four-by-fours owned by senior Chinese officials posted to Tibet, never cars belonging to Tibetans. Once behind the wheel of an all-terrain vehicle, he eluded any attempted pursuit by resorting to routes as apparently impracticable as the one we had taken; no rational driver would consider following. He would then have no trouble selling his spoils in Lhasa. A very jovial bon vivant, he offset his bad karma by offering his services to the monastery where we were headed. Among other things, he took us across a river so deep the water came right up to the windows! How we laughed—once we were high and dry on the far bank.

En route, and again thanks to him, we had the unique opportunity to visit a remarkable group of about twenty nuns living at an altitude of more than 12,000 feet in the Jimnak Trakar hermitages overlooking a breathtaking panorama. They devote most of the year to spiritual practice and then, in the warm season from mid-June to mid-August, come down from the heights to tour the villages and nomad camps, collecting alms in the form of *tsampa*, butter, and dried cheese, which they carry back to their hermitages. They are sometimes invited to spend a few days in the houses or tents to recite prayers or conduct ceremonies. Since that time, we have been helping to improve their day-to-day conditions by providing them with annual assistance.

In 2013, we also went to the village of Seruma, half a day's drive from Yushu, where we had been urgently requested to build a clinic specifically designed for obstetric delivery. A dozen women from the valley had died in childbirth in recent years. We therefore built a five-room health center outfitted with basic medical fixtures so that the doctor—who, as luck would have it, had returned to his native village after retiring from a hospital in Yushu—could assist expectant mothers in better conditions, treat hemorrhages, and perform a few simple surgical procedures. With the villagers' help, the clinic was built in three months. The village head showed us pictures of a snow leopard he had taken with his cell phone from a hundred feet away! It occurred to me that this could cause quite a stir at *National Geographic*, since there were virtually no photos of snow leopards in the wild in those days. Since then, and in that same region, my friend Vincent Munier and other talented photographers have taken splendid pictures of these semi-mythical cats, who rule over the rocky heights above 13,000 feet.

In June 2010, almost twenty-five years to the day after Dilgo Khyentse Rinpoche's first journey to Tibet in June 1985, his reincarnation, Khyentse Yangsi Rinpoche, went to eastern Tibet, accompanied by Rabjam Rinpoche and a few disciples, myself included. So many similarities and so many differences between those two key moments! Like his predecessor, Yangsi was welcomed with a vast procession. This time, horses were replaced by a hundred motorcycles and a few dozen cars that escorted Yangsi on the last six miles to Shechen Monastery. The monastery was jubilant, but our arrival was not as poignant as Khyentse Rinpoche's return after thirty years in exile or his reunion with the survivors had been. Only a few of the elderly monks who had welcomed Khyentse Rinpoche in 1985 were still alive. On the other hand, the enthusiasm and fervor of the crowd were unchanged, and on days when Yangsi Rinpoche and Rabjam Rinpoche offered public blessings, up to ten thousand faithful crowded into the valley, which normally has fewer than a thousand residents.

One morning, a hundred yaks, whose lives their owners had decided to spare in tribute to Yangsi Rinpoche, were herded into a meadow below the monastery to receive his blessing. On another day, it was the turn of a hundred horses to be blessed during a summer festival known as *ta-sang*, literally, "Horses and incense offerings." A towering heap of juniper branches was piled up on a consecrated location on the plain and set afire. Immense aromatic clouds rose into the sky in offering to the local divinities who protect the valley. After the blessing of the horses, horsemen galloped in circles around towering columns of incense smoke. I quickly climbed the hillside to take a few pictures of this spectacular scene.

When Khyentse Rinpoche's first visited in 1985, only a few sections of the monastery's original walls were still standing. In 1988, the monks and the local populace rebuilt the temple in rammed earth, some fifty feet tall. Oddly enough, however, there were only two windows in its five-foot-thick walls! An adjacent building, constructed in the same manner, was completed for Rabjam Rinpoche's visit in 1995. In 2010, Rabjam Rinpoche and all the lamas and monks of the monastery decided to rebuild the complex in cut stone, in accordance with accepted standards, and to build the exact same number of temples that had stood in the original monastery. One of Rabjam Rinpoche's senior assistants, Khenpo Gyurme Tsultrim, who had lived at Shechen Monastery in Nepal since childhood, got down to work. He spent most of each of the next seven years in eastern Tibet, urging the lamas of the valley to work together on the project. Assisted by a German architect, Michael; his wife, Helen; and Pema Dorje, a Chinese architect and practitioner of Tibetan Buddhism, he successfully completed the construction of a splendid five-story stone edifice, whose main temples are adorned with frescoes painted by the best artists of the region.

In 2017, on the day of the August full moon, Rabjam Rinpoche came yet again to eastern Tibet to consecrate the new monastery in the presence of thousands of monks, nuns, and lay faithful from all over Kham. Today, the community is home to two hundred monks, and the college of philosophy, rebuilt in large part with the assistance of Karuna-Shechen, offers a nine-year course of study to six hundred students from eighty monasteries. In this way, Shechen is again playing its role in the preservation of Tibet's cultural and spiritual heritage, despite the constraints imposed by the totalitarian regime that rules over the country.

40

THE SILVER MOUNTAIN AND THE LAKE OF ETERNAL FRESHNESS

Rabjam Rinpoche, a few friends, and I visit Mount Kailash and Lake Manasarovar. On the western border of Tibet, the monumental ruins of the Kingdom of Guge.

Rabjam Rinpoche and I had long wanted to go on a pilgrimage to Mount Kailash. That mythic mountain, rising from the high plains in the far west of Tibet, is one of the most sacred places in the East, venerated by Hindus, Jains, and Buddhists. Mount Kailash, the "Silver Mountain," is known as Gangkar Tise, "White Mountain of the Snows," by the Tibetans, who believe its summit, covered in eternal snow, to be the palace of the deity Chakrasamvara, at the center of his mandala, whereas the Hindus believe it to be the residence of Shiva. To the Jains, it's the place where Rishabhanatha, the founder of their philosophy, was liberated from the cycle of rebirths.

Rabjam Rinpoche wanted to do the pilgrimage incognito. We decided to go in October 1998. He, along with a monk named Pempa who tended to his needs, and I, therefore wore the clothes and trappings of typical hikers. We were accompanied by three friends from Hong Kong: Christian and Maria Rhomberg, and Hon Wai-wai. A Tibetan travel agency in Lhasa organized our expedition. We were expected in Nyalam, the first Tibetan town of any size, some twenty miles from the border, by four Tibetans equipped with two cars and a small truck carrying camping gear, a bottle of gas, and provisions. We entered Tibet by road from Nepal, passing the border-crossing at Dram, and spent our first night in a Tibetan inn in Nyalam. We were careful not to speak Tibetan among ourselves, and Rabjam Rinpoche had asked us not to treat him with any special consideration. But our ruse did not deceive our Tibetan hostess. The next morning at breakfast, she announced, pointing at Rabjam Rinpoche, "That one there is a lama, and the other two are monks, am I right?" There's no escaping your destiny. But aside from that perceptive Tibetan, we managed to go more or less unrecognized for the rest of our journey. It was only near the end of our stay that we revealed Rabjam Rinpoche's identity to the Tibetans who were traveling with us. But they had already suspected anyway.

The landscape of western Tibet, in Ngari Prefecture, is very different from that of Kham. Immense arid plateaus extend for as far as the eye can see, bordered to the south by the snowy peaks of the Himalayas, and divided east to west by endless mountain passes. The denuded landscape is strewn with desiccated bushes and tufts of yellowish grass undulating in the wind. Here and there along the riverbanks, patches of greenery soften the scenery. Most inhabitants have never seen a large tree in their lives. Before heading out for Mount Kailash, I had thought it pointless to bring a walking stick, imagining that I could find one on the way. But once we got there and I asked where I might find a walking stick, they looked at me as if I'd asked for the moon and as if wood was not something found under a tree. I stopped a young man just to make sure they understood what I was saying: "What's a 'tree' [I used the Tibetan word *shing*]?" He pointed to a shriveled bush and was stunned when I showed him a photo of a good-sized tree. During our entire stay, the most we ever saw was a distant little grove of willows in a sheltered, well-watered valley.

In places, mineral deposits gave the land astonishing ochre, bronze, tawny, or purple tones, enhanced by turquoise lakes set into the landscape like jewels of light. Clouds of dazzling white formed and dissolved in the depth of the blue sky. Here and there, we came across a few villages of rammed-earth houses or crossed paths with a smattering of nomads who lived more meagerly than those of Kham. In Kham, the interiors of nomad tents are filled with beautiful rugs and wooden chests painted in multicolored patterns, bespeaking a certain degree of comfort. Entering a few tents along the Kailash road, we were surprised to find nothing but some worn-out carpets and two or three bundles hanging from the tent poles and the central post. The nomads were poorly clad and barely protected against the cold, whose bite was beginning to make itself felt. Their food consisted mainly of a mix of *tsampa* (roasted barley flour) and *chang* (millet beer).

There were few bridges in 1998, and we often had to cross rivers by fording them. In the middle of nowhere, we came upon a brave Japanese cyclist who had ridden all the way from Singapore to Mount Kailash on a three-month expedition. His face smiling and tanned by the high-altitude sunlight, he wore a basic racing outfit even though it was below freezing at night; his bike was equipped with three saddlebags, one in front and two in the back, containing a little sleeping bag and a tiny tent. He ate nothing but two packets of instant noodles a day.

The awesome monotony of western Tibet may be abruptly interrupted by scenery of rare splendor, beyond all expectation, such as the sudden apparition, after three days of desert, of the perfect pyramid of Mount Kailash, capped in eternal snows. It first comes into view at the top of "Prostration Pass" (Chatsel Gang), which gets its name from the fact that it is the first place where pilgrims catch a glimpse of the eternal snows of Mount Kailash and prostrate to the sacred mountain, the object of their journey. Some have spent a good week rattling around in the back of a truck, others have been walking for a month or more, while the most resolute have prostrated the entire way, a venture that can take up to six months, depending on their point of departure. Pilgrims have been making their way here for centuries. "There are mountains which are just mountains and there are mountains with personality. . . . Personality consists in the power to influence others. . . . Above all the sacred mountains of the world the fame of Kailash has spread and inspired human beings since times immemorial," writes Lama Anagarika Govinda in *The Way of the White Clouds*. Lama Anagarika Govinda was first a Buddhist monk in Sri Lanka, and later adopted Tibetan Buddhism and made his first pilgrimage to Mount Kailash in 1932. He returned in 1948 during a lengthy trek. It was done on foot in those days, or on a horse if you were lucky.

At the top of Prostration Pass, pilgrims attach prayer flags to the cairn that has gradually been built up by the faithful there. Soon, another extraordinary view complements that of the Silver Mountain—the vast turquoise-blue expanse of Lake Manasarovar, at an elevation of 15,000 feet. It takes three to four days to circle it on foot. This lake of indescribable beauty is also known by several names: "Invincible Turquoise Lake," "Lake of Eternal Freshness," "Lake of the Divine Lotus." Bordered by marshes covered in orange, dark green, or brick red plants and beaches of black sand, it could also be called the lake of a thousand colors. In the far distance you can also make out the other great lake just beyond, Lake Rakshastal, "Lake of the Demon," filled with brackish water, which is not a destination for pilgrims.[1]

We camped on the shores of Manasarovar that night. Having set out in early October, we were guaranteed a pristine blue sky. In the summer, the rainy season, pilgrims can sometimes reach the end of their visit to this sacred place having had only a passing glimpse of Kailash, cloaked in monsoon clouds. In early autumn, it was certainly beautiful, but very cold at 14°F under the tent that night. In the morning, I found my contact lenses, which I had put out to soak that night, frozen within an ice cube (they were undamaged when thawed, luckily).

At sunrise, I went to sit by the side of the lake and heard the calls of two ruddy shelducks. I looked for them on the surface of the water but couldn't manage to pinpoint them. I finally saw them far off, several hundred yards away. Passing through the perfect silence of the lake, their calls had glided over the calm water, sounding as if they had been emitted right next to me.

The sky, a deep, luminous blue, melted into the turquoise mirror of the lake. The snows of Gurla Mandhata sparkled to the south. To the north stood the perfect pyramid of Kailash. Meditation flourished as easily and naturally in the outdoors as internally. The great Tibetan yogi Shabkar, who visited Kailash in the early nineteenth century, suddenly came to mind. He wrote, "Once when I was relaxing on the bank of the lake, I experienced a state of freedom devoid of any particular object of focus, a state that was clear, vast and open." The experience inspired this song:

The source of all phenomena of samsara and nirvana
Is the true nature of one's own mind:
An immense expanse that is an empty brilliance
Completely free of taking things as real:
This I have realized.

[. . .]
When I dissolve into that vast expanse—
Empty and clear—
Without end, without limits—
There is no difference between mind and sky.
[. . .]
Within that brilliant continuum,
There is no need for effort.
Everything occurs by itself,
Completely at ease, very naturally:
Complete contentment!
[. . .]
Compassion toward sentient beings
Once my mothers, surged up from deep within me—
These aren't just empty words:
Now I'll work to benefit others![2]

As I sat lakeside, thinking of this song, dazzled by the splendor of the scenery and the luminosity of the sky, everything felt to me as if it were in perfect harmony.

After a piping-hot, invigorating breakfast, Christian Rhomberg and I agreed that we could not pass up the opportunity to go for at least one swim in the blessed waters of Lake Manasarovar. Sadhus and entire families of followers make the journey from India on foot (or on horseback for the elderly and less fit) for the privilege of immersing themselves in these sacred waters as they chant full-throated hymns to Shiva. We undressed and, summoning all our courage, ran straight for the lake. When the water was up to our knees, we took the plunge. What a bracing shock— the water could not have been more than 40°F. We swam out some twenty yards, doing our best to ignore the icy cold, turned around, and ran from the water to our towels. Our bodies reacted swiftly, and we were soon enveloped in gentle warmth and delicious euphoria in the morning sunlight. The lake had fully earned its nickname, "Lake of Eternal Freshness."

In addition to the sadhus who come on foot with a little bundle over their shoulders, every summer thousands of Indians apply to make the pilgrimage, the *yatra*, to Lake Manasarovar and Mount Kailash. A few hundred fortunate winners, drawn by lot, are authorized to travel in staggered groups from June to September. Raphaële, who spent several months at Kailash in 1986, told me how she once met twenty Indians on horseback who had crossed 18,000-foot passes in the snow and camped in military tents. They were a fine-looking group: the men, unshaven after their eighteen-day ordeal, wore woolen balaclavas, with a small opening for their eyes and nose, and felt hats; the women were in saris, swaddled in thick sweaters, their heads heavily capped. Having reached their destination after a long journey, they were joyful and full of fervor. But it is not unknown for some pilgrims from the plains of India, unaccustomed to the rigors of high altitudes, to lose their lives on the sacred trek.

The Kailash region is the most elevated part of the western Tibetan plateau and marks its watershed. Four great rivers have their headwaters here. The Brahmaputra flows east, crosses a wide portion of Tibet, then turns south as it crosses the Pemakö region on its way into Assam; the Karnali descends due south to Nepal; the Sutlej flows southwest to India; while the Indus describes a great loop through Kashmir and Pakistan.

It took us three days to circle Kailash on foot. We began in the little village of Darchen, where we spent the night to give our guides time to organize the caravan of yaks that would carry our tents, provisions, and bottled gas. Darchen, "Great Prayer Flag," owes its name to the enormous flagpole farther along on the circumambulation route, to which a giant prayer flag, one yard wide by twenty high, is tethered along its full length. Every year, on the full moon of the fourth lunar month (usually in May)—the anniversary of the enlightenment and death (*parinirvana*) of the Buddha—the pole, which was brought here from central Tibet or Nepal, since there are no trees in the region, is lowered to the ground and a new prayer flag is attached and crowned with a victory standard of multicolored fabrics. It takes fifty pilgrims to lift and delicately ease it back into the hole that keeps it upright. Other flags are also attached to the guy wires that stretch from the top in all directions and are held in place by stakes in the ground. When the great flag has finally been raised, hundreds of pilgrims raise their voices in prayer and wishes of good fortune, burn piles of juniper branches that give off clouds of aromatic smoke, and throw thousands of little squares of thin colored paper into the air, printed with prayers for universal prosperity, which are carried away on the ascending currents.

We set off the next morning before dawn. Our group included us six pilgrims, our three guides, five caravaneers, ten yaks, and the large sheepdogs that traveled with their masters. Circling Kailash, clockwise as required, we walked alongside a river of crystal-clear waters and passed a cliff of ochre earth into whose side dozens of little grottoes had been excavated. It was here, they say, that five hundred arhats, close followers of the Buddha Shakyamuni, came to meditate more than 2,500 years ago. As we advanced at our own pace, a solitary monk caught up with us. He slowed down for a brief exchange. We recognized from his distinctive accent that he was from the Riwoche region of eastern Tibet. He explained that he had circled the mountain thirteen times. He would set out at three in the morning, do one circuit of Kailash during the day and return to Darchen at around eight in the evening. He would then spend one day resting and start all over the next. After chatting with Rabjam Rinpoche, he took his leave, set off like a shot, moving twice as fast as we did, and disappeared over the horizon. As for those who, unlike the headlong monk, prostrate the entire way, it takes them twenty days to complete the loop. Either way, both exploits far exceeded our modest capacities!

In the early afternoon, we reached the north face of Kailash, which offers a magnificent view. Facing the mountain, on the far side of a stream, is a cave where Gyalwa Götsangpa, a great hermit famous for his self-denial and compassion, lived in the thirteenth century. When Götsangpa arrived, the lion-faced *dakini*—a female wisdom deity who dispels external and internal obstacles on the practitioner's path—turned into a *dri* (female yak) and led the hermit to the cave. Once there, she dissolved into the cave wall, leaving nothing but the outline of a horn in the stone.

Located at an elevation of 17,000 feet, the chamber has been known ever since as Dri-ra Phug, "Cave of the *dri* horn." Götsangpa's writings on altruistic love, pure vision, and devotion are especially uplifting.[3] In his youth, he led the life of a talented artist, touring the country with a troupe that performed music, song, and dance presentations on village squares. But he grew deeply weary of the hustle and bustle of ordinary life and decided to devote himself to spiritual practice. One day, he heard someone say the name of Tsangpa Gyare, who would later become his first teacher, and was filled with a profound fervor. When they met face-to-face, the master simply exclaimed, "There you are! How marvelous!"

and that, in a nutshell, was how he became his student. When his teacher died, he carried out his final word of advice to the letter: "Discard all worldly ambition and live in the solitude of the mountains." He spent many years meditating in caves, around Mount Kailash in particular. In the second half of his life, his reputation attracted numerous students and he founded several monasteries. It was this great hermit, Götsangpa, who established the tradition of the pilgrimage around Mount Kailash and laid out the route.

We met the lama who lived in the cave that Götsangpa had once occupied. It turned out that he was the nephew of our friend Lama Chöjor from Jamar. He recognized Rabjam Rinpoche and joined us for the second part of our circumambulation of Mount Kailash.

When they reached Dri-ra Phug, Maria and Wai-Wai decided that the next day's pass and the two days of hiking ahead were too hard for them, and they returned to Darchen with Christian.

We camped that night on a meadow by Götsangpa's cave, and the next day came the most challenging part of the pilgrimage, the crossing of the Dolma La pass. On the way, we stopped at the site of a sky cemetery. A great flat rock there is said to be the mirror of the King of Death, Yamaraja, in which all our past actions and future karma are reflected. To remind ourselves of the teachings on the certainty of death and the unpredictable time of its arrival, we took turns lying down on that great flat stone, in keeping with tradition, while our companion mimicked the act of chopping us into pieces to feed our bodies to the vultures. Pilgrims also leave a piece of clothing as a symbol of their renunciation of both their goods and their bodies. Human remains are left there, out for the vultures, to this day.

As we gradually gained altitude, my breath became more labored and every step of the last two hours of walking cost me a little more than the one before. On the snowbound path near the summit, I had to stop every three steps to regain my breath. At the top of the pass, at an altitude of some 18,000 feet, it occurred to me that if I had not acclimatized myself and trained appropriately I would have been utterly incapable of going any higher if required to do so. Our guides gamboled quite happily and did not seem in the least inconvenienced. Rabjam Rinpoche, who was not in perfect health, rode a yak. We hung prayer flags between the rocks and, having uttered wishes for all beings to be freed of suffering, burned incense, and spent a few moments contemplating the sublime landscape below us, we began our descent, passing on our right a little turquoise lake, the lake of the buddha of compassion, Avalokiteshvara, known also as Gauri Kund to the Hindus. We made camp that night at 17,000 feet. That might seem like a modest altitude to seasoned mountain climbers, but we had had to wait longer than expected in Kathmandu for our permits to visit Kailash and then make haste on the road to the sacred mountain, and had not had enough time to adapt to the altitude. In all my many travels through Tibet, that night was the one and only time I suffered seriously from altitude sickness. After vomiting several times, I began to feel very uncomfortable, lost all strength, and found it harder and harder to breathe. The only solution would have been to descend to a lower altitude, but that was impossible. We were a full day's walk from Darchen, at 14,000 feet—a not inconsiderable altitude—and I obviously couldn't dig a hole to get any lower! Out of desperation, I lay my head on Rabjam Rinpoche's knees for a few moments, called out to my spiritual teachers, and placed my fate in their hands, thinking, "Benevolent teachers, you know! Come what may . . ." Luckily, my condition began to improve, I was able to sleep a few hours, and I was on my feet by morning, ready to head out.

On the southern slope of Mount Kailash, we stopped at a cave where Tibet's most celebrated hermit, Jetsun Milarepa, once lived. A small entryway was later built in front of his cave, containing a wooden altar that held statues and offerings, which partially concealed the cave itself.

Because I had translated his autobiography, I knew that the cave where Shabkar, a great yogi of the eighteenth and nineteenth centuries, had lived was not far from that of Milarepa. But no pilgrim could tell me exactly where it was. I finally met someone who was able to point it out for me, a few hundred yards up the mountainside above Milarepa's cave. We climbed. Unlike Milarepa's, Shabkar's cave was untouched. A stone wall bearing a tiny window and a low doorway protected the entrance. A few steps led down into the sole room, about ten feet by ten. Offerings were arranged in a rocky hollow that formed a kind of niche. To one side, you could still see the smoke-blackened spot where Shabkar had built a hearth to boil his tea, which he mixed with *tsampa*. It felt as if Shabkar had left just the day before. I asked the lama from Götsangpa's cave, who had made the climb with us, to arrange for a statue of Shabkar to be set up in the cave where that great saint and ascetic had lived and meditated. He obligingly agreed. I made him an offering and, once back in Kathmandu, sent him relics of Shabkar that I had been given in Amdo, so that they could be placed inside the statue.

The cave is known as the "White Print," because there was a rock nearby that clearly bore a large white footprint that had been left, it was said, by the Buddha Shakyamuni when he miraculously visited Mount Kailash along with five hundred arhats.

The walking grew easier after our visits to these caves because the path followed a gentle downward slope. We soon reached Darchen, where we had a good night's rest.

A popular saying has it that you attain enlightenment in Kham thanks to spiritual teachers, in central Tibet thanks to textual studies, and in western Tibet thanks to holy places. Why make pilgrimages to these places? First of all, it's the sign of a certain attitude. You set off, often in good company, in a virtuous state of mind, with the intention of becoming a better person, inspired by the sacred nature of a place and an idea of the exceptional beings who lived there. Practicing for one month in a place where great saints of the past have lived is, they say, as beneficial as practicing for a year in an ordinary location. Indeed, by reminding us of the qualities of these teachers, these places send us back to our spiritual practice again and again. Pilgrimage also allows us to heighten our "pure vision," the recognition of the Buddha nature present in all beings and the original purity of phenomena. The world is perceived as a mandala, sounds as mantras, and thoughts as manifestations of enlightenment. As inspiring as it may be, however, outward pilgrimage is validated only by inward pilgrimage, that of the path toward enlightenment, which can be undertaken without moving outside the few square yards of a hermitage.

I had the opportunity to go on many pilgrimages in the Himalayas and in Tibet. Among those that I have described and those that I have yet to relate in this book, my pilgrimage to the Snow Lion Fortress, Senge Dzong, in northeastern Bhutan, was the most arduous, but it was also the one that gave me the strongest sense of being "out of this world." My pilgrimage to Pemakö, in far southeastern Tibet, was the most heavily saturated with blessings and the palpable feeling of the presence of my root teacher, Kangyur Rinpoche. Amnye Machen, in Golok, felt like the most classic—a long hike in the high mountains, punctuated by a visit to the hermitages of Shabkar and nourished by the majesty of the eternal snows that occasionally glimmered through the clouds.

As for the pilgrimage to Mount Kailash, it was unquestionably the most awesome. The immensity of the sky and the landscape, with which the mind fuses, the perfect arrangement of the two lakes, the lofty summits of Gurla Mandhata south of Manasarovar, and the majestic pyramid of Kailash to the north conjured a perfection such as had never been given to me to behold before. Rising like jewels set in the vast, arid plateaus of western Tibet, the natural elements created a world of beauty all their own, imbued with the timeless presence of the hermits who had lived there. The sky, of the deep and luminous blue that is seen only at high altitudes, and the invigorating air, added to the sense of elevation, of completeness. The intensity of those moments feels so unique and holds such a special place in my memory that I have never felt any pressing need to return. Nothing can ever surpass the experience I had there in October 1998, in the company of Rabjam Rinpoche and our fellow pilgrims.

After that unforgettable circumambulation, we pursued our westward journey by car to discover new wonders. The first was Pretapuri, thirty miles from Kailash, a place considered to be one of the twenty-four most sacred sites in Tibet and India, and blessed by Guru Padmasambhava, who left his footprint in the stone. Stunning open-air hot water springs descend in tiers down stepped basins on a broad pyramid. Under an immaculate blue sky, what a joy it was, after eight days on dusty roads and three days of strenuous pilgrimage, to plunge into limpid water whose temperature varied between 85°F and 104°F, depending on the basin. The cold of the air contrasted deliciously with the heat of the water, which penetrated our exhausted bodies down to the very marrow. After this welcome and restorative interlude, we went on our way to the mythic city of Tsaparang, capital of the ancient Guge kingdom, the westernmost point of our journey and of Tibet, not far from the border with Ladakh, in India.

En route, in the middle of nowhere—there was not a single dwelling for thirty miles in any direction—rose a little cabin owned by a couple whose angelic daughter had large blue eyes, a very rare feature in Tibet. Hung on the front of the shack was a large signboard offering "Tea and Yoghurt" in Tibetan. We joyfully consumed both, and I took a portrait of the blue-eyed child, which remains one of my favorites.

In 1948, Anagarika Govinda, a German who was one of the first Western practitioners of Tibetan Buddhism, and his wife Li Gotami, of Parsi origin, spent two years walking from Nepal to Tsaparang, making long halts at Mount Kailash (which Govinda had already visited in 1932) and various monasteries and hermitages.[4] In *The Way of the White Clouds*, Govinda described this long-awaited arrival: "But when, on the last lap of our journey—while emerging from a gorge and turning the spur of a mountain, we suddenly beheld the lofty castles of the ancient city of Tsaparang, which seemed to be carved out of the solid rock of an isolated, monolithic mountain peak—we gasped with wonder and could hardly believe our eyes." Lama Govinda and Li Gotami, both artists, spent six months copying the murals of Tsaparang. The drawings and stories they brought back with them rescued the historic site from oblivion.

It took us only one long day's drive to reach Tsaparang from Kailash, but we were just as stunned by the scale and strangeness of the place. After spending long hours crossing the mineral desert of the high plateaus, we dropped down into the Sutlej River Valley. We drove past endless massifs of high cliffs, rocky sand-colored cathedrals, labyrinthine canyons, and gold-brown bulges sculpted by the currents of the Sutlej, centuries of erosion by wind and the runoff of the rare summer monsoon rains. In the distance, to the south, we could see the summit of Nanda Devi, more than 25,000 feet high. Then we reached Tsaparang—the imposing ruins of the royal palace of Guge, perched on a pyramid-shaped rock some 600 feet tall, a moving reminder of the impermanence of all things. All that remains of the kingdom, which enjoyed its hour of glory in the ninth and tenth centuries, were empty, silent ruins. A village of about a hundred inhabitants, in the upper part of the valley, was the sole evidence that life is still possible in such desolate places.

A visitor to the palace must literally descend into the belly of the mountain then climb a long, steep tunnel bored into its entrails before opening out into a maze of tunnels and grottoes that lead to the royal chambers. On a terrace at the top stands the summer palace, red and solitary, looking out over a vast landscape of yellow ochre selenite—an eloquent reminder of the siege that, according to Tibetan chronicles, King Yeshe-Ö endured in the tenth century, encircled by a Turkish army. The fortress was reputed to be impregnable, but famine got the better of the king and his subjects who had entrenched themselves alongside him— they surrendered after a few months.

On the return journey, about twelve miles from Tsaparang, we stopped at Tholing Monastery, which had once had considerable spiritual influence in Ladakh and Kashmir, located 220 and 300 miles away, respectively. Tholing—which should be spelled Thoding in accordance with Tibetan orthography and means "Soaring in the Sky"—is the oldest monastery in Ngari Prefecture, the westernmost in Tibet. Under the guidance of the famous translator Rinchen Sangpo, who became its abbot, the monastery was built in 997 by King Yeshe-Ö. That monarch played a major role in Tibetan history by inviting the great Indian pandit Atiśa in 1042. The latter spent three years at Tholing before moving on to central Tibet, where he founded the Kadampa tradition, one of the main schools of Tibetan Buddhism. Built on an escarpment above the Sutlej River, the temple is bordered by an array of eight hundred stupas whose dazzling whiteness stands out against the ochre landscape.

A few superb frescoes and statues, some of the most beautiful of the eleventh century, have survived the passage of time and the devastation of the Cultural Revolution. Others were damaged by erosion or disfigured by the Red Guards, who also disemboweled many ancient clay sculptures. As Lama Govinda wrote about the desolation of the place and time's handiwork, "The power vanished, while beauty still hovered over the ruins and in the works of art, which had been created patiently and humbly under the shadow of power."

Our foray in the westernmost region of Tibet concluded this memorable journey. It took us a few days of driving to reach the Gong La pass, more than 16,000 feet above sea level. From there, some of the Tibetan friends who had assisted us with great kindness throughout our journey returned to Lhasa, while the others came with us to the Nepalese border, a two-hour drive south. Rabjam Rinpoche offered his blessing to our traveling companions, and I gave them and their families the red cords that Tibetans tie around their necks, letting them know that the cords had been blessed by the Dalai Lama himself. It was less risky to carry these blessed artifacts than photos of the Dalai Lama, which could have gotten us into serious trouble with the authorities. Our companions accepted the cords with deep devotion. I told them that I would soon be seeing the Dalai Lama and asked if they wanted me to convey a message to him. After a moment of silence, one of them replied, "Tell him we are here."

41

ON THE TRAIL OF SHABKAR

Having translated the thousand-page autobiography of Shabkar, an accomplished yogi, sage, and poet, I travel to eastern Tibet to collect the fourteen volumes of his writings and explore the places where he lived. I stay on Tsonying Island, in Lake Kokonor.

You will remember that, in 1952, on the advice of Dzongsar Khyentse Chökyi Lodrö, Dilgo Khyentse Rinpoche went to Amdo, in northeastern Tibet, to confer the transmission of the sixty volumes of *The Treasury of Precious Termas*. On that trip, he visited Yama Tashikhyil, a little monastery perched at the top of a wooded hill and surrounded by hermitages, in the Rebkong region. This had been the home of Shabkar (1781–1852), an accomplished yogi, sage, and poet, considered throughout Tibet to have been a second Milarepa, the famous eleventh-century hermit. Shabkar spent the last twenty years of his life at Tashikhyil; he especially loved sitting on a large seat made of flat stones under a juniper tree. It was there that he taught and sang the songs of realization that illuminate his autobiography. When Dilgo Khyentse Rinpoche went there, the locals invited him to take his place on that throne and asked him to teach in his own turn. Khyentse Rinpoche improvised some songs of spiritual realization—a rainbow appeared, and fine snowflakes fell like a shower of blossoms. Witnesses to the event came to the conclusion that Khyentse

Rinpoche must be the reincarnation of Shabkar. In telling me this story, Dilgo Khyentse Rinpoche observed, "There was probably some truth to that assumption."

Inspired by Khyentse Rinpoche (as well as by Gene Smith, who had declared that it was the most amazing autobiography he had ever read), I immersed myself in the story of Shabkar's life, excited by the lively, profound, and moving account he gave of his life from infancy to his ultimate spiritual realization. Shabkar was a "bard of enlightenment," crisscrossing Tibet from east to west; like Milarepa, in addition to creating prose chronicles of his life's adventures, he had an incredible ability to improvise beautifully poetic songs for all occasions. He read the exterior world like a guide for his internal life: a white cloud made him think of his spiritual teacher seated, majestic and radiant, on the billows; a bright sky enhanced his realization of the Great Perfection; the fragility of a flower reminded him of life's fragility; the murmuring streams and bird-song resonated with words of enlightenment. With stunning virtuosity, he could build a quatrain using the same initial vowel at the beginning of each verse, or a poem whose every verse began with one of the successive letters of the Tibetan alphabet. The honesty and simplicity with which he related his inner path are enough to convince anyone that sincere fervor combined with undaunted diligence can lead even the least motivated among us to enlightenment.

I became convinced that such a rich and inspiring life story should be translated into a Western language. Since it ran to almost a thousand pages in Tibetan, I recruited some translator friends to prepare a first draft of seven of the book's fifteen chapters, while I got to work on the other eight, simultaneously pursuing the research necessary to achieve a sound understanding of the story, settings, and teachings cited by Shab-kar. I then did several reads of the full-length text to check for accuracy against the Tibetan original and harmonize the style and vocabulary. As I translated, I compiled thousands of notes, six appendices, five indices, a descriptive catalogue of Shabkar's complete works, maps, and family trees of his spiritual lineage, as well as a glossary.

This task took me ten years, because at the same time I was seeing to Dilgo Khyentse Rinpoche's daily needs to the best of my ability. I did, how-ever, benefit from highly favorable circumstances—I was able to consult not only with Dilgo Khyentse Rinpoche to inform my understanding of the text, but also with the many scholars who surrounded him. Coming from all the various regions of Tibet, they were able to clue me in on the places Shabkar wrote about, as well as his occasional use of the Amdo regional vernacular. I put the final touches to the work during the six months of retreat I took in Darjeeling in 1989.[1] Constance Wilkinson, a friend well versed in poetry who lived in Kathmandu, was responsible for the elegance of the text's English, the language in which we did the initial translation.

Shabkar's writings are among the clearest and most elegant in Tibetan literature. All of Buddhism's teachings are laid out over the course of his autobiography. Combining straightforward explanations of these teachings with myriad anecdotes and spiritual songs that manage to offer advice and to describe his meditative experiences at the same time, Shabkar's only concern is to direct people's minds to the Dharma, sustain their resolve and enthusiasm, and prevent any deviation from or stumble on the path of liberation. Although he was immensely knowledgeable, having studied with teachers from every lineage of Tibetan Buddhism, his goal was to make the essence of the teachings resonate within us while never flaunting his theoretical erudition.

The Life of Shabkar: The Autobiography of a Tibetan Yogin was published in 1994, three years after Khyentse Rinpoche's death. It proved quite difficult to find a publisher. One candidate, I was told, merely assessed the manuscript's weight and ruled that it was too heavy to be profitable! I remember one night, after I had racked up several rejections, a BBC broadcast playing on my shortwave radio reported that an American pilot who had once flown helicopters in Vietnam had just received an advance of more than $100,000 for his memoir. I had to ask myself what kind of world we were living in, when one of the most revered masterpieces of Tibetan literature could not find a publisher but the memoir of a pilot who had served in an awful war were snapped up.

It was thanks to the intercession of Matthew Kapstein, an American Tibetologist, that the manuscript was finally accepted by the State University of New York Press.[2] It became a source of inspiration for many practitioners of the Dharma. An abridged version (the English translation, too, ran to a thousand double-columned pages!) was published in French.

Having read Shabkar's writings and compiled their catalogue (most of them are mentioned in the autobiography, and I also obtained several lists of his work from Amdo), I decided to assemble his complete works so as to have them printed in India and made available to all.

Who was Shabkar? He was born in 1781 among the yogis of the Rebkong region. Deeply attracted to the contemplative life from his earliest days, at fourteen he met his first spiritual teacher, Jampel Dorje, "Gentle Diamond Splendor." He relates how, when he listened to his master's teachings, his mind was overcome by weariness and rejection of samsara, the world conditioned by ignorance and suffering. When Jampel Dorje conferred the introduction to the nature of mind, young Shabkar received a complete understanding of that nature, akin to the sky, luminous and free of all duality.

Shabkar went on to meet other spiritual teachers, one of whom advised him to go see the Dharma King—an honorific title for certain teachers who are also "kings" of a province or a tribe, in this case the Mongol community that had settled in the area—Chögyal Ngakyi Wangpo, who lived in the nomad encampment of "Little Mongolia," a district in the Tsekok heights of Amdo, south of Rebkong. At the very moment when he heard the name of that great teacher for the first time, tears of devotion spilled from his eyes, and his only thought was to go find him. The holder of deep spiritual realization and a fine scholar, the Mongol king was revered as an emanation of Guru Padmasambhava.

Having received all the spiritual instruction Chögyal Ngakyi Wangpo had to give, Shabkar set out to put them into practice in a cave in Tseshung, a pleasant place of retreat half a day's walk from Ngakyi Wangpo's camp. It was in that congenial solitude that he deepened his meditative experience and realization. He then returned to his teacher and told him all about the visions and experiences he had had. Most pleased with this account, the Dharma King told him, smiling, "My son, your perseverance through your long retreat has endowed you with renunciation, enlightenment-mind and right view."

A few years later, Shabkar, with his teacher's blessing, deemed it necessary to go somewhere more solitary, such as Tsonying Island, in Lake

Kokonor, or the caves of the Amnye Machen range, to hoist the victory banner of his meditative practice. His description of his final moments in the presence of his revered teacher are especially moving:

The next morning he got up early and, while taking tea, said, "So, renunciate, after drinking this tea you will be off?"

"Yes, master," I replied.

He gave me the rest of his tea, and, when I had finished drinking it, putting his right hand on my head he gave me his blessing and added, "This is my last teaching, my last advice:

[. . .]

While he was saying this, I placed his feet upon my head, and visualized myself receiving empowerment from him.

I thought, "How can I know if I will ever see my guru, my spiritual guide, again in this life? If, after today, I never see him again, what shall I do?"

I wept. Then, looking at his face, I offered this song of good wishes:

[. . .]

While I recited this prayer, I choked with emotion, tears streaming down my face.

As he saw this, some tears came to Chogyal Rinpoche's eyes also and, moved, he took out a fine crystal suffused with rainbow-colored light that he treasured greatly.

"I give you this," he said, "because, owing to your past aspirations and prayers, you are a true disciple. Especially, I give it to you as a sign of the perfect purity of the spiritual bonds between the two of us, father and son. Keep this crystal; there is a special auspiciousness attached to it." Putting it in my hands, he added, "Don't weep, mountain hermit; father and son, we will meet again."

When I crossed the door of the tent and looked up at his face, seeing it filled with tears, I couldn't bear to go any farther. Finally, resolving to go, I went to the tent of Abhe Rinpoche and of their retinue, wished them good health, and offered ceremonial scarves with these words:

[. . .]

Thus, with unbearable regret, I left.

Proceeding down the road, I kept turning my head to look back at Urgeh. When it was finally out of sight, I could not bring myself to continue, and turned to look again: there, bright and vivid, was the tent encampment of Urgeh. I longed to go back.

Then I remembered that I had received all the pith instructions and there was no real need for me to return. Thinking that after staying a while at Tsonying Island I would be able to return to see the precious Dharma King, I prayed over and over that I might meet him in all of my lives.

Again I found myself standing still, unable to go any farther. Finally, I proceeded on, with a heavy heart.

I have never felt greater distress in my whole life. It was a sign that I would never see my guru again.

Shabkar means "White Feet." He was given this nickname because wherever he went, the earth turned white beneath his feet—a metaphor indicating that his teachings inspired all those he met to practice virtue. The nickname may also be linked to the cave in the foothills of Mount Kailash where he settled in retreat, and which I had the good fortune to visit, near the famous "White Print," which is said to be one of the four footprints left by the Buddha Shakyamuni on his miraculous journey to that mountain.

His real name, given to him by the Dharma King, was Tsogdruk Rangdrol, which means "Liberation of the Six Senses." In his autobiography, Shabkar relates how he moved into a cave near the shore of Tsonying Island:

During that year, except for some tea at noon, I didn't cook much. For eight months I maintained silence and only practiced the least elaborate practice, remaining evenly in the natural state of the Radiant Vajra Essence.

Every spring, thousands of water birds make their nests all along the lake shore. While he meditated at the entrance to his cave, Shabkar observed an eagle that preyed every day on three or four baby waterfowl that were not yet able to fly. He writes,

The eagle tore out and devoured their hearts while they were still alive. Feeling intense pity, each year during those two spring months, I tried to protect the small waterfowl from the eagle. They soon understood that I was protecting them and would come and gather near me on the shore of the island. Whenever the eagle approached, they all cried out miserably.

One day I ran after the eagle wielding a slingshot; when the eagle saw me it faltered and fell into the water. It lay there flapping in the water, exhausted, and it began to sink, looking right at me. I felt sorry for it, hauled it out of the water, and put it on the shore. When it had dried a little, I tied the slingshot around its neck and scolded it, saying, "When you're killing little birds you're quite brave, aren't you?" I tapped it several times on its beak and claws with a twig, and just left it there for a while, then freed it. It didn't come back for some time. . . . Protecting them in this manner during those two years, I saved several thousand small birds.

During his retreat on the island, he wrote many texts and poems, including the celebrated *The Flight of the Garuda,* a collection of twenty-three songs on the nature of mind.[3]

Every winter, Shabkar and the other hermits crossed the frozen lake to beg for provisions among the nomads and shepherds who lived in the area. But one year, their supplies ran out before the lake had frozen over, and the hermits had to ration themselves drastically.

His search for important spiritual locations led Shabkar to many sacred sites where he went on retreat: the glaciers of Amnye Machen, the arduous pilgrimage of the Ravines of Tsari, Mount Kailash, and the Lapchi Valley on the border with Nepal. He spent many years in retreat in the caves where the great twelfth-century hermit Jetsun Milarepa and other saints had meditated before him. He also went to Nepal, where he arranged for the spire of the Boudhanath stupa to be gilded with the gold that his followers had donated to him.

Living the life of a wandering yogi, he offered his teachings to all and sundry, from bandits to wild animals. In 1828, at the age of forty-seven, Shabkar returned to Amdo, where he spent the last twenty years of his life teaching, restoring peace to the region and meditating in isolated places, especially in his own village, Yama Tashikhyil, where he ended his days.

How do you go about collecting the works of an itinerant ascetic who spent his life in caves and on pilgrimage, from eastern Tibet to the mineral far west of Mount Kailash, not to mention Lhasa? There are manuscripts of some works by Shabkar in central and western Tibet, where he spent a great deal of time, but it was in his native land, Amdo, that all his works were brought together. I knew that one of his closest students, Sangye Rinchen, had engraved xylographs after his death in Tashikhyil, but I had no idea what had become of them. I asked our friend Raphaële, who fiercely longed to visit that region, to seek out people who could help us carry out this project.

Raphaële had first tried to get into Amdo in 1987, but without success. She was stopped in Serxu the moment she entered that small town in China's Qinghai province, where Amdo is also located. The next year, in 1988, as Dilgo Khyentse Rinpoche's second trip to eastern Tibet drew to a close, she managed to join us for three months, despite the local authorities' various attempts to expel her, which she was always able to outwit. Foreigners were not authorized to enter these regions in those days. When we were on the return journey to Chengdu, Hong Kong, and India, she decided to remain in Tibet and try to get into Amdo once again, following her amazing tour through Kham.

She went off alone, full of zeal but with a heavy heart for leaving Khyentse Rinpoche. It was a good thing she did, because on the next stage of our journey to Chengdu, we learned that the police were looking for her and were determined to arrest her for having stayed in Kham so long without permission. Raphaële had eluded them, yet again.

Still, the Amdo region remained strictly off-limits to foreigners. On this second attempt, Raphaële nevertheless got through, hidden in a bus with the complicity of the driver, and reached her destination in the Rebkong district, Shabkar's birthplace. In the bus station, she looked for someone who could put her on Shabkar's trail. By sheer luck, she ran straightaway into Yudrung Gyal, a colorful character who happened to be the nephew of the famous scholar Gendün Chöphel. He spoke the language of Lhasa—the Amdo dialect being notoriously difficult for outsiders—and invited Raphaële to his home in the village of Shophong Chi, the very house where Gendün Chöphel was born and had spent his childhood. Yudrung Gyal introduced Raphaële to Shabkar's incarnation, the fourth in the lineage, and brought her to Yama Tashikhyil, where Shabkar had lived for many years. They took a steep and narrow path that led in hairpin turns from the riverbank deep in the valley to the top of a wooded hill where a temple-hermitage and a retreat center were being built by a hundred or so busy villagers, monks, and yogis. A vast landscape of forests spread out below, studded here and there by cliffs of red stone topped with verdant meadows.

Raphaële was seduced by the gentleness of Amdo, its inhabitants and yogis with their long hair twisted into buns atop their heads. Compared to Kham and Golok, everything seems a little more comfortable in Amdo; the altitude is lower, between 6,000 and 9,000 feet, and the scenery, customs, and people are more easygoing. A great many sages and scholars have been born in this region, including the fourteenth Dalai Lama, Tenzin Gyatso. Raphaële went on her first retreat in Tashikhyil, a place she would return to often.

Two months later, Raphaële returned to Nepal, excited and bearing great news: the engraved wooden blocks in Tashikhyil had been destroyed in the Cultural Revolution, but almost all of Shabkar's writings had been preserved in print made from those very blocks and in manuscripts in the possession of local yogis. She went back there on pilgrimage year after year, both to go on retreat and to conduct humanitarian projects for our organization, Karuna-Shechen. I now wanted more than ever to walk in Shabkar's footsteps, visit the places where he had meditated and composed his amazingly rich writings, and meet those who safeguarded them.

Not until 2001 was I finally able to get to visit Shabkar's places and collect his writings. Leaving from Shechen, it took me three days by car and bus to reach Amdo and the shores of Lake Kokonor ("Blue Sea" in Mongolian), an immense expanse of salt water 225 miles in circumference located on a high rocky plateau at an elevation of more than 10,000 feet, set in a magnificent landscape bordered to the south by hills teeming with flocks of sheep. Raphaële was to join me there from Rebkong; our plan was to go on pilgrimage to Tsonying Island, in the middle of the lake, where Shabkar had spent four years and where there was a temple that had been destroyed during the Cultural Revolution, then rebuilt in the 1980s. It was now inhabited by a half dozen nuns and a few monks and laypeople. On her previous visit, in 1988, Raphaële, with the help of an old yogi she met on the lakeshore, had managed to cross the lake in a small boat and had stayed to practice on the island for several weeks.

I waited for Raphaële in a little inn on the banks of the lake. One afternoon, as I walked along the beach, I came to a deserted stretch and decided to go for a swim. A few moments before plunging into its transparent waters, I called my mother in France on the very rudimentary cell phone I owned at the time. "Just imagine, dear mother, that as we speak, I'm standing in the waters of Lake Kokonor!" She was mightily impressed. Then I began to run. The water was up to my knees after about fifty yards, and I decided to dive. Bad choice! The hard sandy lakebed rose up sharply and I struck my head very painfully. I lay there for a few seconds on the verge of passing out. Luckily, I did not lose consciousness; otherwise, as I later told my mother to her great horror, that telephone call could have been my last. I got away lightly, with two teeth a little loosened.

Raphaële arrived that night and reunited with the friends she had made on her first visit. With their help, she pulled off the excellent idea of bringing the island nuns a six-foot cement parabola covered in small mirrors that concentrated the sunlight on a container sitting on a movable tripod at the center that could be turned to face the sun. This ingenious system could bring a dozen liters of water to the boil in ten minutes. The parabola weighed more than 200 pounds, and it was no easy job to get it on the boat and transport it to their little temple on the island. The nuns were delighted with this extremely useful gift. Until then, their only fuel had been dried sheep dung and yak patties that they had had to bring in by boat in great quantities.

Raphaële and I visited the little island and moved into two little caves located about a hundred yards from each other, facing the lake. My dwelling was so small I couldn't stand up inside. On top of that, the rock on which I laid my mat and my sleeping bag had a little six-inch indentation in the only place I could lie down. But these Spartan conditions didn't bother me; I was thrilled to be able to spend a few days in this place.

We each had a thermos that the nuns had filled with boiling water when they'd invited us to share their lunch. We were thus able to put together a little breakfast of tea and *tsampa* in our caves.

The island, of which a complete tour on foot takes an hour, is covered in gently rolling grasslands that were once forested before the hermits of yore had the unfortunate idea of introducing sheep. Trees and sheep are now gone. We lingered at length on the lovely meadow overlooking the vast lake, and we visited another cave on the north bank where Shabkar had once stayed. We also paid a visit to a hermit who had spent the past year living in Shabkar's main cave, which opened onto the beach on the south side of the island, not far from ours. A few other practitioners lived here and there in the vicinity.

Every moment spent in that holy place was sheer bliss. One morning, after we'd been there for a week, we heard in the distance the muffled sound of an approaching motorboat. It appeared a half hour later. We went to meet it at the little promontory where it had pulled up and asked when it would next come by. It was now September and autumn was closing in. The captain replied that he was not sure he could make it back in the next few weeks. I had a plane to Nepal to catch in ten days, and it seemed wise not to leave it to chance. We ran back to collect our belongings, said goodbye to our friends the nuns, and hopped on board for the return trip to the continent.

Raphaële and I moved on to the Rebkong district, where we received the warmest of welcomes. I was very pleased to meet the fourth incarnation of Shabkar, who was eighteen years old at the time, as well as his friendly and learned tutor, Jigme Thekchog, who provided me with a list of Shabkar's complete works and pledged his support.

This was in the early days of digital photography. Using a small camera, which nevertheless allowed me to take two-megapixel images, I spent ten days photographing the core volumes of Shabkar's complete works, three folios at a time, wherever they were available. We also made photocopies of some volumes, whenever possible, and borrowed others.

I returned with Raphaële the following year to continue our work, and I suggested to Shabkar's incarnation; to Tsering Gyatso,[4] an especially amiable monk from Tashikhyil who became a good friend; and to a couple of friends from Rebkong that we all go on pilgrimage together to the various places where Shabkar had lived and meditated. It turned out that the *tulku* had not yet been to most of these sites. Thus, for the next fortnight, we hopped from cave to hermitage. We had taken a few volumes of Shabkar's writings with us, and I took advantage of our stops at these holy places to ask the *tulku* to transmit them to us by reading them out loud.

We went first to Jadrön, in Rebkong, a cave set in a cliff near Shabkar's native village, where he performed his first retreat at the age of twenty-five. We then headed for the high plateaus of Tsekok, south of Rebkong, where we stopped at Tseshung, a pretty cave located about a fifteen-minute walk above the river that snakes across an immense plain known as "Little Mongolia," for the Mongol tribes that settled there in the seventeenth century. One of those Mongols was the Dharma King, Chögyal Ngakyi Wangpo, Shabkar's spiritual teacher. We spent the night in Tseshung cave, sleeping on the stone floor, and in the morning, as we were warmed by the light the rising sun, Shabkar's *tulku* read us a hundred pages from one of the volumes. This was truly a lovely place, whose praises Shabkar sang in his autobiography. As he began his retreat, he made the following promise:

In accordance with the words of my guru, I shall not leave this place until definite and genuine meditation experiences and realization arise in my being. At night, I won't sleep in the corpse-like posture of ordinary people but will stay cross-legged and upright. At all times, rather than indulging in idle chatter, I will refrain from speaking. I will eat once a day, at noon. I will live alone. I will think of nothing but my guru's instructions. I will not seek comforts but persevere in the hermit's life and accept its hardships. I will avoid all worldly distractions until I achieve stability in my realization. In short, not letting my body, speech or mind stray into the ordinary, I shall practice day and night.

May the root and lineage gurus grant their blessings that I be able to fulfill these promises!

We spent one day back on Tsonying Island, where we had stayed for ten days the year before, before continuing on our way to other places where Shabkar had gone on retreat. One such place, Takmo Dzong, "Tigress Fort," on the Golok road, was especially impressive. Starting on the main road, we climbed a narrow path for half an hour before reaching a cirque studded with high red cliffs, embellished by a solitary grove of trees at the bottom of the natural declivity. Two caves are embedded in the cliff walls. Shabkar spent four months on retreat in the smaller of the two. We reached it via a steep, narrow ledge and spent the night there.

We pushed on southward until we reached Golok Prefecture and the rocky mountains of Trakar Drel Dzong, "White Rock Monkey Fortress," to the north of the Amnye Machen range. Shabkar composed numerous songs in this place, humorously highlighting the faults and flaws of distracted, arrogant, or misguided practitioners. An ardent champion of vegetarianism,[5] Shabkar imagined a dialogue with an old sheep, advocating on behalf of animals killed for the pleasure provided by their flesh:

One day as I went to refresh myself
In the middle of a meadow,
Many goats and sheep came from all sides
And gathered around me.

Among them, an old sheep spoke:
"Old monk, neither virtuous nor sinful,
I have something to tell you."
"Alright," I said. "Come on, tell me."
He went on: "I have a great favor to request

Of the 'meritorious' lamas
Who come gathering alms in summer and autumn.

"The very moment a short-necked, shiny, chubby monk
Arrives at our village door, leading packhorses carrying a
        lama's red bundles,
He takes a villager with him and comes right
        toward us sheep.

"The 'protection cord' the lama is going to give out
Is for us a noose—
It gets tied around the patrons' necks—
And soon, by our necks, we ourselves are caught.
[. . .]

"You should let us live out this life . . .
Don't let your wisdom, compassion, and
power be so weak!

[. . .]

"So, don't pretend you don't know what's happening,
But come to visit after saying, kindly:
'Don't slaughter your sheep; set them free.'

"When some lamas enter someone's house
And seat themselves comfortably upon the throne,
We are being slaughtered right outside the door—
Don't pretend you don't know what's going on!
When there is nothing on earth
You lamas don't know,
How can you not know about this?

[. . .]

"We pray to you from the bottom of our hearts
That, at that moment, you may say something
        to reprieve us.
When we are gagged and being smothered,
If we could but draw a single breath,
It would be the greatest goodness on
earth.

[. . .]

In answer to this I said:

[. . .]

"By relinquishing this body to sustain a lama's life,
You accomplish something worthwhile.
Is it not noble to give up one's body for the Dharma?"

As I said that, the goats and sheep
exclaimed, with one voice:
"Oh, no! He is one of *those* lamas!"
And, terrified, they all ran away.

As they went off, I added:
"Anyway, I shall take your message to a few lamas.
But when I do so, some of them
May curse or try to kill me!"

Shabkar had become a vegetarian in Lhasa. One day, having prayed with great fervor before the statue of the Crowned Buddha, the Jowo, and abiding in a state of deep meditation, he undertook the long circumambulation around the old city of Lhasa, at the heart of which stands the precious Jokhang Temple, and saw the bodies of myriad sheep and goats that had been slaughtered. This is how he describes the scene:

Feeling unbearable compassion for all animals in the world who are killed for food, I went back before the Jowo Rinpoche, prostrated myself, and made this vow: "From today on, I give up the negative act that is eating the flesh of beings, each one of whom was once my parent."

From then on, although I engaged in many activities to benefit beings, no one ever killed animals as food to offer me. . . . I was fortunate enough to be able to ransom the lives and set free tens and hundreds of thousands of goats, sheep, yaks, birds, and other wild animals, and to save over five hundred people who were on the verge of death—beggars, pilgrims, people coming from afar, people who had long been sick, condemned prisoners, and people who had been trying to kill each other in feuds.

Upon my return to Nepal, bearing all the precious texts that I had photographed and those I had been able to borrow, a team of monks got to work entering all these writings into a computer. The texts were then reread by scholars, formatted in the traditional manner, and printed in Delhi by Shechen Publications. I also prepared a comprehensive catalogue of all Shabkar's work, accompanied by a few photos of places where he had lived. Fourteen 600-page volumes were finally published in 2003.[6] Shortly afterward, Shabkar's *tulku* published in Amdo an edition of the *Complete Works* as books in the Western format.

Shabkar died in Yama Tashikhyil in 1851. Some passages of his story can move you to tears, while others will make you burst out laughing, but

On his second trip to eastern Tibet, in 1988, Dilgo Khyentse Rinpoche crosses the
Gosey La Pass, at 16,400 feet elevation, borne in a palanquin by a dozen people. The
name of the pass means "white hair," because it is said that even if you have dark hair
at the start of the climb, it will be white by the time you reach the top!

In Tibet

On Dilgo Khyentse Rinpoche's trip to eastern Tibet, in 1988, at the annual sacred dance festival celebrating Padmasambhava, the "Lotus Born" master who introduced Buddhism to Tibet.

With Tulku Pema Wangyal and Tsering Phuntsok, one of our Tibetan escorts, we reach the highest of the three sacred lakes above Dzongchen Monastery, more than 16,000 feet above sea level.

Dilgo Khyentse Rinpoche reunites with members of his extended family in Kham, the land of his birth, in 1988. He has not seen some of them for thirty years and is meeting the youngest for the first time, but he cannot stay more than half an hour, as the road ahead is still long.

In 2003, on pilgrimage to the cave of Mount Bahla, at an altitude of more than 15,000 feet, where Dilgo Khyentse Rinpoche spent an entire winter in solitary retreat, cut off from the world by the snow, overlooking the Yangtse (Drichu) Valley.

Transmissions

In December 1985, in Bodhgaya, India, the Dalai Lama confers the empowerment of the Wheel of Time, based on the Kalachakra *tantra*, to the most eminent masters of Tibetan Buddhism, as well as to two hundred thousand followers.

Some of the ten thousand monks and nuns among of the assembled disciples attending the Kalachakara empowerment given by the Dalai Lama at Bodh-Gaya India, in December 1985.

The largest manual printing house in the history of humankind can be found in Derge, eastern Tibet. It houses no fewer than 270,000 woodblocks engraved in Tibetan, containing Buddhist teachings, philosophy, history, and logic. The printing house was saved from destruction by Pewar Rinpoche, a lama who barricaded himself inside for several days when the Red Guards arrived.

Transmissions

At the ancient university of Nalanda—one of the first in the world—on the pilgrimage to India on which I served as guide to Khenpo Wanglo (1927–1992). It was deeply moving to see that renowned scholar sitting in the ruins of that landmark of Buddhist philosophy.

Sengdrak Rinpoche (1947–2005), the Lama of Lion's Rock, whom Dilgo Khyentse Rinpoche once described as his most accomplished student and who was also admired by the Dalai Lama.

Khenpo Pema Wangyal (1929–2019), one of the great scholars and practitioners of Gemang Monastery. I never failed to pay him a visit whenever I was traveling in eastern Tibet.

Final moments with Dilgo Khyentse Rinpoche

Dilgo Khyentse Rinpoche in Dordogne on one of his last trips to France.

At Kathmandu airport in April 1991, the last time I saw Dilgo Khyentse Rinpoche. He is affectionately pulling my ear.

Dilgo Khyentse Rinpoche's reincarnation

A solemn and moving ceremony is held under the vault of the Maratika cave, in Nepal. Trulshik Rinpoche offers Dilgo Khyentse Rinpoche's reincarnation, the Yangsi—"He who returns to life"—a longevity blessing and a new name conferred by the Dalai Lama.

I hold Dilgo Khyentse Rinpoche Yangsi in my arms on his first visit to the Dalai Lama, in Dharamshala, March 1997. To the right, Neten Chokling Rinpoche.

Dilgo Khyentse Rinpoche Yangsi at Shechen Monastery on the day of his enthronement, December 5, 1997.

In 2014, I return to Kangyur Rinpoche's monastery in Darjeeling. Thirty-five years after the fact, I rediscover the hermitage in which I lived from 1972 to 1979. The wood has darkened, and the balcony has been closed in to expand the solitary little eight-by-ten room.

With my father, Jean-François Revel, in Hattiban, Nepal, during the conversations that gave rise to *The Monk and the Philosopher*, whose publication in April 1997 radically changed my life.

In 1997, I met the astrophysicist Trinh Xuan Thuan at the Summer University in Andorra. Three years later, we would publish *The Quantum and the Lotus* together.

In Nepal, 2007, with Wolf Singer, neuroscientist and director of the Department of Neurophysiology at the Max Planck Institute for Brain Research in Frankfurt. Our book *Beyond the Self* was the fruit of our eight years of exchanges.

With the philosopher Alexandre Jollien and the psychiatrist Christophe André during the ten-day dialogue held in Dordogne in January 2015, leading to our book *In Search of Wisdom*.

Photography

On the high plateau of Iceland for the photography book *Émerveillement* ("Wonderment").

In Sologne, 1970, with André Fatras, a pioneer of animal photography in France, who taught me how to use a camera.

In Sologne again with André Fatras, fifty years later, in the same spot as our photograph of 1970.

For the past thirty years, the symposia of the Mind & Life Institute have promoted exchanges among scientists and scholars and contemplatives, mostly Buddhist but including those of other religions as well. I have participated in them regularly since 2000. Here, in 2011.

At Richard Davidson's laboratory in Madison, Wisconsin, in 2001. I have just spent two hours in an MRI machine for a study on the effects of various types of meditation on brain functions.

More than twenty years with the Dalai Lama

I have served as French interpreter for the Dalai Lama since 1989. Here, in Strasbourg on October 23, 2001, at a meeting with European parliamentarians.

His Holiness the Dalai Lama and Archbishop Desmond Tutu, in Dharamshala, 2012, during a week of conversation between those two great moral and spiritual leaders.

From left to right: Khenpo Pema Sherab (a great scholar and former student of Dilgo Khyentse Rinpoche) at eighty-four; Jigme Khyentse Rinpoche (youngest son of Kangyur Rinpoche); and Pema Wangyal Rinpoche (oldest son of Kangyur Rinpoche).

Jetsün Jampa Chökyi, "Amala," wife of my first teacher Kangyur Rinpoche, at seventy-three, posing with her daughter, granddaughter, and one of her great granddaughters, Dechen 1995.

Yahne, my mother, ninety-five and still sparkling with life, 2018.

Karuna-Shechen, an organization serving the neediest

Raphaële Demandre at a teaching session on best practices to reduce mortality rates for mothers and infants at birth, a program that she successfully ran for five years in eastern Tibet.

One of the nine schools that we built out of bamboo in Nepal.

A clinic being constructed in the Dzongsar Valley, eastern Tibet.

A bridge under construction over the Dzachu (Yarlung) River, eastern Tibet.

The most peaceful place of all

Langtang Lirung (23,734 feet) and the Himalayas seen from my hermitage at the Namo Buddha retreat center, Pema Osel Ling, "Lotus Land of Clear Light," Nepal, April 2020.

in any case, as Dilgo Khyentse Rinpoche used to say, "Reading the story of his life, our minds are unfailingly drawn to the Dharma."

On retreat at my hermitage in Namo Buddha, in Nepal, in 2006, as I sat down to meditate one afternoon, wrapped in a heavy cape lined with long strands of red wool, I dozed off for a few minutes and had a dream. A personable yogi of about thirty appeared to me, dressed in a white shawl and a red robe, his long hair knotted at the top of his head. He came toward me. I watched him with respectful curiosity, and he said with a piercing look, "Don't you recognize me?" and then, after a brief pause, "I am Shabkar." I woke up shortly afterward, so I'll never know what happened next! I remained absorbed in that dream a little longer, which was perhaps a little nod of recognition for the sincere devotion that had driven me to translate his life story and publish his work.

42

HIGHER THAN EVEREST?

AMNYE MACHEN

In 2003, I circumambulate Amnye Machen, one of the most sacred mountains in Tibet. I return there in the deep of winter, 2016.

I had long heard about Amnye Machen, the mythic mountain at the heart of the Golok region. Between 1923 and 1946, three explorers estimated its height to be above 29,500 feet, which would have made it the highest peak in the world. During the Second World War, American aviators flying over the Transhimalaya reported that, as they emerged from cloud cover at 29,000 feet, they had seen a peak higher than Everest. The news spread around the world. A mountain higher than Everest! Many years later, one of the pilots confessed that they had played a trick on the British press agencies, which had been hounding them for sensational headlines. Their plane, a propeller-driven DC-3, would in fact have been completely unable to fly at such heights. The truth was, they had never flown above 16,000 feet in that region. The highest peak in the Amnye Machen range reaches the respectable but more modest altitude of 20,600 feet.

In 2003, I decided to go on expedition to Amnye Machen, located halfway between Shechen Monastery in Kham, where I was living, and Amdo, where I wished to return with Raphaële to visit the projects being supported by Karuna-Shechen, which she was managing. In particular, she had been organizing the construction of a large school for eight hundred children since the year 2000. In addition to the pilgrimage to the sacred mountain, I heartily wanted to see Shabkar's hermitages located along the circuit. We drove from the Shechen Valley, in Kham, to Yushu. There, Ato Rinpoche, one of Dilgo Khyentse Rinpoche's nephews, sent his ancient Beijing jeep, its side windows patched with plastic sheets, to drive us to Dzogyen Rawa, where, under the Karuna-Shechen umbrella, we had built a clinic and cared for some twenty orphans and fifty elderly persons housed in state facilities. The project had been instigated by Yeshin, a warm and lively man from the village whose son was a monk at Shechen Monastery, in Kham. Yeshin had called our attention to the precarious situation facing the villagers. He also agreed to serve as our guide throughout the Amnye Machen pilgrimage. Our team was rounded off by a monk from Shechen who happened to be in the region and a nomad who provided us with two yaks, a horse, and a mule to carry our large tent, provisions, and equipment.

The Goloks have long had the reputation of being fearsome bandits who rob travelers. They are rough and ready, to be sure, but also very kind, if somewhat taciturn. As we began our circumambulation of the mountain range, we met a man who was coming down from the highlands and heading for the road we had just left. The dialogue, held in the pure Golok dialect, with its coarse and difficult-to-understand inflections, can be summed up as follows:

"You're heading down?" our guide asked.

"Yes . . . you're going up?"

"Yes."

"Oh . . . that's good," the man concluded.

End of conversation. Tending to confirm the Goloks' reputation for being tight-lipped.

The first night, after five or six hours of hiking, we camped near the north pass, the highest at 15,000 feet, just below the first of the two caves in which Shabkar had lived.

Yeshin lit the fire with a bellows made from a sheepskin. Our friends were thus able to cook us a nice hot dinner. All five of us spent the night lying side by side in our white canvas tent.

The next day, we crossed a broad river south of the mountain. Mules are more sure-footed than horses on steep paths, but they have a hard time fording rivers because they tend to slip more than horses on the wet, rounded rocks. Even so, we had to cross the river on their backs—the water was deep and icy, and the current could easily have carried us off. We crossed one by one, sending our mounts back to the other bank once we were safely ashore. Perhaps because it was tired of this back and forth, or because it had taken a dislike to Yeshin for some mysterious reason, the mule refused to carry him, and he was the last one on the far bank, with no one to help him. I have to admit, it was pretty funny to watch him scramble to get on the uncooperative animal's back. He finally managed to climb aboard and join us on the other side.

On the third day, it rained heavily all day long. There was no shelter to be found anywhere, so we had to continue walking. I was wearing my monastic robes and had brought neither raincoat nor umbrella, neither of which I use very much in normal circumstances. I was drenched from head to toe in no time at all. We had eight hours of hiking ahead of us. Raphaële said that she had never seen me look so miserable!

The rain died down by late afternoon. We raised our Tibetan tent and lit a roaring fire to dry ourselves out. This was early August, the hottest time of the year. And yet, as night fell it began to snow. Our friends declared that they were going to sleep outside.

"But you have all the room you need inside the tent," I pointed out.

"We have to watch over the horses, in case there are thieves about. Anyway, it's the summer!" they concluded with gusto.

They slept under the stars and, come the dawn, shook the accumulated snow off their thick fur cloaks. I later had the opportunity, in 2016, to learn what the rigors of winter really mean in the Amnye Machin range, where temperatures often fall to −25°F. Nothing like our "warm" month of August.

On the fourth day, we finally came in sight of the holiest and highest mountains of the range, Tuk-kar Yeshin Norbu, "Wish-Granting Gem at the Heart's Center," and Tachok Gangkar, "White Mountain, Supreme Steed," referring to the winged horse of Magyal Pomra, the powerful protector of the area. The cloud cover lifted for a few minutes, offering us a brief glimpse of the long-awaited snowy peaks.

We crossed a stream to visit the main hermitage, on the opposite bank, where Shabkar Tsogdruk Rangdrol had spent a year in solitary retreat. The hermitage walls, built of flat stones under a rocky overhang facing the sun, were still standing. After Shabkar and the two assistants who had come with him had finished building this dwelling, which was just large enough for its sole occupant, the assistants departed with their yaks. Shabkar sang this song of jubilation:[1]

Keeping above my head as an adornment
My perfect and sacred master,
I, Tsogdruk Rangdrol, felt yearning
To go to the mountain of Machen.
The white glacier, Mount Machen,
The stone hut fit for one person,
And I, Tsogdruk Rangdrol, have come together . . .
I then persevered single-mindedly in my meditation
practice.

While Shabkar was living here, very little rain fell in the summer months and the lakes, fed only by mountain torrents, dried up. That was the case with one of the two small lakes just below the hermitage. Shabkar went down to the lake's edge and found thousands of tiny creatures, tadpoles and small fry, on the verge of shriveling up and dying. Making some thirty round trips, he carried them in a leather bag filled with water to the upper lake, which had not yet evaporated, saving thousands of lives.

As he was meditating one day, Shabkar had a vision of unfamiliar valleys, countryside, and celestial fields. Then, still meditating, he distinctly saw two yellow ducks on the banks of one of the two lakes. He wondered if these birds were really there. Wanting to make certain, he emerged from his hermitage: the two ducks were on shore, just as they had appeared to him in meditation.

As we sat in front of the hermitage, absorbing the blessings and serenity of the place, I contemplated the scene before me. There were indeed two little lakes, one dried up and the other brimming with water, on which there were swimming . . . two yellow ducks. It felt as if Shabkar had left only a few weeks earlier. I was filled with great joy.

As Shabkar was practicing peacefully one day, a gang of fierce Golok bandits barged into his cave and began rifling through his sacks of provisions: "You don't need to look for my provisions; they are here. One of you can make tea for lunch, and after we have finished drinking it, if you need some provisions let's talk it over." He showed them all his provisions and gave them half of all he had. Then he sang this song:

Surpassing even the wish-granting gem,
Master, remain as the ornament on the
     crown of my head.
[. . .]
Though you have now obtained a human birth,
It is hard to obtain again and again.
No one can say when you will die:
Death may strike tomorrow.
Good and evil actions
Bring their results without fail.
At death, whatever happens accords
With whatever you have done.
[. . .]
If you cannot curtail your cravings and
     learn to be satisfied,
You may take for yourself the wealth of the
     whole country
And still be wanting more.
[. . .]
Today you have been good to me;
You made me practice generosity and patience.
Even ordinary possessions have become supreme.
E ma! This yogin is fortunate!
[. . .]
May everyone who has made some
     connection with me,
Either for good or for ill,
Always be happy and joyful.

When Shabkar had finished improvising his song, the eldest bandit said, "We took your provisions because we didn't have any ourselves. Otherwise, we would never have robbed you." They then asked the hermit to bless them: "A good practitioner is someone like you. May you live for 100 years! . . . Don't forget to keep us under your spiritual protection."

The next day, thirteen more bandits appeared, but they stole nothing. On the contrary, they faithfully and respectfully prostrated themselves before Shabkar and then, after they had asked him to bless them, presented him with fresh provisions. As they were getting ready to leave, he sang them this poem:

You faithful bandits gathered here,
Listen to the song of this yogin.

I am a wandering hermit of the mountains
[. . .]
By the grace of that immensely kind master,
I, Tsogdruk Rangdrol, have understood
        impermanence,
The defects of samsara, and that all
        sentient beings are my own parents.

From deep within me, the yearning welled up
To attain Buddhahood for the sake of all beings;
And, thinking that for attaining this I
        should do spiritual practice,
I completely gave up the concerns of this life.

I wandered from one solitary place to another,
And several years went by.
[. . .]
So, don't live by banditry, O faithful ones! . . .
For now, go in peace;
I shall pray that you all have long lives, free
        of sickness.

When his song was done, one of them cried out, "How fortunate to
have met him just once! This yogin is not one of the usual lot who roam
around here. You can tell just by the way he looks at you. He's not one
to come to the Machen Glacier just because he can't find anywhere else
to stay."

Shabkar also tells how one day when he was walking along one of
the ridges behind his hermitage, facing Mount Machin, his mind fully
relaxed, he swept the horizon with his gaze. In a state of great inner clarity, he sat down, his back straight, and contemplated the immensity of
the sky. His mind melted into space and became one with it. He writes
in his autobiography, "Completely at rest in the natural state of mind—
empty, luminous, without taking things as real—I sang this song, in a
state like space, an unlimited, transparent, all-pervading expanse."

Without a center, without a border,
The luminous expanse of awareness that encompasses all—
This vivid, bright vastness:
Natural, primordial presence.

Without an inside, without an outside,
Awareness arisen of itself, wide as the sky,

Beyond "size," beyond "direction," beyond "limits"—
This utter, complete openness:
Space, inseparable from awareness.

Within that birthless, wide-open expanse of space,
Phenomena appear-like rainbows.
[. . .]
To remain, day and night, in this state
To enter this state easily—this is joy.

He then comments on this experience:

Like the sun shining in a clear autumn sky, the luminous emptiness that is the true nature of mind was laid bare. In a state without center, without limits, empty like space, all phenomena—forms and sounds—were present in spontaneity, vivid as the sun, moon, planets and stars. Mind and phenomena blended completely in a single taste.

Friend and enemy—no difference; gold and stone—no difference; this life and the next—no difference; mind and sky—no difference. Having seen this for myself, I was ready to sit among the glorious sky-like yogins.

Not long after this experience, the snow began to fall day and night without stop for a week, to a depth of two arm-spans, setting the natural boundaries of his retreat. It is customary for a retreatant to set a radius of movement around his place of retreat that he will not go beyond; in this case, the elements themselves had defined that perimeter. He wasn't even able to boil his tea. He drank melted snow mixed with a little barley flour and rested evenly in meditation.

I returned to Amnye Machin in February 2016, and the fact that it was deep winter made it a very different experience. In Golok at that time of the year, the temperature often drops below zero, and sometimes to as low as −30°F. Yaks are known for being highly resistant to the cold, but even their muzzles crack in the winter gales. Lakes and rivers are covered with thick layers of ice that humans, animals, and vehicles can cross without fear. Men and women wear coats made of several sheepskins sewn together. Cheeks burned by the wind glow bright red; lips chap. Inside tents or modest houses, everyone gathers around the stove in the main room, which serves as both kitchen and bedroom, with the family beds lined up along the walls. In the morning, when seven bowls of clear water are offered up to the statue of the Buddha on the family altar, the first has already frozen by the time the last bowl is filled. Fortunately, the sky is usually pristinely clear and the days filled with sunshine.

In fact, I had wanted to come to Tibet in the winter not only to assess firsthand the situation in the schools that Karuna-Shechen had built, but also to experience the extreme cold in the Land of Snows, which is an integral part of Tibetan life and culture. Many explorers, photographers, and inhabitants of the Canadian Great North, Greenland, Finland, and Lake Baikal speak of their attraction to the world's cold places. This fascination with extreme conditions and the endurance and resilience they demand goes hand in hand with the delight of exposing oneself to the rigors of the cold before returning to and relishing the simple pleasures of a warm shelter. I feel just fine at Shechen, in Kham, at an elevation of 12,000 feet, but when I go down to the plains, I feel myself sinking into a state of soggy listlessness. Nothing mystical in that—it's just my personal preference.

That year, we flew directly into the new Yushu airport on the high plateaus, at 13,000 feet. We were met by two monks from Shechen who oversaw Karuna-Shechen's projects in our absence and who had served as our travel guides through Kham.[2] Raphaële was always ready for the next adventure, especially as she was well seasoned against the severe cold. She was already familiar with wintertime Tibet, having spent a winter retreat in the cave of Shak Zimphuk, at Gangri Thökar, an hour's walk below the Shugsep nunnery, in central Tibet. In the fourteenth century, this cave was blessed by the presence of one of the most eminent masters of Tibetan Buddhism, Gyalwa Longchen Rabjam, who lived there on retreat. A nun who was staying in a nearby cave and sometimes assisted Raphaële told us how one morning our friend had washed her hair in a spring that flows even in the deep winter. A few seconds later, her long hair had turned into a mane of filaments rigid with ice. The two or three nuns who lived in the neighboring caves and hermitage came running to see when they heard the news. All of them, Raphaële included, had a good laugh.

As for me, my monk friends had provided me with a thick robe, lined with artificial fur and cinched with a belt over my monk's robe, with an outer woolen cloak lined inside with a thick layer of sheep's wool. The whole thing weighed well over twenty pounds! Still, the cold had no way in, except at the weak spots: the face and the hands.

We toured some of the Karuna-Shechen projects, then hit the road for Amnye Machin. On the way, we stopped in to see the old people who were being cared for by Karuna-Shechen. Our friend Yeshin attended the meeting.

We spent the night at the home of a friend of Yeshin's in Dzogyen Rawa, and the next morning we set out for the road that leads to the entrance to the Amnye Machin circumambulation route. It had been fifteen years since our first meeting, and you could now drive a four-by-four along one-third of the trail that circles the mountain. I wanted to return to the sacred mountains under blue skies and see Shabkar's cave again, west of the range, but we did not have enough time and were not equipped to do the full route on foot, as we had on our previous visit. Instead, we took the liberty of following a small portion of the circuit in the opposite direction from the traditional way. Normally, pilgrims circle sacred mountains, monasteries, and other monuments by keeping them on their right—that is, clockwise—which is considered to be the auspicious way. Only the Bonpos, followers of Tibet's pre-Buddhist religion, circle in the other direction.

We crossed a frozen river and walked another hour to the highest point on the pilgrimage route, across from the two main summits, Tukkar Yeshin Norbu and Tachok Gangkar, whose splendor sparkled blindingly in the sunlight.

We rested in meditation for a few moments before these sublime sacred mountains and offered prayer flags at the location set aside for that purpose at the base of the glaciers. We then crossed the valley on foot to revisit Shabkar's hermitage. There too, we sat for a few minutes and made an offering of juniper smoke. Everything was frozen. The yellow ducks were missing in action this time. They had left for warmer climes.

We retraced our steps and crossed the northern pass, where we stopped to add a few flags to the forest of prayer banners that had been left by other pilgrims. In the meantime, the weather had clouded over and the pale gold disk of the sun shone through the clouds, which hung so low we could almost touch them. A violent wind added to the already glacial temperature, −13°F by the thermometer and even colder with the wind chill. I wanted to take some photos and removed my gloves. In a matter of seconds my fingers grew so numb that I could no longer adjust my camera settings. Even so, I managed to take a few pictures of my monk friends in the blizzard, surrounded by flags.

We went on our way beyond the pass. At the spot where the pedestrian trail forks to go around the mountain chain, we kept going straight until we came to a carriage road that allowed us to reach Pema, in the heart of Golok, by nightfall. Three days later, having visited some of the places where the great teacher Patrul Rinpoche had lived, the last stage of this great loop brought us to Shechen Monastery, the final stop of our winter's journey.

We took this opportunity to look in on the 150 children of the Shechen school, the first of twenty-five that Karuna-Shechen has built in central Tibet. The children were all nicely bundled up in sheepskins and warm hats. They studied joyfully and seemed in no way bothered by the winter, which had always been a part of their lives and did not surprise them. The green pastures of summer were frostbitten, and only a few tufts of yellowish grass stuck up through the patches of snow covering the deep-frozen earth. Yaks can lose up to a third of their weight in the winter, and if there is a late snow they can be decimated by famine. The *dris* calve in the springtime, in March or April, so their little ones can eat well immediately after the thaw and quickly put on weight while it is warm, from May to September, before the cold returns.

As they do every winter, about a hundred nomads and villagers had gathered for ten days in the courtyard of the Shechen philosophical college, under the leadership of Khenpo Pema Dorje, the academy superior. By the end of their stay, accompanied by monks, they would recite in unison no fewer than one hundred million times, collectively, Padmasambhava's twelve-syllable mantra, "Om Ah Hum Vajra Guru Padma Siddhi Hum." At the end of the day, each follower reports to the master of ceremonies the number of mantras he or she has recited that day, which is added to the overall total until the desired number has been reached.

As always when I was in Tibet, I set off for home with a deep sense of regret.

43

HORSEMEN ON THE ROOF
OF THE WORLD

In the summer of 2004, a lively trip to Mani Genkok, a small town in Kham 12,000 feet above sea level. Thousands of nomads and villagers come together on the vast plain for a three-day festival of races, acrobatics, and equestrian games.

One morning in the summer of 2004, as we were on our way to Mani Genkok, a small town in Kham at the edge of a vast stretch of prairie surrounded by mountains, the water in the radiator of our Chinese four-by-four pick-up began to boil. Every ten miles, Tsenor, our regular monk driver, had to carefully unscrew the radiator cap with a rag and quickly step aside as a geyser of boiling water shot into the air. Our radiator was leaking. Tsenor, whose ingenuity knows no bounds, vanished for a few minutes into a meadow carpeted with buttercups, then returned, laughing uproariously, with a hefty lump of horse manure, which he stuffed into the radiator. "A surefire recipe," he told us. A straightforward and apparently ingenious technique to put our mechanics to shame! The "repair" seemed to work for a little while. Our relief was short-lived; six miles down the road, the purée came to a boil, and when Tsenor removed the cap, an interesting concoction erupted from the radiator five feet into the air. We then had to blow into the radiator hole with all our might to flush it out. We had a lot of fun. Meanwhile, a group of Tibetans passed by on horseback, observing us with a look that said, "There's nothing like the old-fashioned means of locomotion, is there?"

Somehow or other we made it to Mani Genkok, at 12,000 feet elevation, in the afternoon. For three midsummer days, we were going to attend a great festival being held for the first time in ten years. Thousands of nomads decked out in their best finery had come from near and far and raised their tents on the vast plain. Each woman carried a large chunk of amber on her head and heavy ornaments of coral, turquoise, and agate inherited from her ancestors. Everyone relished the ephemeral summer warmth, sitting cross-legged or half-lying on beautiful wool rugs spread out in the thick prairie grass, highlighted with yellow and blue flowers. They unpacked colorful leather bags filled with *tsampa* (roasted barley flour) and bricks of *tu* (a mixture of dry cheese, butter, and molasses, dried yak meat, and stewed fruit). They brewed tea in dented aluminum kettles over yak-dung fires.

The festival began. Masked dances performed by monks replayed the highlights of the life of the legendary King Gesar of Ling, who is believed to have been born in the eleventh century in Tsatsa, not far from Shechen. His kingdom encompassed the high plateaus of Ling. Horsemen in sumptuous garb, wearing glimmering helmets in startling configurations, paraded around brandishing victory banners. Gesar was an invincible warrior fighting the most perfidious enemies: hatred, attachment, arrogance, and jealousy. He twirled the sword of knowledge and slashed at the veils of ignorance to conquer inner peace and wisdom.

The episodes of the epic of Gesar have been set down in numerous volumes. More than thirty have been identified, certain passages of which have been translated into French by Alexandra David-Néel, author of *The Superhuman Life of Gesar of Ling*. The story was spread throughout Tibet and all the way to Mongolia by bards able to narrate the sprawling tales of Gesar for hours and even days on end, accompanied by a haunting chant, as if they were reading fluidly from an inner book, even though many bards are simple, illiterate nomads. The gift of declaiming sometimes comes upon them suddenly, as happened to a twenty-year-old man who, without having prepared in any way, began to sing and sing and sing about the exploits of that indomitable monarch, and no one could explain how he did it.

Some bards tour the villages and encampments. These Roof of the World minstrels sometime wear distinctive headdresses to indicate their status and carry a baton covered in ribbons of multicolored silk and silver pendants. They are provided with hospitality for the several days when the community comes together to hear them. Sadly, inspired bards who improvise the epic or declaim it from memory are increasingly rare these days, and most now rely on written texts for their recitals.

Races and horseback games followed one after another for two days. The spectators lined up along the course, sat watching from the slopes of the low hill that flanks the meadow, or perched in clusters on top of every vehicle parked in the vicinity. To get a better view of the spectacle, a police officer, a monk, and a villager shared a narrow barstool on which they stood in precarious equilibrium. The swiftest horses were genuine celebrities known throughout the province. They pawed the ground at the starting line in such excitement that even the most experienced horsemen had trouble reining them in. The moment the signal was given, they surged forward with gusto between the tight ranks of enthusiastic spectators. To take photos, I stepped out onto the racecourse toward the closest horse galloping by. Suddenly, the horse grazed my shoulder at top speed. In long-distance races of two or three miles, you could feel and share the suffering of the horses, whose riders urged them on to exhaustion.

After the races, the elated riders performed all sorts of acrobatics at full gallop, twirling their long black hair braided with threads of red silk. They wore magnificent costumes and brightly colored felt boots, and carried long daggers attached to their belts by scabbards of wood or engraved silver. With their antique muskets, they shot blanks at paper targets hung between two stakes pounded into the ground. When they hit the bullseye, the target disintegrated from the blast of powder that erupted from the barrel in a cloud of white smoke. When they missed, they set off waves of good-natured laughter among the audience.

The horsemen's closing act at the end of the morning was to snatch white silk scarves that had been scattered on the grass in the middle of the course. The exercise required them to lean dangerously far over their saddles, to which they were secured only by a fabric strap wrapped around their thigh. The hardest part was to revert to an upright position with only one calf on the saddle.

When night fell, the horses were set free on the plain. The Khampas have the ability—a completely mysterious one to me—to identify their own mount almost instantaneously among the multitude of black, white, and brown dots scattered across the meadows and hillsides. Bluish smoke rose from the tents, where families reunited for the holiday were boiling soup with fresh noodles and yak meat. The encampment was soon asleep, and the deep silence of the night was disturbed only by growling mastiffs jealously guarding their territory or barking at the least sound.

The next day saw a series of popular dances from every corner of Kham. The folk troupes came out in numbers, very proud of the unique features that distinguished their songs, their dances, and especially their costumes. Men and women started out dancing in separate formations, then came together and mingled, taking turns to sing harmonious melodies. But all good things must come to an end, and in the evening of the third day the tents were rolled away and the crowds evaporated as suddenly as they had appeared. Deep down, some of them surely know that the most beautiful celebration of all is the immutable bliss born of meditation and the transformation of the mind.

44

A TEACHER'S RETURN TO THE VALLEY OF RENEWAL

A visit from Dzongsar Khyentse Rinpoche, the incarnation of Dilgo Khyentse Rinpoche's second spiritual teacher. A great celebration is held and blessings apportioned at Dzongsar, his home monastery. Portrait of Lodrö Phuntsok, the man who rebuilt the monastery and revived the valley's traditional arts and crafts.

"The lama's coming home!" The long-awaited news spread like wildfire, and thousands of peasants and nomads hastened to greet Dzongsar Jamyang Khyentse Rinpoche. Some came from the neighboring valleys, others down from the mountain meadows where they pasture their yak herds at 15,000 feet in the summer months, leaving a few family members behind to tend to the animals. The herders would return to the highlands the next day so that their loved ones could come down in turn and receive the lama's blessing. His 2004 return was an event; it was only the second time, sixteen years after his 1988 visit with Dilgo Khyentse Rinpoche, that Dzongsar Jamyang Khyentse Rinpoche had returned to his predecessor's monastery from India.

Hundreds of tents were set up along the riverbank on a vast plain facing the Dzongsar monastery, located south of Derge, the capital of Kham, eastern Tibet. These tents are woven from thick white cotton and decorated with arabesques made from blue or black strips of fabric that are cut out and sewn by hand. The largest, veritable "big tops," can hold several hundred people. One was of particular interest to the crowd. It was there that the lama would be staying in the days to come.

Some horsemen who had gone off to greet the master came galloping back: "They're coming! They've already passed the Mechö bridge!" Everyone got busy. Some monks got out their fifteen-foot telescoping trumpets while others adjusted the mouthpiece of their *gyaling,* a kind of oboe made of red sandalwood inlaid with gold and silver. The welcoming procession took up its place in joyous chaos. I scrambled up a promontory to photograph the scene from a good vantage point.

A hundred horsemen sitting proudly on their steeds appeared in ceremonial regalia—billowing white trousers of wild silk, coats of brown wool, and scarlet turbans. They brandished standards and banners that rippled in the wind as they galloped toward the tents, cleaving the swells of aromatic white smoke rising from multiple pyres of juniper lit by the faithful. Before the laughing crowd, some horses bucked while others balked—but it takes more than that to unseat a Kham horseman!

"Here he is!" A couple of miles from the encampment, the lama had ditched the all-terrain vehicle he had been riding in for the past three days from Chengdu, swapping it for a brown horse caparisoned in brocade and silk scarves. The animal's mane and tail had been braided with brightly colored ribbons.

The people of the region hold Dzongsar Jamyang Khyentse Rinpoche in such deep devotion because the lama, who was forty-four years old at the time, is the reincarnation of one of the most revered masters of old Tibet, Dzongsar Khyentse Chökyi Lodrö, who lived at Dzongsar; he was one of Dilgo Khyentse Rinpoche's primary teachers, and died in Sikkim in 1959, a year after fleeing the Chinese invasion. In 1988, Dzongsar Jamyang Khyentse Rinpoche, who was born in Bhutan, had accompanied Dilgo Khyentse Rinpoche on his second trip to eastern Tibet and visited his predecessor's monastery for the first time.

The people, lined up on both sides of the road, bowed respectfully when the lama passed by, and threw armfuls of flowers in welcome. During the three days of festivities held in his honor, they literally filled themselves with his presence. The lama, in the middle of the procession led by musicians, was escorted by horsemen who opened a path through the ocean of humanity. He finally reached his tent, where he rested for a few minutes before emerging to meet with all those who had come to pay him tribute and give his blessing to the hordes of the faithful.

By this time, several thousand nomads were sitting in the meadow before the great tent. Dzongsar Jamyang Khyentse Rinpoche took his place on a chair and, using a battery-powered microphone provided by the monastery, offered his best wishes to the assembled crowd. He then related the circumstances of his coming and gave a few teachings and some basic life lessons, urging each and every one to avoid quarrels at all costs, as they are quite frequent among those rugged nomads. He asked if anyone was ready to commit to giving up alcohol, for which half of the members of the audience raised their hands as a pledge; to stop smoking, for which almost all raised their hands; and to quit hunting, protect the environment, and stop littering nature with plastic bags—here too, a majority promised to abide. This exchange was made in a good-natured, humorous mood. As for the crowd, they laughed wholeheartedly to see who had promised and who had not.

It was now time for the benediction. Dzongsar Khyentse Rinpoche recited a sacred text and performed the long-life ritual. He then stood and walked slowly among the people, touching the head of each one with a blessed statue. He was led by a hieratic monk who opened a way through the crowd by waving a stick of incense and a white silk ceremonial scarf to the right and to the left. Paths seemed to open of their own accord through the crowd, and two or three rows of kneeling followers at a time received their blessings. Men, women, children, and the elderly sometimes collapsed onto one another. Their eyes gleamed with joy and reverence. Some recited prayers out loud, wishing happiness to all beings and a long life to the lama.

Throughout the two hours that the blessing ceremony lasted, two monks continuously played the *gyaling*, a traditional instrument somewhere between a flute and trumpet, often richly ornamented. A listener who is unfamiliar with these woodwinds may be astonished at the ability of the monks to draw a continuous tone from them for minutes on end. In fact, the players use a special technique known as "circular breathing," which allows them to blow into the instrument without interruption by gradually expelling a pocket of air created by puffing out their cheeks while they fill their lungs through their nostrils.

We spent most of the day with him in the tent. Our group included Raphaële, two monks from Shechen, and three English volunteer physicians working with Karuna-Shechen, who were astonished by the sophisticated understanding of Western culture apparent in Dzongsar Khyentse Rinpoche's conversation.

The heir of a long line of great spiritual teachers and a refined connoisseur of Buddhist philosophy and the schools of Western thought, Dzongsar Khyentse Rinpoche has lived and taught on five continents and is as comfortable on the high plateaus of Tibet, in Hong Kong, or in London as he is in the old neighborhoods of Delhi. He is the director of several centers and monasteries and of philosophical college, and has written several books, including *What Makes You Not a Buddhist*[1] and *Not for Happiness*.[2] Under the name Khyentse Norbu, he has made several films, including *The Cup*, which premiered at the Cannes Film Festival. He is the initiator of several major projects, including the Khyentse Foundation and Siddhartha's Intent, which work to preserve the spiritual and academic heritage of Buddhism, and the 84000 initiative (84000 being the number of aspects of the Buddha's teachings), whose mission is to translate from the Tibetan, by 2035, the entirety of the *Kangyur*, the collection of the Buddha's words (103 volumes), and that of the *Tengyur*, the commentaries of his Indian disciples (213 volumes) by 2110 (see www.84000.co).

The afternoon was winding down. The lama now headed to the monastery, where he would spend the night. Again, a long procession formed to accompany him the mile and a half from the temporary encampment to the hill on which stood the monastery, which had been restored over the course of the past fifteen years. Shortly before arriving, Dzongsar Khyentse Rinpoche dismounted from his horse and walked the last hundred yards, in a sign of respect for this sacred place and all the great teachers who have lived there. Then, still preceded by musicians and monks waving banners, he took the narrow alleyways that led to his residence. There too, a dozen visitors waited to meet with him in private, share news with him, or ask his advice. It was the same early the next morning, before Dzongsar returned to the festivities taking place over the next two days: equestrian games, folk dancing, and, yet again, the blessing of the crowd.

As occurred pretty much throughout eastern Tibet, beginning in 1985, Tibetans were allowed to rebuild their monasteries, philosophical colleges, and retreat centers. The renaissance man of the Dzongsar Valley is a traditional physician, Lodrö Phuntsok, who, assisted by his wife and six children, spearheaded the reconstruction of the monastery, the preservation of the surviving treasures, the revival of eleven types of traditional crafts, and the publication of dozens of volumes of important texts. In 2001, with the help of our Karuna-Shechen organization, Lodrö Phuntsok, who is also one of eastern Tibet's most accomplished experts in Tibetan medicine, built a large clinic of traditional medicine that sees patients from throughout the region. The clinic also produces dozens of medications from the Tibetan pharmacopeia, in accordance with the highest standards, which are then distributed throughout Tibet and even China. Entering the enormous store room, lined with hundreds of sacks containing medicinal plants and minerals collected in the mountains, one is stunned by the variety of scents. The ingredients are ground and mixed—up to thirty tinctures may go into one medication—and then brought to the adjoining room, where a little water is added to the mixture, which is converted into hard tablets. Two assistants are in charge of making the pills smooth and glossy. They place the pills in long cloth bags, which are then grasped at either end and shaken back and forth for hours to polish the pills. Not all are polished manually; some are placed in a small revolving drum that spins all day long. Tens of thousands of pills are brought up to the clinic's roof to dry on mesh screens. They are then carefully packaged in pretty little bottles for distribution to patients.

For many years, Karuna-Shechen also subsidized an elementary school in Dzongsar, where classes were taught in Tibetan, as well as training for women in various traditional crafts.

A visitor is filled with joy and curiosity to find a series of workshops spread out over eight miles up and down the valley, bringing traditional local craftsmanship to life. A manufactory of *thangka* paintings, led by an excellent professor and staffed by some twenty students, is one of the best in eastern Tibet. In each of the other workshops—pottery, sculpture, wood carving, weaving and embroidery, jewelry, and leatherworking—one or several experts in ancestral techniques pass on their expertise to apprentices who will keep these ancient crafts alive.

On a hillside at the far end of the valley, not far from the Lotus Crystal Cave—Pema Shelphuk—a series of unique hermitages rises in tiers. Almost five hundred hermits—men and women, monks and laypersons—come to undertake meditative retreats there for months, years, or even, for some, the rest of their lives.

With his nonchalant good nature and kindly smile, Lodrö Phuntsok welcomed us every year with unfailing friendliness and accompanied us on our pilgrimages in the vicinity. He also invited us to memorable picnics during the festivals that Tibetans love to hold in the warm days of summer. Although he is lord of the valley and highly respected by all, his humility is ironclad. That is why we have been especially happy to contribute, through Karuna-Shechen, to his admirable work.

45

ENLIGHTENED VAGABOND

Patrul Rinpoche, a great nineteenth-century sage and scholar, wandered as he taught. Having spent thirty years collecting orally transmitted anecdotes of the life of this extraordinary spiritual teacher, I visit the most remote of his retreats.

The air is crisp, the horizon vast and luminous, the wide plains spread out between hills that rise to meet the snowbound glaciers. Just a few solitary farmers inhabit the Dzachuka region, located in northern Kham on the border of Golok—a place of harsh climate and brief summers, inhospitable to crop farming. Most inhabitants of these high plateaus are nomadic herders whose subsistence has depended for centuries on raising yak and, as you head north toward Amdo, sheep. The region is named for the Dzachu River that crosses it and becomes the mighty Mekong as it leaves Tibet.

With no dwelling other than their yak-hair tents, these nomadic pastoralists up camp with the changing seasons, leading their precious cattle from one mountain meadow to the next in search of good grazing.

This was the birthplace, in 1808, of one of the most extraordinary figures in Tibetan Buddhism, Patrul Rinpoche, who bore the name Orgyen Jigme Chökyi Wangpo. From my very first trips to Darjeeling, I heard Kangyur Rinpoche's family speak of that unusual master and was regaled with many anecdotes about his life down the years. What's more, as soon as I began practicing the graduated path, one of the main reference texts used by my companions and me was *Words of My Perfect Teacher*. It had not been translated yet, but one of Kangyur Rinpoche's daughter would explain some passages of it in English for us. This work, Patrul Rinpoche's best known, owes its popularity to its accessibility. It abounds with enlightening stories—often drawn from the Buddha's sutras—and offers a straightforward and immediate presentation of authentic spiritual practice. Patrul Rinpoche is careful to be as direct as possible so as to help beginners launch themselves correctly on the path of liberation from suffering without straying into the byways where their habitual tendencies might otherwise divert them. While on retreat in remote places, he wrote many deep treatises, which, after his death, were collected into six volumes.

The exemplary nature of Patrul Rinpoche's life is a source of ever-new inspiration to practitioners. With ease and detachment, he abandoned the eight worldly concerns. He spent the greater part of his life roaming the mountains and living in caves, forests, and hermitages far removed from the world.

When I first began to read Tibetan, I went in search of a biography of Patrul Rinpoche. I learned that there were two, written by direct disciples of his. The first, about thirty pages long, was written by Dodrupchen Tenpe Nyima; the second, twice as long, is by Khenpo Kunpal, who simply added to Tenpe Nyima's version.

In a culture in which oral transmission plays an important role, Tibetans are renowned for their ability to memorize and orally transmit stories down to their tiniest detail. I particularly recall several evenings spent in Bhutan, recording Nyoshul Khen Rinpoche, a great scholar who had been the student of several teachers belonging to Patrul Rinpoche's lineage in Tibet. He told me any number of stories linked to Patrul Rinpoche's life, with such a profusion of details and such enthusiasm that it felt as if I had been an eyewitness to these events myself. I had a similar experience in Kham listening to masters, many of them eighty years old or more, relate with the same verve what they had learned from Patrul Rinpoche's direct students. I was fortunate enough to be able to record several of them, including Khenpo Palga, who was ninety years old at the time, had lost all his teeth, and spoke the dialect of a Dzachuka nomad. Back in Shechen, with the help of two monks who had come with me, we listened to the transcript several times in order to transcribe it. Dilgo Khyentse Rinpoche also often told impromptu anecdotes about the lives of Patrul Rinpoche and other great sages of the past. When he did, if I didn't happen to have a tape recorder handy, I wrote down his stories immediately after I heard them. Over the course of thirty years, I was able to assemble more than a hundred anecdotes told by eighteen spiritual teachers and scholars, most of whom are no longer alive. This precious oral tradition was in danger of being lost, and I felt that it was important to pass them on to coming generations.

I therefore subsequently endeavored to put these narratives into some sort of order and to set them down in the chronological sequence taking support of Khenpo Kunpal's biography of Patrul Rinpoche. To that end, I catalogued any information that would allow me to place them in their correct geographical and temporal context.

I also used my travels to Tibet to visit the landmarks of Patrul Rinpoche's life and to seek out the places where he lived in retreat, which were not easy to get to. Thanks to Khenpo Dönnyi from Gemang Monastery, I was able to meet with descendants of Patrul Rinpoche's sister, who live in the almost uninhabited valley of Khormo Olu, at 14,000 feet above sea level. It was in that secluded hamlet that Patrul Rinpoche was born in a tent in the middle of the prairie, and it was there that he died. His family retains a few objects that belonged to the wandering hermit: his monastic shawl (he dressed as an ordinary nomad so as not to attract attention, but he cherished and maintained the yellow monastic cape he received at his ordination), a statue of the Buddha, a little, rolled-up picture of his root teacher, Jigme Gyalwai Nyugu, his prayer wheel, and the old metal kettle he took with him everywhere. His begging bowl, one of the objects a monk receives at his ordination, was preserved at a monastery in eastern Tibet near Nangchen; I had the great good fortune of being given this bowl by a leader of that monastery, who now lives in India and had taken it with him from Tibet. I am guarding it dearly for now as a blessing and will eventually offer it to one of my teachers.

Dressed in a thick felt coat known as a *chuba*, or wrapped in a heavy sheepskin in the winter, Patrul traveled alone, and nothing distinguished him outwardly from an ordinary person. He would stop for no particular reason at some point in his wanderings and stay for a while; when he decided to leave, he set out with no specific destination in mind. He stopped wherever he felt like stopping—in a forest, at a cave, in valleys, in snowy mountains, in the middle of nowhere, or in a tent. He stayed in each place just as long as he liked, never lingering too long. He lived in accordance with the wisdom of his predecessors:

Wherever you've stayed, leave nothing behind but the trace of your seat.
Wherever you've walked, leave nothing behind but your footprints.

Whenever he sojourned in the wild open spaces of Tibet, he meditated most specifically on bodhicitta, the wish to liberate all beings from suffering and to lead them to the ultimate freedom of enlightenment. Patrul offered his instruction without prejudice to the followers of all schools of Tibetan Buddhism.

He generally refused the offerings that are traditionally made to a respected teacher or sage. Toward the end of his life, however, at the suggestion of another master, Jamyang Khyentse Wangpo, he accepted them in order to subsidize the needs of stonecarvers working to enlarge an extraordinary edifice, the Palgé Mani stone wall—so called because it was built by a predecessor of Patrul named Palgé. The word "Mani" refers to the mantra *Om mani padme hum*, the mantra of the buddha of compassion, Avalokiteshvara, which is inscribed in many engraved stones. The wall stands on the Plain of the Mamos, a few miles from Patrul's birthplace. They say it was originally a full kilometer long, but it was dismantled during the Chinese Cultural Revolution. As the wall was located in a remote area and made of heavy stones, the slabs were not taken away but simply scattered in the immediate surroundings. The residents of the valley rebuilt it in the mid-1980s. It was subsequently enlarged on a regular basis, and many stonecarvers settled in the area. They added new engraved stones, either commissioned by the faithful or on their own initiative. In the 1990s, a lama sponsored the engraving in stone of all one hundred and three volumes of the *Kangyur*, the collected sermons of the Buddha! The construction of such a wall is said to be the source of great merit for those who sponsor it, those who engrave it, and those who circumambulate it. All such engraved texts and mantras are also intended to contribute to local and world peace. Many stupas have also been built along the entire length of the wall.

The Palgé Mani stone wall, built entirely of engraved stones, is today some 1.2 miles long, thirteen feet high, and as wide as sixty feet in some places. Every time we visit the region, we make sure to walk around it at least once, which takes forty-five minutes at a brisk pace.

Other than the few objects preserved by his sister's descendants, Patrul's entire inventory of property upon his death at eighty consisted of two books: Shantideva's *The Way of the Bodhisattva* and Nagarjuna's *Fundamental Verses of the Middle Way*.

In February 2016, in the dead of winter, my search for places where Patrul Rinpoche once lived led me to Dzagyal Trama Lung, 14,000 feet above sea level, some twelve miles from the Mani wall and accessible by a barely navigable mountain trail. It was here that Patrul Rinpoche received from his primary teacher, Jigme Gyalwai Nyugu, no fewer than twenty-five iterations of the explanations of the preliminary practices of the graduated path of Tibetan Buddhism, which he set down in *Words of My Perfect Teacher*. Ten hermits live there now, including a forty-year-old *khenpo* who had studied at the Larung Gar philosophical college and told me a few anecdotes from Patrul's life that I added to those I'd already collected. When I saw Trama Lung—a barren, desolate spot exposed to fierce extremes of weather (it was well below 0°F by the thermometer, not counting the howling wind) and far from everything—I appreciated the unwavering resolve of practitioners to find perfectly solitary places of retreat!

On my first visit to Khormo Olu in 2017, along with a few monks from Shechen and a group of Western friends who had come to attend Rabjam Rinpoche's consecration of the new Shechen temple, we once again climbed the path leading to the place where Patrul Rinpoche's cremation took place. A solar halo had begun to form when we were leaving Gemang Monastery an hour earlier. When we reached the stupa, the halo had become a radiant, rainbow-colored mandorla directly above it. It remained intact for some time, illuminating our prayers and practices at the foot of the stupa. A gift from Patrul Rinpoche, perhaps?

Over the course of more than thirty years, my readings of Patrul Rinpoche's teachings, the stories of his life, the biographies written by his contemporaries, and my visits to the places where he lived inspired me, in *Enlightened Vagabond*, to gather together everything I was able to learn about him. The few anecdotes that I have not been able to resist sharing below illustrate how the facts and deeds of a sage embody in daily reality the teachings that are found elsewhere in the writings.[1]

THE INGOT AND THE THIEF

One day as Patrul sat on a grass-covered knoll after teaching *The Way of the Bodhisattva* to a large crowd, an old man emerged from the gathering and offered him a big silver ingot. As was his custom, Patrul refused the offering, but the old man was determined. He dropped the ingot at the master's feet and moved off quickly. When it was his own turn to go, Patrul left behind all the offerings that had been brought to him, including the ingot.

A thief heard about the valuable offering that had been made to the master and resolved to relieve him of it. Patrul usually traveled alone and often spent his nights in the open air. Under cover of dark, the bandit approached the sleeping hermit and began to rummage through his meagre possessions. Not finding what he was looking for, the thief patted down Patrul's clothing, which naturally woke him up.

"What are you poking around my clothes like that for?" Patrul Rinpoche cried out sharply.

"Someone gave you a silver ingot! I need it! Give it to me!" the surprised robber demanded.

"*Aho,*" Patrul exclaimed. "Think about what a miserable life you're leading, running around all over the place like an idiot. And you came all this way for a bit of silver? How pathetic! Listen to me. Go back the way you came. At dawn you'll reach the little knoll where I taught. That's where you'll find the ingot."

The thief was suspicious, but he could see that the ingot was not among Patrul's things or in his clothes. Although he doubted that the master could simply have left such an offering behind, he retraced his steps, reached the grassy mound, and eventually found the abandoned ingot.

And yet the man, who was advanced in years, now thought of Patrul's hard words and began to worry about the life he was leading. He lamented long and loud: "That Patrul is an authentic teacher, free of all attachments. I earned myself some awful karma, trying to rob him!"

Tormented by regret, he went off in search of the master. When he finally found him, Patrul shouted,

"Here you are again! Still running up hill and down dale like a knucklehead? What do you want now?"

"I found the ingot and deeply regret having behaved so badly towards you, a true spiritual teacher. I can't believe I was ready to rob you of the little you have! Forgive me, bless me, and take me on as your student!" the tearful robber replied.

"You have no reason to beg my pardon. From now on, practice generosity and invoke the Three Jewels. That will be plenty," Patrul told him.

Circumstances contrived to alert the locals to the bandit's misdeeds, and they showered him with blows. When Patrul got wind of this, he reproached them severely. "When you beat this man, it's me you are beating. Leave him alone!"

Patrul often pointed to all the worries and unsolvable problems caused by possessions. He would say, "If you've got money, you've got money problems. If you have a house, you have house problems. If you have yaks, you have yak problems. If you have goats, you have goat problems." If you want to attain wisdom and enlightenment, the best thing to do is let go of the concept of property.

PATRUL AND THE WIDOW

One day as Patrul was crossing a vast plain on foot, he met a poor woman whose husband had recently been killed by a *dremong*, a huge bear of the steppes. She was heading to Dzachuka with her three children to beg for food. The loss of her husband had left her destitute.

She couldn't stop herself from weeping as she told Patrul her story.

"Don't you worry. I'll help you. I'm going to Dzachuka myself. Let's travel together," Patrul offered.

She agreed, and they walked together for several days. They slept outside at night. One and sometimes two of the children would nestle into the folds of Patrul's sheepskin coat, while the widow cuddled the youngest. During the day, Patrul carried one of the little ones on his back, the mother did the same with another, and the third walked beside them.

When the woman begged in the villages and nomad camps they passed through, Patrul did likewise, soliciting *tsampa*, butter, and cheese. The travelers they met on the way took them for a family of beggars. No one—including the widow herself—suspected the great yogi's true identity.

They finally reached Dzachuka. That day, the woman went off to beg in one direction and Patrul in the other. When they met up again in the evening, the widow noticed the dark look on Patrul's face.

"What's the matter? You look upset," she said.

Patrul brushed her question aside. "It's nothing. I had something I needed to do here, but the people won't let me finish it. They're making a big fuss about nothing."

"What could you possibly have to do here?" the woman asked, astonished.

"Never mind. Let's go," the lama replied.

They came to a monastery on the side of a hill. Patrul stopped. He turned to the widow and said, "I have to go inside. You may come in too, but not now, in a few days."

"No, let's not separate. Let's go in together. You've been so kind to me and the children up to now. Maybe we could get married. But if not, let me stay with you and benefit from your kindness," the widow pleaded in tears.

"That won't work. Up till now, I've done my best to help you, but the people here chatter like parrots. We really can't enter the monastery together. Come back in a few days and you'll find me," Patrul replied.

Patrul climbed the hill to the monastery; the widow and her children stayed down below to beg for food.

As soon as he was inside, and contrary to his usual habit, Patrul ordered that all gifts or provisions offered to him be set aside, as he was expecting a very special guest who would have need of them.

The next day, news of the great master's arrival spread throughout the valley. "Patrul Rinpoche is here! He's going to teach *The Way of the Bodhisattva*!"

All the people came running to receive Patrul Rinpoche's teachings. When she heard the news, the Golok widow was filled with joy. "A great lama has come!" she thought. "This is a golden opportunity for me to make offerings and request prayers for the well-being of my late husband."

Following the crowd, she climbed up to the monastery with her three children. They had to sit all the way at the back of the crowd to hear Patrul's teachings. She was so far away that she could hardly make out the great master's features. When it was over, she rose and joined the other participants in a long line to wait to receive blessings. The moment finally came when she was close enough to see that the great lama in question, Patrul Rinpoche, was none other than her traveling companion in rags.

Moved by amazement and devotion, she approached Patrul: "Forgive me for not having recognized you! Forgive me for having made you carry my children and proposed marriage to you! Please forgive me for everything!"

Patrul brushed off her apologies lightly: "Don't give it another thought! You have nothing to apologize for." And then he turned to the monks of the monastery: "This is the special guest I've been waiting for. Bring all the butter, cheese, and other provisions that were set aside and give them to this woman."

PATRUL IS TAUGHT HIS OWN TEACHINGS

Patrul decided to go to Kathok Monastery and gather merit by circumambulating the stupas of Kathok Kumbum. A few people noticed this shabby lama who stopped in front of every stupa, touching his head to the little central cavity while muttering a prayer or two. Nothing really distinguished him from the other pilgrims, however. He was living at the home of an old lama from Gyarong.

"Have you had any Dharma teaching?" the lama asked.

"Not much. I've received *The Way of the Bodhisattva* and a few other texts. That's about it," Patrul replied.

"You seem to have virtuous inclinations. And since you've come from so far away, you must be a pretty good practitioner. Would you like me to teach you a few rudiments of the Dharma?"

"Sure, I'd like that! Everybody needs the Dharma!"

"There's one teaching called *Words of My Perfect Teacher*, by Dza Patrul Rinpoche. He could really help you. Because if you say your prayers while circling the stupas without the correct attitude and understanding, your efforts will bring you precious little benefit," the old lama went on.

"Oh, I really need those teachings! Be so good as to give them to me!" Patrul exclaimed.

And it so it was that chapter by chapter, the old lama from Gyarong taught Patrul *Words of My Perfect Teacher*. Every so often, the nomad lama, who was apparently simple and illiterate, asked very pertinent questions about the meaning of the text. The lama from Gyarong was puzzled by this very humble student who nonetheless came up with highly probing remarks.

When they were about halfway through the teachings on the text, Patrul left the lama of Gyarong's house and moved in with the old lady who lived next door. Not long afterward, some pilgrims from Dzachuka, Patrul Rinpoche's birthplace, came to Kathok to circumambulate the stupas and happened to notice this scruffy looking lama. His compatriots recognized him immediately. "*Apu!* Apu is here!" they cried out in delight, prostrating before him in devotion. *Apu*, or "uncle," was a nickname often used for Patrul.

Much displeased, Patrul scolded the pilgrims. "I've been living very quietly here, gathering merit. But now you've gone and told the whole world, 'Patrul is here! Patrul is here!' And there go my peace and quiet!"

It all played out just as he predicted. In no time, the word got around that Patrul Rinpoche was in town, even if no one could say exactly where he was.

When Patrul went to the old lama's place to receive his teachings, as he did every afternoon, the latter announced excitedly, "Patrul Rinpoche is here in person! Everybody says so!"

Patrul demonstrated no particular enthusiasm at the news.

At twilight that day, Patrul returned as usual to the old lady's house. She, too, told him breathlessly, "Patrul Rinpoche is here! Just imagine!"

"Why is everyone getting in such a lather! What's so special about this Patrul? He's just one more wandering lama among so many. If you ask me," he want on provocatively, "your Patrul's reputation is overrated! You'd do better with the great lamas of Kathok," he mocked.

The old lady was outraged enough to give him a good tongue-lashing.

"Wretched man! How dare you say such things? You'd feel no reverence even if Patrul Rinpoche, the Buddha himself, came knocking at your door! You'd send him away as a 'wandering old monk!' You accursed little man!" Patrul said no more.

Not long after this episode, Patrul was tracked down. The two high lamas of Kathok invited him to teach *The Way of the Bodhisattva*. Hearing the news, the pious old lady was thrilled at the idea of finally being able to meet the sainted man. The next morning, the tolling of the gong called the people to the teaching. Patrul left the old lady's house, as he did every morning at the same time, as if he were off to his daily circumambulations. As for the old lady, she hurried to the monastery. There, she was astonished to see, sitting on the throne, the raggedy lama who had been living in her home for weeks.

She prostrated at Patrul's feet and said,

"What bad karma I've earned! I scolded you and I was even on the point of beating you. I beg your pardon!"

"There's no harm done," Patrul reassured her gently. "There's no need for you to confess anything. Don't upset yourself. Your mind is pure. A good heart is the root of all Dharma. In fact, it's the very essence of *The Way of the Bodhisattva* that I'm about to teach. It's all anyone needs."

As Patrul began to deliver his teaching, the old lama from Gyarong realized in turn that his faithful student, the penniless lama to whom he had explained *The Way of the Bodhisattva* day after day, chapter by chapter, was none other than its author, Patrul Rinpoche himself. He was deeply abashed, but Patrul comforted him and assured him that he had taught the text very well.

They say that when Patrul expounded the Dharma, the minds of his listeners were totally transformed. As taught by him, an apparently simple point became a kind of doorway into a hundred spiritual understandings. He used direct language that resonated with each individual's inner experiences.

Whatever a person's social status, high or low, Patrul always gave the same advice: "Have a good heart and act kindly. There is no teaching deeper than that." When he was asked to confer a name on someone, he usually chose one that began with *nyingje*, which means "compassion."

He refused to bless people by placing his hand on their head. As he explained, "What's the point of my touching your head with my hands as a benediction? What you really need is to meditate correctly and change your mind from the inside."

Patrul's words were free of hypocrisy and stripped of all pretension. The rectitude of his speech and conduct was irreproachable. He lived a life with no contradictions. His values, his aims, and his behavior were always in harmony with the path. He was never obsequious in the presence of the noble and the powerful or condescending to the humblest among us. He did not waste his time on devious people who displayed affected politeness to mask duplicitous intentions. The affairs of this world had nothing to offer him. His mind was as vast and as fathomless as the ocean. In his preface to *Enlightened Vagabond*, Jigme Khyentse Rinpoche writes,

Patrul Rinpoche is both a reference and an inspiration. I often wonder, "What would Patrul Rinpoche do in this situation?" or "What would he think?" Even though he is not alive, he is still able to make us feel uncomfortable and to cut through the hypocrisy or insecurities that we have as students. This can transform our lives. Even if we try to ignore this uncomfortableness, his compassionate activity continues to haunt us in spite of our thick-skinned ignorance.

Oral tradition has it that Patrul Rinpoche could appear gruff or intimidating at first sight, but that the more time you spent with him, the more you became aware of his perfect equanimity, that is, his total lack of hope and fear. Always open and relaxed, it was actually calming to be around him, as he considered all circumstances, good or bad, to be endowed with a unique savor.

Indeed, it's said that once you found yourself in his presence, you could not bring yourself to leave.

46

A TOWN DEVOTED TO PHILOSOPHY

A winter's visit to Larung Gar, one of the largest academies of philosophy in history, hosting no fewer than six hundred *khenpos*, teaching scholars, and ten thousand monks and nuns.

In February 2016, in the company of Raphaële and two monks from Shechen, I was able for the first time to visit the Larung Gar academy of philosophy, which had long been off-limits to foreigners. Eventually, foreign nationals were allowed to visit but not to stay, so we had to leave before nightfall.

Around the bend of a small pass, a unique panorama lay open before us: the largest Buddhist university in history, apart from Nalanda and Vikramashila, famed institutions that thrived in India two thousand years ago! The Larung Gar academy of philosophy, located in Kham, at an altitude of 14,000 feet, was home to more than ten thousand monks and nuns (who made up the majority of the monastic population), as well as hundreds of lay students. From nearby hilltops, the magnitude of this citadel of the mind is evident. The vista is an immense mosaic of row upon row of tiny student houses covering the valley's three slopes.

Our visit coincided with a prayer week in which the entire community participated. Every day, a nun and a monk took turns leading prayers that took place in the two main temples rising from the midst of the residential neighborhoods. Amplified by loudspeakers, the voice of the nun leading the prayer that day so dominated the chanting of thousands of participants that everyone was able to sing in unison. When we climbed to the top of one of the prayer-flag-covered hills that overlook the valley, and sat for a while on a large boulder, I asked myself, "Where else in the world is there a valley where nothing can be heard all day long, for an entire week, but songs of the Dharma filling space with their serene harmony?"

In 1980, having studied under the best scholars of his time, Khenpo Jigme Phuntsok and a handful of his students founded this academy of philosophy, Larung Gar, in an uninhabited valley near the little town of Serthar, in southeastern Golok. From 1960 to 1980, the most intense period of Chinese repression, Jigme Phuntsok had led the life of a nomad, practicing in mountain hermitages. His charisma and the high quality of teaching at the Larung Gar philosophical academy very soon attracted a growing number of students, coming to form a small city, populated not only by Tibetans but also by hundreds of Chinese, who came to receive teachings in their own language.

In 1989, Jigme Phuntsok went to India at the invitation of Penor Rinpoche, founder of the largest Nyingmapa philosophical college on the Indian subcontinent, with three thousand monks and nuns as students. In 1990, he met the fourteenth Dalai Lama in Dharamshala, then sought out Dilgo Khyentse Rinpoche in Delhi. He prostrated three times before Khyentse Rinpoche, and one of his monks later told me that it was the first time he had ever seen him prostrate before any lama other than the Dalai Lama. Jigme Phuntsok also went on pilgrimage to Bhutan, where he exchanged teachings with Dilgo Khyentse Rinpoche.

On his return to Tibet, he refused to denounce the Dalai Lama, as demanded by the Chinese, which caused him serious problems. The government henceforth denied him all permission to travel. In 2001, several thousand members of the Chinese army brutally stormed Larung Gar academy and bulldozed a third of its residences. This was just one of the many arbitrary actions taken by the Chinese government against the vitality and resilience of Buddhist culture. Thousands of students were expelled and the lodgings of three thousand nuns were destroyed in order to reduce the population of scholars and students. From that point on, access was strictly forbidden to foreigners as the authorities sought to obstruct any witnesses and testimony to the destruction and abuses carried out there. While some people managed to visit in secret, I could not—despite my desire to see this spiritual landmark for myself—take the risk of putting my friends at Shechen Monastery in danger or undermining our humanitarian projects, which were already very challenging, given all the restrictions imposed by the government.

Jigme Phuntsok died in 2004, at the age of seventy, leaving the philosophical academy leaderless but no less thriving in spiritual and philosophical terms.

At Larung Gar, there are no fewer than six hundred *khenpos*, learned "doctors of philosophy" who have completed a minimum of twelve years of study and teach the basic texts of Buddhism to classes of thirty to forty students. The lack of academic and clerical hierarchy is a trademark of the academy's operations. While certain *khenpos*—such as Khenpo Tsultrim Lodrö and Khenpo Sodargye, to name but two—may be highly respected in Tibet and China, the administration is strictly horizontal at Larung Gar, and they have no claim to special treatment or elevated rank. The most eminent *khenpos* live in the same two-room cabins that are assigned to everyone. At major ceremonies, the song master sits on a small throne, needing to remain visible and audible while leading the prayers, while the other members of the monastic community sit in the order in which they arrived and, not, as in the case of most monasteries, according to their seniority or preeminence.

I met Khenpo Tsultrim Lodrö in Chengdu in 2014; he, alongside Khenpo Sodargye, is the senior *khenpo* and spiritual successor to Khenpo Jigme Phuntsok. He was fifty-ish, and I was struck by the simple manner and affability of that great scholar and engaged thinker who, among other things, has made a great contribution to the cause of vegetarianism in Tibet. He cites the Great Parinirvana Sutra, in which the Buddha affirms, "Eating meat destroys the attitude of great compassion." The vegetarian diet has always been popular in Tibet and was promoted by a great number of past masters, although it has never been predominant, no doubt because of the climate (agricultural cultivation is impossible above 12,000 feet and the winters are very long and especially harsh there).

Every year, Khenpo Tsultrim Lodrö and his Chinese students release into the lakes and rivers more than a million live fish, purchased wholesale, that were raised for human consumption.

Over the course of a few months in 2015 and early 2016, the restrictions for foreigners to visit Larung Gar were relaxed, but entry was again forbidden by summer of the same year. The government had instead decided to launch a new phase of destruction of the monastic residences. With that radical measure instituted in the summer of 2016, only those who had been born in the Serthar district were allowed to study in the academic valley; the others were ordered to return to their homelands. To facilitate their ease of access and their "regulation" of the academy's expansion, the Chinese also cut broad roads through the residential neighborhoods. It must be said that this had certain benefits; the truth is, the close proximity of residences was the cause of many fires. In fact, while we stood at the top of the hill, a small fire broke out near the edge of a neighborhood where many dwellings had been torn down in 2001. Within minutes, two hundred or three hundred monks were shuttling back and forth in lines on the hillside with buckets of water. Thanks to their diligence and energy, they managed to extinguish the fire.

We agreed among ourselves that, in the face of a systematic policy of persecution and the elimination of monks and monastic institutions, Larung Gar was an extraordinary example of the resilience of Buddhism and the iron resolve of the Tibetans in that long-persecuted land. Awed and moved by the amazing scenes we had witnessed in the university—unique of its kind in the world, with its ten thousand philosophy students, their prayers rising from the valley to fill the air—we left Larung Gar, a monument to the Tibetan philosophical tradition, with heavy hearts.

On my many journeys to Tibet between 1985 and 2017, I had developed a deep attachment to the Land of Snows. It is the place where I feel most at ease and most powerfully inspired to grow, study, and practice. I am by nature drawn to high altitudes, so the cold and high plateaus of Tibet are an ideal living environment. There are so many other sublime landscapes on our planet Earth, but in Tibet these places of great beauty are imbued with the subtle but palpable presence of my spiritual teachers, the men and women, hermits, monks, nuns, and lay practitioners who, from Padmasambhava's day to ours, have lived in these physically and spiritually special places.

The legacy of Tibetan Buddhist culture is under severe threat, but despite all adversities, its spiritual transmission remains intact to this day. We can only hope with all our hearts that it is able yet again to overcome any obstacles it encounters under the yoke of a totalitarian regime.

VI

IN THE HEART OF THE MAELSTROM

47

THE MONK AND THE PHILOSOPHER

The origins and completion of a book of dialogue with my father, the philosopher Jean-François Revel, marking a turning point in my life. We stay together on a hillside in Nepal and debate the best way to lead our lives.

It all began with a report aired by the weekly television series *Envoyé special* in early 1996. In the summer of 1995, a crew came to Nepal to shoot a segment on the "French monk"—namely, me—who had lived in the Himalayas for the past twenty-five years. We had not yet founded Karuna-Shechen or begun our humanitarian projects. At the time, I was doing what I could to preserve the heritage of Himalayan Buddhism by assisting Rabjam Rinpoche in his efforts to perpetuate the spiritual legacy of Dilgo Khyentse Rinpoche, among other things by translating his oral teachings, which I had recorded, into Tibetan and collecting his writings with a view to publishing them.

Shortly after the story was broadcast on the France 2 channel, the telephone began ringing at Shechen Monastery, where I was then living. The monastery office had just been hooked up with a telephone line, quite a feat at a time when it was practically impossible to secure such a connection in Kathmandu. The call was from France. Out of the blue, a Parisian book publisher was suggesting the idea of publishing a dialogue with my father, the philosopher Jean-François Revel. My first reaction was to tell her, "Ask him what he thinks about it." I had a hard time picturing my father, a well-known intellectual and polemicist, taking the risk of engaging in a dialogue with a Buddhist monk, even if he were his own son. The only interest in spirituality I had ever seen him show was when he had occasionally taken us to admire the architecture of old Romanesque churches on our summer vacations, while my sister and I would have been a lot happier building sandcastles on the beach. After exchanging a few niceties, I hung up the receiver, thinking that that was the last I'd hear of the odd proposal.

To my great surprise, however, the same editor called again fifteen days later to inform me, "Your father said yes!" She had invited my father to lunch at a three-star Parisian restaurant, the kind of offer my gastronome father never turned down. Then, as editors on the lookout for authors sometimes do, she had suggested several book ideas that he had politely rejected, one after the other. Thereupon, she told me, she had asked him over dessert, "How about a dialogue with your son, Matthieu?" His jaw dropped and, after a brief silence, he replied, "How could I say no to that?"

My first reaction was to think, "Now I'm in trouble. With his gift of the gab, he's going to steamroll me." After mulling it over briefly, and drawing on my age-old experience as a soccer player, I said, "Fine, but if we're going to do it, we'll have to have our talk here, in Nepal." It's always best to play on your home turf!

That night, I laid out the proposal for Rabjam Rinpoche, the abbot of the monastery, with whom I am very close. I admitted that I was worried that this might create a lot of disturbances to my peaceful life in Nepal. But he convinced me to agree, saying that such a dialogue could contribute to a better understanding of Buddhism in the West. I accepted the offer.

My father had a literary agent, a common practice in the United States but not yet widespread in France in those days. This agent went to the publishing house with his attaché case and a draft contract that demanded a hefty advance on the author's commission. The editor who had suggested the project was very enthusiastic about the proposed dialogue, but the director of the house had some concerns about the size of the requested advance and pointed this out to the agent: "We all know that Monsieur Revel is an author whose works enjoy a wide readership, but the son . . . who knows? Let's see what happens." His subtext was crystal clear: "Maybe he's just one of those new-agers who go to India to smoke weed." In high dudgeon, the literary agent sputtered dramatically, "How dare you question . . . ?" and so on. He had no choice but to storm off, unsigned contract in hand. As it turns out, I later learned that it had been my mother, Yahne Le Toumelin, who had suggested the idea of the dialogue to the editor, Maren Sell, whom she knew well. She had told her, "Those two should get together and talk."

At the same time, Nicole Lattès, who had founded the publishing house NiL Éditions, among other achievements of her distinguished literary career, had come across a picture of my father and me on a magazine cover following the *Envoyé special* broadcast. She called my father, whose two-volume *Histoire de la philosophie occidentale* ("The History of Western Philosophy") she had successfully republished, and shared her surprise that he had a Buddhist son. With his usual sense of humor, my father replied, "I have another who's Jewish and an Orthodox daughter, so you have the choice!" They agreed to meet for lunch as soon as possible, when she proposed the idea of a dialogue between a philosopher and a monk. My father told her, "That's funny, another editor had the same suggestion, but he's waffling and dragging it out."

Nicole leaped in: "I'm snapping it up! As you know, I've started my own publishing house and I can make you a very reasonable offer. Agreed?" They high-fived in delight and washed down the agreement with a glass of good wine. My father called to inform me of the discussion and that he would be thrilled to come to Nepal.

And so it was that my father, accompanied by his wife, my stepmother, Claude Sarraute, landed in Kathmandu one fine day in May 1996. After showing them around the monastery and introducing them to Rabjam Rinpoche, we went up to Hattiban, a resort twelve miles south of Kathmandu. This charming resort complex is made up of low-slung little houses scattered in a pine forest at the top of a hill overlooking the Kathmandu Valley. But once you leave the main road, getting there involves a bumpy ride in a Jeep up a dirt path that zigzags through the deep forest. After a few minutes, my father couldn't contain his alarm and cried out, "Are you taking us to the end of the world or what?" However, once we reached the pretty main house that served as reception area and restaurant and were welcomed with a necklace of flowers and a fresh lemonade, he was soon soothed by the calm and beauty of the place.

I haven't read all my father's books, but I had prepared for the dialogue by reading his history of philosophy, which has the merit of being extremely clear. He had written it by drawing on his exceptional memory, as if he had found himself on a desert island with no books at hand, leaving blank spaces where he would later insert quotations. Of certain contemporary thinkers whose work was especially abstruse, and whom he held in low esteem, he said, "If they have such good ideas, why don't they express them clearly?" And when I confessed to him that as a teenager, I had been completely unable to understand the writing of certain modern philosophers, he reassured me: "Well, the truth is, that's because there's nothing there to understand."

Ready for any eventuality, I had also drawn up a list of subjects we might discuss. When I showed it to my father, as a way of getting our first conversation started the next day, he gave it a quick look and exclaimed, "Come on! This is all the stuff people have been arguing about for two thousand years!" He took the list with him, and I didn't see it again for the first eight days of our conversations.

We established a daily schedule. We would talk every morning from nine to eleven, then take a walk in the forest, and then have lunch with Claude. In the afternoon, my father would go take his daily nap, and our conversation would resume from three to five.

Despite everything, my father must have had some nervous second thoughts about our discussions, because he sent a fax to Nicole Lattès on the first night, simply saying, "All good."

And indeed, it all went very smoothly. My father led the debates and set out the book's framework. I answered his questions in the light of my experiences with my spiritual teachers over the course of twenty-five years spent in Nepal, Bhutan, Tibet, and India. I was immediately struck and heartened by his open-mindedness. He engaged the full power of his intelligence and knowledge in his questions and responses, but I never once sensed any narrow-mindedness, dogmatism, or cynical irony, which certainly would have poisoned the tenor of our debates. He was ready to discuss anything, to listen patiently to my replies, and to follow up with apposite questions.

On our last morning, my father produced my list of questions. He pointed to a few subjects and said, "So listen, we still haven't touched on these issues."

We left the hills of Hattiban for Kathmandu, our hearts at peace, happy to have been so sincerely open with one another. Some critics have written that our conversations marked a "father-son reunion." It's true that our family ties made our exchanges considerably easier, and yet, except for the brief introduction written by my father, the contents of the book that would emerge from our days in Nepal were focused almost exclusively on the intellectual interaction of our views on the subjects we addressed: Why abandon scientific research for a spiritual quest? Is Buddhism a religion or a philosophy? Is it a science of mind? How does one reconcile a life of contemplation with a life of action? And so on. This was first and foremost about an encounter and dialogue between a Buddhist monk and a Western philosopher.

My father had kicked off our conversations with the following inquiry: "The Greeks asked three big questions: 'What can I know? How should a city be governed? How should I lead my life?'" According to him, science largely answered the first question and democracy the second. As to the third, he believed that the philosophers who came after Spinoza totally cast that question aside in favor of building sprawling intellectual edifices intended to rebuild the world from scratch, as if no one had ever had a thought before them. Faced with this failure of modern philosophy, my father wondered whether the growing interest in Buddhism in the West might be due to the fact that it filled a void by offering pragmatic answers to the question of how best to live our lives. His interest in Buddhism, therefore, was based less on the metaphysics of that spiritual tradition, of which he was no further convinced at the end of our conversations than he had been at the beginning, than on the "art of living" it appeared to offer, and which my father found very attractive. On our book tour through the United States, I was even surprised to hear him sing the praises of Buddhism on several occasions before I'd had the chance to open my mouth.

The outcome of these events developed quickly and smoothly. I went to France in May to meet with Nicole Lattès, with whom I struck up an immediate and lasting friendship. Looking over the contract, I was dumbfounded by the size of my advance (at the age of fifty-one, my personal fortune came to no more than €2,000 or €3,000 at today's rates). I had absolutely no need of the money I was being offered. After steering well clear of red tape of any kind for the past twenty-five years, I felt that the best use I could make of this money would be to contribute it to humanitarian causes and the preservation of the cultural and spiritual heritage of Tibet. After talking it over with Nicole, it was decided that the contract would stipulate that I was to donate all my royalties to the Fondation Padmasambhava, founded in 1979 under the auspices of the Fondation de France and dedicated to the preservation and dissemination of Buddhist cultural heritage. We had to have the document notarized, submit the donation for approval by the prefect, and so on. The funny thing is, it's not so easy to give your possessions away! Later on, Rabjam Rinpoche and I founded our own charitable association, Karuna-Shechen (*karuna* meaning "compassion" and Shechen being the name of our monastery). It is a lay and nonpolitical organization, separate from the monastery, that today assists more than four hundred thousand people yearly in India, Nepal, and Tibet in the fields of health, education, and social services, with a stress on remedying extreme poverty and the empowerment of women. This beautiful venture and all its attendant benefits all got their start with *The Monk and the Philosopher.*

In early June, I reunited with my father at his home in Pleubian, in northern Brittany, to record our concluding chapter. I wanted to lead the debate this time so I could ask him a few existential questions. Regarding death, inter alia, he told me, "I don't think that any human being who knows himself or herself to be mortal and who doesn't believe in an afterlife can experience a feeling of total fulfillment. Relatively, perhaps, it's possible, in terms of some temporary objectives that don't rule out a degree of consummation. But I think that complete solutions to the meaning of life simply don't exist—outside the great transcendent solutions, whether religious, parareligious, or political."

Even so, I tried to nudge him a little out of his entrenched positions: "I think it's possible to acquire wisdom, fulfillment, and serenity, all of them arising from knowledge, or from what could be called spiritual realization. I think that once one's discovered the ultimate nature of the mind, that discovery is timeless. . . . True spiritual realization also transcends life and death, it's the unchanging truth that we can actualize within ourselves—fulfillment that no longer depends on becoming." To which my father replies with the concluding lines of the book: "Well, there you are. And since your hypothesis is more optimistic than mine, I'm sure our readers will feel better if I let you have the last word."

The recordings of our dialogues were soon transcribed. My father, whose command of the French language is incomparably superior to mine, made some quick revisions with his Waterman pen (he never used a typewriter, let alone a computer), while I spent a month laboriously making a few minor improvements to my statements. My mother read the manuscript and told me, "Your father's done for! He's lost all his sparkle. This book is going to flop." I'm very happy to say that her prediction was wrong and that the book has enjoyed a huge success.

Before *The Monk and the Philosopher* came out, I was a complete unknown who had spent twenty-five quiet years in the Himalayas, far from the restless world, without a radio or newspapers (other than those used to wrap vegetables), living with my spiritual teachers in remote regions. When the book was published in April 1997, we made the cover of *Le Point*, among others, and were caught up for three solid weeks in a whirlwind of interviews in every imaginable medium. For someone who had never before set foot in a radio station or on a television set, it was a brutal awakening, to say the least.

Its suddenness at least had the virtue of preventing me from taking myself too seriously; I was the same person who, from one day to the next, went from being completely anonymous to famous and recognizable, thanks to my monastic robes, which make me a walking headline. Fame seems to be based on the appearance of your face on the "boob tube," your voice filling the airwaves, and what the press says about you.

Depending on the way I look at it, *The Monk and the Philosopher* either marked the onset of all my troubles—I was to be caught up in a maelstrom of activity for the next twenty years—or represented an opportunity to share ideas and experiences, the sources of an immensely enriched interior life; to launch humanitarian projects funded by the income from my books and lectures; to engage in other, enthralling dialogues—with the astrophysicist Trinh Xuan Thuan, notably—and to write several books inspired by my diverse encounters. That's how I found myself in the unlikeliest places for a Buddhist monk, such as the World Economic Forum in Davos, to which I was invited ten times, or the United Nations, where I was invited to discuss the implementation of a resolution submitted by Bhutan to place the well-being of peoples, the famous "gross national happiness," on the agenda of that international organization. The motion was adopted by a vast majority. I also began to crisscross the world in response to all sorts of invitations. *The Monk and the Philosopher* was translated into twenty-three languages. It even came out in China, although all references to the Dalai Lama were duly excised from the chapter on Tibet. The official Chinese edition, which sold thousands of copies, was followed by a pirated edition in that country, likewise redacted, that sold one hundred thousand copies!

My father and I have never had any significant disagreements. As he writes in his introduction, "The only clouds that ever passed over our relationship were those of the Asian monsoon." Our travels and colloquies in France, England, and the United States after the book was published reinforced and deepened our affectionate alliance.

We did a book tour in the United States, organized by our American publisher Schocken, with the assistance of Vivian Kurz, a friend and student of Khyentse Rinpoche who managed Shechen Monastery's affairs in the United States. She went everywhere with us. The tour, altogether very pleasant, gave rise to some rather comical scenes.

On the east coast, we were invited to give a talk at Harvard Divinity School. My father had "warmed up" with a couple of Bloody Marys before the conference. He expressed himself with his usual brio and intelligence, but he spoke very slowly, albeit in perfect English. He was widely admired in American intellectual circles; several of his books, *Without Marx or Jesus* in particular, had even been bestsellers in the United States. The audience was therefore hanging on his every word. I made up for it by speaking faster in my own statements. Along with Tibetan, English had become the language I used most. Then came the Q-and-A. After a few preselected questions, someone at the back of the amphitheater called out in a loud voice:

"Monsieur Revel, what do you think of love?"

My father sat silently for a moment, drawing out the suspense, then leaned forward and, weighing each word and hammering it home with a wag of his index finger, announced,

"I am totally in favor of love."

The evening ended with a burst of raucous laughter, including from my friend, the Tibetologist Gene Smith, who was sitting in the first row. In the wings, my father told me, "The Americans make it easy. All you have to do is tell them a good joke." Before leaving, he confessed to Vivian, "I love America."

When my father's dear friend and colleague Olivier Todd delivered his eulogy at the Père Lachaise cemetery in 2016, he noted with affectionate humor, *"The Monk and the Philosopher* was Jean-François's best-selling book. He was well aware of that." Hélène Carrère d'Encausse, permanent secretary of the Académie française, to which my father had been admitted in 1998, told a mutual friend that he had admitted to her that *The Monk and the Philosopher* had meant a great deal to him toward the end of his life. With his typical modesty, he had never told me anything of the kind.

In April 2017, twenty years almost to the day after the book came out, we held a reunion of the main stakeholders of our humanitarian organization, Karuna-Shechen. It was a warm gathering of about thirty of us, including the managers of field projects in Nepal and India and those who helped promote our work by spreading the name of Karuna-Shechen throughout the world; a few of our major donors were also present. Sanjeev Pradhan, who oversaw our projects in Nepal, and I had decided to hold the event in Hattiban. At the close of the first morning's discussions, I led all the participants to one of the Hattiban resort ccurowws and told them, "My friends, this is where it all began. This is where my father and I got together to talk in 1996."

48

FROM ONE BOOK TO THE NEXT

I engage in dialogues with the astrophysicist Trinh Xuan Thuan, the neuroscientist Wolf Singer, and my two "friends in good will," Christophe André and Alexandre Jollien. One book follows another, including three works of advocacy that require years of research.

The way I saw it, *The Monk and the Philosopher* should have marked the beginning and the end of my writing career. My intentions were clear—I wanted to get back to my translations of Tibetan texts as soon as possible. My thousand-page translation of *The Life of Shabkar: The Autobiography of a Tibetan Yogin*, on which I had worked for ten years, had just been published in English by the State University of New York Press, and a few translations of Dilgo Khyentse Rinpoche's teachings had been released by Shambhala Publications. I had no other desire but to pursue this course. But things were to turn out differently.

THE QUANTUM AND THE LOTUS

Following the publication of *The Monk and the Philosopher*, I was invited to the Summer University in Andorra in 1997, where I was very happy to meet the astrophysicist Trinh Xuan Thuan. We got along immediately and engaged in fascinating discussions as we hiked through the magnificent landscapes of the Pyrenees mountains. I was especially eager to clear up certain questions I had about the idea of "limits" in physics. Why is it impossible to imagine a speed faster than that of light, which would contradict the special theory of relativity, and why is that speed 186,000 miles per second and not some other value? Does the Big Bang represent a genuine "beginning"? What about the "quantum vacuum" from which the Big Bang appears to have emerged? Why are the laws of physics as we know them unable to describe the universe in the very first moments after the Big Bang (within Planck time)?[1] Although he was born a Buddhist, Thuan had not had the opportunity to develop his understanding of that philosophy and wished to stack it up against his scientific knowledge. As a Western scientist turned Buddhist monk, I seemed to fill the bill. We also had some rich discussions with Christian de Duve, Nobel Prize laureate in medicine, on the origins of life. In any event, Thuan suggested that we engage in a dialogue on the same basis as that of *The Monk and the Philosopher*. It was hard to turn down such a tempting offer, and we soon met again for a few days in Dordogne to lay out the parameters of the exchange we would pursue face-to-face and in writing.

To the best of our abilities, we debated fundamental issues: Can the universe have a genuine beginning in which "nothing" turns into "something?" Does there have to be a beginning? If, as Buddhism asserts, phenomena are void of independent existence, such questions can no longer be formulated in the same way, since phenomena are not truly "born" but appear and change even as they have no ultimate reality. Every religion and philosophy has stumbled on this problem of creation. To sidestep it, science has eliminated the concept of a god of creation and Buddhism excludes the very concept of a genuine beginning. Buddhism identifies two points of view that are as extreme as they are erroneous: nihilism and material realism. In Buddhism's middle way, there is neither a "nothing" nor a "something" endowed with ultimate reality.

Thuan believes, however, that humankind did not arise at random in an indifferent universe. Indeed, the universe appears to be perfectly organized to ensure the emergence of living beings. It turns out that even a minimal change in fifteen universal "constants"—the gravitational constant, the intensity of the strong and weak nuclear forces, and the speed of light, among others—would entail its sterilization and prevent the nuclear alchemy of the stars from producing the heavy elements, such as carbon, that are necessary to life. It all hinges, therefore, on a very delicate balance. The universe would seem to be governed precisely in such a way as to nurture life and consciousness. That is what we call the "anthropic principle."

For Buddhism, on the other hand, there's no need to invoke the intervention of an organizing principle, a "great watchmaker," or some end purpose that has arranged the universe with the perfect precision necessary to engender consciousness. If, as Buddhism proposes, the universe and consciousness have coexisted since time immemorial, owing to the fact that they are both "primary phenomena," coexisting and interdependent, and cannot have appeared ex nihilo, they are naturally and mutually compatible and cannot exclude one another.[2] Universal constants are thus no more than reflections of their compatibility, without beginning or end. The anthropic principle boils down to examining the two halves of a single walnut and marveling, "It's unbelievable. It's as if the first had been created to allow the second to dovetail perfectly with it."

One of the most fascinating subjects of our discussions was the correspondence between the concept of interdependence, which is central to Buddhism, and the demonstration through quantum physics that reality is not a collection of separate entities endowed with their own intrinsic properties (what physicists call "local properties"), but that it is global and interdependent—"entangled," in the standard formulation. This entanglement is the key characteristic of quantum mechanics. Quantum phenomena do not interact with one another sequentially in time and space within a limited and localizable reality, while losing their ability to coordinate with one another beyond a certain distance; they are essentially connected. An inveterate determinist, Einstein could not accept the primordial role that quantum mechanics attributed to randomness. "God does not play dice," he said. To that end, he designed a famous thought experiment with Boris Podolsky and Nathan Rosen, known as the EPR paradox after the initials of its three authors. In 1982, Alain Aspect and his team carried out a series of experiments on pairs of photons to test the EPR effect. An atom is stimulated in such a way as to simultaneously emit two photons in opposite directions; the electromagnetic fields of these photons should oscillate in strictly orthogonal directions, which the sensors confirmed. It is said that the respective spins of these photons point in opposite directions. It should be noted that a photon's spin is a quantum characteristic of particles intimately linked to their rotational properties. At the quantum level, the spins of these entangled photons have no defined direction before they are detected. It is only once they have been observed that the direction of their spin can be identified. The photons are at that moment separated in space, however, and yet the detection of each clearly reveals two strictly opposite directions, as if they had communicated the direction of their respective spins at exactly the same instant. It is possible to demonstrate experimentally that no information can have been transmitted and that the similarity of their behavior cannot be attributed to a "common cause" that they carry with them as they move through space and time. Thus, there is coordination without communication. This globality flies against Einstein's predictions and contradicts two fundamental laws: the principle of "locality," which states that an object is influenced directly only by its immediate surroundings (regardless of the distance from one another at which the photons are detected, the result is always the same: their spins are determined in relation to each other), and the law of special relativity (if the photons are "communicating" their spin instantaneously, they must be doing so either faster than the speed of light, which has been determined to be unsurpassable, or by "going back" in time). In 1998, the Swiss physicist Nicolas Gisin, with whom I became friends years later, verified this hypothesis over long distances. No matter how far apart they may be, the two particles belong to the same global reality outside of space-time. Physicists call this situation "non-separability." Nicolas Gisin therefore concluded that nature is "nonlocal."[3] This observation should have a powerful impact on the way we ordinarily perceive the world as comprising separate entities, each endowed with independent existence. If phenomena are intimately linked with and dependent on one another, nothing exists in and of itself.

In one of his sermons, the Buddha describes reality as a tracery of pearls. Each pearl reflects all the others, as well as the palace whose façade they adorn and the entire universe. In other words, each element of reality contains all the others. This is only an image, but it eloquently illustrates the concept of interdependence whereby no single entity in the universe can exist totally distinct from the whole.

Is there a reality hidden behind apparent phenomena, or are the latter merely the ephemeral crystallization of an encounter with a certain type of consciousness—in this case, our human consciousness—with a collection of hitherto indeterminate phenomena?

This idea of a real substrate existing independently behind the veil of our perceptions has been long debated within Buddhist philosophy.[4] The way we perceive the world is very specific. If all human beings perceive the world more or less identically, it's because their consciousnesses and their bodies are similarly configured, so to speak. A human's reality differs considerably from that of an ant or a bat, whose perceptual realities remain totally unimaginable to all of us. Buddhist texts offer the example of a jar of water. We generally perceive it as a drink or as a liquid to refresh or wash ourselves with, whereas it is an object of intense dread for someone sick with rabies, a habitat for a fish, and a collection of molecules to a physicist using an electron microscope. A buddha perceives water as a union of emptiness and appearances. Phenomena are indisputably apparent, they "exist," and we therefore cannot speak of "nothingness"; but when we consider the nature of that existence, we see that it is "empty" of independent existence, being neither self-contained nor permanent. Thus, we also cannot speak of an intrinsically existent, hard reality, a belief that arises from what some might call "naive realism," or sometimes "materialism" or "eternalism." According to the Buddhist middle way, there is neither nothing (nihilism) nor something (material realism)—it is only the vision that unites emptiness and appearance that resists analysis.

For Thuan, this affirmation agrees with Niels Bohr's theory that atomic and subatomic objects have no properties exclusive to themselves. When they are not being observed, it is impossible, even in thought, to attribute a determined speed to them or a trajectory along which their precise location can be determined at any moment. The aim of physics is not to describe reality in itself, but to describe the "communicable human experience," that is, the experience of observation and measurement.

Here, we find ourselves again up against the Buddhist notions of relative reality and absolute reality. Relative reality corresponds to the way phenomena appear to us, with identifiable characteristics. Absolute reality corresponds to the absence of independent existence in such characteristics, which suggests that the ultimate nature of phenomena, emptiness, is beyond all description and conceptualization.

Ultimately, we concluded that the main difference between science and Buddhism lay in their end goals. For Buddhism, knowledge is acquired with the therapeutic aim of liberating yourself from suffering, whose primary cause is an erroneous conception of reality and of the self that we imagine residing in the core of our being. Science seeks essentially to describe reality in the most correct way possible and to shine a light on the laws governing observable phenomena and the mechanisms available to explain our observations. But for a scientist, the knowledge acquired thereby does not necessarily entail a change in her way of being or the conduct of her life.

The Quantum and the Lotus (whose French title, *L'Infini dans la paume de la main*, echoes William Blake's "infinity in the palm of your hand"), is a book that attempts to address complex but fundamental questions. And despite the apparent difficulty of its themes, it was very warmly received, which prompted my father to point out that you should never underestimate your readers.

HAPPINESS

My third book, *Happiness: A Guide to Developing Life's Most Important Skill*, was also born of a convergence of circumstances linked to what I felt to be a misunderstanding of the idea of happiness. *The Art of Happiness*, a particularly enlightening dialogue between the Dalai Lama and Howard Cutler that enjoyed worldwide success, was ignored by French critics and somewhat vilified by certain otherwise brilliant and cultured thinkers. The notion of happiness is apparently out of favor in the French homeland.

For Aristotle, however, happiness is the only goal "we always choose for its own sake and never as a means to something else." Along the same line of thought, the Dalai Lama affirms that "Happiness is the aim of life." From that perspective, someone who claims to aspire to other things—freedom, justice, love, friendship, pleasure—is ultimately engaged in the pursuit of happiness by another name, for the simple reason that our thoughts, words, and actions normally tend toward "well-being" and not toward an increase of our suffering or that of others (unless you are caught up in a spiral of self-destruction or animated by malice or perversion). This aspiration, then, extends to life's everyday affairs, ethics, justice, the state of the planet and every other aspect of our existence. This desire so naturally motivates all our actions, words, and thoughts that we aren't even aware of it, like the oxygen we breathe all our lives without noticing it. This is an obvious, even banal conclusion, writes philosopher André Comte-Sponville, "because happiness, almost by definition, is of interest to everyone."[5]

And yet it's common to meet people who insist that they are not looking for happiness, and who may even see such a pursuit as naive. As Pascal Bruckner writes in *Perpetual Euphoria*, "Happiness doesn't interest me."[6] How is it possible to hold two diametrically opposed views on what, for most of us, is a basic building block of our lives? Is there perhaps a major misunderstanding here about the very definition of happiness? The Dalai Lama and those holding the contrary position would seem to be talking about two different things. A magazine asked Pascal Bruckner—whom I consider a friend—and me to engage in a dialogue for a feature article. Upon my return from my hermitage in Nepal, it occurred to me that this subject needed to be explored in greater depth.

From the outset, I was struck by the fact that literature and philosophy offered pretty much every definition imaginable of happiness and its exact opposite. For some, happiness is a life replete with meaning and accomplishment; for others, it's made of up "magical" and elusive moments or ephemeral pleasures; for a few, it is, more prosaically, a good bowl of spaghetti—I swear, I found this definition of happiness in a French weekly in the course of my research!

Has the word been so completely tarnished that we may be excused for washing our hands of happiness altogether, just because we're fed up with "happiness-in-a-box" style consumerism, with advertising that promises perfect bliss at an unbeatable price, with prime-time TV hosts so revved up with happiness that they collapse in exhaustion, with the "crusaders for incandescence," as Pascal Bruckner calls them, and with the thousand-and-one other individualistic and narcissistic quests for happiness—each an illusion that can end only in bitter disillusionment? "Live intensely" has become the leitmotiv of modern humankind, a compulsive hyperactivity in which even the least amount of down time places you at risk of finding yourself alone—with yourself. The meaning is irrelevant, so long as there's intensity. Hence the taste for and fascination with stunts, the maximal stimulation of the senses, the pursuit of violence—pushing yourself to the limit of nowhere, breaking the sound barrier of fecklessness, blowing nothing out of all proportion. There's a full life for you.

But let's not throw out the baby with the bathwater. Just because we might lose our way or go astray on the road to happiness, and sometimes turn our back on it, that doesn't mean it isn't worth achieving.

What is this uncertainty that surrounds the notion of happiness? According to Henri Bergson, "[Happiness] is a word which is commonly used to designate something intricate and ambiguous, one of those ideas which humanity has intentionally left vague, so that each individual might interpret it after his own fashion."[7] From a practical standpoint, allowing our understanding of happiness to remain ambiguous wouldn't be such a terrible thing if it were a fleeting and inconsequential feeling, but given that it is a quality of being that determines every moment of our existence, the problem deserves a little further attention.

Let's look at the question the other way around. Apparently, we can all agree on the fact that no one wakes up in the morning hoping to suffer all day long, much less for the rest of his life. It is therefore desirable to avoid suffering and its causes to the greatest extent possible. That right there is a good starting point to agree on, a basis on which it becomes possible to analyze the causes of suffering, design remedies, and apply them.

We can again refer to Aristotle: "With regard to what happiness is they differ, and the many do not give the same account as the wise."[8] We can indeed look for happiness where it is not and at the same time prolong our suffering. The wise man, however, shows good judgement by correctly identifying the causes of suffering and those that will lead him to *eudaimonia*, a Greek term that signifies "fulfillment" or "flourishing" and that lends its name to eudaimonism, a philosophical doctrine that holds happiness as the sovereign good of existence.

My book was to be a work of interdisciplinary synthesis, taking into account the views of great thinkers of the past, in the West as in the East, as well as research on "well-being" undertaken in the fields of experimental and social psychology and the neurosciences.

It struck me as especially important to highlight the fundamental difference between pleasure, which is a fragile and fugitive sensation, and happiness as a lasting and constant state of being arising from a convergence of various human qualities that have the potential to be cultivated.

"Pleasure is but the shadow of happiness," goes one Hindu proverb. Generated by sensory, esthetic, or intellectual stimuli, the fleeting experience of pleasure depends on circumstances, both of place and of a particular moment. Its nature is unstable and the feeling that generates pleasure can soon turn neutral or unpleasant. The repetition of pleasure generally leads to its fading, and even to disgust. Moreover, pleasure remains an individual experience, essentially focused on oneself, making it readily associated with selfishness and in conflict with the well-being of others. Pleasure can combine with cruelty, violence, pride, greed, and other mental states incompatible with true happiness. As the nineteenth-century French novelist Jules Barbey d'Aurevilly wrote, "Pleasure is the happiness of the fool; happiness is the pleasure of the wise."[9]

Unlike pleasure, happiness is born within. Yes, it can be influenced by circumstance, but it is not entirely subject to it. Far from morphing into its own opposite, it endures and grows the longer it is experienced. It generates a sense of flourishing and fulfillment that, with time, becomes a basic feature of our temperament.

In agreement with many philosophers of ancient Greece (writing about *eudaimonia*) and spiritual traditions, as well as works of contemporary psychology, I saw happiness as an acquired state of plenitude that underlies and pervades every experience and all behavior, and that encompasses all joy and all pain. It entails reduced vulnerability to circumstance, good or bad. An altruistic and resilient fortitude comes to supplant the sense of insecurity and pessimism that afflicts so many minds. I also investigated the different mental factors that contribute to well-being and, contrarily, that undermine it.

I also highlighted the fact that happiness is incompatible with egocentrism, the pursuit of self-centered happiness being doomed to failure since we are fundamentally interdependent on one another. True happiness arises from a tireless good will, without ostentation or ulterior motive, that from the bottom of its heart wants everyone to find meaning in their lives and to flourish to the best of their abilities.

Before launching into this new book, I asked myself seriously, "What is your underlying motivation?" To me, the work would have value only if my one and only goal was to be useful to my peers, even in the most minimal way. Any other reason—in particular, that of writing a best-selling book—seemed futile to me. For instance, one of my favorite books, *Enlightened Vagabond*, which tells the life story of Patrul Rinpoche and took me thirty years to write, on and off, as I collected one hundred anecdotes from oral tradition, was published in an edition of only a thousand copies![10] Not much compared to the three hundred thousand copies of *Happiness*, but it is just as dear to my heart.

LA CITADELLE DES NEIGES ("CITADEL OF THE SNOWS")

In April 2005, I accompanied Rabjam Rinpoche to Senge Dzong, a legendary, extremely remote place in eastern Bhutan. Our four-day trek, including a twelve-hour hike through the jungle that I will describe below, ended 13,000 feet above sea level in a ring of magnificent mountains inhabited by only a handful of monks and hermits. On our return to Paro, where I stayed for two months alongside Rabjam Rinpoche, I decided to write down this unique and spiritually enriching experience in a tale featuring a child, Dechen ("Great Bliss"), who had been drawn to the contemplative life since his very earliest years. When his uncle, who lived with his spiritual teacher in the Snow Lion Fortress, a place "far from men, near to the gods," came down to the village for a few days, the child decided to go with him.

Combining an account of our pilgrimage with historical facts from various times and places, it took me three weeks to write this story, published as *La Citadelle des neiges*, tracing the stages of a spiritual path, describing life with a teacher and the latter's death in "rainbow body." After spending a few years in retreat in a cave, Dechen chooses the life of a wandering bard and takes to the road to share the teachings he has received in the form of uplifting songs, pursuing his own path to enlightenment.

WHY MEDITATE?

At the end of a conference on afflictive mental states, neuroscientific research on mind training, or the inner conditions of authentic happiness, someone has often come up to me to ask, "I'd love to meditate but I don't know how. How do I start?" How could I explain in just a few words? Aware that there was a need here that I was unable to meet, one winter when I was living in my hermitage, I decided to put together a very simple guidebook, based on the wisdom and experience of Buddhism but written for a general audience, practitioners and nonpractitioners alike. I wrote it as if I were explaining the basics of meditation to someone standing right in front of me. Why meditate? How to meditate and on what? To make it as accessible and practical as possible, without reducing my observations simplistically, I described several distinct ways of meditating: on attentive presence; how to cultivate a calmer, stabler and clearer mind; the handling of discursive thought and pain; altruistic love; compassion and impartiality; and so on. The book was based on the teachings received from my teachers, and was rounded out with quotations from their teachings and from Buddhist scripture.

When I was back in France, I showed the manuscript to a close friend who often reread my work for me. He gave it a quick reading and told me, "This thing isn't even a rough draft!" I reworked the text into acceptable shape, and *Why meditate?* was published in 2008. The "thing" was ultimately published in editions totaling more than three hundred thousand copies, so I had reason to hope that it had found its public and successfully met, at least in part, the expectations of aspiring meditators. And yet, one day I found myself on a train, sitting next to someone who said to me, "I've read your book and I think I get it. But tell me, how do I go about *really* meditating?" Back to the drawing board.

This question showed me yet again that nothing can take the place of a live transmission by an experienced teacher or, if possible, an accomplished spiritual master. But I remained confident that at least there was nothing in my little manual that contradicted the more elaborate and deep forms of mind training. For those who wished to move ahead on that path, I later published *On the Path to Enlightenment, Heart Advice from the Great Tibetan Masters*, an anthology of the Tibetan texts that had deeply touched me over the past forty years, and which I had arranged according to the graded order of the Buddhist path and translated into French.

ALTRUISM

I have a special soft spot for the work I want to present to you now. Our times face many challenges. One of our major problems is how to reconcile short-term imperatives—feeding our family, surviving in an economic system of disturbing fluctuations—with the quest for a happy and thriving life in the medium term, and, in the long term, respect for the environment, for the good of future generations and for the eight million species that share the planet with us. Economy and finance follow their own increasingly frenetic and senseless course. We measure the extent of our satisfaction with our own lives against a lifetime plan, a career, a family. It can also be assessed in the quality of every passing moment and in our relationships with others. As for the environment, until recently its evolution was measured in geological, biological, and climatic eras. Nowadays, these changes are happening at an ever-faster pace, spurred by ecological upheavals caused by human activities. When anxious and vulnerable citizens, economists, politicians, and environmental scientists share their hopes and opinions, it is more often than not a dialogue of the deaf. If they ever hope to sit down together around a table to figure out how to work for a better world, they will need first to leave a trail of breadcrumbs. Altruism is the only concept that allows us to naturally connect these three time scales—the short, medium, and long terms—and to bring their demands into a sustainable harmony. Selfishness won't get it done.

If the various economic and financial stakeholders had greater regard for the well-being of others, they would opt for an inclusive system that serves society. If the deciders and other social actors had greater regard for their fellow citizens' quality of life, they would strive to improve their working conditions, family life, social justice, and many other aspects of their existence. They would act with greater resolve to redress inequalities, discrimination, and poverty. They would—we all would—be persuaded to reconsider the way in which we treat animals and stop relegating them to the state of objects for consumption under our blind domination. A pig is not a pile of sausages in waiting. It is a "subject of life." With feelings, emotions, intelligence, the ability to recognize itself in the mirror—in a word, it is a consciousness. Finally, if all of us had greater regard for the generations to come, we would not blindly sacrifice the planet to our transient interests, leaving nothing but a polluted and impoverished Earth to those who will come after us.

Altruism: The Power of Compassion to Change Yourself and the World is the book that required the greatest amount of work for me, by far. It is also the book that represents the culmination of everything I have received in this life in terms of inspiration and knowledge. In addition to what I had learned from my spiritual teachers and science mentors, I devoted five years of relentless work to doing the research that would allow me to draw from the most credible sources possible—the book contains 1,600 references to the scientific and philosophical publications I consulted. I did all this documentation myself, guided by friends from all walks of life, so as to better integrate and interconnect all this information. Over the years, the pieces of the puzzle gradually fell into place. I devoted several months every year to my documentary research and to meeting with scientists, philosophers, social entrepreneurs, and other society stakeholders, then set out for my hermitage to put some order into these ideas and to understand how they all related to one another. Then I started all over again in another field of knowledge.

To define altruism and compassion, and to distinguish them from cognitive and affective empathy, I took inventory of all the many avatars of self-serving altruism that could not be characterized as genuine altruism and strove to highlight the philosophical incoherence of the theory of universal egoism. To that end, I drew in particular on the work of experimental psychology—mainly that undertaken over the past thirty years by Daniel Batson—demonstrating that genuine altruism does indeed exist.

Drawing on the work of Martin Nowak and others, I also had to showcase how cooperation has been critical to the evolutionary process of attaining ever-increasing levels of complexity culminating in social animals, the human species included, and to prove that altruism is not necessarily limited to our loved ones or even to humankind.

Neuroscience and epigenetic data show that we can act for change.[11] Such evidence abounds in the contemplative traditions that have used mind training for millennia to cultivate attention, emotional balance, altruistic love, compassion, and other qualities, and to do so in such a manner as to make these qualities the driving force of our mental states. One key point, which was a true revelation to me, was understanding how, thanks to the evolution of cultures, it is possible to progress from the transformation of the individual to that of society and institutions, and how this process has been at work throughout history.

At the same time, I also had to take stock of countervailing forces: exacerbated individualism, narcissism, violence and its causes, as well as the occasional intellectual movements that champion selfishness. To do so, I had to address the problem of the institutionalized selfishness of certain social stakeholders, such as tobacco companies, which indirectly kill six million people a year, arms dealers and those who deny global warming only to serve their own immediate interests—to cite just these few.

Ultimately, it became necessary to identify solutions allowing us to build a better world and progress toward a more altruistic society. To that end, education must be at the core of our priorities and concerns; we must work to create a sustainable harmony (leading to greater social justice in the present and to respect for the environment in the long term) and to promote an economy that cares for others and governance based on both local engagement and a sense of global responsibility.

My intentions at the outset were modest—demonstrating that true altruism exists and that it can be cultivated. But the deeper I went—as if the field I was working grew larger with every row I plowed—I came to see that most important aspects of our lives are governed by a duality of egoism and altruism. I had no intention of writing a long chapter on the problem of the environment, for instance, but it became clear, here too, that this issue was all about egoism and altruism with respect to future generations. If we don't care about what happens to them, the question of the environment becomes moot because we will not be there to witness their suffering or the sixth major extinction event since the emergence of life on Earth. As my favorite political philosopher, Groucho Marx, used to say, "Why should I care about future generations—what have they ever done for me?" The problem is that so many social stakeholders ultimately hold similar views, albeit in a dignified and serious way. I once heard American billionaire Steve Forbes, speaking about sea level rise, declare on Fox News, "To change what we do because something is going to happen in a hundred years is, I would say, profoundly weird."[12] In other words, *après moi, le deluge . . .*

I took great pleasure in plunging into the research, nailing these ideas down on the page, discovering unexpected correlations among various aspects of altruism, and meeting with the eminent brains whose work provided the foundations of my own. I was sometimes discouraged by the magnitude of the task. I couldn't see an end to it. Sometimes, when I had finished my research for one chapter, I realized that it was more than one hundred pages long! I had to whittle down this mountain of information the way a sculptor chisels away at a block of stone to reveal the contours of a statue and refine its details. This formidable task reminded me, in a funny way and in a completely different field, of the French potter Bernard Palissy, who devoted twenty years of his life to unlocking the secret of the enamel he wished to use to glaze his ceramics, going so far as to burn his furniture and floorboards to fire his kiln. Burning the plank floors of my hermitage would not have been much help to me, but I understood his unwavering resolve to see his work through to the end. Sometimes, a phrase or an idea came to me as I walked in the mountains or awoke at dawn, and I quickly scribbled it down on a scrap of paper before it faded away.

Year in, year out for five years, I worked nonstop. I wrote wherever I could—while waiting for my luggage at the airport at 6 a.m. on my return from India, in the subway, on a park bench, in the plane, in a Hong Kong taxi, in a car on a chaotic Tibetan road, but also in the serenity of my hermitage, where the text began to take shape. I also solicited the help of good friends to reread and improve my somewhat rusty French.[13]

I could see that the book was assuming colossal dimensions, at almost two million characters! I sent the manuscript to Nicole Lattès. She called me a few days later: "We've formatted your book, and guess how many pages it comes to—more than a thousand!" I felt like a kid who's spilled his soup on the tablecloth. What to do? In the bookstore, I was a little comforted to find a few books of more than a thousand pages on sometimes obscure topics. I pared down the text a little, but it still ran to nine hundred pages. A friend I slipped it to told me that she had taken it to the beach and hadn't even made it through the table of contents! But to me, this hefty work of research would at least serve as a basis for exploring certain aspects of altruism and egoism in greater depth. I felt as if I had helped to demonstrate that altruism was neither a luxury nor a utopia but a necessity, the only pragmatic, realistic response to the challenges of our times.

A few good moments reassured me about the usefulness of my work, especially one morning in Paris when a helmeted worker climbed down from a scaffolding to shake my hand and tell me, "Three cheers for altruism!" That very afternoon, a bright red Ferrari stopped, the window rolled down, and the driver called out, "Keep it up for altruism!" I was happy to see that the subject seemed to touch everyone, regardless of their social status. When the book came out in the United States, where it enjoyed critical if not popular success, I received a handwritten letter from Bill Clinton: "Thanks, I'm reading it . . . Bravo!"

My friends Jean-Pierre and Cécile Devorsine decided to make a documentary based on the ideas, research, and initiatives identified in *Altruism* in the fields of education, economics, and the environment. They hired two talented filmmakers, who set out to find researchers and social stakeholders to make an informative film that was as inspiring as it was thoroughly documented.[14] *The Altruism Revolution* was aired on the European public service channel Arte in 2010. My friends had previously produced some hundred documentaries funded by the Centre national du cinéma et de l'image, but when they applied to their regional film commission for financing, they were turned down. Reason: "This project is based on no scientific evidence." Prejudice has a thick skin.

The game is not over—far from it. The epidemic of narcissism is gaining ground, as are demagoguery, populism, and divisiveness. Fake news and conspiracy theories have always existed, but they are now growing in volume and strength. Although the French Parliament, under Louis XIV, issued a decree banning witchcraft trials in 1682, in Europe only two hundred years ago they were still burning witches accused of the most terrible things.[15] Today, however, the volatility of social (or sometimes, "antisocial") networks, the absence of critical thinking and rigor in inquiry, the lack of expertise on complex issues, and our subjugation to unhealthy imaginations are generating a tsunami of confusion.

Now more than ever, therefore, we need altruism, benevolence, generosity, valid knowledge bases, honesty, and cooperation.

A PLEA FOR THE ANIMALS

I was very pleased to have brought my work on *Altruism* to a successful conclusion, but I had promised myself that it was the last book for which I would impose such a burden of research on myself. Even so, I had a little relapse with *A Plea for the Animals: The Moral, Philosophical, and Evolutionary Imperative to Treat All Beings with Compassion.*

As it happens, when I had sent the manuscript of *Altruism* to my editor, Nicole Lattès, she had pointed out that I had devoted seven chapters to the question of animals, ranging from cooperation and the altruism they are capable of demonstrating to our merciless exploitation of other species. In the light of the page limits we had agreed to, she suggested that I retain only one or two of these chapters and that I set the others aside for a book dedicated to the subject of animals. I liked that idea very much, and the following year I took up the seven chapters in question, rubbing my palms together in anticipation, since I had the core material of my new book already there before me. That turned out to be a pipe dream. I couldn't resist the temptation to pursue my research, read any number of books on the history of our relations with other animal species, the vast trade in wild species or the rights of living things. I also delved into the scientific literature on animal intelligence. A year's worth of hard work later, I had a new, expanded, enriched, more strongly supported work on the subject in hand.

Some statistics unearthed by my research were especially eloquent. It is estimated that 110 to 120 billion members of the species *Homo sapiens* have lived on Earth since our species first appeared. Let's not forget that there were still only a few millions of us twelve thousand years ago, when the climate stabilized at the beginning of the Holocene epoch. One hundred and ten billion also happens to be the number of animals that we kill *every two months*, without giving it a second thought, unaware of the enormity of the massacre we are perpetuating and as detached as if it did not raise a massive ethical dilemma for our societies. It also turns out that the second highest source of greenhouse gas emissions, after households and even higher than transportation, is the industrial production of meat, amounting to some 14 percent. It begins with deforestation, followed by the intensive farming of soy and other grains to fatten livestock, and ends with a hunk of plastic-wrapped meat on a tray in a supermarket cooler. In between come various stages of transportation, animal waste and its emission of methane, processing lines, and so on. In a word, there are no winners in the meat trade—everyone loses.

A Plea for the Animals doesn't seek to moralize to anyone; I simply ask the reader to stop turning a blind eye to the key issue of our times. Far from guilt-tripping, I urge each and every one of us to take a sincere and honest look at the false excuses we make to ourselves for looking the other way while animals are being abused, as if these sentient beings were objects of no importance.

In this four-hundred-page work, which I tried to make as complete and well-documented as possible, I devoted a chapter to the positions held or once held by various religions with regard to animals. In that chapter, and that chapter alone, there are just a few pages on the Buddhist perspective— the only reference to that school of thought anywhere in the book, by the way. And yet, to my surprise, one half-page article in a major national daily newspaper, purporting to be a summary of the book, suggested that I had indulged in an "apologia for Buddhism" (four pages out of four hundred!). Its author, a philosopher based in Switzerland, didn't offer a single quotation—which he would have had a hard time finding in four pages out of the book's four hundred—to back up his argument. What's more, he claimed that I was among those who believed that the life of a mouse is as precious as that of a human being, an absurd idea that not even the most extreme champions of animal rights have ever held. (They do maintain, however, that a mouse is in and of itself a "subject-of-a-life" and deserving of respect on that account.) I was a little stunned but had no intention of responding. What good would bickering do? Nicole Lattès, however, decided to do something about it and called the newspaper's editor. He looked into it, and it turned out that the article's author hadn't even read the book! The editor asked well-known philosopher Luc Ferry to write a more objective article, which he did to excellent effect.

This anecdote is emblematic of a certain kind of animosity directed at me by those who find the whole animal issue deeply disturbing. True, it's no fun having our ethical inconsistencies about animals exposed to scrutiny. On one television show, for instance, I was taken to task by two Parisian philosophers. One accused me of having spent my life repressing my inner violence (Really? That was new to me.) and the other snapped at me imperiously: "Isn't it indecent to be so worried about what happens to animals when there's so much human suffering in Syria and other places?"

I was dealing with the "sophism of indecency"—the very thing that Luc Ferry had rightly pointed to in his article: "I'd like someone to explain to me how torturing animals is helpful to human beings. Is the fate of Christians in Iraq improved because thousands of dogs are dismembered every year in China, then left to linger in agony for hours on the cruel pretext that the more unbearable their pain is, the better their flesh tastes? Are we more sensitive to the misery of the Kurds because we mistreat canines here? . . . Each and every one of us can take care of our loved ones, our families, and our jobs, and also be involved in politics or community life, without massacring animals for all that."[16]

How can devoting some of our thoughts, words, and actions to reducing the boundless and unspeakable suffering that we deliberately inflict on sentient beings constitute an offense against human suffering? What about taking time to listen to music, play sports, garden, or tan on the beach? Are those who indulge in such activities, and many others, hateful people because they do not spend every minute of the day relieving famine in Yemen?

From my humble perspective, this mock inquisition is a little incongruous, given that Karuna-Shechen—the humanitarian organization I founded and to which I have donated all my income since its creation—helps hundreds of thousands of human beings every year. To someone who waxed sarcastic about the ultimate utility of her charitable work in Egypt, Sister Emmanuelle replied, "And you, sir, what do you do for humanity?" But I did not have the presence of mind to rebut the "sophists of indecency" like she did. Working to ease the immense suffering of animals in no way diminishes my resolve to mitigate human distress. We have to seek out and assuage all pointless suffering, wherever and whatever it may be. It is up to all of us to foster and keep on fostering impartial justice and compassion for all sentient beings. Goodness is a way of being, an attitude, the intention to do good by all those who come into our field of attention and alleviate their pain. We do not love humans less because we also love animals. On the contrary, we love them more because our benevolence is all the greater and thus more authentic.

I dedicated *A Plea for the Animals* to Pema Wangyal Rinpoche and Jigme Khyentse Rinpoche, tireless champions of the cause of animals who, over the years, have saved the lives of almost ten million animals raised for human consumption. I also want to mention a very dear friend, the lawyer Steven Wise, who has fought in American courts for thirty years to have great apes recognized as legal "persons" and to have the principle of habeas corpus, which forbids the unlawful detention of anyone against his will, applied to them. And of course, I cannot fail to pay tribute to Jane Goodall, who revolutionized ethology in the 1960s by confirming the ability of chimpanzees to use and make tools. Even more importantly, she has demonstrated against all odds that great apes are not statistics in a research paper, but full-fledged individuals endowed with distinct personalities and with emotions that belong to the same evolutionary continuum as human emotions.

All around the world—in Australia, France, and Belgium—I have had several opportunities to meet with Jane Goodall and talk with her.[17] I was even lucky enough to spend a long plane ride in her company. Her apparent frailty, the result of the passage of years that spares no one, contrasted with her rock-solid confidence, reflecting the fearlessness she demonstrated during her years in the Gombe forest. Jane Goodall has, without doubt, fulfilled her mother's admonition: "If you are really and truly determined to work with animals, . . . you will find a way to do it. But you have to want it desperately, work hard, take advantage of an opportunity—and never give up." This tireless resolve shines through in the pellucid clarity of her message, delivered with comity and poise but without concession to the deciders who suffer from a chronic inability to take the measures necessary to save the environment and biodiversity.

To those who would subordinate the preservation of our Mother Earth to some hypothetical mission to conquer outer space and other planets, she replies, "Yes, the best thing for planet Earth would be to send humans to other planets with one recommendation: 'For god's sake, don't come back!'" In her presence, we immediately feel "the serenity of those rare people who, with ethics and integrity, have waged battles larger than themselves on behalf of others. The humility of one who has become an icon, a little bit despite herself, is disconcerting and yet perfectly natural.

Nothing is false, neither her smile nor her gaze, which are open and kind," as one *National Geographic* journalist wrote.[18]

Jane travels three hundred days a year, setting aside two months to rest in the haven of her family home in England. She welcomes each visitor kindly, while maintaining the distance necessary to one who sees new faces every day and cannot possibly enter the personal space of each and every one. She gives her full attention to those who come to see her, but when she speaks of great apes and other species dear to her heart, you feel as if she is "among them," picturing herself over there, in their natural environment.

I once had a similar feeling when I was on a stopover in Hong Kong on my return from Tibet. Some friends invited me to the restaurant of a very chic private club and, as we were chatting, my mind was suddenly filled with visions of the schools we had just built in Tibet and the faces of our young pupils from nomadic families. I couldn't help thinking that the cost of the meal would feed the students of one school for an entire month. Then I pulled back, telling myself that these friends of mine were extremely generous, by the way, and that it was inappropriate to reproach them for their lifestyle just because the price of their car was enough to build a school for a hundred children on the high plateaus of the Land of Snows.

When I had the opportunity to talk with Jane in Brisbane, Australia, in 2011, I asked her if the continuity observed between various animal species and human beings shouldn't lead us to reevaluate our relationship to them. "Of course," she replied, "there's absolutely no question that there is a continuity of feelings and emotions, and in particular that animals feel pain. I don't know how far down the evolutionary ladder this shared feeling persists, but I'm certain that insects feel some sort of pain, since they avoid unpleasant or threatening stimuli. As for animals with more complex brains, they feel not only pain, but also fear and mental and physical distress." At her foundation, the Jane Goodall Institute, the primatologist has launched a program known as Roots and Shoots. Fifteen thousand groups of young people each carry out one project for the benefit of human beings, another for the benefit of other species, and a third for the preservation of the environment. "The only way to raise long-term awareness," she says, "is to work with the young."

Jane believes that the meat industry's practices are especially shocking because they are validated by governments and populations. "Even if they don't approve them consciously, they do so by eating meat. What I find most shocking is that people turn almost schizophrenic as soon as you describe the awful conditions in intensive livestock operations, where so many animals are not even fully stunned before being skinned alive or plunged into boiling water. When I tell all this to people, they often say, 'Oh please, don't tell me. I'm too sensitive and I love animals.' And then I ask myself, 'What's wrong with their brains?'"

I also pointed out the paradox of audiovisual media to her—without batting an eyelid, the networks air the most violent horror movies, but no one wants to broadcast or watch what is happening in our industrial feedlots and slaughterhouses. Furthermore, the slaughterhouses are guarded like military installations, and if you want to record the horrors that are perpetrated there every day, you have to film with a hidden camera, the way the French animal rights organization L214 does, with all the inherent difficulties involved. Jane shared an idea with me in that connection. "I'm thinking of the children. You could make a film showing an adorable child with a chicken, or a chicken saved from a factory farm, with its beak cut off. In the first scene, the chicken is playing in the grass with this cute kid. Then comes the question: 'What happened to its beak?' Then—flashback—we see the severed beak in the henhouse, then quickly return to the peaceful scene so as to not shock sensibilities too much. Then comes another question and another flashback: the chicken loses all her feathers because of being confined in that horrible, narrow space. I haven't found anyone to make the film yet, but I will!"

But of course, there's good news too. Activism on behalf of animals has increased steadily over the past thirty years. This is the work not of a few frenzied "animalists," but of sensible people whose empathy and compassion are focused on animals. It has become more and more difficult to claim to be unaware of the relationship between the suffering of a calf and the veal cutlet on your plate. Public opinion is increasingly turning in favor of protecting animals.

There are now as many vegetarians and vegans in France (between one and two million) as there are hunters (about 1.2 million), and the number of the latter is shrinking by the year, in France and throughout the world.

A growing number of us are no longer satisfied by an ethic that is limited to the way people behave toward one another and believe that benevolence toward all beings is no longer optional, but a core element of who we are. It is incumbent on all of us to continue to promote the advent of impartial justice and compassion toward all sentient beings. Goodness is not an obligation; it is the most noble expression of our human nature.

IN SEARCH OF WISDOM

Delphine, a dear friend whom I regularly visit in the Swiss mountains, had the idea of inviting the physician and author David Servan-Schreiber and the psychiatrist Christophe André, so that the three of us could connect in the serenity of her chalet. Sadly, David's illness and premature death upended her plan. In the meantime, however, Christophe introduced me to Alexandre Jollien, a most uncommon philosopher, both astute and exuberant, capable of the deepest insights as well as spontaneous flashes of irresistible humor, but also someone painfully marked for life, having spent seventeen years in a home for the severely disabled because of his affliction with cerebral palsy. Although he now has a wonderful family, writes magnificent books, and is widely recognized and appreciated, he continues to suffer the effects of his disability. From his home in Lausanne, he always came to spend a day at Delphine's place whenever I was there. On one such visit, we called our friend Christophe and invited him to join us in that charming place.

Following the almost simultaneous publications of our books on happiness, a strong and abiding friendship arose between Christophe, a fundamentally good man, and me.[19] When I was working on *Altruism*, and happened to be passing through Paris, Christophe and his wife Pauline invited over several philosophers whom I wanted to question about altruism.

Alexandre revived the idea of a three-way dialogue. We agreed to meet again in Switzerland in January 2005, but health issues for Delphine and my mother, now in her nineties and living in Dordogne, led us to change the venue to Périgord. We were able to spend fifteen cozy working days deep in the forest, discussing the best way to live our lives, not to dispense lessons, but to share our experience—a fruitful intersection of perspectives on the key issues that touch every human being, a fraternal threesome talking about real life.

We spent our days talking in that unassuming house overlooking the Vézère Valley, where we could watch the rising winter sun gently emerge from the fog and slowly set the landscape aglow. As Christophe explains in his preamble, "Our meals were taken care of—we were provided with succulent vegetarian cuisine—and so we had nothing to do but reflect and sit together by the fireside and have our discussions. To clear our heads, we took long walks in the natural surroundings, shared chatty meals with visiting friends, and visited the Buddhist community at the Chanteloube Study Center." Our conversations centered on themes that we had identified before meeting, and every evening we chose the subject of the next day's discussion so that we had the night to mull it over. We would start by allowing each person in turn to expand on his thinking without interruption, and then we would all offer our own points of view, one by one. Unlike many dialogues in which you can anticipate the answer as soon as the question is asked, I awaited my associates' response with blithe curiosity—they almost always surprised me with the fresh light they shed on the subject of the day. Our editors attended our debates, as did my mother and a few friends, on occasion. Catherine Meyer later did an amazing job of teasing the substance out of more than a thousand pages of transcript.

When it was time to find a title for our book of three voices, our choices were often the subject of gleeful, infectious laughter: *Three Men in a Cote*, *The Cobblers of Compassion*, *The Good, the Bad, and the Ego*, *The Lumberjacks of Altruism*, *The Plumbers of Gratitude*, *The Blabbermouths of Vézère*, *The Garbagemen of Me, Myself, and I*, and so on. There was no shortage of ideas—in quantity, at least.

In Search of Wisdom: A Monk, a Philosopher, and a Psychiatrist on What Matters Most came out in January 2016. Every morning before beginning our discussions, we had expressed the heartfelt wish that this book could be of use to those who would read it, but we had no idea that it would become the widest-read work of nonfiction of 2016 in France. That is surely due to our bonds of affection, our compatibility, and our mutual respect for one another.

BEYOND THE SELF

As Christophe André writes in his preface to the French edition of *Beyond the Self: Conversations between Buddhism and Neuroscience*, "If you've ever gone mountain climbing or hiked in the mountains, you know that getting to the top is a grueling physical endeavor. But you also know the sweet reward of making it there. No one ever regrets the effort they made: the clean air, the windswept summit and the fresh landscapes stretching out before our dazzled eyes make it all worthwhile. Likewise, some books are not easy to climb. We speak of 'demanding' books—they demand all our attention and intelligence if we are to engage, understand, and savor them."

I first met the eminent neuroscientist Wolf Singer, director of the Department of Neurophysiology at the Max Planck Institute for Brain Research (Frankfurt) in London in 2005, at an early symposium on the theme of consciousness. We met again that same year in Washington, DC, this time to discuss the neuronal bases of meditation at a conference organized by the Mind & Life Institute. Over the next eight years, we seized every opportunity to pursue these conversations, in Frankfurt—in a house where Herman Hesse once lived—twice in Nepal, in the tropical forest of Thailand at the invitation of our friend Klaus Hebben, and with the Dalai Lama in Dharamshala, India.[20] *Beyond the Self* is the fruit of colloquies nourished by our friendship and shared interests. The book is an attempt to synthesize eight years of fruitful conversation between Buddhism and neuroscience, bringing together a unique body of wisdom accumulated over thousands of years of practice and objective knowledge subject to experimental proof on subjects as diverse as the effects of mind training on the brain and the corollary idea of neuroplasticity, unconscious processes, and emotions; the way in which we acquire knowledge—how do we know what we know?; an investigation into the concept of the ego; free will and responsibility; and lastly, the nature of consciousness.

Among other areas of common ground, an unexpected convergence emerged between Buddhism and the neurosciences concerning the idea of the "self." Buddhism deconstructs the notion of a unitary and independent self at the core of our being; neuroscience confirms that there is no area of the brain that plays the central role of "command post" in the brain. The idea of such a bandleader is just a convenient fantasy to help us through our daily lives.

Throughout our friendly encounters, our conversations, and our deep friendship, we always kept our minds wide open. The dialogue between Western science and Buddhism stands apart from the often difficult debate between science and religion. It's true that Buddhism is not a religion in the sense generally understood in the West. We might define Buddhism as a path of transformation leading from confusion to wisdom, from suffering to freedom. It shares with science the resolve to investigate the mind empirically. That is what makes the dialogue between a Buddhist monk and a neuroscientist possible and profitable.

We sought to compare the Western and Eastern perspectives, in other words, the differing theories on the makeup of the self and the nature of consciousness as seen from the scientific and contemplative perspectives. Moved by curiosity and mutual friendship, we addressed certain fundamental issues concerning the nature of the human mind. Our intention was to combine our respective areas of expertise and take advantage of two complementary sources of knowledge: the first-person perspective, characterized by introspection and contemplative practice, and the third-person perspective, specific to the neurosciences. From the very start of our exchanges, we knew very well that we would not be able to come up with definitive answers to the profound questions that humanity has asked itself for thousands of years. Nevertheless, we hoped to be able to elucidate certain points of convergence and divergence between our respective areas of knowledge.

Like me, Wolf donated his royalties to Karuna-Shechen's humanitarian work, and he even paid us a visit in Nepal with his wife Francine. I later spent many years collaborating with their daughter Tania, herself a renowned neuroscientist, on research projects seeking to differentiate empathy from compassion.

À NOUS LA LIBERTÉ! ("FREEDOM FOR ALL")

"We're not here to work. We're here to enjoy ourselves, chat and take in the clean air." Now that she was in sound health again, our friend Delphine again invited Christophe André, Alexandre Jollien, and me to her chalet, nestled deep in the Alps, to celebrate our friendship together. For us, it was an opportunity to thank her for having been the muse for *In Search of Wisdom*, which had been published a year earlier. Everything had been arranged for a peaceful and relaxing week in that haven of tranquility. We had planned epic sled races, excursions to neighboring villages, tracking wild animal spoor in the snow. For now, the end of our first afternoon, we found ourselves in the pine-paneled living room whose windows overlooked the mountain peaks. In high spirits as we sat by the fire crackling in the hearth, our conversation took up as if it had never been interrupted. Serious debate kept insinuating itself into the laughter and friendly atmosphere—how to shake our dependency? How do we stay the course when disturbing emotions, sorrowful passions, or oppressive malaise seem to lead us straight into despondency? And of course, the idea took root— what a shame it would be to let all these conversations evaporate into the ether. I innocently left a tape recorder on the table, "just in case." My two partners did not protest. Slowly but surely, we were caught up in the game. The theme of freedom emerged as an invitation to deepen, to build an art of living, to make tools. I admit that we egged each other on, in giddy mutual emulation, to turn off the autopilot, slip from the straitjacket of habit, and try other paths—a broad agenda.

What is inner freedom? What are the obstacles that hinder it? Dependency, fear, discouragement and despair, selfishness, of course, and error. The ecology of freedom: What are the physical, cultural, and human environments conducive to nourishing or stifling it? How do we take the first, cautious steps toward freedom, and, finally, what harvest can we expect from inner freedom? The answers were at hand, arising from our fruitful exchanges: inner peace, serenity in the face of death, a consistent ethic, and unconditional kindness.

I felt a certain apprehension about approaching the subject of death. Christophe and Delphine had both had serious, life-threatening health scares recently, and Alexandre reminded us that one of his heroes,

Spinoza, had died at forty-three, and that he himself was closing in on that milestone—a grim omen, as he saw it. The story of the great Tibetan sage Drukpa Kunley came to mind.

While traveling in the Kingdom of Bhutan, Drukpa Kunley was asked to offer an auspicious prayer for the residents of one home. He said, "The grandparents die, the parents die, the children die." This assertion was met with a respectful if sheepish silence. After a minute or two, the master explained: "You see, if they die in that order, that means the family has been spared any tragic heartbreak." Alexandre, who is the youngest among us, was delighted by this story and, with his usual exuberance, ran around the house shouting, "Matthieu dies, Christophe dies, Alexandre dies!" As the youngest, this worked very nicely for him. The tone was set, and we engaged in edifying conversations on death. One morning at dawn, I suddenly recalled René Clair's tender film *À nous la liberté!* (which litteraly means "freedom is ours!") The title was adopted. The book seemed more accomplished to us than the last, and we felt that we had put the very best of ourselves into it.

And so it happened that, one by one, from first encounter to friendship, from research to discovery, and without ever being a real writer, I ended up creating a fair number of books, supported by my lifelong editors, Nicole Lattès and Guillaume Allary for the books, and Hervé de la Martinière for the photography. My royalties, signed over to Karuna-Shechen in full, funded the development of many projects, which gives me great joy. Writing does not come naturally to me, but I feel great satisfaction in expressing as clearly as possible the ideas that are dear to me and have thoroughly enriched me, sharing them with anyone who wants them, to make his own or not, to draw sustenance from them, to bring them to life and to share them with others in turn.

49

AN UNEXPECTED RETURN TO SCIENCE

In 2000, I take part for the first time in a dialogue organized by the Mind & Life Institute on the destructive emotions. I volunteer to participate in neuroscientific research on mind training. Thirty years after leaving the Institut Pasteur, I again coauthor scientific papers.

THE ADVENTURE BEGINS

In the year 2000, an unusual meeting took place in Dharamshala, India. A few of the world's most eminent specialists on emotions—psychology, neuroscience, and philosophy researchers, as well as Buddhist scholars— got together to talk with the Dalai Lama in the intimate setting of his residence in the Himalayan foothills. The subject of the meeting was destructive emotions. In 1991, Francisco Varela—a renowned neuroscientist who regularly came to Nepal to be with his spiritual teacher Tulku Urgyen Rinpoche, as well as Dilgo Khyentse Rinpoche—had cofounded the Mind & Life Institute with Adam Engle, an American businessman, with a view to organizing encounters between internationally acclaimed scientists and the Dalai Lama, who had been strongly interested in science from an early age.

The Dalai Lama was the inspiration for the Mind & Life Institute, a lay organization comprising representatives from various contemplative traditions, such as the Benedictine monk David Steindl-Rast, Father Thomas

Keating, and Rabbi Awraham Soetendorp, as well as representatives of Hinduism, Islam, and Indian Jainism. Over the years, the institute has organized some thirty encounters between contemplatives and prominent representatives of various fields of knowledge, ranging from quantum physics to the neurosciences, by way of psychology, education, the environmental sciences, and the solidarity economy (the movement that prioritizes the planet and its people over ever-expanding growth and profit). Several Nobel laureates took part in these meetings, including the Nobel laureate in physics Steven Chu and the Nobel laureate in economics Daniel Kahneman, as well as Eric Lander, who, working at the Massachusetts Institute of Technology (MIT), in Cambridge, was a leader of the team that first decoded the human genome.

The Mind & Life Institute's Europe board is today run by Amy Cohen Varela, Francisco Varela's widow. Other members of the board, past and present, have included such neuroscientists as Wolf and Tania Singer—respectively, director of the Department of Neurophysiology at the Max Planck Institute, in Frankfurt, and director of the Max Planck Institute for Human Cognitive and Brain Sciences, in Leipzig—and the philosopher of science Michel Bitbol.

Beyond the intimate encounters that took place over the course of five days at the Dalai Lama's residence in India, Mind & Life also organized two-and-a-half-day public meetings in other countries. The first, convened in 2003 in cooperation with the prestigious MIT, brought together more than a thousand scientists. The last, the Power and Care conference, was held in Brussels in 2016.[1] By that time, I had become a member of the board of the Mind & Life Institute USA, and later, of Mind & Life Europe.

In the year 2000, before I joined that distinguished gathering in Dharamshala, I had had no real contact with the scientific world in almost thirty years; that was when Francisco Varela invited me to participate in a five-day dialogue on the destructive emotions, alongside himself, Richard Davidson, Paul Ekman, Daniel Goleman, and a few other acclaimed researchers.[2] I was to present the Buddhist perspective. The least I can say is that I was somewhat intimidated to launch into this exercise under the watchful eyes of the Dalai Lama, whose knowledge far surpassed mine, and a host of internationally renowned scientists. I felt like a young student taking an oral exam with his most senior professor! But I did my best, and when it was over, the Dalai Lama cheerfully informed me that I had passed my *geshe* test—a title equivalent to doctor of philosophy in the academic tradition. What a relief! This was one of the most memorable conferences ever convened by Mind & Life, so much so that in 2021 we organized a three-day virtual dialogue, with most of the participants from the first event, to commemorate its twentieth anniversary and take stock of the scientific progress that had been made since then.

Now that my "diploma" had been validated, I became a regular participant in Mind & Life's encounters. One morning at the meeting on destructive emotions, the Dalai Lama asked, "All this talk is very interesting, but what concrete contribution can we make to society?" At lunch, the participants excitedly discussed his words and came up with the idea of launching a research program on the short- and long-term effects of mind training—more commonly referred to as "meditation." In the afternoon, in the Dalai Lama's presence, the project was enthusiastically endorsed, marking the birth of a new field of research, that of "contemplative neuroscience." Because of the arc of my life—from research scientist to Buddhist monk whose life had been devoted to spirituality—I happily volunteered to take part in the research.

A spontaneous volunteer, maybe, but a rash one, too! I had absolutely no idea at the time that this proposition would lead me into countless research laboratories, where I would cumulatively spend more than a hundred hours in an MRI machine, and make me the guinea pig of all kinds of experiments for several days every year. I was spared no item on the long list of experiments that can be conducted on a willing volunteer: sudden explosions to study the reflex mechanism, transcranial magnetic stimulation to study brain connectivity, 120°F water and electric shocks on the wrists to determine the mediating effects of meditation on pain, injections of radioactive material to measure the metabolism of an ageing brain—and much more! I sometimes spent ten hours in two days in an MRI machine. As accurately described by Yongey Mingyur Rinpoche, who also participated in this research, the MRI machine has four characteristics: "It is narrow, dark, cold, and noisy." Furthermore, you have to lie on your back and not move your head by so much as a millimeter for the entire procedure. Ideal conditions for meditating, or for napping if you happen to be severely jetlagged! But the truth is, I always took great pleasure in spending time with my scientist friends and carrying out these experiments with them in a spirit of affable cooperation.

The adventure began in Francisco Varela's laboratory at the Centre de recherche en épistémologie appliquée (CREA), at the Salpêtrière Hospital in Paris, following the Dharamshala meeting. At CREA, we undertook only a few preliminary investigations into the phases of synchronization between the various areas of the brain when a visual image is recognized. Francisco had discovered that an increase in gamma oscillations and synchrony between the cortical areas was produced when subjects were able to identify a human face on pictograms. By contrast, if they saw only uninterpretable pictographic outlines in the image, the gamma oscillations were weaker and far less synchronized.

These experiments, which were not publicized, demonstrated that when a meditator was in a state of "open presence," the transitions between the various states were better defined than in untrained subjects, and that the concomitant synchronization was more pronounced.

I immediately appreciated the warm atmosphere of creativity, discovery, and intellectual rigor that I found among my scientist friends, who became a sort of sangha for me—a virtuous community seeking to pool their common efforts on behalf of scientific progress and contribute to the good of society, as the Dalai Lama had hoped they would.

A VISIONARY NEUROSCIENTIST

While the physicist Trinh Xuan Thuan and I were engaged in the dialogue that led to the publication of *The Quantum and the Lotus*, I asked Francisco Varela to read a few chapters, particularly the one on the nature of consciousness. Not long afterward, I ran into Francisco in the lobby of a hotel where we were waiting for the Dalai Lama, who was just arriving for a visit to France. Francisco said to me, "The dialogues on physics and the nature of reality are very interesting on the level of ideas, but you never end up in a physics lab where you could design an experiment that might add to our understanding. From that point of view, you're wasting your time. On the other hand, if you were to go to a neuroscience lab, a collaboration with the researchers there could lead to some thrilling progress."

I was a little blindsided by his forceful opinion, but the events that followed showed just how right Francisco was. He was gifted with rare intellectual insight and a vision that transcended theoretical boundaries and status quos, complemented by the highest standards of scientific rigor. He was the founder of neurophenomenology, which is characterized by a dynamic interaction between the external observation of cerebral phenomena by experimental means—known as "third-person perspective"—and the detailed description of mental states provided by the subject of her experience, an approach that is qualified as "first-person." While a subject's capacities to observe and summarize experiences varies from person to person, these capacities can be strengthened by various methods of focusing the attention, regulating the emotions, and learning to be more finely attuned to mental events. Such practices are followed in phenomenology, psychotherapy, and the traditions of contemplative meditation. Using such methods, subjects can gain access to aspects of their experience that would otherwise have eluded them. In this way, the subject (the meditator, in the case of the research in which I participated) is actively involved in describing her experience and the interpretation of data in the light of that experience—in other words, in reaching an understanding of the specific phenomenological elements of her experience—while the neuroscientist is guided by this first-person information in analyzing and interpreting the physiological data.[3]

In addition to being deeply intelligent, Francisco was an accomplished meditator with boundless respect for his spiritual teacher, Tulku Urgyen Rinpoche, who lived in a little monastery-hermitage overlooking the Kathmandu Valley.

Francisco underwent a liver transplant. He told me that when he awoke from heavy sedation after this lengthy operation, his field of consciousness was immediately filled by the presence of Tulku Urgyen.

In 2016, I myself had to go under general anesthesia in Toulouse for a less serious operation on my knee, having suddenly found myself unable to walk. I was worried about the mind-fog generated by the anesthetic, but contrary to my expectations, when I awoke two hours later, the presence of my spiritual teachers illuminated my mental landscape. I remained for a full hour in a lighthearted and luminous state of mind, filled with undiluted devotion and confidence. I was alone in my room and began to softly sing verses invoking my teacher. I also thought of those most dear to me. I told myself that if things went so well at the moment of death, it wouldn't be such a raw deal. Was anesthesia a kind of dress rehearsal? Did this experience reveal what is present in the deepest recesses of the mind when the cogitation that obscures the field of consciousness goes silent? It is the polar opposite of rumination—perfect simplicity. I felt like a young child discovering the beauty of life with a new and transparent mind. Francisco's account of his own experience came to mind. He had probably gone through something similar.

After a first and brief visit to Francisco's laboratory in 2001, I went to Richard Davidson's lab in Madison, Wisconsin, where he worked with Antoine Lutz, one of Francisco Varela's main students. The plan was to undertake in-depth research to explore the various forms of meditation with a view to identifying those that appeared to be most suited to application in the lay context and those best adapted to a large number of meditators (and an equal number of novices as a comparison group).

A protocol was established. I would begin in a neutral state of mind and then frequently alternate between that neutral state and several specific meditative states involving different attentive, cognitive, and affective strategies. Five types of meditation were selected: concentration on a single point, compassion, awareness, visualization of mental images, and devotion to a spiritual teacher.

Concentration on a single object of attention requires the meditator to eliminate the myriad thoughts that wander through the mind and generate distraction. For this experiment, I chose a point, a rivet in the ceiling of the MRI machine that was in my direct line of sight. I settled my gaze on it and held it there to the best of my ability, "recalling" my mind to attention every time it wandered.

Meditation on love and compassion involves bringing your attention to bear on the afflictions of living beings, recognizing that they all want to be happy and avoid suffering, and then adopting a frame of mind that contains nothing but compassion and love for all beings, family members, strangers or enemies, human and nonhuman. You then commit yourself to unconditional compassion, without ulterior motivation or exclusion. You induce this universal love to the point where your entire mind is saturated in it.

Awareness, sometimes referred to as "open presence" in scientific publications, is a luminous, vast, open, and alert state of mind, free of sequential thoughts and lacking all intentional mental activity. The mind is not focused on anything in particular but remains perfectly lucid, present, and fully aware of everything in a non-grasping mode. When thoughts appear, the meditator tries neither to suppress them nor to encourage them. They arise and disappear without leaving any trace of themselves, like a bird crossing the sky.

Visualization in this context involves reconstituting the precise image of a Buddhist deity in your imagination. The meditator begins by thoroughly visualizing the details of the face, the clothing, the posture, and so on, reviewing them one by one. She then visualizes the deity as a whole and stabilizes the mental image thus created.

In the meditation on devotion, the core element is evoking the qualities of the spiritual teacher. As the recollection of the teacher becomes increasingly present, the mind is filled with profound appreciation and immense gratitude for the qualities he embodies.

These different meditations are among the spiritual exercises that a practitioner of Buddhism cultivates every day in her years on the path to enlightenment. However, although all these forms of meditation deliver interesting results, in our eyes only the first three—focused attention, love and compassion, and awareness—could be used in a secular context and thereby fulfill the mandate assigned to us by the Dalai Lama to work to ensure that our research would ultimately make a useful contribution to society in the fields of education, work, and personal life.

As part of the same process, that year I also went to the laboratories of Paul Ekman and Robert Levenson in San Francisco and Berkeley.

A few days after these first inquiries into the five principal forms of meditation, the Dalai Lama came to Madison to see the neuroscience laboratories. One morning was devoted to presenting him with the very promising results obtained by Richard Davidson and Paul Ekman. Francisco Varela, then on his deathbed, participated in our presentation from his room in Paris, where he was able to follow the proceedings in real time on a monitor. At one point, the Dalai Lama spoke directly to Francisco, looking into the camera and offering his advice and support as he approached his final days. We were all moved to tears.

I went to visit Francisco in Paris a few weeks later, shortly before his death. He told me how pleased he was to see the early results of research that he had earnestly promoted and encouraged. We spoke at length about his imminent death. Francisco was concerned about dying in a state of torpor, of losing the clarity of mind that is so crucial at that critical moment. His wife Amy, who did her best to help him remain upright as he sat in meditation at the moment of his death, told me that Francisco had succeeded in resting in a clear and luminous awareness right up to his last breath.

Illness had taken Francisco prematurely—he and I were the same age. He remains an invisible but smiling mentor, kind and demanding, to all who knew him and now participate in this fruitful collaboration between neuroscientists and meditators. The Dalai Lama himself keeps a little photo of "his friend" Francisco in his prayer book, and always speaks movingly of him.

MONKS IN THE LABS

Once the first results had been obtained in Madison, I returned to Nepal bearing photos of brain imaging that showed considerable differences between the brain of a seasoned meditator in meditation and at rest. I showed them to some monks at Shechen who had undertaken years of retreat. They were immediately intrigued and agreed to travel to Richard Davidson's laboratory so that the effects of meditation could be studied in sufficient number to confirm that the differences observed were due not to individual specificities but mostly to the mind training undertaken by the subjects. Western practitioners, laymen and laywomen of all professions who had completed lengthy contemplative retreats (three to nine years), also took part in the research.

The work revealed that when experienced practitioners began their meditation on compassion, a dramatic increase was observed in the amplitude of rapid oscillations in the 40 Hz frequency range, the gamma frequency identified by Wolf Singer thirty years ago. These oscillations play an important role in cognitive processes. Neuronal oscillation at the gamma frequency allows, inter alia, for the dynamic integration of the activity of a population of neurons that synchronizes upon the emergence of a cognitive function.

This activity, significantly more elevated than that observed in the control group of ten volunteers who had had only one week of meditation training, was, according to Richard Davidson, "of a magnitude never before described in neuroscientific literature."

These results constituted the first serious experimental study of the meditative states. Published in the prestigious *Proceedings of the National Academy of Sciences*, the article was downloaded more than 150,000 times and ranked fifth among the most-read articles on the journal's website a year later. In Richard Davidson's words, "These studies appear to demonstrate that the brain can be trained and physically modified in a way that few people would have imagined."

The contemplative who takes part in such research is not a passive subject, a mere guinea pig, but a true and full collaborator. His contribution is indispensable from the moment the experimental protocol is established. That's why Richard Davidson insisted on including me among the coauthors of the article. In actual fact, it makes little sense to study "meditation" in general. Meditation is training, and everything depends on what you're training for. Tell someone that you're "in training" and he will ask, "For what? Tennis? The flute? Chess?" The same goes for meditation. Every kind of meditation is its own specific training. Moreover, neuroscientific research has clearly shown that every kind of meditation corresponds to a specific signature in the brain by activating or deactivating a different set of cerebral areas. It has also been frequently observed that the repetition of a particular meditation ends up modifying the brain, not only at the functional level during the meditation, but also in long-term structure. The areas of the brain that are regularly triggered end up growing in volume and density.

How, for instance, do you study meditation on compassion? Do you have to wait fifteen minutes while the meditator settles into the meditative state, or are fifteen seconds enough for him to reach the optimal level of compassion commensurate with the degree of his personal spiritual development? Only the meditator himself can answer that question. Interaction between the researchers and the meditator allows them to identify the most appropriate protocol for detecting the effects of meditation on the brain. That is how we went about it from the very first experiments in which I participated in Richard Davidson's laboratory on concentration on a point, love and compassion, awareness, and the visualization of mental images. Even when I was already inside the MRI machine, under the protocol established by the researchers, I would use the microphone to suggest a few modifications to duration, and we would restart the experiment from the beginning. Such constant interaction allowed us to refine the experiment.

But there's more. Once the experiment has been concluded and its results analyzed, the meditator's point of view—known as the "first-person perspective"—is critical to suggesting an interpretation of the data that corresponds to the lived experience. I remember, for example, that when I meditated on compassion, Richard Davidson was puzzled by the fact that the premotor areas of the brain, which are linked to the preparation of movement, were activated along with the areas linked to positive affect, empathy, and the sense of belonging. I suggested an interpretation—that meditation on compassion is accompanied by a readiness to act. When the mind is permeated with unconditional compassion for all beings, we are ready to act for the good of all beings who come into our field of attention and to mitigate their suffering. This is how dialogue between scientist and meditator often facilitates innovative explanations and hypotheses.

We now know that the brain can be profoundly affected by specific training, such as learning to play music or a sport. This discovery suggests that attention, compassion, and even happiness can also be cultivated and are broadly dependent on acquired "know-how."

All competency requires prolonged training. You cannot hope to become a piano virtuoso or a tennis champion without diligent practice. A pianist performing in her first concert will usually have at least ten thousand hours of study under her belt. Some of the meditators tested in the research labs had no fewer than fifty thousand hours of practice behind them. It is entirely conceivable that you can train your mind just as you train your body; you can set aside a certain amount of time each day to cultivating compassion or any other positive quality. In Buddhism, "meditating" means "cultivating" or "growing familiar with." Meditation, in effect, consists of growing familiar with a new way of being, of perceiving the world, and of managing your thoughts and emotions in a more controlled and balanced way. The neurosciences assess these methods and investigate their impact on the brain.

Like any scientific experimentation worthy of the name, our research was undertaken in a spirit of discovery and was never aimed at "proving" the effectiveness of Buddhist meditation, or Christian prayer, in the case of other research projects. The meditator in her hermitage has no need for science to validate a contemplative life whose value she benefits from every day throughout her life. In any case, such an attitude would run counter to the rigor demanded of any valid scientific endeavor.

RECOGNITION OF FACIAL EXPRESSIONS

In 2001, I went to California at the invitation of Paul Ekman, whom I had met at the dialogue on destructive emotions, in Dharamshala. The first series of experiments led by Paul used a system to measure recognition of facial expressions betraying various basic emotions. The protocol involved watching a video on which a series of faces displaying different emotions passed by in quick succession. A neutral face appeared first, followed by one with an identifiable expression that remained on the screen for only one-thirtieth of a second. It went by so fast that you would miss it if you blinked. Every emotional expression was followed by a neutral expression. The test consisted in identifying the facial signals you had just seen for a thirtieth of a second: anger, fear, disgust, contempt, surprise, sadness, or happiness.

The ability to recognize fleeting expressions indicates a propensity for empathy. The seven micro-expressions involved in this experiment are universal, biologically determined, and expressed in the same way throughout the world. There are some cultural differences in the conscious management of emotions, but these natural expressions go by so quickly that they evade the barriers imposed by cultural taboos. Micro-expressions therefore open a unique window on a person's emotional reality.

Ekman's studies of thousands of subjects had taught him that those who obtained the best results in this test proved to be more open, more curious about everything, and more conscientious—both reliable and effective. "So it occurred to me that many years of meditating—which requires both open-mindedness and rigor—would offer a higher aptitude for passing the test," Paul explained to the Dalai Lama at the Madison meeting, also in 2001, when submitting his results.

Indeed, Alan Wallace and I—the only two experienced meditators to take part in the test—both obtained results that were measurably higher than those of the five thousand previously tested subjects. "They do better than police officers, lawyers, psychiatrists, customs agents, judges, and even secret service agents," the latter group having performed the best up till then. "It would appear that one of the benefits of their training is a greater receptivity to these subtle signals of other people's state of mind," Paul noted. I was personally surprised by the results, because when I took the tests, I hadn't felt as if I had done especially well.

THE STARTLE RESPONSE

Among the various experiments in which I took part with Paul Ekman, one conducted at Berkeley was aimed at studying the startle reflex, one of the most primitive automatic reactions in the repertory of human corporeal responses. The startle is the outcome of a cascade of very rapid muscular spasms in response to a resounding and unexpected sound or a sudden, potentially dangerous, event. In everyone, the same five facial muscles contract almost simultaneously at the perception of the stimulus, particularly around the eyes. The entire process lasts one-third of a second and invariably cycles through the same phases; that's how we're made. Like all reflexes, the startle responds to activity in the brainstem, the most primitive, reptilian part of the brain, and is not subject to voluntary control. As far as science was aware till now, no intentional act could change the mechanism that regulates it.

Paul was interested in the startle because its intensity is an indicator of the importance of the negative emotions experienced by the subject, including fear, anger, sadness, and disgust. The more a person startles, the more he is inclined to feel negative emotions; on the other hand, there is no connection between the startle and positive emotions, such as joy.

Paul took me to the psychophysiology laboratory of his colleague Robert Levenson, at Berkeley. The team in charge of the experiment recorded my body movements, pulse, sweat rate, and skin temperature. They filmed the expressions on my face in order to document its physiological reactions to an unexpected noise. Lastly, they identified the maximal threshold of human tolerance—a powerful detonation, equivalent to gunfire next to the ear.

It was explained to me that, at some undetermined moment in the coming minutes, I would hear a powerful detonation and would need to find a strategy to prevent the startle. Some people demonstrate a greater aptitude for this exercise, but no one is able to suppress the startle entirely, regardless of how hard they may try to curb their muscular spasms. Among the hundreds of subjects tested, none had managed to prevent the reflex—not even police sharpshooters, who train every day. Some subjects cry out and others are almost knocked off their chairs by the intensity of the startle. The initial reaction is usually followed by an "aah" of relief, and sometimes by laughter.

I had mentioned to Paul that, among the various types of meditation, awareness or "open presence," in which the mind is perfectly present and available, as vast as the sky, seemed to me to offer the best strategy to adopt in preparing for such an event. In a state of open presence, the mind is like a vast, clear, and luminous sky, free of mental constructions. It does not engage in the perceptions of the five senses, while remaining perfectly lucid.

I therefore chose this meditative state for conducting the experiment. During the detonations, the startle response was either absent or nearly imperceptible. While none of my facial muscles moved, my physiological parameters—pulse, sweat, blood pressure–experienced the same heightening that usually accompanies the startle. This demonstrates that the body does indeed react to the stimulus and records the effects of the detonation, but that the mind is sufficiently vast and free that something it might interpret as a potential threat has no emotional impact on it. According to Paul, with the extent of the startle being proportional to the intensity with which the subject experiences painful emotions, the result indicated a remarkable level of emotional equanimity. In fact, with a meditator in a state of open presence, no relief response is observed following the startle. That is precisely the kind of equanimity that the ancient texts describe as one of the benefits of meditative practice.

To complete the experiment, we repeated it while I was in different mental states, including intense concentration (the mind entirely focused on the imminent detonation), and a state of induced distraction (I imagined myself driving along a mountain road in Tibet). In every other instance, I startled at the moment of detonation, but it was in the state of distraction that my startle was at its most intense.

Paul explained to the Dalai Lama: "When the meditator seeks to control his startle response, he can make it almost disappear. We have never seen anyone capable of doing that. No other researcher has seen it, either. It's a spectacular success. And yet we haven't the slightest understanding of the anatomical characteristics that allow him to suppress his startle reflex." Paul pensively added this observation: "I thought this was an enormous long shot, that it was so unlikely that anyone could choose to prevent this very primitive, very fast reflex. Yet from what we know about meditative practice, it seemed worth a try."[4]

Here, too, our dialogue with the scientists proved to be very useful. My interpretation was that a distracted mind is "elsewhere," and that even when it is intensely focused on the imminent detonation, it is engaged by that focalization and not really "available." When the detonation occurs, it abruptly returns the mind to the present moment—which is a survival reflex in response to a threat. With open presence, on the other hand, the mind rests continuously in the present moment, devoid of all mental fabrications and objects of focus, and when the explosion occurs, there is no need for that mind to return to the present moment because it has never left it. The detonation is nonetheless clearly perceived. In fact, immediately after the detonation—I went through a whole series of them over the course of two days—I always felt my state of mind to be even clearer and more limpid than it had been before the detonation, like an immaculate sky, perfectly aware and empty of all discursive thoughts.

DEFUSING CONFRONTATION

We also conducted experiments on the physiology of confrontation with aggressive persons. Paul Ekman and Robert Levenson were overseeing research on conflict resolution. Paul proposed that I debate a contentious subject with two very different personalities. In this particular case, the issue at hand was understanding why a former research scientist in molecular biology had chosen, on the one hand, to become a Buddhist monk and, on the other, to subscribe to such ridiculous notions as the continuity of consciousness and reincarnation. We were covered in sensors to record our heartbeat, blood pressure, respiration, skin conductance, perspiration, and body movements. Our facial emotions were recorded on video, the data to be thoroughly analyzed to detect micro-expressions revealing psychic reactions. My first interlocutor was Professor Donald Glaser, a Nobel laureate in physics who had pivoted to neurobiological research. He was extremely affable and very open-minded. We greatly enjoyed our discussion, and when our ten minutes of conversation were over, we were both sorry not to have more time to pursue it. Our physiological parameters indicated a calm, conflict-free attitude. The researchers then brought in a second person known for his belligerent personality—he was not informed of the reason he had been asked to participate, naturally. We were expected to get into an argument. My detractor came ready to rumble and went straight to the heart of the matter. His physiological parameters immediately skyrocketed. As for me, I did my best to remain calm and to offer him reasonable answers in a friendly way. His parameters soon began to flatten out and, after ten minutes, he told the researchers, "I can't argue with this guy. His ideas all make sense, and he smiles all the time. Plus, he radiates a kind of friendly aura." It takes two to quarrel and, as the Tibetan saying goes, "You can't clap with one hand."

Paul Ekman concluded his presentation by stressing that each of the studies undertaken with the first meditator (me) had yielded results that he had never seen in his thirty-five years of research. Over the course of our different experiments, Paul and I became great friends, and I visited him often in California. He, Richard Davidson, Alan Wallace, and I wrote an article published in a science journal, comparing the Western and Buddhist perspectives on emotions and well-being.[5] I subsequently cosigned a dozen scientific publications with my research colleagues.

SLEEP AND STRESS IN MEDITATORS

When I was staying at my hermitage in Nepal, I took some notes on the sleep habits of retreatants. Richard Davidson and Antoine Lutz had asked me to collect, once a week for a month, saliva samples from meditators on three-year retreats. For the sake of comparison, I also collected samples from local Nepalese, especially the staff at the retreat center, who lived in the same tranquil place but did not practice meditation. The volunteers had to deposit their saliva samples in tubes as soon as they woke up, thirty minutes later, and on three other occasions throughout the day. I noticed that most of them naturally slept less than the norm. Some slept only from 10 p.m. to 2 a.m., without experiencing either fatigue or drowsiness during the long day that followed.

I myself had noticed that, whenever I was on a retreat of several months, my need for sleep gradually diminished, dropping to six hours of rest a night. My conjectural interpretation is that while my days are certainly filled with sustained spiritual practice, they are perfectly orderly, consistent, and free of disturbance. Nor are there any parasitic or useless thoughts or memories—all those elements born of the many, often chaotic activities, perceptions, impressions, and experiences of an ordinary, hectic day—to be voided during sleep. Meditators train their minds, but they do so methodically and consistently, day after day, without having to assimilate new events or external circumstances.

Furthermore, at a neuroscientific conference in Washington, a sleep specialist reported that a person turns from fifteen to twenty times a night during sleep. My personal impression is that my body is less restless when I am on retreat. I go to sleep on my right side and, if I happen to wake up in the night, I always check the time on the little alarm clock I keep close by, on the night table to my right. I always wake up in the same position, the alarm clock before my eyes. All these observations are worth looking further into.

A VISIT TO FRANÇOIS JACOB

In the early 2000s, I had the urge to return to the Institut Pasteur to see François Jacob and some of my old friends again. François Jacob received me warmly and repeatedly insisted that I "looked so well!" I suppose he meant that I didn't seem too unhappy with the path I had chosen. I told him about the neuroscience research I was involved with and about the Mind & Life Institute. But just as he had been back in the days when I'd known him well,

François Jacob was still a reserved individual. He seemed interested, asked me a few questions about the research I had taken part in, but his responses were far from expansive. We saw each other briefly once or twice in subsequent years, including at the BIOVISION World Life Sciences Forum in Lyon. I regularly sent him my modest writings, and he sent his condolences on the death of my father, whom he knew from the Académie française.

THE CRUCIAL DIFFERENCE BETWEEN EMPATHY AND COMPASSION

Among the various research projects on which I have collaborated, one that most opened my eyes to a new way of understanding mental states was led by Tania Singer. It established a clear distinction between empathy and altruistic love and compassion. Affective empathy allows you to enter into resonance with someone else's affective state. If the person across from you is happy, a smile will soon rise to your lips; if she is suffering, you will feel and share in her pain. Empathy is directed inward; it is the effect that other people's emotions have on you. If you are an empathetic person whose work brings you into affective resonance with the suffering of others on a daily basis, the cumulative impact of negative emotions will ultimately lead to emotional exhaustion—burnout. That is how it is, for example, for those who spend their days with the homeless, migrants, or a troubled family member. For lack of better, one remedy that is generally recommended for such empathetic distress is to keep your distance to protect yourself emotionally. But we all know that remaining distant from others is far from an ideal solution, as it can lead to indifference.

The experiments conducted by Tania Singer demonstrated that, in broad terms, while empathy can lead to burnout, altruistic love and compassion, contrarily, regenerate our capacity to care for our fellow beings with serenity, benevolence, and courage. Such emotional states do not lead to "compassion fatigue," as it is sometimes referred to in medical circles, but, more correctly, to "empathy fatigue." In the United States, one study has shown that 60 percent of health-care workers suffer or have suffered from burnout and that one-third are so severely affected that they have to leave their jobs.[6] This rate has been assessed as reaching 80 percent in the hospitals of Singapore, which are very well equipped.

I had begun working with Tania in 2007, in Maastricht, in the laboratory of Rainer Goebel, who had developed a new functional magnetic resonance imaging (fMRI) technology allowing changes in brain function to be monitored in real time, whereas data is usually analyzed once the procedure is over. Tania asked me to generate a powerful feeling of empathy by visualizing people afflicted with terrible pain. I was asked to alternate some twenty times between periods when I generated a state of affective empathy and periods of emotionally neutral rest. In previous studies, the experiment had involved asking subjects to watch a person sitting close by the scanner who was administered painful electric shocks to the hand. Tania had found that a part of the brain network associated with pain was activated even though the subjects were only watching someone in pain; they effectively experienced pain by witnessing the suffering of others.[7]

When the first series of meditations ended, Tania asked me, "What is it you're doing? This doesn't look anything like what we usually observe in people feeling empathy." I explained that I had meditated on unconditional compassion, striving to experience a powerful feeling of love not only for people in pain, but for all sentient beings.

Tania asked if I could generate nothing but empathy for the suffering of another person, a loved one for instance, without bringing altruistic love or compassion into it. It was not something I was used to doing, but I tried to concentrate intensely on the feeling of empathy. The night before, I had seen a disturbing documentary on the BBC concerning mentally handicapped children in a Romanian institution. Appallingly thin, they had been essentially left to their own devices. One had been so frail that he had broken his leg just by walking. The orderlies had merely put a splint on him and left him to waste away on his cot. When they were washed, most of the children moaned in pain. Another skeletal child, sitting naked in a corner of the room, nodded his head over and over again, his eyes blank. I also imagined a loved one injured in a car accident, lying in a pool of blood by the side of the road at night, far from any assistance. I found myself in the grip of dismay mixed with aversion before this gory scene.

I spent an hour in resonance with all this suffering before the experience became unbearable. I felt an incapacitating distress that prevented me from turning spontaneously to the children. This brief but intense experience of empathic distress, disassociated from compassion, had already led me to burnout.

Tania told me through the headphones that if I was inclined to continue the experiment, we could do an extra session in the scanner and go straight to the meditation on compassion, which had originally been scheduled for the afternoon. I greeted this proposal with relief. As soon as I redirected the focus of my meditation onto love and compassion, my mental landscape changed dramatically. The images of suffering children remained clearly in my mind, but instead of generating a feeling of distress and powerlessness, I felt a boundless love for these children, as if I had opened a dam and let loose a flood of positive emotions crashing over the children's pain. Each atom of suffering was replaced by an atom of love. My sense of impotence and grief over the feeble child who moaned at the slightest contact, or over the blood-soaked accident victim, were then replaced by the benevolent strength I projected on them; I mentally swept them up delicately in my arms, bathing them in affection. I was convinced that, if all this were real, I could have enwrapped these children in tenderness and solicitude that could only have brought them comfort.

I also saw that compassion and benevolence strengthen resolve and the desire to come to the aid of others. While affective empathy resides in the capacity to reactively experience and share the feelings of others, compassion and altruistic love are directed outward; they are active. These active states are constructive and have a dimension that is entirely warm-hearted; for that reason, they are far more powerful than empathy. It strikes me as obvious that if a person who assists the suffering is infused with benevolence, she radiates an appeasing calm. Her attentiveness will shine through, and the patient will be comforted. In essence, love and calm neither grow tired nor wear out; on the contrary, they help us to overcome and heal our emotional wounds. They can serve as antidotes to the emotional exhaustion of burnout.

The full analysis of the data confirmed that the brain networks activated by the meditation on compassion were not the same as those linked to empathy that Tania had been studying for years. In particular, the network linked to negative emotions and distress remained inactive during the meditation on compassion, while those areas of the brain associated with positive emotions and maternal love were activated.[8]

These three affective dimensions—love of the other, empathy (emotional resonance with the suffering of others or becoming cognitively aware of their situation), and compassion—are naturally connected. If affective empathy, which is the capacity to enter into resonance with someone else's feelings, occurs within the sphere of altruistic love when we are confronted with suffering, it should, in consequence, engender compassion—the desire to alleviate that pain and its causes. Thus, when altruistic love passes through the prism of empathy, it emerges as compassion. But empathy on its own, without altruism and compassion, is like an electric pump operating without grease—it inevitably burns out.

THE RESOURCE PROJECT

Following this three-dimensional study, Tania Singer and her colleagues completed a longitudinal study (which observes changes in a subject over the course of months or even years).[9] The project, named ReSource, was aimed at training a group of volunteer beginners in various forms of affective and cognitive capacities for a whole year. To start with, Tania Singer and her colleagues divided about a hundred subjects into two groups. One meditated on love and compassion, while the other worked only on empathy. At the end of a week of meditation on altruistic love and compassion, the subjects perceived the video excerpts of suffering people that were shown to them in a more positive and benevolent light. "Positive" does not mean that the observers considered suffering to be acceptable, but that they reacted to it with constructive mental states, such as courage or the desire to ease the suffering, and not with "negative" mental states, which generate distress, despondency, and avoidance.[10]

On the other hand, when the subjects devoted a week to cultivating empathy alone by entering into resonance with the suffering of others, they continued to associate empathy with negative values and demonstrated a heightened perception of their suffering, sometimes to the extent of being unable to control their emotions or their tears. This group of participants also experienced more negative feelings about regular scenes of everyday life. One participant attested that when she watched the people around her while riding the tram in the morning, she saw suffering everywhere and tears rose to her eyes.[11]

Conscious of these potentially destabilizing effects, Tania and her colleague Olga Klimecki gave the second group an additional training in altruistic love (one hour a day) after the week devoted to empathy. She noted that this addition counterbalanced the negative effects of the empathy training; the negative affects fell back to their initial level and the positive affects increased. These results, too, were associated with corresponding changes in the brain networks involved.[12] Furthermore, the researchers were also able to demonstrate that a week of compassion training increased prosocial behaviors in a virtual game designed to measure the subject's propensity to help others. By comparison, a week of memory training entailed no improvements in prosocial behaviors.[13] Following this preliminary study, Tania and her team monitored a group of 190 volunteers who undertook three months of mindfulness meditation, three months of meditation on taking other people's point of view into account (putting oneself mentally in the other's place), and three months of meditation on altruistic love, to the tune of forty minutes a day in each case. This longitudinal study, the longest of its kind to date, demonstrated that each type of meditation induced specific structural changes in different areas of the brain. Furthermore, while mindfulness meditation did heighten attention, only meditation on altruistic love induced an increase in prosocial behaviors.

MODULATING LEVELS OF CONSCIOUSNESS

I have participated in many other research programs, but I will cite just two others that offer very groundbreaking prospects. I met the Belgian neurologist Steven Laureys at a conference in Paris, and we soon became fast friends. He had done cutting-edge research in the identification of different states of coma. In some cases, the patient remains conscious and, to a certain extent, accessible to communication; for instance, if she is asked to imagine that she is playing tennis with her right hand, activity in the motor area of her brain corresponding to the use of that hand can be detected. Steven invited me to his laboratory at the Liège University Hospital Center to participate in a procedure to verify the theory that a meditator can modulate the clarity of her consciousness, the level of which is assessed by measuring the brain's reaction to transcranial magnetic stimulation (TMS)—such reactivity being thought to indicate the level of consciousness. We were joined by Marcello Massimini, another expert in consciousness and in the TMS technique we intended to use. Depending on the circumstances, the level of brain reactivity in a given subject normally varies fairly little—around 5 percent—in the waking state. That level drops significantly in states of unconsciousness: deep sleep, fainting, anesthesia, and coma. The question was, could a meditator deliberately modulate her level of consciousness? I suggested that we compare two extremes: open presence, which for a meditator represents the state of greatest possible clarity, and a kind of meditation that I invented for the occasion: "self-induced cognitive opacity"—the most stupid mental state imaginable. I was very proud of my innovation!

I allowed my mind to sink into the most amorphous, stolid state possible, with a minimum of mental activity, with no content other than lethargy itself—a state of mind almost entirely stripped of clarity. The mentality stagnates in torpor, as if it had fallen into thick mud, feeling nothing, perceiving nothing, almost at a complete standstill. This state is neither pleasant nor unpleasant, has no qualities, and corresponds to a minimal perception of the world around it. Thoughts occasionally arise like bubbles that form slowly in the mud and are immediately reabsorbed. One more step in this direction and you fall asleep.

The procedure seemed to have worked in that, between open, lucid, and luminous awareness and induced opacity, brain reactivity clearly varied at a much higher rate than normal, at around 30 percent, as the researchers informed me.

Antoine Lutz had come to join in our experiments. He had left Richard Davidson's laboratory in Madison to establish his own at the French National Institute of Health and Medical Research (Inserm), in Lyon. This series of experiments, conducted over the course of two very busy days, was typical of the challenges encountered by the practitioner when meditating in a laboratory environment. The TMS apparatus weighs heavily on the crown of the head. The stimulations send several powerful shockwaves per second through the skull; 126 electrodes from an electroencephalography machine are also connected to the TMS machine. To prevent the noise of the TMS stimulations from interfering with the measurements, "white noise" is transmitted to the meditators through headphones. The noise is a high-intensity hissing that has nothing "white" about it. While I did my best to rest in "open presence," research assistants and a team filming the experiment came and went through my field of vision. Because I was unable to hear those who wished to talk to me, at one point Antoine held up a whiteboard on which he had written, "Try not to blink."

The electrical activity generated by the muscles used in blinking does indeed disrupt the electroencephalogram recordings. Another whiteboard read, "Go into open presence."

I almost burst out laughing. This went on for more than an hour. Toward the end, Antoine wrote out another message: "Can you try to sleep?"

The researchers wanted to compare my brain reactivity levels in the sleeping and waking states.

"I can try," I replied.

With all that paraphernalia on my head, my nap promised to be not very restful. I asked that the lights be lowered and that my seat be lightly tilted. The hammering of the TSM and the hissing of the white noise went on unabated. I finally managed to snooze for a few minutes; everyone was satisfied, especially me, as it meant the experiment was over. We started all over again the next day, with the same protocol. In the meantime, I spent two hours in an MRI machine and did a PET scan to measure the brain metabolism of a meditator at rest, which appears to differ from that of untrained subjects.[14] A scientific paper was published upon conclusion of the research.[15]

I had only one more step to go in my career as guinea pig—to study brain aging in meditators before the brain in question disappears entirely.

PROJECT SILVER SANTÉ

In 2006, Gaël Chételat, of the Cyceron PET Center, and Antoine Lutz, now at Inserm, asked me to recruit people with at least three years of meditative retreat experience to undertake a pilot study to secure funding from the European Commission for a much larger program, Silver Santé ("Silver Health"), to study the effects of the meditative lifestyle and meditation on the aging process. Six experienced meditators volunteered for this inquiry, and the results were compared to those of 186 subjects who had never practiced meditation. Significant differences were observed in the volume of certain areas of the brain and in the brain's metabolism. While scientists are cautious about drawing attention to such statistics, according to the published graphs, the brains of meditators—compared to the control group of 186 subjects—present certain characteristics equivalent to those of people fifteen years younger.[16] Still, this is only a pilot study, and the data need to be confirmed by studying a larger number of meditators for an extended period.

These early results nevertheless earned the project the endorsement of the European Commission, and an eighteen-month longitudinal study was launched with 180 volunteers over sixty-five years of age. Half of them, chosen at random, practiced meditation every day, while the other half learned or improved their mastery of English in similar conditions (regular practice sessions, group meetings, coaching by motivated instructors, and so on).

My visits were the occasion of some funny incidents. In addition to the tests conducted during the daytime, the researchers also investigated the quality of the subjects' sleep. Sometime around 7 p.m., therefore, I returned to the lab to be fitted with a skullcap rigged with thirty-two electrodes, then went to Gaël's for dinner. Her children were only mildly surprised when I showed up decked out in this headgear. On the other hand, as I returned to the hotel, hoping to sneak quietly up to my room, I ran into a group of tourists in the lobby, who stared at me in shock, and in some cases with pity. They must have thought I'd come straight from the hospital.

The next afternoon, I boarded a train shortly after I had gone through the PET scan, which measures brain metabolism by monitoring radioactive isotopes injected into the bloodstream. The man in charge of radioactive security took me to the train station by car. During the drive, his jacket pocket emitted a persistent peep. I asked him what it was. "It's you," he replied.

His Geiger counter was reading my radioactivity. Charming. I asked him how long I could expect to sizzle like this.

"Oh, it will all be discharged in the urine within twenty-four hours." I prayed that the antiterrorist bomb squads that sometimes patrol train stations were not equipped with Geiger counters. Once in Paris, I took care not to say anything to alarm anyone, but I was careful not to give my friends a radioactive hug.

The findings of this longitudinal study, the largest ever undertaken on the effects of meditation on aging, are being analyzed now. In the light of the pilot study, we can reasonably expect that persons who have practiced meditation for eighteen months will show a slowing of the aging of the brain and body cells, the latter measured by the activity of the telomerase enzyme. Telomeres are sequences of DNA located at the end of a chromosome. They ensure the stability of genes during cellular division but are shortened each time the cell divides. When the length of a telomere falls below a critical threshold, the cell can no longer divide and gradually enters senescence. Telomeres are protected by the enzyme telomerase. Thus, the aging of our bodies' cells, our health, and our longevity are affected by our telomerase activity rate. Several studies have shown that telomerase activity is markedly higher after three months of retreat devoted to six hours of meditation a day.

BUDDHISM AND SCIENCE

The partnership between Buddhism and science can sometimes be surprising, but it obeys a sound logic. In point of fact, science can be defined as an empirical and rigorous investigation of reality, aimed at discovering and explaining natural phenomena and predicting their function. Its realm is not limited to external phenomena, as studied in physics and biology. The functioning of the mind, which falls within the cognitive sciences, and of the nature of lived experience, which belongs to the field of introspection, phenomenology, and understanding the nature of our own mind, is also a domain of scientific research and knowledge. Science, therefore, lends itself neither to blind faith and dogma, nor to hypotheses that cannot be empirically refuted.

A scientific hypothesis must be able not only to be verified experimentally, but also to be refuted by facts that, if produced, will prove its error. Now, if a theory is formulated in such a way that it is always verified, regardless of the observed facts, it does not advance the state of knowledge. As Karl Popper demonstrated, a theory that cannot be falsified is not science; it is ideology.

As a result, the majority of religions that are founded on unverifiable dogma, such as the creation of the universe, do not fall within the competence of science. It is that dogmatic dimension that makes most of the dialogue between science and religion so difficult and vexing.

Buddhism is a little different. Its mission from the very beginning has been to bridge the gap between appearance and reality, that is, between the way we see things and their true nature. In particular, we tend to see certain things or entities as being permanent and endowed with independent and intrinsic existence, which is a misrepresentation of reality, since they are in fact impermanent and interdependent, that is, devoid of independent existence. Such distortions of the underlying foundation of being are not purely intellectual matters, since they are heavy with consequence. They cement the duality between self and the rest of the world, generating impulses of attraction and aversion, which then generate a variety of mental toxins: hatred, obsessive desire, lack of judgment, jealousy, pride, and all their possible variants. This delusion ultimately leads to suffering.

The history of science broadly undervalues the contribution of Buddhist philosophers or ignores them altogether, as if the thinkers of ancient Greece were the first and only ones ever to consider the fundamental questions. And yet, long before the Christian era, Buddhism posited a refutation of the existence of indivisible particles far more sophisticated than the theory of "curved atoms" proposed in ancient Greece by Leucippus and Democritus.

The Buddhist philosophers reasoned along these lines. If we assume that matter is composed of indivisible particles, such particles must combine. But how would two "indivisible" particles come into contact with one another? If they have one dimension, the western side of a particle, for instance, would first touch the eastern side of another. But if these particles have western and eastern sides, they must have different parts and therefore cannot be said to be indivisible. If we then say that they have neither sides nor parts, it follows that they have no dimensions. In that case, the only way for particles to come into contact with one another is to fuse together. If two particles can fuse together, why not three? A mountain or an entire universe could fuse into a single particle. Basic reality would be unable to assemble or deploy itself. This reductio ad absurdum led the Buddhist philosophers to theorize that point-like and indivisible particles cannot give rise to the universe. If we reply that particles do not need to touch one another to form matter, that would mean that there is empty space between two particles and that, since they have no dimensionality, an infinite number of particles, and ultimately the entire universe, could fit between two particles. This refutation of the notion of an indivisible particle overturns our mental conceptualization of nonbreaking, permanent, and independent particles, with no causation other than themselves, as the building blocks of reality. This reasoning was developed in the sixth century BCE, then reviewed and discussed up to the seventh century CE in numerous philosophical treatises.

Toward the first century CE, Buddhist philosophers compiled a great many, surprisingly modern, theses on perception. Moreover, one branch of Buddhist philosophy based on an elaborate system of logic—known as *pramana* (a Sanskrit term meaning "proof" or "means of knowledge")—sought to identify a "valid knowledge" of reality. That is the very definition of science.

Because of these rigorous intellectual foundations, Buddhism was comfortable in its dialogue with science from the outset. The main point of contention between these two disciplines remains their investigation of the nature of consciousness, the most complex question of all. According to Buddhism, as well as phenomenology, consciousness is a "primary fact" that is not necessarily linked to brain function, which is obviously not the opinion of the vast majority of neuroscientists.

Nevertheless, as Richard Davidson told me, no one had ever seen scientists so gung-ho to secure a front-row seat for the annual meeting of the Society of Neuroscience, held in Washington, DC. And yet, that is exactly what happened on November 12, 2005, when the doors of the vast auditorium were flung open in anticipation of the Dalai Lama delivering the opening statement before that yearly gathering of more than thirty thousand scientists. The Dalai Lama spent thirty minutes emphasizing the pragmatic and investigational nature of Buddhism, which seeks to eliminate suffering through a better understanding of the nature of mind. He asserted that where the knowledge acquired by science contradicted some ancient Buddhist writing, the latter could be considered outdated, adding, "On the other hand, Buddhism can share with modern science the knowledge it has acquired over 2,000 years of mind-training."

The Dalai Lama affirmed that if science were able to demonstrate irrefutably that certain Buddhist propositions were false, they would have to be rejected. He therefore declared that traditional Buddhist cosmology—itself based on a Hindu cosmology prevalent more than two thousand years ago—had been rendered obsolete by current scientific knowledge. To appreciate the magnitude of such a statement, it would be as if the Pope had questioned the creation of the world in six days.

The Dalai Lama often says, "By exercising their minds, people can become more calm, serene, and altruistic. That's my primary goal. I'm not trying to promote Buddhism, but the way in which the Buddhist tradition can contribute to the good of society."

DON'T UNDERESTIMATE THE POWER TO TRANSFORM THE MIND

All this research confirms that consistent mental training can help develop and increase many human qualities. Other research also shows that you don't need to be an expert practitioner to benefit from the effects of meditation, and that twenty minutes of practice a day contributes significantly to reducing not only anxiety and stress, but also the disposition to anger (whose harmful effects on health are well established). Eight weeks of mindfulness meditation (such as mindfulness-based stress reduction, MBSR), thirty minutes a day, yield a marked strengthening of the immune system and concentration, along with reduced blood pressure in hypertensive subjects and accelerated recovery from psoriasis.[17] Hundreds of scientific papers on this subject are published every year. Thirty years of research confirm, inter alia, that six months of mindfulness-based cognitive therapy (MBCT) reduce by 30 to 40 percent the risk of relapse in patients who have experienced at least two episodes of serious depression, and continue to protect them for several years following therapeutic intervention.[18]

The most important thing in practicing meditation is not the time you devote to it but its regularity. If the brain is engaged every day, some thirty days should be enough to see significant change in neural functions. Once considered fanciful, the study of the influence of mental states on health has increasingly moved to the forefront of scientific research.[19]

The Dalai Lama often describes Buddhism as being above all a science of the mind. That should come as no surprise, since Buddhist texts particularly insist on the fact that all spiritual, mental, physical, and ethical practices seek, directly or indirectly, to transform the mind. What's more, there are entire tractates devoted to establishing a taxonomy of mental states. These works enumerate and describe fifty-eight major harmful states, break down their nuances and by-products, and cite other mental modalities that can be associated with them.

Only forty years ago, one tenet almost universally accepted in the neuroscientific community was that the brain contained all its neurons at birth and that their number was not modified by lived experience. Today, however, we know that new neurons are created right up until death, and the term "neuroplasticity" has been coined to reflect the fact that the brain is constantly changing in response to our experiences and that its structures can be profoundly modified by specific training, be it in the arts, physical performance, or personal qualities. Attention, altruism, and all the basic human qualities can be cultivated and largely draw on skills that can be acquired.

As Yongey Mingyur Rinpoche writes, "One of the main obstacles we face when we try to examine the mind is a deep-seated and often unconscious conviction that 'we're born the way we are and nothing we can do can change that.'"[20]

Underestimating the power to change our mind is a mistake heavy with consequence. Our character traits will persist so long as we do nothing to control or correct them. And it will be impossible to activate the best of ourselves so long as we allow our habitual propensities and automatic behaviors to sustain or even reinforce themselves thought after thought, day after day, year after year.

Studies maintaining that 40 to 60 percent of our character traits are determined by our genes are contested both by neuroscientists working in the field of neuroplasticity and by experts in epigenetics—a booming branch of research that studies how genetic expression is activated or inhibited. Let us recall that the genes are a kind of "blueprint" that may or may not be put into effect and that is no way definitive; even in adults, the expression of genes can be heavily influenced by our life circumstances.

We find it perfectly normal to spend years learning to walk, read, write, and complete professional training. We spend hours working out to get in shape, sometimes pedaling furiously on an exercise bike going nowhere.

To perform a task of any kind, we must muster a minimum of interest and enthusiasm and always keep its potential benefits in mind.

There is absolutely no reason why the brain should be exempt from that logic or be able to change without effort, simply because we wish it to do so. That would make no more sense than hoping to learn to play a Mozart concerto by tinkling at the piano keys once in a while. The only secret is "Practice, practice, practice."

A GOOD JOKE: "THE HAPPIEST MAN IN THE WORLD"

A good joke, sure, but one that I have been no more able to shake than Captain Haddock was able to rid himself of his pesky band-aid in *The Calculus Affair*. One night in January 2007, I received a call in Nepal from the Shechen clinic, then another from France, informing me that the BBC World Service, the British international radio service, was urgently trying to get in touch with me. I was given a number to call, and around 11 p.m. found myself talking live on *News Hour*. They asked me how I felt about being named "the happiest man in the world." An article, published the next morning on the front page of the newspaper the *Independent*, repeated this odd rubric now attached to my name. My response, essentially, was, "We can all be the happiest man or woman in the world if we look for happiness in the right place. This designation has no basis in science, and it takes only a few seconds of thought to see how impossible it is to know the degree of happiness of seven billion human beings. In any case, the brain has no lobe devoted to happiness. It's better than being called the unhappiest man in the world, and it certainly offers a good hook for reporters, but it's really just 'the biggest joke in the world.'"

What had happened? Two or three years earlier, the Australian television channel ABC had aired a documentary series on anger, fear, and happiness. They had come to film our experiments in Madison when I was at Richard Davidson's laboratory, and then in Nepal. In one of the final scenes of the documentary, I can be seen on a little path descending a mountain as a narrator says, "Here is perhaps the happiest person in the world." And that's where it ended—for a while. But then one day, a very friendly journalist who was interviewing me for the publication of *Altruism* in the United Kingdom, and who had seen the documentary, headlined his front-page article "The Happiest Man in the World?" From that moment on, events spun out of control. Far from vanishing, as I had hoped, the word was spread in dozens of newspapers from Chile to Thailand and continues to this day to pop up in the press now and then, journalists being unable to resist the temptation of using such a grabby slogan. The following month, I was interviewed by another reporter from the same newspaper, the *Independent,* and tried to set things straight, but the headline was again splashed across the page in large type: "Meet Mr. Happy."

What had led the reporters from ABC and the *Independent* to come up with such a catchphrase? When they came to Madison, Richard Davidson and Antoine Lutz had recently completed research showing that seasoned practitioners who engage in meditation on compassion generate gamma oscillations of unprecedented intensity. I was only one among some fifteen long-term meditators who had participated in this research and achieved similar results. One zone activated by the meditation on compassion is also associated with positive emotions. That's all the press needed to proclaim that they'd found the world's happiest man. I confessed my embarrassment to my scientist friends and did I all could to remedy the effects of this journalistic hyperbole. But my efforts were largely in vain. I've resigned myself to taking this rumor with a grain of salt and good humor, and to learn a little humility from it.

50

SERVING THE NEEDIEST
KARUNA-SHECHEN

In the year 2000, my royalties from *The Monk and the Philosopher* and an encounter with a philanthropist allow me to launch some forty humanitarian projects in Tibet, Nepal, and India. This activity leads us to establish the Karuna-Shechen organization.

In 2001, having launched our first humanitarian projects in eastern Tibet the year before, one of my trips brought me at twilight, after a two-day drive from Shechen, to the little village of Dzogyen Rawa, in Golok, 13,000 feet above sea level. Even in the summer, it gets cold as soon as the sun sets. The next day, we visited some nomad communities. Under a yak-hair tent, a twelve-year-old girl stirred a large wooden spoon in a cauldron set on a clay hearth. She was cooking *dri*-milk cheese over a low flame. Rays of sunlight played in the whorls of smoke rising slowly through an opening in the tent roof. Sitting in a corner, the little girl's grandmother whispered her prayers, silently sliding her *mala* beads between her fingers. At one end of the tent, Lhamo, the mother, lay on a pallet, frail, her eyes too big for her emaciated face, her gaze oddly static.

When Lhamo had fallen ill, they had taken her on horseback to a little hospital a day's ride away. She had been diagnosed with tuberculosis of the bone, but her family could not afford the medication, which was far too costly. The disease had progressed. Lhamo had been bedridden for three months. Her husband had died a year earlier. Her old mother and her daughter were responsible for all the household chores and for the herd.

Happily, through the doctor at the Dzogyen Rawa clinic, for which we had built a new wing, we were able to offer her appropriate treatment. We carefully explained to her daughter how to administer her medicine. She listened closely, and on her face there appeared a gleam of hope mingled with disbelief. Muttering her prayers while holding back her tears, the grandmother thanked us effusively.

We returned to Golok the next year and found Lhamo, who had moved on to new grazing land, as the nomads regularly do. We had heard from Yeshin, our friend and the local coordinator, that she had survived her illness, but we were not expecting to find a woman with a radiant smile, almost unrecognizable. Lhamo had gained weight; she walked with two wooden canes, beside her daughter beaming with joy and gratitude.

A life saved. One among 1.5 million patients being cared for by our organization, Karuna-Shechen. In twenty years of operation, we certainly saved many others! Twenty years of heart-warming success.

BEGINNINGS

It all began in 1997. When *The Monk and the Philosopher* came out, I suddenly found myself facing the prospect of having money that I had no use for. During the book tour, a journalist asked me if I had any regrets in life. I thought of myself as having been incredibly lucky in my life, I replied, but I would have liked the opportunity to make greater use of the compassion I had done my best to cultivate during twenty-five years of meditative practice, guided by my teachers. As it happened, that wish was going to be fulfilled. Up until then, I had had to sit by helplessly before the problems faced by those among whom I lived and worked in India, Nepal, and Tibet. I had had no financial means to do anything useful for them.

Dilgo Khyentse Rinpoche had wanted to build a clinic near Shechen Monastery, in Nepal. This ambition began to gel when Rabjam Rinpoche called me one day to say that he, like me, was powerfully inspired by the statements issued by His Holiness the Dalai Lama, calling on Buddhist communities to become more actively involved in assisting the local populations that had welcomed them when they had arrived from Tibet in a state of utter destitution. Rabjam Rinpoche also greatly admired Mother Teresa and all those who devoted their lives to others. He was very eager for us to do charitable works. Things were falling into place.

In 1999, we considered various options, first in Nepal, near Shechen, but also in Bodhgaya, India, where we were building a monastery. Rabjam Rinpoche had met with some stonecutters in a remote village and had been deeply distressed by the tenuous public health conditions there. He came up with the idea of organizing a mobile clinic consisting of a doctor, a nurse, basic medical equipment, and medicinal supplies; the clinic itself was a simple four-by-four that did regular rounds in several villages. This first initiative was followed by the decision to set up a clinic in Nepal. We went out in search of the funds necessary to build it. These were provided by, among others, the Oltramare family of Switzerland, who had ties to the Dalai Lama and Bhutan. Delphine Oltramare's grandparents, Fritz and Lisina von Schulthess, had become friendly with the royal family in the 1950s. It was they who had arranged for the Swiss farmer, Fritz Maurer, to go to Bhutan with his Helvetic cows. All these donors became good friends of ours, especially Delphine, the friend who had invited Christophe André, Alexandre Jollien, and me to her Swiss chalet for the discussions that turned into our book *À nous la liberté!* She has since served as president of Karuna-Shechen Switzerland. Japanese and American patrons also contributed to the construction of the Shechen clinic in Boudhanath, near the monastery, which opened its doors in 2000 and was enthusiastically run for many years by Dominique Marchal, a former professional pilot turned humanitarian, and then by Isabelle Pastor and Dany Laigret.

Things would soon pick up steam. In 1999, not long after the publication of *The Monk and the Philosopher*, I received an invitation from Thubten Wangchen, a Tibetan monk who runs Casa Tibet in Barcelona with great resolve and steadfast good humor. He asked me to lead a conference commemorating the fifth anniversary of the establishment of Casa Tibet. That cultural and spiritual organization enjoyed the support of a German patron, Klaus Hebben, who had also financed projects in India sponsored by the Dalai Lama, including two homes for the elderly in Ladakh and Shimla. He had read *The Monk and the Philosopher* and wanted to meet me. We met in Barcelona. As we dined and strolled together through the streets of the Catalan capital, a strong and enduring friendship arose between us. This was the start of an unusual adventure, to say the least.

Klaus asked me if there were any possibility of undertaking humanitarian projects in Tibet. "The repression is still very harsh there," I told him, "But we could try and start with a school and a small dispensary near Shechen Monastery, in Kham, which would help us oversee the projects."

Klaus agreed on the spot and sent funds to a trusted friend in Hong Kong. I returned to eastern Tibet in 2000, and with the help of two Shechen monks who would work alongside us for the next twenty years, we brought these first two projects to fruition. We were a little nervous about how the Chinese government would react, but the following year we noted with relief that the school and the clinic were functioning optimally and that the authorities approved of our initiative.

When I returned to eastern Tibet in 2001, there were about a hundred students—including a large number of girls, as we had wished—happily studying at the school (which offered the five-year elementary curriculum), and the clinic was seeing thirty patients a day. I came away reassured, bearing a report and photographs for Klaus.

"We can do more. Tell me what," Klaus said.

The following years were a little like the Old West as far as our humanitarian projects were concerned. We had not yet founded the organization and it was not easy to arrange money transfers to China. Despite it all, we managed to build dispensaries, schools, bridges, and homes for the elderly. When I visited the sites, I often discovered the need for some new project; I would then call Klaus for his thumbs-up and get it done then and there. Sometimes at six in the morning, two or three strapping Khampa lads would throw open the door to my bedroom, ask me with broad smiles if I'd slept well, sit on the floor, and beg me to come visit their village, where they had great need for a school or a clinic. I usually told them that I would need to consult my "boss" and then, with the help of my collaborators, we took down the information about the village in question and locals who could oversee the project on site. We would visit the location later and make our decision.

We were sometimes also accompanied by doctors. Jean-Noël Cheveau, notably, went to Kham four times and greatly helped improve our health services, and Christopher Hillman, a congenial physician of Native American origins, came several years in a row to spend months at a time at Shechen. In particular, he saw to the health-care needs of the schoolchildren. On one of his visits, he decided to stay the winter. I warned him that the winter conditions were merciless. One morning, Christopher spilled a glass of hot tea that he had just filled across the table. By the time the tea had stopped flowing, it had already turned to ice. Our doctor decided it was time to be off. Doctors from Switzerland, Argentina, Israel, and Korea also spent time with us, in conditions that were often demanding.

We were able to complete forty projects in our first four years of operation in Tibet, building twenty clinics and the same number of schools. On the other hand, we had not expected to have to build bridges, a task that usually falls to the government. Nevertheless, in response to the repeated and insistent requests of the villagers, who returned to appeal to us year after year, we built eighteen of them! Bridges significantly improve the daily lives of local populations. In 2005, for instance, we built an eighty-foot suspension bridge over the Yangtse (known as the Drichu in Tibet) in a region where there had been no place to cross the river for forty miles. In the summer, locals crossed its turbulent waters on fragile crafts, and lives were lost every year. One group of villagers informed us that three children had been killed the previous winter when the ice that covered the river by their village cracked under their weight. Three suspension bridges were also built over the Dzachu (Mekong), as well as more modest structures straddling perilous ravines and gorges. For instance, to reach the Tsedrön Monastery, where we had built a school and a clinic twelve miles from the main road as the crow flies, you had to take a narrow footpath that wound through steep gorges spanned by nine catwalks and little wooden bridges. Several of these were on the verge of collapse, despite the locals' ongoing efforts to reinforce them. Without these bridges, it was a day's walk along the ridgeline to reach Tsedrön, a dangerous route that was impassable to horses and yaks carrying trade goods. We built five bridges whose wooden decking was supported by solid concrete pillars, while the locals were in charge of upgrading the path. Today, it takes only four hours on horseback or motorcycle to reach Tsedrön from the main road on the banks of the Drichu River.

In Tibet, journeys are measured in hours, not miles, since it all depends on the state of the roads. These have gradually been improved over the years, but even today it's very often impossible to travel more than twenty miles an hour on bumpy trails or poorly paved roads riddled with potholes.

KARUNA GROWS

As our projects in Asia had expanded considerably by 2004, the French-woman Pascale Sevault suggested that we establish an organization to promote our activities and receive donations in a legal framework. I had considered naming the organization Compassion in Action, but someone pointed out that the phrase had a "very religious" ring to it. We called it Karuna—"compassion" in Sanskrit—which means more or less the same thing without saying so outright, and tacked on the name of our monastery, Shechen, since there were already several organizations named Karuna around the world. I was promoted to "president," even though such titles don't really feature on the list of my ambitions. The founding members also included Michael Tardieu, an alumnus of the HEC business school in Paris, who has worked in the humanitarian field his entire life, in addition to his professional activities, and continues to support us indefatigably. Pascale organized several conferences on behalf of Karuna-Shechen in the hope of persuading major companies to underwrite us. In particular, she organized one dinner at which I spoke of happiness and altruism to half a dozen senior executives. After a brief introduction, I went into detail about our humanitarian projects. Everyone seemed thrilled. A few days later, Pascale received a note informing her that, as a sign of their gratitude, this small group of businessmen were gifting me a small portable printer. I've found it to be most useful.

Thankfully, in addition to my book royalties and the income from my conferences, which have always been allocated in their entirety to Karuna-Shechen projects, philanthropists, family foundations, and countless people around the world have joined the ranks of the Karuna family. In order to receive donations that are deductible from donors' taxes, Karuna-Shechen branches have been opened in the United States, Hong Kong, Canada, and Switzerland, while Karuna-Shechen France has now become simply Karuna-Shechen, as the central hub for all our activities.[1]

In Nepal, in addition to our clinic, which has treated almost forty thousand patients a year for the past twenty years, we have undertaken multiple projects, including the construction of nine schools built entirely from bamboo and able to accommodate 1,000 to 1,500 students each, under the leadership of the ingenious, resourceful, and passionate Uttam Sanjel. The cost of schooling was highly competitive—parents paid only €1 a month per child.

Uttam was a consummate communicator. Raising his index finger to resemble the letter I (as in "me"), he would explain that this "I" was like a wall that separated people and tripped them up again and again. Then he would lower his finger to the horizontal position and say, "If we lower the 'I,' it becomes a bridge between people." He also had a very novel way of recruiting. If he needed fifty teachers for one of his schools, he would put an ad in the papers and receive up to a thousand applications. He would choose about 150 candidates, then ask three teachers to teach for one week in each of the school's fifty classrooms. At the end, he asked the children to choose the teacher they had most enjoyed studying with! This method might be hard to persuade our French Ministry of Education to adopt. But despite his genius, Uttam was a maverick in school management, and we left him free to pursue his own initiatives some ten years ago. He didn't care to bow to the management requirements of charitable projects approved by the authorities of donor countries.

Back in Nepal, Karuna-Shechen—first under the leadership of Nadine Donnet, then of the visionary Sanjeev Pradhan for seven years, followed by Shalav Rana—extended its activities to many poor districts. Two major earthquakes ravaged the country in 2015. In close cooperation with Shechen, every day for two months a team from the Shechen clinic and some thirty monks set out on two trucks to distribute food, blankets, and other necessities in the affected villages and to provide treatment to their residents. In so doing, and in cooperation with several local organizations, we assisted two hundred thousand people in 220 villages, delivering six hundred tons of rice and fifteen thousand tents, among other things. There was even an article on the front page of the *Kathmandu Post*, the largest daily newspaper in Nepal, with a photograph of some monks in a village. The headline was "They Walk the Talk." Ever since, in the twelve districts hardest hit, we have pursued a program of school reconstruction, food security (sustainable and profitable organic agriculture), training women in how to convert their villages to solar electricity, training in first aid and the prevention of human trafficking, mostly affecting girls and women, and organ trafficking. We also rehabilitate government schools neglected by the authorities, providing material assistance and motivating teachers and villagers. Navaraj Sodari, for instance, teaches at the Jamuna elementary school in Begu, in the Dolakha district. In a conversation filmed for Karuna-Shechen, he says, "When I was selected to become a teacher here that was one of the happiest days of my life. Another very happy day was when our school started to receive the support from Karuna-Shechen. All the teachers feel motivated now because of the wonderful changes the support has brought."

It is often difficult for our affluent societies to grasp the difference that even modest aid can make. The cost of converting an entire house to solar energy is approximately €400, and the day-to-day lives of its inhabitants are completely changed by it. Sadikshya is a bubbly little girl in the sixth grade of a school in the Nepalese countryside. She lives with her mother. "I don't remember my father's face," says Sadikshya, smiling for the camera at a filmed encounter with Karuna-Shechen's partners. "He left us when I was a baby, and I have grown up with my mother, and my neighbors. . . . We may not be rich, but we have enough to eat and wear, and my mother loves me very much. That is all that matters." For the previous two years, Sadikshya and her mother had been living in complete darkness every night. "After the earthquake," she continues, "We were given solar lights, and we used it for six months, before the battery died. Since then, we have been living with only a torch light. At night, I often go to my neighbor's home to do homework." Since that time, Sadikshya's house is one of a hundred in the village of Walthing, in the Kavre district, selected for solar installation. "Now, because of this solar light, I can study, and help my mother with household work."

In India, our projects have progressed significantly under the expert and creative leadership of Shamsul Akthar and continue to spread throughout the two poorest states of the country, Bihar and Jharkhand. We have built medical centers from which mobile clinics head out for distant villages and to which patients from hundreds of neighboring villages come for treatment. More than a hundred thousand patients benefited from these services in 2019. In 2020 and 2021, we came to the assistance of tens of thousands of those most at risk from the COVID-19 pandemic: the elderly, the handicapped, and the malnourished.

We have also established seventy literacy centers for women, some of them more than fifty years old. The Small Money, Big Change program sought to promote the creation of sixty thousand gardens to help families become self-sufficient, at a cost of €120 per vegetable garden. The fact is that, because of the prevalence of monoculture, peasants rarely grow the fruits and vegetables they need to sustain themselves and instead buy them at the market. We supply them with plants, a substantial cross section of food grains, and organic composting techniques to provide them with a certain degree of independence. We also dig waterways for irrigation. Moreover, we build job-training centers for women in basketry, embroidery, the manufacture of decorative candles, sanitary napkins, and so on. We support dozens of education centers for young children, the equivalent of nursery school in France. We train facilitators to teach them the meaning of cooperation through game-playing and apprenticeship. We donate toys and school furniture to these little state-run country schools. We have equipped hundreds of village homes with rainwater collection systems and planted thousands of trees.

Up until 2008, I made on-site visits to all our projects every year and launched new initiatives. Raphaële and I would take pictures, then I would do the accounts and lay out a selection of images. I would print twenty copies of the thirty-page annual report on the monastery's printer and send them to our major benefactors. When Patricia Christin, whose assistance has become invaluable to me, became president of Karuna-Shechen France, we decided to rotate the presidency every eighteen months.[2] Thanks to the efforts of Jean Timsit, Quentin Durand, and the current president of Karuna-Shechen, Erick Rinner, we recently established a system of governance based on the idea of interdependence embodied in "circles of competence" dedicated to field projects, communications, legal and financial aspects, the vision of a more altruistic society, our relationship to our benefactors, and so on. The circles allow those of us with specific competencies to make optimal use of them to the benefit of our projects, regardless of their geographical location. The system is inspired by the principles of self-management devised by Frédéric Laloux—with whom we held a very productive seminar—in his book *Reinventing Organizations*.

Karuna-Shechen now boasts a dynamic team of collaborators who have spurred its growth in a way we could never have imagined when we were first starting out. For the first time in twenty years, we have an office in Paris and have also decided to support charitable works in France and Europe, alongside the humanitarian emergency service SAMU Social and an organization that serves the homeless.

All those who participate in Karuna-Shechen projects are convinced not only of the importance of altruism, but also of the need to cultivate kindness, integrity, resilience, dedication, humility, and joie de vivre in our own lives. Indeed, it is often human weaknesses—ego conflicts, corruption, and so on—that give rise to the collapse of some charitable organizations, and not a lack of projects or resources.

I am confident that our present and future partners will perpetuate those values. I therefore wish from the bottom of my heart to thank the teams, volunteers, and generous benefactors who were members of the Karuna-Shechen family throughout our years of growth and those of today.[3] This synergy is a fine example of the idea of interdependence that is central to Buddhism: interdependence among populations in need, our dedicated staff in the field, the various chapters of Karuna-Shechen that publicize our activities and raise funds, and our loyal benefactors. All of them, each in their own way, make our work possible and sustainable.

Our approach has always been pragmatic and focused on the field and the needs identified by the beneficiaries themselves, keeping their lived experience in mind and without preconceived ideas.

We now help more than four hundred thousand people a year in the areas of health care, education, and social services. Our chief focus is on remediating extreme poverty. Cobbled together by a handful of passionate amateurs, Karuna-Shechen has become an organization capable of having a major impact on the well-being of the people of the places where we work. Because my royalties underwrite almost all our running costs, 100 percent of donations go to the implementation of our projects.

Is it really possible to make a difference in the world merely through our own individual deeds? Would it have been better for me to stick to my monk's life, my retreats in Himalayan hermitages, pursuing my spiritual path with all my heart, far from the bustling world and the dissipation of energies inevitably generated by nonstop activity? A few months ago, these questions came to me with acute poignancy far above Central Asia, on a return flight to Nepal, as I watched Yann Arthus-Bertrand's moving film *Human*.

Love and happiness are the most universally shared aspirations. And yet, inequality is rampant, and the gap continues to widen between the poorest and neediest and a handful of privileged people amassing billions at the top of the pyramid. What are our ideals of goodness and altruism against that? How can we contribute to the happiness of all amid the confusion that seems to reign over our world?

To be sure, my choices and initiatives—and, far more important, those of Karuna-Shechen—have been able to do a little good and save many lives, for which I am profoundly grateful. And it occurred to me as I watched *Human* that this, perhaps, is the heart of the matter, the spark that gets things moving.

We must never underestimate the power of ideas and of those who put them into action! By transforming our mind and the way we see the world, we can gradually begin to contribute actively to changing priorities and transforming our cultures. Many major shifts in societies seemed unlikely at first glance. Satyagraha, the principle that inspired the nonviolent resistance launched by Gandhi, means "the power of truth." That is what drives actions and moves mountains.

All change is begun by a few people aware of the need to strive for a better world. They have the inner conviction that they can make their wishes and dreams come true. They may sometimes be labeled idealists, or even agitators, and be pilloried by the advocates of the status quo, but little by little others will open their eyes and join their cause. When their numbers achieve critical mass, public opinion is swayed. As Gandhi said, "First they ignore you, then they laugh at you, then they fight you, then you win."

On my many field visits to complete projects dear to my heart, I have met countless inspiring people contributing with admirable dedication, each in their own way, to that sea change. We might call them the unsung heroes of compassion. Gurmit Singh is one such hero.

On the road from Bodhgaya to Nepal, Shamsul Akhtar, who oversees Karuna-Shechen's projects in India with gusto, introduced me to this everyday saint, whose authenticity and simplicity dazzle me whenever I think of him.

What makes Gurmit Singh who he is is perfectly simple and requires only the heartfelt impulse that is present in each of us, but which we allow to shine forth all too rarely. Gurmit, however, is graced with uncommon spontaneity and commitment. For the past twenty-five years, every night around 9 p.m. he has closed up his clothing store in Patna, Bihar state, purchased hot meals, flatbread, vegetables, eggs, yogurt, and sweets, and ridden his overloaded moped to the two main hospitals of the capital of one the poorest states in India, home to the ill, the destitute, and the marginalized. They are known as *lawaris*—the unclaimed—because they have no one to turn to for help. A rundown, filthy, and fetid room is set aside for them.

Until after midnight, Gurmit distributes food and comforts those lying on the hospital's cement floor or on rudimentary benches, the decent beds being occupied by the more affluent patients. Nurses come to see them twice a day, and they are served a meagre, barely edible meal. Rats are everywhere and sometimes bite them. But when Gurmit Singh arrives with his provisions to feed, often with his own hands, those who are unable to feed themselves, smiles return to faces ravaged by suffering.

Thus, Gurmit assists a very poor pregnant woman who had been struck by a train and had a leg amputated. She had also lost most of her memory. Gurmit has managed to locate a member of her family by posting her photo on the social networks. He also pays for medicine that the hospital does not provide for free and that the patients cannot afford to buy for themselves. He regularly gives blood and encourages his friends to do the same.

Gurmit expects nothing for his care, and yet the two hospitals, to which he goes every single day, have twice denied him access. This inconceivable wrong-headedness may perhaps be explained by a feeling of guilt on the part of those who run these institutions like businesses and fear for their reputation. They don't care to be reminded day after day that goodness must always be their first concern. Resolute, Gurmit has managed each time to persuade someone to step in and allow him to continue his work.

His greatest fear is missing one of his daily visits. "Who will take care of them if I don't come?" And in fact, he has not had a vacation or left Patna in thirteen years for fear of forsaking the unclaimed, except on one single occasion, when the Sikh expatriate community in England honored him for his commitment.

To defray their expenses, Gurmit and his five brothers, who all live in modest lodgings in the same building, put 10 percent of their income in a donation box. In their family, birthday parties and gifts have been replaced by contributions to the kitty.

It all began twenty-three years earlier, when a woman who made her living selling plastic bags door-to-door showed up at the store in tears carrying her little boy, who had been badly burned. Gurmit took them to the hospital, but the doctors were on strike. Indignant, he arranged for the child to receive first aid, then decided to return to tend to others who were neglected by the hospital and society.

What surely touches us and moves us most is the "banality of good" and the "blinding proximity to goodness" embodied by Gurmit Singh. It is a revelation of generosity in its purest form, without affectation or pretension.

We all need object lessons to inspire our lives, role models who exemplify goodness in its undiluted essence. Quality has nothing to do with quantity. We all need the Gurmit Singhs of this world to light our path and restore our trust in human nature.

I wrote a book trying to prove that genuine altruism exists. Gurmit Singh sums up the eight hundred pages of *Altruism* in a few brief words: "Happiness is helping others." Someone else once wrote, "The only ones among you who will be really happy are those who have sought and found how to serve." That was Albert Schweitzer, 1952 Nobel peace laureate, who built a hospital in the equatorial forest. We can't all be Nobel laureates, but we can all be Gurmit Singh. All we need to do is open our hearts wide.

THE BAREFOOT COLLEGE

Sanjit "Bunker" Roy is another exemplar of compassion in action. We first met in Zurich in 2010, in the presence of the Dalai Lama, at a Mind & Life Europe seminar on the theme "Altruism and Compassion in Economic Systems."[4] I felt an immediate bond with this strong and jovial man, concerned for others and astonishingly creative. In 2013, with a small group of colleagues from Karuna-Shechen, I went to Tilonia, in Rajasthan, India, to visit his Barefoot College. Bunker and his team welcomed us with open arms. Everyone there lives very modestly, in the style of Gandhi's communities, and no one is paid more than €100 a month. After lunch, everyone lines up at the cold-water faucet to wash their own dishes. On our first morning there, we planted a symbolic tree and then went to the training workshop for "illiterate grandmothers," women from around the world whom the school pledges to turn into solar engineers in six months. Bunker had observed how the men who took these courses left for the cities and never came back. They were useless to their villages. "Men are hopeless," he liked to say mischievously. It came to seem obvious to him that it was better to educate women, most especially young grandmothers from thirty-five to fifty years old, who had more free time than mothers. It seemed to him that even if they were illiterate, they could still be trained as "solar engineers" capable of building solar panels. Plus, there was little risk that they would leave their village.

How did such an inspiring man, more Indian patriarch than Rajasthani farmer, end up in Tilonia, deep in the Rajasthan desert? The scion of an upper-class Indian family, Bunker Roy was educated at one of the most exclusive boarding schools in India, in Dehradun. His mother pictured him becoming a doctor, an engineer, or maybe an official at the World Bank. In 1965, when Bunker had just turned twenty, a terrible famine broke out in Bihar state, one of the poorest in India. Inspired by Jayaprakash Narayan, a great moral leader of India and friend of Gandhi, Bunker Roy decided to go to Bihar with several of his friends. He returned a few weeks later, utterly transformed, and told his mother that he wanted to go live in a village in Rajasthan. After a moment of dismayed silence, his mother asked him,

"And what do you plan to do in this village?"

"Work as an unskilled laborer digging wells."

"My mother almost fell into a coma," Bunker recalls, laughing. The other members of his family tried to reassure her: "Don't worry, it's just a little crisis of idealism. He'll be disillusioned in a few weeks and come home." But Bunker didn't go home; he spent the next forty years moving from village to village. He spent six years digging wells in the Rajasthani countryside with a jackhammer. His mother didn't speak to him for years. When he finally settled in the remote little village of Tilonia, far from everything, the local authorities were equally baffled about what he was doing there.

"Are you running away from the police?"

"No."

"Did you fail your exams?"

"No."

"Couldn't you get a job in the civil service?"

"Nope."

Someone of his social background and education was out of place in a village like that, but he felt at home there. He knew he had to do more than just dig wells, especially since most of the wells in the local villages frequently dried up. In a deep ravine at the foot of a hill that rose from the desert floor, he discovered the ruins of what seemed to be an ancient dam. Rain is rare in Rajasthan, but when it comes it falls in violent torrents. The water rushes down the hillsides, forms short-lived rivers that flow into local waterways, and disappears within a few days without having had enough time to soak into the earth. He mobilized the villagers to rebuild the dam. The earthworks were fully restored. When the rainy season arrived, they retained a great deal of water, creating a little lake that was gradually absorbed into the subsoil, refilling hundreds of wells in the neighboring villages with drinking water. From that day forward, women no longer had to trudge miles every day to fetch often polluted water and carry it back in heavy jars on their heads or hips.

At the Barefoot College, rainwater collected on house roofs is channeled and stored in 25,000-gallon cisterns that supply the college with water throughout the year. Bunker has installed rainwater-collection systems in every village of the region. Following his lead, Karuna-Shechen has developed a widespread rainwater-collection program in Bihar and Jharkhand.

We also visited a few of the 110 night schools that Bunker has set up, which are attended with infectious enthusiasm by village children who can now learn to read and write in a playful atmosphere, sometimes until 10 p.m.! The pupils of these "shepherd schools," as Bunker calls them, have formed a "children's parliament" of forty representatives, most of them girls. It is the only one of its kind to operate all year long and to meet once a month to discuss issues affecting the lives of the youngest. They learn about their rights and do not hesitate to raise the most sensitive questions when abuses are perpetrated against any of them. The parents take this "institution" very seriously and send a delegation to attend the parliament's deliberations (silently), along with the village heads. Every two years, the children campaign for election in the villages, thereby learning the principles of democracy. The Rajasthan children's parliament has proven to be more effective than first foreseen and has succeeded in greatly improving conditions for local children. The parliament even won an award in Sweden, and its prime minister, a thirteen-year-old girl, met with the queen. The latter was impressed with the village girl's poise and serenity in the midst of an assembly of adult dignitaries, and asked her, "How is it you have such self-confidence?" To which the young peasant replied, "I am the Prime Minister, Your Majesty."

Bunker was long ignored, and then criticized by local authorities and international organizations, including the World Bank. He has reconciled with his family, of course, which is now proud of him. What had seemed to his relatives to be a senseless sacrifice was for him a success that filled him with enthusiasm and contentment. Far from discouraging him, the obstacles that he encountered on the way only stimulated his intelligence, compassion, and creativity, and the same was true for his wife, Aruna Roy, who is renowned in India for her work on behalf of the most vulnerable, especially the peasant class. Over the past forty years, Bunker has carried out a multitude of amazing projects in twenty-seven countries. Hundreds of illiterate grandmothers have installed solar electricity in almost a thousand villages in India and Africa. His work is now funded by the Indian government and other charitable organizations.

The teachers at the Barefoot College have no degrees, but share their experience based on years of practice, drawing on the age-old savoir faire of peasants and artisans.

To make their teaching entertaining to the peasants, they stage performances with large papier-mâché marionettes. With a wink to those watching them from on high, the puppets are made from recycled World Bank reports.

UNPARALLELED DETERMINATION IN THE SIMPLEST OF GUISES

Another hero of the heart I've had the good fortune to know is Fazle Abed. We met over a cup of tea in Vancouver at a peace conference organized around the Dalai Lama. He asked me what work I did, and I told him that I ran a humanitarian organization that had built around fifty schools and thirty clinics. I knew nothing about him and asked him the same question. He replied with no affectation of any kind: "I've built thirty-five thousand schools." I felt very small. I ran into him again sometime later in Delhi and asked him how he had managed to accomplish his projects on such a vast scale. He answered with a laugh. "It's easy. Just multiply what you do by a hundred!" That, in any case, is how he did it.

Born in East Pakistan, Fazle studied chartered accounting in London. Back in his country, he was hired by the Shell Oil company, where his skills helped him quickly climb the corporate ladder. In 1970, he was working at company headquarters in London when a cyclone devastated his country, claiming three hundred thousand victims. Fazle decided to quit his high-paying job and return to East Pakistan, where, with a few friends, he founded HELP, an organization to provide assistance to the devastated people of the island of Manpura, which had just lost three-quarters of its population. But he was compelled to leave the country a few months later because of the fighting that led to the rupture between West Pakistan and East Pakistan. When the war of independence ended with the birth of Bangladesh in 1971, Fazle sold his apartment in London and returned home with all he owned, resolved to devote his finances and skills to his country.

The former East Pakistan was emerging from a devastating war, and the ten million people who had sought refuge in India were now returning.

Fazle chose to begin his work in a remote rural area in the northeast and founded the Bangladesh Rural Advancement Committee (BRAC). Thanks to his organizational genius and clear-sightedness, BRAC became the largest nongovernmental organization (NGO) in the world. It has assisted seventy million women and, all told, more than 110 million people in sixty-nine thousand villages. It is no exaggeration to state that BRAC has changed the Bangladeshi landscape. There is nowhere in the countryside where the NGO's logo can't be seen on the side of a school, a training workshop for women, or a family planning center. Fazle Abed rose to the challenge. He increased his activities not by 100 percent but by 100,000 percent in a dozen countries, while maintaining all his effectiveness and all his humanity.

We met again in 2010, at the World Economic Forum in Davos, where many attendees fly to Zurich by private jet, then take a helicopter or limousine to the famous Swiss resort. When the forum ended, I was preparing to board the 5 a.m. bus for Zurich airport when I saw Fazle sitting alone all the way in the back. To me, that said a great deal about the simplicity and modesty that concealed the undaunted resolve that allowed him to do so much good.

Ever discreet, avoiding the limelight and shining the spotlight on the work of his partners, Fazle Abed was truly "larger than life." He died in 2019.

BEAUTIFUL TURQUOISE OCEAN, SYMBOL OF OUR HUMANITARIAN ACTION

In 2005, we went to a remote area of eastern Tibet to assess the progress being made on a clinic we had built a year earlier. I walked into the dark kitchen adjoining the clinic. Near the hearth stood a girl with a pure face, matted hair, eyes simultaneously laughing and serious, an honest smile, and a direct gaze with no trace of timidity. She lit up the room. I took a snapshot of her before she went back to her bowl of *tsampa*. I saw her again a few minutes later with her uncle, one of the clinic's doctors, who was taking her pulse. Again charmed by her ingenuousness, I took a picture of them together.

These images remind me of the raison d'être of our mission in the fields of education and health care, especially for women. A few years later, I thought of that little girl and asked her uncle if he could track her down for me. A meeting was set up without my being told that, to reach us, she would have to walk half a day down from the high-altitude pastureland where she was spending the summer with her nomad parents.

Eight years after our first meeting, she glowed with the same simplicity and radiance as those of the little girl I had met in 2005. Her name is Druk-kar Tsho. In Tibetan, *druk-kar* is a poetic phrase for a kind of "beautiful turquoise," and *tsho* means "ocean." Thus, her name can be translated as "Beautiful Turquoise Ocean." But it was by the name of Karuna Girl that the thirteen-year-old whom I photographed on our second meeting became the symbol of our humanitarian vision. Her portrait has featured on the front pages of our website, brochures, and posters ever since.

I showed her the photo and thanked her for having become, through her smile, the ambassador for our humanitarian projects. "This picture has been seen by tens of thousands of people around the world," I told her. She looked at me sweetly, but my words meant nothing to her. Why would thousands of people want to see her photo? Thank you, Druk-kar Tsho, for donating your gracious smile, a symbol of so many children living in poverty throughout the Himalayas!

AMATEUR DIPLOMAT

In 2008, a few months before the Olympic Games in Beijing, demonstrations erupt throughout Tibet and are ruthlessly suppressed. President Sarkozy summons me to the Élysée Palace to discuss the situation of the Tibetan people. He wants to arrange a dialogue between China and the Dalai Lama.

The Tibetans saw the 2008 Olympic Games in Beijing as their last chance to be heard by the world, which for too long had been deaf and blind to the oppression they had endured for half a century. Beginning on March 10, the anniversary of the 1959 Lhasa uprising, demonstrations broke out in Lhasa and soon spread throughout Tibet. Martial law was declared in many districts. The Chinese police and army shot at the demonstrators and killed more than two hundred. Faithful to the Dalai Lama's injunctions, the Tibetans committed no acts of violence against the occupier.

Fifty years earlier, on March 10, 1959, nearly thirty thousand Tibetans had massed around the Dalai Lama's summer residence, the Norbulingka, to prevent him from being kidnapped by the Chinese. The repression was merciless. Nearly fifteen thousand Tibetans were killed in a few days. On March 17, the Dalai Lama, accompanied by his family and an escort of resistance fighters, fled in the night. Two days later, the Norbulingka was shelled and its occupants massacred. The Chinese searched in vain among the corpses for the Dalai Lama's body. Walking and riding practically day and night, the exhausted Dalai Lama managed to reach the Indian border on March 31.

In March 2008, foreigners who were visiting Lhasa were confined to their hotels and then expelled. All of Tibet was closed to travelers. The only information available was provided by the reports of the government's Xinhua News Agency and Chinese journalists. In Nepal, however, we received text messages from Tibetans who were able to use their cell phones in between the many service interruptions. Several French radio stations reached out to ask me what was going on, and I shared these few eyewitness accounts on the condition that the source remain strictly anonymous so as to as keep my chances of returning to Tibet open. Following one of these interviews, one radio station got a call from the Chinese embassy in Paris, demanding to know who this "Shanghai-based French businessman talking about the situation in Tibet" was. Beijing's surveillance stretched far and wide.

In early April, I went to France, where Sofia Stril-Rever, a good friend of the Tibetan cause, wanted to call a press conference. Weighing the pros and cons, I decided that these events were too serious to be passed over in silence, regardless of the personal cost to me. Some fifty journalists attended, including my friend Olivier Weber from the weekly news magazine *Le Point*. I explained, to the best of my ability, what we knew about the situation in Tibet.

On April 10, I went to Tania Singer's neuroscience lab in Zurich. In the middle of a meeting with the researchers, the lab secretary entered the room, phone in hand. There was a call for me from France, from the Office of the President of the Republic. I have no idea how they tracked me down. President Sarkozy, they said, wished to see me to talk about Tibet. I was to return to Paris the next day, and a meeting was arranged for the morning of Saturday, April 12.

I walked to the Élysée and was admitted into the presidential palace. Nicolas Sarkozy met me at the top of the stairs on the second floor, and we went to a small salon where we talked for three-quarters of an hour, along with Jean-David Levitte, the diplomatic adviser to the president, and his assistant. The president was sincerely concerned about the situation in Tibet. I briefly outlined some features of that very special country, which is seven times bigger than France, the source of most of the great rivers of Asia, and very rich in minerals, and shares more than 1,200 miles of border with Myanmar, Bhutan, Nepal, and India. I then told him what we knew about developments in Tibet, highlighting the frequency with which the military had fired at unarmed civilians, including in Gêrzê, in eastern Tibet, where hundreds were killed. Tanks had taken up positions in the streets of Tibetan cities. Men in chains were paraded down the streets of Lhasa and portrayed as criminal enemies of the nation. Between five thousand and ten thousand people were sent to distant prisons, where they languished for years without trial of any kind.

I also reiterated the position of the Dalai Lama, who had insisted over and over again down the years that he was calling not for independence for Tibet, but for a mutually acceptable solution that would give Tibet some form of autonomy within China—one country, two systems—allowing it to govern its own internal, cultural, and religious affairs, as well as the teaching of the Tibetan language, while leaving external relations, defense, economy, and so on to China.

The president then asserted with conviction, "I will go to Beijing to speak with President Hu Jintao and tell him that he should meet and hold constructive talks with the Dalai Lama to resolve the issue of Tibet." The president's adviser, visibly anxious about the possible outcome of such an appeal, pointed out that both parties, France and China, would need to get something out of the meeting. Perhaps the president could begin by talking to his Chinese counterpart by phone, he suggested. "Not good enough," Nicolas Sarkozy shot back. "We need to talk face-to-face." I rather admired the president's readiness and resolve. His adviser told him that he would be meeting with a senior Chinese official the following week and that he would raise the issue with him then. That's where things remained.

On April 24, marking the first anniversary of his presidency, Nicolas Sarkozy was interviewed on television by Patrick Poivre d'Arvor and David Pujadas. The foreign policy questions began with Tibet. Patrick Poivre d'Arvor, who had gotten wind of my audience at the Élysée, asked the president if he was in direct or indirect contact with the Dalai Lama. The president said he was. "We're talking about Matthieu Ricard, aren't we?" "Yes," the president conceded. Hearing that, I kissed my visas, visits, and projects in Tibet goodbye!

Not long afterward, Sarkozy conditioned his attendance at the opening of the Beijing Olympic Games on the improvement of the situation in Tibet and the launch of talks with the Dalai Lama. This bold position, in addition to the mishap with the Olympic torch, which had been briefly doused on the streets of Paris by demonstrators for the Tibetan cause, led to a mass boycott of French products in China. Some Chinese taxis, which usually displayed the injunction "No dog" on their rooftop signs, changed it to read "No dog, no French." We were in disgrace.

A few weeks later, Bernard Kouchner, the foreign minister, whom I knew well, called to ask me to propose to the Dalai Lama the idea of an event, hosted in Brussels by all twenty-seven members of the European Union, at which they would issue a declaration calling on the Chinese to begin constructive negotiations on the fate of Tibet. The idea was quashed for fear of annoying the Chinese.

In late July, I found myself in Croatia with Rabjam Rinpoche, who was scheduled to deliver a weeklong teaching there. Having traveled a great deal in Asia and across the Atlantic in the preceding months, and by dint of being hunched over in a seat for long transcontinental flights, I developed a Baker's cyst at the back of my knee, which burst, causing acute and persistent pain and making me unable to bend my swollen leg. Fearing phlebitis, a doctor attending the teachings took me to a hospital in Zagreb. I was laid out on a table and a doctor came to examine me. He took out a yardstick and began taking measurements. "What are you measuring for?" I asked him curiously. "The size of your coffin," the doctor replied, and burst out laughing. I found the joke funny, but the friend who was with me did not, and he recommended that my leg be given a Doppler scan to see whether I was at risk of phlebitis. "Okay, I'll come back tomorrow morning," I told the doctor. "Only if you sign a waiver that I'm not responsible if you die overnight," he replied. "Fine, I'll stay," I said.

I was placed in a room with an old Croatian gentleman who insisted on chatting with me, although I took pains to make him understand through gestures that I didn't speak his language.

I had a cell phone with me, but as I spent very little time in France, I was using a reloadable payment card that only had a handful of credits left on it. Suddenly a text popped up: "The President wants to talk to you. Can he call you in ten minutes?" It occurred to me that as I was abroad with only €3 of credit, the call would be cut off within two minutes. I quickly replied that I was in hospital for observation. Would it be possible to talk tomorrow? We set a time.

I was discharged the next day. Nothing serious to worry about. I explained to Rabjam Rinpoche that we would have to take a break in the teaching (I was translating from Tibetan into English) because of the important call I was expecting. I had given the telephone number of a Croatian friend of mine so we could talk without fear of being interrupted on mine.

The telephone rang. I took my leave and slipped off to an adjacent room. Jean-David Levitte was calling to let me know that the president wanted to meet with the Dalai Lama on his trip to France, which was scheduled from August 11 to 23, a few days before the opening of the Olympic Games in Beijing. He added that he did not think that this was the best time for such a meeting, and that the Dalai Lama's advisers were of the same opinion (which turned out to be not at all the case). The president wanted to hear my thoughts on the matter.

A few minutes later, the president called me, as friendly as he had been at our first meeting, and asked me the question I had been told to expect. I told him, in essence, "Mr. President, my heart tells me that you should meet with the Dalai Lama, but if your advisers and his believe that it would be wiser to wait until the Olympic Games are over, I can hardly advise you otherwise." After a brief conversation, the president ended by telling me that he would ask his wife to go see the Dalai Lama and that he would meet with him himself at a later date. Jean-David Levitte called back very courteously to thank me.

The Dalai Lama came to France and delivered five days of teachings at Nantes, the primary reason that the Federation of Tibetan Buddhism had invited him. I served as his interpreter, as usual, now sitting on a chair instead of a cushion because I was still unable to bend my leg. He was received at town hall with great pomp by the deputy mayor of Nantes, Jean-Marc Ayrault, who had ordered the Tibetan flag to be flown next to the French. The socialist leader Ségolène Royal also came to see the Dalai Lama. Before leaving France, the Dalai Lama briefly toured a few Buddhist centers that had invited him, including the Lerab Ling Center in Lodève for the inauguration of a new temple. It was there that First Lady Carla Bruni-Sarkozy came to meet him, accompanied by Foreign Minister Bernard Kouchner, a long-standing friend of the Dalai Lama, and Secretary of Human Rights Rama Yade. Former Prime Minister Alain Juppé was also among the high-ranking guests.

On December 6, 2008, President Sarkozy at last met the Dalai Lama, in Poland, on the margins of the ceremonies commemorating the awarding of the Nobel Peace Prize to Lech Wałęsa, hero of Polish emancipation from the USSR. In retaliation, Beijing postponed an annual summit with the European Union that was to have been held in Lyon.

In late May 2009, I went to Hong Kong, where I generally went through the process of requesting a visa for China on my way to the high plateaus of Tibet. I was traveling with a doctor on his way to visit the clinics that Karuna-Shechen had helped build in Tibet. The reply came the next day. Visa denied. Reason? "No reason has been provided," we were told by the travel agency acting as our intermediary. My doctor friend got his visa and left without me to meet up with our local colleagues in Tibet.

What could I say? What could I do? I had done nothing wrong and traveled to Tibet only to serve its people.

The following night, I had a very powerful dream about Khyentse Rinpoche, in which it felt as if he were truly present. He smiled and told me that all would be well. He suggested a practice for my next retreat, focused on a particular wisdom deity. I also heard the sublime melody of a mantra being sung by a female voice. I awoke in the middle of the night, my mind filled with intense bliss. I sang the mantra for a few moments with the same melody I had heard, convinced that I would remember it in the morning. But alas, when I woke up, the mantra and the melody had both dissolved into the ether of forgetfulness.

I returned to Nepal, my mind at peace, and went on a two-month retreat at my hermitage in Namo Buddha, following the instructions that Khyentse Rinpoche had given me in the dream.

I figured that my days of traveling to Tibet were over, as I was now certainly on a list of undesirables. But the next year, to my great surprise, I was granted a visa thanks to a friend with professional connections in China. When my friend handed me my passport with the precious stamp in it, I couldn't believe my eyes and had to sit for a while on a bench in the Tuileries Garden, basking in the fresh air and morning sunshine, watching the children play and the older people stroll. Then I returned skipping and jumping to the place I was staying, overcome with joy at the idea of being able to return to the Land of Snows.

52

THE CLARION OF FAME

I deliver my message of altruism and benevolence throughout the globe, both to general audiences and to the greats of this world, including in Davos. I give more and more interviews and question the real beneficial effects of public speaking.

When *Altruism* was published, I spared no effort, pushing myself to the brink of exhaustion, to promote the ideas it set out for the common good, which I cared passionately about. For instance, I recall participating in an evening conference in Geneva, followed by an early-morning departure for Rennes, where I spent a fun afternoon as "editor-in-chief for the day" for the daily newspaper *Ouest-France*, before ending up at another conference that very same evening. On the drive from the *Ouest-France* offices to the conference venue, I almost passed out, and realized that I had bitten off more than I could chew and that it was time to take a break. I remembered what David Servan-Schreiber had told me shortly before he died of a brain tumor: "I've put everything I recommend in my books into practice, except when it comes to 'positive stress.'" He was referring not to the kind of negative stress that builds up when you are weighed down by an unchecked excess of activity, but to the fatigue that comes from doing too much of what you love.

I've often found myself in such situations, in which knowing where to draw the line can be very difficult. In the fall of 2016, I was invited to participate in a three-day seminar on environmental issues at the Garrison Institute, in the forested countryside of the Hudson Valley, an hour by train from New York City. I was coming directly from Nepal, requiring twenty-four hours of travel in three planes and a train. On my last night there before the seminar ended the next day, my telephone, which I had unwisely left turned on, woke me from a sorely needed sleep at three in the morning. A writer from a French weekly magazine was working on a piece about animals and industrial slaughterhouses and wanted to interview me. Feeling dutybound to bring these issues to public attention, I replied that I could certainly talk with her at 7:30 a.m., but that jetlag required me to get a few more hours of sleep. We scheduled the interview for early that morning, before the seminar came to a close at lunchtime. I then had to fly to San Diego, California, to take part in a three-day symposium organized by the Mind & Life Institute. More than a thousand scientists and clinicians would be there to present their work on the short- and long-term effects of mind training, also known as "meditation."

Reaching the hotel in San Diego at nine that evening, with another four hours of time difference (being still on Nepal time, it was 8 a.m. for me), all I wanted was to lay my head on one of those soft pillows on my bed and sleep the sleep of the just. Foolishly, I checked my computer just in case there was an urgent message about the symposium or another pressing matter to attend to. Bad idea—there was an email from the aforementioned journalist containing the completed interview; the magazine had to go to print in a few hours, and any corrections I wanted to make would have to be done immediately. I spent a whole hour, my head nodding with exhaustion, correcting a rehash of my statement that, as often occurs, put words into my mouth that I had never said, which can sometimes be too reductive or even partially contradict what I had been trying to convey. I returned the amended text, hoping that it would get there before the deadline, which it did, to my great relief.

Clearly, the journalist had done nothing wrong; on the contrary, she had taken the initiative of giving a soapbox to a champion of the cause of animals. Furthermore, it's a tough job to summarize someone's spoken argument, and she had had the open-mindedness and professionalism to let me vet her article, which is not always the case.

We write books to share and promote the ideas they contain. We can only be grateful when they appear to strike a chord, when so many books by excellent authors conveying important ideas do not get the readership they deserve simply because the press ignores them.

I had been a complete unknown the day before *The Monk and the Philosopher* came out; after the first few television shows, people began to come up to me on the street and invite me out for coffee. Once, a car even stopped in the street and the driver asked, "Can I drop you off somewhere?" I said that I'd already reached my destination. "Never mind. Get in and let's drive around a little and talk."

When the commotion around *The Monk and the Philosopher* eventually died down, I was tempted to cut and run from all the fanfare. Passing through Dordogne, I was able to meet Pema Wangyal Rinpoche, the eldest son of my first teacher, Kangyur Rinpoche, who had undertaken a four-year solitary retreat in a little one-room house in the woods. He nevertheless was kind enough to see me. He did not speak, having taken a vow of silence, but scribbled a few notes. I explained my new circumstances to him and asked his advice.

"Accept everything!" he wrote.

So, I played the game and agreed to everything I was offered, never suspecting where my commitment would lead. Things snowballed fast. Several books and countless travels ensued—eighty-four boarding cards in one year. Not especially eco-friendly or restful. Useful? A little, I hoped.

The ideas that I champion often attract a sympathetic response when people approach me in public places. Those who consider me a total moron are polite enough not to say so to my face.

More than once, Alexandre Jollien, Christophe André, and I have each been approached on the street by a stranger who has told us, "You have changed my life" or even "You have saved my life." It's enough to give you the chills. You feel completely confounded by the gap that has suddenly opened between the impact you may have had on someone's life and the fact that you know nothing about him. What a responsibility! What can you say? I tend to reply that I'm deeply moved by his words and that if my book has been of use to even a single person, it was worth writing. I sometimes hug him and wish him all good things in life. And then we both go on our way, mostly likely never to see each other again. This kind of occurrence is both disorienting and encouraging.

It's obvious that this kind of visibility is largely due to the media hype surrounding the release of my books. Talk show hosts have sometimes asked me what a monk is doing on a television set. I've told them that I was there because they'd been kind enough to invite me and that I enjoyed sharing ideas that are important to me. And when I've been given the time, I've taken care to point out that I had nothing to win and nothing to lose by coming on television, and that if I hadn't been asked, I would have been perfectly happy back in my hermitage overlooking the Himalayas.

One January morning in 2006, I left my hermitage in an old Jeep for the Kathmandu airport, two and half hours away. I was headed for the World Economic Forum in Davos, Switzerland, for the first time. What did I think I was going to do there? The transition could not have been more abrupt.

The year before, a forum organizer had reached out to invite me. I thanked her but replied that it was hard to see what kind of a role I could play at such a happening. She didn't give up, but contacted me the next year, stressing that in addition to the sharing of ideas, the forum was an excellent place to raise funds for humanitarian projects.

At my earliest events, French journalists asked me what I was doing there. Good question. I generally replied that I could have been outside with the anti-globalization demonstrators who, the first time I was in Davos, protested naked with the kind of colorful, gas-filled balloon that kids hold with a string as props, but since I had been given the floor and was free to express my opinions, there may be some use in my having a voice in the debates. A voice that some people seemed to find disturbing, since at other conferences sponsored by major international organizations, I have been warned before going on stage with the injunction, "Don't say a word about Tibet," even when my proposed statement was on a completely different subject.

I was invited to speak at the forum ten years in a row. It was there, in fact, that I met certain people who would go on to become loyal friends and benefactors of our humanitarian projects. Which only goes to show that it's sometimes good to leave your "comfort zone." When I plunged into the hustle and bustle of its venues, with more than two thousand attendees coming or going among the multiple conferences and presentations taking place simultaneously in the various conference halls, it made my head spin. Every year, you can freely rub shoulders with thirty or forty heads of state at Davos, and if you have any interest in world affairs, it's fascinating to see up close how these people operate and, every so often, to participate in a roundtable with them. More than anything, you come across hundreds of high-level scientists, activists of all kinds (Jody Williams, for instance, or Jane Goodall), "young social entrepreneurs," inventors, and so forth. I have met some eminent scientists, some of whom have become friends, such as Johan Rockström, one of the world's great experts in environmental science. All were critically helpful to me when I was writing *Altruism*.

At the Davos Forum, other than events on economics and finances for which I hadn't the least competence, I took part in panel discussions on the emotions, the nature of mind (with Steven Pinker and the philosopher Daniel Dennett, among others), and animal testing (with Francis Collins, director of the United States National Institutes of Health). Issues of all sorts were addressed. To give just a few examples, there were discussions on the novel topic "From Gross National Product to Gross National Happiness" with Daniel Kahneman, Nobel laureate in economics, and on global mental health with the editor-in-chief of the science journal *Nature*. At events with titles such as "Ancient Wisdom on Modern Questions," I had the opportunity to talk with Ecumenical Patriarch Bartholomew I of Constantinople, Rabbi David Rosen, the Archbishop of Dublin, and the Grand Mufti of Bosnia. Some of the regular sessions we held with these religious leaders allowed me to spend time with Desmond Tutu, whom I was thrilled to get to know.

At one of these meetings of religious leaders at the 2012 Forum, Tutu declared, "I know of no religion that claims it is permissible to kill." I took the liberty of suggesting to the assembled dignitaries that we issue an unequivocal joint statement on this opinion, targeting the faithful of all religions. I added that, coming from a simple Buddhist monk, such an idea would carry little weight, but coming from Archbishop Tutu, Nobel peace laureate, and supported by the representatives of all major religious, there was some chance it would be heard. The other religious dignitaries sidestepped the issue under the pretext that there were "various points of view on the subject." I also enjoyed meeting with Sheikh Abdallah bin Bayyah, who was born in Mauritania and is highly respected for his wisdom; he has openly denounced terrorism and said that we must go to war against war itself.

For almost thirty years now, requests have continued to pour in from all over, and one of the good and beautiful events that I have been fortunate to participate in has been the Journées Émergences. These "days of emergence" have been held in Brussels every year since 2009, and I have attended every year for the past twelve, often alongside my dear buddies Christophe André and Alexandre Jollien. Organized by Ilios Kotsou, Caroline Lesire, and an enthusiastic team of volunteers, the event brings together thinkers, scientists, men and women of commitment, eyewitnesses to history—such as the son of a couple murdered in a concentration camp and the son of a Nazi officer, who became dear friends—and artists, around such timely topics as "change yourself, change the world," "happiness and adversity," "in the heart of fear," "transmission," "evoking death to illuminate life," and so on. The ethologist Frans de Waal; the neuroscientists Tania Singer and Steven Laureys; the founder of the Mindfulness-Based Stress Reduction course, Jon Kabat-Zinn; the educator Céline Alvarez; the blind explorer Jean-Pierre Brouillaud; the champion of "happy sobriety," Pierre Rabhi; and the spokesperson and director of the animal rights organization L214, Brigitte Gothière, who campaigns for an end to the useless suffering inflicted on billions of animals every year through industrial farming; among others, come together during these rich and compelling days of exchange and dialogue. Alongside the veteran pacifist Satish Kumar—who, in the 1960s, spent two years walking from India to Europe, through Russia, with no money, only to be arrested in front of the Élysée Palace by order of General De Gaulle—we too led a silent march for peace and climate justice through the streets of Brussels, accompanied by thousands.

The atmosphere at the Journées Émergences, generally attended by more than two thousand people, is one of great warmth, and attendees often come from far away. Profits are donated to charitable organizations, and all speakers volunteer their services.

The presentations are interspersed with musical interludes. That is how I had the great joy of meeting the wonderful pianist Maria João Pires. A friendship sprang up between us that has only grown deeper every time we meet, and I even had the opportunity to visit Maria in Belgaïs, Portugal, at the serene arts center where she hosts young musicians who wish to learn from and be inspired by her profound and fascinating method of teaching. Maria João played several times between speeches, choosing a different work suited to each theme. As we relived these moments, we came up with the idea of holding a concert dedicated to our respective charitable organizations—a marriage of music and meditation.

The first two took place at a meeting organized by the Mind & Life Institute between the Dalai Lama, scientists, and philosophers on the topic "Power and Altruism." It was held at the Center for Fine Arts in Brussels. For the topic "The Art of the Fugue and the Art of Meditation," we alternated Bach preludes and fugues with guided and progressive meditations, going from attentive presence to unconditional love. To preserve the quality of the silence within which both music and meditation are born, I asked the audience to applaud as much as they wished between pieces, but to do so with only one hand. They were free to use both at the end of the meditative concert.

Later, Maria João included Schubert impromptus in her musical interludes, and we gave six more concerts. One of the most memorable was the one held in Arles, where, two nights in succession at sunset, Maria played in the open air in the ancient Roman theater in front of a thousand listeners, accompanied by birdsong that gradually dimmed as night fell.

I am a monk; I have been, remain, and will remain a monk and need nothing more than the many blessings that this life has brought me. If my activities have somehow benefited anyone, they are in and of themselves the greatest of rewards I could have hoped for. Everyone should see that contributing to the happiness of others is the greatest of all achievements.

On this topic of great importance, to say the least, the notion of a nation's "happiness" was taken up at the United Nations, where a debate led to the adoption of a resolution submitted by Bhutan based on the concept of Gross National Happiness. It called on governments to take the idea of their citizens' happiness seriously into account in their decisions. The government of Bhutan asked me to invite representatives of the major religions; we were joined by Brother Thierry-Marie Courau on behalf of Christianity, Rabbi Awraham Soetendorp for Judaism, Faouzi Skali for Islam, Bhikkhu Anil Sakya for Theravada Buddhism,[1] and Swami Armapriyananda for Hinduism. Secretary-General Ban Ki-moon opened the meeting. I participated, inter alia, at the first roundtable, chaired by Helen Clark, the prime minister of New Zealand. My task was to explain "the inner conditions of genuine happiness" in four minutes. Sometime later, Helen Clark, whom I ran into again at the Davos Forum, reminded me of something I'd said: "If a country is the richest and most powerful on Earth, but everyone there is unhappy, what's the point?"

If the list of speakers in the debate is anything to go by, the topic was taken very seriously; these included the prime minister of Bhutan, Jigme Thinley, an eloquent champion of the concept of Gross National Happiness in Bhutan; several Nobel laureates in economics, including Joseph Stiglitz and Daniel Kahneman; as well as Lord Richard Layard and John Helliwell (authors of the annual *World Happiness Report*). The resolution, adopted by a large majority, is part of the framework of the seventeen Sustainable Development Goals that define United Nations projects in the current decade.

Once, at the close of a conference on the island of Réunion, I found myself surrounded by a group of very genial people wishing to ask me questions or have me sign books. I felt a little overwhelmed. A man who had been watching this scene unfold said to me, "You look as if you no longer belong to yourself." When there's a real need to be of service to others, like a medic on a battlefield or a rescue worker at a natural disaster, it can be a good thing not to belong to yourself. Even so, at that moment I could rightly ask myself whether I was truly being useful or whether I hadn't merely fallen into a futile and endless cycle in which not a minute of my life belonged to me.

This question has dogged me throughout these past twenty years since the release of *The Monk and the Philosopher*. Another time, when I was really beginning to question the point of making a spectacle of myself all over the world, I came across a two-part article written by my father titled "The Ordeal of Renown I and II," published in the review *Commentaire*. Reading it came as a great relief to me, punctuated with laughter; my father had a wit and a way with words that I, alas, did not inherit. I wished he were still alive so I could tell him how much I saw myself, howsoever modestly, in his words:

"Oh, not long, two pages, maybe three," but of course it's "urgent," due two days from now at the latest. How can you turn it down, so long as the cause is a noble one, the topic connected to something you're involved in, even a controversy that you've just begun to address? I've never been afraid of work. But it's precisely because I have a lot of it that it absolutely must be well organized.

Either the journalist hasn't read the book that he has asked to meet with the author to discuss, or he's only had the time, he claims, to "skim" it. That means he's thrown a hasty glance at the flap copy on the dust jacket. . . . In short, what the visitor calls "interviewing" the author is to get him to summarize his work with a few basic platitudes for the readers of his publication.

He's asked to give a second-rate parroting of something he went to great pains to write with precision and nuance, and to boil it down to a few summary and simplistic soundbites.

I've also met any number of excellent journalists who have engaged with the issues very fruitfully and had a gift for bringing out the best in their subject.

But fame, even when it's very relative, as in my case, also attracts criticism. Some is constructive; it can help you move ahead when it's well-founded and welcome. Some critiques are based on a lack of information or perhaps on a certain animosity toward your ideas or what you may represent in the eyes of those who disagree with you.

I've mentioned the case of a philosopher who wrote a critique of *A Plea for the Animals* in a major newspaper, putting words in my mouth that I had never said. I've been in many other situations of this kind. I've been called a "new age Buddhist" (my Buddhist friends consider me to be rather traditional); I've been accused of surreptitiously trying to propagate Buddhism in the West, although I've never had the least inclination to proselytize. For that matter, I have always thought that the Dalai Lama's advice to a small group of teachers of Tibetan Buddhism in France to be very wise (although I myself am not a teacher): "Don't try to disseminate Buddhism; just encourage people to be good human beings."

According to some people, I am also a champion of mindfulness meditation. I have great respect for the good done by Jon Kabat-Zinn and mindfulness teachers in developing the Mindfulness-Based Stress Reduction program. But I've written almost nothing about mindfulness as a secular technique. All I have done is to suggest, always with diffidence, that training in altruistic love and compassion should be clearly embedded in any meditation in order to avoid any potential egocentric and deviant manipulation of meditation that is extraneous to its primary purpose.

According to various journalists, I have also promoted the quest for pleasure—hedonistic happiness—and the gratification of the senses, thereby reinforcing selfishness in my readers. In a word, the exact opposite of what I've always written and defended. In *Happiness*, I devoted an entire chapter to the distinction between pleasure and happiness. I demonstrated that true happiness cannot be equated with an uninterrupted sequence of pleasant sensations, which is more like a highway to exhaustion. The chapter explains that happiness is a way of being that arises from the flowering of a range of human qualities, including altruism, inner freedom, and the development of inner resources allowing us to navigate life's highs and lows with resilience and kindness. I have repeatedly analyzed the harmful consequences of selfish individualism and demolished the concept of the ego as a singular, independent, and lasting entity. In other words, I am an "ego-terminator," as Alexandre Jollien puts it!

Apparently, I have also promoted an instrumental vision of altruism mainly as a vehicle for being good to oneself, whereas, on the contrary, I strove in *Altruism* to show that this form of "self-interested altruism" is fundamentally different from true altruism. I used supporting scientific references to explain precisely and in detail how a feeling of deep satisfaction may "also" be derived from acts inspired by authentic altruism, but that such a feeling can never be the primary reason for benevolent behavior, the ultimate aim of which is to increase the well-being of others and ease their suffering, not to achieve one's own well-being or to promote one's own short- or long-term personal interests.

No one is under any obligation to read my books, indeed, but attributing words to someone that they have never said is, at best, an error of judgment, and unfortunately may sometimes reveal a lack of intellectual honesty. There's nothing new in any of this; it has always been easier to imagine what an author has written than to read his work!

"PURE VISION" IN THE FACE OF EVIL

Among the messages and principles of Buddhism that I am especially eager to share with the greatest number of people—again, without ever seeking to "convert" anyone, but to introduce the universal teachings they contain that can contribute to the well-being and happiness of all—is that of "pure vision." According to Buddhism, this consists of seeing the Buddha nature in every being. How can this be reconciled with the horrors that are perpetrated throughout the world every day? Children killed in front of their parents, or vice versa; women and children raped by mercenaries or abused in private by members of their own families, teachers, or other authority figures in sports institutions, schools, churches, Buddhist centers, orphanages, or forced labor camps in the Kolyma gulag, all the way to the reeducation camps for Uyghurs, where rape is par for the course. Humans are apparently capable of the best and the worst. We are the only species capable of consciously doing both great good and great evil. The suffering of the victims is terrible and lasting, and caused by the appalling aberrations of their predators.

Pure vision is not, however, an escape hatch to an angelic vision of the human being. It does not ignore the suffering of victims or minimize the gravity of crimes, but it does necessarily go hand in hand with unconditional benevolence. Abuses of all kinds must be prevented, in particular by making it easier for victims to entrust themselves, without fear or shame, to those who can free them from their oppression in care facilities where they will be warmly welcomed and heard. Schools should also include in their curricula sensitization to the precursor signs of abuse and encourage children to report them as soon as they appear.

Pure vision in the face of cruelty involves keeping ever in mind the potential for transformation that is in each of us and not succumbing to "mean world syndrome." As painful as the tragedies they have experienced may be, victims can rise from the ashes and flourish in life. As dreadful as their behavior may be, criminals have the potential to reform themselves, which is to the benefit of society as a whole.

In 1995, I was invited, at the request of the prisoners, to speak at the Muret Detention Center, south of Toulouse, where detainees serve long sentences. I spent an entire afternoon talking with some twenty inmates. The contrast between the many security gates I had to pass through to get to them and the congenial atmosphere of our dialogue was quite confusing. Among other things, I spoke to them of the fact that every human being has a gold nugget deep within his mind that may long remain hidden in its own seam or sink into the mud following a given incident, but that it is always possible to extract that nugget, polish it, and restore it to full luster. The gold itself is never degraded.

One detainee told me that he took this as a message of hope. "Too often," he said, "we're told right from the beginning that we're born stained with original sin, and when we go on to commit a crime that we're doubly bad. And then, on top of that, we're in jail." The prisoners saw no way out of this threefold straitjacket. Stressing their potential to bring forth the best part of their humanity is like showing them a light at the end of the tunnel. This was a matter not of "absolving" them of their crimes or ignoring the fate of their victims, but simply of highlighting the possibility of doing good to right a wrong. The death penalty, which paradoxically kills to expose the atrocity of killing, excludes any possibility of redemption. Aside from one or two prisoners who scowled as they listened—one of them told me at the end that he was in a constant rage and that he was only waiting to get out so he could settle things with the guy who had ratted on him—my conversation with the detainees was more like a gathering of friends than a prison visit.

Pure vision, then, can be compared to "original goodness"; it embodies the idea that the ultimate nature of our mind is not altered by any mental poison that may invade it temporarily, which can be neutralized. The opposite of pure vision is the belief that the world and human beings are fundamentally evil. This tendency leads to a blanket condemnation of the entire human community just because a few individuals behave abhorrently. This "mean world syndrome" is therefore what we might call an "impure vision" of human beings. In essence, we must respond to the atrocities too often committed by the human race with transformation and kindness, not with hatred and vengeance.

As a rule, I have no taste for engaging in polemics that soon turn bitter and generate nothing good. Moreover, we know that, because of "confirmation bias," the more we demonstrate to someone that his arguments are unfounded, the more he becomes entrenched in his position and rejects any information that might undermine his convictions. Such contentiousness creates a wretched state of mind. I remember, too, what my father once wrote: "There is no polemic; there are only good arguments and bad arguments." And I would dare to add, "There are only facts and fictions." I prefer to remain at peace, let false statements fade away, and heed the advice of Patrul Rinpoche:

"All talk is like an echo," said the buddhas,
But these days it's more like the re-echo of an echo.
If your actions conform with Dharma, you'll antagonize everyone;
If your words are truthful, most people will get angry;
If your mind is truly good and pure, they will judge it a defect.
Now is the time to keep your own way hidden.

My teacher Dilgo Khyentse Rinpoche comments on this verse from *The Heart Treasure of the Enlightened Ones*, which I translated from Tibetan:

The happiness and suffering created by praise and criticism are ephemeral. When you are complimented, instead of feeling proud just regard the praise as if it were something you were hearing in a dream or a fantasy. Tell yourself that it is not you that is being praised but the good qualities you may have developed through spiritual practice. In fact, the truth is that the only people really worthy of praise are those who have attained liberation.

When you are criticized, accept it as an opportunity to acknowledge your hidden faults and increase your humility. As it is said, "Blame and ill treatment are the roots of the meditation flower." They are your teacher, destroying attachment and craving. If brought to the path, harsh words and blame will inspire your practice and strengthen your discipline. How can you ever repay such kindness?

For a Bodhisattva who has realized the dreamlike nature of speech, criticism and abuse can only enhance his meditation practice. It does not matter whether he encounters good or bad circumstances, as both help to increase his merit and wisdom. He is never swept away by worries and desires because his mind remains undisturbed in the perfect view. Having let go of all worldly values, he obtains the esteem of others without seeking it.

As for us, even if we were to single-mindedly put everything we have into achieving fame throughout the world, there would always be someone to denigrate us. And even were we to succeed, whatever fame we might achieve, whether for our courage, physical beauty, or power, would only be temporary.

For several years now, the only reason that I have come down from my hermitage in Nepal—other than for reuniting with family and friends—has been to ensure the continuity of Karuna-Shechen's humanitarian projects. Since 2019, thanks to the heartening commitment of everyone at Karuna-Shechen and to a solid and effective system of governance and operations drawing on the expertise of qualified people, I have gradually stepped aside, confident that the good that Karuna-Shechen has been doing for the past twenty years will go on for many more years still.

53

DORDOGNE, FORTY YEARS ON

The Chanteloube Study Center in Dordogne has been growing and thriving since 1970. I went there for twenty-four years in my capacity as translator. I go there now to spend time with Kangyur Rinpoche's family, my mother, my sister, and my spiritual friends.

The Buddhist adventure in Dordogne began in the early 1970s when Bernard Benson, a student of Kangyur Rinpoche's, offered land to a few groups of Tibetan lamas who, in time, built four teaching and retreat centers in the Vézère Valley. I have known many members of this remarkable community from the time we studied together in India with Kangyur Rinpoche and Dilgo Khyentse Rinpoche. They now live there, united by their spiritual quest, focused on practice, study, and translation, with equal parts resolve and humility.

Following the death of Khyentse Rinpoche, I spent more time in Dordogne to receive teachings from the sons of Kangyur Rinpoche; enjoy the company of his widow, Jetsün Jampa Chökyi; and spend time with my elderly mother, my sister Ève, and my spiritual brothers and sisters. A kind of salutary and regenerating return to the source, to the family of my root teacher and to my oldest spiritual friends.

Tulku Pema Wangyal, Kangyur Rinpoche's eldest son, had been invited to France in late 1975 by his father's Western students. He saw this as an opportunity to accomplish his father's vision and to work for the good of beings in places where the understanding and practice of Buddhism were still very limited. In the late 1970s, he made Dordogne his permanent domicile, brought his family over from Darjeeling, and invited a number of great masters to teach there, including Dudjom Rinpoche, Dilgo Khyentse Rinpoche, Trulshik Rinpoche, Tenga Rinpoche, Penor Rinpoche, His Holiness the fourteenth Dalai Lama in 1991, His Holiness Sakya Trizin, Dzongsar Khyentse Rinpoche, Yongey Mingyur Rinpoche, and many others.

It is his tireless determination that has allowed the Chanteloube Study Center and its three retreat centers to thrive over the past forty years—as I write this, in 2022, a ninth three-year retreat is under way—along with the Padmakara Translation Group, the summer seminars, and the "parallel retreats." The latter allow students to pursue their professional or family lives while taking a course of nine years or more that is similar to a three-year retreat, attending a three- or four-day seminar twice a year.

On his initiative, too, 108 granite stupas, in which precious relics, texts, and mantras dedicated to world peace are embedded, were built near the main Chanteloube retreat center. Several hundreds of thousands of molded, consecrated statuettes have been carefully set out within their perimeter walls—a patient task that took five years to complete.

Pema Wangyal Rinpoche is also the initiator of several charitable associations: Maison 24 in Dordogne, and Casa in Portugal and Brazil, caring for the homeless and the food insecure, as well as Friends of the Earth and Siddhartha in India. He works tirelessly for the cause of animals and has released into their natural environment more than ten million animals that had been destined for slaughter by humans. Moreover, it is to him that I now turn for instruction and guidance when I go on retreat.

Through his spiritual accomplishment and influence, Pema Wangyal Rinpoche, now seventy-five years old, inevitably recalls his father to the minds of all who knew him. Completely indifferent to worldly considerations, his only concern is to ease the suffering of human beings and animals and to safeguard the authenticity of Buddhist teachings.

Kangyur Rinpoche's wife, Jetsün Jampa Chökyi, better known as Amala, moved into the Chanteloube community with her family in the late 1970s, devoting most of her time to spiritual practice. She did not give formal teachings but offered precious counsel to all who sought it from her; her light shone on all who came to her, and many people, me included, considered her to be a spiritual master. Inseparable in my mind from Kangyur Rinpoche ever since we met in 1967, she was always an immutable reference point for me through the quality of her presence, her humility, and her gentleness—reflections of authentic spiritual realization.

She spent the last two years of her life in the Algarve mountains, in Portugal, where many practitioners now go on retreat. Every so often, she would ask to be taken to the nearest town, Portimão, where she would set herself up in a cafeteria in the middle of a crowded supermarket. Sitting quietly at a table, Amala was there not just for a cup of tea, but to immerse herself in the throng, among the teeming people, and to pray for each and every one of them, connecting with them in a salutary way. Passersby sometimes came up to her, intrigued or attracted by her serene presence. They would chat for a while through one of her daughters.

When her health began to deteriorate in the winter of 2003–2004, I left Nepal to go see her one last time in Portugal. I found her in bed, breathing with difficulty. She was barely able to talk, but when I was admitted into her presence and she raised her eyes to me, she gave me one of the most beautiful gifts I have ever received: a celestial, ineffable smile that lit up not only her face, but the entire room. While her condition certainly caused her what we call "pain" at the physiological level, she did not experience it the same way we do. Her serenity radiated immutably through the disintegration of her body. It is also said that in enduring affliction, a highly accomplished person takes on the suffering of the world. Amala must have borne more than her share.

Amala died shortly after our last encounter, on February 15, 2004, at the age of eighty-four. After forty-nine days of special prayers and rituals, Trulshik Rinpoche flew from Nepal to Portugal to preside over the cremation ceremony, which was held in front of the house where she had spent her final years. The simple fact of thinking of her and recalling her face always calls me back to what is essential.

Pema Wangyal Rinpoche recently asked his younger brother, Jigme Khyentse Rinpoche, to take over most of his teachings. You will remember that, before his death, Kangyur Rinpoche had confirmed that Jigme Khyentse Rinpoche would ensure the continuity of his spiritual line.

Jigme Khyentse Rinpoche's teachings are able to break through the defenses of even the most weary and overloaded among us. One of the major obstacles facing practitioners is the risk of becoming jaded and impervious to the teachings. When we hear them, we say, "Oh, I've already heard that somewhere." As they say in Tibet, we become like a leather bag that spends years in contact with butter but never absorbs it, or a rock lying at the bottom of a river without ever soaking up a single drop of water.

Like a brilliant musician improvising on a theme while adhering perfectly to the rules of harmony, Jigme Khyentse Rinpoche opens unimagined windows in our understanding of teachings that we have heard again and again without ever having been able to extract their essence. I am constantly dazzled by the way he introduces key points of Buddhist thought in a light in which I have never seen them, while impeccably maintaining their authenticity.

To cite just one example among many, we generally identify three phases on the path to enlightenment: individual liberation (*pratimoksha*), the wish to achieve enlightenment for the good of all beings (*bodhicitta*), and the pure vision that recognizes the unity of emptiness and appearance in all things. One might understand the first phase as the "individualistic" desire to free oneself alone from suffering, a goal that would seem more suited to a timorous mind than that of devoting oneself to freeing all beings. What's more, it's obvious that unless you have freed yourself from samsara, you will have a very hard time liberating others from it, as the blind cannot lead the blind. But Jigme Khyentse Rinpoche defines the concept of *pratimoksha* as the need to break from the very notion of the individual. Indeed, so long as we remain attached to the real existence of an individual entity—a unitary, independent, and permanent "self"—we will have no chance of breaking away from samsara, much less of freeing others from it. This illumination corresponds perfectly to one characteristic of arhats—practitioners of the basic vehicle who have achieved an end to suffering, or limited nirvana—that of having freed themselves from attachment to the existence of an individual "self," even if they have yet to recognize the absence of identity in phenomena as a whole.

Jigme Khyentse Rinpoche sometimes relied on memorable catch-phrases to better spark the imagination. At a summer seminar, attended by a friend who was fiercely interested in the topic of happiness, he asserted, "What you generally call happiness, we call suffering." This was his way of bluntly recalling that we seek happiness where it cannot be found—in the afterglow of endless gratification, in profit, praise, fame, physical beauty, power, and so on—while blithely running after the very causes of suffering.

Jigme Khyentse Rinpoche may often spend an entire morning teaching on an apparently anecdotal theme, inspired by topical circumstances that he imbues with broad and profound meaning. At a seminar organized in Mexico City by Shechen Monastery, Rabjam Rinpoche and Jigme Khyentse Rinpoche, who have been very close since childhood, were both scheduled to teach. Rabjam Rinpoche's plane was late, and he was unable to get there in time for the opening of the event. Jigme Khyentse Rinpoche began his teaching as follows (I'm quoting from memory): "We're waiting for Rabjam Rinpoche, right? But the truth is, we're always waiting for something in life. Sometimes it's something specific, sometimes it's some vague thing that's supposed to answer some unspoken desire. This chronic state of waiting nourishes the fear and hope that disturb our mind and generate a nagging sense of dissatisfaction." For the rest of the morning, he delivered a thrilling teaching in the form of variations on the theme of waiting.

I myself have come to see that some of the most gratifying moments of my life have occurred in the total absence of hopes and fears of any kind. A few years ago, I was about to take off from Kathmandu airport, hoping to reach Amsterdam the next evening for a conference that had been meticulously planned by its organizers. From there, I was to go on to France. Suddenly, the departures board announced that the flight to Delhi, where I was to make my connection, had been cancelled. I quickly made the rounds of all the airlines operating out of Kathmandu; it was just not going to be possible to reach Amsterdam by the following evening. I felt very bad for the organizers and called to inform them of the situation. I took my luggage and went to sit on a bench outside the airport. It was a late spring afternoon. No one was expecting me, either here or anywhere else. I had said my goodbyes at the monastery; they thought I'd already left. With serene contentment I watched the travelers come and go, the sparrows searching for crumbs on the ground, the sun bowing toward the mountains as it set; there were all sorts of sounds that had no special meaning for me and no effect on what happened to me. Free of ruminating thoughts, I delighted in the freshness of the moment. "Might be a nice thing," I thought to myself, "to be in such a state of inner calm all the time." That led me to thinking about the wandering hermits who, like Patrul Rinpoche, roam from one place to another without anyone paying them any mind. They can't get lost because they have no specific destination; they can never be late because no one's waiting for them. After half an hour, I got up, grabbed by bag, and returned to the monastery at a leisurely pace.

It's every bit as rewarding to get to know the other members of Kangyur Rinpoche's family, each in her or his own way. Rangdrol Rinpoche, Kangyur Rinpoche's middle son, was recognized by Dilgo Khyentse Rinpoche as the reincarnation of Tsawa Rinchen Namgyal, a master of the late nineteenth century. Alongside his older brother Pema Wangyal Rinpoche, he studied at the Central Institute of Higher Tibetan Studies, in Sarnath, and then received many teachings from the great masters of our time. He regularly teaches at the three-year retreats. An exceptional practitioner, he spends a good part of the year on retreat.

Rigdzin Chödrön, Kangyur Rinpoche's eldest daughter, now very advanced in years, learned traditional Tibetan medicine from her father and has cared for countless patients in France and elsewhere. Her younger sister, Yangchen Chözom, a nun, is one of the best exemplars of devotion and diligence I know. She seems to be a whirlwind of industry, day and night, completely devoted to her father's vision and Pema Wangyal Rinpoche's activities. The youngest sister, Pema Chökyi, works at her side and, like her, spends a great deal of time on retreat.

As they did when we first met in 1967, Kangyur Rinpoche's entire family—now including Rigdzin Chödrön's two daughters, who were only two or three years old back then, Dawa Tsedrön and her husband Étienne, and Dekyi Lhakpa—continue to set an edifying example of consistency between teachings, spiritual practice, and action. They inspire the entire community of students who live spread out across the valley and hills of Vézère and come together for communal practice, teachings, and a variety of tasks.

In 1994, Tulku Pema Wangyal asked Rabjam Rinpoche to teach *The Treasury of Precious Qualities*, detailed explanations of which the latter had received from Dilgo Khyentse Rinpoche. For three years in a row, ten days straight, Rabjam Rinpoche explained the early chapters of the treatise, whose text fills two 700-hundred-page volumes. When he reached the ninth chapter, which addresses the philosophical aspects of the middle way (*madhyamaka*), he asked Khenpo Pema Sherab, one of the best scholars of our time, to teach that and the following chapters. Khenpo Pema Sherab was a student of Dilgo Khyentse Rinpoche in Tibet and was with him on his hectic flight from the Chinese invasion. Once in India, he studied with scholars who had managed to escape from Tibet and lived in refugee camps. He became a *khenpo* (doctor of philosophy), then went to southern India to run the Namdroling monastic institute (at Penor Rinpoche's monastery), where three thousand monks and nuns study. He accepted Rabjam Rinpoche's request on the condition that I serve as his interpreter (I had been close to Khenpo Pema Sherab for forty years and was familiar with his way of speaking and teaching).

Khenpo, whom we call Khen Rinpoche ("Precious Scholar") out of respect, has taught at the Chanteloube Study Center for three weeks every summer since 1997, which comes to a total of one year and three months of daily teachings and translations. Having completed *The Treasury of Precious Qualities* over the course of thirteen years, Khen Rinpoche taught other important texts from the Nyingmapa school.[1]

It was a privilege to act as his interpreter, but it was also a unique challenge. Until just a few years ago, he taught four hours straight in the morning and two in the afternoon. I would quickly go over the text early in the morning, then Khen Rinpoche would teach from 9 a.m. to 1 p.m., with a fifteen-minute break in the midmorning. As translator, I could not relax my attention for more than a few seconds without running the risk of missing a part of the teaching. Khenpo would speak for stretches of five to ten minutes, then I would reconstitute his explanations to the best of my ability in French or English. Because he was explaining a text, I had to keep my eyes riveted on the page while also memorizing his explanations. If I had taken notes, I would have lost the thread of the text, and any attempt to catch up would have interfered with my listening. Khen Rinpoche would pick up his explanations again the moment I was done. I have to admit that I avoided looking at my watch for a good part of the morning session, for fear of seeing how much time I still had left to translate—not that I was reluctant to serve this outstanding teacher, but because of the intense concentration required by the task. My resilience was put to the test. But I did notice that it went best when I entered a state of flow, the optimal experience described by the psychologist Mihaly Csikszentmihalyi, and that both the listening and the translation proceeded in a calm and open space within which words and the meaning of the teachings meshed with one another like the notes of a symphony.

Luckily for me, Khenpo Pema Sherab's always perfectly structured and lucid teachings made my job easier. As I read the text before the teaching session, I anticipated having to struggle with certain especially difficult passages, but his explanations were so clear that I rarely had any problems.

In 2001, Khenpo Pema Sherab gave his annual teaching at a center in the Algarve hills, in Portugal. One morning when I met him for breakfast, he pointed at his mouth, signaling that he was unable to speak. He had been struck with cerebral ischemia, a temporary interruption of blood flow to the brain that alters its functioning. He later told me that the first thing that came to mind when he realized he'd lost the power of speech was that his teaching of *The Treasury of Precious Qualities* would be abruptly cut short. He was not especially concerned for his own fate. He was hospitalized for a few days and, fortunately, gradually recovered his power of speech over the next few weeks. Since then, the members of his entourage have convinced him to limit his teachings to two or three hours a day.

In 2019, having spent twenty-two years interpreting for Khenpo Pema Sherab—whom we now called Khen Rinpoche ("Precious Khenpo") or Khenchen ("Great Khenpo") in view of his seniority and the respect he commanded throughout the Tibetan Buddhist world—I asked a brilliant young scholar, Khenpo Sonam Tsewang, to take over from me. He had studied Buddhist philosophy for thirteen years, then taught for several more under Khen Rinpoche's guidance. On other occasions, I had noticed that he was an outstanding translator, combining a perfect knowledge of the texts with an excellent command of English. As for me, my brain is not as vibrant as it once was, and I am losing my hearing. On top of that, despite how much care I take preparing for and translating the teachings, I am well aware that, although I am constantly speaking in Tibetan, I inevitably make mistakes, since it's not my native tongue. I do, however, continue to provide simultaneous translation in French for the few listeners who speak no English.

Khen Rinpoche retired from most of his duties at the Namdroling institute at the age of eighty-four and now (in 2022) lives part of the year in Dordogne, right next door to my mother's house. The very model of a man who has devoted his life to study and practice, always even-tempered and kind, he radiates a soothing calm. Satisfied in all things, he has very few needs. When his students from the Namdroling monastic institute—which counts one thousand students, in addition to the three thousand monks and nuns in the monastery—wanted to buy him a car in Mysore, he made it very clear to them that he did not want one. He begins practicing long before dawn, then spends his days reading texts and walking in the forest, which gives him particular pleasure. Whenever I'm in Dordogne, I accompany him on his afternoon walks every day, along with Khenpo Sonam and Ani Pema, a nun from Tibet who has seen to his personal needs for the past twenty years.

It was also thanks to Khenpo Pema Sherab's explanations that the translators of the Padmakara Translation Group have been able to translate the texts he teaches and to publish them in French, through the Éditions Padmakara publishing house, and in other languages abroad. These translators, who have been working tirelessly in the quiet of the Périgord forests for the past thirty-five years, are among the most competent of our time. Over the years, they have published some fifty volumes of major texts of Indian and Tibetan Buddhism. These include such classics as Shantideva's *A Guide to the Bodhisattva's Way of Life*, with three volumes of commentary; spiritual practice guides like Patrul Rinpoche's *Words of*

My Perfect Teacher; philosophical treaties like Shantarakshita's *Ornament of the Middle Way*; and biographies like *The Life and Visions of Yeshe Tsogyal*. There are also such canonical "summations" as the five-thousand-page *Soutra de l'entrée dans la dimensions absolue* (the Gandavyuha sutra, the "Entering the Dharma Realm" sutra, translated from the Chinese into French), which starts off with a five-hundred-page introduction, as well as transcriptions of oral teachings translated from Tibetan, such as Dilgo Khyentse Rinpoche's *The Heart of Compassion*.[2] Many of the group's translations have come out directly in English through Shambhala Publications, as well as in Spanish, Portuguese, and German. Over the years, I have translated seven volumes of Dilgo Khyentse Rinpoche's teachings from Tibetan into English or French, as well as texts written by other authors.[3]

My old friend Gérard Godet, whom I saw a great deal of when I still lived in Paris before definitively leaving for Darjeeling, and whom I thought of as a second uncle, had also joined the Dordogne community and retired from his professional activities. He took monastic vows, did three consecutive three-year retreats, then spent the last years of his life practicing in a little house very near my mother's. He was the very embodiment of a modest and sincere practitioner, well-liked by all. At his death in 2010, he spent ten days in a state that the Tibetans call *thukdam*, a sort of postmortem meditation seen in some advanced practitioners, as I've previously mentioned in the case of Sengdrak Rinpoche. The mayor granted a special waiver for his body to be left untouched throughout that time. When the ten days were up, the doctor who legally certified his death noted that the body showed no sign of decomposition, no odor, and no rigor mortis. Gérard simply looked as if he were sitting in meditation, his eyes closed, his limbs and skin supple. When this special state eventually ended, his body began to exhibit all the ordinary signs of death. That day, the migratory common cranes that usually flew straight overhead made a broad circle above the house. In an auspicious coincidence, a double rainbow appeared at the very moment when Gérard's body left the house for the crematorium.

Here too, events did not proceed as usual. I wasn't there, but several friends have described the scene for me on several occasions. The complete cremation of a body usually takes twenty minutes. But after fifteen minutes, the man in charge of the crematorium came out to tell Pema Wangyal Rinpoche that the body had not yet been consumed. He couldn't understand what was going on. Pema Wangyal Rinpoche advised him to press on. He emerged ten minutes later, visibly upset. He invited Pema Wangyal Rinpoche and a close associate to come look through the little viewing window that opened onto the furnace. The body remained visible in the midst of the flames. "Do something!" said the distraught official. Pema Wangyal Rinpoche muttered a few prayers and suddenly, like a match thrown into a puddle of gasoline, the body shot up in flames and was reduced to ashes in moments. The attendant asked us to kindly keep the incident to ourselves, lest anyone suggest that his equipment was defective. Furthermore, when the cremains went through the machine that processes the ashes, it got jammed: the heart had not burned.

When Gérard died, many people we had never heard of, and charitable institutions, came forward to attest to the help he had offered them without letting any of us know about it. The discretion of a pure heart.

Up until two or three years ago, I regularly went to the Chanteloube Study Center to interpret and assist at the summer seminars, which gave me an opportunity to visit with my mother, Yahne Le Toumelin. She had taken part in the second three-year retreat in Dordogne and had then moved to the Vézère Valley to live among her spiritual teachers. I also spent time with her whenever I was in France. As she grew older, I began spending more and more time with her in Dordogne. The one-story house—a large room and her little bedroom—that she has been granted use of for life is an open place where friends know that they will be very warmly welcomed for a meal, a moment of sharing or comfort, or even a quick painting lesson. The large room used to serve as her studio. When I'm there, I usually stay in a little 150-square foot wooden cabin adjoining her house.

At ninety, she still had all her faculties and continued to regale us with her clever witticisms. I wrote down a few when she came up with them. For instance, never having gotten her driver's license, she has used a bicycle and liked to say, "I'm not an autodidact; I'm a cyclodidact." She liked to write on a Christmas card, "Born is the Holy Instant, Immaculately Free of Concepts." One morning when her rheumatism had given her a bad night, she quipped, "How can I complain about my bones? They were so good to me for so long!" Concerning Xavier Emmanuelli, the cofounder of Doctors Without Borders, Samu, and Samusocial International, with whom I held a conference in Périgueux to benefit people living with food insecurity and supported by Maison 24, she said, "He has a heart in each hand." At ninety-four, she joked, "More and more, I'm becoming less and less" and "Silence is the language of the future."

In January 2016, under the auspices of the city of Bordeaux, a grand retrospective of her work, covering seventy years of painting, was organized in the historical venue of the chapter house of the Mably courtyard by two Bordelais friends, Christian Jean dit Cazaux and Patrice Géraudie. Seventy canvases were exhibited. Friends from all walks of life came to the vernissage for a joyful celebration. She stopped painting a few years ago, having gradually lost her mobility and the use of her left hand.

Before her memories vanished for good, I interviewed my mother about her life and photographed several hundred of her paintings at my sister's house in Dordogne, where many of them are stored, and also among the collectors I was able to track down. In the fall of 2016, Éditions La Martinière published *Lumière, rire du ciel* ("Light, the Laughter of the Sky"), an album retracing the highlights of her life and work, with texts by one of the fathers of Surrealism, André Breton, and the poet Jean Markale and philosopher Michel Bitbol. Somewhat earlier, in 2011, she had published a little study of painting under the same name (the title inspired by the Italian Renaissance philosopher and poet Marsilio Ficino), with Éditions Pauvert.

Her cognitive powers have been gradually declining since 2017, but she continues to this day to say her prayers and read out loud, four hours a day, the books we choose for her. She sings a lot, her voice still retaining its strikingly crystalline timbre—not only Buddhist chants, but Schubert's "Ave Maria," Charles Trenet's "La Mer," or songs her mother and aunt sang her in the 1930s and the 1940s, which we had never heard, such as André Perchicot's "Si t'es dans la purée, reviens vers moi" ("If you're in the soup, come back to me"). Short-term memory gives way to scenes, people who have been gone for fifty years, and distant details that resurface in her mental landscape.

Now, in 2023, my mother is one hundred years old and may well outlive me. In the meantime, assisted by two friends from the Buddhist community in Dordogne who take turns attending to her, I do my best to support her and have stayed at her side most of the time for the last two years.

My sister Ève also lives a part of the year in Dordogne. She has a pretty house about three miles from my mother's. Stricken at the age of forty-two with early onset Parkinson's disease, she has reacted courageously, as we read in her moving accounts *Parkinson Blues* and *Une étoile qui danse sur le chaos* ("A Star Dancing on Chaos").[4] Young Parkinson's patients do not enjoy the same social assistance provided to other disabled workers (such as part-time worker's compensation and so on) because it's a disease that primarily affects older people, most of whom have already left the labor market. Despite her condition, Ève continued to work at her profession as a speech therapist and to devote herself full time to what she calls "the bad kids, the ones you never see at birthday parties."

Despite her thirty-six years of service at Saint-Anne's and other City of Paris institutions, and her devotion to the disadvantaged children she took care of, Ève was kept on as an independent contractor—no paid vacations and a newcomer's contract at the start of every school year. Under the law, she should have been made a permanent staff member after two years, but the administration declined to consider her requests. Finally, and in an ironic twist of fate, she was made permanent only two years before retirement! In order to finally secure this status, at the age of fifty-eight she had to sit an exam before a panel of young therapists who had far fewer years of professional experience than she did. One of the examiners asked,

"What do you believe is the main quality a speech therapist must possess?"

"Personally, or professionally?"

"Personally."

"To be loving."

Ève noted that the reply had come to mind instantaneously and seemed to her to be perfectly obvious.

One day, she realized that a child she had been treating for a year had finally learned to read but was pretending to still be illiterate. The reason for his deception was simple and touching: he didn't want to give up the warm, loving, and comforting presence that was otherwise so lacking in his life.

The hope for a way in is always there, as it was with the child who wrote nothing but profanity but who, with Ève at his side, one day discovered the beauty of words. Finally, he put down his pencil and declared, wonder-struck: "One day, I want to be a *poem*."

"The word lady" is how she was known to children for whom words remain a mystery and who suffer from their inability to use them in more or better ways, from being cut off from reading, writing, and a whole, vast world. The nickname also became the title of the book Ève wrote to share her experience of working with them. An early editor rejected the manuscript of *La Dame des mots* a few days after receiving it, explaining that "the author clearly understands nothing about children and that you can't build a book on good intentions." My editor and friend Nicole Lattès had the wisdom to publish this richly instructive book. It seems to me that Ève understands children in a way that one would like to see more of in the world, and that you can build not only a book but an entire life on "good intentions."

The most beautiful tribute to Ève undoubtedly came from Lala, one of her former pupils, who tracked her down years later, after having made a professional and family life for herself, living a stable and happy life. She said simply, "We've come a hell of a long way together."

Ève and her husband, Yann, offer me a solid life lesson, taught by example at every moment, with simplicity, perseverance, and dignity. Ève teaches me courage, Yann solicitude. Ève's courage lies not only in coping resolutely with a grueling disease from which she will not recover, but in having adopted and relentlessly maintained a positive and resilient vision and attitude to her affliction. "I know that I have a disease," she says, "but I am not that disease and I never will be." In refusing to identify with her illness, she has opened a space of freedom in which she can live, create, and love. Ève is also blessed with two loving sons, Raphaël and Guillaume, and her delicious grandchildren Amaya, Akiko, Elio, and Esther, and I am their great-uncle.

Whatever suffering and often intense physical pain she has had to endure—she underwent serious spinal surgery and broke both hips in the space of six months—I have never seen Ève give in to mood swings, anger, or discouragement. She is devoid of the least trace of resentment. "You have taken this disease in hand," I wrote in the preface of *Une étoile sur le chaos*, "like a musician who comes across a damaged instrument and learns to draw a beautiful melody from it that surprises and transports us all."

I have a wealth of marvelous family and friends, and I draw great joy from them. I have met countless people leading "good," constructive lives, people who do good all around them and manifest praiseworthy, even exceptional human qualities. It is possible to work together for a more altruistic world, a society rooted in greater solidarity, and a human race more keenly aware of the stakes involved in the future of the planet and biodiversity as a whole. This more ethical and responsible samsara is infinitely better than a world in which animosity, selfishness, and indifference reign.

As desirable as it may be, however, this best of worlds can be even better if we learn to remediate the deep causes of suffering. In the light of what I have seen of my spiritual teachers and of the teachings I have received, I don't see how it could be possible to come up with a revised and corrected samsara that would nonetheless remain samsara—that is, the world conditioned by suffering. Samsara is not reparable and there is no point in painting it in a flattering light, any more than there is a point in repainting a wall that has fallen into ruin. It is eminently commendable and desirable to be a good human being and to behave with dignity, generosity, honesty, simplicity, and intelligence, but if you fail to act on the roots of suffering, although you may find legitimate satisfaction in the success of your altruistic actions, you will soon be caught in the rising tide of dissatisfaction and frustration. At one of the summer seminars led in Dordogne by Jigme Khyentse Rinpoche, as the seasonal heatwave was at its worst, a woman made the following remark: "I have to admit that rather than sit here listening to teachings, the only thing I want to do is take my canoe down to the river and find a quiet place to go swimming."

Jigme Khyentse Rinpoche replied more or less as follows: "I should think that your very understandable attraction to the cool river water is driven by a desire to feel better. But behind that immediate wish, what's pushing you in that direction?" "The desire for well-being," she answered after a moment's thought. "Very good. And couldn't that well-being take on different aspects, levels, and durations? What, then, is the purpose of the Dharma's teachings?" And for the rest of the morning, Jigme Khyentse Rinpoche laid out various facets of a crystal-clear teaching on the distinction between tangible but ephemeral well-being, linked to the senses, and the broader, more lasting well-being generated by eliminating the latent causes of the endlessly renewed frustrations and suffering of existence. "In essence," he concluded, "the Dharma's teachings are a fundamental remedy for suffering." Volumes can be and are written on the way to live a "good" life. That is an eminently critical task in these troubled times, and the general-interest writings that I have humbly shared with the world are a few more drops in the ocean. But it is essential to identify reference points for what could be true emancipation from the primary causes of suffering, a path that I have chosen to take and on which I still have a long, long way to go, even as I sense that my direction will allow me to actualize my potential and make the very best use of the time I have been given in this life. I tried to summarize this point of view in the conclusion of *Happiness*:

Everybody (or almost everybody) is interested in happiness. But who is interested in enlightenment? The very word seems exotic, vague, and distant. And yet ultimate well-being comes from fully eliminating delusion and mental toxins, and thus suffering. Enlightenment is what Buddhism calls the state of ultimate freedom that comes with a perfect knowledge of the nature of mind and of the world of phenomena. The traveler has awakened from the sleep of ignorance, and the distortions of the psyche have given way to a correct vision of reality. The divide between subject and object has vanished in the understanding of the interdependence of all phenomena. . . . The sage has come to see that the individual self and the appearances of the world of phenomena have no intrinsic reality. He understands that all beings have the power to free themselves from ignorance and unhappiness, but that they don't know it.

How could he fail to feel infinite and spontaneous compassion for all those who, spellbound by ignorance, wander lost in the trials of samsara?

While such a state may seem very far removed from our daily concerns, it is certainly not beyond reach. . . . Milk is the source of butter, but it won't make any if we simply leave it to its own devices; we have to churn it. The qualities of enlightenment are revealed through transformation at the far end of the spiritual path.

The fact is, each stage is a step toward fulfillment and profound satisfaction. The spiritual journey is like traveling from one valley to another—beyond each pass lies a landscape more magnificent than the one behind it. . . . At the heart of enlightenment, beyond hope and doubt, the word "happiness" itself has no meaning. The shadows cast by concepts dissolve in the dawn of nonduality. . . . She who understands the true nature of things is like a navigator landing on an island made entirely of pure gold; even if she looks for ordinary pebbles, she won't find any.

Some people have told me, "You live the easy life in your hermitage: no family, no household to run, no schedule to keep or difficult professional environment to endure. You're privileged." Privileged perhaps, but in what sense? I'm no golden boy, no scion of wealth lazing poolside in California; at twenty-six I made a choice to quit my profession, inspired by a new way of living, and to throw myself into this new, different life, with no sense of what my material future held in store, and aspiring only to share my spiritual teacher's daily life.

I do indeed feel privileged to have met those who have guided my life and to have taken my decision at an age young enough to have allowed me to put my aspirations fully into practice. This choice was not about taking the easy way out; objectively, my years in Darjeeling, in a ten-by-ten-foot room without electricity, running water, or heating, were austere, to say the least. And yet, from my perspective, those were fine and happy years, rich and fruitful. In giving it all up, I had taken the plunge without a safety net; I had very little to fall back on, and things could easily have gone less well than they did.

I couldn't say whether I've been on a perpetual vacation since 1972 or have had no vacation at all. I live day to day. Whether I am devoting myself to spiritual practice or working on some project, there is no Saturday or Sunday in my week. I do what I love doing and what has meaning for me, without tallying my efforts but at my own pace.

As atypical as such a course of life may seem, could my own experiences and all that I have witnessed be of some use to my peers? The fact that I have felt a great deal of joy in living my life could certainly be attributed to my having a carefree and accommodating temperament, but I feel that such inner contentment is born of a certain number of factors that are within reach of each and every one of us, if we wish to grasp them.

Above all, I believe that it's essential to live consistently with that which most inspires us. Circumstances may appear to obstruct the realization of our aspirations, but with resolve and perseverance it is possible in most cases to overcome the obstacles and attain our goals. Whatever the prevailing conditions may be as we start out, if the right direction is clear in our mind, anything is possible. As the old saying goes, where there is a will, there is a way.

VII

A RETURN TO THE SOURCE

54

SNOW LION FORTRESS

<hr>

Rabjam Rinpoche takes me on a pilgrimage to Senge Dzong, the most legendary site in northeastern Bhutan. After an arduous trek through the semitropical forest, we reach the cirque of the Snow Lion Fortress, more than 13,000 feet above sea level.

There was one other place, more legendary than anywhere else in Bhutan, that Rabjam Rinpoche and I dearly wanted to see: Senge Dzong, the "Snow Lion Fortress." This pilgrimage was especially important to Rabjam Rinpoche, as he wanted to fulfill Dilgo Khyentse Rinpoche's repeatedly expressed desire to visit the site. Given the extreme hardships necessary to reach that high-altitude location, known for abrupt changes in weather that make flying hazardous, the only means of getting there available to him would have been by helicopter. Concerned for Dilgo Khyentse Rinpoche's safety, the king of Bhutan had respectfully discouraged him from making the trip.

We made the journey in April 2005, with the king's permission, which in those days was required if you wished to visit that especially sacred and remote place in eastern Bhutan, in the Kurtoe region, hard by the border with Tibet.

It took us three days by car to cross central Bhutan from Paro, through the Bumthang district, the Ura Valley, and awe-inspiring first-growth forests of immense trees teeming with birds, some of them endemic. Tigers, which can be found as high as 13,000 feet, sometimes pass through these dense forests. This unique opportunity to observe tigers in their pristine habitat is owing to the exceptional circumstances in that country, whose constitution requires no less than 60 percent of the national territory's natural ecosystem to be preserved untouched, which allows these big cats to move unhindered, from the subtropical forests along its southern border with India all the way to the eternal snows in the north.

Our travel by road ended at the Lhuentse Dzong, in Mongar district. The *dzong* is perched on a wooded promontory overlooking the Kuri Chu River. Our small group of pilgrims set off on foot the next day at dawn. It included Rabjam Rinpoche, of course, accompanied by two of his monks, three young Bhutanese from his entourage, a Chinese student who spoke fluent Tibetan, and me. Crossing an ancient-looking suspension bridge, we passed through the little village of Khorma, consisting of some fifty houses. A few locals recognized Rinpoche and asked for his blessing. As we left Khorma, we met a village woman who, seeing us happily traipse along with our little backpacks, exclaimed, "Poor things, how will they ever manage? They're carrying next to nothing." She was certainly familiar with the rough outing awaiting us, but what she didn't know was that fifteen minutes behind us was a caravan of ten mules laden with tents and victuals, led by five or six soldiers whom the king had sent to watch over Rabjam Rinpoche and his traveling companions.

We walked for two hours, following the banks of the turbulent Khorma Chu River, then plunged into the dense jungle. The immense trees formed an emerald vault through which streams of light poked here and there. The thick undergrowth, strewn with decomposing tree trunks, moss, and orchids, was riddled with streams that branched out and extended to form endless bogs.

A walking stick in each hand, my monastic robe raised to midcalf, and clad in hiking boots, I had to jump from rock to rock—hoping that they would not roll out underfoot—quickly leap onto a narrow and half-rotten tree trunk, and, before it collapsed under my weight, identify the next trunk or some barely visible stone and reach it with my outstretched foot. Distraction was not an option! This hazardous gymnastic course went reasonably well; stones and logs had been set up in convenient places in the mud over the years by countless travelers and shepherds.

The forest was busy with odd-voiced birds: toucans, whose resounding calls echoed in all directions; Himalayan magpies with their discordant cries, whose immense tails undulate, like a stole of blue feathers gliding above the greenery, when they suddenly take flight nearby. Large butter-flies passed us like flowers wafting on the breeze. Bears, no less beautiful but more dangerous to those who encounter them unexpectedly, also live in the vicinity; fortunately, we didn't run into any.

The truth is, we feared leeches far more. They swarmed by the thou-sands. Like slim black tongues, they raised their heads and swayed on leaves overhanging the path or on the grass underfoot, as if they sensed our approach, or else they dropped from the tree branches onto our heads. Every morning found some of us rubbing salt into our feet and calves to prevent these predators from latching on to our flesh. But some always managed to wriggle their way into our clothing. Their bites were painless, and we became aware of their presence only when the blood began running down our legs or drenched through our shirts. We pulled them off by gently running our fingernails under the attachment point so as not to kill them. At night, we searched for stragglers that had got-ten into our clothes. Nothing serious—at worst, the bite itches a little for a week or so; leeches aren't dangerous and transmit no parasites to humans. As for the mules, they had no way to defend themselves and soon found themselves dripping with blood, especially where their skin is thinnest, on their legs, around their eyes, and in their nostrils. For the next twelve hours, the jungle floor seemed to rise and fall forever. The low parts, sometimes leading to the banks of a raging stream, offered no relief; beyond the precautions necessary on sometimes slippery slopes, every descent reminded us of the lost altitude we would need to recoup.

Night fell and it began to rain. We had found nowhere to stop and make camp since we had first entered the forest, but in the twilight a clearing suddenly opened in the vegetation and small terraced fields appeared. Below, a deep gorge cleaved the wooded valley with a dizzying gash. On the opposite slope, a stream dropped in a great waterfall, a scarf of white silk slowly waving against the dark rock wall.

We came across a hamlet with a grand total of three cottages. A tall stack of wood was piled up under the awning of a barn. The peasant householder, a woman named Am Phurba, eagerly welcomed Rabjam Rinpoche and his entourage.

She made superb textiles of brightly colored silk, known as *kishuthara*; depending on the intricacy of the pattern, a large piece can take anywhere from three months to a year of work. Their sale provided for the family's modest needs. A revitalizing supper was served, then Am Phurba draped a broad cloth over her loom, her husband damped the embers with ash, and the household was soon asleep. Only the distant roar of the river and the tick-tock of a fat Indian alarm clock, keeping very approximate time, disturbed the profound silence of the night.

Everyone was up and about at the first glimmer of dawn, except the two newborns asleep in their parents' bed. They all got straight down to their daily chores: the fire had to be revived, offerings set out on the little domestic altar, wood and water fetched, breakfast prepared, and the animals let out.

Am Phurba lost no time in sitting down at her loom. Her shuttle went back and forth with such fluid movement that it seemed to be moving on its own, by magic. From time to time the weaver seamlessly tied on new vibrantly colored threads of silk, her fingers bringing to life the complex pattern she kept in her head. She chatted with us as she worked.

But it was time to take our leave of the charming family that had welcomed us so warmly into their home, and we set off again after leaving a few presents. That morning, in this sanctuary lost deep in the heart of the semitropical forest, we came across some yaks tromping through the swampy undergrowth. How had they gotten there, these animals that normally live in the mountain pastures, the land of the nomads? We soon spotted a few cabins, inhabited by two Tibetan families. The parents had fled the Chinese invasion more than thirty years earlier with a dozen yaks and settled here, living a simple and austere life in rickety huts. They offered us some whey, of which they had an excess in summer, when they churned butter all day long.

As night fell, we set up camp in a clearing on the riverbank. Our guides gathered dead wood to start the fire and prepare a hot supper. We covered the ground with several layers of pine twigs, whose long needles formed a soft carpet. Every so often, a horned owl broke the silence with her prim and solemn "who?"

We finally emerged from the forest on the morning of the third day and struck out at a right angle to the west, following a stream whose foaming spume broke against enormous black stones it had polished smooth over the centuries. Eddies formed around invisible troughs, bursting in a silvery mist that vibrated with all the colors of the rainbow. We came across our first patches of snow in the next few hours. The path grew steeper, zigzagging between huge boulders. Our ascent lasted most of the afternoon, and I had to stop frequently to catch my breath.

The flora was changing quickly. Yellow and blue gentian, edelweiss, and juniper replaced the tropical scents. We reached a green plateau crossed by a stream that we had to ford several times by playing tightrope-walkers over tree trunks thrown across its path. At last, we climbed a gentle slope and reached the summit, Prostration Pass, where, as tradition required, we prostrated three times, in reverence and wonder, in the direction of Snow Lion Fortress. Fifty or so prayer flags, attached to long bamboo poles, fluttered in the wind. We then descended into the majestic cirque, a vast bowl surrounded by rock walls crowned with crests of eternal snow. It was in this remote and holy place, in all its untouched splendor, that in the ninth century Padmasambhava meditated while Yeshe Tsogyal, also known as "Victorious Ocean of Wisdom," his heart student and spiritual consort, lived ascetically in a cave lost among the snows, even higher up in the mountains. The cirque forms an almost perfect circle around a plain of heather and pine forests at an altitude of 15,000 feet. A sparkling blue river snakes its way across the expanse. Some two miles away to the right, a little temple sparkled in the sunlight atop a stony spur, a gold nugget against the dark scrim of mountains, built to enshrine Padmasambhava's cave.

The climb had been painful, but now I walked with a light step, buoyed by renewed joy. Every stone, every tree, seemed perfectly present, partaking of a more lively and intense reality. The snow-capped peaks were lined with promontories that bent toward the center of the plain. They looked like recumbent elephants offering their backs to anyone who wished to clamber aboard, or proudly steadfast lions defying the intrepid traveler. The plain itself formed an eight-petaled lotus, and above the white mountain crests the sky was outlined like a *gakyil*, a "wheel of joy." Creeks crisscrossed the meadows and a little turquoise lake rested within, like a cup of ambrosia offered by nature itself. Patches of fog enveloped the slopes and hung from the canopies of tall pines. Crenelated peaks and craggy aretes reached up to the sky, breaking waves turned to stone. The entire landscape was a vision of peace and immutable majesty. I have never, anywhere, had such a clear feeling of being at the "end of the world." Every rock, every cave, every river here has a history going back to the beginning of time. The land is sacred, the sky is sacred. As we walked, from time to time we disturbed mottled pheasants that flew off in a flurry of wings. A scant twenty hermits lived in the cirque. Snow leopards, furtive and rarely visible, haunt the rocky heights.

The sky clouded over from one moment to the next, and it began to snow. We quickly set up our tents, and as we huddled around the wood fire a dozen red silhouettes emerged from the falling snow. These were the valley's retreatants who, having heard the news of Rabjam Rinpoche's arrival, had come to meet him. They sat around him in a circle and asked him for a teaching to establish a spiritual link between them. As Rabjam Rinpoche spoke, the snowflakes accumulated on their clothing until the white of the snow overwhelmed the red of their robes. They then said goodnight and disappeared behind the curtain of snow.

That night, I was flattened by a high fever; luckily, it lasted only one night, but it was a cause of some concern to Rabjam Rinpoche. The next morning, an immaculate blue sky shone over the cirque, and we set off, crossing the meadows that led, within a half hour's walk, to the little temple on the hillside, within which was the opening to Padmasambhava's cave. An altar held some clay statues whose colors had faded, and sacred texts before which offerings had been left. A play of shadow and light was reflected in the patina of the dark wood floorboards. The walls were hung with a few *thangkas*, framed by brocades in discolored patterns. A light scent of pine and juniper wafted through the air, mingled with incense. We recited our prayers and meditated in silence.

An incense offering was prepared on the banks of the little crystalline lake, whose mirrored surface reached almost to the foot of the temple. Juniper branches dipped in lake water were piled onto a wood fire on which sizzling barley flour, butter, honey, and molasses were being cooked. Thick, sweet-smelling whorls rose into the air, in which we were able to visualize countless multicolored flowers, sparkling jewels, delectable foodstuffs of all kinds, perfumes and music filling the skies with offerings to buddhas past, present, and future—gifts without number, all imbued with the desire to ease the suffering of an infinite number of beings and to bring them peace and felicity.

We also hoped to be able to make it up to the Black Lake and the White Lake, at an altitude of more than 16,000 feet, to visit the cave where Yeshe Tsogyal attained the supreme realization of the nature of her mind. But the hermits told us that it would be impossible at this time of the year—the path was covered by more than three feet of snow and the climb was steep.

Having spent two nights and enjoyed all the splendors on offer, we set off on the return journey, our hearts and footsteps buoyed. It's always easier to head downhill, and the way back felt more relaxed—or was it the beneficial effects of that celestial place that gave us wings?

By the time we reached Khorma two days later, the villagers had gotten wind of Rabjam Rinpoche's pilgrimage and came out to ask him for a long-life blessing, which he provided. He then paid a visit to a close student of Dudjom Rinpoche, Lama Namdröl Sangpo, known as Khorma Rinpoche, whom I had met in Nepal and who had lived in a bamboo hermitage above the village for the past ten years. He had asked that Rabjam Rinpoche visit him in his hermitage, and I was able to go along. We spent some spiritually rich and humanly warm moments with that hermit monk, who exuded serenity ripened by many years of practice. At his request, Rabjam Rinpoche offered him a long-life blessing.

After a good night's rest at Lhuentse Dzong, we took the return road to Paro. My heart brimming over from this fruitful pilgrimage, when we reached the tranquility of Rabjam Rinpoche's home in Satsam Chorten, I was inspired to write a little spiritual tale, *The Snow Citadel*, which I completed in the following weeks.[1]

55

PEMAKÖ
THE PLACE SHAPED LIKE A LOTUS

I make a very moving visit to the Indian part of Pemakö, a sacred land where Kangyur Rinpoche lived for four years—the only person in the twentieth century to reach its most inaccessible site, the Yang Sang.

Pemakö is a vast region, covering an area of almost 12,000 square miles, straddling southeastern Tibet and the north of Arunachal Pradesh state, India. Originating at the foot of Mount Kailash, in the far west of Tibet, the Brahmaputra crosses the high plateau and bypasses the eternal snows of Namchak Barwa (24,900 feet), then reaches the sacred land of Pemakö. There, this majestic river becomes a huge torrent that plunges nine thousand feet between the mountains and emerges through tumultuous gorges twelve miles downstream. Not until 1998, following amazing adventures and eight expeditions to this almost impossibly remote region, did three explorers—Ian Baker and Hamid Sardar, who had long lived in Kathmandu and were students of Chatral Rinpoche, and Ken Storm—finally reach the legendary "hidden falls" at the great bend in the Brahmaputra. To get to this mythic place, they had had to blaze a trail through leech-infested forests and negotiate the steep cliffs of the Brahmaputra gorges. Although the falls were known to local inhabitants, the exploit of these three was announced as the last great geographical discovery of the twentieth century.[1]

I had been dreaming for fifty years of being able to go to Pemakö one day, see it with my own eyes, and develop a personal rapport with its spiritual power. Kangyur Rinpoche and his family often spoke of the great blessings of the four years they spent there, from 1956 to 1960, during the final phase of their exile from Tibet into India. A place apart from the world, a "hidden land," a *beyul*—which, in Tibetan, refers to highly sacred places whose powers of benediction are amplified by their remoteness. It is said that some parts of these "hidden lands" are known as "very secret"—*yang sang*—and accessible only to those endowed with profound spiritual realization. Ordinary beings can spend days in their vicinity, searching without finding them and encountering insurmountable obstacles. To those who have the good fortune of discovering and entering them, these lands have great powers to transform—it helps them progress speedily toward enlightenment if they have not already attained it. Pemakö is one such special place.

According to one prophecy, Kangyur Rinpoche's spiritual teacher, Jedrung Rinpoche, was meant to visit the Pemakö *yang sang*. Circumstances did not allow him to fulfill that prediction, however. Kangyur Rinpoche promised him that he would go in his stead, which he did twice, once alone and one with an old attendant. He told his family that the place was imbued with ineffable serenity. Wild animals approached him without fear, and some even died at his side, as if in meditation. Every day, rainbows forged a luminous bridge between earth and sky. On another expedition, Ian Baker and a small group of explorers were able to reach the most sacred site accessible to pilgrims, Dorsem Phodrang—the "Palace of Vajrasattva"—an awe-inspiring monolithic mountain of black rock surrounded by eight lakes, all sacred like the mountain. He had hoped to be able to reach the "very secret" land—the *yang sang*—from there, but Kangyur Rinpoche alone was able to gain entry there in the twentieth century.

Raphaële, who is unstoppable, managed to reach the Tibetan side of Pemakö on her own in 1994. Leaving from Lhasa, she surreptitiously crossed the Kongpo region of southern Tibet in the back of a potato truck. As they approached a checkpoint, her traveling companions hid her in a potato sack. When they reached Pe, the last village before the Doshung La Pass, which leads into Pemakö, she met a short, good-natured man who was making the journey on foot and agreed to let her travel with him. This welcome guide turned out to be fond of the drink, and Raphaële struggled to wake him up in the morning! Even so, she managed to cross the pass and spent ten days in the village of Hami, near which were three caves that had been blessed by Padmasambhava: Marpung, Pema, and Shelri. She was unable to go any farther, however. A few hours away by foot, the Yarlung Tsangpo Grand Canyon—the longest and deepest in the world—could be crossed only by a bridge guarded by the Chinese army. An American hiker who had tried to cross had recently been arrested.

When China established its stranglehold over Tibet in 1959, extending to its very remotest corners, Pemakö was cut in half. The higher part, to the north, now belongs to Chinese Tibet, while the lower section is in the Indian state of Arunachal Pradesh, north of Assam. It was the Indian sector that I had an opportunity to visit in January–February 2020.

Because of its proximity to the Chinese border, the Indian part of Pemakö was long off-limits to foreigners. Even today, you need a permit that is difficult to obtain. I therefore had little hope of seeing my wish granted until one day in 2019, when Rabjam Rinpoche was invited by Khenpo Tsering Dorje, founder of the chief monastery of the region, located in Tuting, the last significant village before the Tibetan border, fifteen miles to the north. My friend, the English monk Sean, was able to accompany Rabjam Rinpoche, but I was on retreat at Namo Buddha at that time and unable to join them. The following year, however, I was overjoyed to be invited in turn, alongside the great eighty-five-year-old scholar Khenchen Pema Sherab, a student of Dilgo Khyentse Rinpoche, for whom I have worked as interpreter for many years at the seminars he leads every year in Dordogne. Khenpo Sonam and two nuns were also members of our group.

Getting to Tuting, a small town in northeastern Arunachal Pradesh, is an adventure in itself: sixteen hours by car from Dibrugarh, the closest airport, the last eight of which in a four-by-four on a bumpy and muddy dirt road. This track, which follows the course of the Brahmaputra, is a succession of ups and downs through great semitropical forests, from which the snowy peaks to the north can already be glimpsed. We reached Tuting after nightfall, and Khenchen Pema Sherab was welcomed by a beautiful procession of monks and locals.

The next morning, as I was going around Tuting Monastery, which houses some precious relics, and wandering about the precinct, I was immediately struck by the very particular atmosphere of the place. It was the very picture of the image of the mythical Shangri-La, the paradise on earth of James Hilton's novel *Lost Horizon*, later adapted for film by Frank Capra. A place set apart from the world, where everything feels simple, peaceful, and harmonious, and where there is nothing to do but no one seems to feel the slightest need to keep busy. A place replete with blessings unchanged since time immemorial, where every atom of earth, water, and air seems to quiver with the presence of timeless wisdom and compassion.

During my stay in Pemakö, I grasped, more than anywhere else, the meaning of the "pure perception" of a place or environment. I felt quite clearly that the only barrier between my mental state and pure vision was the one I set up myself through my habitual tendencies. All I need do was tear down these artificial barriers to perceive the primordial purity of the infinite nature of phenomena, such as it is and has always been. Of course, all I managed to do was draw a little bit closer to such a realization, but more than ever before I had a sense of how it must feel, which filled me with unalloyed bliss and great inner exuberance, as if the solidity of ordinary appearances were melting little by little under the sunlight of this pure vision. Without actually "seeing" anything at all (unlike the great yogis who have had extraordinary visions), I continuously sensed that the land, the forest, and all space teemed with *dakas* and *dakinis*, those male and female beings of wisdom who symbolize and embody the qualities of enlightenment.

To deepen my inspiration, on this trip I undertook to translate a text taught in the twelfth century by the teacher and hermit Gyalwa Göt-sangpa. In 1983, Dilgo Khyentse Rinpoche had asked Sengdrak Rinpoche to give him the oral transmission of Götsangpa's three volumes of writings, and I was fortunate to receive it on the same occasion. The following instructions are to be found in the text:

Since the body, speech and mind
Of all sentient beings
Are of one taste with the enlightened body, speech and mind of the teacher,
Within the continuum of ultimate truth,

I take refuge respectfully.
In the beings of the six realms who are naturally the teacher

The minds of all sentient beings
Are luminous yet ungraspable.
Their own awareness, great bliss, free of concepts,
Is the buddha nature.
I respectfully take refuge
In the beings of the six realms, in the luminous absolute dimension.

Earth, water, fire, wind, and space
Are the five female deities of the five buddha families.
In those elements, endowed with the nature of female deities,
I respectfully take refuge.

In the morning, I visualized all the space above Pemakö suffused with a golden light, at the center of which was my root teacher, Kangyur Rinpoche, surrounded by rainbow haloes and a cloud of *dakas*, *dakinis*, deities of wisdom, and spiritual masters of the past. While I have little gift for visualization, I managed to maintain this one clearly all morning, in a state of profound joy.

Even if Kangyur Rinpoche was no longer present in his physical body, he was everywhere. My teacher assumed a thousand different forms to reveal his presence in all things. Sounds, the whisper of the wind, the babbling of streams, birdcall—they all rang with the teacher's voice. Even the deep silence of the night was saturated with his presence. The teacher's mind gleamed behind each thought.

We spent our first dozen days in Tuting in a house immediately adjacent to the monastery. This was the season of the Pemakö New Year, which takes place a month before the Tibetan New Year, even though the cycle of major annual holidays is based on the same lunar calendar. We joined in the various celebrations—offering ceremonies in the temple and sacred and popular dances in the monastery courtyard, all unfolding in a festive and congenial atmosphere.

We also went to several pilgrimage sites in the vicinity of Tuting. One of the most astonishing was two dark boulders in the shape of eagles, considered to be male and female *garuda*, a mythical bird that symbolizes the teachings of the Great Perfection because it hatches from the egg ready to fly, just as the Great Perfection leads directly to enlightenment. We went to another pilgrimage site on the banks of the Brahmaputra, where there is an impressive formation of dark boulders in all shapes and sizes, dotted with water basins containing vermillion and bright orange puddles of mud. This sacred place is dedicated to the Eight Herukas, deities symbolizing the enlightened aspects of the body, speech, mind, spiritual qualities, and beneficent activities of the buddhas.

For the rest of the day, alongside Khenchen Pema Sherab, we performed many circumambulations of the nine stupas set out in a circle, commemorating the nine major events of the Buddha's life, in a large field where novice monks and village children were at play, between the monastery and the slope down to the Brahmaputra. The calm that reigned over that place felt immutable.

The time came to leave on a pilgrimage to the most sacred Indian sites in Pemakö, not including those in Tibet, located in a valley a five-hour drive from Tuting. But what a drive! We could only cling tightly to the Indian four-by-four handgrips as we were tossed in every direction by the jolting vehicle. The road was mostly one long quagmire in which we found ourselves repeatedly bogged down. Luckily, we were traveling in two cars, so one was always available to haul the other out of trouble.

When we reached Yoldong, a little hamlet of few houses, we were suddenly greeted by the sight of the lush valley that is home to several sacred places, including Devikota, the largest among them. On the slope of the pass that overlooks the landscape, a young lama had built a little temple and a cluster of hermitages in which we sheltered for the night. At dawn, the rays of the rising sun played among the clouds floating above the valley. Through this silvery mist, we caught a glimpse of the snow-capped peaks that mark the border with Tibet: Pema Shelri, "Lotus Crystal," home of the buddha of infinite light; Amitabha, symbol of the *dharmakaya*, the absolute body; Riwo Tala, also known by the mythical name of Potala, rising in the Pure Land of the buddha of compassion, Avalokiteshvara, the *sambhogakaya*, the subtle body; and Cittapuri, "Heart-Mind Fortress," the palace of Guru Padmasambhava, the *nirmanakaya*, the emanation body.

These mountains, interspersed with lakes, are also pilgrimage sites. No one lives on them because they are too high, and while they can be climbed in about two weeks of hiking in the summer, the snow makes them inaccessible in the winter. Beyond these mountains, some twenty miles away as the crow flies, lies Tibet. Between Devikota and the mountains, the valley is dotted with other places of meditation, such as Tashi Chöling and Pema Drepung.

We walked down from Yoldong through the little village of Munkotra. We crossed the "Secret River" (Yang Sang Chu), which flows from sacred mountains, on a bamboo bridge that gave us the cold sweats. It took a certain sangfroid to cross the bridge, which is a "bridge" in name only—three bamboo poles, rotten in certain places, lashed together and flanked by two thin rails to help you maintain a precarious balance above the turbulent waters of the torrent roaring barely three feet below.

At the top of the hill on the far side of the bridge was a temple big enough to hold about a hundred people. It was there that, at the age of seventeen, circa 1921, Dudjom Rinpoche conferred for the first time the sixty volumes of *The Treasury of Precious Termas*, the *Rinchen Terdzö*, which he bestowed no fewer than ten times in his life. The memory of Dudjom Rinpoche, a teacher from whom I had the privilege of receiving many teachings, in Nepal and in France, where he passed away, is omnipresent in Pemakö a century later. He was the most influential teacher in the region, as well as regent for several years, as the government in Lhasa was unable to administer every far-flung province of Tibet.

The memory of Kangyur Rinpoche's four-year sojourn in Pemakö in the late 1950s is also very much alive in the minds of the older inhabitants. Two of them, respectively eighty-one and eighty-two years old, had helped Kangyur Rinpoche transport the precious treasures he had saved from Tibet (mostly books) from Rinchenpong, in the Tibetan part of Pemakö, to the Indian zone. I was deeply moved to hear them share their memories of my teacher. In accordance with a prophecy he had received in a vision, Kangyur Rinpoche had considered settling in a place called Pema Pong, "The Lotus Heap," farther north up the valley from Devikota. If he had, I would no doubt have led a very different life and would not now be compiling my *Notebooks of a Wandering Monk*. But a testy local official obstructed the fulfilment of this wish, and Kangyur Rinpoche decided to proceed to India, first to Assam and then to Darjeeling, where I met him.

Pemakö is populated by Bhutanese and Tibetans, most of them from Kham, who have preserved their identity and customs, including their dress. Even so, most inhabitants (some 60 percent) belong to the Lhopa people, whose villages of houses built on stilts made of wood or braided bamboo fibers dot the forest. The interiors of their dwellings, fitted with very small windows and without electricity, are dark. The family gathers around a fire that burns continuously at the center of the single, large room. Other than this spacious living area, the house has only one entrance, a sort of veranda, and one or two tiny rooms for storing goods and provisions.

Most inhabitants of Pemakö lead a simple life and provide for their own needs. They cultivate the land but do not sell the fruits of their harvest, mostly rice and a few varieties of vegetable. If they have a rice surplus, they set it aside for the following year in little wooden sheds on stilts, well protected from rodents, and donate a portion as offerings to neighboring monasteries during the seasonal ceremonies.

One monk, who grew up in Munkotra before leaving to study at a monastery in southern India, told me that, when he was a child, they also gave food surpluses to the fish of the river that flows by the village. No one engaged in trade and the villagers coveted no possessions. The only things they bought in the little town of Tuting, located a long day's walk from Munkotra even via shortcuts, was fuel for the kerosene lamps they used at night, matches, and some clothing. To make these modest purchases, they used the little money they earned by selling livestock and wood. The children at the little school studied by the feeble light shed by these lamps. The household fire was lit with a flint and oakum. Most of the villagers had no shoes. The monk who described the inhabitants' day-to-day lives in his childhood got his first pair at the age of fifteen. The calluses that formed on the soles of their feet protected them from the rough soil and thorny plants. The monk added that the Lhopas, who would spend several days at a time hunting in the dense primordial forests that blanket the mountainsides, complained that they had trouble getting around in shoes, which they found more slippery than their bare feet. Even today, when the Lhopas go hunting for several days, they sleep in the forest without shelter or blankets.

Any family that cleared a small patch of land and cultivated it became its de facto owner. To this day, there are no property deeds for the land located around a village. The tribal peoples also shared various sections of the teeming streams and rivers where they fished. A couple generally had between five and eight children who, as soon as they were old enough, helped in the fieldwork, which was all done by hand, the slopes being too steep to be worked by plough animals. Everyone went to bed early at night. The only entertainment was village feasts and religious ceremonies.

Nowadays, the monks added with a hint of nostalgia, much of this land is no longer cultivated and people often go back and forth to the plains to engage in trade. To a foreign observer, however, these changes seem minimal. There may be a few solar panels to generate electricity, but there is neither telephone service nor stores, and the windy, muddy, and rocky trail from Tuting to Yoldong requires almost five hours in a four-by-four to cover a distance of thirty miles. The Lhopas still live in near self-sufficiency, almost entirely cut off from the world. But the city is closing in—a road is being built.

The young monk's words reminded me of my 2012 stay at Shey Monastery in Nepal, in the high Dolpo region, some 14,000 feet above sea level, near the Crystal Mountain (Shelri). Rabjam Rinpoche had been invited as guest of honor to a festival celebrated there every twelve years in the Year of the Dragon. On that occasion, more than a thousand mountain-dwellers, who had walked between three and fifteen days from the surrounding districts, converged on Shey, which usually has fewer than a hundred inhabitants. One of the villagers who had come out to greet Rabjam Rinpoche happened to mention that money was of no use to them at Shey—the landscape was vast and the land free; yaks reproduced every year, so there was no need to buy any; there was no road, so no need to buy a car; and there was no electricity, so no point in owning a television or other electric appliances.

Following this charming pilgrimage, on our return to Tuting, at the request of village communities that wished to host Khenchen Pema Sherab, we stopped off at a few little temples in the north. In the last village, the motor road ended a twenty-minute walk from a low pass where a stupa marked the border with Tibet, strictly guarded by the Chinese army. No one and nothing gets by. A few Lhopas, who wander for days on end, heedless of borders, during their hunting expeditions, probably cross back and forth undetected, hidden in the almost impenetrable forests known to them alone.

At the end of three weeks, we regretfully left this most marvelous of places for the plains of India.

In this late phase of my life, discovering Pemakö gave me a deep sense of completeness. I had finally seen the place that Kangyur Rinpoche had told me so much about, and been able to immerse myself in an almost palpable way in the spiritual power of his timeless presence.

56

HERMITAGE OF THE MORNING CALM

My precious hermitage at Namo Buddha, Nepal, built on a site chosen by my teacher Dilgo Khyentse Rinpoche, who, when he first saw it, wrote to someone, "How good it would be to end my days in such a place!" It has been my preferred home since the year 2000, providing me upon awakening every morning with a 120-mile view of the Himalayas.

In 1969, Dilgo Khyentse Rinpoche went on pilgrimage to Namo Buddha, Nepal, where, it's said, in a past life the Buddha offered his body to a tigress and her starving cubs. From that vantage point, Khyentse Rinpoche saw the site on a neighboring hill where, twenty-five years later, Pema Osel Ling, "Lotus Land of Clear Light," was built as the retreat center of Shechen Monastery, where I have my hermitage. Back in Kathmandu, he wrote to a spiritual friend, "How good it would be to end my days in such a place!" Whenever I stay at my hermitage, the memory of that letter strengthens my conviction that this place, blessed by my teachers, is very well suited to spiritual practice.

At Namo Buddha, the stars are still visible when the first glimmer of dawn appears. The Himalayas are silhouetted against a bluish-gray sky. The mountains turn a crimson pink; then comes the magic moment when the first peak, more than 26,000 feet high, hooks the rays of the rising sun and bursts into orange flame. The entire chain is soon ablaze, and then the raking light illuminates the sea of clouds spread out at the foot of the mountains, covering the valleys, which will remain deep in fog for the next hour.

It's the dawn of a tranquil morning.

From the terrace of my hermitage, I embrace the majesty of the Himalayas, which extend before my eyes for more than 120 miles. The immensity and ever-changing beauty of this sublime landscape pervade the mind like a nectar. The silence is so complete that I can identify the least sound—the voices of Nepalese peasants several hundred yards away on the opposite hillside, a crow rehearsing his repertory of caws at the top of a tree, the distant response of a fellow crow not wishing to be outdone, and, during the summer monsoon, the patter of rain falling on trees and ground that slowly gathers in intensity as a rainstorm approaches.

A setting like this strengthens your ability to observe the thoughts that arise from emptiness and dissolve back into it, like the sound of a bell that fades into the silence from which it emerged.

How can I describe the very particular sense of fulfillment I feel in my hermitage? Upon my arrival, I need only a few moments to set aside all the preoccupations encumbering my mind. I take a cold shower in the little water closet outside the single ten-by-ten-foot room of my hermitage, as if to get a fresh start after having escaped the pollution of the city. I make myself a strong cup of tea and sit on my balcony, which offers a view of the valleys and mountains that seems to go on forever. I stay there, thinking nothing in particular, breathing in the pure air and allowing my gaze to melt into the immensity of space and land beyond the bluish veil that blurs the boundary between sky and earth. I allow my mind to rest in limpid simplicity, in the calm of the natural state that clearly emerges when the mind is no longer clouded by incessant mental fabrications. I savor a delicious freedom that I would exchange for nothing in the world. Feeling close to all those I love without the imperious need to be in their presence, I am satisfied without having to fire up the engines of some imaginary paradise. What more could anyone wish for? Everything is here, there are no complications, nothing to lose or to gain.

There is nothing I need, nothing I miss. This motionless journey excites and fulfills me far more than any expedition to the sources of the Orinoco or the summit of Kilimanjaro. Inner freedom and the joy of nourishing devotion to one's spiritual teacher, of resting in the mind's natural state and of cultivating altruistic love for all beings are more precious than any possession.

When we contemplate the mind's natural simplicity, naked, crystal-clear, free of all artifice, it seems almost perverse that at other moments we have been prey to animosity, obsession, and all other opaque and troubled mental states. Forgetting this pure awareness, losing sight of the fact that all our thoughts and perceptions are manifestations of that presence, is a kind of fundamental ignorance; the moment our judgment and fixations reify those manifestations, they create a veil that conceals the mind's basic nature, pure awareness free of concepts.

When we feel a moment of perfect wholeness, it encompasses everything we could possibly wish for. The very notion of desire or want evaporates.

When we withdraw into such serene solitude, external silence opens inner doors. The purity of the present moment dominates the flow of time and suffuses the heart with salutary qualities. Outer peace and inner peace become one.

For a meditator who is able to maintain her inner freedom in all situations and is never distracted from her understanding of the nature of her own mind, it makes little difference whether she dwells in the solitude of a Himalayan hermitage or is stuck in a Parisian traffic jam. But until we have attained a minimal level of stability in our practice, we will be unable to maintain the same state of mind in a Parisian traffic jam as we could in a place where everything around us nurtures inner peace. It is therefore helpful to seize every possible advantage when choosing a place conducive to contemplation. Our initial state of weakness precludes us from resorting to unfavorable conditions as catalysts of spiritual progress. It behooves us to take the time to cultivate our inner resources in circumstances that will further our training.

Many texts describe in detail the characteristics of places conducive to spiritual practice and of those that hamper it. It's important to avoid places that could strengthen our mental toxins, disturb our mind, and muddle our discernment. That includes social and family settings, which are sources of endless tension and distraction. If possible, we should choose a site blessed by teachers of the past and the present, where we will have little trouble procuring provisions and a few elements essential to a prolonged stay (such as fresh water), a place with no hazards and that is accessible to those who may occasionally come to offer guidance to retreatants.

The texts also identify the characteristics of places conducive to specific practices. When meditation is focused on peaceful abiding—*shamatha*—we should seek out forests or some other sheltered and remote place. To cultivate deeper insight—*vipassana*—which apprehends the ultimate nature of things, and to meditate on awareness, a practice centered on the luminous, yet empty aspect of the mind, we should choose an elevated space overlooking broad landscapes, with an unobstructed view of the sky. If we are training to master strong emotions, we should seek out rugged terrain, gorges and ravines traversed by powerful watercourses and busy with wild animals. In Tibet, practitioners wishing to cut off the ego at its roots go to meditate in open-air cemeteries in the mountains, special places where the bodies of the dead are left out for the vultures. We need to use our judgment in choosing the *place that is most conducive* to the particular spiritual practice undertaken at any given moment.

As to the specific characteristics of a good site to build a retreat center or monastery, ideally it should be built facing south, open to an unobstructed view, and east to welcome the rising sun. The location must include a gentle elevation to the west and a higher mountain to the north. In a valley dotted with low-lying hills forming a kind of string of heaps of gems, it is useful to have a river flowing east to west. Contrarily, it is not advisable to be facing a rampart of mountains with a summit rising behind them like a menacing tooth.

Furthermore, it is especially inspiring to undertake a retreat in a place where spiritually accomplished beings have lived and meditated. It is said that one month of meditation in such a place will generate more progress than a year of retreat in an ordinary place. There are several reasons for this. Thinking of and immersing oneself in the lives of great sages in the very places where they have lived is a source of inspiration that imparts special intensity and clarity to meditation. The holy site also reminds us of the tireless resolve demonstrated by these sages in pursuing the path of enlightenment and of the qualities they cultivated.

Their invisible presence suffuses your meditation sessions, the interludes between them, your rest, your mealtimes, and all other activities.

In 2006, I spent an entire year in retreat in my hermitage. The retreat was, however, interrupted for a few weeks when I went to France to be with my father as he lay dying in the Kremlin-Bicêtre Hospital. I was able to spend the last fifteen days of his life at his side. He was calm and serene, which was not his dominant trait, and effusively thanked all those taking care of him. My sister Ève, my brother Nicolas, my stepmother Claude Sarraute and her other children, Martin and Laurent, came to see him regularly. They had their professional responsibilities to attend to, however. Having traveled all this way to be with him, I spent the larger part of every day at his bedside. On his last days, I was there night and day. The deeply caring nurses allowed me to sleep in his room on a foam mattress on the floor. In the morning, I would go take a shower and breakfast at the home of my philosopher friend Michel Bitbol, who lived across from the hospital. Tulku Pema Wangyal also came to see him. My father greeted him politely. Pema Tulku Wangyal had given me a *yantra*, a diagram made of mantras written to ease the passage of the consciousness in the *bardo*, the intermediate stage following death, which I slipped into the pocket of his pajamas. The nurse noticed the folded slip of paper and asked me if it was a "love letter" for my father. I nodded with a smile. One morning, my father informed me, "I think I'm going to die," adding shortly afterward, "We're on a boat to Argentina, aren't we?" The nurses told me that the dying often evoke the theme of a journey. A very long journey indeed. One morning, his blood pressure dropped precipitously. He more or less sank into unconsciousness. His nurses advised me to call in the family, which I did. My mother Yahne, his first wife, came too, whispering a few sweet nothings into his ear. My father lived another four days. One nurse quipped, "Yes, these older models just keep on running!" I did my best to make my father's final days as comfortable as possible.

A little after midnight on Saturday, April 29, 2006, as I lay on my mattress on the floor, having barely slept for the past two days, I suddenly awoke and realized that the room was abnormally quiet. My father had stopped breathing. The nurses would not be doing their rounds until 3 a.m., and once the death had been confirmed they would have to attend to the body immediately. I took advantage of the delay to spend a peaceful half hour in the dark, praying and practicing with all my heart in communion with him. I then called the family. They came quickly and we all spent a few moments together around my father's deathbed. After noting that his face was handsome and calm, Claude—who a few days earlier had forcefully informed me that "Of course, there's nothing after death"—asked me, "Where do you think he is right now?" I refrained from hypothesizing. My sister kissed his forehead.

Tulku Pema Wangyal had told me that it would be good to let the corpse lie for twenty-four hours, with as little touching as possible, which is hardly standard procedure in hospitals. After these few family moments with my father, the nurses asked us to let them take charge of the body. But then one of them clarified: "Tomorrow is Sunday and May 1 [a public holiday in France], so we won't touch the body. We'll just put it into refrigeration until Monday." Tulku Pema Wangyal's advice was thus heeded without my having to do a thing.

The news was announced on Sunday morning. That night, we all gathered at my brother Nicolas's place. On the eight o'clock news, the first item was, "The philosopher Jean-François Revel has died. With him we have lost what may have been the last of the independent thinkers. He will be remembered principally for his book of dialogue, *The Monk and the Philosopher*, with his son, the Buddhist monk Matthieu Ricard." They then ran a few photos of our encounter. I kept my thoughts to myself, because Claude believed that my father had done *The Monk and the Philosopher* just to please me and that the book was just a "bump in the road" of his career.

My father was buried in the Père Lachaise Cemetery. Claude chose a sun-drenched plot and Olivier Todd gave a moving eulogy. My sister goes regularly to leave flowers on his grave. My father had lived his life to the full and died without too much suffering; I had been able to get there in time and we had all enfolded him in our affection. I was able to say my farewells with an untroubled mind. Aware of the impermanence of all things and the fragility of life, I never felt as if I went through a period of mourning, strictly speaking. My feeling was, instead, one of gratitude—it was he who had given me life. At his deathbed, I had suggested to my sister Ève and my brother Nicolas that the best way to pay tribute to my father was not to indulge in sorrow, but to do beautiful things in the time remaining to us.

A few days after my father's death, I briefly traveled to Belgium to interpret for the Dalai Lama, who also advised me again to focus my practice on compassion, and I returned to my retreat in my hermitage in Nepal for the rest of the year, which proved to be blissful from start to finish. I enjoyed every moment of practice with unalloyed delight, and the idea of having months of meditation before me filled me with simple joy, like a peasant who is offered a fertile field to cultivate.

I had few "signs" of accomplishment such as those described in the texts, other than that of "experiencing extreme joy in spiritual practice and feeling light, physically and mentally, as if learning to fly." It was a time of unparalleled riches.

In the course of time, a few little dwellings had been built not far from mine, so I had another, more remote hermitage built in a tranquil setting, and also smaller (eight by ten feet inside, but with an open balcony), on a slope overlooking a pine forest where few people passed by other than the occasional villager collecting dead wood. Ever since, that is where I go whenever I am lucky enough to be on retreat. It's a place endowed with every condition conducive to practice.

I am sometimes asked if I ever get bored in my hermitage. I have never experienced such a state of mind—quite the contrary. Unlike ordinary times and activities, which can often be insipid, when you are fully committed to a spiritual practice that external distractions can neither disturb nor interrupt, time assumes an entirely different value. Every moment is like a drop of pure gold that, as the hours pass, becomes a golden river that flows slowly through the valley of time, a healing elixir that nourishes every fiber of your being in bountiful solitude.

The solitude of the meditator is unlike the loneliness suffered by those living amid the multitudes, such as in a big city. Questioned by researchers, about one in five Americans admitted that they had experienced a deep sense of loneliness during the two weeks preceding the survey.[1]

They felt cut off from others, unseen, and said that they had no one to confide in or ask for help. Such social isolation is the source of many ills, physical and mental.

By contrast, those who benefit from rich and friendly social ties enjoy better mental health and a more efficient immune system; they are less reliant on various dependencies (tobacco, alcohol, drugs); they suffer less from heart disease and senile dementia; and, ultimately, they live longer on average.

At the same time, there is another way of being alone, the soothing experience of wide-open spaces that strengthens the sense of communion with nature and all beings. Such solitude is, in fact, deeply fulfilling. It is also the hermit's free choice of temporary isolation that allows her to deepen her spiritual practice without distraction. Far from cutting us off from the world, it becomes a powerful means of opening oneself to others, to becoming aware of the interdependence of all things, and to generating boundless love for all beings.

Even more, the very idea of solitude becomes meaningless when our mind melts into the ultimate dimension that encompasses everything—the infinite multiplicity of phenomena and of all beings, no matter how many they may be. Can we label as "solitude" an inner state in which there is no notion of "separation"? In this solitary practice, free of all hindrances, we become one with every singing bird, with the branches swaying in the breeze, with the grass and the sky, with every atom in the universe, and with the silence and murmurs that fill it. A very simple, joyful, and serene state of union. A retreat in a solitary place gives us the time and space to understand that authentic happiness is a state of lasting plenitude.

How does a retreatant's typical day of unfold? She rises long before dawn. Upon awakening, she chants a melodious song invoking her spiritual teacher:

Primordially pure space of the ultimate dimension,
Oh, benevolent teacher, turn your mind to me! [. . .]
Far from my native land, severing the attachment to the self at the heart of absolute nature,
May I soon attain Buddhahood.

In this way, she draws from within a deep fervor that often brings tears to her eyes. She then rekindles her diligence by thinking of the impermanence of all things, the fragility of human life, and the need to give it meaning. There are billions of living people, but how many of them even take account of the value of their existence? And of those who engage in practice, how many persevere and attain enlightenment? The latter are as few as the stars at dawn. The meditator then reflects on the importance of the laws of causality—what needs to be done and to be avoided to mitigate suffering—and on the imperfections of samsara, the round of existence. She then devotes herself to the various stages of preliminaries that I have already described: taking refuge, the altruistic vow to attain enlightenment for the sake of beings (*bodhicitta*), purification through meditation on Vajrasattva, the offering of the universe mandala and Guru Yoga, union with the mind of the teacher. These practices are repeated until the mind is deeply impregnated with them.

The meditator then begins her daily practices, based on the main teachings and transmissions she has received. Now, she sets out on the core practice on which, on the advice of her spiritual guide, she will focus during the days, weeks, or months of her retreat. When she has finished, she dedicates the benefits of her meditation to all beings.

Now it's time for breakfast. In my case, that's a cup of tea and a bowl of Nepali muesli or *tsampa* on my hermitage balcony. This basic platform without rails overhangs a steep slope, at the foot of which extends a pine forest ridged with misty glens and, in the distance, magnificent snow-capped mountains.

In the morning, in accordance with the instructions issued for each retreat, I generally devote myself to visualizing deities symbolizing various aspects of enlightenment and to reciting mantras. This teaches me how to develop a pure vision of the phenomenal world and of beings. Each form becomes a deity, each sound a mantra, and each thought a reflection of wisdom.

After the midday meal, I read inspiring texts and sometimes write a little or push ahead with a translation under way. The retreat center was connected to a power line a few years ago, but blackouts are frequent, sometimes lasting for hours, which requires me to adapt to the whims of technology. After that, I devote myself to observing the nature of mind—that is, clear and luminous awareness—that emerges once the fog of discursive thought dissipates and evaporates into the sky of simplicity. As night falls, I say prayers for the well-being of all beings, then fall asleep uniting my mind with that of Kangyur Rinpoche and Dilgo Khyentse Rinpoche, who are one at the ultimate level. The latter wrote,

Thus, little by little with the passing days and months, your mind will become clearer and more stable. It will no longer be carried away on the waves of unwholesome thoughts that undermine your inner peace. It will be free of the flow of mental constructs that impel us, helpless, towards greed, hatred, and suffering.

One day, I sat and watched a butterfly perched on a flower bobbing in the breeze. It foraged for pollen and then, for no apparent reason, flew off, flitting here and there, only to return, fluttering its lovely blue wings over the orange pistil. This cycle, repeated several times, reminded me of the instructions on how to stabilize the mind: "When you notice that you have been distracted by new thoughts, return again and again to your object of focus. If your mind grows tired and your concentration lax, let it simply rest in its natural state, maintaining that inner freedom, without encouraging thoughts or trying to suppress them. Observe the very nature of your mind. Does it have a shape, color, location? Finding nothing, remain at ease, relaxed, in that "unfound." Allow your thoughts to break down as they form, like a drawing traced with your finger on the surface of the water."[2]

I am no kind of poet, but one day I wrote these lines about my wandering mind:

Tired of struggling with my thoughts, I asked them:
"Can't you leave me alone?"
Like a gang of cheeky kids
They burst out laughing.
I tried to run away,
But they followed, taunting me even more.

Exhausted, I sat on a hillside.
"Will I ever get away from them?"
I thoughtfully gazed at the sky.
Suddenly I had an idea:
"I just have to become invisible,
Like a little sliver of sky!"

As I gazed into space, my mind
Gradually began to melt into it.
"That did it!" I thought,
And laughed and laughed at the idea of my forlorn thoughts.
But I soon stopped laughing
Because "I" was no longer there.

When I look back at the years I spent in retreat in Darjeeling, and later at Namo Buddha, each represented a stage of maturation and of deepening compassion and understanding of the nature of mind. When I lived in Darjeeling, after Kangyur Rinpoche's death in 1975, I spent four years in my hermitage above the monastery, some in periods of strict retreat, seeing only Pema Wangyal Rinpoche to receive instruction. Then, beginning in 1979, I had the privilege of living with Dilgo Khyentse Rinpoche for thirteen years. When his time came to leave this world, in 1991, I returned regularly to my hermitage in Namo Buddha, Nepal, where I spent all of 2006. I spent a total of five years in solitary retreat in Darjeeling and Namo Buddha, which were hands down among the most fruitful of my life.

In 2014, I returned to Orgyen Kunzang Chökhorling, in Darjeeling. I spent a long, emotional moment in Kangyur Rinpoche's room. I also revisited my hermitage, forty-two years after its construction. The wood had darkened considerably, and the balcony had been enclosed to enlarge the tiny room. Three young monks lived there. They appeared to take me for a madman when I told them I had spent seven years living there.

I recall a BBC interview in which I was asked what contribution the hermit makes to society. Isn't it fundamentally selfish? But how can you accuse a practice of being selfish when one of its primary goals is to eliminate selfishness? Selfish concerns reign all too often over our lives. Attempting to eradicate them is clearly an altruistic undertaking. You may favor action over contemplation, but if that action is steeped in selfishness, it's a good bet that it will generate little good to anyone. As one Buddhist saying goes, "Whatever is not done for the good of beings does not deserve to be undertaken."

The hermit is no way indifferent to the fate of humankind, but she clearly understands that, in her current condition, not only is she incapable of accomplishing the well-being of others, but she is just as powerless to rid herself of her own suffering. If she chooses to live apart for a time, it is to deepen her practice and devote the years necessary to cultivate the inner resources that will allow her to contribute in an enlightened manner to the well-being of others. The wounded stag hides in the forest until he recovers, then returns to capering over hill and dale. The hermit is like a doctor who, well aware that he can't perform emergency surgery in the street, commits to building a hospital that will care for countless patients more effectively, even if, in the meantime, the masonry and plumbing work will heal no one.

One of the great lessons I have learned from my years spent, on the one hand, on retreat in mountain hermitages, meditating and contemplating untamed nature and, on the other, immersed in the chaos of modern life, is that of simplicity.

As I sat on my hermitage balcony one day, I had this thought: "If a fairy offered me three wishes of a purely material nature, what could I possibly ask for?" Given the size of my hermitage, my options were limited: no room for a stereo system, or even a tabletop computer. I have an altar on which I keep some statues, about twenty books, a few scraps of clothing, and some useful tools. After a while, I burst out laughing. I could think of nothing that would be of any use to me and that would not simply get in the way, so I came up with a mantra that brings me a great sense of relief when I chant it a dozen times: "I need nothing! I need nothing! I need nothing!" Long live blissful simplicity!

I love these words by Henry David Thoreau: "Simplify! Simplify! Simplify!"[3] Simplifying our thoughts, simplifying our words, and simplifying our actions does not diminish our creativity or restrict our lives; it is the intense appreciation of the unparalleled serenity of a mind at rest in its natural state. It is to set down the long-borne burden of the artificial and distorted constructions that ceaselessly fester in our mind, disturb it, spin it around and around, fragment it, squeeze it, shackle it—in a word, torment it.

Simplicity is allowing our thoughts to rest in the nature of mind, like leaves that break free of the tree and fall naturally to earth; it is the sun rising above the sea of clouds; it is the mirror of a lake of transparent waters; it is the crisp, pure mountain air; it is the gaze that melts into a cloudless sky or sweeps to a distant chain of wooded hills; it is the inner eye that rests on the pristine nature of the mind.

I have no desire other than to be able to die in my Namo Buddha hermitage or some other, similar place in Tibet or elsewhere, and to retain until my final breath the lucidity necessary to unite my mind with that of my root teacher Kangyur Rinpoche, which is one with that of Khyentse Rinpoche, and to rest in the immutable simplicity of the nature of mind, in accordance with the latter's guidance:

Even if death should strike today like a lightning bolt, be prepared to die without sorrow or regret, without the least attachment to what you leave behind. Resting in your recognition of the ultimate vision, leave this life like an eagle flying away into the blue.

EPILOGUE

As these recollections come to a close, two themes strike me as especially salient.

First, on the personal side, my life since I was twenty has been inspired by the wisdom and kindness of my spiritual masters and their teachings. They have guided my path, and while I may be a poor walker, each step has been lighter than the one before, and always joyful, rewarding all my efforts. The unfathomable depth of these teachings and of Buddhist philosophy continues to spur my boundless admiration and wonder.

Second, on the general level of ideas, having pondered this issue my entire life, I have come to the conclusion that altruism is the most essential concept for contributing to the good of human beings and the eight million species with which we share the planet, today and in the future.

"Nothing is more powerful than an idea whose time has come," wrote Victor Hugo. Now more than ever, altruism seems to me to be that force for change.

Altruism, taking care of others, should not be dismissed as a utopian theory espoused by a few soft-hearted naïfs. If these were just the rantings of a monk from his Himalayan hermitage, the idea would be of little importance. But this idea has been gaining ground for the past twenty years in many schools of thought, from psychology to the evolutionary sciences, not to mention the realms of social entrepreneurs and environmental experts. The need to foment cooperation, solidarity, fraternity, respect for the other, consideration for other species and future generations encourages me to contribute to the spread of this mutation in our societies. The changes may be slower than we would like, but they are under way, and I am happy to be an enthusiastic participant in this vast movement, which reminds me of the first flowers of spring: one flower blooms, then two, then four, and soon the meadow is carpeted with blossoms of many colors.

Now, having shared the ideas that are most dear to me and translated the Tibetan texts that have most inspired me, I feel as if the time has come to focus on the spiritual path—the very reason that induced me to leave for India at the age of twenty. If it were up to me, I would prefer to die in my hermitage, my mind clear and serene, rather than in an airport.

I picture with joy the days, months, or years that I may have left to immerse myself in spiritual practice, accompanied by my teachers, who are alive in my mind. I can always rely on the inspiration of this prayer by Gyalse Ngulchu Thogme, author of the *Thirty-Seven Practices of a Bodhisattva*, which allows us to expand the space of our equanimity:

If I remain in good health,
I will use my strength to devote myself to spiritual practice.
If I fall sick,
I will use my affliction to increase my compassion for those who suffer.
If I live long,
I will use every moment to do good for others and for myself.
If my life comes to its end,
I will die as best I can so as to be reborn auspiciously in search of enlightenment.

I still have the greater part of the path to freedom and enlightenment ahead of me, but the distance I have come so far reassures me that it is possible to transform oneself and eventually reach it. Indeed, my modest progress has already led me from the state of cranky teenager—a "little jerk," as my friend Dédé likes to say—to that of elderly monk who delights in every moment spent on the path to liberation.

I have sometimes hurt those I have met, through ineptitude, negligence, or, worse yet, under the influence of lack of kindness, or of irritation or attachment. That would not have occurred if I had been sufficiently attentive to and concerned for their well-being. I apologize from the bottom of my heart to all of them, and vow to humbly contribute to the good of others in this life and all those to come. I have no excuse other than my own delusion. May it one day be fully dispelled!

My last one-way ticket. In a few months, a few years perhaps—who knows?

A few snowflakes swirl 12,000 feet above sea level. Shechen Monastery, in Tibet, rises in tiers up a green hillside. The eye is drawn higher up the slope to the little hermitage where Shechen Gyaltsap, Dilgo Khyentse Rinpoche's teacher, lived and meditated. After a half hour's steep climb, I reach the retreat center, a hundred yards below the hermitage.

With a broad, toothless grin, an old monk welcomes me with the standard greeting: "Welcome! Glad to see you back home. May you live a hundred years!"

As long as space remains,
As long as sentient beings remain,
Until then, may I too remain
To dispel the miseries of the world.

Shantideva, *A Guide to the Bodhisattva's Way of Life*

XINJANG
LADAKH
Srinagar
JAMMU AND KASHMIR
Pathankot
Dharamsala
LAHORE
Indus
NGARI
TIBET
Sutlej
Tsaparang
Mount Kailash
HIMACHAL
PRADESH
Lake Manasarovar
PENDJAB
Dehra Dun
Haridwar
UTTARAKHAND
Karnali
Yarlung Tsangpo (Brahmaputra)
Dolpo
Sakya
NEW DELHI
NEPAL
Ganges
Nyalam
Thangboche
UTTAR
PRADESH
KATHMANDU
Mount Everest
Yamuna
Lumbini
Namo Buddha
SIKKIM
Jaipur
Ghaghara
Gandaki
Darjeeling
Maratika
Gomti
BIHAR
Ganges
Varanasi
Patna
Bodh Gaya
INDIA
JHARKHAND
N
100
400 km

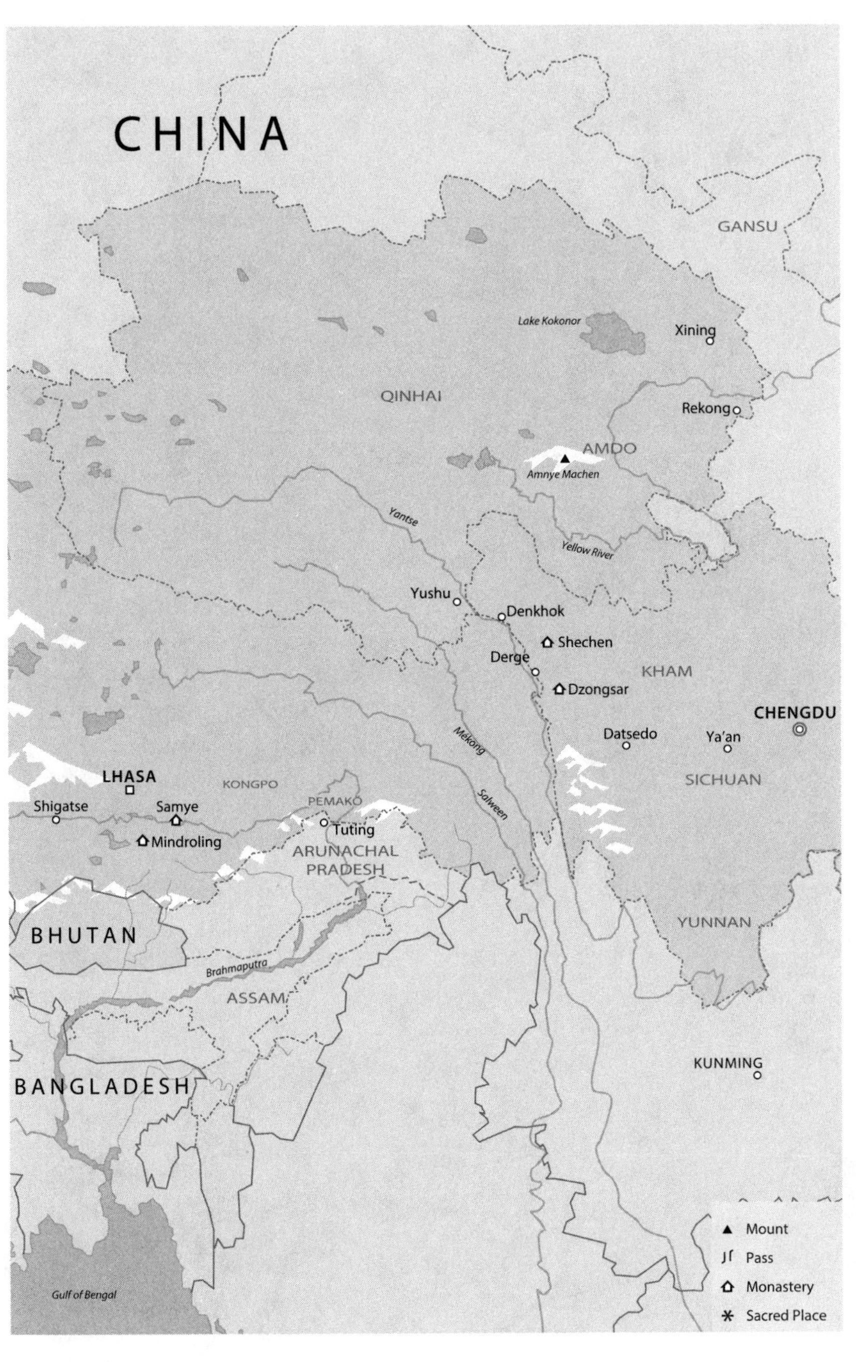

CHINA
GANSU
Lake Kokonor
Xining
QINHAI
Rekong
AMDO
Amnye Machen
Yantse
Yellow River
Yushu
Denkhok
Shechen
Derge
KHAM
Dzongsar
CHENGDU
Datsedo
Ya'an
Mekong
SICHUAN
LHASA
KONGPO
Shigatse
Samye
PEMAKO
Salween
Mindroling
Tuting
ARUNACHAL
PRADESH
YUNNAN
BHUTAN
Brahmaputra
ASSAM
BANGLADESH
KUNMING
Gulf of Bengal
Mount
Pass
Monastery
Sacred Place

N
50
150 km
Lac Hara
GANSU
Lake Kokonor
Tsonying Mahadeva
Xining
Kumbum
CHABCHA
TRIKA
Takmo Dzong
MANGRA
AMDO
Amnye Getho
REKONG
Shophon Chi
Yama Tashikhyil
Labrang
Tsö
Drakar Treldzong
TSEKOK
Dzogyen Rawa
Tseshung
Lake Kyaring
MATO
SOGPO
Lake Ngoring
Amnye Machen
MACHEN
Machu (Yellow River)
MACHU
DZOGE
TIBET
Nyempo Yurtse
NGAWA
Dzagyal Trama Lung
PADMA
MEWA
Palge Mani
Yalong
Gemang
Karchung Khormo Olu
Rivière Do
GOLOK
Serchu
Juniong
Dodroub
DZAMTHANG
YUSHU
Drichou (Yangtsé)
Arik Dza
DZACHOUKA
Benchen
Tsatsa
SERTHAR
BARKHAM
Ku La
Sakar
Denkhok
Larung Gar
Lingtsang
Shechen
Zurmang
Dzogchen
Muri La
KHAM
Chaîne de
Mani Genkok
Sinda
Tro Sitrön
Lake Yilung
DERGE
Tro La
GANZE
Palpung
Dzongsar
TRANGO
Wolong
JOMDA
Kawaluhgring
GYALMORONG
Siguniang
Khampagar
Dzong Shö
Riwoché
Kathog
Nyoshul
TAWU
PELYUL
Adzom
THROMTHAR
CHAMDO
Ngul River
Thromgo
NYAKRONG
CHENGDU
Lhagong
GONJO
Gu-nye La
Minyak Rabgang
Dzachou (Mékong)
MINYAK
Gye La
DATSEDO
YA'AN
DRAYAB
Chazam
Pomda
MARKHAM
LITANG
Erhlan Shan
BATANG
Getse
Kala
GARTOK
Minyak Kangkar
Ngajuk La
Drichou (Yangtsé)
Chaktreng
KARPO
Dungri Karpo
GYEZIL
Demo La
DABPA
Dagpa Lhari

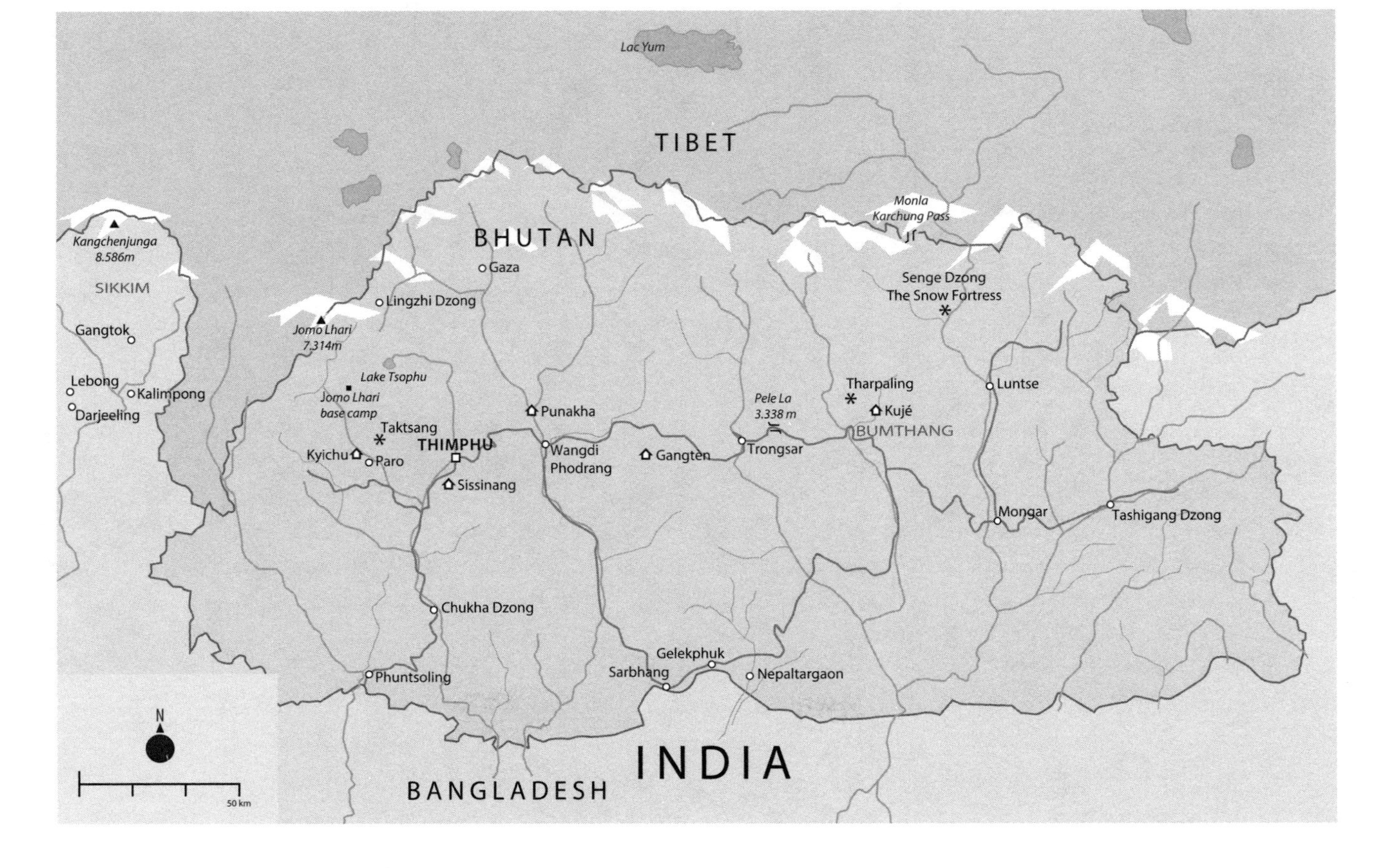

TIBET
Lac Yum
Monla
Karchung Pass
Ji
BHUTAN
Gaza
Kangchenjunga
8.586m
SIKKIM
Senge Dzong
The Snow Fortress
Lingzhi Dzong
Gangtok
Jomo Lhari
7.314m
Tharpaling
Luntse
Lebong
Kalimpong
Lake Tsophu
Pele La
3.338 m
Kujé
Darjeeling
Jomo Lhari
base camp
Punakha
BUMTHANG
Taktsang
THIMPHU
Gangten
Trongsar
Kyichu
Paro
Wangdi
Phodrang
Mongar
Tashigang Dzong
Sissinang
Chukha Dzong
Gelekphuk
Sarbhang
Nepaltargaon
Phuntsoling
N
INDIA
BANGLADESH
50 km

ACKNOWLEDGMENTS

I am infinitely grateful to the spiritual teachers whose memory I evoke in this book. They guide every moment of my life and give it all its meaning. This work is a modest testimony to a life lived in their presence.

Rabjam Rinpoche, Pema Wangyal, and Jigme Khyentse Rinpoche have advised me to put down in writing a testimony about my teachers, and I am very happy to have been able to do so, howsoever imperfectly, with their blessing.

With all my heart, I thank Nicole Lattès for having spent years encouraging me to write this book. Her suggestions for and guidance of the manuscript of these *Notes* were invaluable to me.

My profound gratitude goes to Carisse Busquet and her late husband, Gérard, for having reread the book so deeply and so carefully, helping me to put it in good order and to improve it in both style and format. I can never thank Carisse enough for her faithful help to me over the past twenty years, rereading my work and translating into French *The Life of Shabkar* and *Enlightened Vagabond*, texts that I translated from Tibetan into English.

My thanks to my publisher Guillaume Allary and to Stéphane Desa for their key role in developing this book through their close readings and wise counsel, which helped me to better structure these recollections and improve the clarity, style, and fluidity of my writing.

Wholehearted thanks to Raphaële Demandre, who reread the chapters on our shared adventures in Tibet and refreshed my memory on many points.

Many thanks to Witty Wahida Léon, Anne and Gérard Tardy, and Cécile and Jean-Pierre Devorsine, who knew my teachers, for their generosity in checking the manuscript and offering pertinent suggestions.

I am indebted to Luciana Chiaravalli-Benson for having prepared the maps so thoughtfully and expertly.

Thanks, too, to the good friends who suggested some very fine titles, such as *Never Without My Begging Bowl*, *Bye-Bye Samsara*, *A Bee in the Garden of the Buddhas*, *The Sun of Devotion*, and *A Gyrovague Monk*, to name but a few. Stubborn Breton that I am, I preferred to stick with the title that came to mind when I first had the idea of putting this account to paper, since a monk can wander—that is, take to the road—with no particular ties to anything, without being lost, thanks to the guidance of his beloved teachers. One who, as one Tibetan text puts it, "leaves nothing behind him when he sets off but his footprints."

I indeed owe a deep bow of gratitude to Jesse Browner for his elegant and precise translation, which faithfully retains the spirit of my testimony, and for his having been so careful in checking many points of places, names, and so on. This comes as the continuation of a warm and friendly collaboration that began with his translating "*Happiness: A Guide to Developing Life's Most Important Skill*."

The present translation would not have been possible without the support of my dear friend Barry Hershey, who has also extended his admirable generosity for many years to the humanitarian projects that we have been doing our best to carry on in Tibet.

Countless thanks as well to the whole team at MIT Press, who have kindly given themselves wholeheartedly to the publication of this book and brought it to fruition.

As with all my writing, all royalties from this book go to the Karuna-Shechen organization, which I cofounded twenty-two years ago to assist the neediest in India, Nepal, Tibet, and, more recently, Europe.

NOTES

CHAPTER 1

1. Kangchenjunga. The spelling used in India is a distortion of the Tibetan words Khang Chen Dzö Nga (Wylie: *khangs chen mdzod lnga*).

2. "Mantra" is a Sanskrit word. One of its meanings is "that which protects the mind." Indeed, chanting a mantra protects the mind from distraction and error and allows it to rest in the awareness that is always present behind the whirlwind of thoughts.

CHAPTER 2

1. There were five documentaries in total: *The Message of the Tibetans*, in two parts; *Le Lac des yogis* ("Lake of the Yogis"); *Les Enfants de la sagesse* ("Children of Wisdom"); and a film shot in Bhutan, *Au royaume du Bhoutan* ("In the Kingdom of Bhutan").

2. F. Leboyer, *Birth without Violence*, 4th ed. (New York: Healing Arts Press, 2009).

3. The equivalent of $75 at the time, or around €400 today.

4. A ghat is a flight of steps or tiers built on riverbanks to allow access to the water, usually a sacred river, such as the Ganges in Haridwar and Varanasi.

5. In the Hindu tradition, the word *darshan*, a Sanskrit term for "view" or "vision," has two different meanings. In the first meaning, it refers to the faithful seeing the face of a sage or divinity with a view to absorbing their qualities and saintliness; in the second, it identifies a philosophical movement within Hinduism.

6. Lilian Silburn, *Le Vijñana Bhairava* (Paris: Éditions E. de Boccard, 1961).

7. Vedanta, a term signifying "end of the Vedas," is a school of Hindu thought comprising various traditions, including Advaita Vedanta, which addresses the

nonduality of the individual self (*atman*) and undifferentiated ultimate reality (Brahman).

8. The Sikhs are a community of northern India whose monotheistic religion, Sikhism, was founded in the fifteenth century by Guru Nanak. Among other distinctive practices, members of the community wear beards and allow their hair to grown long.

CHAPTER 4

1. The "Mexican suitcase" contained 4,500 photographic negatives taken by Robert Capa, David Seymour, and Gerda Taro, covering the entire span of the Spanish Civil War. It was safeguarded by Cziki Weisz, who, before escaping to Mexico, confided it to an employee in the Chilean embassy in France. Thought to be lost in 1939, these invaluable negatives reemerged in Mexico in 2007 in the possession of the heir of a Mexican general who had been ambassador to the Vichy government.

2. Yahne Le Toumelin, *Lumière, Rire du ciel* (Paris: Éditions de La Martinière, 2001).

CHAPTER 6

1. Among the important treatises on the graded path that have been translated into English, I would cite *The Treasury of Precious Qualities*, by Jigme Lingpa and Kangyur Rinpoche, vols. 1 (rev. ed.) and 2 (Boulder, CO: Shambhala Publications, 2011–2013), and *The Light of Wisdom*, commentary by Jamgön Kontrul (Boulder, CO: Ranjung Yeshey Publications, 2013–2018).

2. The concept of Buddha-nature (*tathagatagarbha* in Sanskrit) refers to the fact that all living beings have the potential or the capacity to achieve full enlightenment.

3. Jedrung Rinpoche, of the Riwoche Monastery, also known as Trinle Jampa Jungne (1856–1922).

4. Among these students was Trogawa Rinpoche, a doctor lama, who later established a center for traditional Tibetan medicine in Darjeeling; the scholar Khenpo Palden Sherab, also from Riwoche, who taught at the Central Institute of Higher Tibetan Studies, in Sarnath, accompanied by his father and his brother, Lama Gyurdrak, a yogi particularly beloved by Kangyur Rinpoche; Kangyur Rinpoche's family; and Anne Benson.

5. Including Frédérick Leboyer, Olivier and Varenka Marc, Arnaud and Denise Desjardins, Gyurme Dorje, my mother Yahne Le Toumelin, Laurent and Sylvie Tremblay, Etienne and Georgina De Swarte, Pema Yeshey (Michal Abrams), Martin Watten, Dharmadipo, Keith Downman, Bernard Benson, his wife Maryse, and those of his six children who came to Darjeeling (Peter, Anne, Juanita, Kit, and Jenny), Helena Blankleder, Jill Heald, John Canti, Charles Hastings, Steve and Larry Gethin, Gérard Godet, Ronald Crossley, Loren and Ziska Stanlee, Sabina and Gerald von Minden, John Giorno, Craig Musser, Kim and Mary-Ann Hegan, Christophe Bureau, Vivian Kurz, Patrice Collet, and Patrick Planquette and a few others I might have met too briefly

6. Professor Gérard Buttin was also a member of the jury.

CHAPTER 7

1. Unlike the kind of beds we are used to, Himalayan "beds" are usually banquettes without box springs, made of two large hard, square cushions stuffed with bran (which can be folded on one another for ease of carrying) and covered with woolen rugs. Blankets are folded up at the head of the bed or rolled against the wall against which the "banquette-bed" is usually pushed.

CHAPTER 8

1. This nonsectarian movement, known as Rimey in Tibetan (*ris med*), has been active throughout Tibetan history, but reached its acme in the nineteenth century in Tibet. Under the guidance of such great spiritual masters as Jamgön Kongtrül Lodrö Thayé and Jamyang Khyentse Wangpo, its aim was to counter the sectarianism dividing the various philosophical schools and to launch a spiritual renewal. See chapter 17, "Jam gon Kong sprul and the Nonsectarian Movement," in E. G. Smith, *Among Tibetan Texts: History and Literature of the Himalayan Plateau* (Somerville, MA: Wisdom Publications, 2001), 235–270.

2. The Sanskrit terms *siddha* and *mahasiddha* (meaning, literally, "one who is accomplished") refer to highly realized ascetic masters, who were sometimes monks or yogis but also laypersons practicing various trades. The term applies equally to ascetics of certain Hindu, Jain, and Tibetan Buddhist schools of thought.

CHAPTER 9

1. Dudjom Rinpoche and Pawo Rinpoche, as well as the fourteenth Karmapa, Dodrupchen Rinpoche, Nono Rinpoche, and Kalu Rinpoche the following year.

2. *The Treasury of Precious Qualities*, vol. 1, chap. 5. For the condensed extracts offered here in this book, I have drawn from English and French translations, as well as from the Tibetan original.

3. "Times of decadence" refers to the "five degenerations" or the "age of five residues" (*snyigs ma lnga* in Tibetan). These are the degenerations of lifespan, of afflictive mental states (the emergence of the five poisons), of sentient beings (the difficulty of helping them), of time (increase in wars and famine), and of views (the spread of erroneous views).

4. Jamgön Kongtrül Lodrö Thayé (1813–1899). Excerpt from Matthieu Ricard, *On the Path to Enlightenment: Heart Advice from the Great Tibetan Masters* (Boulder, CO: Shambhala Publications, 2013). Translated by the author from *bla med nang rgyud sde gsum gyi rgyab chos padma'I zhal gdams lam rim ye snying 'grel pa ye shes snang ba*, published in English in a different translation, as *The Light of Wisdom*, commentary by Jamgön Kontrul (Boulder, CO: Ranjung Yeshey Publications, 2013–2018).

5. Drikung Kyobpa, also known as Jigten Gönpo. Quoted in many works, including Patrul Rinpoche's *Words of My Perfect Teacher* (*rdzogs pa chen po klong chen snying thig gi sngon 'gro'I khrid yig kun bzang bla ma'I zhal lung*).

6. This commentary by Khenpo Yönten Gyatso (*mkhan po yon tan rgya mtsho*), a great scholar from Gemang Monastery in eastern Tibet (who lived from the second

half of the nineteenth century into the early twentieth, and was a student of Patrul Rinpoche), was written in two volumes: *yon tan run po che mdzod kyi 'grel ba zla ba'I sgron me* (for the section on the sutras) and *nyi ma'I 'od zer* (for the section on the Vajrayana) and was taught by Dilgo Khyentse Rinpoche in Bhutan, and then by Rabjam Rinpoche and Khenpo Pema Sherab in France, over the course of thirteen consecutive years. The extract here has been abridged and paraphrased.

CHAPTER 10

1. P. Bruckner, *L'Euphorie perpétuelle* (Paris: Librairie Générale française, 2002), 107.

2. The English philosopher Herbert Spencer wrote, in *Definitions*, "Time: that which man is always trying to kill, but which ends in killing him."

3. Victor Cousin, *Oeuvres completes*, 1841.

4. Victor Cousin, *Nouvelle revue encyclopédique* (Paris: Firmin-Didot frères libraires, 1847), 33.

5. On this subject, see M. Csikszentmihalyi, *Flow: The Psychology of Optimal Experience* (New York: Harper Perennial Modern Classics, 2008).

CHAPTER 11

1. Although these three major Buddhist schools of thought are considered to be "one path" (Ekayāna), there are significant differences among them. Theravada, the "school of the Elders," defines itself as the orthodox representative of original Buddhism, as taught by the Buddha Shakyamuni in the fifth and fourth centuries BCE. It stresses the strict observance of discipline (*vinaya*) and individual liberation (*pratimoksha*) from suffering. Mahayana, the "Great Vehicle," stresses the idea of compassion. Drawing from the words of the Buddha (*sutra*), the *bodhisattva*—"hero of enlightenment"—vows to attain Buddhahood to free all sentient beings from suffering. Lastly, Vajrayana, the "Diamond Vehicle," which emerged in India and was more broadly developed in Tibet in the eighth and ninth centuries under the aegis of the great master Guru Padmasambhava, integrates the philosophical ideas and sacred texts of the two earlier schools and adds a multiplicity of meditation techniques allowing the practitioner to advance rapidly on the path to enlightenment. Theravada is based on renunciation, Mahayana on compassion, and Vajrayana on pure vision.

2. To be more precise, in Tibetan Buddhism pure vision (*dag snang* in Tibetan) essentially consists of recognizing that all phenomena appear but are empty of independent existence, and that this applies to all phenomena without exception. It is therefore necessary to recognize the union of appearance and emptiness, and then to perceive all forms, sounds, and thoughts as manifestations of the body of the Buddha or the teacher, of his voice, or of the sound of mantras, and thoughts as movements of *dharmata*, the ultimate nature of mind. Ultimately, it requires recognizing the Buddhahood of all sentient beings and to perceive the aggregates of the body as the five *dhyani* buddhas, the five elements as the five female buddhas, the eight aspects of consciousness as the eight bodhisattvas, and their objects as the eight offering goddesses.

3. Ratna Lingpa's *termas*, in nineteen volumes; the thirteen volumes of Gyalwa Longchen Rabjam's *Nyingthig Yabshi*; the complete works of Jedrung Trinle Jampa Jungney in eight volumes; the seven volumes of Rigdzin Jatsön Nyingpo's *termas* and annexed texts; and a half-dozen other volumes.

CHAPTER 12

1. One of the three buddhas who preceded the fourth, the Buddha Shakyamuni. According to the cosmology of Great Vehicle Buddhism, and in particular to the Bhadrakalpikasūtra, we live in a "fortunate aeon," that is, a *kalpa* in which a buddha has arisen and taught. A *kalpa*, or aeon, covers the duration of the formation, existence, and destruction or disappearance of a particular universe. Buddhism speaks of a succession of countless *kalpas*. It is also said that in our *kalpa*, 1,002 buddhas will appear, attain perfect enlightenment, and turn the wheel of the law. Shakyamuni is the fourth Buddha of our era, preceded by Kashyapa and to be followed by Maitreya.

2. K. Dowman, *The Legend of the Great Stupa and the Life Story of the Lotus Born Guru* (Cazadero, CA: Dharma Publishing, 1973), p. 24.

3. Furthermore, in the case of the teachings of Dudjom Lingpa and Dudjom Rinpoche, most of these cycles are *termas* that, as we have seen, are teachings conferred by Guru Padmasambhava on his close disciples, then concealed in various ways until they could be rediscovered over the course of the centuries by lama *tertöns* (lama "discoverers" of these teachings) at a time when their practice will be of greatest use. These *termas* ("hidden treasures") are focused on various deities of wisdom: Guru Padmasambhava, Amitayus (the buddha of "infinite life"), Vajrakilaya (a wisdom deity whose practice allows the practitioner to eliminate all external, internal, and hidden obstacles on the path to enlightenment), Manjushri (the buddha of wisdom), Yeshe Tsogyal (who symbolizes the female aspect of wisdom), and many others.

4. Padmasambhava and Jamgön Kongtrul Lodrö Tayé (commentaries), *L'Essence de sagesse primordiale*, four volumes (Le Plantou, Plazac: Éditions Padmakara, 2011).

5. Khyentse Rinpoche also conferred the transmission of empowerments linked to the Great Perfection, from the thirteen volumes of the *Nyingthig Yabshi* (*snying thig ya bzhi*) by Gyalwa Longchen Rabjam Drime Öser (*rgyal ba klong chen rab 'byams dri med 'od zer*, 1308–1364).

CHAPTER 13

1. In the 1960s, at the Bhutia Busty Monastery in Darjeeling, Dilgo Khyentse Rinpoche received from Kangyur Rinpoche the transmission of the Nyingma Gyubum ("The Hundred Thousand Tantras of the Nyingma tradition"), as well as volumes of spiritual treasures discovered by Taksham Nuden Dorje (*stag sham nus ldan rdo rje*), also known as Samten Lingpa (*bsam gtan gling pa*), born in the seventeenth century. In return, he requested from Khyentse Rinpoche the transmission of Gyalwa Longchen Rabjam's Nyingthig Yabshi.

2. Guru Padmasambhava was the great Indian master who, along with Abbot Shantarakshita, introduced Buddhism to Tibet in the eighth and ninth centuries.

3. The Golden Milk Lake of Gyalgyam lies at the foot of Dothi Kangkar mountain, in eastern Tibet, a six-hour drive from Patang Valley, near Yushu. It is a sacred site for longevity practices. While he fervently prayed for the longevity of his teacher, Khyentse Chökyi Lodrö, and performed an offering ceremony centered on Amitayus, the buddha of infinite life, his mandala appeared with great clarity on the surface of the lake. Shortly afterward, he saw in a dream a text written in the hand of the first Khyentse, Jamyang Khyentse Wangpo. The text appeared to him as a "visionary treasure" (*dgongs gter*), and he set it down in writing.

CHAPTER 14

1. The five regions are central Tibet (currently known the Tibet Autonomous Region), Kham, Qinghai, Gansu, and Yunnan.

2. Jamyang Khyentse Wangpo (*'jam dbyangs mkhyen brtse'i dbang po, padma 'od gsal mdo sngags gling pa, rdo rje gzi brjid*, 1820–1892) was a great scholar and discoverer of treasures (*tertön*); he was also one of the main drivers of the nonsectarian Rimey movement, which advocated respect for the principal schools of Tibetan Buddhism.

3. *The Treasury of Precious Instructions* (*gdams ngag rin po che'i mdzod*), published in Tibetan in e volumes by Shechen Publications in 1999.

4. Jamyang Khyentse Wangpo had five emanations corresponding respectively to his body, his speech, his mind, his qualities, and his enlightened activities for the benefit of all beings. The concept of reincarnation is already confusing enough to Western culture, without the added complication of one "person" having several incarnations or emanations. Indeed, the idea of reincarnation makes Westerners think of the perpetuation of an "individual identity," whereas from the Buddhist perspective it is about the continuity of a flow of consciousness, stripped of all unitary and independent identity. When several incarnations are identified, as has occurred several times in Tibetan history, this has nothing to do with an individual entity divided into five sub-entities, but reflects the continuity of various aspects of enlightenment and the manifestation of the various ways in which the good of sentient beings can be propagated, just as a single moon—in this case, the enlightened consciousness of a spiritual master who has transcended the concept of individuality—can be reflected on the surface of any number of bodies of water, spontaneously and effortlessly. At this enthronement ceremony, Shechen Gyaltsap Rinpoche conferred a new name on Rabsel Dawa: Gyurme Pema Thekchok Tenpe Gyaltsen, "Immutable Victory Banner of the Supreme Vehicle."

5. Most of Guru Padmasambhava's teachings, which were hidden as "spiritual treasures" (*gter ma*) to be rediscovered in the following centuries at a time when they would be most useful, were almost all hidden by Yeshe Tsogyal, Padmasambhava's main student and spiritual consort. To establish the auspicious bonds that will allow the *tertön* to discover the treasure that he is destined to find, in accordance with Guru Padmasambhava's prophecy, he should take a spiritual consort. In some cases, the mere act of seeing her, even at a distance with no physical contact, is enough to establish these auspicious bonds, and some *tertöns*, such as Jatsön Nyingpo and Jamyang Khyentse Wangpo, remained monks.

6. Tibetan Buddhism counts several "lineages" of masters who are the holders of the major texts of the different schools of Tibetan Buddhism. Historically, the Khyentse lineage begins with Rigdzin Jigme Lingpa (*rig 'dzin 'jigs med gling pa*, 1730–1798), who notably discovered the Longchen Nyingthig, "The Heart Essence of the Vast Expanse."

7. "Salga" is a family nickname for Rabsel Dawa, formed by adding the suffix "ga" to one part of a person's name (in this case, the "sel" of "Rabsel"), a common practice among the Khampas.

CHAPTER 15

1. These are the Centre d'études de Chanteloube, founded by Tulku Pema Wangyal; the Urgyen Samye Chöling dharma center, established by Dudjom Rinpoche; the Dhagpo Kagyu Ling, established by the sixteenth Karmapa and Lama Gendun; and the Nenang Samten Chöling, founded by Pawo Rinpoche.

2. Dilgo Khyentse Rinpoche, *The Heart of Compassion: The Thirty-Seven Verses on the Practice of a Bodhisattva* (Boulder, CO: Padmakara Translation Group, 2007).

CHAPTER 17

1. 

2. In Tibetan Buddhism, the so-called fierce or wrathful forms that some representations or deities of wisdom assume in no way indicate anger or malevolence, but instead represent an enhanced mode of compassion, as well as the power that removes any external and internal obstacles that may be found on the path of liberation from suffering and ignorance.

3. Machig Labdrön (*ma gcig lab sgron*, 1055–1153). She is considered to be a *dakini*, a woman who is fully realized spiritually. She is the source of the practice of Chöd, or Tcheu, literally meaning "cutting through," in the sense of cutting through attachment to the ego and the solidity of phenomena in order to sever suffering at its very root and realize the true nature of mind, the union of emptiness and luminosity. This tradition and its teachings are found in all schools of Tibetan Buddhism.

4. The Drukpa Kagyu tradition is a branch of the Kagyupa school, one of the main currents of Tibetan Buddhism. The Kagyu school has been founded by Marpa the translator and by the great yogi Milarepa in the eleventh century. The Drukpa branch was founded by Tsangpa Gyare (*gtsang pa rgya ras shes rdo rje*, 1161–1211),

a disciple of Lingje Repa (*gling rje ras pa, padma rdo rje*, 1128–1188) and teacher of Gyalwa Götsangpa Gonpo Dorje (*rgyal be rgod tshang pa mgon po rdo rje*, 1189–1258).

5. A *mala* is a Tibetan rosary traditionally consisting of 108 beads made of a variety of wood species (rudraksha or *Elaeocarpus angustifolius*, sandalwood, longan, or similar), crystal, or semiprecious stones.

CHAPTER 18

1. The four main branches of the Kagyu lineage of Tibetan Buddhism are those established by the disciples of Gampopa (1079–1153), himself a student of Milarepa. The Drikung Kagyu lineage is one of the eight "minor" lineages founded by the disciples of Phagmo Drupa (1110–1170). The founder of this lineage was Kyobpa Jigten Sumgön Rinchen Pal (1143–1217). The thirty-seventh Drikung Kyabgön Chetsang (*'bri gung skyabs mgon*, born in 1946) is the current head of the lineage.

2. *The Eight Great Chariots of the Practice Lineage* denotes the eight major practice lineages of the old and new schools that transmitted the Buddhist teachings from India to Tibet. These are the Nyingmapa, Kadam, Sakya, Marpa Kagyu, Shangpa Kagyu, Kalachakra, Shyijé and Chö, and Orgyen Nyendrub lineages.

CHAPTER 19

1. *Ro mnyam*, or one taste, refers to the ability to perceive all events impartially, experiencing no reactions of attraction or repulsion.

2. More than ten thousand of these images have also been made available on the website www.himalayanart.org.

CHAPTER 20

1. The mantra of the Buddha of compassion, Avalokiteshvara, which is very commonly recited in Tibet, by laypeople and monastics alike.

2. Advice drawn from volume 3 (GA) of *The Collected Writings of Skyabs-rje Dil-mgo Mkhyen-brtse Rin-po-che*, 25 volumes (Kathmandu: Shechen Publications, 1994), p. 192

3. Roland Barraux, *Histoire des Dalaï-lamas—Quatorze reflets sur le Lac des Visions* (Paris: Albin Michel, 1993).

CHAPTER 21

1. The Three Baskets are respectively composed of the Sutras (the Buddha's sermons), the Vinaya (the rules of monastic discipline), and the Abhidharma (the categories of mental events, the composition of the universe, cosmology, and so on).

CHAPTER 22

1. Gyalwa Götsangpa Gonpo Dorje (*rgyal be rgod tshang pa mgon po rdo rje*, 1189–1258) was a great yogi of the Drukpa Kagyu lineage. He spent many years living in caves, particularly in the vicinity of Mount Kailash, and was renowned for his

complete renunciation. Over the years, he made twelve pledges to strengthen his commitment to maintaining an authentic spiritual practice and compassionate behavior. One of those pledges was to treat all those he met with the utmost respect. As a result, whenever he traveled in the company of students or pilgrims, he always offered the best place to sleep, the best food, and the tastiest drinks to others. As he explains in his autobiography, "I was not content to make these commitments in theory, but I put them into practice, and whoever came before me—dogs, beggars, wild animals, and so on—I considered them my meditation deity. In this way, the horns of my pride were radically broken."

CHAPTER 23

1. One 700-page volume on the preliminary practices of Vajrayana, *rdo rje thegs pa'i thun mong gi sngon 'gro spyi la sbyar chog pa'i khrid kyi rgyab yig kun mkhyen zhal lung rnam grol shing rta*, vol. 6, *The Collected Works of Že-chen Rgyal-tshab Padma-rnam-rgyal* (Kathmandu: Shechen Publications, 1975–1994). Translated into English as *A Chariot to Freedom, Guidance from the Great Masters on the Vajrayana Preliminary Practices*, by Shechen Gyaltsap Gyurme Pema Namgyal (Boulder, CO: Padmakara Translation Group, Shambhala, 2022).

2. Dilgo Khyentse Rinpoche, *The Heart Treasure of the Enlightened Ones* (Boulder, CO: Shambhala, 1993).

CHAPTER 24

1. The Mind & Life Institute, an organization founded in 1990 by the neuroscientist Francisco Varela and American lawyer Adam Engle, with the blessing of the fourteenth Dalai Lama, seeks to promote meetings and exchanges between Buddhism and science. Such dialogue fosters a better understanding of the nature of reality and the mind in order to spark a positive change in the world.

2. Paul Ekman and His Holiness the Dalai Lama, *Emotional Awareness: Overcoming the Obstacles to Emotional Balance and Compassion* (New York: Times Books, 2008).

3. Chinese and Vietnamese Buddhists are strictly vegetarian. While the Buddhist texts do not unanimously condemn the consumption of meat, some Mahayana (Great Vehicle) sutras are quite unequivocal. Notably, the Buddha says in the Great Parinirvana Sutra, "Eating meat destroys great compassion," and counsels his disciples to avoid consuming meat "just as they would the flesh of their own children." Many Tibetan masters have also rejected the consumption of animal flesh.

4. The activity of the amygdala and the anterior insular cortex is notably weaker in meditators than in novices.

5. A. Antoine Lutz, Daniel R. McFarlin, David M. Perlman, Tim V. Salomons, and Richard J. Davidson, "Altered Anterior Insula Activation during Anticipation and Experience of Painful Stimuli in Expert Meditators," *Neuroimage* (January 2013); and David M. Perlman, Tim V. Salomons, Richard J. Davidson, and Antoine Lutz, "Differential Effects on Pain Intensity and Unpleasantness of Two Meditation Practices," *Emotion* 10, no. 1 (2010): 65–71.

CHAPTER 26

1. The Tibet Autonomous Region includes the central and western regions of Ü-Tsang and Ngari, including the capital, Lhasa. Greater, or historical Tibet, has thus been cut off from the regions of Amdo, adjoined to Qinghai, and Kham, adjoined to Sichuan with parts in Yunnan and Gansu.

2. A new translation is to be published by Éditions Padmakara in 2023 under the title *Le Seigneur du Lotus*.

CHAPTER 27

1. The name has been changed to protect his identity, as he is still alive.

2. The biographies of these two masters have been translated into English as *Enlightened Vagabond: The Life and Teachings of Patrul Rinpoche* (Boulder, CO: Shambhala, 2017), and *Lion of Speech: The Life of Mipham Rinpoche* (Boulder, CO: Shambala, 2020).

3. As recounted in *Enlightened Vagabond*.

4. Khyentse Rinpoche wrote a short biography of Kunga Palden that is included in volume 1 of his *Collected Works*. He was a student of Patrul Rinpoche, Jamyang Khyentse Wangpo, and, especially, Önpo Tendzin Norbu (1851–1900).

5. The common raven (*Corvus corax*) is very widespread in Tibet, although it has become quite rare in France, where sightings of the smaller rook and crow are much more common.

6. This book first appeared in the United States under the title *Journey to Enlightenment: The Life and World of Khyentse Rinpoche, Spiritual Teacher from Tibet* (New York: Aperture, 1996).

CHAPTER 29

1. Emperor Ashoka ruled from 265 to 238 BCE or 273 to 232 BCE.

2. *The Life of Shabkar: Autobiography of a Tibetan Yogin*, ed. Constance Wilkinson, trans. Matthieu Ricard et al. (Albany: State University of New York Press, 1994; Ithaca, NY: Snow Lion, 2001).

CHAPTER 30

1. The lineage of Panchen Lamas dates from the seventeenth century and was instituted by the fifth Dalai Lama (1617–1682); the title is given to the successive incarnations of the abbots of the important Tashi Lhunpo Monastery, belonging to the Gelugpa school.

2. Unlike the Dalai Lama, who was able to escape to India and avoid imprisonment, the Panchen Lama remained in Tibet. In 1960, after his Tashi Lhunpo Monastery was sacked, several monks were executed, and many more imprisoned, he declared his allegiance to the Dalai Lama and, in 1962, addressed to Chinese Premier Zhou Enlai his famous "70,000 Character Petition," in which he described the "misery and desolation" caused by the Chinese invasion.

In 1966, he was abducted by the Red Guards with his entire family, brought to Beijing, and severely beaten. At his trial, he was beaten every day with a belt, but kept his lips sealed the entire time. He was incarcerated from 1968 to 1977 in a prison not far from Beijing. Kept in solitary confinement in a tiny cell, every day he wrote a letter to the government protesting the abuses committed in Tibet. He was regularly taken from prison to be subjected to public humiliation before thousands of spectators in stadiums around Beijing.

During the last year of his life, the Panchen Lama sought to restore the use of the Tibetan language in public administration and schools. On a trip to Australia as a member of an official Chinese delegation, he was able, unbeknownst to his guards, to speak by telephone with the Dalai Lama for over an hour—their first verbal exchange since 1959. In a speech delivered a few days before his death, he said, "If we compare the price of the sacrifice we have made with the development that we have seen, my feeling is that the value of our sacrifice has been far greater. Our sacrifice far outweighs our development." In Tibet, the Panchen Lama remains a powerful symbol of the hopes of the people, and his portrait—whose display is tolerated, unlike that of the Dalai Lama—can be found hanging in a prominent place in most Tibetan homes.

3. *Corvus corax tibetanus*, the largest subspecies of raven.

4. *The Three Classes of the Great Perfection* (*rdzogs chen sde gsum*) constitute volume 62 of the new edition of *The Treasury of Precious Termas*, the *Rinchen Terdzö*, published under the title *The Great Treasury of Rediscovered Teachings, rin chen gter mdzod chen mo* (Boulder, CO: Shechen Publications, 2007–2018).

CHAPTER 31

1. The word *khenpo* (*mkhan po*) is a title accorded to a monk who has studied Buddhist philosophy in a monastic college, or *shedra* (*shes grwa*) for nine to twelve years or more, after which he is qualified to teach in monastic and lay communities.

2. They were students of the renowned Khenpo Thubten Chöphel (better known by the name Khenpo Thubga) (*mkhen po thub sten chos dpal*, 1896–1956), with whom Khyentse Rinpoche had himself studied in his youth.

3. https://fr.wikipedia.org/wiki/Université_de_Nalanda.

4. "Root text" refers to an author's original text, most often accompanied by one or more commentaries written by the author himself or other scholars.

5. In Tibetan, *sems kyi chos nyid*, literally "the very nature of mind."

CHAPTER 32

1. The poem is included in the *Collected Works* of Khyentse Rinpoche, volume 3 (Boulder, CO: Shambhala, 2011).

2. "Teacher" refers to Kangyur Rinpoche; Orgyen Kunzang Chökhorling is the name of his monastery. "Kunzang" refers to the primordial buddha Kuntu Zangpo (Samantabhara in Sanskrit).

3. I was translating the autobiography of Shabkar at the time.

4. One of Khyentse Rinpoche's principal names.

CHAPTER 33

1. Some of these texts have already been translated. They include

Shechen Gyaltsap, *Zurchungpa's Testament: A Commentary on Zurchung Sherab Trakpa's Eighty Pieces of Advice, with Commentary by Dilgo Khyentse* (Boulder, CO: Padmakara Translation Group, Shambhala, 2007).

Shechen Gyaltsap, in *Vajra Wisdom: Deity Practice in Tibetan Buddhism* (Ithaca, NY: Dharmachakra Translation Committee, Snow Lion, 2013).

Shechen Gyaltsap, with commentary by Shechen Rabjam Rinpoche, *The Great Medicine That Conquers Clinging to the Notion of Reality: Steps in Meditation on the Enlightened Mind* (Boulder, CO: Shambhala, 2007).

Shechen Gyaltsap, *Practicing the Great Perfection: Instructions on the Crucial Points* (Boulder, CO: Padmakara Translation Group, Shambhala, 2020).

At the request of young Khamtrul Rinpoche, the incarnation of a teacher who had been very close to Khyentse Rinpoche, the latter also conferred the transmission of the six volumes by Jatsön Nyingpo ("Rainbow Essence"), an eminent teacher of the sixteenth and seventeenth centuries, whose seven volumes of teachings I printed in Delhi in the later 1970s.

2. Long-life ceremonies, a Vajrayana practice, are intended to increase the longevity of a master or anyone threatened by disease or other obstacles. Several specific deities are invoked in these rituals, most particularly Amitayus, the buddha of infinite life, and White Tara.

CHAPTER 34

1. These volumes include the *Five Great Treasuries*, in more than ninety volumes, which Jamgön Kongtrul Lodrö Tayé collected and edited throughout his life in the nineteenth century, as well as the *Tantras of the Nyingma School* (thirty-two volumes), the *Lama Gongdu* corpus by Sangye Lingpa (thirteen volumes), the three main cycles of the *Kagye* (seventeen volumes), the *Complete Works* of Rigdzin Jigme Lingpa (thirteen volumes), and the works of Lama Mipham (twenty-seven volumes), Shechen Gyaltsap (thirteen volumes), Shabkar (fourteen volumes), and many others.

2. https://rtz.tsadra.org/index.php/Main_Page and https://www.tbrc.org/#!footer/about /newhome.

3. Jamgön Kongtrul redacted the *Rinchen Terdzö* at the monastery-hermitage of Dzongshö Deshek Dupa, a secluded mountain retreat located between Dzongsar and Kathok, in eastern Tibet. Woodblocks (xylographs) were then engraved at Palpung Monastery, in sixty volumes. Later, a new set of xylographs were engraved in sixty-four volumes at Tsurphu Monastery by the fifteenth Karmapa, Khakyab Dorje. We ultimately published two editions at Shechen. The most recent, a definitive version in seventy-one volumes, is titled *The Great Treasury of Rediscovered Teachings (rin chen gter mdzod chen mo)* (Shechen Publications, 2005–2018), and was completed with the generous support of the Tsadra Foundation.

4. For over a hundred *yantras* (sacred diagrams) and *chakras* (circular, wheel-shaped diagrams, *chakra* in Sanskrit) intended to accomplish various activities for the good of beings, including to mitigate illness, obstacles, conflicts, and so on; to enhance prosperity and spiritual qualities; to promote favorable circumstances in daily life; but above all to progress toward enlightenment and eliminate internal and external obstacles.

5. www.himalayanart.org.

CHAPTER 35

1. Matthieu Ricard, *Monk Dancers of Tibet* (Boulder, CO: Shambhala, 2003).

2. *Moines danseurs du Tibet*, a fifty-five-minute film by Jean-Pierre and Cécile Devorsine, Via Découvertes Films.

CHAPTER 36

1. Among them, Penor Rinpoche and Mindrolling Trichen Rinpoche, heads of the Nyingmapa lineage; Chogye Trichen Rinpoche, an eminent Sakyapa lama; Drikung Kyabgön, head of the Drikung Kagyu school; as well as the reincarnations of Dilgo Khyentse Rinpoche's two primary teachers, Shechen Gyaltsap Rinpoche (from Shechen Monastery, Tibet) and Dzongsar Khyentse Rinpoche (incarnation of Jamyang Khyentse Chökyi Lodrö).

2. Trulshik Rinpoche conferred all empowerments and explanations, while the oral transmission was done by Dzongsar Khyentse Rinpoche and Rabjam Rinpoche.

3. At the heart of the Buddhist world stands Bodhgaya, the "diamond throne of India" where Prince Siddhartha attained enlightenment under the Bodhi Tree, becoming the Buddha Shakyamuni. Three other sites are considered to be major destinations for pilgrims: Lumbini, Nepal, where the Buddha was born; Sarnath, near Varanasi, where he gave his first teachings; and Kushinagar, where he died and entered *mahaparinirvana*, the great transcendence and complete cessation of suffering.

Four other sites are also considered to be important holy places: Shravasti, Rajgir, Sankissa, and Vaishali. The Buddha spent more time in Shravasti than anywhere else. Among other things, he led the annual rainy season retreat twenty-two times there. He also performed a series of miracles there to convince the skeptics. At Rajgir, the Buddha taught the Prajnaparamita, the "Perfection of Transcendent Wisdom," which establishes that all phenomena are empty of inherent existence. At Sankissa, the Buddha returned to earth from the heavenly realm of Tusita, where he had offered teachings to his late mother during the three months of the summer retreat. At Vaishali, the Buddha ordained the first nun, Mahaprajapati Gotami, his aunt and foster mother, and many other women. It was here, too, that a monkey made him an offering of honey.

CHAPTER 38

1. Paul Ekman, personal communication. See also Daniel Goleman, *Destructive Emotions: A Scientific Dialogue with the Dalai Lama* (New York: Bantam, 2004).

2. Available on YouTube, https://www.youtube.com/watch?v=ZZiQ2dGNVgE.

3. *Le Monde*, October 31, 1993, "La visite du Dalaï-lama en France—Un moine tibétain chez les Chartreux."

4. The Dalai Lama, Desmond Tutu, and Douglas Carlton Abrams, *The Book of Joy: Lasting Happiness in a Changing World* (New York: Avery, 2016).

5. At the dialogue-interview conducted in Paris by Claudine Vernier-Palliez for an article published in *Paris Match* in 2017, Henri Cartier-Bresson joined us and took our pictures. I met Pierre Ceyrac one other time at the home of Henri Cartier-Bresson and Martine Franck, again with Claudine.

6. From a private communication with the author.

CHAPTER 39

1. He is also known as Barjung Khenpo, "Master of philosophy at Barjung Monastery."

CHAPTER 40

1. In Tibetan, the lake is known as *lag ngar mtsho*, literally, "Lake in the shape of a forearm," because of its elongated shape.

2. *The Life of Shabkar*, ed. Constance Wilkinson, trans. Matthieu Ricard et al. (Albany: State University of New York Press, 1994; Ithaca, NY: Snow Lion, 2001).

3. I am translating some of these texts, which will eventually be published by Shambhala Publications and Éditions Padmakara.

4. The Parsis are a community whose members practice Zoroastrianism, or Mazdayasna, with a dualistic cosmology of good, embodied by Ahura Mazda, and the evil spirit Ahriman. Originally from Persia (Iran), they were forced to emigrate after the Arab conquest from the sixth to the eighth centuries. In India, they are mainly settled in the state of Gujarat and in Mumbai (Bombay).

CHAPTER 41

1. Constance Wilkinson edited the English text with great elegance and made an important contribution to its poetic qualities, while Carisse Busquet translated the English version into French

2. *The Life of Shabkar*, ed. Constance Wilkinson, trans. Matthieu Ricard et al. (Albany: State University of New York Press, 1994; Ithaca, NY: Snow Lion, 2001).

3. *Le Vol du Garouda*, a French translation with commentary by Dilgo Khyentse Rinpoche, was published by Éditions Padmakara in 2021. An English translation will be published by Shambhala Publications

4. Not his real name. For their own security, we must protect the identities of those who work on projects with us in Tibet.

5. Shabkar wrote several spirited defenses of vegetarianism, two of which have been translated into English under the name *Food for Bodhisattvas*, Padmakara Translation Group, Shambhala Publications, 2011; *The Wonderous Emanated Scripture* (SH 54, *rmad byung sprul pa'i glegs bam*), in *Collected Writings of Shabkar Tsogdruk Rangdrol*

(Boulder, CO: Shechen Publications), vol. 8 (Nya), and *The Nectar of Immortality* (SH 65, *legs bshad bdud rtsi'i chu rgyun*), vol. 12 (Na).

6. *The Collected Works of Zhabs dkar thsogs drug rang drol*, 14 vol. (New Delhi: Shechen Publications, 2003). I have also drawn up a catalogue raisonné of Shabkar's writings, Matthieu Ricard, *The Writings of Shabkar, A Descriptive Catalogue* (New Delhi: Shechen Publications, 2003).

CHAPTER 42

1. This song and the two that follow are abridged versions of those found in *The Life of Shabkar*, ed. Constance Wilkinson, trans. Matthieu Ricard et al. (Albany: State University of New York Press, 1994; Ithaca, NY: Snow Lion, 2001).

2. For their own security, it is best not to name these two monks.

CHAPTER 44

1. Dzongsar Jamyang Khyentse, *What Makes You Not a Buddhist* (Boulder, CO: Shambhala, 2006).

2. Dzongsar Jamyang Khyentse, *Not for Happiness: A Guide to the So-Called Preliminary Practices* (Boulder, CO: Shambhala, 2012).

CHAPTER 45

1. These stories, retold in Matthieu Ricard, *Enlightened Vagabond: The Life and Teachings of Patrul Rinpoche* (Boulder, CO: Shambhala, 2017), have been abridged here.

CHAPTER 48

1. Planck time is the time it takes a photon in a vacuum to travel a distance equal to a Planck length, a unit of scale defined in terms of the universal constants of relativity, gravity, and quantum mechanics.

2. On this idea of primary phenomena, which would take too long to develop here, we may refer to Michel Bitbol, "Is Consciousness Primary?" *NeuroQuantology* 6, no. 1: 53–72; Michel Bitbol, *La conscience a-t-elle une origine?* (Paris: Flammarion, 2014); as well as chapter 6 of my dialogue with Wolf Singer, *Beyond the Self: Conversations between Buddhism and Neuroscience* (Cambridge. MA: MIT Press, 2018).

3. Nicolas Gisin, *Quantum Chance: Nonlocality, Teleportation and Other Quantum Marvels* (Göttingen: Copernicus, 2014).

4. See, for instance, John W. Pettit, *Mipham's Beacon of Certainty: Illuminating the View of Dzogchen, the Great Perfection* (Somerville, MA: Wisdom Publications, 2002).

5. André Comte-Sponville, *Le Bonheur, désespérément* (Nantes: Pleins Feux, 2000).

6. Pascal Bruckner, *L'Express Magazine*, May 23, 2002; and *Perpetual Euphoria: On the Duty to Be Happy* (Princeton, NJ: Princeton University Press, 2010).

7. Henri Bergson, *The Two Sources of Morality and Religion*, trans. R. Ashley Audra and Cloudesley Brereton (Notre Dame, IN: University of Notre Dame Press, 1977).

8. Aristotle, *Nicomachaean Ethics* (1, 4), trans. W. D. Ross, www.gutenberg.org.

9. This quotation is usually attributed to Barbey d'Aurevilly and drawn from his *Journal*, p. 127, but the Chevalier de Boufflers wrote almost exactly the same thing in a poem several decades earlier: "Pleasure is the happiness of madmen. Happiness is the pleasure of wise men."

10. Ricard, *Enlightened Vagabond*.

11. Epigenetics is a branch of biology that studies the nature of the mechanisms that, in a reversible, transmissible, and adaptative manner, modify the expression of genes without changing their nucleotide sequence.

12. Stephen Forbes, statement made in a debate on Fox News, October 18, 2009.

13. Christian Bruyat, Marie Haeling, and Carisse Busquet, as well as Françoise Delivet, who edited the book for the publisher.

14. Sylvie Gilman and Thierry de l'Estrade. The documentary, produced by Via Découvertes Films, was aired on Arte in 2015, and subsequently on other channels.

15. The last woman to be burned as a witch in France was killed in the Lot-et-Garonne department in 1826. Alleged sorcerers and witches were recently executed in Saudi Arabia.

16. *Le Figaro*, November 6, 2014.

17. Recently, we did an in-depth online conversation that can be viewed at https://www.youtube.com/watch?v=EFOLtXEKoN4&t=22s.

18. https://www.nationalgeographic.fr/animaux/jane-goodall-il-y-deux-jane-il-y-licone-et-il-y-moi.

19. Christophe André, *Vivre heureux: psychologie du bonheur* (Paris: Odile Jacob, 2003).

20. Herman Hesse (1877–1962), German, later Swiss, novelist, poet, painter, and essayist. When published in the United States in 1951, his philosophical novel, *Siddhartha*, enjoyed worldwide renown, especially during the opening to Eastern spirituality of the 1960s.

CHAPTER 49

1. Matthieu Ricard, Tania Singer, and K. Karius, *Power and Care: Toward Balance for Our Common Future—Science, Society, and Spirituality* (Cambridge. MA: MIT Press, 2019).

2. Daniel Goleman has described these meetings in his book *Destructive Emotions: How Can We Overcome Them?* (New York: Bantam, 2004).

3. See, in particular, F. J. Varela, "Neurophenomenology: A Methodological Remedy for the Hard Problem," *Journal of Consciousness Studies* 3, no. 4 (1996): 330–349; A. Lutz and E. Thompson, "Neurophenomenology Integrating Subjective Experience and Brain Dynamics in the Neuroscience of Consciousness," *Journal of Consciousness Studies* 10, no. 9/10 (2003): 31–52; E. Thompson, "Life and Mind: From Autopoiesis to Neurophenomenology, A Tribute to Francisco Varela," *Phenomenology and the Cognitive Sciences* 3, no. 4, (2004): 381–398.

4. Goleman, *Destructive Emotions*.

5. P. Ekman, R. J. Davidson, M. Ricard, and B. A. Wallace, "Buddhist and Psychological Perspectives on Emotions and Well-Being," *Current Directions in Psychological Science* 14, no. 2 (2005): 59–63.

6. J. S. Felton, "Burnout as a Clinical Entity—Its Importance in Health Care Workers," *Occupational Medicine* 48, no. 4 (1998): 237–250.

7. More precisely, two areas of the brain—the anterior insula and the cingulate cortex—are strongly activated by this empathetic response, and their activity can be correlated with negative affective experience of pain. For a synthesis of the thirty-two studies on empathy and pain, see C. Lamm, J. Decety, and T. Singer, "Meta-Analytic Evidence for Common and Distinct Neural Networks Associated with Directly Experienced Pain and Empathy for Pain," in *Neuroimage* 54, no. 3 (2011): 2492–2502.

8. The strengthening of positive response by drawing on compassion is associated with the activation of a brain network that includes the medial orbitofrontal cortex, the ventral striatum, the ventral tegmental area, the brainstem nuclei, the nucleus accumbens, the medial insula, the pallidum, and the putamen. All these areas of the brain have previously been associated with love (maternal love in particular), affiliation, and gratification. With respect to empathy, it is the anterior insula and the middle cingulate cortex that are involved. O. M. Klimecki, S. Leiberg, C. Lamm, and T. Singer, "Functional Neural Plasticity and Associated Changes in Positive Affect after Compassion Training," *Cerebral Cortex* 23, no. 7 (2012): 1552–1561; O. Klimecki, M. Ricard, and T. Singer, (2013), op. cit.; O. M. Klimecki, S. Leiberg, M. Ricard, and T. Singer, "Differential Pattern of Functional Brain Plasticity after Compassion and Empathy Training," *Social Cognitive and Affective Neuroscience* 9, no. 6 (2013). For a neural distinction between compassion and empathy fatigue, see O. Klimecki and T. Singer, "Empathic Distress Fatigue Rather Than Compassion Fatigue? Integrating Findings from Empathy Research in Psychology and Social Neuroscience," in B. Oakley, A. Knafo, G. Madhavan, and D. S. Wilson, *Pathological Altruism* (Oxford: Oxford University Press, 2011), 368–383.

9. B. Bornemann and T. Singer, "The Resource Study Training Protocol," in *Compassion: Bridging Practice and Science—A Multimedia Book*, ed. T. Singer and M. Bolz (E-book, 2013).

10. O. M. Klimecki et al., "Functional Neural Plasticity" (2012).

11. At the neural level, research has found that training in empathic resonance increases the activity of a network that is involved in both empathy for pain and in the experience of personal pain. This network includes the anterior insula and the anterior mid-cingulate cortex; T. Singer and M. Bolz, eds., *Compassion: Bridging Practice and Science*.

12. More precisely, these regions include the orbitofrontal cortex, the ventral striatum, and the anterior cingulate cortex. In their training, participants took a course on the concept of *metta*, a word meaning "altruistic love" in Pali. The instruction received by participants focused above all on kindness and kind wishes ("May you be happy, in good health, and so on"). Training included a full day spent with a teacher, followed by group practice for an hour every evening. Participants were also encouraged to practice at home.

13. O. M. Klimecki et al., "Functional Neural Plasticity" (2012).

14. PET stands for positron emission tomography. A PET scan first requires the injection into a vein of a mildly radioactive substance.

15. O. Bodart, M. Fecchio, M. Massimini, S. Wannez, A. Virgillito, S. Casarotto, M. Rosanova, A. Lutz, M. Ricard, S. Laureys, and O. Gosseries, "Meditation-Induced Modulation of Brain Response to Transcranial Magnetic Stimulation," *Brain Stimulation: Basic, Translational, and Clinical Research in Neuromodulation* 11, no. 6 (2018): 1397–1400.

16. G. Chételat, F. Mézenge, C. Tomadesso, B. Landeau, E. Arenaza-Urquijo, G. Rauchs, C. André, R. de Flores, S. Egret, J. Gonneaud, G. Poisnel, A. Chocat, A. Quillard, B. Desgranges, J.-G. Bloch, M. Ricard, and A. Lutz, "Reduced Age-Associated Brain Changes in Expert Meditators: A Multimodal Neuroimaging Pilot Study," *Scientific Reports* 7, no. 1 (2017): 10160.

17. Mindfulness-Based Stress Reduction (MBSR) is a secular training course in mindfulness meditation, based on Buddhist meditation practices, that has been developed in the United States hospital system by Jon Kabat-Zinn over the past thirty years and is now being successfully used in hundreds of hospitals to diminish postoperative pain and pain associated with cancer and other serious diseases. See Jon Kabat-Zinn et al., "The Clinical Use of Mindfulness Meditation for the Self-Regulation of Chronic Pain," *Journal of Behavioral Medicine* 8 (1985): 163–190.

18. Z. Segal, M. Williams, and J. Teasdale, *Mindfulness-Based Cognitive Therapy for Depression*, 2nd ed. (New York: Guilford Press, 2018).

19. A. Lutz, J. D. Dunne, and R. J. Davidson, "Meditation and the Neuroscience of Consciousness: An Introduction," chap. 19 in *The Cambridge Handbook of Consciousness* (Cambridge: Cambridge University Press, 2007), 497–549.

20. Yongey Mingyur Rinpoche, *The Joy of Living* (New York: Harmony, 2008).

CHAPTER 50

1. Karuna Asia is headed by Ingrid Kwok; Karuna USA was founded by Vivian Kurz and is currently overseen by Alexandre Lippens; Karuna Canada was founded by Charles-Mathieu Brunelle and Pascale Demers; Anne and Gérard Tardy oversaw Karuna-Shechen projects in England. In Switzerland, Karuna-Shechen projects were initially undertaken under the auspices of the Tashi Paljor Foundation, established by Ursula and Daniel Vollenweider with Rabjam Rinpoche, and in 2016 we created a new Karuna-Shechen branch run by Delphine Oltramare and Catherine Lalive. The Émergences organization is our partner in Belgium.

2. Marc Jelensperger took over from Patricia Christin, and I took over from him, for a second time, followed by Jean Timsit. Karuna-Shechen now has an international board; a president, Erick Rinner; and an executive director, Quentin Durand; who are reelected every two years.

3. The active members of the various branches of Karuna-Shechen can be found on our website. I apologize for not being able to name them all. I will limit myself to naming the current senior stakeholders above and beyond those already referred

to: Sébastien Pais de Figueredo, Javed Miri, Catherine Lalive, Tarek Toubale, Michel Tardieux, Philippe Ricard, Barend Von der Vorm, Delphine Oltramare, Jon Schmidt, and, at the international level, in Hong Kong, Ingrid Kwok and David Baverez.

4. A seminar co-organized by Tania Singer, Diego Hangartner, and me. The edited transcripts of this meeting were published in a book, T. Singer, and M. Ricard, *Power and Care: Toward Balance for Our Common Future-Science, Society, and Spirituality*, MIT Press, 2019.

CHAPTER 52

1. Theravada Buddhism, also known as Fundamental Vehicle Buddhism, defines itself as the original branch of Buddhism, and emphasizes the personal liberation of the practitioner. The Mahayana, deeply imbued with the concepts of love and compassion, stresses the need to achieve enlightenment for the sake of helping all beings attain the cessation of suffering.

CHAPTER 53

1. In later years, he also taught the basic texts of Gyalwa Longchenpa, *The Wish-Fulfilling Treasury (yid bzin rin po che'I mdzod)*, for four years and, since 2018 and possibly until 2024, *The Precious Treasury of Essential Instructions (man ngag rin po che'I mdzod)*, with the help of a 750-page commentary.

2. These translators include, among others, Anne Benson, Helena Blankleder, Christian Bruyat (deceased in 2018), Christophe Bureau, Carisse Busquet, John Canti, Patrick Carré, Changchup, Étienne Horeau, Luciana Chiaravalli-Benson, Drupchen (Hélios Hildt), Wulstan Fletcher, Steve and Christine Gethin, Charles Hastings, Maria Jesus Hervas, Witty Léon, Sabina von Minden, Anne Tardy and me. The younger translators currently being trained to take up the cause include Ananda, Coralie, Pem, Rigzin, Sarah, and a few more besides!

3. The catalogue of excellent translations offered by Éditions Padmakara can be found at https://www.padmakara.com/fr/. In English, the translations of the Padmakara Translation Group are published by Shambhala Publications, Boulder, CO.

4. E. Ricard, *Parkinson Blues* (Paris: Editions Arléa, 2004). Ève has also published *La Dame des mots* (Paris: NiL Éditions, 2012), recounting her career as a speech therapist; *Une étoile qui danse sur le chaos* (Paris: Albin Michel, 2015); and a collection of poems, *Éclats de vie* (Geneva: Éditions Jouvence, 2021), with a preface by Christian Bobin.

CHAPTER 54

1. M. Ricard, *La Citadelle des Neiges* (Paris: Nil Éditions, 2005).

CHAPTER 55

1. See I. Baker, *The Heart of the World* (London: Penguin Press, 2004).

CHAPTER 56

1. S. Cacioppo and J. T. Cacioppo, "Social Connections Matter," chap. 2 in *Introduction to Social Neuroscience* (Princeton, NJ: Princeton University Press, 2020); L. C. Hawkley and J. T. Cacioppo, "Loneliness Matters: A Theoretical and Empirical Review of Consequences and Mechanisms," *Annals of Behavioral Medicine* 40, no. 2 (2010): 218–227.

2. Translated from the Tibetan from an oral teaching by Dilgo Khyentse Rinpoche.

3. Henry David Thoreau (1817–1862) was an American philosopher, artist, writer, essayist, and poet. He insisted on walking in nature for three or four hours a day. His best-known work on the simple life is *Walden; or, Life in the Woods.*

PHOTO CREDITS

In order of appearance

Cover photo © Raphaële Demandre

FIRST PHOTO INSERT:

1. Plate 1 © Matthieu Ricard
2. Plate 2 (upper left) © Frederick Leboyer
3. Plate 2 (upper right) © Arnaud Desjardins
4 and 5. Plate 2 © Matthieu Ricard
6 and 7. Plate 3 © Matthieu Ricard
8 and 9. Plate 4 © Matthieu Ricard private collection
10 and 11. Plate 5 © Le Toumelin family collection
12 and 13. Plate 6 © Matthieu Ricard private collection
14. Plate 7 © Matthieu Ricard
15. Plate 8 © Shechen Archives
16. Plate 8 © Marilyn Silverstone / Magnum Photos
17 and 18. Plate 9 © Matthieu Ricard
19. Plate 10 © Shechen Archives (photo Marilyn Silverstone)
20 and 21. Plate 10 © Matthieu Ricard
22 to 30. Plate 11–15 © Matthieu Ricard
31 and 32. Plate 16 © Matthieu Ricard

SECOND PHOTO INSERT:

33 to 36. Plate 17–19 © Matthieu Ricard

37. Plate 19 © Raphaële Demandre

38 to 43. Plate 20–21 © Matthieu Ricard

44. Plate 22 © Matthieu Ricard

45. Plate 22 © Raphaële Demandre

46. Plate 23 © Matthieu Ricard

47. (lower left) Plate 23 © Raphaële Demandre

48. (lower right) Plate 23 © Shechen Archives (photo Greg Rabolt)

49. Plate 24 © Raphaële Demandre

50. Plate 25 © Marilyn Silverstone / Magnum Photos

51 and 52. Plate 25–26 © Raphaële Demandre

53. Plate 26 © Yeshe Philipe Danais

54. Plate 27 © Jean-Pierre Devorsine

55. (lower left) Plate 27 © Collection André Fatras

56. (lower right) Plate 27 © Yves Lanceau

57. Plate 28 © Mind & Life Institute

58. Plate 28 © Antoine Lutz

59. Plate 29 © Manuel Bauer

60. Plate 29 © Tenzin Choejor

61. (upper left) Plate 30 © Matthieu Ricard

62. (upper center) Plate 30 © Sue Greenop

63. (upper right) Plate 30 © Raphaële Demandre

64. (lower left) Plate 30 © Martine Franck/Magnum photos

65. (lower right) to 70 Plate 30–32 © Matthieu Ricard

Chapter 17, note 1 © Matthieu Ricard

Matthieu Ricard donates all of his income—royalties from all his books, photographs, and conferences—to the humanitarian projects run by the Karuna-Shechen Association, which he cofounded twenty-two years ago to alleviate the suffering of the most destitute in India, Nepal, and Tibet.

Carrying on the ideal of "altruism in action," Karuna-Shechen has benefited more than 400,000 people every year in the fields of health, education, food security, women's literacy and professional training, and environmental preservation.

In concrete terms, the book you are holding in your hands allows a child in Nepal to go to school for a week, two people with disabilities to receive a medical procedure, or a family to benefit from an organic vegetable garden for a season.

Thank you!

contact@karuna-shechen.org

www.karuna-shechen.org

The Karuna-Shechen family: some of the volunteers, field workers, full-time workers, and benefactors who work for Karuna-Shechen.